BUSINESS-TO-BUSINESS
MARKETING MANAGEMENT

BUSINESS-TO-BUSINESS MARKETING MANAGEMENT

A Global Perspective

Jim Blythe
Alan Zimmerman

THOMSON

Australia • Canada • Mexico • Singapore • Spain • United Kingdom • United States

THOMSON

Business-to-Business Marketing Management

Copyright © Thomson Learning 2005

The Thomson logo is a registered trademark used herein under licence.

For more information, contact Thomson Learning, High Holborn House, 50–51 Bedford Row, London, WC1R 4LR or visit us on the World Wide Web at: http://www.thomsonlearning.co.uk

British Library Cataloguing-in-Publication Data
A catalogue record for this book is available from the British Library

ISBN 1-84480-001-6

First edition 2005

Typeset by J&L Composition, Filey, North Yorkshire

Printed in Italy by G. Canale & Co.

CONTENTS

18 ETHICAL CONSIDERATIONS FOR BUSINESS MARKETERS 356

19 THE FUTURE OF BUSINESS MARKETING 384

PREFACE

The aim of this book is to give the student a comprehensive overview of the current state of academic and practitioner thinking on managing business-to-business marketing. Most marketing writing centers on the consumer, which is perhaps unsurprising as all of us are consumers: as a way of introducing marketing thought, consumer marketing is undoubtedly the easiest place to start. Yet business-to-business marketing accounts for larger markets, greater expenditures and greater scope for developing long-term relationships between buyers and sellers. It also carries its own dangers and rewards, and presents problems that do not exist in consumer marketing.

Both authors are experienced teachers and researchers, with work published in the US and the UK, but more importantly both authors have extensive business backgrounds, and are thus able to speak authoritatively from a wealth of practical experience. The book is therefore focused on business marketing management, full of practical examples taken from direct experience of business-to-business marketing.

The text is aimed at students in every part of the world whether they are undergraduates in specialist marketing courses, MBA students, or practitioners who would like to acquaint themselves with current academic research. The text is also suitable for those studying for professional qualifications such as the Chartered Institute of Marketing Diploma or American Marketing Association Professional Certified Marketer examinations.

Structure and plan of the book

A major theme of the book is that business-to-business marketing cannot be carried out in anything other than a global context. Even companies who do not trade outside their national borders cannot be immune from the inroads of foreign competitors entering their home markets.

Part 1 of the text provides the foundation for later chapters. The overall purpose of this section is to improve the student's understanding of the business buyer. The book assumes some knowledge of marketing but Chapter 1 outlines the main differences between B2C and B2B marketing and, in so doing, touches on some basic marketing theory. Chapter 2 looks at business buyer behavior, again covering some basic decision-making theory but putting it into a B2B context. Chapter 3 introduces strategic planning, which sets the scene for the rest of the book. The first three chapters, taken together, establish the environment within which B2B marketing decision-making takes place.

Part 2 gives a strategic underpinning to the tactical chapters to come in Part 3, including the issues around evaluating B2B market opportunities in global markets. Chapter 4 describes information gathering techniques including using secondary and primary sources. Chapter 5 introduces B2B segmentation, perhaps the most critical strategic management decision any firm must make, and Chapter 6 covers market entry, considering new markets in general as well as international markets.

Part 3 builds on the first sections by focusing on the tactics of B2B marketing. Chapter 7 looks at product strategy and development, especially global aspects of the product lifecycle and the entire process. Chapter 8 is a unique chapter in a B2B text, which describes services marketing and includes the important relationship between product and services in business marketing. Chapter 9 discusses pricing, showing the benefits and pitfalls of good pricing management. Chapter 10 describes supply-chain management and is concerned with the conceptual and theoretical aspects of managing supply-chains, while Chapter 11 is focused on the physical act of delivering goods to customers. Chapter 12 is about managing customer relationships: personal selling, key-account management and relationship marketing, which many would describe as the heart of B2B marketing. Chapters 13 to 15 are about the tactics of B2B marketing communications: advertizing, sales promotion, exhibitions and trade fairs, and corporate reputation management. The discussion of trade fairs in chapter 14, so vital to international B2B marketing, is another unique aspect of this book.

Part 4 deals with integrating the organization's marketing efforts. Chapter 16 revisits the strategic issues raised in Chapter 3 and shows how suitable planning, implementation and control will help resolve the strategic problems faced by the firm. Chapter 17 is about preparing the organization for new approaches: staff empowerment, organizational structuring and change management. Chapter 18 examines some of the ethical issues faced by B2B marketers in an international context, including cultural problems associated with ethical behaviour in a global setting. Few B2B texts have devoted an entire chapter to the critical question of ethics, so this text makes an important contribution here. Finally, Chapter 19 considers some of the future possibilities in B2B marketing, both in terms of academic theory and in terms of the practical, social, legal and economic forces that are shaping business in the 21st century.

The book also includes an Appendix, giving students a basic primer on exchange rates. Using the material provided, students can convert currencies. This is especially useful in some cases, such as Ackley Industries.

Pedagogical features

- **Case studies.** Throughout the book we have made liberal use of case studies and real-life examples. Each chapter has its own brief case study, and each section ends with a large case study that encapsulates the section. The case studies have their own review questions, intended to encourage readers to apply the content of the chapter to a real situation: in some cases, the questions address application of theory; in others, they give students the opportunity to make recommendations for the company studied.
- **Boxed examples and Talking Points.** Within each chapter there are boxed examples and also Talking Points, which are controversial statements intended to provoke thought and class discussions.
- **Review questions.** Each chapter also has its own set of review questions, designed to ensure that readers have understood the concepts presented and can apply them in practice. These questions can be used in class exercises or discussions, or can be used by the student studying alone: answers are available on the companion website.

Website

The website contains the following features:

- PowerPoint slides to accompany each chapter.
- Specimen answers to chapter and case study questions.
- Course outlines for 12-week and 26-week teaching programs.
- Class exercises for use in tutorials.
- Practical exercises.
- Internet exercises.
- Essay questions for each chapter.
- Specimen examination questions for each chapter.

The intention of the website is to provide lecturers with most of the materials they need to run an effective course based around this textbook. Lecturers are able to 'cherry pick' the features they need to fill gaps in their own existing materials, or to use the website materials in their entirety. The website also includes a very long comprehensive case, Frankfurt Pump, which may be used throughout the course or as a final project.

Overall, this book and its accompanying website should provide a comprehensive course in business-to-business marketing in a global context. It offers concise, easy-to-use coverage of an important area of marketing, one that is growing in importance as the century unfolds.

ACCOMPANYING WEBSITE

Visit the *Business-to-Business Marketing Management* accompanying website at www.thomsonlearning.co.uk to find further teaching and learning material including:

For Students
- Internet projects
- Multiple choice questions for each chapter
- Additional cases with accompanying questions
- Related weblinks
- Sample essay questions

For Lecturers
- Instructors manual – including a lecturers' plan, how to use the text and answers to the questions within the text and on the open access website
- Downloadable PowerPoint slides
- Case study teaching notes to accompany cases within the text
- Extra questions including exam questions, practical assignments for each chapter, tutorial topics/exercises for each chapter, sample practical assignments and extra MCQs

WALK-THROUGH TOUR

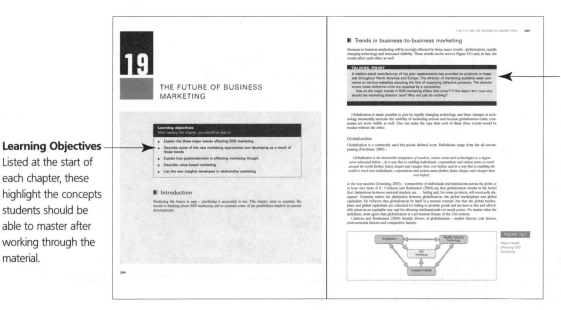

Learning Objectives
Listed at the start of each chapter, these highlight the concepts students should be able to master after working through the material.

Talking Points
Challenges to received wisdom, which are meant to spark critical thinking and discussions in class.

Summary
Bulleted list at the end of each chapter reviewing the main concepts covered.

Review Questions
Short questions which encourage students to review the material and to show their mastery of it.

Spotlight on B2B Marketing
Short cases designed to demonstrate the material discussed within the chapter. Questions related to each case are also included.

Case Study

Major cases at the end of Parts 1, 2 and 3, which are constructed to allow students to integrate all the material learned in those sections.

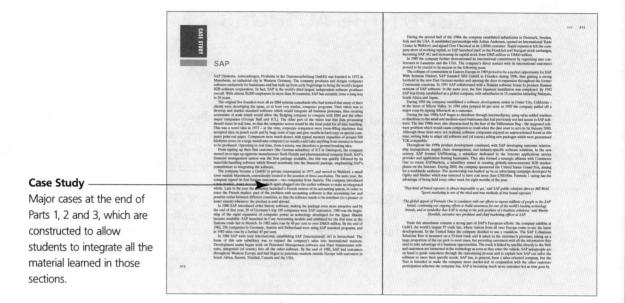

ABOUT THE AUTHORS

Alan Zimmerman is Associate Professor of Business at the City University of New York – College of Staten Island where he leads the international business program. He has written an Export Marketing guide book, as well as a number of journal articles and conference proceedings. He is also founder and president of a business and market research and consulting firm.

Jim Blythe is Reader in Marketing at University of Glamorgan. He is the author of seven textbooks on various marketing topics, as well as having an international reputation for his research on trade fairs and on sales management. He is a former company director with a wide experience of business and has carried out consultancy work both for major corporations and small enterprises.

ACKNOWLEDGEMENTS

▌ Dedication and Acknowledgements from Alan Zimmerman

Dedication

To my late parents, Alice and Roy Zimmerman, whose love of learning and world view inspired my intellectual curiosity.

Acknowledgements

First, I would like to acknowledge my friend and co-author, Jim Blythe, who made this process so rewarding. He has many talents including the ability to quickly grasp any concept and to convert it into understandable (even if British) English. Thanks to Sue Blythe for her hospitality and genuine fish and chips. I would like to especially thank my wife, Lori, for her consistent love and encouragement as well as her endless supply of brownies for quick energy. Kathleen Riley made outstanding contributions, not only in the transcription of the manuscript, but also in the design of the diagrams and research of basic concepts.

Special thanks to Michael Szenberg at Pace University who showed me the scholarly approach to problems and Laura Nowak, Chair of the Business Department at City University of New York – College of Staten Island, whose advice helped me realize my academic goals. Also to my colleagues in the Business Department and at the College for their support. Special recognition to Wilma Jones and her staff at the CSI Library for their diligent work in finding sources whenever I needed them.

Of all the business people I have known, I would like to single out Michael Ferrara, CEO of X-Rite Corporation, at various times a colleague, boss and client, whose observations are reflected in many areas of this text. I would like to thank as well all of my current and past students at the College, including Nick Orlando who performed some special research.

▌ Dedication and Acknowledgements from Jim Blythe

Dedication

To Sue, with love as always, and to the unknown inventor of the wheel, surely the first-ever component not specified by an original equipment manufacturer.

Acknowledgements

First my friend and co-author, Alan Zimmerman, whose attention to detail and solid experience of business made it unnecessary for me to apologize for too many errors in the text. Second, my students past and present, who have often asked me awkward questions which made me re-think what I was telling them and sometimes even forced me to look up the answers – truly, the best way to learn is to teach.

Finally, Lori Zimmerman for her friendship, guided tours, patience, encyclopedic knowledge and of course brownies.

And from both of us . . .

Thanks to our editor at Thomson, Anna Carter, and her colleague Jen Pegg for all their support, help, and good humor. We are also indebted to the reviewers of the text who made very valuable critical contributions and helped us improve the material and who remained positive even while correcting our mistakes.

Any errors that remain are ours alone.

▋ Acknowledgements from Thomson Learning

Thomson Learning would like to thank the following reviewers who have commented on this edition.

Mark Attride, Institute of Technology, Carlow, Ireland
Haydn Blackey, University of Glamorgan
Ross Brennan, Middlesex University
Nigel Caldwell, University of Bath
Lau Geok Theng, National University of Singapore
Paul Mattyssens, University of Limburg and Erasmus University

THE BUSINESS MARKET ENVIRONMENT

This part is intended to provide the background to the contexts in which business-to-business (B2B) marketing takes place. It provides a framework for understanding the motivations of industrial buyers, the differences between B2B marketing and consumer marketing, and provides a framework for the strategic planning which is needed to carry out B2B marketing in global markets.

Chapter 1 provides an introduction to B2B marketing, emphasizing the conceptual differences between businesses and consumers as customers. The relationship between businesses is intrinsic to B2B marketing, so this chapter devotes space to ways of fostering these relationships. Since business relationships are usually much longer lasting than the relationships between businesses and consumers, the potential gains from setting such relationships on a sound footing from the outset cannot be over emphasized. This chapter also looks at the structure of B2B markets and defines what constitutes a business market: the overall aim of the chapter is to provide an overview of the unique features of B2B marketing.

Chapter 2 looks at the tactical issues of how businesses actually buy. This chapter includes a section on non-profit organizational buying, and the effect of group influences on the buying process, since few decisions in organizations are ever made in isolation. The types of buying organization affect the decision-making process, so the different types of organization which exist in a globalized world are examined in some depth. The key aim of this chapter is to enable you to understand what makes business buyers tick: understanding their motivations, needs and decision processes, is as important as understanding the procedures the firms lay down for purchasing.

Chapter 3 examines the development of strategy for global business markets. Strategy is affected by the environment in which the firm finds itself and also by the organizational culture: the purpose of strategy is to provide a direction for the organization's activities. This chapter looks at the global business environment as well as some of the macro trends in B2B strategic planning. It includes value-chain analysis, added value, obtaining competitive advantage (which is usually the basis of virtually all commercial strategies) and of course competition and hypercompetition issues. Value networks and strategic alliances are also covered in some detail – few firms in the global business environment are able to function without forming alliances with partner firms.

Overall, this part provides the foundation for later chapters, in which the emphasis is on studying the techniques that marketers use in order to approach markets. The overall purpose of this part is to understand buyers better – which is, of course, the basis of all marketing.

INTRODUCTION TO BUSINESS-TO-BUSINESS MARKETING

Learning objectives

After reading this chapter, you should be able to:

- Define the B2B market

- Discern the differences between real marketing and 'trappings'

- Understand the size and scope of the market

- Describe the differences between B2B and consumer marketing

- Explain B2B goods classifications

- Understand the importance of relationships in B2B marketing

■ Introduction

Marketing has its roots in understanding consumers and because we are all consumers it has become altogether too easy to concentrate on using consumer-based examples and theories when discussing marketing concepts. However, business markets are far larger: businesses buy and sell more goods than consumers and the transactions that take place between organizations have a greater impact on the economy and the welfare of people, than the transactions between businesses and consumers. Understanding the differences between marketing to consumers and marketing to professional buyers in commercial organizations is the first step in developing a successful business marketing program.

■ Defining the business-to-business market

The business market has been defined to include organizations that buy goods and services for use in the production of other products and services that are sold, rented or supplied to others. It also includes retailing and wholesaling firms that acquire goods for the purpose of reselling or renting them to others (Kotler and Armstrong 2001). But this definition is far too narrow for our purposes. The full B2B market includes customers who are institutions like hospitals and charities and all levels of government. This is especially true across the globe where quasi-government operations, like the Mexican oil supplier Pemex, may be the biggest customer in a country. The business market not only includes physical products but services as well. In fact, as we will see, large institutions, governments and businesses buy virtually every product and service.

Based on many years' experience, it is clear to the authors that business buyers generally buy to increase their profits. Institutional buyers have the same concerns but they may be focused on providing an adequate surplus. There are only two basic ways to increase profits (or surplus): boost sales or lower costs. These objectives may be achieved by increasing efficiency or purchasing lower-cost products/services. Sometimes B2B buyers also buy to avoid penalties from government regulators or negative publicity from activist groups. We have concluded that the most effective marketing programs directed at business buyers are always based on one of the following three basic appeals:

1 increasing sales
2 reducing costs
3 meeting government regulations.

Especially when taking a marketing strategy from a domestic to an international setting, experience shows that the appeal must be simple to explain. Appeals that do not fall into one of the three basics above often fail when translated to foreign markets.

Exhibit 1.1 is an advertisement which clearly shows how the use of a rather uninteresting looking product can improve company productivity. The message is simple and can easily be translated to any number of languages.

EXHIBIT 1.1

Advertisement focused on improving employee productivity

TALKING POINT

A product known as an auto diode is a key component in the alternators used in virtually every automobile in the world. One old line electrical products manufacturer was supplying an attractive product at a cost of nearly one US dollar per unit. Competitors developed a much simpler product which eliminated the outer layer of packaging and could be offered to automotive manufacturers at less than US$0.20. The engineers at the older firm were convinced that buyers at General Motors, Ford, and Toyota would be willing to pay more for the better packaged product, even though both met the same functional requirements. One engineer even remarked, 'they can see the better quality – it looks better!'

Is price the only consideration in B2B markets? Are we living in a world where manufacturers can only survive by being the cheapest? Or is the real issue value? And how do you define that?

Trappings versus substance

As is illustrated by the Talking Point above, many B2B firms *appear* to adapt the marketing concept, but more often than not, they are stuck in what has been called the 'Rugged Engineering Trap'. This is a warmed-over version of production orientation where a firm is convinced (usually by its engineers) that if 'we build a better widget, the world will beat a path to our door'. These firms are only giving lip service to the marketing concept especially where technology is emphasized over customer needs. This disease is chronic in B2B marketing and endemic among many firms. Michael Porter (2001) recently wrote that some companies 'have used Internet technology to shift the basis of competition away from quality features and service toward price', because they forgot to satisfy customers. Many B2B firms adapt what appears to be a marketing orientation, but they are simply using the 'trappings' of marketing rather than the substance. Trappings include activities like:

- declarations of support from top management
- creating a marketing organization complete with product management
- new strategic or marketing planning approaches
- complete marketing information (MIS) systems
- increasing marketing expenditures for advertising, research and training.

Adapted from: Ames 1970

The trappings do not address the central need for a B2B firm to focus on the critical purpose of its existence. More than 30 years ago, Peter Drucker said that 'there is only one valid definition of business purpose: to create a customer' (Drucker 1973). But Lou Gerstner stated that IBM's major problem when he took over was that the firm had forgotten to satisfy customers and was more interested in promoting technology (Gerstner 2002).

No amount of sparkling technology, management dictums, new plans or systems can replace the basic understanding exhibited by the most effective B2B firms. The key task doesn't sound very exciting, but it is absolutely vital to success. It is to determine what customers really want and to put all the resources of the firm on the task of delivering it. A firm that can accomplish this (no mean feat) is really a marketing-oriented firm, not one with just the 'trappings' of marketing.

As we shall see, there are major differences between consumer and B2B marketing. Yet, the basic concept of satisfying customers' needs remains the same. Experience has shown that B2B marketers must be generalists. They are far more involved with customers' individual needs and must often adapt their product and service offerings to meeting those needs. Salespeople for B2B firms frequently need to have the same skills as general managers, for they often select the most important customers or customer segments, design products and service packages to satisfy those customers, develop marketing plans for them, set the prices and perform the follow-up service required to keep the customers happy.

The consumer sale in most products consists of only one transaction compared to the many transactions that take place before that one final sale is made in the B2B world. The conversion sequence shown below gives an idea of the number of steps required to make any product.

Since businesses, institutions and governments buy every product, simply looking at a product cannot tell us whether it is a consumer or B2B product. Consider the humble hairdryer. If we trace this product through the stages in the production chain, we will see that many B2B transactions must take place in order for a final sale to a consumer to happen.

Now, let us apply the hairdryer to this process.

If we examine the hairdryer, we can see that it is made up of about five major elements, including:

- a plastic shell
- a heating element
- a motor and fan
- controls and switches
- a wire and plug.

The diagram below (Table 1.2) shows how many possible transactions there are from the original gathering of the raw materials to the final sale to the consumer. We can count 18 transactions which fall into the B2B category as compared to one final transaction to the consumer. To make this simple electric hairdryer requires raw materials from oil, steel, aluminium and rubber producers, materials processors who turn the raw ores into usable products, manufacturers of parts and sub-assemblies who put together materials of various kinds and deliver several components to another firm who would be a final assembler. In this case, we have assumed the final assembler is in Taiwan. The final assembler then delivers the product to the distributor, a private brander who may be a firm like Clairol. This firm then sells the product to a wholesaler, who in turn sells to a retailer and only then does the consumer have the opportunity to purchase it.

TABLE 1.1 Conversion sequence

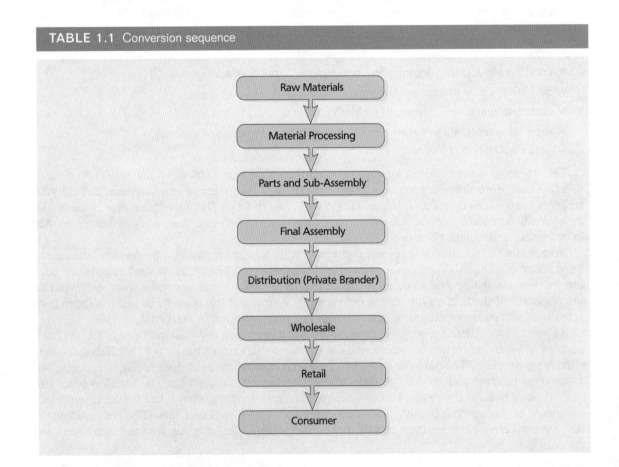

TABLE 1.2 Transactions to make a hairdryer

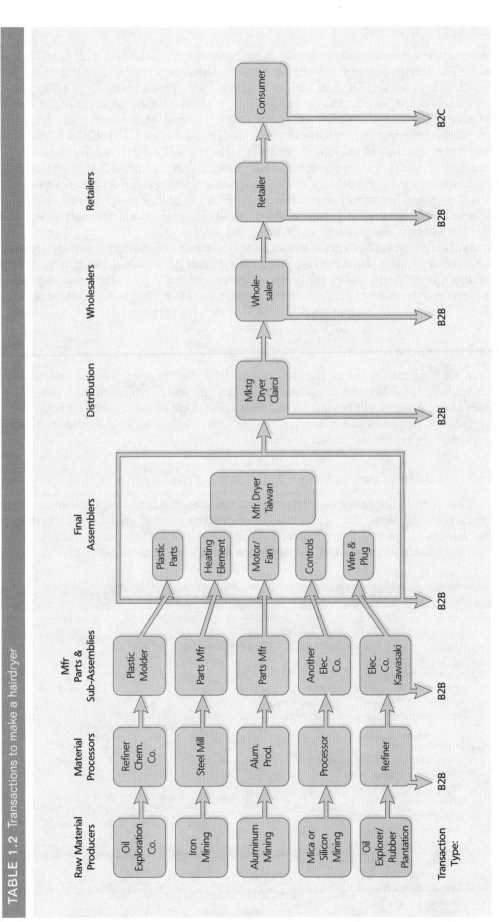

Impact of the Internet

The advent of the Internet is fundamentally changing the way firms address their production or supply chain. The IBM group buys 95 per cent of its requirements using e-procurement. In 2000, Daimler-Chrysler, Ford and General Motors launched a joint procurement service. Since that time, this service, now called Covisint, has grown rapidly from about 22,000 users at the end of 2001 to over 77,000 users at the end of 2002 (Covisint.com 2003). General Motors reported spending nearly US$100 billion in the first eight months of 2001 through this service (Line 56.com 2003). Both IBM and Ford report hundreds of millions of dollars in savings by using e-procurement methods.

While there seems to be some concern about electronic procurement, it appears that it is being heartily accepted by many firms and will soon be a requirement laid down by large firms on smaller suppliers. The major reasons why some firms are hesitating to plunge completely into e-procurement include unsolved technological problems, concerns about security and managerial and technical obstacles (for instance, see Marston and Baisch 2001).

A study of corporate facilities managers shows they are far more willing to purchase low-risk products like supplies via the Internet than expensive capital items. This study shows, that on average, only 3 per cent of capital items, but 10 per cent of maintenance and repair supplies were purchased by these buyers over the Internet (Tellefsen and Zimmerman 2004). The study also showed that buyers are more likely to use the Internet for data gathering than order placement.

Size of the market

As we can see from the number of transactions that take place to provide our simple hairdryer, the B2B market is far larger than the consumer market. The purchases of governments alone dwarfs the purchases of any collection of companies and consumers. One of the largest buyers in the world is IBM, whose total purchases added up to more than US$42 billion in 2001. Fujitsu spent nearly half of that just on components and materials (*Purchasing* 2002).

Conceptual differences between B2B and consumer marketing

While on the surface the basics of marketing are the same for attracting consumers, businesses, governments or institutions, there are a number of differences which make the marketing of products and services in the B2B market quite different from marketing to consumers. The 12 major differences in consumer versus B2B marketing are spelled out in the table below.

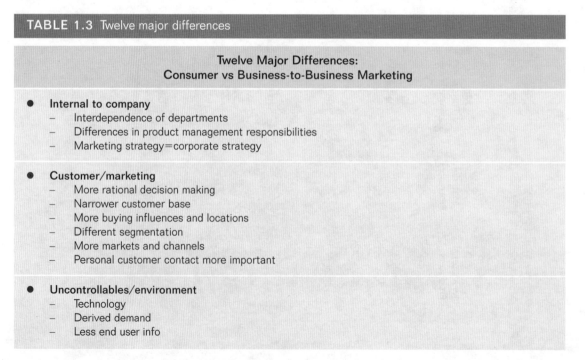

TABLE 1.3 Twelve major differences

Twelve Major Differences:
Consumer vs Business-to-Business Marketing

- **Internal to company**
  - Interdependence of departments
  - Differences in product management responsibilities
  - Marketing strategy=corporate strategy

- **Customer/marketing**
  - More rational decision making
  - Narrower customer base
  - More buying influences and locations
  - Different segmentation
  - More markets and channels
  - Personal customer contact more important

- **Uncontrollables/environment**
  - Technology
  - Derived demand
  - Less end user info

Internal to company

In business marketing, it is not possible for one department alone to develop or make a change in an offering and gain the approval in a large number of customers. In a business marketing firm, a product manager usually must act like a mini general manager. Every product manager faces the problem of responsibility without authority. The business marketing manager must be able to gain cooperation from all the other functions including engineering, information resources and manufacturing. Especially in the manufacturing of B2B products there are often long lead times.

An office furniture product manager takes the needs of the marketplace gained from market research and, working with an internal or external industrial designer, develops concepts for a product. At the same time, the product manager must involve engineering, finance and manufacturing, to develop initial feasibility studies and cost estimates for the product. The lead time for tooling (the forming equipment used to make the product pieces) may be close to one year. The product manager must make decisions, finalize the design, gain cooperation from all other departments and then approve the order for the tooling, while planning to introduce a product one year in advance. While consumer product managers are usually graduates of advertising agencies or corporate advertising departments, business product managers often have technical backgrounds. The reason for this is that advertising plays such a small role in business marketing when compared to consumer marketing. In addition, product managers are frequently required to make customer visits. These visits not only give these managers important feedback, but the product managers are active members of the sales team, providing expertise and the authority from headquarters on pricing and special packages of product and service.

In business marketing, the marketing strategy often is the same as the overall corporate strategy. For reasons already cited, many of the firms' functional areas must be involved in the marketing strategy. For instance, a small security division of a large corporation was faced with an opportunity to develop special security equipment for the White House in Washington DC. The sales person presented his ideas to engineering, manufacturing and the finance department and the entire division decided to pursue this large opportunity, changing the corporate strategy from commercial to governmental target market segments. The investments required to make this product were significant. In addition, other departments had to change their priorities with the new product forcing a new strategy. The gestation period from time of suggestion to actual sales involving this large government contract was well over two years and therefore, the entire division had to change its strategy to be successful.

Customer/Marketing

While emotion plays some role in the purchasing process, generally speaking, buying decisions are more rational in non-consumer markets. It is hard to justify the purchase of a new company-wide computer system based on the color of the machine housings or the social relationship between the purchaser and the salespeople. Some rationale must be developed in order for this decision to be accepted by all members of the purchasing firm. This rationale will be described in more detail in Chapter 2.

Consumer markets generally consist of millions of individuals. Far fewer customers make up most non-consumer markets. For instance, a provider of jet engines may need to call on only a few potential customers such as Airbus and Boeing who manufacture the majority of commercial airliners. In business marketing, Pareto's Law is often strongly in effect. In other words, a small percentage of the customers account for a very large percentage of all the business in a particular segment. For instance, in the United States, about 4 per cent of all corporations account for 70 per cent of all exports. This narrow base means that in many markets, the buyers have more power than the sellers.

Whereas in consumer marketing, families and other reference groups play key roles in the purchasing decision, in business markets, the decision-making unit or buying center is the key. There are a number of individuals who take specific roles and make decisions based on these roles. This will be discussed in detail in Chapter 2. In addition to a number of individuals in this decision-making unit, there are a number of locations involved. One large credit card firm assembled a team who were located in various cities throughout North America, Europe and Asia. These individuals rarely met, but communicated by e-mail, voice mail and fax. In making a buying decision about a new computer software program, these people took various roles and came to the decision without physically ever being in the same room.

Business buyers are characterized in different ways than consumer buyers. Consumers can be segmented by demographic or psychographic methods while customers in business markets are segmented by factors such as industry classification codes, product applications, price sensitivity, location, importance of product to the buying firm and customer size. This segmentation is discussed in far more depth in Chapter 5.

While consumer goods are often sold directly or through only one or two steps of distribution, business equipment and services providers often use many different channels. Most large producers sell directly to large customers, while also selling through various other channels at the same time. For instance, a roofing shingle firm is likely to sell directly to large home builders, contractors and 'big box' retailers like Home Depot in the US or B&Q in the UK, while at the same time selling through distributors who in turn sell to smaller lumber yards and other outlets. Each effort through different distribution channels reaching different customers requires a different marketing strategy.

The largest portion of a business marketing budget is accounted for by the salesforce. Personal contact is extremely important to the success of a business marketer. In some firms, highly trained salespeople with engineering or medical degrees are required to make a convincing case to sophisticated customers. In consumer markets, television, newspaper and other non-personal information sources are critical. Proprietary research completed with architects over the last ten years shows that they consistently place the highest value on the manufacturer's salesperson as a source of information, compared to advertising, catalogs, the Internet or any other source.

TALKING POINT

Now that the Internet has become so important in business procurement, some firms believe understanding customer needs doesn't seem to matter as much as it used to. Simply put up a price when a customer asks for it and, if you have the lowest number, you get the order. You don't need salesmen to talk to the customers and you surely don't need any market research. This is certainly a lower cost approach to marketing.

So why don't we all go through this route? If dropping the price to rock bottom is the way forward, why shouldn't we all do it? Why NOT focus on just one need – the need for a low price?

Or maybe we're in business for more than just doing the customer a favor?

Uncontrollables/Environment

While some final consumers find technology exciting, it is not usually their telling attribute. With business customers, the application of proper technology often has significant effects on the financial results. You only need to imagine the production line of a firm manufacturing computers to see the importance of particular circuit boards. A circuit board provider would need to be intimately familiar with the technology used by a Dell, Acer or Hewlett-Packard in order to serve these firms most effectively. Should an error be made and the wrong type of board either physically or electrically be provided, these computer manufacturers' assembly lines would shut down and the loss of revenue would be significant. Technology is also very important in improving the sales success ratio. Since salespeople can carry laptop computers into a customer's location, they can often make very effective presentations and at the same time tap into head office databases to answer important questions on the spot.

Perhaps the most well-known difference between consumer and business marketing is the concept of derived demand. This simply means, as we have seen in the hairdryer example, that the demand for business marketers' products is derived from sales to the consumer. A firm supplying personal security systems to home builders would be affected significantly by the number of new homes or apartments built in a particular area. Should demand for these homes slacken, no amount of convincing marketing will force a home builder to purchase more personal security systems than needed for installation in newly built residences. Business marketers must look beyond their own customers to the ultimate consumer to understand trends which may have a significant effect upon their business. The disposable income in a particular market has a significant effect on the demand for automobiles. A firm supplying seats or stereo equipment to automobile manufacturers would do well to review the disposable income trends in a particular market to predict future sales of their products.

In consumer markets, there are well-established government and private firms supplying specific market data. For instance, in the United States, the AC Neilsen Company supplies frequent data about supermarket sales by product and brand. In addition, models exist which can predict the success of a consumer marketing activity based on small experiments. For instance, exposing a test market to advertising, then examining the results, can allow a firm to predict nationwide sales since well-established formulas are commercially available to make this prediction. No such formulas exist in B2B markets and frequently, the data required by a particular business marketer is difficult to find. A firm which manufactures access flooring (a product which provides a false floor on top of an original floor to allow a plenum for housing wiring and passing air conditioning) was attempting to determine the size of its market in the Far East. The firm looked first at the United States and found that no government data was available which specifically identified the sales of this type of product. The closest identification was 'metal fabricated products, nec'. The meaning of 'NEC' is 'not elsewhere classified', the bane of any marketing researcher. This means that data concerning many kinds of fabricated metal parts was included in the category and the access flooring manufacturer could only know the absolute largest possible size of its market, but was really no closer to identifying the real size. In looking for data in Hong Kong, China and even Japan, the manufacturer ran into the same problem. No data of this definition was available. This kind of problem is often true for business marketers and the solution is described in further detail in Chapter 4.

TALKING POINT

Consumer marketing is almost the same as B2B marketing. After all, aren't there customers and multiple buying influences and environmental forces in each market? Shouldn't a person who was in charge of marketing for toothpaste be able to adapt to selling oil-well drilling equipment?

Or are we saying that people stop being human when they become industrial buyers?

Relationship building

An extremely vital part of success in business marketing is the development and maintenance of customer relationships. Instead of simply looking at a series of transactions between a customer and a supplier, the successful marketer attempts to establish a relationship. This is not always a long term relationship, but the interchange should be seen as more than a simple transaction. In fact, one definition of marketing is 'to establish, maintain, enhance and commercialize customer relationships so that the objectives of the parties involved are met. This is done by a mutual exchange and fulfillment of promises' (Gronroos 1990). The seller gives a set of promises related to products, services, financing, administration, information, social contacts and other commitments. The buyer gives a set of promises related to payment and use of the product. When the promises are kept on both sides, both parties gain benefits and the relationship is enhanced. Once past promises are fulfilled new sets of promises can be made on both sides to continue the building of the relationship (Calonious 1986 and 1988).

Recent research shows that not every customer either needs or desires a long term relationship (Day 2000 and Cannon and Perreault 1999). Some business marketers should segment their customers according to their relationship needs. For a fuller explanation of this, see Chapter 12.

Business goods classifications

There are a number of ways of classifying B2B goods. All are entirely different than consumer goods, which are usually divided into convenience, specialty and shopping goods. From a B2B point of view, goods are divided by the use to which they will be put. The most widely accepted classification of business products is as follows:

Entering goods and services – products and services that become part of other products – raw materials, component parts and materials. Examples of these kinds of products are taillights for an automobile, lumber or metallic ores, formed parts of aluminum or plastic or electronic products like integrated circuits. These are usually expensed rather than capitalized.

Foundation goods and services – products that are used to make other products. This includes installations and accessory equipment. The former are items like offices and buildings and the latter, machine tools. Foundation goods do not become part of the finished products. While most of them are capital items, some foundation goods can also be expensed.

Facilitating goods and services – products and services that help an organization achieve its objectives. These goods also do not enter the product or even the production process. Generally speaking, facilitating goods and services are expensed rather than capitalized. Examples of facilitating goods and services are market research services, cleaning supplies and services, copiers and small hardware. Facilitating goods are usually divided into supplies and business services. In this category are items which are often characterized as MRO (maintenance, repair and operations).

As will be seen, the goods classification aids in developing strategy for the business marketer. While it is only one important aspect of strategy development, the type of good gives basic direction to the strategy.

■ Road map through the text

As you read through the text, you will see it is uniquely oriented, with a global perspective. While the text introduces the student to all the basics of B2B marketing, including the latest research in various areas, our goal has been to focus on the entire world since most B2B marketers must take advantage of opportunities wherever they arise. In addition, we believe that marketing is essentially a practical discipline. So, while theory is introduced, we attempt to focus the student on real tools which can be used in the day-to-day management of a B2B firm.

The book is organized into four parts. First is the Business Market Environment. This part provides the context for B2B marketing and includes the current chapter as well as a discussion of business organization buying behavior and strategic planning for global markets. We have purposely placed strategic planning at an early stage in the book since this overview is necessary to put the rest of the text into proper context.

The second part, called Evaluating Market Opportunities, includes market research and information systems, discussing ways of gathering information which are unique to the B2B marketer; segmentation, targeting and positioning, which is designed to show marketers how to group customers across the world into like segments; and market entry tactics describing how the strategic planning you have accomplished in the earlier portions of the text can be applied to ways of entering new markets with an emphasis on foreign markets.

The third part is Formulating the Marketing Mix, which focuses on the specific tactical activities involved in B2B marketing. First is a discussion of product strategy and development, which describes new product development for the global B2B market, the product lifecycle and the management of products for business markets. Next is a discussion of business services, describing the differences between the marketing of products and the marketing of services. Chapter 9 describes pricing in a global context. Here we will review the basics of business product pricing and the major issue of transfer pricing. Next is supply chain management, the strategic management of distribution channels. The discussion here includes power relationships in distribution and the special problems of global distribution of B2B products. Chapter 11 deals with logistics and physical distribution, getting goods to the right location in the right quantities and in the right condition. Here the text includes Internet delivery of services.

Chapter 12 examines current communications theory as it applies to B2B marketing. Customer relationships and key account management is a critical aspect of B2B marketing and Chapter 13 will review this in a global context. Chapter 14 focuses on sales promotion, especially on the often neglected area of exhibitions and trade fairs, so important especially to B2B marketers throughout the world. Chapter 15 discusses corporate reputation management, the most up-to-date way of looking at this, which includes public relations and corporate advertising as well as crisis management.

The final part of the text, Managing the Marketing Program, describes the specific management issues faced by B2B marketers. Chapter 16 is on marketing planning, implementation and control which discusses combining the elements of a marketing mix in the correct way and overcoming difficulties of implementation. Next, Chapter 17 describes various ways of organizing the marketing function, including staff empowerment and management of functional groups within the firm as well as change management. Chapter 18 reviews ethical issues for business marketers, especially important when dealing with the global marketplace. The final chapter describes the future of business marketing, including the continued rise in importance of the Internet and other communications technologies and possible changes in globalization and the impact of Post-Modern philosophy on marketing thinking.

SUMMARY

Business-to-business marketing is substantially larger and very different from consumer marketing. The business market includes all businesses, institutions and governments who buy virtually every product and service to help them in turn provide products and services to other businesses and to consumers. Marketing to these customers requires a different orientation than that used in consumer marketing.

The key points from this chapter are as follows:

- The most effective B2B marketing programs focus on one of three basic appeals: increasing sales, reducing costs, meeting government regulations.

- 'Trappings' such as new technology, planning approaches or management dictums cannot substitute for a true customer orientation – finding out what customers really need and focusing the organization on providing it to them.

- There are far more B2B than consumer marketing transactions and the B2B market is far larger than the consumer market.

- The Internet is changing how customers buy but the need for a basic marketing orientation remains.

- There are 12 major differences between B2B and consumer marketing which include those that are related to the company, customers and the environment.

- Building relationships is critical to the business marketer since an in-depth understanding of the customer processes is the main ingredient in B2B processes.

- Business goods/services are classified as entering – items which become part of the product/service of the customer company, foundation – usually large capital items that are used to make products and facilitating – which help the customer's organization achieve its objectives.

REVIEW QUESTIONS

1 What are the main characteristics of B2B marketing?

2 What are the most important tools B2B product managers would use to achieve their objectives?

3 What are the 12 major differences between B2B and consumer marketing? How would these differences affect formulating a B2B strategy?

4   How can a manager avoid the 'trappings' of marketing?

5   What defines the relationships which are so important to B2B marketers?

6   What are the major goods classifications of B2B products?

SPOTLIGHT ON B2B MARKETING

Toyo Ichiura had recently been transferred from the Consumer Electronics to the Business Solutions Divisions of Rising Sun Electronics. The firm is a US$10 billion company, manufacturing every kind of electronic product from TVs to portable CD players. Rising Sun is a household name throughout the world, known for quality consumer electronics products. Recently they have also become interested in serving business markets and established the Business Solutions Division to take their electronic know-how into business markets. Their first segments will be related to business communications and on-site security. Last year they sold about US$500 million in products and services to business markets, but top management expects these markets to grow in excess of 20 per cent per year. In addition, the margins on business products are at least double those in the consumer markets.

After only about three months on the job as vice president of marketing for Business Solutions, Ichiura was wondering how he could carry out his assignment from the CEO. When the CEO hired him, he had said 'the marketing in our B2B operations just isn't what it should be. Since you have extensive experience in marketing for consumer electronics products, I assume you will be able to determine what we can do to improve our marketing for Business Solutions'.

As Ichiura began to study the Business Solutions Division, he had come to a few tentative conclusions. First, advertising and promotion received little emphasis in this division. Second, marketing for each business seemed to be relevant only to that business, a self-contained unit. Third, the product managers in these businesses were deeply involved with their customers, sometimes spending weeks at a time working on one large customer rather than focusing one common appeal to the largest number of consumers.

Ichiura decided to discuss his observations with some of his more experienced B2B colleagues at RSE. When he described his tentative conclusions, his colleagues surprised him by disagreeing with them. So he decided to speak to a fellow graduate of Tokyo University he knew was now working in a B2B position in the steel industry. He was in for another surprise. After some reminiscing, Ichiura broached his subject with his friend Yoichiro Watanabe. He reiterated his three major conclusions and asked for advice. Watanabe took a moment to look at the busy traffic in the Tokyo streets below before responding:

'Well, it is difficult. While marketing is called marketing with consumers and is also called marketing in the B2B world, there are so many differences it is hard to know where to begin. The kinds of tools you used in your previous position are just the opposite in many cases to what should be done in your current position. It might be prudent to put off your deadline for reporting to your CEO and spend some time with the major customers of your division. I believe I know you very well and I know you will be able to learn the nuances of this new field.'

Questions

1   Was Watanabe wrong? Were the B2B marketing executives at RSE just protecting their past decisions?

2   What major differences do you think Ichiura will find if he follows Watanabe's advice?

3   Is it a good idea to promote consumer marketing executives to senior B2B marketing positions?

4   Why do advertising and promotion play a subsidiary role in B2B marketing?

5   What are the major differences between B2B buyers and consumer purchasers?

REFERENCES

—— http://www/covisint.com, accessed 3/18/03

—— http://www.line56.com, accessed 3/18/03

—— 'Best Practices at Big Blue Three Years Later', *Purchasing* 131: 3: 11.

—— 'Fujitsu Cuts Procurement Costs and Suppliers', *Purchasing* 131: 3: 30.

Ames, B. C. (1970) 'Trappings vs Substance in Industrial Marketing', *Harvard Business Review* 48: 4: 93–102.

Bonoma, T. V. (1982) 'Major Sales: Who Really Does the Buying?', *Harvard Business Review* 60: 3: 111–119.

Cannon, J. P. and Perreault, W. D., Jr (1999) 'Buyer-Seller Relationship in Business Markets', *Journal of Marketing Research*, Vol. 36, 439–460.

Colonius, H. (1986) 'A Market Behavior Framework', in K. Moller and M. Paltschick (eds) *Contemporary Research in Marketing*, Proceedings from the XV Annual Conference of the European Marketing Academy, Helsinki, Finland.

Colonius, H. (1988) 'A Buying Process Model', in K. Blois and S. Parkinson (eds) *Innovative Marketing – A European Perspective*, Proceedings from the XVII Annual Conference of the European Marketing Academy, University of Bradford, England.

Day, G. S. (2000) 'Managing Market Relationships', *Journal of the Academy of Marketing Sciences* 28: 1: 24–30.

Drucker, P. F. (1954) *Management: Tasks Responsibilities Practices*, New York: Harper & Row.

Gerstner, L. (2002) *Who Says Elephants Can't Dance*, New York: Harper Collins.

Gronroos, C. (1990) 'Relationship Approach to Marketing in Service Contexts: The Marketing and Organizational Behavior Interface', *Journal of Business Research* 20: 3–11.

Kotler, P. and Armstrong, G. (2001) *Principles of Marketing*, Upper Saddle River, NJ: Prentice-Hall.

Marston, L. and Baisch, L. (2001) 'The Overdue Promise of E-procurement', *Health Management Technology* Nov 2001: 22: 11: 32–35.

Porter, M. E. (2001) 'Strategy and the Internet', *Harvard Business Review* 79: 3: 62–78.

Tellefsen, T. and Zimmerman, A. (2004) 'The Impact of Buyer Perceptions and Situational Factors on Internet Usage', *International Journal of Internet Marketing and Advertising*, July/Sept: 1: 3.

HOW BUSINESS ORGANIZATIONS BUY

▊ Introduction

Organizational buying is often supposed to be more rational and less emotional than consumer purchasing behavior. However, it would be wrong to assume that organizational buying is always entirely rational: those responsible for making buying decisions within organizations are still human beings and do not leave their emotions at the door when they come to work, so it seems unrealistic to suppose that they do not have some emotional or irrational input in their decision-making.

■ The decision-making unit

There are very few cases where industrial purchasing decisions are made by only one person. Even in small businesses it is likely that several people would expect to have some influence or input into purchase decisions. Because of this, the decision-making process often becomes formalized, with specific areas of interest being expressed by members of the decision-making unit (DMU) and with roles and responsibilities being shared. This group which cannot be identified on any company organization chart, also called the Buying Center, varies in make-up from one buying situation to another. Individuals may participate for a brief time only, or be part of the group from conception to conclusion.

The decision-making unit is thought to contain the following categories of member (Webster & Wind 1972):

Initiators: These are the individuals who first recognize the problem.

Gatekeepers: These individuals control the flow of knowledge, either by being proactive in collecting information, or by filtering it. They could be junior staff who are told to visit a trade fair and collect brochures, or personal assistants who see their role as preventing salespeople from 'wasting' decision-makers' time.

Buyers: The individuals given the task of sourcing suppliers and negotiating the final deal. Often these are purchasing agents who complete the administrative tasks necessary for buying. These people often work to a specific brief and may have very little autonomy, even though they may be the only contact suppliers' salespeople have at purchasing organizations.

Deciders: These are the people who make the final decisions and may be senior managers or specialists. They may never meet any representatives of supplying companies. Deciders generally rely heavily on advice from other members of the DMU.

Users: These are the people who will be using the products which are supplied: they may be engineers or technicians, or even the cleaning staff who use cleaning products. Their opinions may well be sought by the deciders and in many cases the users are also the initiators.

Influencers: These people 'have the ear of' the deciders. They are trusted advisers, but from the supplying company's viewpoint they are extremely difficult to identify. Influencers may be employed by purchasing firms (for example, engineers, information systems managers or research managers) or they may be consultants (for example, architects, acoustics and safety consultants). Influencers might even be a decider's golf partner, old college friend, or teenage son.

These categories are not, of course, mutually exclusive. A User might also be an Influencer, or a Gatekeeper might also be an Initiator. The categories were originally developed to explain purchasing within families – which may be an example of the apparent similarities between B2B marketing and consumer marketing.

In fact, the members of the decision-making unit are affected both by rational and emotional motivations. Salespeople are well aware that buyers are affected by their liking or dislike for the suppliers' representatives and buyers will often be working to their own agendas: for example, buyers might be seeking a promotion, or might feel threatened in terms of job security, or may be conducting a vendetta with a colleague. Any of these influences might affect the buyers' behavior, but all of them would be difficult or impossible for a supplier's salesperson to identify correctly and act upon.

In general, members of a decision-making unit tend to be more risk-averse than consumers. This is because the Buying Center (DMU) members have more to lose in the event of a wrong decision: for consumers, the main risk is financial and even that is limited since most retailers will replace or refund goods purchased in error. For industrial purchasers, however, a serious purchasing mistake can result in major negative consequences for businesses as well as loss of face at work, in shattered promotion dreams, or even in dismissal in serious cases. The professional persona of industrial buyers is liable to be compromised by purchasing errors, which in turn means that buyers will feel a loss of self-esteem.

Determining the relative power of each member of the Buying Center (DMU) for each purchasing situation is a difficult task. Ronchetto *et al.* (1989) identify those characteristics of individuals who may be most influential in a DMU:

- important in the corporate and departmental hierarchy
- close to the organizational boundary

- central to the workflow
- active in cross-departmental communications
- directly linked to senior management.

It should be obvious that purchasing managers are most important in repetitive purchases, while the CEO will become heavily involved in unique, costly and risky buying decisions.

As a result of this increased risk, industrial buyers use a variety of risk-reducing tactics (Hawes and Barnhouse 1987). These are as follows and are presented in order of importance:

1 Visit the operations of the potential vendor to observe its viability.
2 Question present customers of the vendor concerning their experience with the vendor's performance.
3 Multisource the order to ensure a backup source of supply.
4 Obtain contract penalty clause provisions from the potential vendor.
5 Obtain the opinion of colleagues concerning the potential vendor.
6 In choosing a vendor, favor firms that your company has done business with in the past.
7 Confirm that members of your upper management are in favor of using the vendor as a supplier.
8 Limit the search for, and ultimate choice of a potential vendor, only to well-known vendors.
9 Obtain the opinion of a majority of your co-workers that the chosen vendor is satisfactory.

Buyers are affected by individual, personal factors as well as environmental and organizational factors. Personally they exhibit many of the same influences on the buying decision that consumers have: the desire to play a role, for example, may cause buyers to be difficult to negotiate with as they try to drive a hard bargain. The desire for respect and liking may cause buyers to want to give the order to salespeople who are exceptionally pleasant or helpful and to deny the order to salespeople who are regarded as being unpleasant or pushy. Figure 2.1 and its explanatory notes, shows why business buyers are likely to be affected by some or all of the following environmental influences (Loudon and Della Bitta 1993):

1 Physical influences. The location of purchasing firms relative to their suppliers may be decisive, since many firms prefer to source supplies locally. This is especially true in the global marketplace, where purchasing companies may wish to support local suppliers, or may prefer to deal with people from the same cultural background. In many cases, buyers seem almost afraid to source from outside their own national boundaries, even when rational considerations of cost and quality would make the foreign supplier the better bet.
2 Technological. The level of technological development available among local suppliers will affect what buyers can obtain. The technology of buyers and sellers must also be compatible: in global markets this often presents a problem, since international technical standards remain very different for most products. Despite efforts within the European Union to

FIGURE 2.1

Environmental influences on buyer behavior

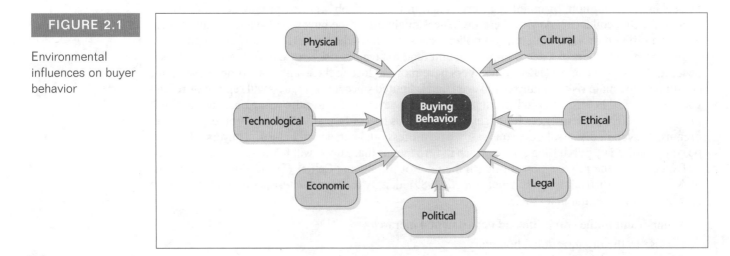

harmonize technical standards, Europe still does not have standardized electrical fitting plumbing fittings or even computer keyboards. Many European firms find it easier to tra with former colonies thousands of miles away than deal with countries within the EU, sim because the technical standards of the former colonies are identical with their own.

3 Economic influences. The macroeconomic environment is concerned with the level of demand in the economy and with the current taxation regime within buyers' countries. These conditions affect buyers' abilities to buy goods as well as their need to buy raw materials: if demand for their products is low, the demand for raw materials to manufacture them will also be low. On a more subtle level, the macroeconomic climate affects buyers' confidence in the same way as it affects consumer confidence. For example, a widespread belief that the national economy is about to go into a decline will almost certainly make buyers reluctant to commit to major investments in stock, equipment and machinery. In a global context, the fact that countries enter and leave recessions at different times will affect the timing of marketing efforts on the part of vendors. At the microeconomic level, firms experiencing a boom in business will have a greater ability to pay for goods and a greater level of confidence.

4 Political influences. Governments frequently pass laws affecting the way businesses operate and this is nowhere more true than in international trade. Trade sanctions, trade barriers, specifically non-tariff barriers, preferred-nation status and so forth all affect the ways in which buyers are permitted or encouraged to buy. In some cases, Governments specifically help certain domestic businesses as part of an economic growth package. The political stability of countries is also a factor that vendors need to take into account.

5 Legal influences. Laws often lay down specific technical standards, which affect buyers' decisions. Buyers may be compelled to incorporate safety features into products, or may be subject to legal restrictions in terms of raw materials. Often, vendors can obtain competitive advantage by anticipating changes in the law.

6 Ethical influences. In general, buyers are expected to act at all times for the benefit of the organization, not for personal gain. This means that, in most cultures, the buyers are expected not to accept bribes, for example. However, in some cultures bribery is the normal way of doing business, which leaves vendors with a major ethical problem – refusing to give a bribe is likely to lose the business, but giving a bribe is probably unethical or illegal in the company's home country, especially now that the OECD Anti-Bribery Convention has been widely adapted. As a general rule, buyers are likely to be highly suspicious of doing business with salespersons whom they perceive as acting unethically – after all, if salespersons are prepared to cheat on their employers, they cannot be trusted not to cheat on the buyers.

7 Cultural influences. Culture establishes the values, attitudes, customary behavior, language, religion and art of a given group of people. When dealing internationally, cultural influences come to the forefront: in the UK it might be customary to offer a visitor a cup of tea or coffee, whereas in China it might be customary to offer food. Dim Sum originated as a way for Chinese businessmen to offer their visitors a symbolic meal, as a way of establishing rapport. Beyond the national culture is the corporate culture, sometimes defined as 'the way we do things round here'. Corporate culture encompasses the strategic vision of the organization, its ethical stance and its attitudes towards suppliers among other things. In addition, many business people act in accordance with their professional culture as well (Terpstra & David 1991). Each of these will affect the way business is done.

Organizational factors derive from the corporate culture, as well as from the strategic decisions made by senior management within the firm. Organizational policies, procedures, structure, systems of rewards, authority, status and communication systems will all affect the ways buyers relate to sales-people. Figure 2.2 shows the main categories of organizational influences on the buyers' behavior.

Buying tasks differ greatly between firms, but may also differ significantly within firms. For example, the buying task for supermarkets clearly differs from that for manufacturing companies, since supermarkets intend to sell-on the vast majority of their purchases unchanged, whereas manufacturers are largely concerned with sourcing components and raw materials. Within this generalized structure supermarkets have other variations in the buying task: the buyers' approach to buying canned goods will be totally different from the approach used to buy fresh produce such as vegetables or fresh fish.

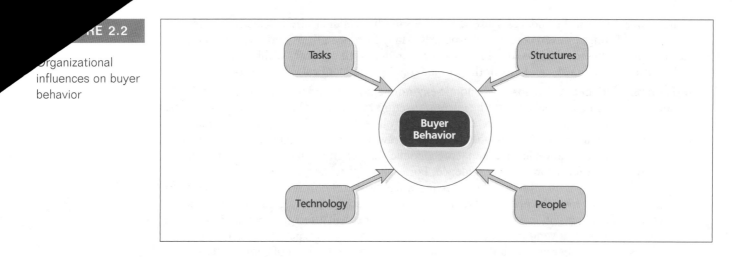

Equally, manufacturers will have a different approach when buying basic raw materials as opposed to buying components and a different approach again when buying lubricating oil or business services or new factory premises. The purchasing tasks will affect the buyers' thinking and negotiating approach, usually so seriously that firms will have separate buyers for each type of buying task.

Structure of the organization falls into two categories: the formal structure is what shows on the organization chart and the informal structure which is actually what dictates staff behavior in most cases. The informal structure is the network of social obligations, friendships and internal liaisons which influence day-to-day behavior. The formal organization structure determines such issues as the degree of centralization in purchasing decision-making, the degree to which buying decisions follow a formal procedure (i.e. how constrained by rules buyers are) and the degree of specialization in buying for different purposes or different departments in the organization. The informal structure dictates such issues as rivalry between buyers, 'brownie points', (recognition by management for jobs done well) cooperation between buyers in maintaining each other's status in the eyes of the boss, and so forth. The maze of informal relationships can be extremely complex, especially for salespeople observing from the outside, but often forms a key element in the success or failure of key-account selling. In the global context, the informal structure is subject to many cultural influences – the Oriental concern with gaining or losing face, for example, can be a crucial factor in doing business. The informal structure is also important in determining who will be the influencers in the decision-making unit; some colleagues' opinions may be regarded as more trustworthy than others, for example.

The technology within the organization may act to control or circumvent much of the buyers' role. For example, computer-controlled stock purchasing, particularly in a just-in-time purchasing environment, will prevent buyers from being able to negotiate deals and in many cases removes buyers from the process altogether. Models for inventory control and price forecasting are also widely used by buyers, so that in many cases the negotiating process is virtually automated with little room for maneuver on the part of buyers. In these circumstances the selling organization needs to go beyond the buyer to the other members of the DMU in order to work around the rules.

The characteristics of the people involved in the organization will, in part, determine the organization's culture, but will in any event control the interpretation of the rules under which purchasing departments operate. At senior management level, the character of the organization is likely to be a function of the senior management, and in many cases organizations' founders will have set their personality firmly on their organization's culture. Virgin is clearly an offshoot of Richard Branson's personality, as Bodyshop is an offshoot of Anita Roddick's.

We frequently hear about the global village, about the convergence of cultures and about a new world order in which we accept and understand each other's cultures. So why is it necessary to consider cultural issues when we are marketing products and services? Surely the goods speak for themselves – does crude oil have a cultural value, or does a stamp mill have a cultural connotation?

Shouldn't buyers be prepared to accept and understand cultural differences? Otherwise how are we to do business? Or perhaps buyers arrogantly believe that sellers should adapt their approach to meet the buyers' culture – thus possibly missing out on getting the best deals for their organizations.

If we get clashes between corporate cultures within the same country, how much worse will the clashes be in globalized markets?

◼ Classifying business customers

A business customer is one who is buying on behalf of an organization rather than buying for personal or family consumption. For the purposes of discussion, we usually talk about organizations as the purchasers of goods, but of course this is not the case: business customers, in practice, are human beings who buy on behalf of organizations.

Organizations might be classified according to the types of buying and end-use they have for the products. Table 2.1 shows the commonly accepted classifications.

Business and commercial organizations

Business and commercial organizations can be segmented as original equipment manufacturers (OEMs), users and aftermarket customers. OEMs buy foundation, entering and facilitating goods including machinery and equipment used to make products and which are incorporated directly into

TABLE 2.1 Classification of buying organizations

Type of organization	Description
Business and commercial organizations	These organizations buy goods, which are used to make other goods and those that are consumed in the course of running the organizations' businesses. These organizations buy foundation goods and services used to make other products, facilitating goods and services, which help organizations achieve their objectives and entering goods and services, which become part of another product.
Reseller organizations	Resellers buy goods in order to sell them on to other organizations or to final consumers. Typically, resellers will be wholesalers or retailers, but they may also be agents for services, for example travel agents or webmasters who act as facilitators for other firms.
Governmental organizations	Governments buy everything from paperclips to aircraft carriers through their various departments. Because national and local government departments operate under specific rules, a different approach from that for businesses is usually required.
Institutional organizations	Institutional organizations include charities, educational establishments, hospitals and other organizations that do not fit into the business, reseller or government categories. These organizations may buy any of the products but they are used to achieve institutional goals, usually to provide services.

the final product. For example, computer manufacturers may buy machine tools to make computer cases and also buy silicon chips from specialist producers: the chips are incorporated into the final product, but the same type of chip might be incorporated in computers from several different OEMs. The Intel Pentium chip is an example.

For OEM buyers, the key issue will be the quality of the products or services. Such buyers are usually operating to fairly exact specifications laid down by their own production engineers and designers: it is unlikely that the supplying firm will be able to do very much to have the specification changed. This means that introducing a new product to an OEM will be a lengthy process, since the supplying company will need to establish a long-term relationship with the customer in order to become involved at the design stage for the new products.

User customers buy products, which are used up within the organization, either as components in their own equipment or to make the equipment perform properly, for example lubricating oils or cleaning products. These products are not resold, but may be bought in considerable quantities. Obviously some of these are service products – accountancy or legal services, cleaning services, maintenance or building services are all contained within the firm and not resold.

Aftermarket customers are those involved in the maintaining, repairing and overhauling (MRO) of products after they have been sold. For example, in the elevator business, independent contractors not affiliated with the original manufacturer perform most MRO. These contractors buy the components, supplies and services they need wherever they can find them.

The classification split between OEM, users and aftermarket customers is only relevant to the supplier. OEMs can also be user customers for some suppliers. For example, a plastic molding company may sell components to an OEM and plastic tools to a user as well as plastic replacement parts to an aftermarket organization: in some cases these may even be the same organization. Buying motivations for each type of purchase are clearly very different.

Reseller organizations

The majority of manufactured goods are sold through reseller organizations such as retailers and wholesalers. Intermediaries provide useful services such as bulk breaking, assortment of goods and accumulation of associated product types: due to increased efficiencies resulting from these services, intermediaries tend to reduce overall prices for the final consumer. Cutting out the middleman usually reduces efficiency and tends to increase prices as a result; although there is a popular view that disintermediation reduces prices by cutting out the intermediaries' mark-ups.

Reseller organizations are driven almost entirely by their customers. This means that they will only buy products which they perceive to have a ready market: there is therefore a premium on employing buyers who have a clear understanding of marketing. Unlike the OEM buyers, there is little need for resellers to understand the technical aspects of the products they buy – they merely need to feel confident that the ultimate consumers will want the products.

Reseller organizations carry out the following basic functions:

1 Negotiate with suppliers.
2 Promotional activities such as advertising, sales promotion, providing a salesforce, etc.
3 Warehousing, storage and product handling.
4 Transportation of local and (occasionally) long-distance shipments.
5 Inventory control.
6 Credit checking and credit control.
7 Pricing and collection of price information, particularly about competitors.
8 Collection of market information about consumers and competitors.

For manufacturers, this places a premium on establishing close long-term relationships with resellers. Shared information, as part of an integrated channel management strategy, becomes crucial to forward planning.

Government organizations

Government and quasi-government organizations are major buyers of almost everything. In some markets the government is heavily involved in industry. For instance, all insurance in India has until recently been a government monopoly and the oil industry in Mexico is controlled by PEMEX, a quasi-government entity. Governments are thought to be the largest category of market in the world, if all levels of government are included in the equation. The structure of government varies from one country to another: for example, in Spain there is the national government based in Madrid, the regional governments (e.g. the Junta de Andalucia), the provincial governments (e.g. Provincia de Granada) and the local town halls (e.g. Ayuntamiento de Ugijar). Sometimes these local town halls group together to form an alliance which carries out mutually beneficial activities such as tourism marketing or funding a local swimming pool, but frequently they act independently of one another within the frameworks of their own jurisdictions.

Because of the strict rules under which most government organizations operate, special measures are often needed to negotiate deals. In particular, government organizations are characterized by the tendering system, in which firms are asked to bid for contracts, which are then usually offered to the lowest bidder. From a supplier's viewpoint, this can be seriously counterproductive since the lowest price is also likely to be the least profitable, so selling firms will often try to circumvent the process by ensuring that they become involved before the tender is finalized. In this way it is often possible to ensure that the tender is drawn up in a way that favors the proactive firm over its competitors, thus ensuring that competitors either do not bid at all, or bid at too high a price.

In some cases, governments need to purchase items which are not available to the general public or to other businesses. Military hardware is an obvious example: clearly ordinary businesses are not allowed to buy tanks or fighter planes. On a more subtle level, goods such as handguns are not permitted for private organizations in the UK, but can be sold to the Army or the police force. Some types of computer software are only appropriate for use by the tax authorities and academic research is, in general, paid for entirely by the government in the UK. From a marketing viewpoint, these specialist markets present an interesting challenge, since in some cases the products need to be tailored to a specific government or a specific government department. This may mean that there is considerable scope for negotiation, but since the contract might still have to go out to tender, the company may find that it has merely wasted time unless it can demonstrate that no other company can carry out the work.

In some circumstances, governments may issue a 'cost-plus' contract, in which the organization is given a specific task to carry out and bills according to the cost of the contract plus an agreed profit margin. In the early days of space research this type of contract was common, since it was impossible to predict what the costs might be when dealing with an unknown set of circumstances. More recently these contracts have fallen into disrepute since they reward inefficiency and waste.

Institutional organizations

Institutions include charities, universities, hospital trusts and non-profit organizations of all types, for instance schools and so forth. In some cases these are government owned but independent for purposes of purchasing and supply (for example, secondary schools), in other cases they are totally independent (for example registered charities). The traditional view of these organizations is that they are chronically underfunded and therefore do not represent a particularly munificent market, but in practice the organizations actually have a very substantial aggregate spending power.

Because budgets are almost always very tight, the marketing organization may need to be creative in helping the institution to raise the money to buy. For example, a firm which produces drilling equipment may find that it has a substantial market at Oxfam, since Oxfam drills wells in many arid regions of the Third World. However, since Oxfam relies on public generosity to raise the money to buy the equipment, the manufacturer may find it necessary to part-fund, or even manage a fundraising campaign, in order to make the sale.

Suppliers are often asked to contribute to charities, in cash or in products. This may not always be possible, since the supplier's only market might be the charities, but in some cases firms may find it worthwhile to supply free products to charities in order to gain PR value, or sometimes in order to open the door to lucrative deals with other organizations. For example, a Third World charity might be prepared to field-test equipment which could then be sold to a government department in the same country.

We are often told that marketing is about managing the exchange process, yet government departments and many institutions seem to lay down the ground rules from the start. Marketers have to play by the buyer's rules to be in the game at all – so how can they possibly be managing the process? Pushed from one set of constraints to the next, it would seem that the average marketer is just a pawn in the buyer's hands!

Yet maybe that is how it should be, if customers are at the center of everything we do. Not to mention that the management process itself could be construed as a clearing-house for pressures rather than as a directive force – in a sense, no manager is actually in control, so why should marketers be any different?

Buyers' techniques

Buyers use a wide variety of techniques according to the buying situation they are faced with. The buying situations are generally divided into three types:

1 *Straight rebuy*. This is a situation where the buyer is buying the same product in similar quantities from the same supplier. For example, an engineering company might buy the same quantity of components from its suppliers each month. In these circumstances the buyer needs no new information and does not need to engage in much negotiation either. Prudent buyers may occasionally look at other possible sources of components in order to ensure that no new technology is available or that other suppliers are not able to supply the same components cheaper, but in general, the order placement is automatic. In many cases the buyer establishes an electronic data interchange (EDI) link with a supplier or establishes automatic buying procedures through the Internet and orders are handled without any human interface. If the product is of minor importance, or represents a low commitment in terms of finance or risk, the buyer will not undertake any information search and will probably simply order the goods. This is called causal purchasing, because it results automatically from a cause such as low stock levels. For example, a buyer for a large engineering firm probably spends very little time deciding on brands of paper for the photocopier. On the other hand, buying copper cable might be a routine purchase, but the buyer might occasionally monitor the market for alternatives. Such buying is called routine low-priority buying because it has a lower priority than would be the case if an entirely new situation were being faced. The company is unlikely to get into serious trouble if it pays 10 per cent more than it should for cable, for example.

2 *Modified rebuy*. In this situation, the buyer re-evaluates the habitual buying patterns of the firm with a view to changing them in some way. The quantities ordered, or the specification of the components, may be changed. Even the supplier may be changed. Sometimes these changes come about as a result of environmental scanning, in which the buyer has become aware of a better alternative than the one currently employed, or sometimes the changes come about because of marketing activities by the current suppliers' competitors. Internal forces (increases or decreases in demand for components) might trigger a renegotiation with suppliers or a search for new suppliers. In any event, the buyer is faced with a limited problem-solving scenario in which some negotiation needs to be carried out with existing or new suppliers and new information will probably need to be sought out as well. In a modified rebuy situation a buyer may well require potential suppliers to bid against each other for the business: the drawback of this approach, however, is that it often results in damaging the relationship with existing suppliers that may have been built up over many years.

3 *New task*. This type of buying situation comes about when the task is perceived as being entirely new. Past experience is therefore no guide and present suppliers may not be able to help either. Thus the buyer is faced with a complex decision process. Judgmental new task situations are those in which the buyer must deal with technical complexities of the product,

complex evaluation of alternatives, and negotiating with new suppliers. Strategic new task situations are those in which the final decision is of strategic importance to the firm – for example, an insurance company in the market for new record-keeping software will be investing (potentially) hundreds of thousands of dollars in retraining staff and in transferring existing records, not to mention the risks of buying software which is unable to cope with the tasks it is required to carry out. In these circumstances, long-range planning at director level drives the buying process and the relationship with suppliers is likely to be both long-term and close.

From the viewpoint of the business marketer, the main chance of winning new customers will come in the new-task situation. The risks for buyers involved in switching suppliers are often too great unless there is a very real and clear advantage in doing so: such an advantage is likely to be difficult to prove in practice. In the new-task situation, potential suppliers may well find themselves screened out early in the process and will then find it almost impossible to be reconsidered later.

The buygrid framework

Organizational buying can be seen as a series of decisions, each of which leads to a further problem about which a decision must be made (Cardozo 1983). From the viewpoint of the business marketer, it is possible to diagnose problems by examining the sequence of decisions – provided, of course, the decision sequence is known to the marketer. Marketers can identify the stage at which the firm is currently making decisions and can tailor the approach accordingly.

The industrial buying process can be mapped against a grid, as shown in Figure 2.3.

The most complex buying situations occur in the upper left portion of the framework and involve the largest number of decision makers and buying influences. This is because new tasks require the greatest amount of effort in seeking information and formulating appropriate solutions, but will also require the greatest involvement of individuals at all levels of the organization, each with their own agenda.

The buygrid framework has been widely criticized, however. Like most models it tends to over-simplify the case. As in consumer decision-making, the sequence may not be as clear-cut and events may take place in a different order in certain circumstances. For example, a supplier might approach a firm with a solution for a problem which it didn't know it had, thus cutting out several stages of the process: the firm may well recognize the need and the problem, but will probably not

Stage	Buying Situations		
	New task	Modified Rebuy	Straight Rebuy
Anticipation or recognition of a problem (need) and a general solution			
Determination of characteristics and quantity of needed item			
Description of characteristics and quantity of needed item			
Search for and qualification of potential sources			
Acquisition and analysis of proposals			
Evaluation of proposals and selection of supplier(s)			
Selection of an order routine			
Performance feedback and evaluation			

FIGURE 2.3

The buygrid framework

Adapted from the Marketing Science Institute Series, *Industrial Buying and Creative Marketing*, by Patrick J. Robinson, Charles W. Faris, and Yoram Wind. Copyright 1967 by Allyn and Bacon, Inc. Boston.

need to acquire proposals and select a supplier since the supplier is already on board with a solution. Secondly, suppliers go to great lengths to differentiate themselves from competitors as effectively as they can, so that the buyer may not have any other potential suppliers of the exact product on offer. Thirdly, the model assumes a rational approach to purchasing which is often simply not there. Finally, the boundaries between new task, modified rebuy and straight rebuy are by no means clear-cut.

Because buyers are influenced by both rational and emotional considerations, the potential supplier needs to be aware of the buying motives of each member of the decision-making unit. What is more, each member of the DMU will apply different criteria for judging which suppliers should be included and which excluded (Kelly and Coaker 1976): the finance director might emphasize low prices, whereas the chief designer might be concerned with product quality and the production engineer with reliable delivery. The buyer might be concerned with the relationship with the supplier's salespeople.

In the case of key-account management, this problem of dealing with different members of the DMU is often overcome by taking a team approach to the sale. While the key-account manager handles the initial contact and the management of the process, other specialists are brought in to deal with financial aspects, technical aspects and so forth. In this way each member of the DMU is speaking to someone with the same common language and a common understanding of the conceptual environment within which each specialty operates. In some cases the number of people working on the account can become large: when IBM were dealing with Lloyd's Bank (one of the Big Four UK banks) they had over 100 people working on the account and set up a special branch office in the Canary Wharf area to be near Lloyd's head office.

Value analysis

Value analysis is a method of evaluating components, raw materials and even manufacturing processes in order to determine ways of cutting costs or improving finished products. Value-in-use is defined as a product's economic value to the user relative to a specific alternative in a particular application (Kijewski and Yoon 1990). Value-in-use is the price that would equalize the overall costs and benefits of using one product rather than using another.

For example, consider long-life light bulbs. These bulbs are usually between five and ten times as expensive as ordinary tungsten-filament bulbs to buy, but last five times as long and use only 20 per cent of the electricity. For a domestic consumer, this represents a considerable saving, more than enough to cover the initial outlay for the bulbs, but for a business customer the saving is even greater, since the cost of paying someone to replace the bulbs is significant. Assuming the life of a tungsten-filament bulb as being 1000 hours on average, compared with 5000 hours for a long-life bulb, the calculation would run as shown in Table 2.2.

Using this calculation, the company can make an immediate saving of just under £700 a year by switching to long-life bulbs. In fact, the capital cost of changing all the bulbs in the building would be recovered in the first year, although in practice the firm would probably only replace the tungsten-filament bulbs as they fail in use: in this way the labor cost of replacing the bulbs would be no higher than normal.

TABLE 2.2 Long-life bulb vs tungsten-filament bulb

1 *Annual cost of existing product:*	
250 replacement light bulbs × 45p	£112.50
Cost of electricity: @ 6.7p per kilowatt × 60 watts × 150 bulbs:	£603.00
Cost of replacing bulbs assuming 10 minutes per bulb @ £10 per hour:	£416.00
TOTAL COST PER ANNUM:	**£1131.50**
2 *Cost of using long-life bulbs:*	
50 replacement bulbs per annum × £5 =	£250.00
Cost of electricity @ 6.7p per kilowatt × 11 watts × 150 bulbs =	£110.50
Cost of replacing bulbs assuming 10 minutes per bulb @ £10 per hour =	£83.20
TOTAL COST PER ANNUM:	**£443.70**

Because some buyers do use this type of calculation to assess alternative solutions to existing problems, the astute marketer will be prepared with the full arguments in favor of the new solution, including all the relevant factors, which make the product more attractive. On the other side of the coin, astute purchasers will involve potential suppliers in the discussions and in the value analysis process (Dowst and Raia 1990).

Evaluating supplier capability

Purchasers also need to assess the capability of potential suppliers to continue to supply successfully. This is a combination of assessing financial stability, technical expertise, reliability, quality assurance processes and production capacity. In simple terms, the purchasing company is trying to ensure that the potential supplier will be in a position to keep the promises it makes.

Table 2.3 Illustrates some of the ways in which buyers can assess potential suppliers.

While these methods are better than nothing, in most cases they rely on judgment on the part of the purchaser, who may not in fact have the necessary expertise to understand what the supplier's capability really is.

TALKING POINT

The methods of assessment shown in the table all rely on some kind of judgment on the part of the buyer. Even the financial figures filed at the company record office require interpretation – and may even have been 'massaged' to make the company look more financially viable than it actually is.

So why bother with what is, after all, a somewhat time consuming exercise? Presumably a rogue supplier would have little difficulty in pulling the wool over the eyes of a buyer who probably lacks the engineering training to understand what is in front of him or her. On the other hand, an honest supplier would probably provide the 'warts and all' picture that might well lose the contract. Maybe buyers would be better advised to go for the supplier who looks the worst – at least we know they are being honest with us!

Evaluating supplier performance

Even after the contract is awarded, the purchasing company is likely to periodically need to review the supplier's performance. In some cases, suppliers have been known to relax once the contract is awarded and of course the circumstances of the buying organization are likely to change considerably in the course of what will be a lengthy relationship.

The basic evaluation methods are as outlined in Table 2.4.

TABLE 2.3 Assessing suppliers

Attribute	Assessment method
Technical capability	Visit the supplier to examine production equipment, inspect quality control procedures and meet the engineering staff.
Managerial capability	Discuss systems for controlling processes, meet the managerial staff and become involved in planning and scheduling supplies.
Financial stability	Check the accounts filed at Companies House or other public record office, run a credit check, examine annual reports if any.
Capacity to deliver	Ascertain the status of other customers of the supplier – would any of these take priority? Assess the production capacity of the supplier, warehouse stocks of the product, reputation in the industry.

TABLE 2.4 Evaluation approaches

Approach	Explanation
Categorical plan	Each department having contact with the supplier is asked to provide a regular rating of suppliers against a list of salient performance factors. This method is extremely subjective, but is easy to administer.
Weighted-point plan	Performance factors are graded according to their importance to the organization: for example, delivery reliability might be more important for some organizations than for others. The supplier's total rating can be calculated and the supplier's offering can be adjusted if necessary to meet the purchasing organization's needs.
Cost-ratio plan	Here the buying organization evaluates quality, delivery and service in terms of what each one costs. Good performance is assigned a negative score, i.e. the costs of purchase are reduced by good performance: poor performance is assigned a positive score, meaning that the costs are deemed to be greater when dealing with a poor performer.

All these methods involve some degree of subjectivity, in other words each method requires buyers to make judgments about the supplier. The fact that the outcomes are expressed in numbers gives each method a spurious credibility: those involved in evaluation exercises of this nature should be aware that the evaluation exercise itself should be evaluated periodically and the criteria used by the various individuals involved needs to be checked.

TALKING POINT

Much of the emphasis in the preceding sections has been on the purchaser's evaluation of suppliers. But what about the other way round? Customers are not always plaster saints – some are late payers, some impose unreasonable restrictions, some reject supplies for the flimsiest of reasons and some are just plain unpleasant to deal with.

So should suppliers have their own systems for assessing purchasers? Should we just grovel at the feet of any organization willing to buy our goods – or should we stand up and be counted? After all, without supplies no company can survive – so presumably we are equally important to one another.

Maybe this is really the purpose of segmenting our markets – and what is really meant by segmentation.

SUMMARY

Buyers have a large number of influences on their decision-making. At the very least, buyers have their own personal agendas within the companies they work for: in the broader context, a wide range of political, environmental and technological issues will affect their decision-making. The end result is likely to be a combination of experience, careful calculation and gut feeling.

The key points from this chapter are as follows:

- Buyers are subject to many pressures other than the simple commercial ones: emotions, organizational influence, politics and internal structures are also important factors.

- The decision-making unit (DMU) or buying center is the group of people who will make the buying decision. Roles and composition of DMUs vary widely.

- Business and commercial organizations are likely to be swayed most by past experience with a vendor, product characteristics and quality.

- Resellers are driven by their customers.

- Government markets are large and almost always use a tendering system.

- Institutional markets may need special techniques to help them afford to buy the products.

- Markets can be divided into those buyers who buy products designed to make other products or who will incorporate the purchase into their own products (original equipment manufacturers, OEMs); those who consume the product in the course of running their businesses (user markets); or those who serve the aftermarket.

- A purchase may be a straight rebuy, a modified rebuy, or a new task. These are given in order of increasing complexity and do not have discrete boundaries.

- A team approach to buying usually dictates a team approach to selling.

REVIEW QUESTIONS

1 How would you expect a government department to go about buying a new computer system?
2 How might internal politics affect a buyer's behavior?
3 What factors might be prominent in the buying decision for cleaning materials?
4 What factors might a supplier take into account when evaluating a purchasing company?
5 How might the directors of a company go about setting standards for evaluating suppliers? What objective criteria are available?

SPOTLIGHT ON B2B MARKETING

In January 2003 the UK Government announced that the £2.8bn contract to build two new aircraft carriers for the Royal Navy would be split between British company BAE Systems and Thales, its French arch-rival. When maintenance work and upgrades are considered, the deal is worth approximately £9.2bn over the lifetime of the vessels.

Celebrations were, however, somewhat muted at BAE. The company will be getting two-thirds of the business, but will (under the terms of the deal) have to build the ships to Thales' designs. In other words, BAE are taking the lion's share of the risk, since they will be responsible for any cost overruns and design corrections, but will not have the power to vary the designs. Even though the UK taxpayer will pick up 10 per cent of cost overruns, this still leaves BAE vulnerable in some respects. The situation is worsened by the fact that the companies who were involved in the bidding process were told that the outcome would be a 'winner takes all' contract. On the other hand, BAE may be lucky to have been offered anything at all. In December 2002 the company's shares dropped dramatically after it announced cost overruns on other Ministry of Defence deals, then on January 15th Geoff Hoon, the Defence Secretary, announced that he thought BAE was 'no longer British'. Then as late as January 21st the national organizer of the Transport and General Worker's Union, Jack Dromey, revealed that senior civil servants were recommending that the contract should be awarded to Thales in its entirety.

Final details need to be worked out, and it is fairly certain that BAE will be pressing for a better deal on the overruns, since the company is already in dispute with the Ministry of Defence about cost overruns of up to £1bn on the Nimrod aircraft and Astute submarine deals. Industry reaction to the deal was one of astonishment – one senior defence executive said 'Thales won this on design and price, but BAE got the prime contractor role because of politics'.

The political issues are by no means simple. Under European Union rules, contractors throughout the EU must be given the opportunity to bid on government contracts within any of the Member States – in other words, national governments are not allowed to play favorites by awarding contracts to their own suppliers. The problem is that this law is more honored in the breach than in the observance – although Thales have apparently come in with a lower price and a better design, it would be impossible for a UK government to award the contract entirely to the French, knowing that there is no possibility of the French allowing British companies to compete on an equal footing in France.

Defence secretary Geoff Hoon dismissed such allegations as being, 'the kind of anti-European, anti-French rhetoric that's come to characterize the modern Conservative party. . . It's a disgrace'. Meanwhile Lord Bach, the procurement minister, and Sir Robert Walmsley, chief of defence procurement, were examining the extent to which the taxpayer would carry the risk in terms of cost overruns. Government policy has been to move these risks away from the taxpayer and towards the contractor, but of course the higher the risk the contractor is expected to take, the higher the overall cost of the contract, so the government will almost certainly need to compromise.

City analysts believe that the contract represents a Pyrrhic victory for BAE. Although the contract will contribute £30m to annual profits, this is a relatively small amount of money – the total contract only represents 2 per cent of sales for BAE. In exchange for this, the company has given Thales a stronger foothold in the UK, building on its acquisitions of defense companies such as Racal, Pilkington Optronics and Shorts Missile Systems. Some City analysts believe that BAE would have been better off if the company had lost the prime contract to Thales and had instead concentrated on low-risk subcontracting work at its shipyards.

Meanwhile, the Royal Navy eagerly awaits delivery of the ships. Captain Simon Williams, assistant director of strategy at the naval staff, says that the current carrier fleet is designed primarily for protecting the Navy from attacks while at sea. The new carriers will have the capability to attack shore installations. 'If you put one of these carriers in international waters off another country it becomes a very flexible tool and it focuses the mind of the people we are trying to influence', he said. The ships will be equipped with the new F–35 fighters, the replacement for the Harrier Jump-jet, now nearing the end of its useful service life.

Whatever the outcome, the Unions are pleased. Bill Morris, general secretary of the Transport and General Workers' Union, said, 'I believe our quality British workforce will deliver a quality British product. The challenge is now for BAE Systems to deliver on time and on budget'.

Questions

1 How has the political environment affected the purchasing process?

2 Who were the influencers, deciders, buyers, gatekeepers and users in the DMU?

3 What effect does the UK government's previous experience of the suppliers have?

4 If the potential profits on the deal are so low, why would BAE be interested in bidding for the contract?

5 What effects might the deal have on the long-term relationship between BAE and Thales?

REFERENCES

Cardozo, R. N. (1983) 'Modelling organisational buying as a sequence of decisions', *Industrial Marketing Management* 12 Feb: 75.

Dowst, S. and Raia, E. (1990) 'Teaming up for the 90s', *Purchasing* 108, Feb: 54–59.

Hawes, J. M. and Barnhouse, S.H. (1987) 'How purchasing agents handle personal risk', *Industrial Marketing Management* 16 Nov: 287–93.

Kelly, P. and Coaker, J. W. (1976) 'Can we generalise about choice criteria for industrial purchasing decisions?', In K. L. Bernhardt (ed.) *Marketing 1776–1976 and Beyond,* Chicago: American Marketing Association: 330–33.

Kijewski, V. and Yoon, E. (1990) 'Market-based pricing: beyond price-performance curves', *Industrial Marketing Management* 19 Feb: 11–19.

Ronchetto, John R., Jr., Hutt, Michael D. and Reingen, Peter H. (1989) 'Embedded Influence Patterns in Organizational Buying Systems', *Journal of Marketing* 53: 4: 51–62.

Terpstra, V. and David, K. (1991) *The Cultural Environment of International Business*, Cincinnati, OH: South-Western Publishing Company.

Webster, F. E. and Wind, Y. (1972) *Organisational Buying Behaviour*, Englewood Cliffs, NJ: Prentice Hall.

3

STRATEGIC PLANNING FOR GLOBAL BUSINESS MARKETS

Learning objectives

After reading this chapter, you should be able to:

- Explain the main dimensions of strategy as they apply in B2B markets
- Describe how strategy is developed
- Explain the importance of the planning process
- Explain the relationship between strategy and tactics
- Describe ways of maintaining competitive advantage in a global economy

■ Introduction

Strategy is concerned with moving the organization from where it is now to where we would like it to be. It is the business process concerned with planning the long-range activities, character and underlying values of the organization.

Strategy differs from tactics in that strategic decisions are far more difficult to reverse, they usually involve the decision-makers in rejecting other options and they tend to dictate the long-term nature of the organization as well as its activities.

■ Strategic planning process

Strategic planning starts with the firm's full understanding of the business it participates in. No better approach has been developed than that offered by Peter Drucker (1973). Drucker advised businesses to ask three basic questions:

- What is our business?
  - Who is the customer?
  - What is value to the customer?
- What will our business be?
- What should our business be?

Asking 'what is our business?' is the way to get to the firm's vision and business mission and two of the most important questions in determining the answer to that first question are 'who is the customer?', and 'what is value to the customer?'. These we have shown in later steps of the strategic planning process (choice of segments). Answering the question 'what will our business be?' means to project the current trends and business practices into the future with no change – how will the business look if it keeps operating the same way for years into the future? The third question is where strategic planning really takes place. In this case, management thinks about what the business should look like and what changes need to be made so that the business will be addressing the proper markets with the proper products and services at a future time.

Figure 3.1 shows an overview of the strategic planning process

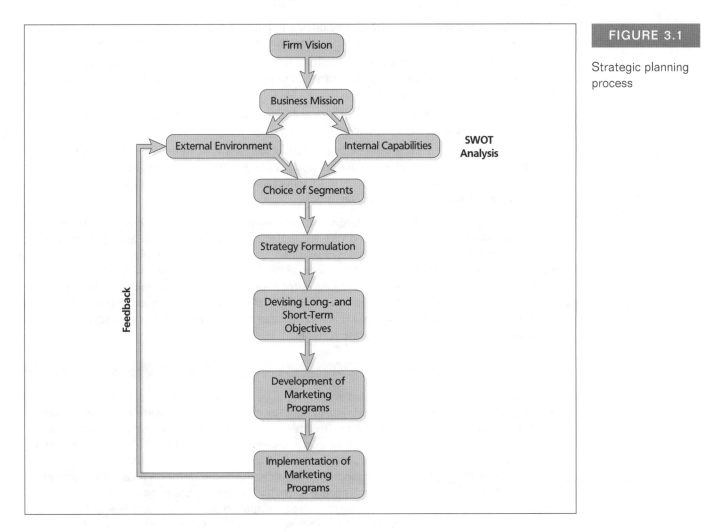

FIGURE 3.1

Strategic planning process

Mission, vision and objectives

All organizations need to coordinate the attitudes and activities of staff. In order to do this, most firms try to develop a corporate culture in which the overall strategic direction of the organization is the driving force. This strategic direction is most often communicated via a corporate vision, a corporate mission and corporate objectives. Some firms have only one of these: some have all of them. In other words, they are not mutually exclusive.

The corporate mission is the over-riding reason for the organization's existence. It is the purpose of the organization. The mission statement is the formal document which outlines the reasons for the organization's existence, but frequently it is no more than a set of corporate platitudes which do little to inform staff, customers and other stakeholders of what the organization is about.

A corporate mission statement has five characteristics (Ackoff 1986):

1 It contains a formulation of objectives that enables progress towards them to be measured.

2 It differentiates the company from its competitors.

3 It defines the businesses that the company wants to be in, not necessarily the ones it is already in.

4 It is relevant to the stakeholders in the organization, not just to shareholders and managers.

5 It is exciting and inspiring.

Mission statements must reflect corporate values in order to be of use in coordinating corporate activities (Campbell 1989). Campbell goes on to argue that there are four key issues involved in developing a useful mission:

1 Clarification of the purpose of the organization. Is it the organization's purpose to maximize shareholder value – or is the purpose to (for example) develop a worldwide network?

2 Description of the business and its activities and the position it wants to occupy in its field. For example, the business might want to 'offer supreme value for money' or 'be the industry leader in quality engineering'.

3 Statement of the corporate values. This would include the company's intentions towards its employees, customers and suppliers.

4 Organizational behavior should be controlled in such a way as to match with the mission statement. If this is not the case, the mission becomes mere empty rhetoric – it would be better to amend the mission statement to reflect actual behavior than to have a mission statement which does not match outcomes.

Examples of good or poor mission statements are easy to find. David and David (2003) found that a majority of the 95 firms they studied did not address several of the nine essential components required of a mission statement. As shown in Figure 3.2, IBM's mission statement meets some of the requirements described by Ackoff and Campbell while that of a UK firm seems not to.

Mission statements have become an essential part of corporate life in the past 20 years or so. Banks expect companies to have mission statements, staff are often asked to explain how their activities relate to the corporate mission and mission statements are often found in corporate end of year statements as a justification for corporate activities.

TALKING POINT

'If we don't know where we're going, any road will do to take us there.' This well-known saying implies that knowing where we want to be allows us to choose a route – yet the analogy with road transport is not a good one. Business life is infinitely more complex than driving between cities: the cities do at least stay in the same places relative to each other and the roads do not suddenly turn to marshmallow or get taken over by competitors.

So is there really any point in spending much time putting together a mission statement? Can we realistically set out a corporate direction years in advance? If we make the statement less rigid and therefore much more vague, does it have any value? Striking this balance may be the hardest part of producing a mission statement!

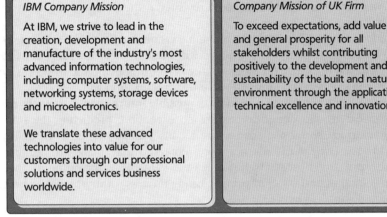

FIGURE 3.2

Comparing mission statements

Vision is the management's view of what the organization should be. Often the vision comes from the founder of the organization: charismatic individuals such as Anita Roddick of Body Shop, Richard Branson of Virgin and Sam Walton of Wal-Mart have imprinted their personalities on the companies they founded. Everyone within those companies shares the corporate vision, at least in some degree, and understands the intended 'personality' of the organization – it is not necessary to produce a vision statement, although many firms do this.

The lack of a vision statement does not mean that there is no vision. The characteristics of an organization can be very clear to its members without having anything at all in writing. One of the difficulties faced by a company led by a visionary such as Roddick or Branson is that there is a lack of continuity. If the founder leaves, retires or dies the company can easily lose its way.

Planning

Going through this process requires looking at both the external environment and the internal capabilities of the firm and performing a SWOT Analysis (strengths, weaknesses, opportunities, threats). The environment must be examined for opportunities and threats while the firm's internal capabilities are looked at for strengths and weaknesses. Here, managers must be entirely honest with themselves so the company's true capabilities can be assessed. The next most important step is the choice of market segments which is covered in depth in Chapter 5. This step is the most important strategic step a manager can take. Then comes strategy formulation, developing objectives, marketing programs and implementation. A feedback loop must be established so that results can be compared with plans throughout the process.

Objectives are about where the company wants to be. An objective needs to be measurable and specific, however: many corporate objectives are couched in vague terms, perhaps talking about 'providing products of the highest quality'. This is not measurable, since it is impossible to say what is the highest quality – judgment of this will differ from one person to another. In other words, there is a difference between an aim (which is a general direction and is not measurable) and an objective, which is a destination point and is therefore measurable.

Long-term objectives relate to the desired performance and results on an on-going basis: short-term objectives relate to the near-term performance targets that the organization desires to reach in progressing towards its long-term objectives (Thompson and Strickland 1980). Some firms use management by objectives as a way of controlling and directing activities of staff members, but this can lead to a lack of initiative: what is not measured is not managed and is therefore not done.

The main advantage of setting objectives is that the organization has a clear direction and also a clear coordinating mechanism. Everyone in the organization either knows what they should be doing to achieve the objective, or can work out what they need to do when faced with new circumstances. The major drawbacks of objectives are firstly, that achieving the immediate objective becomes paramount, at the cost of responding to environmental changes or to the overall direction of the firm and secondly, the difficulty of finding a new direction once the objective has been achieved. For example, if a firm has the objective of 'becoming the world's largest supplier of ball bearings' written into its mission statement, the statement would have to be revisited if the firm actually becomes the world's largest supplier of ball bearings.

Strategy formulation involves three strands: planning, vision and emergent strategies (incremental changes to the pre-determined plan). The strategy will need to steer a course consistent with the environment within which it operates, the values of the organization and the firm's resources (EVR). The closer this EVR congruence, the more effective the organization will be.

Planning is the process of formulating responses to possible future events. Virtually everyone plans to a greater or lesser extent and organizations are no exception: predicting the future, however, occurs with varying accuracy, so most plans require a considerable degree of flexibility in order to work successfully. In fact, Dwight Eisenhower once remarked that 'plans are nothing, planning is everything'. In other words, the process itself is at least as valuable as the output of that process.

Plans can be considered as part of an ongoing learning process within the organization (Idenburg 1993). It is possible to distinguish between:

1　Formal planning systems, through which clear objectives should lead to intended strategies. These systems are best suited to industries where change is slow and the environment is stable.

2　Learning or real-time planning, which represents a formal approach to adaptive strategy creation. Regular meetings between managers will occur, in which new responses to environmental changes will be discussed and new strategies formulated.

3　Incremental change and logical incrementalism. The organization operates within a clear mission, but with the recognition that there is a need for flexibility. Managers are encouraged to experiment.

4　Emergent strategies, in which the organization in effect 'muddles through' by reacting to environmental changes as they occur. This mode apparently involves little or no planning, but in fact the organization which follows this approach will have structures in place for coping. For example, an organization which exists in a turbulent environment in which rapid change is endemic is likely to adopt an organismic organization structure, is likely to have recruitment and training policies which allow for rapid shifts in personnel tasks, is likely to have administrative systems which are flexible and is likely to have enhanced systems for monitoring the environment. Such organizations are therefore not as disorganized as they may at first appear.

Planning within a global environment is, of course, extremely complex due to the near impossibility of monitoring every aspect of the global environment. Virtually all firms operate in a global context, even those which do not intend to operate outside their own national borders – unless the firm's home country operates in a protectionist manner, the firm is open to competitors entering the market from overseas. This can easily upset the most carefully laid plans, since the EVR congruence will be lacking in circumstances where the environment has undergone a sudden shift.

TALKING POINT

It seems as if planning ahead is so difficult it is hardly worth bothering. The world is changing so fast, we can hardly keep pace – so why bother? Why not just take each day as it comes? After all, we can't predict the future – or can we?

Yet many things remain the same. Firms still need the same raw materials as they have for the past hundred years, they still need to produce things and sell things: even in fast changing areas such as electronics the principles of physics on which circuitry works has not changed. Anybody who reads science fiction could have predicted the cellular telephone (from 1951) the communications satellite (1947) and the rise of conservationism (1950). Maybe what we should be doing is planning around the near certainties and letting the uncertainties take care of themselves!

■ Value-chain analysis

Organizations operate by adding value to their inputs in order to create wealth. The outputs of a firm should be more valuable than the inputs, or there is really no point in carrying out the activities and equally there is unlikely to be much chance for the firm to survive in the long run. This applies equally to non-profit organizations and even governments: a government which does not spend tax money in such a way as to improve the lives of its electorate is quickly voted out of office. Likewise a charity which does not contribute anything worthwhile to the community will find that its contributions from the public rapidly dry up.

Value creation will only happen if the suppliers, producers, wholesalers, retailers and indeed everyone involved in moving from raw materials extraction through to consumers, can cooperate in an effective manner. Along the way the basic raw materials acquire market values much greater than their original cost: crude oil extracted for US$25 a barrel becomes plastic items worth 50 or 100 times as much, for example. Negotiation is the mechanism by which this wealth is divided among the various organizations involved.

The implications of this are as follows:

1 Value creation requires cooperation from all the members of the chain. Whether this comes about through negotiated coordination of activities or through market forces does not matter: the organizations rely on each other either way.

2 Those in the chain must consider the needs of other chain members if the process is to work to mutual advantage.

3 Cost improvement and efficiency improvements will benefit everyone in the chain in the long run, but most especially will benefit the individual member because there is no need to renegotiate with other members in order to reap the benefits.

4 There is therefore a premium on managing the value-chain within the firm itself.

5 There is a fundamental reliance on the contribution of people.

Within the firm, the basic structure of the value-chain is as shown in Table 3.1 (Porter 1985).

Each of the activities in the value chain might lead to competitive advantage. In some firms, it is only the marketing that really distinguishes the product: for example, lubricating oil is produced to standards laid down by engine manufacturers, so a trucking company will need to buy oil of a specific standard. All the oil companies supply oil to the same standard, so the only real difference is going to lie in the marketing of the product. In other firms, the reliability of the outbound logistics might be the deciding factor for customers (especially if the customer operates a just-in-time production system).

The value-chain is supported by four activities, as follows:

1 *Procurement*. This is the function of acquiring the inputs used in the value chain and applies to inputs used at any stage. In other words, procurement is not only connected with the inbound raw materials or components: it is also concerned with anything used in the course of providing marketing inputs, servicing inputs, or materials used for outbound logistics.

2 *Human resource management*. This is the function of recruiting, training and rewarding staff members in the organization.

3 *Technology development*. This includes know-how, research and development, product design and process improvement work.

4 *Infrastructure*. This includes the working spaces (factories, offices, mines, etc.), the organizational structure of the firm, the financial and operational control systems and the feedback systems used by management.

From a marketer's viewpoint, one of the problems with the value-chain concept is that it relegates marketing to a functional position. Obviously marketing has a function, but marketers believe that marketing should be the pervading philosophy of the successful firm, rather than simply a subsidiary function. For a marketer, marketing is everything the firm does, from inbound logistics right through to after-sales service.

TABLE 3.1 Value-chain

Primary activity	Explanation and examples
Inbound logistics	Inbound logistics is the study of movement of factors of production. For example, a manufacturer of outboard motors needs to ensure that stocks of component parts are always on hand. A failure to have sufficient carburetors in stock means that production would cease, even if pistons, propellers, cylinder blocks, gears and everything else needed were ready at hand.
Operations	These are the processes which convert inputs into finished products. For the outboard motor manufacturer, this would mean machining raw castings, manufacturing engine covers, painting, assembling motors, testing the finished motors, packaging the products.
Outbound logistics	Outbound logistics is concerned with the movement of finished products. It involves the shipping of products in a timely manner to customers in order to meet their needs: in the case of the outboard motor company, this means ensuring that boat builders are supplied on time, since they are in turn unable to complete the boat unless they have the motors. It also means ensuring that boat chandlers and repair yards have supplies of replacement motors as necessary.
Marketing and sales	These activities ensure that customers are aware of the products and favor them over competitors' products. For the outboard motor manufacturer this falls into two phases: firstly, the company needs to persuade boat builders, repair yards and the like that their motors are best, but also they need to persuade the final consumer, the boat owner, of the same thing. In a sense this is part of the same process: boat builders are unlikely to specify a motor that boat owners have never heard of or distrust.
Service	After-sales activities for an outboard motor manufacturer would include supplying spare parts as necessary (and preferably promptly), warranty work on failed motors, training of service engineers at boat repair yards and helplines for boat owners.

Value networks

The concept of the value-chain has a close relationship with supply chain analysis, with the addition of the support functions within the firm. Unfortunately, the dynamic nature of 21st century markets means that supply chains are constantly breaking or changing their natures so that supply chain and value-chain analysis is insufficient to describe the complex relationships that exist between firms in a given market. The implications of partnerships, strategic alliances and relationship marketing need to be considered as well.

Value-chain analysis implies a linear process, ignoring inputs from outside the chain – many firms may input into the process at various stages. The reality is therefore that the value-chain becomes a value network, a group of interrelated entities which contribute to the overall creation of value through a series of complex relationships.

For a firm in a global market, this means that many relationships in many different countries need to be considered. The value network may be different for each major customer – for example, an international construction company such as Taylor Woodrow may form alliances with many other companies in order to carry out a major construction project. Perhaps the best example of this is the Channel Tunnel Project, in which Taylor Woodrow, Costain, Wimpey, Balfour Beatty and Tarmac joined together with five French construction companies (Bouygues, Dumez, Spie Batignolles, Societe Auxiliaire D'Entreprises and Societe Generale D'Entreprises) to form Transmanche Link. Eurotunnel was, and still is, the largest construction project in history and involved many hundreds of companies in a complex network of responsibilities, each having to make its own contribution at the right time and in the right way. Each of the companies involved in the Transmanche Link consortium also had other construction projects in process: for example, Wimpey was at the time

Britain's biggest house builder and also owned Morrison Homes, the United States' biggest house builder.

Smart firms know when to compete and when to collaborate. Marketing alliances of all kinds have been developed to serve customers. These may focus on product or service, promotion, logistics or joint pricing (Kotler 2003).

Competitive advantage

The purpose of almost any strategy is to create competitive advantage. Porter (1985) identified three basic competitive positioning strategies which are shown below as Figure 3.3.

1   *Cost leadership.* In this strategy, the company minimizes its production, distribution and/or marketing costs so that it can compete on price without sacrificing profits. The low cost approach may be aimed at the entire industry across the world or to a particular segment (either global or local). This means sourcing factors of production from the cheapest possible sources, which may mean moving production to developing countries in order to save costs, or moving production closer to the markets the company serves.

2   *Differentiation.* If the company's products stand out from competitors by being substantially different (from the customer's viewpoint) the firm is able to charge a premium. The firm may concentrate on differentiation across the entire industry or in just one segment. This relies on having strong segmentation and targeting strategies.

3   *Focus.* Here the company concentrates on a few tightly defined market segments, with low cost or differentiation strategies avoiding the temptation to try to please everybody. Sometimes these markets are exclusive in the sense of involving very expensive or highly technical products. For example, Novo Nordisk of Denmark specializes in producing industrial enzymes. Alternatively, the firm might provide for a given customer type – Wild Well Control Inc. of Texas specializes entirely in putting out oil well fires.

The least effective approach is to try to be both a low cost and differentiated firm, which results in a firm being 'stuck in the middle'.

An alternative view of strategic positions was taken by Treacy and Wiersema (1993). This approach identifies three value disciplines aimed at increasing customer value. These are as shown in Table 3.2.

The main difference between Treacy and Wiersema and Porter is that the former categorization is not mutually exclusive. A company can be a product leader while also having high customer intimacy – in fact, the two stances would probably be mutually supportive.

In the global context, competitive advantage can be achieved in different ways for each market the firm operates in. A company which is the cost leader in its domestic market might very well find itself to be a differentiator in a foreign market, perhaps because its products are unknown there. Firms are unlikely to achieve customer intimacy in a foreign market, at least in the early stages of market entry: establishing a rapport with customers takes considerable cultural sensitivity and even those firms which employ largely local workforces have difficulty in establishing themselves as 'local' firms.

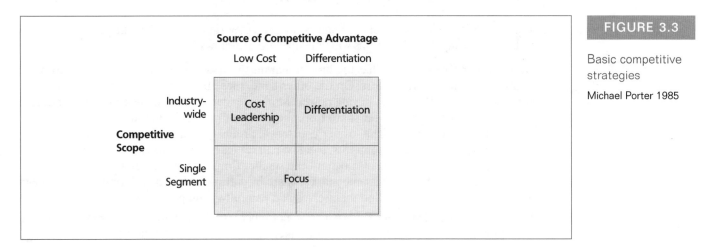

FIGURE 3.3

Basic competitive strategies

Michael Porter 1985

TABLE 3.2 Value disciplines

Title	Explanation
Operational excellence	Industry leadership in price and convenience. This approach is similar to Porter's Cost Leadership, but includes the idea of general efficiency. The focus of this approach is on efficient systems, reducing staff input to the minimum.
Customer intimacy	Precise segmentation and attention to customer needs. The company seeks to develop close long-term relationships with customers, which implies empowerment of staff, good market research and careful attention to segmentation and targeting policies.
Product leadership	Offer leading-edge, state-of-the-art products and services. Companies following this strategic alternative aim to make competitors' products (and indeed their own) obsolete. These companies have high R&D expenditure, staff innovation programs and systems for bringing new products to market quickly. Such companies are common in the electronics industry, but 3M also have a vigorous new product development system.

Occasionally firms will try to carry out more than one strategic approach because of disagreements among senior managers. Consensus among managers tends to improve performance at the strategic business unit level (Homburg *et al*. 1999) but conflict is not necessarily a bad thing: it sometimes leads to creative solutions being developed, or to new ideas being generated.

TALKING POINT

The competitive positions outlined by Treacy and Wiersema, Porter and others seem to offer firms a fine choice of approaches. Yet many firms (if we believe their mission statements) try to offer more and more to customers. Statements such as, 'We seek to offer the best products at the most realistic prices' imply a conflict in the strategic position – and one which, if Porter is to be believed, is likely to prove fatal.

So where does that leave us? Are the mission statements mere idle rhetoric, promising things which the firm has no intention of delivering, or are firms trying be all things to all people and thus heading for the bankruptcy court? Or can the firms take the universal get-out clause of adopting Treacy and Wiersema's categorizations, which are not mutually exclusive anyway? Does this give the firm's managers permission to do whatever they want to do and claim that it is part of a very clever combination strategy?

■ Competition and hypercompetition

Competitive positions within markets become established over time, particularly in markets which are fairly stable. The competitive positions which evolve are as follows:

1 *Market leader*. This company has the largest market share, which may make it subject to the scrutiny of monopoly regulators. On the other hand, these firms can control the market because they have the largest buying power. Market leaders have two basic strategic options: they can try to win even greater share from the smaller firms in the market, or they can try to expand the overall market. The former course will probably lead to retaliation and/or investigation by monopoly regulators, so most market leaders seek to expand the overall market, even though this will also benefit the smaller firms. Some market leaders will try to squeeze more profit from the same market share by cutting costs, which is of course bad news for suppliers, who may well find themselves in a painfully weak bargaining positioning.

2 *Market challengers*. These are firms which seek to increase their share of the market, either at the expense of the market leader or (more likely, given the power relationships involved) at

the expense of the smaller firms in the market. In order to attack the market leader, the challenger must have a substantial competitive advantage, whereas attacking smaller competitors may only involve running a powerful promotional campaign, a short price war, or a takeover policy.

3 *Market followers*. Market followers usually try to avoid any direct confrontation with the market leaders, since they are unable to sustain a competitive battle in the long run. The usual strategy for a follower is to allow the market leader to make most of the investment in developing a new market, then pick up any segments which are too small for the market leader to bother with. Although market followers will never become marketing leaders, they often have much the same profit levels since they do not have the expense of developing the markets (Haines *et al*. 1989).

4 *Market nicher*. These companies concentrate on small segments of the market, seeking to meet the needs of those customers as closely as possible. Since nichers operate on a low-volume, high-margin basis, they are often small- to medium-size companies (Clifford and Cavanagh 1985). The competitive strategy of a nicher is to get to know the segment so well that competitors are effectively shut out, so the key to success is to specialize.

Market leaders frequently need to defend their positions, as do other suppliers, albeit on a less frequent basis. Defense strategies are as shown in Table 3.3.

In most markets, the market challenger's best strategy would be to attack the market leader, unless of course the market leader can defend its position effectively. This means that market leaders need to be constantly vigilant and must be able to mount a vigorous defense. More importantly, the market leader needs to make it clear to competitors that it has the capability to mount a vigorous defense, or even attack if circumstances warrant it.

Market challengers might use any of the strategies outlined in Table 3.4.

So far, this section has been about monopolistic competition in which firms jockey for position in a fairly gentlemanly manner dividing up the market into neat segments in which each company operates with little risk of attack from other companies. In some markets this has given way to hyper-competition in which 'anything goes' (D'Aveni 1994).

TABLE 3.3 Defense strategies

Strategy	Explanation
Position defense	This involves building barriers which prevent or restrict competitors from entering the market. These barriers may be related to inputs – for example, cornering the market in raw materials – or to outputs, for example using a patent to protect a particular process.
Flanking defense	Since market leaders often ignore parts of the market which they feel are not worth approaching, competitors can sometimes find an opening without directly confronting the market leader.
Pre-emptive defense	The market leader will sometimes attack the other companies before they can move in, for example by using a massive price cut to stave off a threat of entry.
Counter-offensive defense	When attacked, the market leader launches an instant counter-attack. This can take the form of a promotional campaign, a price war or the development of a 'me-too' version of the competitor's product.
Mobile defense	The market leader moves into new markets before the competitors can do so. In effect, the market leader takes a proactive approach.
Contraction defense	Sometimes the market leader finds itself unable to defend all its markets and withdraws to its core business. In some cases this does not prove sufficient and the company continues to retreat until it has nowhere left to go.

TABLE 3.4 Market challenger strategies

Strategy	Explanation
Frontal attack	In a frontal attack the market challenger attacks the target company by matching its efforts across the board. The challenger attacks the competitor's strengths rather than its weaknesses, in effect entering into a war of attrition. The company with the greatest resources will usually win in these circumstances, but such frontal attacks are costly for all concerned.
Flanking attack	The flanking attack concentrates on the competitor's weaknesses, seeking out areas where the competitor is unable to compete effectively. The challenger will identify areas of the business which the competitor is serving badly. Sometimes the company under attack will simply retreat rather than fight for a market which is marginal for it, so this can be an effective strategy for a small firm attacking a larger one.
Encirclement attack	This strategy involves attacking from several directions at once. It works best when the attacker has more resources than the defender.
Bypass attack	Here the challenger bypasses the other firms entirely and targets totally new markets. This is particularly effective in a global context, where a new market may open up in which the leading competitors are not represented.
Guerrilla attack	The challenger makes occasional attacks on a larger competitor, using different tactics each time in order to confuse the target competitor. The constant switching of tactics does not allow the competitor time to formulate a response, in effect forcing the competitor to become a follower.

To cope with this new reality, managers look for new ways to out-compete rivals. This goes further than merely staking out a claim in the market: in any market in which there is room for four companies, five or six will be competing and the weakest will eventually disappear – only to be replaced by a newcomer. The philosophy underpinning hypercompetition is that managers need to concentrate on a new 7-S framework, rather than the Peters and Waterman (1980) 7-S framework popularized in *In Search of Excellence*. The new 7-S's are shown in Table 3.5.

The 7-S framework presented in Table 3.5 is not intended to be read as a series of generic strategies. It is a set of key approaches that might carry the organization in many different directions. The framework also encompasses three factors for effective delivery of tactical disruptions of the market: vision, capabilities and tactics.

Within the hypercompetitive environment, traditional sources of strength no longer apply. Giants of industry are frequently brought down by relatively small competitors able to adapt to new situations, or able to bring new ideas to bear. Much of the success in a hypercompetitive environment is based on the strategy of finding and building temporary advantages through market disruption rather than sustaining advantage and building for equilibrium. In other words, success comes from initiating changes in the market rather than from responding to changes.

Of course, not all disruptions are successful. For a disruption to be successful, it must fulfill the first S – the creation of a temporary ability to serve stakeholders better than the competition can. Successful firms may well prioritize the customer as the most important stakeholder: customer satisfaction becomes the instrument by which the company seeks satisfaction of other stakeholders such as employees and shareholders.

For example, Intel have a process of concurrent engineering in which Intel designers visit every major computer manufacturer and every major software house around the world to ask them what they want in a chip. The company also provides early software simulations to computer manufacturers, thus allowing these customers to gain a first-to-market advantage over competitors. Also Intel produces software compilers which they supply to software companies in order to make the transition to the new chip run more smoothly. The ability to predict future trends in markets is clearly crucial

TABLE 3.5 The new 7-S framework	
Factor	Explanation
Superior stakeholder satisfaction	The ability to satisfy the firm's stakeholders more effectively than competitors are able to offers clear advantages. Customer satisfaction, much beloved by marketers, is only part of this process, since other stakeholders must also be kept happy or even delighted by the firm's activities.
Strategic soothsaying	This is about understanding the future evolution of markets and technology. Success in predicting future trends is clearly linked to success in making or responding to changes.
Positioning for speed	Preparing the company for a rapid change of approach is crucial to the firm's ability to initiate and respond to competitive shifts.
Positioning for surprise	Being able to make changes rapidly enough to take the competitors by surprise is a useful capability, as is being flexible enough to cope with surprises.
Shifting the rules of the game	As firms learn how to break down entry barriers quickly and cheaply, the 'gentlemen's agreements' to avoid direct competition are breaking down. A firm which is successful at shifting the rules is likely to catch competitors flat-footed and thus gain competitive advantage quickly.
Signaling strategic intent	Letting competitors know what will happen if they follow a particular course may be a good way to slow down or negate their strategic actions.
Simultaneous and sequential strategic thrusts	Either carrying out a number of different competitive initiatives at once, or carrying them out in a rapid sequence, can confuse and disorient competitors. Often, a 'false start' along one course followed by a rapid change of direction to another course will be highly effective.

to a firm such as Intel: the company not only needs to predict trends in its own business-to-business markets, but also needs to predict trends in the consumer markets that its customers serve.

To an extent, soothsaying is linked to vision: the corporate vision is likely to include some assessment of possible future trends and opportunities for disruption.

The capability for disruption is dependent on the next two factors. A company's ability to act fast and its capacity for surprising its competitors are crucial in causing disruption: if two companies see the same opportunity together, the one which is able to act the fastest will win the day. Equally, the firm which is able to create new opportunities which its competitors are unable to foresee will drive the market.

The final three elements are concerned with the tactics for disruption. Actions that shift the rules of competition will catch competitors out, but of course such changes are subject to retaliation as competitors readjust. Most planning takes account of possible competitor responses, but it is far less common for managers to attempt to shape the responses of competitors so as to maximize competitive advantage. Signaling the firm's likely competitive responses to competitors in advance can delay their plans while they consider the consequences and can sometimes create surprise.

Simultaneous thrusts or a sequence of rapid moves can confuse and create surprise among competitors. Moving in several different directions at once makes it difficult for competitors to formulate a suitable response, since the competition is unlikely to be able to coordinate across all fronts in the same way as the initiating firm can coordinate.

In a hypercompetitive market, competitive advantage is gained by achieving four key goals, as shown in Figure 3.4.

FIGURE 3.4

Key goals of
hypercompetition

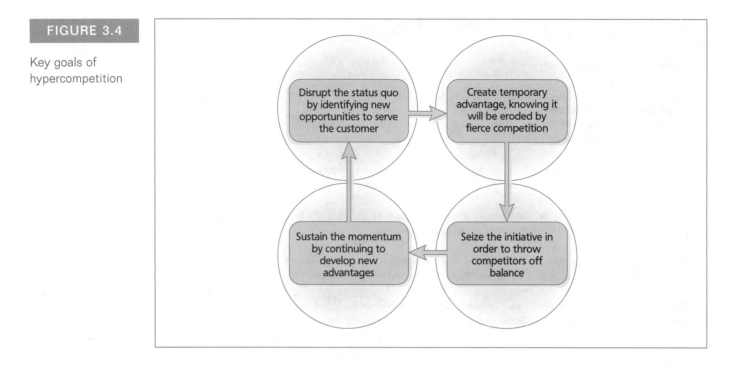

TALKING POINT

Frequently marketers use the language of warfare to describe what they do. We defend markets, we run advertising campaigns, we establish territories, we conquer a market, we attack a target. At the same time we talk about nurturing the customers – rather like a military commander who claims to be liberating the people he's killing.

So how do we reconcile this apparent discrepancy? Do we change our terminology to reflect the nurturing side of our nature? Or do we change what we do, so that instead of battling with our competitors for the pawns we call customers, we start to cooperate with our competitors to meet customer needs?

Or is it perhaps nearer to the truth to admit that actually we are out to please the share-holders – the customers are merely a means to an end?

In hypercompetition it is not sufficient to be able to build a static set of competencies, as has been the case in the past. It is also important to know how to use those competencies to seize the initiative and maintain the flow of disruptive changes in order to maintain a lead. Successful hypercompetitors do not wait for a competitive response – they continue to innovate and upset the market equilibrium, keeping ahead by maintaining a balancing act which the competitors are unable to match.

Companies need to consider trade-offs, as with any other analysis pattern or scheme. However, the approaches are not mutually exclusive, and companies can (and do) select more than one approach at a time. There are of course many trade-offs (D'Aveni 1995) and Table 3.6 shows a few examples.

Because firms have limited resources, they will be unable to acquire all the 7-S elements at once and will therefore need to consider which ones to prioritize. This requires analysis of the competitors in order to play to the weaknesses of the competition. The trade-offs mean that firms cannot use all the elements at once anyway, although it is perfectly feasible to combine a few elements at any one time.

Hypercompetition should not be seen as a universal formula for all firms in all circumstances. Many firms operate in stable industries where competitive pressures are relatively low – the oil industry is an example. Change is slow in such industries, and the type of rapid disruption of the

TABLE 3.6 Trade-offs in the new 7-S framework	
Trade-off	**Description**
Speed vs stakeholder satisfaction	Companies may sacrifice product quality (thus affecting customers) or may push employees too hard in order to increase speed of change. Rushing new products to market without proper testing may also reduce customer satisfaction.
Surprise vs stakeholder satisfaction	Sudden changes of direction are unsettling for employees and may well confuse customers. Shifting the rules and simultaneous strategic thrusts also lead to confusion among staff and shareholders, and may weaken brand values which have taken years to establish.
Speed vs soothsaying	Speed can easily leave too little time for reflection on future events, especially since the effects of change cannot be estimated if the changes themselves are happening too fast. The same is true of simultaneous strategic thrusts.
Shifting the rules vs speed	Shifting the rules often requires strategic alliances to be formed with other firms (either competitors or members of the value-chain) which means that negotiations will reduce speed. These negotiations also reduce the possibilities for surprise, since any such negotiations are likely to be public.
Sequential thrusts vs surprise	Sequential thrusts commit the firm to a predetermined course of action which may be surprising in itself, but which will rapidly lose the element of surprise as the plans leak out.

market described in hypercompetition is unlikely to be of any relevance. In the longer run, if all firms in a given industry adopt the hypercompetitive approach, anarchy is likely to be the result and a new paradigm will need to be found to establish an element of stability. The model also assumes that rapid change will continue indefinitely and that the speed of change is increasing: both of these assumptions are subject to debate.

■ Globalization strategy

Firms which adopt a global strategy will usually try to develop international competitive strengths that would not have been available to them had they remained purely domestic firms. They will also perceive key opportunities and threats on a worldwide basis. This does not, of course, preclude the firm from having a national strategic orientation in some areas of its operations.

There are four main strategic options open to the globalizing company (Grosse and Kujawa 1992).

1　Aim for a high share of a global market.
2　Aim for a niche in a global market.
3　Aim for a high share of a national market.
4　Aim for a niche in a national market.

The firms seeking a high share of a global market will need to begin by identifying high volume segments which exist globally, in other words segments which cross national boundaries. Examples are the global computer business and the global telecommunications market. Secondly the firm will need to produce a wide range of products to meet the needs of that market segment or those market segments. In order to compete against global niche marketers, the global high-share company must seek those benefits which come from being able to supply a wide range of products. These include inbound logistics advantages such as being able to use the same raw materials to produce many products and the ability to offer a wider range of choice to customers.

Global niche strategists target a single industry or a single type of problem. For example, Microbiological Systems Ltd. supply biologically-based environmental pollution detection systems to the chemical industry. The firm is at the cutting edge of research in the area and is able to supply systems which are cheaper, more sensitive and more reliable than anyone else's. Such firms protect their market niche by holding the key patents on the processes they use and by spending large amounts on R&D in order to stay ahead of the competition.

Global nichers usually want to avoid head-on competition with the major firms, typically because they do not have the resources for a long drawn-out battle. The policy works best for firms which have a global advantage (i.e. an advantage over all other firms in the industry wherever they are located) and which do not have to adapt their product to meet local conditions.

National high share strategists target countries where they think they can obtain a high share of the market. This may come about because of tariff barriers which prevent other foreign firms from entering the market (as in the case of a customs union or common market), or it may be that local firms are unable to supply the demand for the products. In some cases the production facilities for a firm may be located in a country where the raw materials are easily available: for example, Rio Tinto Zinc produces aluminum in Australia and New Zealand, copper in Papua New Guinea and uranium in Namibia. In each case the company is well-placed to supply local or regional demand for the end product.

Choosing one country from another can be a difficult problem with more than 200 to pick from. A number of researchers have proposed using an adaptation of the well-known GE matrix. This market choice matrix is shown in Figure 3.5.

The Market Choice Matrix compares product/business strengths with a particular market's attractiveness. On the vertical axis, the product/business strengths relate to a specific set of factors which may be varied by a manager depending upon the analysis for a particular firm. A suggested list of factors for this axis include:

- business size
- financial strength
- technology superiority
- brand perceptions
- personnel.

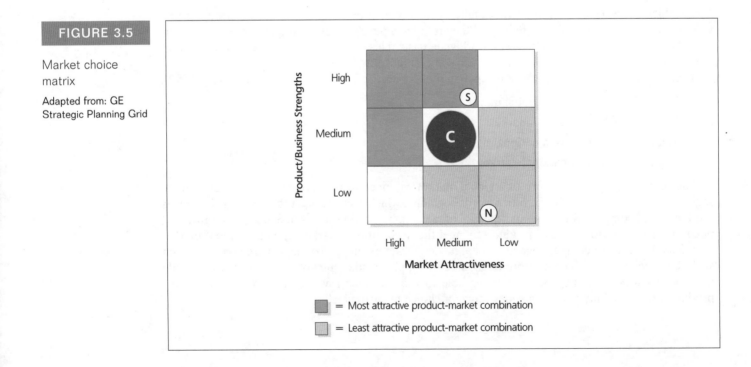

FIGURE 3.5

Market choice matrix

Adapted from: GE Strategic Planning Grid

The horizontal axis, market attractiveness, would include factors such as:

- trade barriers
- competition
- cultural acceptance
- technological readiness
- previous corporate establishment
- availability of distribution.

Each of the factors for product/business and market attractiveness should be given a weight and then each sub-factor rated. When the weights and ratings are summarized, an overall number can be developed. From this number, the placement on the country market portfolio grid would be determined. The relative size of the market can be shown by varying the size of the circles representing each country market.

On the example above, we have shown a firm with medium business strengths and medium market attractiveness for China which is represented by a large circle since the market potential is large. Sweden is represented as a market where the business has high strengths, but the attractiveness is only medium since the market is crowded with competition. The size of the Swedish market is shown with a smaller circle. Finally, a medium-sized circle is shown in the lower right-hand corner for Nigeria where this firm has little strength and the market attractiveness is rather low. For this product, the market size in Nigeria is about the same as that of Sweden.

In some cases national high-share strategists are favored because they are prepared to allow the national government a share in the firm. This type of joint venture is favored in Sweden and in many third-world countries, where the governments find it a useful way to raise revenue without increasing taxation.

National niche strategists exploit the advantages of specialization on a national basis to help defend their segments against local and international rivals. This approach works best where global product strategies are not compatible with local demands and where a large amount of product adaptation is needed from country to country. Competitive advantage derives from the firm's ability to adapt to local needs: for example, a truck manufacturer will need to adapt the vehicles for climatic differences and infrastructure differences – the quality of the roads is likely to make a difference to suspension specifications, gear ratios and so forth.

Garten (2000), in reviewing the requirements for global strategy advises:

- Rethink everything about the strategy – even what the strategy means – in a fast and brutally competitive environment.
- The best strategies are developed by organizations who can gather and process massive amounts of information.
- Companies that succeed globally are constantly innovating.
- To succeed globally, firms need to create a culture which allows for extensive internal and external collaboration.
- Global change offers unprecedented opportunities to capture markets.

In general, globalization generates economies of scale and allows firms to spread risk. The downside is that it creates problems of adaptation of strategy to meet local conditions in the target markets.

SUMMARY

Strategy is the guiding force of any organization. It allows every member of the organization to understand where the organization is heading, which means that decision-making by junior managers and even grass-roots workers becomes much easier. The framework created by an effective, and effectively communicated, strategy is essential for the smooth running of the organization.

However, strategic planning is not a straightforward matter. Competition, hypercompetition, and the rapidly changing environment all affect the firm's ability to plan ahead.

The key points from this chapter are as follows:

- Mission statements, vision statements and objectives are all ways of communicating the overall strategy of the organization.

- Strategy revolves around environment, resources and vision: the more congruent the EVR, the more successful the strategy.

- Value-chains are not sufficient to analyze global businesses: the value network, containing all the partner organizations, also needs to be considered.

- Basic strategic approaches are cost leadership, differentiation and focus: attempts to combine these strategies are unlikely to be optimal.

- Positions within the market are market leader, market challenger, market follower and market nicher.

- Hypercompetition is about disrupting markets in order to out-compete other organizations.

REVIEW QUESTIONS

1 Why should firms not try to mix Porter's strategic approaches?
2 How might a firm apply basic defense strategies in a hypercompetitive environment?
3 What is the difference between vision and mission?
4 How might a firm plan for entering a former communist country such as China?
5 What would be the most appropriate competitive strategy for a small firm wishing to enter a well-established national market?

SPOTLIGHT ON B2B MARKETING

Rio Tinto, despite its Spanish-sounding name, is in fact a British company. The company's roots go back to the 19th century, when the Rio Tinto Company was formed to mine for copper at Rio Tinto in southern Spain. The company merged in 1962 with the Consolidated Zinc Corporation (founded in 1905) to form Rio Tinto Zinc.

Growing largely by merger and acquisition, the company is now among the world's largest mineral extraction and smelting corporations. Between 1968 and 1985 the company made acquisitions in cement, chemicals, gas and oil and manufacturing, but in the late 1980s the firm conducted a major review of its strategy and divested itself of its non-mining interests. By 1994 the company was almost entirely out of any business not directly concerned with mining and from 1995 onwards the company has refocused its R&D expenditures on a global basis.

On the company's website there appears a statement of the corporate vision.

Rio Tinto is a world leader in finding, mining and processing the earth's mineral resources.

In order to deliver superior returns to our shareholders over many years, we take a long term and responsible approach to exploring for first class orebodies and developing large, efficient operations capable of sustaining competitive advantage.

In this way, we help to meet the global need for minerals and metals which contribute to essential improvements in living standards as well as making a direct contribution to economic development and employment in those countries in which we invest.

Wherever we operate, we aim to work closely with our hosts, and strive to respect laws and customs, minimise adverse impacts, and ensure transfer of benefits and enhancement of opportunities.

We believe that our competitiveness and future success depend not only on the unrivalled quality and diversity of our assets but also on our record as good neighbours and partners around the world.

Accordingly, we set ourselves high environmental and community standards.

Our commitment to health, safety and the enhancement of the skills and capabilities of our employees is second to none in mining.

We seek to make lasting contributions to local communities and to be sensitive to their culture and way of life.

The company owns 22 gold mines in Australia and is listed on the Australian stock exchange, although control is exercised from London. Copper and gold account for nearly 40 per cent of the company's sales, iron ore and industrial minerals for 35 per cent, aluminum and coal for roughly 10 per cent each, and the other operations the remainder.

Despite the company's remarkable success, the path has not always been smooth. Often attacked by environmentalists, the company has spent a great deal of effort and money in establishing environmentally-friendly policies, but still remains the target for frequent attacks and accusations of causing environmental damage and not respecting the rights of local inhabitants of the areas in which it operates. By its nature, mineral extraction causes some environmental damage and working in the industry is almost always hard, dirty and dangerous, but Rio Tinto seems to have come in for more than its share of the blame.

On March 27th 2003 the company's South African subsidiary, Palabora Mining Company Ltd., announced that it was in financial difficulties and needed to increase its current borrowing from US$185m to US$275m. Rio Tinto stepped in with a temporary loan in order to shore up Palabora, but the strength of the Rand made the firm's future problematical. At the same time, Australian aluminum exports were predicted to be stagnant and the cost of electricity in New Zealand was forcing up production costs: aluminum smelting uses very large amounts of electricity, since it is an electrolytic process. In general, falling demand for metals on world markets affected Rio Tinto seriously in the first half of 2003.

The company states its overall strategy as follows:

Rio Tinto takes a long term and responsible approach to mining, our proven area of expertise where we have competitive advantage.

Our strategy is to focus on large scale, long life and cost competitive mining operations and to invest throughout their lives so that they maintain their competitive positions. We always pay attention to the quality of projects not to particular geographical areas or commodities.

Our operating practices are geared to long term economic value and we constantly seek efficiency improvements.

Rio Tinto's planning horizons and existing operations ensure that present reserve and production levels of essential minerals and metals should be sustained for 20 or more years.

We have a portfolio of quality projects, currently under development or appraisal and a clear and focused exploration programme to seek out and secure quality new opportunities for further profitable expansion.

Overall, Rio Tinto's strategic plan seems set to take the company ahead into the 21st century.

Questions

1 How does Rio Tinto's vision equate to the attacks by environmentalists?
2 To what extent does Rio Tinto appear to be customer-oriented, judging from the company's official statements?
3 What might Rio Tinto do about the problems of exporting minerals?
4 How does the vision statement relate to the strategy?
5 What type of globalization strategy do you think Rio Tinto is adopting?

REFERENCES

Ackoff, R. L. (1986) *Management in Small Doses*, New York: John Wiley.

Campbell, A. (1989) Research findings discussed in Skapinker, M. (1989) Mission accomplished or ignored? *Financial Times*, 11 January.

D'Aveni, R. A. (1994) *Hypercompetition: Managing the dynamics of strategic manoeuvring*, New York, Free Press.

D'Aveni, R. A. (1995) 'Coping with hypercompetition: the new 7-Ss framework', *The Academy of Management Executive*: 9: 3: 45–67.

David, Forest R. and David, Fred R. (2003) 'It's Time to Redraft Your Mission Statement,' *Journal of Business Strategy*, 24: 1: 11–14.

Drucker, P. F. (1973) *Management Tasks, Responsibilities, Practices*, New York: Harper & Row.

Garten, J. E. (2000) *World View: Global Strategies for the New Economy*, Boston: Harvard Business School Publishing, xiii–xiv.

Grosse, R. and Kujawa, D. (1992) *International Business*, Homewood Ill: Irwin.

Idenburg P. J. (1993) 'Four styles of strategic development', *Long Range Planning* 26: 6.

Kotler, P. (2003) *Marketing Management*, Upper Saddle River, NJ: Prentice-Hall.

Peters, T. J. and Waterman, R. H. (1982) *In search of excellence: lessons from America's best-run companies*, Harper and Row.

Porter M. E. (1985) *Competitive Advantage: Creating and Sustaining Superior Performance*, New York: Free Press.

Thompson, A. A. and Strickland, A. J. (1980) *Strategy formulation and implementation*, Homewood, Ill: Irwin.

Treacy, M. and Wiersema, E. (1993) 'Customer intimacy and other value disciplines', *Harvard Business Review* Jan-Feb: 84–93.

HEALTH RESEARCH COUNCIL OF NEW ZEALAND

During the late 1990s a sea change ran through New Zealand Government purchasing policies, at least as far as purchasing research goes. Up until the mid–1990s, research had been funded on the basis of its worthiness, from a small budget which often only part-funded the research. The research outcomes were generally made public knowledge and were not especially targeted at New Zealand, so the knowledge gained was effectively given away to anyone who cared to exploit it. New Zealand is a small country, with less than four million people: its entire government budget is less than that for the city of London, so it is essential that research is purchased which will directly benefit the people of New Zealand. This thinking led to the Blueprint for Change document, published in May 1999, which laid down the new rules for purchasing research on behalf of the Crown.

The Ministry of Research, Science and Technology (MoRST), which works at the highest level of policies, strategies and statistics, is the lead agency responsible for allocating funds for research. MoRST's mission is 'to inspire and assist New Zealanders to achieve a better future through research and innovation'. MoRST's Maori name, Te Manatu Putaiao, literally means 'the Ministry for the foundation of the world' and MoRST certainly takes this name seriously.

The forerunner to Blueprint for Change was the Foresight Policy. The minister for Research Science and Technology, Maurice Williamson, had this to say about it:

The Foresight Project provided a framework for thinking about the sort of future New Zealand wants, and defined the context for the Government's research, science and technology investments. The Government invests in research, science and technology to generate new innovative, economic, environmental and social capacity. In this way, the Government underpins innovation throughout all sectors of New Zealand. It cannot work in isolation, however. Innovation must be focused on the needs of end-users – whose lives, environments and enterprises will be affected by new knowledge and technological change.

The Government needs confidence that its research, science and technology investments will be rapidly and effectively exploited to achieve stated innovation goals. This is more likely where sectors demonstrate their strategic thinking about the future, through bold and dynamic innovation strategies.

Because the world economy, particularly in the developed world, was undergoing rapid changes there was a view in New Zealand that the economy should be moved towards a knowledge-based society. Manufacturing, mineral exploitation and agriculture are being carried out far more efficiently by Far Eastern and Third World countries, so the Western countries have moved towards a research and education based economy, in which know-how is exploited to develop the national wealth. Blueprint for Change expressed this view as follows:

For New Zealand, the successful development of a knowledge society will involve moving to systems, services and products with higher levels of value added by knowledge. Government aspirations for New Zealand focus on building an enterprise economy, creating a culture of innovation, enhancing the roles of individuals, families, communities and the private sector, maintaining and enhancing environmental quality and building national identity and cohesion. Collectively, they create a vision for New Zealand's future as a knowledge society.

The Blueprint for Change was prepared by encouraging a wide range of groups across New Zealand to:

- think strategically about future directions for their sectors
- identify their innovation needs and the contributions that RS&T can make to them and
- make commitments to developing their own competencies and research capabilities.

These groups contributed to the development of the target outcomes through a consultation process that involved:

- public conferences in July and November 1998
- analysis of the sector foresight strategies received in October and November 1998
- publication of draft target outcomes in December 1998 and
- analysis of submissions on the draft target outcomes received in February 1999.

Approximately 140 sectors submitted strategies to MoRST in 1998. The target outcomes listed below reflect the key aspirations which emerged across this set of submissions.

A draft set of target outcomes published in December 1998 drew approximately 130 responses from individuals and groups. These submissions enabled MoRST to reduce the number of target outcomes and to sharpen their focus and clarity.

Four science envelope goals were identified: the innovation goal, the economic goal, the environmental goal and the social goal. These were defined as follows:

Innovation goal: Accelerate knowledge creation and the development of human capital, social capital, learning systems and networks in order to enhance New Zealand's capacity to innovate.

The first goal recognizes the importance of building a culture of innovation in New Zealand to underpin all other economic, environmental and social outcomes. RS&T should generate new knowledge, help develop human and network capacities and stimulate an entrepreneurial culture so that New Zealand can be a full participant in the global knowledge age.

This goal links directly to the Government's aspirations to create an enterprise economy and to value innovation. It reinforces the Government's strategic priority on expanding the country's knowledge base and technological capabilities.

Economic goal: Increase the contribution knowledge makes to the creation and value of new and improved products, processes, systems and services in order to enhance the competitiveness of New Zealand enterprises.

The second goal stresses the importance of new knowledge and technological change as a driver for value-creation, innovation, and productivity gains across the economy.

This goal identifies the contribution that knowledge makes to economic competitiveness. It provides a context for Government investment in RS&T consistent with the policy that investment should generate widespread net benefits over time, without displacing or otherwise creating disincentives for investment by others.

A focus on the knowledge base behind new and improved products, processes, systems and services will ensure that Government investment in RS&T complements the role of private sector investment in generating wealth for New Zealand. This goal links to the Government's aspiration to develop an enterprise economy.

Environmental goal: Increase knowledge of the environment and of the biological, physical, social, economic and cultural factors that affect it in order to establish and maintain a healthy environment that sustains nature and people.

The third goal emphasizes how knowledge of environmental states and processes underpins our ability to improve environmental quality and integrity. It picks up ideas related to New Zealand's environmental heritage expressed in Government's aspirations and Government's strategic priority on biodiversity.

This goal focuses on improving understanding of the web of interconnected factors that determine the state of the environment. The knowledge gained will underpin sustainable management of all New Zealand's environments (terrestrial, marine and atmospheric) and will contribute to minimizing hazards and risks associated with our unique environments. This will in turn contribute to better economic and social outcomes.

Social goal: Increase knowledge of the social, biological, environmental, cultural, economic and physical determinants of well-being in order to build a society in which all New Zealanders enjoy health and independence and have a sense of belonging, identity and partnership.

The outcomes were to be achieved through smart purchasing, relationship contracting and contestability. Portfolios of research were to be constructed through a process of negotiation between the research institutions themselves (universities, commercial institutions, teaching hospitals and so forth), potential users of the research (health services, social services, industry, etc.) and the purchase agents, which are the government bodies set up to fund research in each sector. The Health Research Council is the body responsible for allocating government research funding to research into health within New Zealand and is therefore one of the purchasing agents for research on behalf of MoRST.

All purchase agents are required to have a transparent and contestable process for making investment decisions. Any individual, public or private enterprise or organization can negotiate a portfolio of research and indeed the more organizations and individuals pitch for research grants, the higher the quality of the outputs is likely to be. Purchasing agents are also required to provide information to MoRST on the effectiveness of their investments, via an annual analysis which is then fed into the budget decision-making process. Research portfolios are also expected to be designed to meet the needs of the Maori population, whose cultural divergence from white New Zealand society means that they have special needs: there is a legal obligation on the New Zealand Government to make these special provisions as a result of various treaties with the Maori. There is therefore considerable pressure on purchasing agents such as HRC to obtain high-quality research with measurable outcomes which will benefit the people of New Zealand fairly directly.

The overall strategy proposed by MoRST was intended to result in specific research outcomes and the Blueprint for Change document outlined some example target outcomes. Two of the sample target statements proved highly relevant to HRC.

TARGET OUTCOME STATEMENT

Health for all. Individuals, families and communities throughout New Zealand enjoy high health status and independence. New Zealand's unique and innovative health delivery systems combine international best practice with local experience and knowledge of needs.

Examples of the contributions RS&T could make towards this target outcome:

- *Expanding knowledge and understanding of factors influencing health status, including disparities, of New Zealanders.*

- *Developing technologies, products, processes and services for improving health status and reducing health disparities among New Zealanders.*

- *Fostering networks and collaborations for increasing global access to health care knowledge and technologies.*

- *Developing knowledge management systems for integrating health information and disseminating new health care technologies and services.*

TARGET OUTCOME STATEMENT

Maori development. Maori achieve well-being, self-sufficiency, prosperity, equity, justice and political effectiveness.

Examples of the contributions RS&T could make towards this target outcome:

- *Developing Maori intellectual capital and capacity through participation in the RS&T system.*

- *Enhancing the ability of Maori to develop and manage their resources by developing science and technology skills and networks to enable economic self-sufficiency.*

- *Developing an understanding and appreciation of Matauranga Maori and Tikanga Maori.*

- *Building an infrastructure relevant to robust Maori development. For example, understanding governance structures.*

- *Understanding the social, cultural and economic determinants of well-being.*

The result of this thinking was the development of the Rangahau Hauora Maori portfolio. This portfolio of research projects seeks to encourage Maoris themselves to carry out research into health issues, developing specifically Maori research methodologies and methods, so that new health research is carried out by Maoris for Maoris. The main projected outcome for the research is the development of a critical mass of Maori researchers, operating under Maori philosophies and paradigms, who will develop solutions to Maori health problems such as heart disease and diabetes.

The project went out for general discussion during 2002, being published on HRC's website along with several other projects. The HRC already had investments in Ngai Tahu Maori Research Unit and Tomaiora Maori Health Research Unit (both at Auckland University) and also in the Te Pumanawa Hauora at Massey University. The purpose of the discussion document was to encourage other research organizations and individuals to come forward to participate in the project.

Other projects include research into non-communicable diseases (in which Maori research is included also), mental health, injury and rehabilitation (a key issue in New Zealand, since the Government operates a central no-fault compensation scheme for accidental injuries) and health and independence of population groups. In all, nine research portfolios have been initiated to date, most with at least some reference to Maori issues and all with a distinct New Zealand flavor.

Total funding available in 1999/2000 was NZ$42.4m, which could be allocated for up to five years. The research is fully funded, so applicants do not need to find matching partners to meet the cost: this has the advantage that the HRC has full ownership of the research outcomes and can therefore control the uses to which the research is put, at least to some extent: presumably in some cases there may be commercially exploitable outcomes, although in most cases the purpose of the exercise is not commercial, but is rather aimed at improving life for New Zealanders.

During 2001/2002, the HRC received 221 applications in its annual project round and awarded a total of 58 contracts. These were chosen in a two-step process involving local and overseas expert referees who work in the same research area and intense scrutiny by specialized assessing committees. The total amount for new contracts was NZ$33.39m (excluding GST). Projects ranged from 'The pathogenesis and treatment of preterm brain injury' a project intended to take three years at a cost of NZ$2,054,000, to 'Maori quantitative research methodologies and methods', a two year project costing NZ$200,000.

For a small country, New Zealand has made a great impact on the world. This innovative approach to purchasing research is likely to prove beneficial not only to New Zealanders, but also to the rest of the world: new insights taken from the ancient Maori culture, new research outcomes obtained as a result of full funding and especially, the exciting possibility of research outcomes which come from interdisciplinary contacts are all major contributions to the welfare of people everywhere.

Case study questions

1 How do the research projects relate to the strategy of HRC and in turn to the strategy of MoRST?
2 How would you go about preparing a research proposal for HRC?
3 What are HRC's needs as an organization?
4 How might a research institution operating outside New Zealand obtain some funding from HRC or MoRST?
5 What type of buying situation is represented by HRC's policy?
6 Who are HRC's customers?
7 Who are MoRST's customers?

PART

2

EVALUATING MARKET OPPORTUNITIES

Part 2 will introduce you to the practical issues involved in evaluating market opportunities and making the correct strategic choices. In Chapter 4 we will introduce market research from a B2B perspective. Here we will discuss techniques for gathering information from secondary sources and how to design custom or primary research. We will also discuss the role of market research in determining market potential and developing sales forecasts. Chapter 5 will show you how to segment business markets and points out the differences between using segmenting techniques for consumer markets and business markets. The chapter ends with a full discussion of positioning and targeting of key market segments. In Chapter 6 you will learn about market entry tactics, focusing on finding ways to enter new markets, whether domestic or international. This chapter gives special emphasis to blocked markets and strategic alliances.

MARKET RESEARCH AND INFORMATION SYSTEMS

Learning objectives
After reading this chapter, you should be able to:

- Understand the need for market research

- Differentiate between B2B and consumer market research

- List recent changes in the field including new pitfalls researchers face

- Understand how to develop a market information system and describe the research process

- Describe the role of market research in determining market potential and developing sales forecasts

- Recognize when there is a need for and pinpoint the appropriate time for using outside specialists

- Explain how to use each of the market research methods

- Understand the uses of benchmarking

■ Introduction

Market research is at the heart of any effective marketing program especially when a manager is planning to enter a foreign market. Research is the starting point for determining who the best customers are, how they go about making buying decisions and what the potential sales might be to each of them. Market research also helps a manager determine what competitors are doing and what they might do. It is critically important to develop as much information as possible before making financial commitments. While business decisions can never be made with absolute certainty, developing as much information as possible reduces the uncertainty to a manageable level.

■ The need for market research

Market research is 'the systematic and objective identification, collection, analysis and dissemination and use of information for the purpose of improving decision making related to the identification and solution of problems (and opportunities) in marketing' (Malhotra 1999). While other and more detailed definitions have been given, especially by the American Marketing Association, this definition is concise and focuses on the fact that information needs to be developed as it relates to specific business problems or opportunities. In B2B settings, market research is heavily used for forecasting, developing trends, finding market potential, studying the competition and developing sales forecasts and sales quotas.

Differences between consumer and business market research

While consumer and business marketers both conduct research related to product attributes and product acceptance, most consumer research focuses on these areas. Consumer market researchers also spend a good deal more on advertising and packaging research than do business marketers. Most business market research is aimed at market potential and determining members of the buying center (DMU). In addition, business market researchers are often faced by a different set of problems than are consumer researchers. Table 4.1 below is an overview of these differences.

Changes in market research

While the basic techniques for completing market research have remained the same, the advent of the Internet has had a major impact on the gathering of both primary and secondary data. As more and more decision makers become familiar with using the Internet, it is possible to survey them without the use of telephone or mail techniques. The danger of an unqualified respondent completing the survey is about equal for the Internet and mail techniques. The Internet has also made it possible to develop secondary data much more rapidly and efficiently. Virtually any data source is available to anyone in any part of the world once that person has made the connection to the web. This allows faster, more accurate development of information and the ability to compare sources at very low costs.

Developing a marketing information system

A marketing information system is a fully integrated approach to developing, storing and using information from all sources to help develop the most effective marketing strategies and plans. Figure 4.1 describes the entire marketing information system.

Marketing information systems use information not only developed by market research but also information that exists both in internal and other data sources. All this information is placed in a so-called 'data warehouse'. The development and maintenance of the data warehouse is a key task for

TABLE 4.1 Consumer versus B2B marketing research

Consideration	Consumer	Business-to-Business
Universe	Large. Dependent on category under investigation but usually unlimited.	Small. Fairly limited in total population and even more so if within a defined industry category.
Respondent accessibility	Fairly easy. Can interview in malls, at home, on the telephone, via the Internet or using mail techniques.	Difficult. Usually only during working hours at plant, office, or on the road. Respondent is usually preoccupied with other priorities.
Respondent cooperation	Over the years has become more and more difficult, yet millions of consumers have never been interviewed.	A major concern. Due to the small population, many respondents are being over-researched. The purchaser and decision-makers in the business firm are the buyers of a variety of products and services from office supplies to heavy equipment.
Sample size	Can usually be drawn as large as required for statistical confidence since the population is in the hundreds of millions.	Usually much smaller than consumer sample, yet the statistical confidence is equal to the relationship of the sample to the total population.
Respondent definitions	Usually fairly simple. Those aware of a category or brand, users of a category or brand, demographic criteria, etc. The ultimate purchaser is also a user for most consumer products and services.	Somewhat more difficult. The user and the purchasing decision-maker in most cases are not the same. Factory workers who use heavy equipment, secretaries who sit on office chairs, etc., are the users and, no doubt, best able to evaluate products and services. However, they tend not to be the ultimate purchasers and in many cases do not have any influence on the decision-making process.
Interviewers	Can usually be easily trained. They are also consumers and tend to be somewhat familiar with the area under investigation for most categories.	Difficult to find good executive interviewers. At least a working knowledge of the product class or subject being surveyed is essential. Preferably more than just a working knowledge.
Study costs	Key dictators of cost are sample size and incidence. Lower incidence usage categories (for example, users of soft moist dog food, powdered breakfast beverages, etc.) or demographic or behavioral screening criteria (attend a movie at least once a month, over 65 years of age and do not have direct deposit of social security payments, etc.) can up costs considerably.	Relative to consumer research, the critical elements resulting in significantly higher per-interview costs are: the lower incidence levels, the difficulties in locating the 'right' respondent (that is, the member of the correct buying center) and securing cooperation, time and concentration of effort for the interview itself.

Adapted from: Katz, Martin 1979

any marketing department. It requires excellent planning and organization and dedication to keep it up to date and usable. In order to use the information in the data warehouse, many firms have developed decision support systems. A decision support system (DSS) is an interactive computer-based tool used by decision makers to help answer questions and solve problems. The function of a DSS is to change data (simply statistics about some particular item) into information which may show the relationship between one event and another.

Here again, diligence is required to develop and maintain the most effective DSS. A true competitive advantage can be developed through an effective marketing information system and an easy to use DSS.

FIGURE 4.1

Elements of a complete marketing information system

Perreault & McCarthy 2000

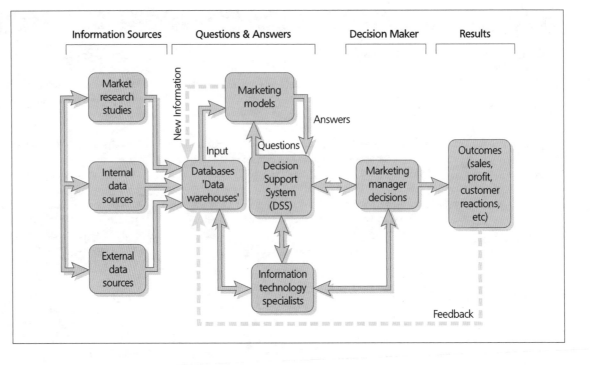

The marketing research process

The marketing research process follows six major steps outlined in Table 4.2.

TABLE 4.2 The marketing research process
Determine information requirements Define the problem Determine appropriate managerial level requiring information Decide on type of decision 　　Strategic 　　Tactical
Research design Establish clear research objectives Consider unit of research analysis 　　Regions 　　Countries 　　Sub-units within countries Determine sources of information Select appropriate research technique 　　Design and/or adapt to each country
Develop secondary data
Develop primary data Domestic In-country
Analyze data
Present findings

The first and most important step is to clearly determine what information is needed. In order to do this, a firm must determine what use the information will be put to. Will the decision be strategic or tactical? Will it have major or minor cost ramifications? At this point, a quick review may suggest that the cost of potential research exceeds the cost of a mistaken decision. Especially in the marketing of services, it is often less costly to simply try out an idea to see whether the market reacts positively rather than spend the time and money fielding research. Within this step, the researcher must also decide what kind of presentation will be required, whether highly technical or managerial in approach.

Clearly, the most important aspect of this stage of research is the definition of the problem. This is the step which causes the most problems and can lead a firm down an expensive path towards poor results. Specific discussions must be held with all decision makers to clearly understand the problem. In this step, managers often confuse symptoms with the problems. A symptom might be declining sales in a particular product line, but more work must be done to focus on what might be causing sales to decline before research is undertaken.

Once the problem is defined, we move to the next step – research design. The most important part of this step is to establish clear research objectives. Like any objectives, research objectives must be measurable. 'To determine why sales of laser printers are declining' would be a poor research objective. A more specific research objective might be; 'to determine why buyers of laser printers are failing to trade in their printers for new ones', or 'to determine the market potential of a specific office chair in the UK for next year'.

Research will be designed differently if it is to be conducted across a number of countries. More careful design must be undertaken to be sure results are comparable from one culture to another.

Next, the researchers must determine where the information will be developed. The sources vary widely from secondary information to primary research techniques which will be discussed later in this chapter.

Once the first two steps have been completed, researchers should develop secondary data before moving ahead to custom or primary research. Secondary data is defined as that which has already been developed for some other purpose. These data are available from many sources, including governments, trade associations and publications. Nearly all of it has been put on the Internet in some place. A good starting point is often a Meta search engine such as Google. The main reason for proceeding with secondary data before embarking on primary research is quite simple: it costs less and is faster to complete than custom research. Once this step is completed, it may be that the researcher has developed all of the information necessary for a decision to be made. Therefore, no primary research would be undertaken.

However, especially when dealing with international research, one may find that secondary sources do not give a full and accurate picture. To begin with, secondary data is often out of date. It is often unclear how the data were collected and whether the respondents were relevant to the problem faced by the researcher. Especially using Internet sources, it would be prudent to have several independent sources of information giving the same relative answer before proceeding confidently. A list of sample B2B information sources on the Internet is shown in Table 4.3.

TABLE 4.3 Sample Internet business information sources

- www.corporateinformation.com – Select a country and/or an industry and develop in-depth information about companies, country and/or industry.

- www.findsvp.com – Market research information especially related to technology. Clients include: Abbott Laboratories, American Express, JC Penny, Kmart Corporation, NBC Television Network, Radio Shack, Saatchi & Saatchi, DFS, and Showtime Networks, Inc.

- www.frost.com – Frost & Sullivan; provides research information and consulting services.

- www.intelliquest.com – Millward Brown Intelliquest provides technology and Internet companies with information-based marketing services.

TABLE 4.3 *(cont.)*

- www.uspto.gov – United States Patent and Trademark Office, non-commercial federal entity. Provides info. on all aspects of patents including trade-related intellectual property issues.

- www.census.gov – United States Census Bureau, provides massive amounts of information including population facts and estimates.

- www.stat-usa.gov – STAT-USA, an agency in the Economics and Statistics Administration. Provides economic, business and international trade information produced by the U.S. government, through low-cost subscription services like STAT USA/Internet(r) and USA Trade(r) Online.

- www.dnb.com – Dun & Bradstreet supplies business information; they have information on 75 million companies worldwide.

- www.comscore.com – Designed for obtaining market intelligence regarding an online category including Internet audience measurement.

- www.topica.com – E-mail discussions, newsletters and publishing solutions.

- www.wilsonweb.com/webmarket – Internet marketing information center; provides on web marketing.

- http://fita.worldbid.com – Federation of International Trade Association (FITA); Trade leads, International Buy/Sell exchange, business to business marketplace that helps a company find more business.

- www.worldbizmedia.com – Access to international business-to-business media for advertising agencies and their clients; has a database of 4,000 international business-to-business publications.

- www.fita.org/tshows.html – Database of hundreds of trade shows, conventions, seminars and meetings worldwide. One can search by city, state, country, industry or month.

- www.bizweb.com – Index of company websites; search by category.

- www.business.com – search engine for business information; contains more than 400,000 listings.

- www.intbit.com/products/gbd.htm – Global Business Directory; more than 350,000 major global companies, businesses and services are included covering all industries. Also included are more than 300,000 e-mail addresses. Fax number, telephone number and other contact information also available.

- www.tgrnet.com – Thomas Global Register; a directory of 500,000 manufacturers and distributors from 26 countries, classified by 10,500 products and services categories.

- www.europages.com – The European Business Directory; search for information on a supplier or service provider. A business-to-business directory published in six languages in three media versions: Website, Printed version and CD-ROM.

- www.economist.com/countries – Basic info. including economic data, political profiles, links to newspapers and government offices, for many countries.

- www.census.goc/foreign-trade/www – US Foreign Trade Statistics; State Exports (by country or commodity), press releases and trade highlights, updated Foreign Trade Web News.

- www.globaledge.msu.edu/ibrd/ibrd.asp – Provides an outline of the business climate, political structure, history and statistical data for more than 190 countries. A directory of international business resources categorized by specific orientation and content, glossary of definitions and descriptions of terms and acronyms used in international business.

- www.ustr.gov – Office of the United States Trade Representative; Provides the latest news, reports and publications, speeches and testimony, National Trade Estimate Report on foreign trade barriers, published annually and written by USTR staff, surveys significant foreign barriers to US exports.

- www.library.uncc.edu/vibes – VIBES (Virtual International Business and Economic Sources); provides over 1,600 links to Internet sources of international business and economic information.

- www.unctad.org – United Nations Conference on Trade and Development based in Switzerland. Aims at the integration of developing countries into the world economy, schedules of events and meetings.

- www.odci.gove/cia/publications/factbook – the CIA World Factbook, a thorough annual compilation of history and data about every country in the world.

TABLE 4.4 Primary data methods

Survey
Personal interviews
Focus groups
Mail surveys
Telephone surveys
Internet surveys or focus groups

Observation
Watching how products are used, for example how factory workers use machine tools
Analyzing websites and other communications tools
Observing employee behavior

Experimentation
Test marketing
Trials of new systems or products at selected customers' premises

There are three major ways to develop primary data: through surveys, observation or experimentation.

Experimentation is not often used in B2B research. It involves developing matched sets of respondents and varying stimuli to each to determine what reactions might be obtained. This method is more often used in consumer market research. Test marketing is probably the main way in which experimentation might be used in B2B research, but asking selected customers to use a product for a trial period is also a possibility, particularly when a close relationship exists between the firm and its customers.

Observation simply means 'watching' either users or decision makers. A B2B firm might, for instance, use time-lapse photography in a factory to determine how workers use a color measuring device in a production line. Some firms have also been known to observe the number of containers flowing out of a competitor's factory to measure their sales rate.

By far the most common form of research is the survey. In business marketing, personal interviews (also known as desk-side interviews) are often used for determining customer requirements or to forecast future needs of key customers. Where questions are complex, personal interviews are often the best method.

If respondents are geographically concentrated, it can be less costly to conduct focus groups with five to ten individuals. Focus groups are best used with respondents who identify more readily with their profession than with their employer. For instance, placing marketing directors of competing firms in one focus group will usually yield no useful information, whereas assembling a group of architects who work for various companies can be quite successful. Focus groups are less costly per respondent than are personal interviews, while maintaining many of the advantages. Frequently, business marketers need to show potential customers what a product looks like or how it works. Both personal interviews and focus groups allow for this and both allow for the gathering of a great deal of information in a limited amount of time. The key advantages to both interviews and focus groups is the ability to obtain answers to probing questions that get to the heart of a customer's thinking process. In addition, focus groups often give researchers special insight into the influence others have on the decision-making processes of all the members of the buying center.

The disadvantages of both focus groups and personal interviews are the cost and relative time required to collect, analyze and report the data. Since the number of persons interviewed must be limited by the market research budget, projecting results to a national or world market is problematic. Focus groups and in-depth interviews are particularly useful for finding out why people behave the way they do, however, surveys generally only tell us what people do or intend to do.

Telephone surveys are frequently used to get information from business respondents. When respondents are easy to identify and reach by phone, this method is far less costly than either focus groups or personal interviews. Telephone interviews can also be completed quickly and, if the sample is chosen properly, the results are projectable to the overall market. As must be obvious, it is difficult to ask in-depth, probing questions on the phone and there is a limit to the length of interviews. Some interviewer bias may creep into the discussions, so that the opinions recorded reflect the interviewer's personality and beliefs more than that of the respondent. In addition, it is not always clear that the respondent is identified correctly and so the respondent may be misrepresented. One major disadvantage of telephone surveys is that the researching firm would be unable to show products, concepts or advertising to the respondents unless special arrangements are made to send information to them in advance of the interviews.

Mail surveys are the least expensive approach to gaining information through research. Just about any respondent is a possible target for mail research and this method can completely eliminate interviewer bias. The major disadvantages to mail surveys are the low response rate and the complete lack of control over who actually responds. In other words, business marketers may receive surveys completed by secretaries or administrative assistants rather than the actual targeted individual. Mail surveys are also relatively slow and eliminate the possibility of showing products or concepts with a live demonstration.

Recently, the Internet is being widely used for both surveys and focus groups. The major advantages of using the Internet in this way, as shown in Figure 4.2 below, are speed and cost reduction of the survey itself. Internet surveys are far less expensive than telephone surveys and Internet focus groups are equally less expensive than 'live' focus groups. The ability to show some products or advertising or software to respondents is an advantage for the Internet approach. However, there are some disadvantages. For B2B research the total cost of an Internet project can be the same or higher than

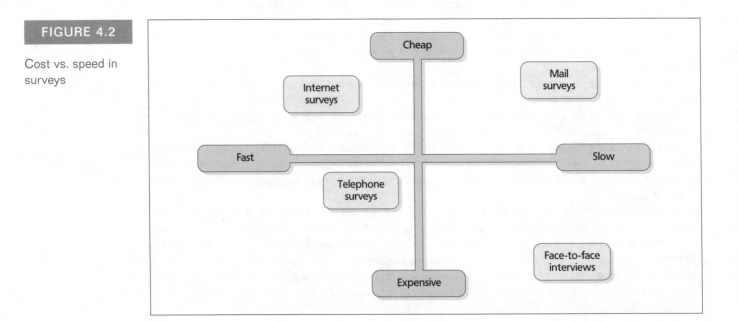

FIGURE 4.2

Cost vs. speed in surveys

for a telephone project because of the lack of sources for e-mail addresses of respondents and the necessity to pay each respondent an incentive for participation. Since e-mail addresses of respondents in specific B2B segments do not exist, the approach is to recruit each respondent by telephone and then send them to a website to complete the survey. This requires an incentive be paid, which can often amount to the same or more per respondent as the cost of a completed telephone interview. The additional cost of telephone recruiting can easily make the total cost prohibitive. In addition, many firms do not allow complete employee access to the Internet. This automatically limits the sample and may bias the results. Both Internet surveys and Internet focus groups have the disadvantage that it is not clear who is responding and misrepresentation may occur. Internet focus groups have an additional disadvantage in that the face-to-face reaction and ability to read body language is eliminated.

Some firms also undertake customer visits by firm personnel (rather than professional researchers) to gather various kinds of data. With this method, firm personnel may visit a customer's site or invite a key customer to the firm's headquarters. Customer visits can reveal current and potential problems related to products or service, uncover unknown customer needs which may lead to new market opportunities and also solidify customer relationships. This method can be as effective as formal market research using the methods described above if care is taken in the selection of respondents and capturing of data. Firm personnel must be given training in interviewing techniques and given discussion guides or questionnaires to manage the visits. When these precautions are not undertaken, this method is best used as a sales aid. One firm invited customers to view a new product at its plant. Customers were flown to the plant on the company's aircraft and given extensive hospitality. While touring the models of the new product, the visiting customers made many useful comments. Unfortunately, the host company made no provision to capture the comments and the visits were far less valuable than they should have been. Table 4.5 presents the overview of survey methods.

Applying all of these research techniques to the international setting requires an increased level of sensitivity. While in the past some felt that qualitative research techniques such as personal interviews and focus groups could not be applied in many markets, studies by one of the authors show this not to be the case (Zimmerman and Szenberg 2000). Nearly every qualitative research technique is employed in nearly every country, from the People's Republic of China to Mexico and desk-side interviews are employed nearly as frequently. Cost for business research varies widely by country, with the most expensive country Japan, where a typical project may cost twice as much as one completed in the US.

An important concept in international research is the debate between the so-called 'emic' and 'etic' schools of thought. The emic school believes that attitudes and behaviors are unique to a particular culture while the etic school attempts to find universal culture-free measures which may be applied across various markets. Differences of this nature tend to be minimized in business marketing since questions more often relate to technical problems rather than emotional and personal motivations. Nevertheless, a business marketer must be aware of these two schools of thought and carefully apply measures used in one culture to others using suitable tests to be sure the measures are appropriate.

TALKING POINT

In reviewing secondary data, it is important to maintain a somewhat skeptical attitude, especially as it relates to data from various international and Internet-only sources. Key questions to ask are:

- Who collected the data?
- What methods were used to collect the data?
- Who were the respondents?
- When was the data collected?

So if secondary data is so fraught with risk, why use it at all? Why not go straight to collecting our own primary data, where at least we can maintain some semblance of quality control? Or would this just get us in trouble with the finance director?

TABLE 4.5 Comparing B2B survey methods

Research Method	Characteristics of Respondents	Advantages	Disadvantages
Personal (Desk-Side) Interview	• Few • Geographically dispersed • Difficult to reach	• Can ask complex questions • Can show/demonstrate product or concept • Get qualitative (why) answers • High response rate	• Most costly method • Relatively slow • Risk of interviewer bias • Results usually not projectable to entire market
Focus Groups	• Moderate number • Geographically concentrated • Somewhat difficult to reach • Identify with profession rather than employer	• Cost efficient compared to personal interviews • Can show/demonstrate product or concept • Faster than personal interviews • Can get qualitative (why) answers • Interaction can simulate real-world decision-making	• Relatively costly, though less per respondent than personal interviews • Possible moderator bias • Dominance by one/few respondents • Usually not projectable to entire market
Telephone Surveys	• Few or many • Geographically dispersed • Relatively easy to identify and reach	• Lower cost than personal interviews or focus groups • Fast • Projectable with large enough sample	• Limits types and length of questions • Possible interviewer bias • Possible misinterpretation of respondent • Inability to show concept or demonstrate product
Mail Surveys	• Any respondents who can receive mail	• Least costly of all methods • Eliminates interview bias	• Control of exact respondent • Low response rate • Relatively slow • Inability to show concept or demonstrate product
Internet Surveys	• Respondents with access to Internet	• Low cost • Fast • Ability to show some concepts or products	• Possible invalid sample • Control of exact respondent
Internet Focus Groups	• Moderate number • Geographically dispersed • Difficult to reach	• Lower cost than personal focus groups • Fast • Ability to show some concepts or products	• Control of exact respondents • Lack of face-to-face interaction • Others, same as groups above

Sampling and validity

A key part of gaining useable answers from research is developing the proper sample. In business markets, the number of individuals is usually limited. In addition, Pareto's Law often applies (simply put, about 80 per cent of the results come from about 20 per cent of the entities). So, in many markets a handful of corporations will buy most of the product. Because of this, random sampling, often used in consumer research where each individual is looked upon as a relatively equal customer, is not a frequently used sampling approach in business markets. Generally speaking, business marketers use stratified random sampling where a specific subset of potential respondents is selected and then of this subset specific respondents are chosen by chance. In some markets there are so few potential respondents who may purchase the product that a 100 per cent review of the population is possible. For instance, a firm which sells products to the commercial air frame manufacturing business could interview Boeing, Airbus, Embraer and Bombardier and have the answers covering most of the market potential.

Validity means a particular research measurement actually measures what it is supposed to measure. Problems with validity arise when questions are vague or misleading, or respondents attempt to be especially cooperative and answer questions even when they have no information. Pre-tests of research instruments can help improve validity.

Internationally, these questions are even more difficult because respondents in various cultures may give a different interpretation to a perfectly 'obvious' concept. For instance, the word 'family' is interpreted in Africa to include all of the extended family, while in Western societies it is often interpreted to include only the immediate family. Similar problems can arise in business markets and therefore survey instruments and focus group moderator guides must be pre-tested before being used across many cultures. Often it is useful to have interviewers define terms for respondents before proceeding with the interviews. Also, in some cultures respondents do not wish to disappoint the interviewer. This means that respondents may give an answer even when they have no idea what the true situation is, or may provide answers which they think will please the interviewer.

Developing questionnaires

To write a good questionnaire is an art as well as a skill. First, questions should be placed in a logical order, with the most sensitive questions at the end of the questionnaire. All questions should relate to research objectives. If questions are being asked which don't help produce the desired result, they add time and should be eliminated. For focus groups and personal interviews, open-ended questions (those that cannot be answered by a simple yes or no) are best because they start discussion and lead to explanation by the respondent. For telephone and mail surveys, closed-ended questions are best. These are questions which can be answered by selecting a measurement such as 'always, sometimes, never' or by a yes-no or some other simple choice. Avoid double-barreled questions, that is, questions that ask for two answers at the same time. This is a common failing of even some sophisticated researchers. A question such as 'have you bought electronic equipment from us and are you satisfied' might be answered yes. But in analyzing the results, one would not know whether the respondent was saying 'yes, we have bought equipment' or 'yes, we are satisfied with the equipment' or both. Do not use wording or jargon that the respondent may not know. This is especially a problem in business marketing where assumptions can often be made about those within the market. Often, respondents are not familiar with the terminology the manufacturer considers quite basic. Rather than admit ignorance, respondents will often give answers which are completely misleading or uninformed.

Provide a succinct, but convincing introduction which tells respondents why they should help the researcher gather the information needed. In some cases, respondents may be promised a summary of the results. If this isn't possible, simply stating that results will be used to help improve service can be effective. Allow for 'don't know' responses rather than make respondents answer questions they are unqualified to answer. Avoid hypothetical questions or examples which may confuse respondents. Specifically asking respondents if they would buy a product if it were priced at a particular level usually yields useless results. To estimate true buying potential, trade-off or conjoint (sometimes also called forced-choice) analysis is usually used. This is a much more reliable indicator of future buying behavior. Asking respondents for specific suggestions for new products is also usually unproductive. It is more effective to ask respondents what problems they face in order to elicit ideas for new products or product improvements.

Analyzing the data

In analyzing quantitative data, researchers will assemble the information into cross-tabulated tables which allows the examination of the answers to questions by sub-segment, such as years' experience

FIGURE 4.3 Sample of a cross-tabulated page of research   Architectural Research Associates

— ELECTRONIC AND PRINT PRODUCT INFORMATION —   DECEMBER 1999

Q. 13 Internet usage classification

	Total	Region				Firm Type			Firm Size		Title			Work Type			Single Family Res.		Internet Usage		
		West	Mid-West	North East	South	Gen. Contr	Home Bldr	Dsgn Bld	Med	Large	Cons. Mgr	Esti-mator	Super/Pres/VP	Mostly Renov.	Mostly New	50-50	<25%	25%+	Never Use	5 hrs/less	5+ hrs
Total	404 100%	90 100%	72 100%	85 100%	157 100%	289 100%	38 100%	77 100%	277 100%	127 100%	133 100%	151 100%	120 100%	67 100%	286 100%	51 100%	343 100%	61 100%	49 100%	183 100%	139 100%
Heavy User	139 34.4%	29 32.2%	25 34.7%	28 32.9%	57 36.3%	94 32.5%	15 39.5%	30 39.0%	85 30.7%	54 42.5%	47 35.3%	53 35.1%	39 32.5%	25 37.3%	101 35.5%	13 25.5%	119 34.7%	20 32.8%	–	–	139 100%
Light User	204 50.5%	43 47.8%	38 52.8%	44 51.8%	79 50.3%	149 51.6%	16 42.1%	39 50.6%	146 52.7%	58 45.7%	62 46.6%	80 53.0%	62 51.7%	31 46.3%	145 50.7%	28 54.9%	177 51.6%	27 44.3%	–	183 100%	–
Never Use	49 12.1%	15 16.7%	7 9.7%	10 11.8%	17 10.8%	36 12.5%	7 18.4%	6 7.8%	37 13.4%	12 9.4%	15 11.3%	18 11.9%	16 13.3%	8 11.9%	34 11.9%	7 13.7%	37 10.8%	12 19.7%	49 100%	–	–
Don't Know/ Refused	12 3.0%	3 3.3%	2 2.8%	3 3.5%	4 2.5%	10 3.5%	–	2 2.6%	9 3.2%	3 2.4%	9 6.8%	–	3 2.5%	3 4.5%	6 2.1%	3 5.9%	10 2.9%	2 3.3%	–	–	–

or geographic location. Figure 4.3 is a sample of a cross-tabulated page of research from a study of architects.

Figure 4.3 shows respondents' answers to a question about their Internet usage. As can be seen, the total of all respondents' answers is given as well as answers by region, by type of firm, size of firm, title of respondent, type of work and whether they are heavily or not heavily involved in designing single-family residential homes. Three Internet usage columns are the same as the classification columns on the far left. From the bold numbers, we can see that 42.5 per cent of respondents who work in large firms can be classified as heavy Internet users as against only 30.7 per cent of those who work in medium-sized firms.

Results may be analyzed using available software programs which describe data or help to develop forecasts. Significance tests (t tests) are extremely important in determining how likely it is that the results from the sample represent the opinions and beliefs of the entire population. Sophisticated researchers also undertake factor analysis in order to determine whether one factor being measured is simply the same as another measured factor. The goal is to establish a list of important factors which would be independent from each other. Software available for personal computers allows fairly sophisticated statistical analysis to be performed quite simply and at low cost.

Qualitative data analysis is by necessity more subjective. Usually, transcripts are made of focus groups or recorded interviews made during the interviews on focus groups. Computer programs now allow an analysis of words or phrases used to aid the researcher in the analysis. Although there are more than 24 software packages now available to help the qualitative researchers (Barry 1998), Table 4.6 shows some of the leading ones with a brief explanation of each.

In general, qualitative research can explain the thinking respondents are using to arrive at conclusions, but conventional wisdom dictates that qualitative results are not projectable because of the small sample sizes. However, as we have seen in some business markets dominated by very or few major players, a limited sample will deliver highly projectable results.

The final step is to present the findings. In most cases, a firm will request a written report as well as an oral presentation. The advent of the Internet and presentation software allows a firm to receive electronic copies of the written report and to view a presentation electronically which can then be used for further presentation within the firm. Experience shows that presentations must be carefully honed to keep the attention of top management. The use of graphics and even integrated 'sound

TABLE 4.6 Analysis tools for qualitative data

Program	Description
ATLAS.ti	Theory building. Features VISE: Visualization, Integration, Serendipity and Exploration. Can map out relationships between data and theory on screen and move between them.
QSR NUD*IST	Indexes, searches and supports theorizing; will handle textual records such as photographs and tape recordings. Connects categories, and is good at generating taxonomies (showing how concepts relate).
QUALPRO	Researcher has to segment and code, then QUALPRO will find and assemble the indicated segments.
The ETHNOGRAPH	Does what QUALPRO does, but can also find text that has been coded two or more ways.
Longman Concordance	Creates a KWIC (key word in context) file by searching for the key word identified by the researcher and abstracting it with the words around it so as to develop a list of places where the key word appears.

bytes' or video clips from focus groups or interviews (if available) enhances the impact of the presentations. The most effective presentations last no longer than one hour, should concentrate on the conclusions to be drawn from the research and should suggest potential actions resulting from these conclusions.

Market potential and sales forecasts

Frequently, market research is used by business marketers to estimate the market potential for a particular product or product line and then to develop sales forecasts and quotas for the salesforce. Two overall strategic approaches to sales forecasting exist; 'break-down' and 'build-up'. The break-down approach begins with the overall market for the product category and seeks to predict what the firm's share of that market will be. For example, a bank may have access to government economic forecasts which can be used to calculate the total loans market for the following year. The bank forecasters will know what the bank's share of the market was in previous years and can use this information to make a reasonable estimate of what the bank's total lending will be in the ensuing year.

Obviously, the first and most important step in the build-up approach is to define the market segment. This has been discussed at length in an earlier chapter. In order to develop sales forecasts, one must develop market potential. In order to develop market potential, various methods should be combined. The use of both primary and secondary data is usually essential to arrive at a meaningful answer. Figure 4.4 describes the development of the market potential for an office furniture firm.

Assuming the firm was examining the potential in several foreign markets, the first step would be to determine how many workers there are in each market, then reduce that number to administrative workers and further reduce it to desk workers who might be able to use the office furniture. Next, a percentage of desk workers who would be given new furniture each year must be determined. The resulting number would then be multiplied by a dollar figure spent per employee and this would yield the market potential in a particular market for office furniture. Market potential is the maximum possible sales of all firms of a particular kind of product in a market during a particular period, usually one year. The market forecast is a somewhat lower number management uses as a realistic basis for planning.

Starting from the market forecast, the sales forecast can then be developed. In order to do this, the market forecast would be multiplied by the company's expected market share in this particular country. This then yields the sales potential. The sales potential could then be reduced to territorial quotas by using the geographic market share. For example, let us assume a market forecast of US$200 million was developed for office seating in Japan. This figure would then be looked at based on the market share for the firm developing the sales forecast. If this market share were 25 per cent, sales potential would be US$50 million. In order to assign sales quotas, management might increase the sales forecast over the sales potential, assuming that extra efforts by the salesforce might increase market share. However, for this example, let us assume that US$50 million would be used as a sales potential. If it is determined that Tokyo is 50 per cent of the market, the sales quota for Tokyo would be US$25 million.

FIGURE 4.4	
Development of market forecast and sales forecast	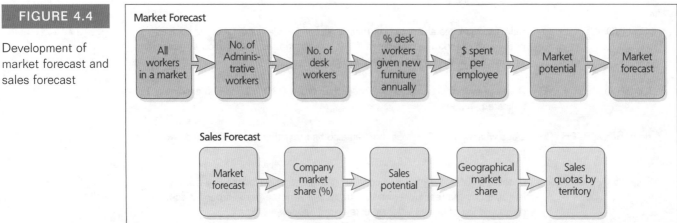

As might be expected, some of this data is easily obtained through secondary sources. However, other data would need to be developed though other methods. Often, primary research is used to develop an estimate of these unknowns, such as the percent of desk workers to be supplied with new furniture annually or the dollars to be spent per employee on new furniture. The method is called the Chain-Ratio Method of developing a forecast. However, other methods are also used. Some firms have been able to use statistical series for comparison with sales of a particular product, for instance, one might determine that for every US$10-million worth of automobiles shipped, US$500,000 in brake lights will be sold. These kinds of relationships can be developed through time series analysis (see Table 4.7). Here again, a usage factor may need to be developed through primary research.

Some firms use the Delphi technique to forecast the future, especially for new products with no historical data. In the Delphi method, opinions of a panel of experts are gathered. Once all the opinions have been summarized, they are circulated to the panel through several rounds with the goal of developing a consensus among the experts.

In most forecasts, an important input is executive judgment. Frequently, senior managers who have been working in a particular industry or country for many years have very good ideas about the sizes of markets or the penetration of a particular product. Their input should be used in developing the final forecast.

Many firms also use the salesforce composite method to develop a sales forecast. This is a bottom-up approach where individual salespeople estimate their sales for the following year. Each of these forecasts is then summarized to develop territorial and national as well as international forecasts.

TABLE 4.7 Time series analysis

Type of Analysis	Description
Trend analysis	Focuses on aggregate sales data collected over a long period to determine whether sales are rising, falling, or staying level.
Cycle analysis	Here the forecaster examines the sales figures from a number of years to see whether there is a cyclical pattern; perhaps a response to the economic boom and bust cycle. This method has been largely discredited for most markets, since the cycles do not follow a regular pattern.
Seasonal analysis	Sales figures are analyzed on a monthly or even weekly basis to see whether there is a seasonal cycle operating.
Random factor analysis	In any analysis there will be figures that do not fit the pattern; random factor analysis seeks to attribute explanations for these abnormal findings. For example, a spell of unseasonal weather might have affected one month's figures.

TABLE 4.8 Common sales forecasting techniques

Technique	Explanation
Customer survey	Typically, customers would be asked about their buying intentions over (say) the next 12 months. Often buyers would be unable to answer with any degree of certainty, but the average of the responses is often fairly accurate, depending on the industry involved.
Salesforce survey	Salespeople are asked how much they expect to sell. This has the drawback that they may be over-optimistic, or (on the other hand) may fear that they will be held to their forecast and will deliberately under-estimate.
Distributor survey	A variation on the salesforce survey, used when the company has a substantial network of distributors.

TABLE 4.8 *(cont.)*

Technique	Explanation
Delphi approach	This is a method of eliciting expert opinion from a panel of those involved (sales managers, marketing executives, distributors etc.).
Time-series analysis	Using the company's past sales records to predict the future. Time-series is unable to take account of the unexpected and of course looks at comparing the current situation with the past, rather than comparing the current position with a projection of where the company should be.
Test marketing	Launching the product in a limited market, either geographically or in terms of customer groups, can be very effective in developing an estimate of overall sales following roll-out to all customers. The main drawback is that it telegraphs the company's intentions to its competitors.

While this is a valuable tool to be used in developing the final forecast, experience has shown that salesforces tend to be too optimistic. Using the sales composite forecast alone usually yields territorial objectives which turn out to be nearly impossible to achieve. In short, the best method for developing a sales forecast is the combination method, that is, using the results of several methods both quantitative and qualitative (see Table 4.8 above). This usually yields the most accurate market potential and sales forecasts.

In international research, some firms have turned to scenario analysis, recognizing that developments in international markets are often discontinuous (witness the fall of the Soviet Union). In this approach, scenarios are developed by experts through the Delphi technique and by senior management. Scenarios encourage firms to develop contingency plans should the selected sales forecast prove unreliable because of unpredictable events.

Organizing for market research

Many different approaches to organizing the marketing information system have been attempted by various firms. A basic decision must be whether all functions are to be performed within the firm or whether some will be contracted to independent vendors. The obvious advantage of holding all work within the firm is the absolute certainty that none of the information will be given to unauthorized people. A major disadvantage is the high cost, keeping on staff who may not be fully employed all of the time.

Some large firms maintain a centralized research function through which all projects are implemented. Others have decentralized their research functions so that SBUs are completely in charge of all of their own projects. The obvious benefits for the decentralized organization is that all research projects tend to be relevant to the specific needs of the divisions. However, the major drawback is that no corporate-wide studies (such as image studies of the overall corporation) are ever undertaken. Therefore, many large firms have opted to have a centralized research function with localized, divisional researchers as well.

One fact is absolutely clear and that is no market intelligence unit can be successful without the support of top management. While the market intelligence function often reports to the marketing function, one might argue that it should report to an executive rather than a functional area. In some firms, the information function reports to the financial organization.

A key question is the 'make or buy' decision for market research. As mentioned before, some firms prefer to hold all information in-house and will continue to keep all research functions within the firm. However, this requires experts such as focus group moderators to be employed either at running focus groups throughout the year or in some other way. Very few industrial firms require the number of focus groups or interviews which would keep moderators or interviewers busy all the time. Therefore, most business marketing firms opt to use outside vendors. Throughout the world there are experts in every aspect of market research ready to serve. Organizations like ESOMAR can provide lists of vendors by specialty and location.

FIGURE 4.5   Sample research proposal

ACME COMPANY

SYSTEM FOLLOW UP STUDY

INTRODUCTION

Recently completed focus groups indicated some buyer interest in a new computer-based System to be offered by Acme Co. But there were several reservations expressed by respondents. The firm has now advanced the development of the concept.

The firm has also improved the demonstration of this service and wishes to further test the general viability of the concept.

OBJECTIVES

- To test the acceptability of the new system with buyers.
- To help select participants for the in-market test.

METHODOLOGY

- Because we want detailed reactions to the new system and may want the participants to have hands-on experience, we recommend mini-focus groups be held to accomplish these objectives.
- Eight mini-focus groups will be held, four in London and four in New York. Each is planned for 1½ hours.
- ABC Research will develop all recruiting guides for the mini-focus groups, subject to the approval of Acme management. Individuals will be screened for size of firm, industry and other criteria to be determined.
- Lists for recruiting will be provided by Acme Co. and will be obtained by ABC Research.
- ABC Research will recruit seven (7) individuals for each group according to the requirements in the recruiting guide. We recommend that participants be paid an honorarium of $100–125 for their time. (Note: We have budgeted for five respondents per group, at $125.)
- John Smith will serve as impartial moderator at all groups.
- ABC Research will make all arrangements for focus group facilities.
- ABC Research will develop a detailed focus group discussion guide subject to the approval of Acme management. The discussion guide will be designed to elicit:

  - General reaction to the concept.
  - Insight into sellers and products most suited for the new system.
  - Perception of benefits of and objections to the new system.
  - Customer requirements for system tools including installation, training, ease of use and reporting.
  - Perspectives on fee structures and data security.

- An ABC researcher will be present at all groups to aid in arrangements and take notes.
- Acme _will_ be mentioned as the sponsor of the research.
- After the focus groups are completed, ABC will develop a complete report summarizing the findings. This report will emphasize conclusions and recommendations based on our findings and experience.

NEEDED FROM ACME

- Proposed system concept statement and computer demo as agreed.
- Lists for recruiting.

DELIVERABLES

- Complete report of focus groups – two copies (one bound and one unbound) or via email.
- PowerPoint presentation of findings (optional at extra cost).
- Audio tapes (if requested).
- Transcripts of focus groups (if requested).
- Video tapes (optional).

TIMING

Action	Complete By
Approval	January 10
Arrangements/Logistics	January 17
Approved Recruiting Guide	January 17
Discussion Guide	January 24
Recruiting	January 31
Focus Groups: (Recommended Schedule)	
London	February 4 (Noon and 6:00 p.m.) February 5 (8:30 a.m. and Noon)
New York	February 6 (8:30 a.m. and Noon) February 7 (8:30 a.m. and Noon)
Debriefing	February 14
Complete Report	February 28

FIGURE 4.5 *(cont.)*

BUDGET

Professional Services		$ 16,350
Expenses (billed at cost)		$ 14,800

Facility rental (8 @ $450)	$ 3,600
Food (8 @ $100)	800
Travel	3,000
Transcripts (8 @ $175)	1,400
Incentives (8 × 5 × $125)	5,000
Telephone/copies	500
Clerical	500

TOTAL BUDGET $ 31,150

Videotaping available at $350 per group additional (billed at cost).

TERMS

One half of budget less incentives due upon approval (January 10)	$ 13,075
Incentives due one week before first group (January 31)	$ 5,000
One quarter of budget less incentives due at midpoint of project (January 31)	$ 6,538
One quarter due upon completion of project (February 28)	$ 6,537

APPROVAL

_____   _____
John Smith, President   Date
ABC Research

_____   _____
Joe Jones,   Date
Manager, Market Research
Acme Co.

An ongoing analysis is necessary to determine the level of centralization and in-house completion required. But a successful project requires one point of contact within the firm. Usually this individual should know something about market research in order to manage the project successfully. Outside vendors will present specific proposals which should include the objectives of the study, methodology, completion schedule and costs as well as deliverables.

Figure 4.5 (above) is an actual example research proposal adapted for this text.

Not having a specific proposal can lead to misunderstandings and disappointment for the researching firm. One large, multinational firm commissioned a study from a large consulting firm in Japan. At the conclusion of the study, the consulting firm presented the results on overhead slides then scooped up the slides and left. The multinational firm had no written report and no record of the findings, except for notes taken during the presentation of the overhead slides. A clear definition of deliverables would have avoided this problem.

Managing research projects

To summarize, the best way to manage a market research project is to clearly understand what the project is to accomplish. Research objectives should be clearly specified before any research is undertaken. At that time, the firm should identify what it knows and what it doesn't know and then do a thorough secondary data search. Once primary research is decided upon, research vendors should be

TABLE 4.9 Managing research project (guidelines)

- Anticipate actions resulting from findings
- Clarify/specify research objectives
- Identify knowns vs unknowns
- Develop secondary data first
- Choose research providers carefully
  - References – check
  - Knowledge of industry
  - Knowledge of market
- Review detailed proposals
- Do not underfund
- Manage domestically and in-country

carefully chosen. The firm should check the references of any research vendor and that vendor should know both the industry and the market. Written proposals should be reviewed and a vendor chosen. Research, especially including many national markets, should not be underfunded. It is preferable to limit the scope of research rather than to complete partial research across many topics and markets. Finally, the research project must be managed in the domestic market as well as in-country markets. Table 4.9 lists these project management guidelines.

■ Benchmarking

Many firms see benchmarking as an important aspect of their overall information gathering program. Benchmarking began as a result of the re-engineering movement and has often been focused heavily on processes such as engineering, purchasing, manufacturing and human resources. But benchmarking

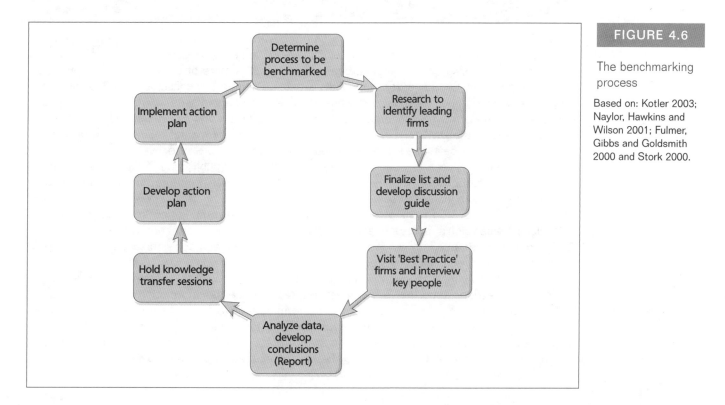

FIGURE 4.6

The benchmarking process

Based on: Kotler 2003; Naylor, Hawkins and Wilson 2001; Fulmer, Gibbs and Goldsmith 2000 and Stork 2000.

can also be put to fruitful use by business marketers. The essence of benchmarking is identifying 'best practices' for particular processes or functions, then learning from these practices and adapting them to the needs of your firm. Firms who wish to benchmark usually identify potential sources for information in non-competing industries where the processes involved show some commonality. The process is described in Figure 4.6.

The first step is to determine the processes to be benchmarked. Naylor *et al.* (2001) identify a method for choosing marketing processes which might be benchmarked by placing them on a matrix that attempts to measure each function's importance to business success and the urgency for the need for improvement. Once the processes to be benchmarked have been determined, a secondary research program should be undertaken to find firms that may be candidates for cooperation and to develop general knowledge about these processes. The next step is to finalize the potential partner list and to develop a discussion guide to be used during site visits. The firm should arrange visits where representatives of the benchmarking firm would visit firms known for best practices and ask pre-developed questions. Here a guide more like a focus group moderator's guide would be best since the questions should be framed in an open-ended manner. The next step is to analyze the data and develop the conclusions, providing a report for all interested firm personnel. Following this, the benchmarking team should arrange for knowledge transfer sessions either by one-on-one discussions within the firm or by meetings. Fulmer *et al.* (2000) describes a two-day knowledge transfer session in which management as well as the best-practice interviewees in addition to the benchmarking team all participate. Next would be to develop an action plan using the information learned from the benchmarking process. In this plan, Stork (2000) recommends setting goals then identifying work steps necessary to achieve these goals and methods of measurement to see whether progress is being made toward the goals. He also suggests a plan for 'recalibration', as the action plan might have to be changed as a result of changing environments. He warns about writing a report and simply filing it. While the action plan is implemented, there should be a feedback mechanism to start the process over should that be required.

While benchmarking is certainly popular, with some reports of more than 70 per cent of the 500 largest US firms practicing it (Naylor *et al.* 2001), Quinn (1999) warns against simply meeting best practices. He identifies 'figures of merit which set targets above the normal so that the firm develops competitive advantages in its most important core competencies', thereby taking benchmarking one step further.

SUMMARY

Market research is critical to developing an effective business marketing program. Research used properly helps marketers identify and solve problems. While consumer research focuses most on advertising and packaging, business research is more often focused on developing market potential. Consumer research deals with large numbers of consumers, each of whom is generally looked upon as equal, while business research generally deals with very small populations where a few respondents affect the largest portion of sales volume. Understanding the makeup of the DMU or buying center is a critical task of market research and once this understanding is developed, market research can be far more effective. The Internet has made developing secondary data far easier since virtually all published information is available somewhere on the web. However one must be careful in using Internet information without confirmation from many sources.

Most sophisticated firms attempt to develop a complete marketing information system, including a decision support system to help managers use the information to make decisions. Developing both an effective marketing information system and decision support system is a difficult project requiring consistent effort.

When developing market research, the most important step is to define exactly what information is needed. To do this, a firm must decide what use the information will be put to and who will be making decisions based on the information developed. Clear research objectives are critical if a research project is to be successful. After reviewing all secondary research, the firm then decides whether to move ahead with primary research. The Internet allows focus groups and interviews to be completed far less expensively. However it may be impossible to draw a representative sample through the Internet. Since there are far fewer members of any particular population in a market segment, it may be possible to interview a small number of individuals to develop realistic and projectable results using focus groups, desk-side or telephone interviews. The advantage of the personal approach is that products can be demonstrated and more in-depth questions can be used. Firms must be careful that instruments such as questionnaires or focus group moderation guides can be used in various markets across the world. While all qualitative market research techniques have been used successfully in various countries, pre-testing of these instruments is necessary to be sure of the validity of the responses. When analyzing quantitative data, cross-tabulated tables are used to show the differences between various sub-segments of the respondent pool. Qualitative research is analyzed using software which can identify words or groups of words used frequently or by old fashioned reading and discussion methods.

Market research is used often by business marketers to develop market potential. Once a market segment is developed, research is often used to develop critical ratios, such as the percentage of individuals who may decide to buy a new software product within the next year. These ratios are then applied to known data to develop a market potential. Once the market potential is developed, sales forecasts and sales quotas are usually determined. Since in business marketing the salesforce is so critical, developing attainable sales quotas is important. Some firms use the Delphi technique to forecast the future, requiring a group of experts to give their opinions in several rounds. Firms also use the salesforce composite method, using a bottom-up approach from the salesforce. However, this approach tends to give very optimistic forecasts. Scenario analysis is also useful, especially in international research where unpredictable events happen quickly.

While a few firms hold all market information functions within the firm, most outsource at least data collection, hiring focus group moderators or telephone or Internet researchers when required. Keeping all research within the firm obviously protects sensitive data. However, the extremely high cost of keeping specialists on staff who may not be fully employed deters most firms from doing this. Many firms have a combined centralized and decentralized approach to research, the centralized function developing projects affecting the entire firm and the decentralized function completing research which focuses only on a particular division or product line. When hiring an outside research vendor, specific proposals must be obtained. A firm must qualify the vendor as to expertise in market, product and method. When commissioning a research project, a firm must be careful not to underfund the project. To be successful, a project must have the support of top management. The most successful projects are completed where management understands the role of market research and the costs involved.

Benchmarking is the process of identifying best practices in organizations and then attempting to emulate these to improve the way things are done within a firm. The benchmarking process resembles the market research process in many ways and care must be taken to select the proper candidates and to develop the correct research instruments. Once best practices are identified, the firm must have an action plan to make sure these practices are implemented. The most successful firms try to exceed these best practices to establish real competitive advantage in their core competencies.

REVIEW QUESTIONS

1 What are the major differences between consumer and B2B market research?

2 What are the advantages and disadvantages of using the Internet for market research?

3 What are the key components of a marketing information system?

4 If you were the marketing director for a keyboard manufacturer whose major customers are personal computer manufacturers, how could you design the most effective market research program? What are the key steps in the process for you?

The NG Electronics corporation was a $250-million manufacturer of various electronic components Headquartered in Seoul, Korea. The firm had embarked on a long-term program of research and development with two university professors and had finally perfected a new high-speed, high-efficiency motor. Upon testing this small electrical motor, NG discovered that it was far more efficient than those of its competitors. The firm wished to move ahead quickly and turned to Lonny Cho, the director of marketing, to determine whether or not they should commit to building a new production facility.

The bulk of NG's sales were to large OEMs, with the rest (about 25 per cent) sold to small manufacturers and distributors. Lonny thought about the problem and realized that the firm could easily determine the acceptability of the new product with the larger OEMs, but the hundreds of other potential customers for this firm around the world presented a different picture. No one on Lonny's staff, including himself, had any experience with market research. However, there was no budget for this, so they decided to move ahead on their own. After some thought, Lonny determined that the key questions were:

1 How many units would a particular customer wish to buy?
2 How big was each customer segment?
3 What were the customer segments?
4 Who at each firm made the buying decisions for these motors?
5 What were the most popular sizes?
6 From whom did they usually buy?
7 How did they learn about new products?

Lonny knew enough to perform some secondary data work on his office computer and determined that the key end use market segments for this product were:

- pumps
- industrial sewing machines
- aircraft auxiliary equipment
- fluid meters.

Lonny thought about the sample. Since NG already sold to two of the end-use segments, he had customer lists of the larger OEMs, but he would have source lists of the smaller ones and the distributors. Because there was no budget, Cho selected a few of his junior employees who spoke English very well for telephone interviews. He then developed a questionnaire (which is included as Exhibit 4.1). In addition to developing the survey and starting his employees on the project, Cho also thought about the possibility of calling-in an outside market research firm to handle the project.

Questions

1 What is your overall assessment of Lonny Cho's approach to his information needs?
2 Will the questionnaire Cho designed elicit the information he is seeking?
3 What modifications would you make on this questionnaire
   a if it were used as an Internet or mail survey, or
   b to be used as a telephone survey?
4 If you were Lonny Cho would you prefer to use your own employees or attempt to get a budget to hire a market research firm? Why would you? How could you justify the use of an outside firm?

5 When would you choose the personal interview method versus the focus group method to gather data?

6 Suppose you were to be assigned to develop a sales forecast for tempered glass to be used in office buildings in Singapore. What are the major steps you might take to get to an acceptable forecast?

7 What are the advantages and disadvantages of in-house versus outside vendor performance of market research?

8 Suppose you were the marketing communications manager for a company in India developing software. What steps might you take to implement a benchmarking program to improve your department's results?

REFERENCES

Barry, C. (1998) 'Choosing Qualitative Data Analysis Software: Atlas/ti and Nudist Compared', *Sociological Research Online* 3: 3. http://www.socresonline.org.uk/socresonline/3/3/4.html

Fulmer, R. M., Gibbs, P. A. and Goldsmith, M. (2000) 'Developing Leaders: How Winning Companies Keep on Winning', *Sloan Management Review* 42: 1, Fall: 49–59.

Katz, M. (1979) 'Use Same Theory, Skills for Consumer, Industrial Marketing Research', *Marketing News*, January 12: 16.

Kotler, P. (2003) *Marketing Management*, Upper Saddle River, NJ: Prentice-Hall.

Malhotra, N. K. (1999) *Marketing Research: An Applied Orientation*, 3rd ed. Upper Saddle River, NJ: Prentice-Hall.

Naylor, J., Hawkins, N. and Wilson, C. (2001) 'Benchmarking Marketing in an SME: The Case of an Italian Kitchen Furniture Manufacturer', *The Marketing Review* 1: 325–339.

Perreault, Jr., W. D. and McCarthy, J. E. (2000) *Essentials of Marketing : A Global-Managerial Approach*, New York: McGraw-Hill.

Quinn, J. B. (1999) 'Strategic Outsourcing: Leveraging Knowledge Capabilities', *Sloan Management Review* 40: 4: Summer: 9–21.

Stork, K. (2000) 'Getting Payback from Benchmarking', *Purchasing*: 22 December: 30.

Zimmerman, A. S. and Szenberg, M. (2000) 'Implementing International Qualitative Research: Techniques and Obstacles', *Qualitative Research: An International Journal* 3: 3: 158–164.

EXHIBIT 4.1 Customer market survey

Customer Market Survey

Company Name _____ Industry Category _____

City _____ City and Country _____

Individual Interviewed _____ Title _____

Good morning/afternoon. I'm _____ , calling for NG Electronics. We are conducting a survey among knowledgeable executives like yourself about small, high-speed motors and I'd appreciate your cooperation. I'll be as brief as possible.

1. To what extent are you involved in the _____ specifying _____ purchase of small, high-speed electric motors? (Check which ones)
   _____ Very involved
   _____ Somewhat involved
   _____ Not involved (Ask to speak to the person most involved in that location and start interview again)
   _____ Terminate
   _____ Refused

2. What is the primary use of high-speed motors you buy?

   _____
   _____

3. What volume of small, high-speed motors would you normally purchase over 12 months?

   _____ Current purchases   _____ Peak   _____ Purchase activity next year

   Units:
   _____ Less than 100
   _____ 100–300
   _____ 300–500
   _____ Over 500

4. What price do you usually pay?

   _____
   _____

5. What size high-speed electric motors do you mostly purchase?

   _____
   _____

6. What RPMs do you require?

   _____
   _____

7. What is the average life of the small, high-speed motors you build into your original equipment?

   _____
   _____

8. Where do you usually buy your small, high-speed motors? (Prefer names and locations if possible)

	Name	Location
From a distributor		
Direct from the factory		

9. What is the primary reason you would select one supplier over another?
   _____ Competitive pricing   _____ Technical capability
   _____ Response time to quotes   _____ Fabrication capability
   _____ Inventory availability   _____ Location
   _____ Other (quality, service, delivery) _____

EXHIBIT 4.1   *(cont.)*

10. Do you usually buy your high-speed motors packaged with other components, or do you buy only the motor?

   _____ Package   _____ Motor   _____ Both

11. In making your purchasing or recommendation decision for high-speed motors, please describe how important the following are (check the appropriate items):

Factory:	No Importance		Somewhat Important		Very Important
	1	2	3	4	5
_____ Manufacturer's reputation	_____	_____	_____	_____	_____
_____ Distributor reputation	_____	_____	_____	_____	_____
_____ Availability	_____	_____	_____	_____	_____
_____ Service after the sale	_____	_____	_____	_____	_____
_____ Price	_____	_____	_____	_____	_____
_____ Warranty	_____	_____	_____	_____	_____

12. Which of the following is most important (Check one)

   _____ Manufacturer's reputation
   _____ Distributor reputation
   _____ Availability
   _____ Service after the sale
   _____ Price
   _____ Warranty

13. How do you receive information on the products you consider? (May check more than one, but not more than three)

   _____ Mailings from manufacturers
   _____ Mailings from distributor
   _____ Trade publications
   _____ Internet
   _____ Salespeople – distributor
   _____ Salespeople – manufacturer
   _____ Word of mouth
   _____ Other _____

14. How would you prefer to receive information on new products? (Check no more than three)

   _____ Mailings from manufacturers
   _____ Mailings from distributor
   _____ Trade publications
   _____ Internet
   _____ Salespeople – distributor
   _____ Salespeople – manufacturer
   _____ Word of mouth
   _____ Other _____

15. For purposes of classification, how many employees are at this location? _____

16. What is the approximate age of your manufacturing facility at this location? (in years) _____

5

SEGMENTATION, TARGETING AND POSITIONING

Learning objectives

After reading this chapter, you should be able to:

- Understand the importance of market segmentation

- Differentiate between consumer and business segmentation techniques

- Describe the segmentation process

- Differentiate between segmenting by identifiers and by response profile

- Understand the basics of segmenting across countries

- Explain how market targeting may be used to implement market segmentation

- Describe the positioning process

- Describe the relationship between positioning, market targeting and segmentation

■ Introduction

Choosing the most rewarding market segments has been called the most important strategic decision a business marketing firm must make. It is also perhaps the most demanding of decisions. When a firm chooses the market segment(s) it wishes to pursue, by necessity it is also eliminating a number of potential market segments it will not attempt to serve. Segmentation is a basic marketing tool used by consumer products firms that is often used ineffectively by business marketers.

▉ Importance of segmentation and targeting

Even the wealthiest firm cannot afford to serve all potential customers in the same way and most firms don't have unlimited resources. Since 1956 when Wendell Smith described the idea of market segmentation, firms have known that they should choose the most profitable groups of customers to target. As we have seen in Chapter 3, unless a firm chooses overall cost leadership as its basic strategy, strong segmentation is required for success in both differentiation and niche strategies. Sophisticated marketing managers have developed the idea of 'cost to serve'. This simply means determining what it costs to provide products and services to particular market segments. It may seem obvious that supplying many small customers with small quantities of custom made product is more costly than supplying a few large customers with large quantities of standard product. But often this simple truism may be lost in an avalanche of data. The basic tenet behind the idea of segmentation is to find and serve the most rewarding customers. If a firm is able to offer a unique set of benefits to a particular market segment it will have achieved a significant competitive advantage.

Effective segmentation offers a number of advantages to a firm that successfully completes the task. Firstly, the very act of analyzing all potential customers and narrowing the list to those deemed potentially most responsive is in itself a worthwhile undertaking. By doing this, the firm can develop specific marketing strategies for one or a number of identified segments, meaning the product/service offering, the pricing, the promotion and the distribution will be tailored to satisfy each segment. By identifying the most rewarding segments a firm will be able to properly allocate its budgets, placing the largest expenditures in activities designed to serve the most lucrative and responsive market segments. Once the segments are clearly identified and the marketing process begins, the firm can monitor the success of these efforts and reallocate resources or re-segment as necessary.

The work in developing market segments is hardly glamorous. It often consists of detailed analysis of market research and sales data of specific product lines. But the importance of doing this job cannot be overstated. Focusing limited resources, especially the salesforce, on customers who are most likely to respond is the most important task any marketing manager can undertake.

Many firms define a market segment by product type or product size. This overly simplistic approach can have dire consequences, because it is product-focused rather than customer-focused. In the US computer hard disk drive (HDD) industry, suppliers identified customers for 14-inch drives as mainframe computer manufacturers, users of 8-inch drives as mini computer makers, customers for 5.25-inch drives as personal computer manufacturers and for 2.5-inch drives as portable and laptop suppliers. Many firms focused on one or few segments and were unable to move into new segments as technology converged. A number of leading US HDD firms such as Memorex, Control Data and DEC were eventually forced to leave the HDD business.

As will be seen in the next chapter, the ability to correctly define an emerging market segment and to master the resources to pursue it is a vital skill. In the HDD Business, the leading Japanese firms have continued to be the major suppliers for the past 20 years (Chesbrough 2003).

Another common error business marketers make in segmenting is simply accepting the definition of an entire industry as one segment. For instance, a manufacturer of train control equipment might say 'we sell to electrified railroads' and classify the Santiago Subway or London Underground in the same category as a surface electrified railroad in India. The most obvious differences such as the product being used underground versus in full exposure to the elements would thus be ignored. Some managers err on the other side of the spectrum, thinking about their segments in too narrow a fashion. They may think only about a particular industry dominated by a few major firms and not about new segments which could use their product that are entirely unrelated to the primary target segment.

TALKING POINT

If a whole industry is not a segment, then what is? If we define our segment as smaller than the whole industry, how do we decide who we are NOT going to sell to?

And isn't that a little stupid anyway? If another firm in the same industry wanted to buy our products, are we going to throw them out on their ears?

Or if a firm from another industry wants to buy, what do we say? Do we tell them their money isn't good enough for us? Obviously not – so what are we saying?

Is segmentation about who spends their money with us – or is it about how we spend our money?

Consumer versus B2B segmentation

According to Kotler (2003), the major segmentation variables for consumer markets are geographic, demographic, psychographic and behavioral. While the geographic sub-categories are obvious, the demographic includes age, family size and lifecycle, gender, income, occupation, education, religion, race, generation, nationality and social class. The psychographic variables include lifestyle and personality characteristics while the behavioral variables include occasions, benefits, user status, usage rate, loyalty status, readiness stage and attitude toward the product. Some of these variables can be applied in business marketing as we shall see. Certainly the geographic variables are important as are the demographics of the firm and in some cases, the demographics of the buyers. There is far less importance in the race, religion or nationality of buyers of business products while psychographics are generally inapplicable in business markets. Of the behavioral variables, some can be adapted to business markets and this has been done with some success. Business marketers should be careful about applying consumer segmentation techniques directly to business markets. Unrefined use of consumer segmentation techniques can lead a business marketer in the wrong direction.

Relationship between segmentation, targeting and positioning

Segmentation, targeting and positioning are part of a single process as shown in Figure 5.1.

The first step is to group customers together along common variables. Specific operational variables are identified later in the chapter. The second step is to choose the most attractive segments for the marketing effort. Criteria for determining whether segments should be approached are described in detail in the forthcoming pages. The third step is to develop a position which attempts to place the marketing firm uniquely in the mind of the buyers. The firm will then implement its marketing strategy around this position it has developed.

FIGURE 5.1

Segmentation/
Targeting/
Positioning process

Adapted from Kotler
2003

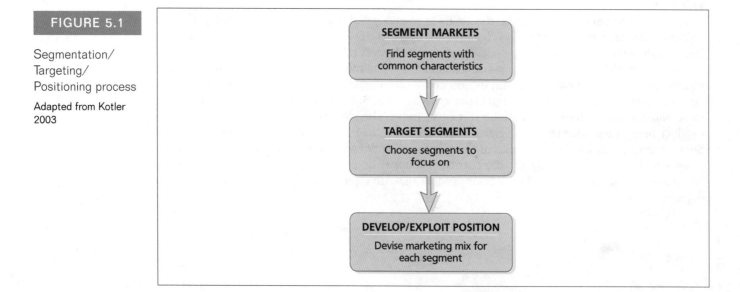

Effective segmentation

What is a market segment? Most simply, a market segment has been defined as a group of customers who can be reached with a distinct marketing mix. That is, these customers have certain traits in common which helps to explain (or predict) their reaction to a firm's marketing program. Since, of course, the marketing mix consists of the four P's of marketing – price, product, promotion and place – a market segment would react to a unique mix of these marketing stimuli. This will be further explained in the targeting section.

While segmenting is always a possibility, it is not always a most rewarding course to follow. For example, a security firm might segment its customer base into supermarkets and drug store chains. However, if there were no difference in the requirements of these customers nor in their reaction to the firm's offerings as represented by the marketing mix, this kind of segmentation would be unproductive. Hlavacek and Ames (1986) warn that firms may find themselves in one of two extreme situations, either they might not have identified enough market segments or they have found way too many. The tests of a good market segment are listed in Table 5.1.

First of all, a segment must be measurable. That is, specific information about the size and expenditures and characteristics of any segment can be determined through primary or secondary research. Second, the market segment must be substantial, that is, large and profitable enough to justify a firm's expenditures of manpower and capital. From this point of view, the most effective segment is the largest homogeneous group that can be established. Third, the segment must be accessible. The firm must be able to reach the segment through marketing efforts. For instance, it would be of no use to know that left-handed purchasing managers are more inclined to buy cleaning solvents from a particular firm, since there is no clear way to reach this segment through sales effort or established media. Some analysts add the term 'actionable' to this list of segmentation tests but accessible and actionable are really two words essentially describing the same attribute. A good segment must be differentiable which means it is homogeneous within and heterogeneous between. In other words, the group targeted reacts in a particular way to marketing stimuli and that reaction is different from the reaction of other segments. This variable should also be reviewed for the level of response. If a segment is more responsive than another, it may make it more attractive for a particular marketer. Finally, the best segments are somewhat stable. Although segments can change as product offerings and marketing stimuli are changed, the best segments are relatively stable justifying the investment by a firm in targeting that particular segment.

Competition

A critical aspect of segmentation involves the analysis of competition. Certainly, when a firm chooses the segment to serve it is in essence choosing its competitors as well (Zahra and Chaples 1993). Competitive analysis consists of finding the relevant market segment, identifying competitors, determining their strengths and weaknesses and attempting to anticipate their future actions. Since segmentation defines the competition, some firms have been surprised by the unexpected entry into a particular market by competitors who were not identified as serving that segment. Looking carefully at competition could help to define the market segment. Since competitors may define a segment in a different way, it is rewarding to attempt to understand the competitor's definition of segments and then to re-examine the segmentation chosen for new insights.

TABLE 5.1 Tests of a good segment
Measurable
Substantial
Accessible
Differentiable
Stable

Segmentation variables

Business marketing segmentation variables can be divided into two main categories as shown below in Table 5.2.

In the first category called *identifiers* by Day (1990), firms attempt to pre-establish segments *a priori*, that is before any data is collected. These are the more traditional segmentation variables because the data is easier to obtain through observation of the buying situation or from secondary sources. Some researchers call these macro variables. As can be seen from Table 5.2, they include demographic, operations, product required and purchasing situation variables related to current or potential customer market segments. Day (1990) also identified *response profile* characteristics, 'unique to the product or service . . . based on attributes and behavior toward the product category or specific brands and vendors in that category'. These include specific vendor attributes such as overall value offered, product quality, vendor reputation, on-time delivery and so on. In addition, customer variables such as the makeup of the decision making unit (or buying center), the importance of the purchase to the subject segment and the innovativeness of the firms in this potential segment are examined. Another important aspect of the response profile technique is to review applications to determine how products are used. Finally, personal characteristics may be included to define a particular segment. These include variables related to individuals in the buying center such as risk tolerance, loyalty, age, education and experience.

These variables are often referred to as *a posteriori*, or after the fact variables in which a 'clustering approach' is used to gather like customers together based on their particular needs. Some researchers call these micro variables.

Looking at the usefulness of the two basic segmentation approaches as measured against the tests for a good segment, Malhotra (1989) claims the identifier approach is better than the response profile approach in terms of measurability and accessibility since it is easy to find and reach the segments which already have established data classifications. He feels this method is particularly good for institutional markets where the number of establishments is small and the number of variables is large. On the other hand, Malhotra believes that using the response profile or clustering approach will produce more responsiveness from a particular segment since the marketing mix will be closely tailored to the specific needs of the segment identified.

TABLE 5.2 Segmentation variables

Identifier (a priori)	Response Profile (a posteriori)

Demographic
    Industry classification
    Firm type – OEM, End User, Aftermarket (MRO)
    Company size
    Geographic location
    Financial info/credit rating
	Vendor Product Attributes
	    Overall value
	    Product quality
	    Vendor reputation
	    Innovativeness
	    On-time delivery
	    Lowest cost

Operations
    Technologies used
    Level of use – heavy, light, non-user
    Centralized/decentralized purchasing
	Customer Variables
	    DMU (Buying Center) makeup
	    Purchase importance
	    Attitude toward product
	    Corporate cultural characteristics (innovativeness)

Product Required
    Custom ↔ Standard
	Application
	    End use
	    Importance of value in use

Purchasing Situation
    Buying situation – new task, modified rebuy, straight rebuy
    Current attitude toward our firm
    Relationships
	DMU/Buying Center Personal Characteristics
	    Risk tolerance
	    Loyalty to current vendor
	    Age
	    Experience
	    Education

Adapted from: Kotler 2003, Day 1990, Rao and Wang 1995, Malhotra 1989, Cardozo 1980.

Generally speaking, business marketers have used identifiers in segmenting their customers. The major reason for this is simplicity. With the Internet, it is easy to get the kinds of information needed to segment markets using the identifier approach.

The use of the response profile approach is a subject of much discussion in the literature. While there is general agreement that the customer's view of vendor attributes or how the decision-making unit is constituted or the risk tolerance of key members of the DMU is invaluable segmentation information, there is little agreement about how widespread this approach is.

Dibb and Simkin (2001) point out that although much has been written about segmentation, there is limited guidance for managers attempting to implement a true market segmentation process. They identified three major categories of barriers to segmentation: infrastructure, process and implementation. These can be further sub-divided into culture, structure and resources.

Infrastructure barriers include the support (or lack of support) from senior management, lack of intra-functional communications, entrenched organizational structures and the lack of financial and human resources. Process issues include the lack of practical advice on how to actually implement segmentation, the unwillingness to share ideas and data, the lack of a fit with corporate strategy, and the misuse of the process because there is poor understanding of it. Implementation barriers include the difficulty of changing present segmentation in the firm. Since industries are often organized around product categories or distribution channels it is extremely difficult to develop segments which are not congruent with those existing divisions. These barriers also include poor identification of responsibility and poor communications and lack of senior management involvement. In the end, the test is aligning budgets and assignments with the segmentation solutions. If this isn't accomplished, the entire process is a waste of time. A summary of the key segmentation barriers and recommended treatments is included as Table 5.3.

TABLE 5.3 Diagnosing and treating key segmentation barriers

Problems	Infrastructure	Process	Implementation
Culture	• Inflexible, resists new ideas • Not customer focused • Doesn't understand segmentation rationale	• Not committed to sharing data/ideas • Lack of 'buy in' • No fit with corporate strategy planning	• Product focus • Insufficient belief in the process • Unwillingness to change current segmentation
Structure	• Lack of intra-functional communications • Low senior management interest or involvement • Entrenched organizational structures	• Misuse of segmentation process	• Poor demarcation of responsibility • Ineffective communications of segmentation solution • Poor senior management involvement
Resources	• Too few or untrained people • Insufficient budgets	• Inadequate data available • Insufficient budgets • Too few or untrained people	• Lack of alignment of budgeting with segmentation • Insufficient time allowed
Solutions	Prior to process • Find available data • Identify people/skills • Get senior management support • Develop communications • Establish adequate budgets • Train people – basic segmentation skills	During process • Specify segmentation steps • Fill gaps in education/skills • Collect data – internal and external • Establish regular communications meetings • Review for fit with corporate strategy	Facilitate Implementation • Identify and communicate findings • Make changes to plans and programs • Identify changes required to culture and structure • Specify budgets, responsibilities and timing to roll-out solutions • Develop method for monitoring roll-out

Based on Dibb and Simkin 2001

Dibb and Simkin recommend treatments or solutions to the problems identified. As can be seen from Table 5.3, prior to the process it is important to find important data, identify the people and the skills required to get the segmentation process done. Senior management must strongly support the process, develop the proper communications channels, establish adequate budgets and set up training for people who will be assigned to do the process but may not have the necessary education or skills.

During the process, it is important to identify the segmentation steps, get the education gaps filled, then collect the data through internal and external sources (here a firm may employ a number of secondary and primary data techniques). It is also important to establish regular meetings for communications or progress and for senior management to be sure that the segmentation is going to fit into the overall corporate strategy.

Finally, to facilitate implementation the authors recommend identifying the specific audiences to whom the findings will be communicated and then to do that, to make changes to plans and programs congruent with the new segmentation solutions, to identify changes that are required in the culture and the structure of the firm, then to specify responsibilities, budgets and timing to make the segmentation work and finally to set up a monitoring process to see whether the segmentation process is being implemented and whether this implementation is effective.

■ Segmentation process

While the process can be described, there is no one correct way to go about segmentation. Finding customers who can be served with a particular marketing mix is both an art and a science. Creative marketing executives will see combinations of firms which their competitors may not see. This alone yields a strong competitive advantage. A mix of data analysis and judgment based on industry experience is often necessary to achieve really effective segmentation.

The most widely accepted approach to segmentation is that proposed by Bonoma and Shapiro (1984). They describe the nested approach, starting with very general, easily available information and moving to the most specific variables which, incidentally, are the most difficult to obtain information about (see Figure 5.2).

The first and most obvious step is to group companies by industry classification. In the United States, the most common industry classification has been the Standard Industrial Classification (SIC), which was replaced in 1997 by the North American Industrial Classification System (NAICS). The NAICS was created to rationalize data among the three NAFTA countries – United States, Canada and Mexico. Other classification systems include the SITC System established by the United Nations in 1950. The US also participates in the Harmonized Commodity Description System, known simply as the Harmonized System which is used to classify goods in international trade since January 1st 1989. This system is in common use in more than 50 countries.

Industry classifications give a firm a start on a grouping of customers and prospective customers into potential segments.

Many firms simply divide their customers into heavy, medium and light users, the so-called A-B-C division. This may be useful for assigning sales persons to particular accounts, but is a poor substitute for the full segmentation process. Using firm demographics, as shown in Table 5.4, also includes dividing customers into types (OEM, end user, and aftermarket (MRO)) and also to group them by company size, geographic location and by specific financial factors such as credit worthiness.

Classifying customers according to OEM, end user or aftermarket (MRO) gives important clues to their commonalities. An OEM buys components, systems, equipment and materials. In the case of components, these enter the OEM's final product while materials are consumed in the manufacturing of their products. Systems and equipment are used to make the products. Original equipment manufacturers often purchase many different items to develop a particular product (see the hairdryer example in Chapter 1) and frequently brand the product with their own name. Users obviously put the product to use. For instance, John Deere tractors are used by farmers while Deere itself is an OEM (Hlavacek and Ames 1986). The aftermarket, also called MRO, includes firms who offer add-on products, repair services or replacement parts. Often, a producer may sell products or services to all three of these firm types, but each is a separate and different segment since requirements will probably be quite different.

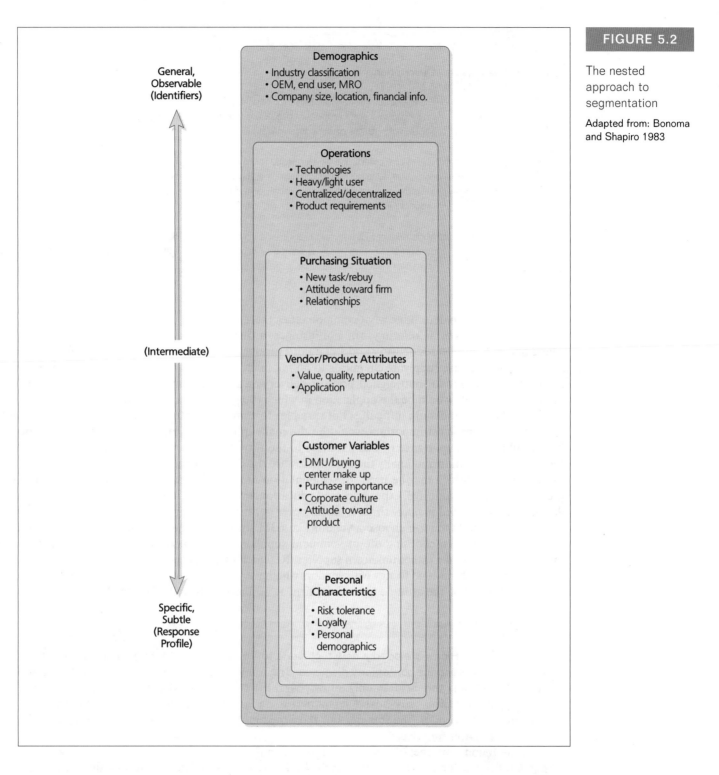

FIGURE 5.2

The nested approach to segmentation

Adapted from: Bonoma and Shapiro 1983

A second step involves more understanding of customer operations. In this step, the marketer would determine what technologies potential customers are employing, whether they are heavy or light users of the product to be offered, whether they purchase in a centralized or decentralized way and specifically, what product requirements customers have, ranging from standard to custom products.

A third step is to look at the purchasing situation – whether for this firm this purchase is a new task, a straight rebuy or a modified rebuy, whether the potential customer has positive attitudes toward the firm and what relationships have been established by the marketing firm with potential customers.

TABLE 5.4 Classification of customers	
Type of Customer	**Description**
OEM	Original Equipment Manufacturer. These customers buy manufacturing equipment, raw materials and components to make into finished products. Examples would be car manufacturers or consumer durables manufacturers.
End user	These customers use up the product entirely in the course of running the business. For example, a company will use cleaning materials, energy, copier paper, office furniture and so forth without incorporating any of these items into the finished products which it sells.
Aftermarket (MRO)	Maintenance, Repair and Operations companies provide services to companies and consumers. For example, a computer repair company will use spare parts, tools and transport to repair or replace defective parts.

A fourth step is to determine what commonalities there are among potential customers related to particular attributes by an offering firm. For instance, a customer group may be quite price sensitive where another emphasizes delivery and still a third product quality defined in some specific manner. As an example, a firm supplying chemicals to an ink maker found that color consistency was of primary importance and far outweighed price or delivery as a purchasing attribute. Another aspect of the vendor attribute would be the application in which the product may be used.

A more refined and more difficult set of variables to gain are identified in Figure 5.2 as customer variables. First and most important would be the makeup of the buying center or DMU. Included here would be the importance of this purchase to the firm, the corporate culture including the attitude toward innovation and finally the attitude toward the product area. A final and most difficult set of characteristics which may be used for segmentation are personal characteristics of individuals in the DMU. These include age, experience and education, loyalty to current vendor and risk tolerance. A common saying used in many firms is 'no one ever got fired for buying IBM'. Individuals with low-risk tolerance would tend to choose a vendor like IBM since the chances of negative consequences for an individual when choosing the pre-eminent supplier in any market are far lower than if that individual had chosen a rather unknown supplier. Research by the authors shows that in nearly every industrial market, firms tend to stay with vendors who have satisfied them. So, important segmentation characteristics will be the attitude toward the firm as well as loyalty and tolerance for risk.

TALKING POINT

A firm in Costa Rica developed a new technique for inexpensively testing blood samples for a number of potentially contagious diseases. The founder of the firm is a doctor with extensive experience in this field. In only a few years, the firm had established itself as the leading supplier to large, city-based hospitals in its native country as well as Venezuela, Colombia and Ecuador. The founder felt the firm should continue to serve large, city-based hospitals in Latin America.

Is the founder correct? Does the identifier segmentation approach give the firm its best competitive position? Would it be worth the effort for the firm to try to use the response profile approach as well?

Since the firm is so small and is in such a niche market anyway, why not let the world beat a path to its door? Why worry about segmenting at all?

Robertson and Barich (1992) proposed a simple approach to segmentation based only upon the purchase decision process. In this case, the authors claim identifying potential customers as first time prospects, novices and sophisticates, yields all the segmentation information needed. First time prospects are firms who see a need for the product, have started to evaluate possible suppliers, but have not yet purchased. Novices are customers who have purchased the product for the first time within the last 90 days and sophisticates have purchased the product before and are ready to rebuy or have recently repurchased.

First time prospects are seeking honest sales reps who know and understand their business, a vendor who has been in business for some time and wish to have a trial period. Novices are looking for technical support, training and knowledgeable sales reps. Sophisticates are seeking compatibility with existing systems, customized products, a successful record from the vendor, speed in fixing problems and post-sales support. The main advantage of this simplified approach is the ability to implement it with the salesforce, which is often the major hurdle for effective segmentation implementation.

Segmenting by customer benefits is recommended as the most effective approach and Rao and Wang (1995) found that identifiers do not correlate very well with profile or benefit-sought variables. While these authors endorsed the nested approach to segmentation, they emphasized the importance of understanding specific customer benefits for the most effective segmentation.

Selecting the best segments

Freytag and Clarke (2001) offer a segment selection process illustrated in Figure 5.3.

This process requires that a firm compare potential segments it may serve, estimating future attractiveness, resource demands and fit with firm strategy. First, the firm should decide whether this particular segment will be growing at a suitable rate, is large enough and profitable enough to serve. In addition, the firm should assess the competition and the risk, understand any governmental or environmental concerns, what demands customers may have and how serving this particular segment may affect present and future relationships with current and future customers. Second, the firm must look at demands on its resources in technology, relationships, human resources in each of the functional areas, image, capital investment and product development required. Finally, the firm should

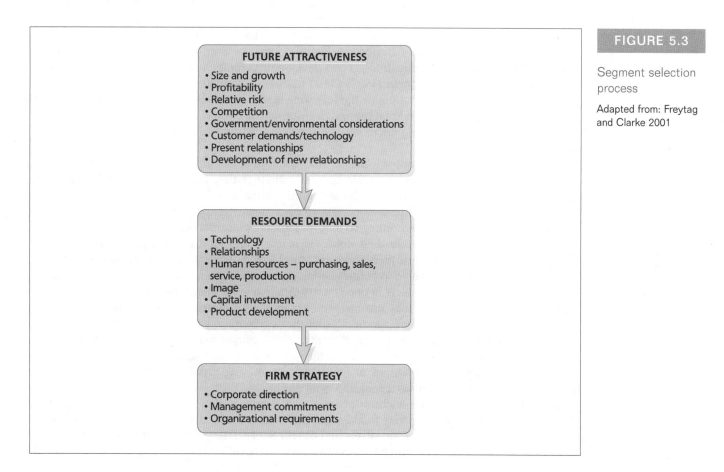

FIGURE 5.3

Segment selection process

Adapted from: Freytag and Clarke 2001

examine whether this new segment is congruent with its present or future strategy related to the overall corporate direction, management's commitment and organizational requirements required to implement the strategy.

Bonoma and Shapiro (1983) recommend choosing segments using two major criteria: Customer Conversion Analysis and Segment Profitability Analysis. The first simply means a manager should determine how many of potential prospects in a particular segment can be converted to customers and how large that served segment will be. This is based upon the number of prospects in a market (the density) which can be reached for a particular marketing expenditure.

Segment Profitability Analysis is an attempt to determine the contribution margin per dollar invested to serve that segment. They recommend combining these approaches to determine which segments a firm ought to serve.

Need to re-segment

Since business market segments change quickly, it is important to re-segment frequently. Some have suggested re-segmenting at the beginning of a new stage of the product lifecycle, but this is too difficult to determine. Nevertheless, changes in competition, technological advances, economic downturns or upswings and consolidation of an industry make re-segmentation very important. Once a firm begins to look at its existing segmentation on a regular basis, it may find it necessary to establish new segments for the most effective use of its marketing efforts. Management should avoid being 'married' to the current segmentation and hold open the possibility of re-segmenting. It is a management task to consistently ask questions, re-examining the basic assumptions which underlie the current segmentation.

Global segmentation

Segmentation strategy is not limited to any one country. Sophisticated business marketing firms look across countries for commonalities of market segments. For instance, ICI Nobel Explosives offers mining explosives across various countries to similar customer types, coordinating its activities in each country by segment and offering product and sales activities accordingly (Gillespie et al. 2004). The same segmentation procedure described in Figure 5.2 can be used across various countries except that the data is much more difficult to get and developing common measures is often a real obstacle. Despite this, Schuster and Bodkin (1987) found that more than 40 per cent of firms they surveyed gathered segmentation information for the following macro variables: geographic location, company size, usage, buying strategy, end market and decision-making stage. More than 40 per cent of firms gathered data for the following micro variables: product attributes, purchase importance, attitudes and personal characteristics.

In business markets, it is not unusual to find commonalities among customers throughout the world. Electric utilities require the same products whether they are located in Kuala-Lumpur or Caracas. A firm selling switchgear to electric utilities must look to a worldwide customer base in order to get the economies of scale necessary to be a global competitor. According to Yip (2003), customers can be segmented according to their purchasing patterns. *Global customers* are quite willing to purchase products outside their domestic markets and tend to have global control of purchasing from headquarters. Another important variable for segmenting these customers is the way in which the products are used. Yip defines *national global customers* who use suppliers from around the world but employ the products in one country. *Multinational global customers* also buy from suppliers in many countries, but they use the products in many countries as well. Management should look for commonalities among customers using the segmentation process described in the earlier part of the chapter rather than accept that minor differences make serving one segment across countries too difficult to achieve. There are many benefits to serving multinational customer segments not only including economies of scale, but also moving rapidly to world class product and service offerings, making further expansion even easier.

A study of the purchasing decision process in a region of the United States, Sweden, France and five southeast Asian countries found some differences in the decision-making process and the structure of the buying center (Mattson and Salehi-Sangari 1993). This study also found differences in the most important purchase decision variables used by the decision-making unit for the same products. In short, this study serves as a caution that care must be taken in segmenting markets across countries. However, the benefits of international segmentation are worth the effort required.

Market targeting

Once the segmentation process is nearly complete, the firm must choose the target market segments it wishes to serve. A target market is a set of buyers with common characteristics which a company decides to serve. To decide on which market segments to target, a firm would decide whether a segment is attractive and whether the firm has the resources to serve that segment and whether serving that segment fits with the company's overall objectives.

A firm may choose to apply *undifferentiated marketing* which means focusing on commonalities among all segments, but in essence attempting to serve the entire market with only one marketing mix. This is found most often in the earliest stages of a product lifecycle when undifferentiated products will be accepted by customers because there is no other choice. Think for a moment of the early days of the personal computer market industry. Early personal computers were very heavy, very slow and had limited software capabilities. Yet many firms purchased large numbers of these personal computers because the productivity increases of their employees outweighed the difficulties of finding specific computers which satisfied their corporate needs. Undifferentiated marketing usually only lasts as long as competition is limited.

When a firm decides to use *differentiated marketing*, it designs specific marketing mixes to serve each segment. Obviously, differentiated marketing costs more than undifferentiated marketing and can only be justified when the results outweigh the cost. The easiest way to picture differentiated marketing is to conceive of the marketing machine as shown in Figure 5.4.

In this machine, each lever represents one of the 4 Ps. In using differentiated marketing, these levers would be set to best satisfy a particular segment. For the next segment, the levers would be set differently. However, it is important to remember that not all levers have to be changed to serve each segment. In many cases the same product, price and promotion may serve two different segments where the only variation required is distribution or service (included under place).

For firms with very limited resources the only choice may be *concentrated marketing*. In this case a firm concentrates on one or very few segments. The idea is to build a dominant position in that segment. For example, a firm manufacturing highly sensitive, low-light level television cameras focuses its efforts on industrial applications of unauthorized entry or pilferage. Here again, the marketing machine must be carefully set to serve the specific segment(s) chosen. This is perhaps the most risky targeting strategy since the possibility exists that the segment(s) may experience economic difficulties or choose to use a substitute product. Firms using the concentration strategy must be vigilant about the possibilities of new segments.

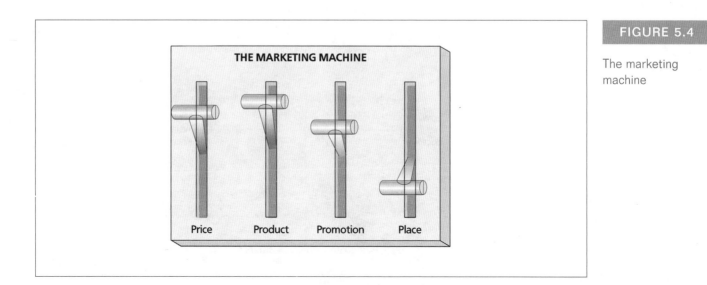

FIGURE 5.4

The marketing machine

Positioning

Positioning essentially means developing a theme which will provide a 'meaningful distinction for customers' (Day 1990). The concept of positioning was strongly advanced by Ries and Trout (2001). They state that many products already have a distinctive position in the mind of the customer. These positions are difficult to dislodge. For instance, IBM would be thought of as the world's largest and most competent computer company. Trout and Ries say that competitors have three possible strategies they may follow. First, the firm may choose to strengthen its current leadership position by reinforcing the original concepts that lead to the first position in the mind of the customer. Second, to establish a new position – 'cherchez le creneaux' – looking for new openings in a market. Third, to attempt to de-position or re-position the competition. Ries and Trout claim that customers establish a ladder for each product category in their minds. On these ladders, buyers establish possible suppliers as first, second or third level. This can offer an opportunity for positioning. Their most famous example of this comes from the auto rental business and the rental company, Avis. When Avis entered the market, Hertz held an unassailable position as the premier car rental firm. Avis was one of many other competitors, but Avis chose to position themselves as '#2' which at that time was an unoccupied position. This immediately catapulted Avis to a position as an important competitor despite the reality that it was no larger than any of the other competitors fighting for a piece of the market with the pre-eminent Hertz. Avis established itself as the first alternative to Hertz in the minds of customers. This is also known as establishing the 'against' position – Avis placing themselves against Hertz.

As mentioned in Chapter 3, Treacy and Wiersema (1993) offer three value disciplines – operational excellence, customer intimacy or product leadership. They recommend a firm becomes a 'champion' in one of these areas while simply meeting industry standards in the other two.

Often, positioning is based upon a series of perceptual maps. An example is shown in Figure 5.5.

This example shows two important variables, the horizontal axis for initial price and the vertical axis for technical assistance. It is obvious that the lower right hand corner of this matrix is probably a poor position to be in. In this quadrant, a firm would be offering a high initial price with only adequate technical assistance.

Let us assume that three firms are in the market. Firm A is a low-priced firm offering little technical assistance. Firm B is a higher-priced firm with very good technical assistance. The management of Firm C may see an opportunity to stake out a position as a somewhat lower price offering than B with somewhat better technical assistance than A. (It might be noted here that a firm which could occupy the upper left quadrant offering low initial price and very good comprehensive technical assistance might win many more customers than either A, B, or C. However, for the purposes of this example, we assume that it is not possible in the industry to offer this combination.)

FIGURE 5.5

Perceptual map

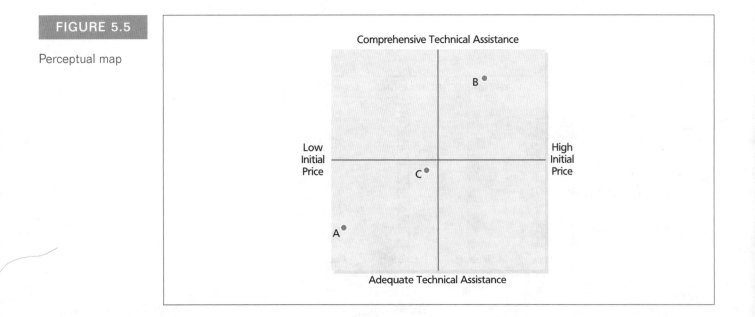

A critical point is that customers must place value on the variables being examined. In our example, if the customers had no particular need for technical assistance this perceptual map would be virtually useless. However, if Firm C's market research shows that technical assistance and initial price are critical variables in the decision-making process this map is quite useful in helping develop a position which can be clearly communicated to potential customers.

A special consideration for international positioning is the country of origin effect. Buyers have already established perceptions of country capabilities, i.e. 'German engineering' develops positive associations. An office furniture firm decided to make products for the EU in a new, state-of-the-art factory in Kells, Ireland. The products were equal in quality in every way to those produced in the US factory, yet continental buyers often rejected the Irish-made product for inferior brands made in their home countries. Country of origin effect seems to be reduced as buyers become more informed, but it is important a manager know what perceptions already exist so that they can be addressed.

Re-positioning

If a current position has been rendered useless by competitor pressure or customer indifference or because the results of the firm are less than expected, new positioning is necessary. Day (1990) offers the four-step process for reassessing a positioning theme shown in Table 5.5.

The main test in this approach is to be sure that alternatives are meaningful to customers, and feasible and superior to what competition offers or may offer.

Designing the programs to implement the chosen position can be a complex task requiring cooperation from all functional areas in the firm and sometimes requiring product and service modifications as well. Once a position is chosen, a firm must clearly communicate this position in a consistent way. The best positioning is simple to communicate – 'the fastest, the oldest or the most technically competent' – are easy messages to communicate through advertising, public relations and especially through the salesforce. It is especially important that a simple position be established when a firm is to communicate in many languages and across many cultures. Reducing the position to its irreducible simplest form will make it easy for the salesforce to communicate what the company stands for and this is a critical ingredient in global success. Choosing the right position is the culmination of all the market segmentation and targeting work which has been discussed in this chapter.

TABLE 5.5 Developing a new positioning theme	
1	Identify alternative positioning themes
2	Screen each alternative according to whether it is: • Meaningful to customers • Feasible given the firm's competencies and customer perceptions of the firm • Superior/unique vs competition; difficult for them to match • Congruent with company objectives
3	Choose the position that best satisfies the criteria, and generates the most enthusiasm and commitment within the organization
4	Design the programs needed to implement the position. Compare costs of these programs with likely benefits

Adapted from: Day 1990

SUMMARY

The most important strategic decision a business marketing firm must make is choosing the most rewarding market segments. Segmentation is the first of the three step process, followed by choosing the most effective segment, called targeting and positioning the firm in the most attractive way toward that market segment.

The key points from this chapter are as follows:

- Consumer marketers segment by geographic, demographic, psychographic and behavioral characteristics. Only some of these are applicable to business market segmentation.

- It is dangerous to simply apply consumer marketing segmentation techniques to business markets.

- A good segment is measurable, substantial, accessible, differentiable and stable.

- Identifiers fall into demographic, operations, product and purchasing situation variables.

- Response profile variables include product attributes, customer application and buying center personal characteristics.

- Infrastructure barriers, process issues and implementation barriers are the major problems encountered by firms attempting to segment their markets effectively.

- Segmentation should be continually re-examined to be sure that market conditions have not changed.

- Each group requires different capabilities from a firm.

- Future attractiveness of the segment, demands on the resources of the firm and the fit with the firm strategy are the three major tests to be applied.

REVIEW QUESTIONS

1 What are the major differences between consumer and B2B segmentation techniques?
2 Describe how segmentation, targeting and positioning are related to one another.
3 Enumerate the tests of a good market segment.
4 List identifier segmentation variables and response profile segmentation variables.
5 What might be the problem of applying segmentation across different cultures and countries?
6 Apply the nested approach to segmentation to a multinational bank.
7 In selecting a market segment, what are three major criteria?
8 How do the settings on the 'marketing machine' and the identification of market segments tell you whether a company is using undifferentiated, differentiated or concentrated marketing?
9 How do perceptual maps help in positioning?
10 What obstacles might a firm expect in implementing its segmentation, targeting and positioning procedures?
11 Assume you are the marketing vice president for a firm selling interior lighting equipment. How might you go about segmenting your markets on a worldwide basis?

SPOTLIGHT ON B2B MARKETING

Hewlett-Packard is a US$72-billion corporation with 15,000 sales reps and 65,000 service and support personnel. The company sees itself as a market leader in notebook and desktop computers as well as PDAs. Since this firm includes the word 'invent' in its logo, they concentrate heavily on product innovation, introducing more than 100 new products and adding 1400 patents in 2002 alone. Hewlett-Packard sees itself as the number one IT company in the small- and medium-sized business market.

Matt Mazzantini, manager for the commercial marketing team for Hewlett-Packard, was in charge of introducing a computer product in a new product category called the Tablet PC. In this product category, the computers are about the size and weight of a notebook but function more like a writing pad. The user employs a stylus to write notes just as you would with a pen and paper. The new product, called the TC 1000, might have many possible market segments. But which to focus on? Assuming Mazzantini wished to choose business customers as an initial target since HP often uses new technology as a door opener with large scale commercial customers, which segments should he choose and how to group them?

A first cut might be to think about customer demographics. Would industry classification mean anything here? How about operations? Purchasing situation? Or vendor/product attributes? Or would customer variables be the key? Or personal characteristics of the buyers? Would this product be purchased centrally or by individuals in target firms?

The main product attributes which are superior to competition are the long battery life and the ability of the TC 1000 to work with a keyboard or as a tablet. Price was set 3–7 per cent lower than competition. After some research, it was determined that users who use a lot of forms and documents or who go quickly from one meeting to another would get the most benefit from the new product.

Mazzantini doesn't feel that it's more difficult to market high-tech products. He says, 'it's even easier than launching traditional packaged goods. Once customers have an opportunity to see the product, they fall in love with it. It sells itself and makes my job a lot easier'.

This case adapted from Krauss (2003) and Hewlett-Packard 2002 Annual Report

Questions

1 How can the nested approach to market segmentation be applied to the Compaq TC 1000 project?

2 What is the most important of all segmentation variables for success in this product launch?

3 How can Mazzantini evaluate the various possible segmentation/positioning strategies he might use?

4 How could Mazzantini use positioning to make the most effective use of the segmentation work? Where should the levers of the marketing machine be set?

5 What positioning message might be the most effective in this product launch?

REFERENCES

Bonoma, T. V. and Shapiro, B. P. (1983) *Segmenting the Industrial Market*, Lexington, M.A.: D.C. Health Co.

Bonoma, T. V. and Shapiro, B. P. (1984) 'Evaluating Market Segmentation Approaches', *Industrial Marketing Management* 13: 4: 257–268.

Cardozo, R. N. (1980) 'Situational Segmentation of Industrial Markets', *European Journal of Marketing*. 14: 5/6: 264–276.

Chesbrough, H. W. (2003) 'Environmental Influences Upon Firm Entry into New Sub-Markets: Evidence from the Worldwide Hard Disk Drive Industry Conditionally', *Research Policy* 32: 659–678.

Day, G. S. (1990) *Market-Driven Strategy: Process for Creating Value*, New York: The Free Press.

Dibb, S. and Simkin, L. (2001) 'Market Segmentation: Diagnosing and Treating the Barriers', *Industrial Marketing Management* 30: 8: 609–625.

Freytag, P. V. and Clarke, A. H. (2001) 'Business to Business Market Segmentation', *Industrial Marketing Management*: 30: 6: 473–486.

Gillespie, K., Jeannet, J-P and Hennessey, H. D. (2004) *Global Marketing: An Interactive Approach*, Boston: Houghton Mifflin Company.

Hlavacek, J. D. and Ames, B. C. (1986) 'Segmenting Industrial and High-Tech Markets', *Journal of Business Strategy* 7: 2: 39–50.

Kotler, P. (2003) *Marketing Management*, Upper Saddle River, NJ: Prentice-Hall.

Krauss, M. (2003) 'New Tech Still Suffers Old Marketing Woes', *Marketing News* 37: 5: 12.

Malhotra, N. K. (1989) 'Segmenting Hospitals for Improved Management Strategy', *Journal of Health Care Marketing* 9: 3: 45–52.

Mattson, M. R. and Salehi-Sangari, E. (1993) 'Decision Making in Purchases of Equipment and Materials: A Four-Country Comparison', *International Journal of Physical Distribution and Logistics Management* 23: 8: 16–30.

Rao, C. P. and Wang, Z. (1995) 'Evaluating Alternative Segmentation Strategies in Standard Industrial Markets', *European Journal of Marketing* 29: 2: 58–75.

Ries, A. and Trout, J. (2001) *Positioning: The Battle For Your Mind*, New York: McGraw-Hill.

Robertson, T. S. and Barich, H. (1992) 'A Successful Approach to Segmenting Industrial Markets', *Planning Review* Nov-Dec: 4–48.

Schuster, C. P. and Bodkin C. D. (1987) 'Market Segmentation Practices of Exporting Companies', *Industrial Marketing Management* 16: 2: 95–102.

Smith, W. R. (1956) 'Product Differentiation and Market Segmentation as Alternative Marketing Strategies', *The Journal of Marketing* 21: 2: 3–8.

Treacy, M. and Wiersema, F. (1993) 'Customer Intimacy and Other Value Disciplines', *Harvard Business Review* 71: 1: 84–93.

Yip, G. S. (2003) *Total Global Strategy II*, Upper Saddle River, NJ: Prentice Hall.

Zahra, S. A. and Chaples, S. S. (1993) 'Blind Spots in Competitive Analysis', *Academy of Management Executive* 7: 2: 7–28.

6

MARKET ENTRY TACTICS

Learning objectives
After reading this chapter, you should be able to:

- Understand the key considerations in market entry decisions
- Explain the role of management in an internationalizing firm
- Describe the foreign market entry strategy alternatives
- Show how foreign market entry decisions are made
- Prescribe the cure for blocked markets
- Describe the special characteristics of strategic alliances

■ Introduction

Entering new markets is both challenging and rewarding. A manager must weigh a number of variables to get the decision right. This is especially true when a firm is thinking about getting into international markets. Segmentation, which we discussed in the last chapter, is an important prerequisite for determining the best new market to enter. Once the decision is made, there are many choices for market entry. These are based on specific considerations which will be described in this chapter.

■ Market entry considerations

Many factors in the environment affect the market entry decision. As described in Figure 6.1, these so-called uncontrollables include economic, demographic, competitive, political/legal, technological and social cultural aspects.

Obviously the economic environment has a major impact on the market entry decision. Growth in an economy or particular segment will attract competitors and may make an entry decision more difficult. On the other hand, an economy or segment that isn't growing may cause firms to leave the market and enter new, more promising segments. The demographic trends include shifts and growth in population. These trends have major effects on consumer spending which in turn affects derived demand in business markets.

The competitive environment both in a firm's current served segment and in a market under consideration has an important effect on the entry decision. Firms already in the target market will need to be dislodged, but at the same time the firm entering the market cannot afford to neglect its existing markets.

Changes in the political/legal environment may cause a firm to see a new market as attractive or a current market as unattractive. A new government planning to expand military spending might cause an electronics firm to pursue the government market for the first time.

The technological environment has a profound effect on market entry decisions. Some believe technology is the major driving force pushing firms into new markets.

Finally, the social/cultural environment is important to entry decisions. Changes in social mores have a major effect on B2B marketers, since their demand is derived from consumer markets. For instance, the addition of women to the workforce has meant more meals eaten in restaurants creating major markets for producers of restaurant equipment and suppliers of every type.

Ansoff's Matrix (Figure 6.2) helps firms to decide whether they wish to provide current products to current markets or to take those same products to new markets. The other basic alternative is to take new products to current markets or new products to new markets (Ansoff 1957).

Market penetration and product development strategies are outside the scope of this chapter. Market development occurs when a firm uses its current products to approach a new market segment.

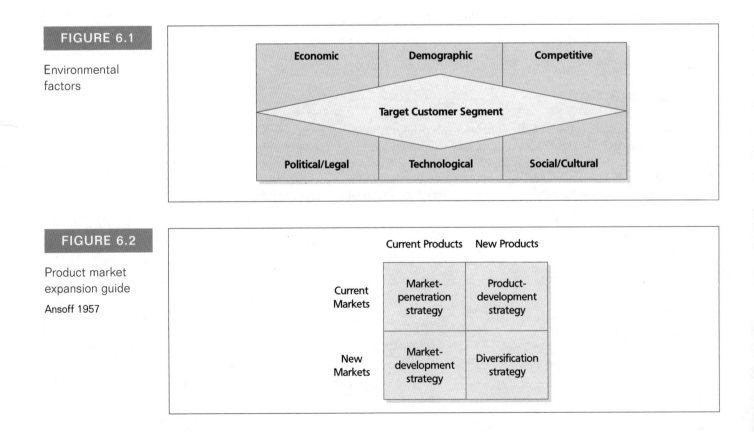

FIGURE 6.1

Environmental factors

FIGURE 6.2

Product market expansion guide

Ansoff 1957

A market segment is a group of customers who react in a specific way to a marketing mix (see Chapter 5). So, while market development allows a firm to take its current products to a new segment, it will more than likely be required to change other aspects of the mix – pricing, promotion or distribution.

Day (1990) adds a third alternative (Related) to each axis. This is placed between Current and New on each axis of the grid – products and markets. Taking Related products to Present or Related markets through product improvements or line extensions is a less risky way to expand than Market Development or Diversification. Needless to say, Diversification into markets completely unrelated to the firm's current segments with products or services completely new to the firm is the riskiest path to take. If a firm excels in some activity, management might feel it can expand into new areas to exploit these skills in some new way, but as Day says, 'in practice these prospective synergies are often illusions'.

An example of this can be seen in the business interiors industry. Hauserman, Inc. was the dominant producer of ceiling-high movable metal walls, primarily used as room dividers in offices. Hauserman decided to move into a new but related product area, manufacturing less than ceiling-high panels with essentially the same function of space division and storage. The firm had well-established customers in most of the largest corporations in the US, Europe and Asia and believed it would be easy to sell additional products to these current customers. While Hauserman thought it was pursuing a market penetration or possibly a product development strategy, the truth turned out to be quite different. The market segment the firm was approaching included an entirely different Buying Center (DMU). Instead of selling to plant engineers and maintenance people, the firm now found itself addressing architects, interior designers and facilities managers employed by these same large firms. While it was not clear to Hauserman when their planning was taking place, the company wound up in a diversification strategy, facing a completely new set of customers and competitors with new products. After a prolonged, expensive and unsuccessful effort, the firm chose to leave this market segment.

As mentioned in Chapter 3, a firm should completely examine a proposed market segment for EVR congruence, that is, the firm should enter an environment where its values and resources make success likely.

Success factors

Chesbrough (2003) examined variables related to entry of sub-markets in the hard disk drive industry. He concluded that a number of factors are important to success when moving into a new market segment. These are presented in Table 6.1.

The capital structure of the firm seems to have an influence on success in new market entry. Firms with more traditional capital sources tend to focus more on current markets than on new markets. He also identified the importance of securing the required technical skills through acquisition, licensing

TABLE 6.1 New market entry factors
Capital Structure
Technical Skills
Customer Relationships
Competition in New Market
Competition in Current Market
Forecast Growth of the New Market
Management Attitudes

Adapted from: Chesbrough 2003

or hiring of highly skilled employees as an important factor in successfully moving into a new segment. Another important factor is forecast growth of the new market. Firms who move quickly into markets where the growth was forecast to be significant had more success. The need for customer relationships is also a key success factor. A firm can use its existing customers to try out new technologies and gain rapid feedback to improve its offerings. As might be expected, management attitudes are also important to the success of a firm moving into a new market. As we will see, this is especially true in international market entry.

The competition in both new and current markets has an effect on a firm's entry. That heavy competition in a current market would make a firm wish to move to a new segment is obvious. A lack of competition in a new market would make it attractive.

Role of technology

Geroski (1999) points out that technological competence combined with good planning is essential to successful market entry. An example can be taken from the airline industry in the US where the replacement of older DC9s and Boeing 737s (which were unable to fly coast-to-coast) by newer aircraft allowed low-cost airlines to compete with established carriers on these very profitable, long-haul routes. He also points out that technology alone will not guarantee success. Other competencies are prerequisites for success in new markets – improved customer service, developing new products, strong brand names or reputations or better management of suppliers are all examples.

TALKING POINT

For many years, research showed that firms who got into a market first were the most successful firms. The well-known PIMS database showed a correlation between firms who were first movers and had a high market share. Consulting companies like Boston Consulting Group pushed the idea of getting into a market first with low prices to keep out the competition.

But what happened to the old saying, fools rush in where angels fear to tread? What happens if all the predictions are wrong, and the product flops? Why not let someone else take all the risk and make all the mistakes, then come in with a better product that builds on their experience?

First movers versus followers

When moving into a new market, a firm would consider whether it wishes to be a first mover or a follower. Many of the same new market entry factors identified by Chesbrough (2003) would be relevant to this decision. First movers usually end up with the largest market shares. They erect high barriers to entry for other firms through early establishment of their brand name, or economies of scale in production or marketing, commitment of distribution channel members and customer loyalty (compounded by high switching costs). First movers are often believed to have a head start that cannot be overcome by later entrants into a market (Varadarajan *et al.* 1999). They learn about their customers' preferences and can even shape their customers' beliefs as the market develops.

On the other side of the ledger, pioneers incur large cost disadvantages compared to firms who follow them into a market. Boulding and Christen (2001) found pioneers to be substantially less profitable than followers in the long run. Specifically in their study, the ROI of first movers was more than 4 per cent lower than followers in industrial markets. Later entrants learn from the first movers, avoid costly mistakes and may be more flexible in their processes. Varadarajan *et al.* (1999) suggest that firms use a contingency approach to the first mover decision – that is, consider factors such as product type, advertising intensity or minimum scale required in the industry before deciding to be a pioneer in a market. One need only think back to the Sony Betamax for a good example of a pioneer who did not reap ultimate real rewards by being first.

◼ Entering foreign markets

Of all new market entry decisions, a foreign market entry decision is the most difficult. Long-term commitment on the part of management is essential – without commitment of resources and manpower the market entry will fail, since existing competitors in the target country are often totally committed to what is, for them, the home market.

Czinkota and Ronkainen (2001) present major motivations to globalize as shown in Table 6.2.

A firm with proactive motivations especially looking for additional profits will often 'stay the course' when expected profits take longer to be realized. According to one experienced international manager, global business 'takes longer, is harder and costs more' than everyone in the firm expects.

A firm with real or perceived advantages in technology or product may achieve long-term success. Having exclusive information about customers, distribution or competitors in foreign markets can also be a proactive reason to move ahead internationally. Since we have already discussed the importance of management commitment, a management which wishes to push a firm in an international direction will certainly do so and will have a lasting effect as long as that management is employed by the corporation.

Governments frequently offer tax breaks to exporters, but these can easily be removed by subsequent finance ministers, so they usually only provide a temporary incentive. For instance, in the United States, Foreign Sales Corporation provisions were in conflict with World Trade Organization agreements, because they were seen to be an unfair subsidy on US exports. The WTO requested that the US Congress amend the tax laws to bring them into compliance with WTO regulations, as a result of which some firms withdrew from export markets.

Economies of scale are another proactive motivator. The home market, especially in a small country, may not be large enough to support the company.

Reactive motivations usually do not have long-lasting effects. A reactive motivation such as competitive pressure makes a firm think internationally simply to coopt its competitors from a foreign market. Some firms move too quickly into these situations and find themselves unprepared for the difficulties they encounter. Overproduction, declining domestic sales and excess capacity are similar reactive kinds of motivators. The underlying idea is that when the domestic market declines, the foreign markets are used as 'safety valves' to take up the slack for declining domestic sales. In these cases, the effects are not long-lasting and when domestic market activity improves managements not committed to international business often reduce or terminate their foreign market activities.

This can lead to negative feelings and reluctance to purchase again from any of those same corporations in the future. A specific example occurred in Chile where Westinghouse Electric Corporation sold heavy equipment to the Chilean copper mining industry. After Westinghouse withdrew to the USA following an upswing in demand there, some Chilean firms took the attitude 'You left us when things got better in the US, how do we know you won't do it again?'.

TABLE 6.2 Major motivations to globalize	
Proactive Reasons	**Reactive Reasons**
Profit advantage	Competitive pressures
Unique products	Overproduction
Technological advantage	Declining domestic sales
Exclusive information	Excess capacity
Managerial commitment	Maturity/decline stage of PLC
Economies of scale	Proximity to customers and ports

Adapted from Czinkota and Ronkainen 2001

When a product reaches the end of its lifecycle in the home market, some managers become tempted to sell the product in what they perceive as a less sophisticated market. This tactic might have worked 20 or 30 years ago, but satellite TV, the Internet, improved education and travel opportunities mean that prospective buyers have seen, and want, the latest technology and are often offended by a lesser offer. Even in cases where the older technology would be more appropriate, buyers want the latest model.

A final reactive motivation is closeness to customers and ports. This is often given as the reason why US companies trade more heavily with Canada than with any other country.

Generally speaking, the most successful firms in international markets are those with proactive motivations. They attempt to secure a market position internationally rather than simply react to orders from outside their domestic market.

Choosing foreign markets

Experience has shown that a marketing program in a new location has the best chance of success if the firm can simply present one clear advantage. A number of these are summarized in Table 6.3.

A firm will have the easiest time convincing customers to try its product if there is a clear reason to do so. Lower cost is obviously a most compelling reason. In the table we have specified lower *landed* cost. It is important for a firm to understand all customer costs, including import duties and VAT, when comparing what a customer would pay to acquire its product or service versus the competitive offering.

More cost-effective technology means a purchasing firm will realize savings through reduced labor or increased output, either in production or marketing. Some firms succeed because they have a certain cachet, either through strong branding or through the reputation of the country of origin. In some markets, American, German or Japanese technology may be perceived as the best. Whether this is true or not isn't important to the success of the firm if it can successfully position itself as providing the latest for the technologically advanced culture. Another obvious benefit which can be easily communicated is higher quality. Quality must be defined in customer terms for each product or service. Some customers may see quality as durability while others may feel quality relates to the appearance of the final product. The only definition of quality which matters is that of the customer. The final, simple to explain, competitive advantage is environmental acceptability. In the EU where environmental concerns are more important than in the US, recyclability or biodegradability may be a key selling point.

The major considerations in choosing a particular market are shown in Table 6.4. These fall into two major categories, macro (or country-specific considerations) and micro (or market-specific factors).

Of critical importance are the needs of the customer, the exact relationship which the customer requires for successful sales and service by the marketing firm.

The choice of which foreign market to enter cannot easily be separated from the choice of entry mode. Most firms will perform an iterative process looking at the attractiveness of a particular market and thinking about ways of entering and weighing factors in each area before making a final decision. We have chosen to present the considerations related to particular markets first

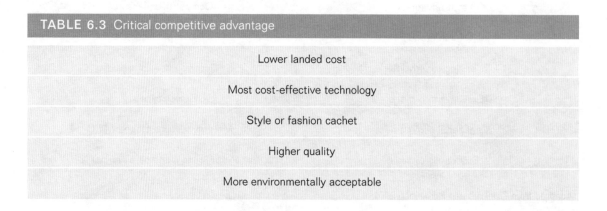

TABLE 6.3 Critical competitive advantage

Lower landed cost
Most cost-effective technology
Style or fashion cachet
Higher quality
More environmentally acceptable

TABLE 6.4 Major considerations in choosing a particular international market

Macro	Micro
Country	Market

<ul><li>Economic</li><li>Political/Legal</li><li>Cultural</li><li>Technological/Infrastructure</li><li>Geographic</li></ul>	<ul><li>Customer
	  – Key segments
	  – Purchase criteria</li><li>Market size and growth</li><li>Competition</li><li>Product acceptance</li></ul>

followed by the entry mode choices to more clearly delineate the considerations a firm must make when choosing foreign market entry. An overview of the considerations in this complex decision is presented in Figure 6.3. It should be noted that some of the factors described relate to the markets under consideration, some relate to company capabilities and still others relate to the benefits or drawbacks from particular entry strategies. This diagram is intended as an overview, describing all the factors which affect the final decision to enter a foreign market through a particular entry strategy.

Figure 6.1 described most of the environmental factors which affect a market entry decision. These same economic, demographic, competitive, political/legal, technological and social/cultural factors are at work in any foreign market. But some specific characteristics of the overseas market should be mentioned here. Obviously, countries differ in their economic situations. In some particular locations, there may be a number of well-financed firms who are looking for a product offered by a particular firm. But in others, the weak finances and/or lack of hard currency may force a marketing firm to offer an unusual approach to a market. In some cases, a particular market may be extremely small and a firm may not be able to serve it profitably.

In the political/legal arena, a firm may encounter obstacles both in the home country and the host country. For instance, the Foreign Corrupt Practices Act, in effect in the United States since the 1970s, forbids company payments to government officials for securing a favorable decision on product sales or other possible advantages. In countries where bribery is the normal way of doing business, this may handicap US firms.

Host country governments often impose trade barriers of various kinds. These may take the form of tariffs or non-tariff barriers which may make the market difficult or impossible to enter. A special section on these so-called 'blocked markets' is included at the end of this chapter.

Technologically, markets vary widely. Appropriate technology for groups of markets may be required, or (as stated earlier) buyers may demand the latest technology even when it is not appropriate.

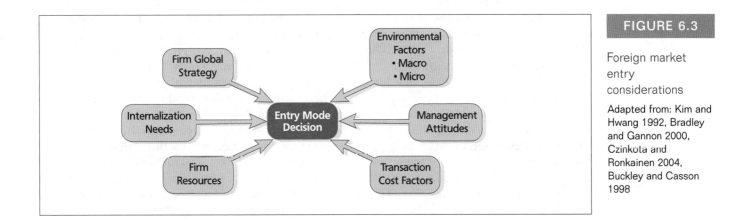

FIGURE 6.3

Foreign market entry considerations

Adapted from: Kim and Hwang 1992, Bradley and Gannon 2000, Czinkota and Ronkainen 2004, Buckley and Casson 1998

In some cases, cultural differences can make doing business in a particular place quite difficult. Terpstra and David (1991) describe the triple socialization of managers, meaning they are operating in three different cultures – national, professional and corporate – and they must balance the values they hold in each of these cultures while functioning in a foreign market.

Terpstra and David also introduce the concept of 'frontstage' and 'backstage' culture. Frontstage culture is the normal ways of doing things that insiders are willing to share with outsiders, while backstage culture is the normal ways of doing things that insiders are not willing to share with outsiders. A marketer attempting to enter a new market should find a mentor who is willing to reveal the commonly accepted ways of doing things, whether they are part of the frontstage or backstage culture.

Geographic considerations are often overlooked. For instance, a shipment of high-tech X-ray equipment was held in storage at a port in Saudi Arabia. Because the shipping firm did not consider the very high temperatures to be experienced by this equipment while it was being shipped, some of the machines literally exploded before the shipping containers could be opened.

Micro factors focus on the particular market or markets under consideration. Firstly, of course, the segment or segments need to be identified. As we have seen, some segments transcend national borders, especially in business markets. If this is the case, a firm may consider a number of national markets while looking at these micro factors. Secondly, the most important factor here is determining market size and growth. Many of the techniques described in Chapter 4 would be used here. Competition is a critical factor in deciding whether or not to enter a market. One additional variable which may be present especially in smaller international markets is the ability of competition to dominate the distribution channels. In many industrial markets, there are very few knowledgeable, qualified distributors for particular products. If a firm were marketing scientific instruments for laboratories, it would be surprising to find more than one or two qualified distributors in smaller or emerging markets. This may mean a marketing firm reconsiders its approach to a particular market, or the firm may consent to using a competitor's distributor since there is no other entry strategy. We have described product acceptance in various sections of this chapter. Suffice it to say that individuals must be comfortable with the technology required to operate equipment being offered or knowledgeable enough to take advantage of services being offered.

∎ Foreign market entry strategy

There are three schools of thought about how firms enter international markets. The first is the gradual involvement or Uppsala model which believes that firms enter international business at first using low resource commitment modes such as licensing or exporting. As the firm gains more knowledge and experience, it moves to higher levels of market entry alternatives in terms of resource commitment and accepts higher levels of risk.

A second approach is based on transaction cost analysis. In this approach, firms keep to themselves functions which they can perform at lower cost and contract out to other firms activities which can be completed by those other firms at lower cost. Firms consider all costs when making these decisions including the costs of checking quality and managing marketing, production, sourcing and so on.

The third approach focuses on location specific factors as described above.

Pan and Tse (2000) showed that in the People's Republic of China, firms made discreet decisions in two main steps. Firstly, they chose between equity (joint and sole venture) and non-equity (export and contract) alternatives. In this decision, country specific factors are most important. Secondly, managers made the decision about the kind of equity venture they would pursue and here, firm-specific factors are more important than country (or environmental) factors.

Buckley and Casson (1998) developed a comprehensive model summarizing the effect of a number of variables on the market entry decision. Their variables included: location costs, internalization factors, financial variables, cultural factors (trust and psychic distance), market structure, competitive strategy, adaptation costs and the costs of doing business abroad. They conclude that firms take into account different sets of variables in deciding upon local production or local distribution activities. In addition, they emphasize the importance of competition and market structure in the entry decision.

Many researchers have found that 'cultural distance' between home market and target market is an important factor for choosing one particular market instead of another. A new study calls into question the importance of cultural distance as a determining factor in the choice of foreign markets.

Mitra and Golder (2002) found that, in the large multinational consumer products companies they studied, knowledge gained by the corporation from working in similar cultural and economic environments around the world was a most important determinant for firms choosing to enter particular markets. In other words, firms learn from operating in countries which are close culturally or economically to a particular target market and then use that knowledge to increase their confidence for moving forward into a selected market. In this study executives placed more importance on economic than cultural factors. These executives felt they could hire or transfer managers with experience in similar foreign markets to overcome any cultural problems.

Emerging markets such as India and China offer large opportunities but also special problems. In these markets, the legal system is often underdeveloped and corruption can pose a major hurdle to success. The infrastructure – both physical and financial – may be inadequate for a modern multinational. Brand recognition may be minimal for products which are well established in more advanced countries. In fact, all the uncontrollable or environmental factors may be quite different in these emerging markets. A manager must assess these factors more carefully in emerging markets and then tailor a marketing mix which will be successful in each emerging country.

Comparing the entry strategy alternatives

There are three basic ways to enter foreign markets: exporting, investment or contract. While much has been made in international marketing literature about a step-by-step process of international market entry, many of the most sophisticated firms do not move in a step-by-step process, but instead they see themselves as 'born global'. Especially for services or technology firms where 'brick and mortar' investments are often not required, firms tend to use the most effective entry strategy rather than moving through a step-by-step approach (often described as moving from licensing to exporting and finally to some form of investment). The necessity to establish economies of scale quickly or to capture market share have led to immediate acquisitions by firms in the telecommunications business, to name one example.

Experience has shown that before moving into a foreign market, a firm should ask itself at least two key questions. Firstly, why have we succeeded domestically? (What are the critical success factors that have made our firm successful?) Secondly, can these key success factors be duplicated in foreign markets?

Examining each of the alternatives more closely, let us first look at exporting. As Table 6.5 shows, there are a number of export alternatives with various names.

Indirect exporting means selling a product to an intermediary located within the same domestic market. Direct exporting means selling that product to an intermediary located in a foreign market. The table also shows the difference between agents and merchants. Rather than the specific

TABLE 6.5 Export alternatives

Domestic (Indirect)	Foreign (direct)
Agents	
Brokers	Brokers
Export agents	Manufacturer's reps
Export management companies	Factors
	Managing agents
Merchants	
Domestic wholesalers	Distributor/dealers
Export trading companies	Import jobbers
Export management companies	Wholesalers/retailers

Zimmerman and Fitzpatrick 1985

terminology used for each type of firm, this is a most important distinction. Agents are firms which aid in finding and selling to customers but do not take ownership of the product. Merchants do take title, own the product and can resell it. The importance in this difference relates to control. A manufacturing firm selecting an agent will have far more control over the agent's subsequent marketing activities than it will over a merchant. While selling to a merchant is attractive, since a firm will receive payment and no longer have the risk of loss of a product, merchants can sell products in unauthorized markets leading to the problem of 'gray goods', the unauthorized shipment of products from their intended market.

In reviewing Table 6.5 it should be noted that export management companies are listed twice, once under indirect agents and then again under indirect merchants. Export management companies are generally small firms with expertise in a particular industry or geographic area or both. They can serve as agents in finding customers and distributors without buying and reselling products. But they can also serve as merchants where they take on an ownership role and they do buy and resell. The same export management company may perform both roles for the same client in different markets.

The second and third foreign major market entry strategies are shown in Table 6.6.

Using investment, a firm may choose to pursue a sole venture in which it owns all aspects of the foreign business entity or establish a joint venture or enter into a consortium. Wholly owned or sole venture entry modes may be so-called greenfield enterprises in which the firm establishes a branch office or subsidiary from the ground up. Or a firm may choose to make an acquisition of an existing firm. This is often a fast way to buy market share and expertise in a foreign market. Of course, the investing firm would expect to pay a premium for the speedy entry afforded by the acquisition process. A firm may choose to establish a joint venture. Some researchers see equity investment joint ventures as one form of strategic alliance but strictly speaking, a joint venture occurs when two firms invest to start up a third, new entity. A consortium is a group of firms formed to complete a particular large project. A consortium of engineering, train equipment and construction firms was formed to build the Rio De Janeiro subway, for instance.

The third major form of market entry is contract, which takes many forms. In licensing, one firm lets another use its intellectual property for a fee, usually a royalty on sales. Franchising, related to licensing, takes place when a franchiser grants the franchisee the right to do business in a particular way in exchange for a similar fee. More popular and important today are non-equity or non-investment strategic alliances. In this case, two firms decide to work together in a particular area, setting limited objectives which are usually spelled out in a memorandum of understanding. For instance, two pharmaceutical firms recently signed a strategic alliance which allowed a US firm to market in the US a Japanese firm's blood pressure medicine while allowing the Japanese firm to market in Japan the US firm's ulcer medicine. Strategic alliances take many forms and may just focus on production, marketing, or research and development. A special section on Strategic Alliances is included in this chapter.

TALKING POINT

A Japanese manufacturer of fiber optic cable had developed several proprietary techniques which were patented in its home country. The firm saw a huge potential in the People's Republic of China. After some preliminary research, a local Shanghai firm was found which wished to help the Japanese firm market the product in China. Since the Chinese Government had not yet adopted all the WTO rules, the government insisted on a joint venture form of organization for this fiber optic activity.

In view of the Chinese Government's attitude, what was the right decision for the Japanese firm? Should they enter the market or wait until the WTO rules are fully enforced so they do not have to share their secrets with the local joint venture partner? Why would any firm want to give away its secrets to a potential competitor – is any market worth the risk?

TABLE 6.6 Investment and contract alternatives

Investment	Contract
Wholly owned or sole venture	Licensing
● Greenfield	Franchising
– Branch offices	Strategic alliances (non-equity)
– Subsidiaries	Management contract
● Acquisitions	Contract manufacturing
Joint ventures/strategic alliances	
Consortia	

Finally, contracts for manufacturing or management are also an alternative. Under a management contract, a firm asks another to manage an effort for them. This could be the management of marketing or production and there would be a fee paid by the contracting firm to the manager. In contract manufacturing, one firm simply issues a purchase order to another to make products. For example, an office furniture firm wishing to serve a local market in Mexico chose a supplier to make desktops and assemble other simple furniture products. This was an arms-length arrangement, not a joint venture or even a strategic alliance, but simply the selecting of one firm to manufacture products for another.

The most important considerations for each of the major market entry alternatives are presented in Table 6.7.

TABLE 6.7 Comparing selected market entry alternatives

Entry Mode Consideration	Indirect Export	Direct Export	Licensing/ Franchising	Minority Joint Venture	Majority Joint Venture	Sole Venture	Contract
Resources Required	Very little	Minimal capital – must manage effectively	Minimal capital – human resources may be significant	Significant, but less than majority joint venture or sole venture	High for capital and human resources	Highest level of any alternative	No capital – can be significant human resources
Potential Risk(s)	Low risk of any kind	Low risk of loss	Risk of establishing competitor (licensing)	Significant for investment – differences between partners	Significant for investment – differences between partners	Assume all risk for investment	Low
Experience Gained	Limited	Some experience in foreign market(s)	Limited	May be limited – take advantage of local knowledge	High – some local knowledge	High – no local knowledge in ownership position	Limited
Return on Investment	Limited	Good	High but gross margin limited	May be good	May be excellent	May be excellent	N/A
Host Government Reaction	None	Limited	May be unfavorable	Generally favorable	May be unfavorable	May be unfavorable	None

TABLE 6.7 *(cont.)*

Entry Mode Consideration	Indirect Export	Direct Export	Licensing/ Franchising	Minority Joint Venture	Majority Joint Venture	Sole Venture	Contract
Control Capabilities	Limited	Possible loss of control of marketing	Possible loss of control of quality and/or marketing	Less than majority joint venture or sole venture	High	Highest possible	High
Other Considerations	Easy way to explore international business	Good first learning step	May be only way into market – need to keep intellectual property registered	May be required by government	Many firms prefer this	Protect company secrets	Meets specific needs

As can be seen, indirect export is an easy way to begin to explore international business which requires little in the way of resources, either capital or human. Risks are low as are returns and a firm would gain little experience in an international market using this approach. Direct export gives a firm somewhat more experience while requiring more in the way of people. Direct export also allows for less control by the firm. Licensing can yield excellent returns since the investment is small. Licensing requires some human resources to be sure that intellectual property registrations are kept up-to-date and that the licensees are performing properly. This is also true of franchising. While licensing presents a rather attractive picture since royalties seem to go right to the bottom line of the licensor's financial statement, there are a number of hidden costs as described above. The key worry of the licensor is the possibility of establishing a competitor. This happened to a manufacturer who had licensed a large Japanese electronics firm to make elevators according to specifications from the US company. After ignoring the licensee for many years, the US firm was surprised to see the Japanese company bidding on contracts in Saudi Arabia. Some vigilance is required to be sure that the licensee is meeting quality and marketing standards and audits are required of the books to be sure that the proper royalty payments are being made.

Minority joint ventures require less investment than majority joint ventures and in some countries may be the only way to enter through investment. The minority partner may be a much larger firm and may feel uncomfortable in a minority position. The relationship between the minority owners and majority owners is the key to seeing that local knowledge is used to the fullest extent while the possibly more experienced and larger minority partner can also bring its skills to bear. Host governments generally favor minority positions for large multinationals. It should be said that host governments in many markets have the right to review both license and joint venture agreements and to reject those they consider unfair as to up-front payments or royalty levels. Some firms that take the minority position do not use the possibility to gain experience about a local market. A minority partner must be proactive to get as much knowledge and experience as possible in this situation.

Many multinationals favor the majority joint venture approach in which they enter into business with a minority partner who has the local knowledge to help develop a particular market. In some cases host governments are displeased by that kind of arrangement, but this does give the multinational control over all aspects of the business. The danger is that the majority partner may impose its will on the minority partner, thereby losing the valuable local input. Both majority joint ventures and sole ventures pose the highest possible risk, since the investments are usually the largest and most inflexible of any of the alternatives.

When a firm decides to go it alone and to create a sole venture, it has complete control of all aspects of a business. This approach may provide the highest return on investment. Of course the risk of this approach is higher than any other alternative since the firm is basically entering a foreign market by itself without any input from local ownership partners.

Contracting will be used to meet specific needs in a particular market. Since very little or no capital is invested, risks are generally low. Host firms can protect their intellectual property by not sharing very much with a contract manufacturer or manager. On the other hand the firm will gain little experience from this kind of arrangement unless it is extremely proactive in seeking it out. The firm can exercise the highest possible control with this kind of arrangement.

■ Virtual market entry

The maturing of the Internet and communications technologies has opened a new entry possibility – virtual market entry (Jeannet and Hennessey 2004). In this case, a firm can take advantage of its ability to establish a detailed website, plus its own Intranet, the ability to share files among employees and selected members of the distribution channel, e-mail and sophisticated cell phones and PDAs. Using all of these communications devices, a firm may choose to enter a market without a physical presence. This can be an effective way to avoid government restrictions.

It should be noted that the simple establishment of a website does not make a business successful. Evidence shows that significant conventional promotional efforts are required to direct customers toward a site. In addition, while the cost of establishing a website is relatively low, the cost of updating and maintaining the site, especially if the firm is planning to take orders directly, can be significant. Underfunding of websites is a chronic problem in business markets.

■ Strategic alliances

A strategic alliance is a formal or informal arrangement between two or more companies with a common business objective (Czinkota and Ronkainen 2004). There are many ways in which firms cooperate with one another covered by this definition, including joint ventures and other contractual arrangements. But often these alliances are less formal and involve the agreement by two firms to pursue particular objectives in order to help one another. At a time when the cost to serve all markets throughout the world has become prohibitive, smart managers are deciding where and when to compete and where and when to cooperate.

These alliances may be formed within a country or across diverse, international markets. One leading thinker on the subject, Kenichi Ohmae (1989) said, 'with enough time, money and luck you can do everything yourself. But who has enough?' Recently, British ship-maker UBH International formed an alliance with a Chinese firm, China International Marine Containers (CIMC) (*Professional Engineering* 2003). In this alliance, CIMC wants to establish a strong position in gas and liquid tank containers while UBH, recently rescued from receivership, needs an infusion of cash. UBH is providing intellectual property, helping the Chinese firm set up a large new facility near Shanghai. The firms are working closely to gain contracts in their targeted market.

Keegan and Green (2003) identify three characteristics of strategic alliances.

1 The participants remain independent after forming the alliance.
2 The participants share the benefits of the alliance as well as control over performance.
3 The participants make on-going contributions in technology, products and in other key strategic areas.

Alliances are growing rapidly in popularity. According to Booz-Allen & Hamilton, a US based consulting firm, alliances in the United States have grown by 25 per cent a year over the last decade and by more than that in Europe and Asia (*Economist* 2001). In fact, that same firm estimated that 32,000 alliances had been formed around the world from 1995 to 1998 and that three-quarters of these alliances had been across national borders (*Economist* 1998). Alliances take many forms. They often focus on joint R&D or marketing efforts. The main reasons for the popularity of strategic alliances are shown in Table 6.8. As can be seen in the Table, strategic alliances are often used to develop global markets. No one firm has the ability to develop every market simultaneously around the world and so frequently it will agree to local help in one or a number of particular markets. The very high cost of developing new products and producing them for

TABLE 6.8 Reasons for strategic alliances

Develop markets/especially global
Spread very high cost/risk of R&D/production
Block or co-opt competitors
Enhance important skills
Control critical resources
Cost-effective procurement
Sharing technology

Adapted from Varadarajan and Jayachandran 1999, Czinkota and Ronkainen 2004, Banks and Baranson 1993

worldwide consumption also leads firms to establish alliances for completing research or setting up production.

Sometimes, it may be a good idea to cooperate with another firm who may be ready to establish a dominant position in a particular market. This can be done by developing a strategic alliance with a competitor or with a third firm who would be able to block your competitor. Some alliances are developed on the basis of learning new skills. Some firms wish to acquire technology. This is particularly true in the biotechnology business where the larger pharmaceutical firms have often partnered with very small but highly skilled biotechnology firms. In some cases, a particular resource may be critical to the success of a firm and it may be necessary to develop an alliance to protect the supply of that resource. Alliances are also formed to procure products around the world, in order to reduce the cost of doing so and in some cases alliances are formed so that firms can share technology rather than develop it on their own.

In choosing an alliance partner, it is important to take the time to be sure the firm you wish to work with will prove reliable over time. Table 6.9 is a profile instrument which allows assessment of a potential partner based on the most important characteristics a firm may establish for selection. This instrument may also be used in choosing one local distributor or agent over another.

The main areas to be assessed relate to past performance of the firm, its current capabilities, the reputation and relationship that the firm has established, the goals and strategies and overall compatibility of the firms. It might be noted that this partner profile may be used for potential distributors, agents or joint venture partners as well as alliance partners. Using this approach, a firm can choose one potential partner from another. First, management would establish weights for each characteristic and then rate each potential partner on these characteristics. The weights and ratings would be multiplied, the total tallied, then divided by the total weights to gain an overall rating for a particular firm.

The factors for the success of one alliance versus another have been studied by a number of researchers. Generally speaking, success factors have been summarized in Table 6.10.

First and most important is careful selection of both the partner and the projects. A recent study has found that similar organizational cultures are more important than similar national cultures (Pothukuchi *et al.* 2002). Also important is a relative balance of power and management between the partners. This will be discussed below in some detail. Clear leadership is necessary so that all members of the alliance know what is expected of the organization and of the relationship. Also important is communications, not only at top management, but at the operational and the worker level of the organization. Very important is the careful negotiation of the agreement. The more formal the alliance may be, the more time must be given to negotiations. In other words, the negotiation of a joint venture agreement would take far longer than the negotiation of a simple letter of understanding between two firms for a strategic alliance. Research also shows that successful alliances are based on complementary skills. If each firm has the same skills, the reasons for alliance are often hard to

TABLE 6.9 Partner profile

Characteristics	Weight (1–10)	Rating (1–10)	Total
Past Performance			
Profitability			
Sales growth			
Market share			
Cooperation with other partners			
Experience with market/product			
Financial strength			
Capabilities			
Facilities			
Marketing/sales			
Design/technological			
Size of firm			
Language			
After-sales			
Knowledge of local business customs			
Reputation/Relationships			
With suppliers			
With customers			
With financial institutions			
With government(s)			
Goals and Strategies			
Short term			
Long term			
Compatibility			
Product lines			
Markets			
Style/personalities			

Adapted from: Moriarty and Kosnik 1989

TABLE 6.10 Alliance success factors
Careful selection of projects and partners – similar organizational cultures
Relative balance of power/management between partners
Clear leadership
Communications at all levels of organization
Careful negotiation of agreement
Clear 'divorce' provisions
Complementary skills in each partner
Built-in flexibility

Adapted from: Czinkota and Ronkainen 2004, Varadarajan and Jayachandran 1999, Pothukuchi *et al*. 2002, Bleeke and Ernst 1995

sustain. Researchers recommend built-in flexibility since markets develop quickly, technology changes and, especially looking at worldwide industry, the ability to change quickly is vitally important. In addition, it is important that clear separation provisions be included in any agreement between two parties. Internet technologies have helped foster cooperation in an alliance since it is easy for people around the world to share their work or store information.

Bleeke and Ernst (1995) warn that joint ventures formed for the wrong reasons often fail and end up with one partner selling itself to another. They reinforce the point that alliances of complementary equals is the only path that leads to a 'marriage for life'. This requires partners who have different product, geographic, or functional strengths.

An example of a firm using many strategies at once can be seen in Dow Corning (Baker 2003). The firm's overall strategy for growth proceeds in four main ways:

- increased market penetration
- new product introductions
- geographic expansion
- acquisition/alliances.

The firm has developed an alliance with Genencor to develop silicon-based biotech materials, bringing together two very different sciences to create new technologies and products such as biosensors. Dow Corning wishes to offer total solutions to its customers rather than just be a materials provider and has developed at least eight alliances in the last year and a half. The firm is also adapting technologies to the local conditions through its R&D labs, especially in China.

■ Selecting the entry strategy

In making the decision about which investment alternative to use, Dunning (2001) developed the eclectic paradigm (also known as OLI) in which he identified three important considerations for making decisions:

- ownership advantages
- location advantages
- internalization considerations.

According to Dunning, firms look at a particular market to decide whether this location has the right environmental conditions for success. This would include characteristics like *per capita* income, size of market, political risk, cultural affinity and so on. Ownership advantages derive from what is also called transaction cost analysis, meaning that some forms of ownership give higher returns to a firm and therefore that firm does not wish to contract with another firm to perform these functions. A third consideration is internalization. Here a firm is considering the need for keeping proprietary information within the firm. For instance, the company may own patents or have developed specific ways of doing business which it does not wish to share with a partner. This would preclude the use of export or joint venture forms and focus the firm more strongly toward a sole venture entry strategy.

Root (1994) developed a strategy decision rule for choosing the most appropriate entry alternative: maximize profit over the strategic planning period subject to constraints imposed by company resources, risk and non-profit objectives. These considerations are summarized in Table 6.11. Obviously, profit will vary with each alternative. Risk is a critical alternative. Various kinds of risk must be faced, ranging from the risk of starting a competitor through licensing through the risk of a loss of investment because of political changes in a particular market. Non-profit objectives may include market share or reversibility of a decision as well as other corporate considerations. One of these might be the need to market a particular product in a market in order to secure orders for a more important product. In one instance, a division of a large multinational was asked to market office furniture in South Korea despite a 200 per cent import duty so that this firm would be able to secure large contracts for nuclear power plants. Considerations like this for large multinationals do not fall into the control, profit or risk categories, but can be important in the decision process. Control is also a key consideration in choosing the correct strategy. If a firm must control information or quality or manufacturing processes or even marketing strategies to be successful, several of the possible entry strategies would be unsuitable.

Blocked markets

Governments often erect trade barriers to protect local industry. These barriers can range from tariffs to restrictions on operations or entry through various forms of discriminatory rules and regulations called non-tariff barriers. These non-tariff barriers are especially common in services industries. Kotler (1986) described 'blocked' markets as those with high entry barriers caused by governments, labor unions and other interest groups. He prescribed the use of 'megamarketing' to overcome blocked markets, adding two Ps (power and public relations) to the familiar four Ps of marketing. He recommended a firm influence critical decision makers in its favor – through reward, coercion, special expertise, legitimacy and prestige and that executives map the existing power structure, develop a strategy and an implementation plan. The firm should choose one of three broad strategies: neutralize opponents, organize allies or turn neutral groups into allies. Kotler also specifically mentioned 'at home' lobbying – using the home government to pressure a foreign government into opening a market.

Dahringer (1991) suggested five key management actions which can be taken to combat barriers to services. These are:

embodying – including services in physical goods, to move the total product toward the more tangible domain

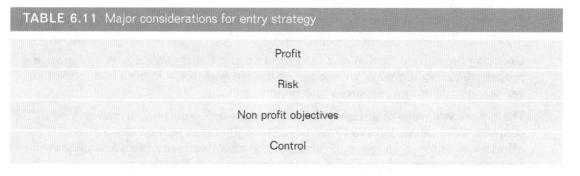

TABLE 6.11 Major considerations for entry strategy

Profit
Risk
Non profit objectives
Control

Adapted from: Root 1994

superior management – developing strategic alliances, most particularly franchising, which permit a partnership between a locally knowledgeable partner and the foreign organization

customizing – developing the most attractive package of benefits so that customers will pay a higher price or move to the service rather than have the service brought to them

technology – using communications and computer technologies (technology transfer is another way of overcoming barriers)

macromarketing – working with governments to relieve discrimination through government actions.

A study by one of the authors (Zimmerman 1999) found that successful managers take a long-term view when confronted by a blocked market. The manager may engage in some of the activities highlighted by Kotler or Dahringer, beginning a long-term process to break into a market. Those who begin the process early can be rewarded. One large insurance firm worked for ten years to wedge its way into the Japanese property and casualty insurance market. When a crack appeared in the government barriers, the firm was first to establish itself and gained brand recognition and a large share over the long-term.

SUMMARY

Perhaps the most perplexing decision a manager must make is when and how to enter new markets. Managers must first clearly decide upon the segments to be addressed and then, taking into account all the environmental factors and their company's resources, choose the most effective market entry strategy.

The key points from this chapter are as follows:

- A range of environmental factors, including economic, demographic, competitive, political/legal, technological and social/cultural are all at work affecting the new market entry decision.

- Firms can take their current products to current or new markets or develop new products for their current or new markets. The latter is the riskiest strategy. Firms who do not realize which alternative they are choosing can often experience severe difficulties.

- Technology is often a key factor in driving firms to new markets and is also a critical success factor.

- While traditionally first movers into markets have been seen as gaining major benefits, they also experience major cost disadvantages when compared to followers. A follower strategy can be successful as well.

- Firms who are successful in moving into foreign markets usually have proactive reasons. Rather than simply reacting to declines in their domestic market, they see foreign markets offering new opportunities. Positive management attitudes toward foreign market entry is critical to success.

- The most successful firms in foreign markets have at least one clear competitive advantage they can translate to their new market.

- Choosing the correct market and the correct market entry strategy is an iterative process requiring thorough knowledge of the environmental factors in a market as well as the company's resources and requirements.

- The three basic ways of entering foreign markets are exporting, investment or contract. While some believe firms move through stages in their international efforts, newer research tends to reinforce the idea that many firms just choose the proper strategy even if they have no past international experience.

- Deciding on the correct entry strategy requires a firm to decide how it can maximize profit subject to company resources, risk, control requirements and non-profit objectives.

- Many firms encounter blocked markets and need to take a long-term approach to opening these markets.

- Strategic alliances offer firms an opportunity to work with other firms who have complementary strengths without the need for a formal relationship like a joint venture. But careful selection of the partner and clear goals and communications are prerequisites to success.

REVIEW QUESTIONS

1 What are the key environmental factors to be considered when entering a new market?

2 Describe the product market expansion guide using both Ansoff's and Day's approaches.

3 What are the advantages and disadvantages of being a first mover into a market?

4 Describe the proactive and reactive reasons for entering foreign markets.

5 Why is it important to have a clearly communicated competitive advantage in a foreign market? List those given in the text.

6 What are the major macro and micro considerations in choosing a particular market?

7 What are the three schools of thought about how firms enter international markets? Describe each in detail.

8 What are the three basic ways to enter foreign markets?

   a What are the main differences between agents and merchants?

9 Describe the advantages and disadvantages of the various investment and contract market entry strategies.

10 What is the strategy decision rule for choosing the most attractive foreign market entry alternative?

11 If you were faced by a blocked market, what actions would you take?

12 What are the main reasons for strategic alliances?

   a What are the critical factors in choosing one partner over another?

   b What are the most important factors for success in an alliance?

SPOTLIGHT ON B2B MARKETING

Wilhelm Bender looked out the window of the Lufthansa flight back to Frankfurt and reviewed the events leading up to the disappointing week he had just experienced. Bender's company, Fraport AG, had made the decision to write off its complete investment in the Philippines as a result of the failure of the final negotiations undertaken by him.

Fraport is a Frankfurt-based company whose main business is to operate the Frankfurt airport. With sales of about US$2 billion, the company had recently gone public and decided to expand internationally. In 2003, Fraport was operating airports in Hanover and Saarbrücken as well as in Turkey and Peru. As part of its aggressive international expansion, Fraport decided to target Manila in the Philippines. In wanting to operate an airport in the Philippines, the company would have considered a number of market entry strategies. They finally decided on a joint venture and formed the Philippines International Air Terminal Company with one of the smaller and less prominent ethnic Chinese trading families that play a central role in the Philippine economy, the Cheng family.

In order to make this project work, the joint venture needed to gain a contract from the Philippine Government and was awarded one by then President Fidel Ramos. He was succeeded by President Joseph Estrada and the contract was expanded in size and scope. Unfortunately, Mr Estrada had to leave office after a popular uprising in 2001. He was succeeded by Gloria Macapagal Arroyo, who gained prominence by promising to fight corruption.

The project had been accused of bribing some officials under the Estrada regime. Mrs Arroyo requested that the contract be changed significantly. Especially important to the success of Fraport's joint venture were provisions giving them exclusive rights to operate duty-free shops in the new terminal, requiring that all airlines move to the new terminal and pay higher fees than they had paid with the old terminal. The joint venture built a huge new Terminal Three at a cost of nearly US$400 million. But the joint venture was constantly suffering from a shortage of capital. Most of the money was put up by Fraport. At one point, Fraport was told that the agreement they had made with the government had been declared null and void. The current government, especially, disputed the rights to the duty-free stores and higher fees charged to airlines. The new terminal has not opened.

Bender wondered whether there had been a better way to enter the Philippine market or whether his choice of partner had been flawed. For now, he only knew his firm had taken a US$318 million charge, resulting in an overall US$132 million loss for 2002.

This case is based upon Landler, M. 'A Bitter Exit From a Philippines Airport', *New York Times*, April 30, 2003:W1.

Questions

1 What environmental considerations would Fraport need to have carefully examined before deciding to move ahead in the Philippines?

2 What other market entry strategies might have been available to a firm like Fraport in the business they are in?

3 What are the key considerations one might use in choosing a potential joint venture partner?

4 How is the role of government different in international markets?

5 If you were Mr Bender, what would your next step be?

REFERENCES

—— (2001) 'Just Good Friends', *Economist* 360: 8235: August 18: 12–14.

—— (1998) 'The Science of Alliance', *Economist* 346: 8062: April 4: 69–70.

—— (2003) 'Chinese Alliance to Revive UK Vessel Maker', *Professional Engineering* 16: 5: 4.

Ansoff, I. (1957) 'Strategies for Diversification', *Harvard Business Review* 35: 5: Sept–Oct: 113–124.

Baker, J. (2003) 'Broader Horizons', *European Chemical News* 24–30 March: 26–27.

Banks, P. F. and Baranson, J. (1993) 'New Concepts Drive Transnational Alliances', *Planning Review* 21: 6: Nov/Dec: 28–31.

Bleeke, J. and Ernst, D. (1995) 'Is Your Strategic Alliance Really a Sale', *Harvard Business Review* 73: 1: 97–105.

Boulding, W. and Christen, M. (2001) 'First Mover Disadvantage', *Harvard Business Review* 69: 9: 20–21.

Bradley, F. and Gannon, M. (2000) 'Does the Firm's Technology and Marketing Profile Affect Foreign Market Entry?', *Journal of International Marketing* 8: 4: 12–36.

Buckley, P. J. and Casson, M. C. (1998) 'Analyzing Foreign Market Entry Strategies: Extending the Internationalization Approach', *Journal of International Business Studies* 29: 3: 539–562.

Chesbrough, H. W. (2003) 'Environmental Influences Upon Firm Entry into New Sub-Markets: Evidence from the Worldwide Hard Disk Drive Industry Conditionally', *Research Policy* 32: 659–678.

Czinkota, M. and Ronkainen, I. A. (2004) *International Marketing*, New York: Harcourt, Inc.

Dahringer, L. D. (1991) 'Marketing Service Internationally: Barriers and Management Strategies', *Journal of Services Marketing* 5: 3: Summer: 5–17.

Day, G. S. (1990) *Market Driven Strategy*, New York: The Free Press.

Dunning, J. H. (2001) 'The Eclectic (OLI) Paradigm of International Production: Past, Present and Future', *International Journal of Economics of Business* 8: 2: 173–190.

Geroski, P. A. (1999) 'Early Warning of New Rivals', *Sloan Management Review* 40: 3: Spring: 107–116.

Jeannet, J-P. and Hennessey, H. D. (2004) *Global Marketing Strategies*, New York: Houghton-Mifflin Company.

Keegan, W. J. and Green, M. C. (2003) *Global Marketing*, Upper Saddle River, NJ: Prentice-Hall.

Kotler, P. (1986) 'Megamarketing', *Harvard Business Review* 64: 2: March/April: 117–124.

Landler, M. 'A Bitter Exit From a Philippines Airport', *New York Times* April 30 2003: W1.

Mitra, D. and Golder, P. N. (2002) 'Whose Culture Matters? Near-Market Knowledge and its Impact on Foreign Market Entry Timing', *Journal of Marketing Research* 39: 3: August: 350–365.

Moriarty, R. T. and Kosnik, T. J. (1989) 'High-Tech Marketing: Concepts, Continuity and Change', *Sloan Management Review* 30: 4: 7–18.

Ohmae, K. (1989) 'The Global Logic of Strategic Alliances', *Harvard Business Review* 67: 2: March/April: 143–154.

Pan, Y. and Tse, D. K. (2000) 'The Hierarchical Model of Market Entry Modes', *Journal of International Business Studies* 31: 4: 535–554.

Pothukuchi, V., Damanpour, F., Choi, J., Chen, C. C. and Park, S. H. (2002) 'National and Organizational Culture Differences and International Joint Venture Performance', *Journal of International Business Studies* 33: 2: 243–265.

Root, F. R. (1994) *Entry Strategies for International Markets* New York: Lexington Books.

Tepstra, V. and David, K. H. (1991) *The Cultural Environment of International Business*, Cincinnati, OH: South-Western Publishing Co.

Varadarajan, R. P. and Jayachandran, S. (1999) 'Marketing Strategy: An Assessment of the State of the Field and Outlook', *Journal of the Academy of Marketing Science* 27: 2: 120–43.

Zimmerman, A. S. (1999) 'Impacts of Services Trade Barriers: A Study of the Insurance Industry', *Journal of Business and Industrial Marketing* 14: 3: 211–229.

Zimmerman, A. S. and Fitzpatrick, P. (1985) *Essentials of Export Marketing*, New York: AMACOM.

ACKLEY INDUSTRIES

The problem

Ackley Industries, located in Cleveland, Ohio, is a US$8-billion multinational corporation, manufacturing many industrial and consumer products. About 10 per cent of total sales is in Europe and the Middle East. The firm is especially strong in the industrial electrical components business.

One of Ackley's many operating units is the office furniture division. This division grew from a metal-forming capability and an internal need for office furniture.

From humble beginnings in 1971, the division has grown to a significant size. During the 1990s the furniture division returned excellent profits with operating margins often exceeding 20 per cent. Despite the growth of this division, it remains a relatively small piece of the overall corporate pie and rather different from the other businesses in the corporate family. The division operates relatively independently but must rely on corporate efforts for sales outside the US.

One hot-selling Ackley item in the US is Ack-Tec, a well-priced, high-quality desk, designed to be used with desktop personal computers. Thus far, Ackley's office furniture division has sold its products only in the US.

Frank Selvy, the manager of European/Middle Eastern sales, is stationed in London. He receives the following email:

Ackley management has decided to introduce Ack-Tec as our first office furniture product in your area. Please submit rough outline of marketing plan including your recommendations for initial pricing.

US list price, EXW Cleveland is:

Quantity	List Price
	$
1	320
2 – 50	299
51 – 500	275
over 500	negotiated

These products are sold by us in the US through local dealers. Dealers normally purchase at 50 per cent off list price. The dealer then marks up its price to whatever is competitive in the market (final price is usually 20–35 per cent off list price or 30–40 per cent dealer mark up). Direct product cost on this desk for our first year's domestic sales was 60 per cent (gross margin, 40 per cent). Need your first-cut plan within two weeks.

Regards,

John Holloway

President

Market considerations

The market for furniture of this kind is growing rapidly in the US – an annual rate in the last three years of 20 per cent. Total US sales in 2003 of specialized, computer-related furniture was US$250 million. Data for Europe and the Middle East are less firm but the market is estimated to be in an earlier stage than the US. Europe may be two to three years behind in market development. Selvy estimated the market for 2003 at nearly US$80 million in Europe and only about US$6 million in the Middle East.

Customers for this furniture appear to be large multinational firms, especially US-based companies with a large numbers of desktop computers. But purchase patterns vary. In some firms, all furniture is specified by headquarters purchasing or office facilities management. In others, local managers can choose brand and type. Independent architects and interior designers influence purchases as well, with some firms relying heavily on homebased advisors and others using local specifiers.

White collar workers' unions influence decisions in some European countries while no such organizations exist in the Middle East. Questions of personal taste and prestige of the buyers are also at work in the purchase of office furniture.

There remain many standards questions still to be resolved for office furniture in the European Union. But Selvy thinks this is an attractive product-market.

Product considerations

The most interesting feature of the Ack-Tec desk is the built-in electrical receptacle at desk height for plugging in the various items which computers require. In the current design, these are obviously US-type receptacles.

Selvy is already well aware of the differences in electrical requirements in various countries, such as the 50Hz, 240 volt current in the UK. But with this product, he must also recognize the differences in receptacle format. France, the UK and Germany each have their own format and none is the same as the US. In the Middle East both UK and US standards are seen. In addition, all electrical apparatus must be approved by local government sanctioning organizations and within Europe must carry the CE safety mark.

One other problem with the product is also bothersome. Europeans use A4 sized paper for correspondence, making their requirements for files, and hence desk drawers, different from that of the US. In the Middle East, some countries such as Saudi Arabia do use the US paper sizes.

Selvy has also become aware that other office products like telephones seem to succeed and fail as frequently on design, appearance and color as on features and longevity.

Competition

Major competitors overseas are Compu-Furniture, a UK-based firm; Mobilier de la France, a French firm; and Brinzini, an Italian division of General Steel, a US-based firm.

The only overseas firm Ackley encounters domestically is General Steel, the leader in the US office furniture business with office furniture sales of US$2.5 billion in 2002. General Steel has almost 25 per cent of the office furniture market in the US while Ackley estimates their own share at about 10 per cent.

Another competitor, US Automation Company, is a multi-product firm with total sales of more than US$5 billion in 2002. Their furniture division holds about 15 per cent of the US market. While many US divisions not in the furniture business are presently exporting, the furniture division has thus far concentrated only on the US market.

Estimated sales of specialized computer desks for key competitors in Europe for 2002 are as follows:

Compu-Furniture	£20 million (U.K.)
Mobilier de la France	€12 million
Brinzini	€8 million
All others	$23 million (U.S.)

Sales in the Middle East are probably proportionally the same.

Compu-Furniture is a small firm which is primarily engaged in computer peripherals. Total sales of the company were £60 million during 2002. Their sales are primarily in the UK. Mobilier de la France is mainly a wood furniture firm with total sales of €75 million. They are concentrating on Europe and the Middle East. Brinzini is a full-line furniture company, with total sales of €52 million, which has concentrated in Europe, but has a strong relationship with Al Qatar and Co., a large, financially powerful importer in Saudi Arabia.

One additional interesting development has come to light in the initial research. It appears that Mobilier de la France is negotiating with General Steel to be acquired by GS, or for some kind of joint venture.

Selvy's response

Selvy is not surprised by requests for instant response. He feels his first task is to determine the best target markets. He uses the latest information he can find. He knows that he doesn't have figures on locally produced PCs.

He then quickly checks out the competition and finds several similar products available in the UK. These are manufactured in France, Italy and England. He develops a competitive pricing chart:

End user price quotes			
Quantity	US$ Compu-Furniture	US$ Mobilier de la France	US$ Brinzini Division of General Steel
1 – 5	189	205	195
6 – 100	179	198	185
over 101	negotiated	185	173

He also determines that the duty into the European Union on this product is 7.5 per cent and freight and insurance from the US will average about 6 per cent. These would be applied to the dealer purchase price. VAT would be added to each stage where value is added, but VAT is recoverable if the products are for business use.

For the Middle East, import duties range from 20 per cent in Saudi Arabia to 100 per cent in Egypt. Freight and insurance from the US average 15 per cent.

To serve the Middle East from Europe would reduce freight and insurance costs from 15 per cent to 8 per cent but import duties would remain the same.

Selvy has good contacts with government and industry officials in the UK, Europe and the Middle East. He confirms that the market is growing rapidly.

Selvy weighs the various possibilities for establishing Ackley's market position. He outlines them as follows:

- not enter
- acquisition
- ackley sole venture
- licensing of a European or Middle Eastern manufacturer
- joint venture or strategic alliance with dealer or competitor
- direct/indirect export
- contract manufacture.

He knows from past experience that headquarters management usually wants to take a step-by-step approach with a minimal start-up investment and some results within the first year. He also knows that management will be willing to invest significantly if he can make a strong case.

Case study questions

1 What is Ack-Tec's competitive position in Europe and the Middle East?

2 What additional information should Selvy plan to get?

3 What strategic options should Ackley consider for the furniture division in the Middle East and Europe?

4 What would your first-cut marketing plan include?

5 What would you recommend to the home office if you were in Selvy's position?

FORMULATING THE MARKET MIX

This Part gives you the tools to organize the tactical activities involved in global B2B marketing. This Part builds upon Part 1, the Business Market Environment which described the motivations of industrial buyers, the differences between B2B and consumer marketing and the strategic planning framework. It also builds upon Part 2 in which you were introduced to market research techniques, segmentation and market entry strategies.

In Part 3, Chapter 7 defines product and describes the product lifecycle. It shows how a product strategy may be developed and how the product lifecycle relates to global marketing. The chapter also describes an effective product development process for a global B2B firm, discusses the make or buy decision and global outsourcing.

Chapter 8 focuses on B2B services, showing the difference between services and tangible products. This chapter points out the relationship between product and services in business marketing and the importance of managing marketing, operations and human resources together. The chapter reviews e-services and discusses barriers to services erected by foreign governments. It also describes the difference between a product-centric company and one which is attempting to provide customer value.

Chapter 9 discusses the all important aspect of pricing, showing that in business markets, vendors usually face a 'stepped demand curve' and can demand higher prices than they may think possible. Exceptions in high-tech markets are also described. Pricing objectives and strategy and customer perceptions of price are discussed. The misuse of the experience curve is described in addition to costing methods. Special emphasis is given to international pricing, including price escalation in international markets. Transfer pricing and dumping are described as is competitive bidding.

Chapter 10 describes distribution channels, showing the proper way to ensure that goods arrive in the right condition at the right time in the right place. The chapter describes relationships between buyers and sellers, conflict within distribution networks and how managers can manage this conflict. The action of reducing steps of distribution is also described.

In Chapter 11 tactics and logistics are described, showing how the entire supply chain is managed for optimum cost and service level. The positives and negatives of 'just-in-time' purchasing are described as well as international transportation methods along with the transportation mode.

Chapter 12 is about communications in B2B markets. First, this chapter describes the major differences between B2B and consumer marketing communications and shows how buyers seek information. A discussion of cultural differences in communications is included as well as steps in attitude change. The chapter describes cognitive dissonance and standardization versus adaptation in international marketing communications.

In Chapter 13 personal selling is described. Personal relationships are critical in business marketing and the salesperson plays a far more critical role in business markets than in consumer markets. A full discussion of the sales presentation is included in this chapter, discussing preparation, presentation and closing the sale.

Chapter 14 discusses sales promotion, exhibitions and trade fairs. Since trade fairs are especially important in international B2B marketing, special attention is given to this very important topic including objective setting, strategic issues and evaluation of activities. Legal and regulatory issues of sales promotion are also discussed in this chapter.

Chapter 15 reviews corporate reputation management. Corporate reputation is the aggregate perceptions of outsiders about the salient characteristics of a firm. This chapter identifies the features that characterize an organization's reputation, explores the events and characters that create that reputation, shows the role of public relations in ordinary and crisis times and discusses sponsorships.

Overall, this Part reviews the most important tactics marketers use in B2B markets around the world and gives you the tools to implement the most effective marketing program possible.

7

PRODUCT STRATEGY AND PRODUCT DEVELOPMENT

Learning objectives
After reading this chapter, you should be able to:

- Differentiate between business-to-business and business-to-consumer product strategy

- Understand the product life cycle and how it applies to B2B and global markets

- Describe the diffusion of innovation process

- Outline and explain the new product development process

- Discuss the considerations in global brand strategy

- Understand the make or buy decision and how global sourcing and subcontracting relate to this decision

▮ Introduction

No market remains the same forever and marketing managers are always looking for new and better ways of doing things to generate satisfaction for their customers and increase return to their shareholders. Competitors lurk in every market trying to think of more attractive products and services. All of this means a firm must engage in a formal new product development process. The firm needs to develop an overall product strategy and then manage a process which will keep its offering as attractive as possible to customers.

◼ Definition of product

A product is an offering of the firm which satisfies the needs of customers. Customers are seeking to purchase benefits and they are willing to part with items of value including funds and their time in exchange for gaining these satisfactions. This includes the core product and benefits, essentially the value the customer is actually purchasing, plus the product attributes which include the brand name, the design, country of origin, price and packaging as well as support services like delivery, installation, warranty and after-sales service. Since many business marketers began their careers as engineers they often focus too strongly on the tangible core product and functions, rather than the total package that the customer considers when he/she buys.

The customer looks at the total product as shown in Figure 7.1.

◼ Product strategy

The product strategy of a firm relates to making decisions about the features, quality and the entire offering shown in Figure 7.1. In addition, product strategy involves developing a rational relationship between and among product offerings. For instance, an office furniture product manager must decide upon the features, functions and benefits of a particular seating line, the quality level which will affect the pricing and all the ancillary items under his or her control including packaging, design, country of origin, delivery, installation, warranty and after-sales service. He or she also has to make decisions about the brand. If one assumes that this product manager is employed by Steelcase, the world's largest office furniture manufacturer, he or she may choose to offer the product as a Steelcase-branded product, or to develop a new brand name not associated with Steelcase so that this product stands on its own. A third choice might be to private-brand the product for some other outlet such as Office Depot or Staples. These three choices are illustrated in Figure 7.2.

The issues involved in this type of trade-off are complex, since the marketing manager is unable to predict the future accurately. The balance between investment and risk is always a difficult one for managers, since there are few ways to obtain a high return without taking some risk. On the other hand, taking risks does not, of itself, generate high returns. Usually these conflicts are resolved by internal negotiations between marketing and other functional managers within the firm. In deciding upon the entire product offering, the manager must distinguish between an individual product which has a unique set of the attributes seen in Figure 7.1, a product line, which is a group

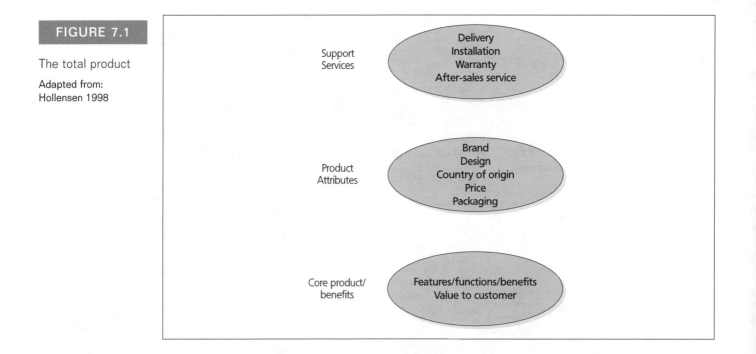

FIGURE 7.1

The total product

Adapted from:
Hollensen 1998

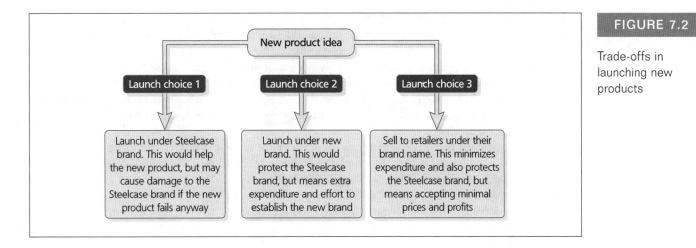

FIGURE 7.2

Trade-offs in launching new products

of these individual products that are related to one another and the overall product assortment, which is all the product lines together.

In the global context, product lines tend to expand to accommodate the different requirements of national markets. Each country requires slightly different product characteristics, leading to a proliferation of models. It is critical for a manager of the product line to attempt to limit the number of products and product lines to the minimum which will satisfy the requirements of most of his or her customers. Pruning the product line to remove unprofitable or underperforming products is a critical skill a manager must vigorously employ.

While consumer product strategy is similar to business product strategy, there are a few major differences. Firstly, consumer product strategies focus more heavily on brand identity and product appearance than do strategies related to business products. Since most business products are sold with related services like installation, training, after-sales service and maintenance, in almost every case a business product must be offered as a total package. As mentioned earlier, business buyers attempt to minimize the emotional content of their decisions. In most cases, they are concerned with specific tangible benefits which can be measured when they make a buying decision. Therefore, designing a business product requires a full understanding of the customer's value-creating activities so that the product can be positioned as an important contributor to the customer's value chain.

The well-known product lifecycle concept dictates that a firm engage in a dedicated product development process (see Figure 7.3).

The product lifecycle posits that there are four major stages which most industries advance through. The first is *Introduction* marked by start-up sales growth. Generally in this stage a firm is

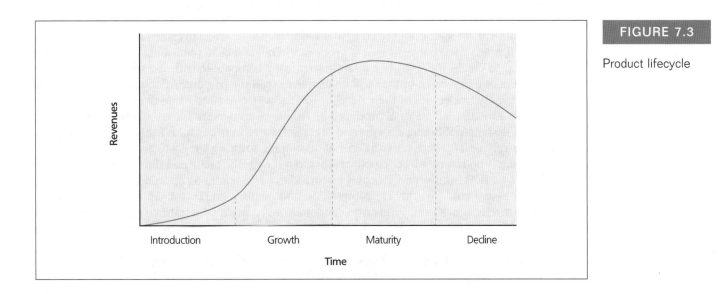

FIGURE 7.3

Product lifecycle

spending more on producing and marketing the product than it is receiving in revenue from sales. In the *Growth* stage the product begins to be accepted and sales climb, with a consequent improvement in the relationship between revenue and expenditure. The initial investment in developing the product and preparing to produce it have probably been met and the firm should begin to see a positive return on the investment. The longest period is the *Maturity* stage in which sales begin to level off since penetration in the market is high. Even though sales level off, so that revenue remains fairly constant, profits can continue to rise throughout this stage, depending upon competitive pressure and efficiencies the firm may realize.

The *Maturity* stage is the point at which the investment really pays off. Expenditure on marketing is usually relatively low as a percentage of the revenue received and the initial start-up investment should have been recouped. The final stage is *Decline* in which sales of the product gradually fall off as it is supplanted by some newer solution. Here profits may continue to be positive even though sales revenue may decrease sharply. Eventually, the product will cease to be viable as competing products enter the market, or as newer versions of the product are produced by the firm.

The product lifecycle concept has been criticized because it presents too specific a pattern of stages for industries which don't always follow a smooth curve. In addition, those who are marketing the product seldom know what stage the product is in. A key criticism is that the product lifecycle may be the result of marketing efforts rather than a course followed by products regardless of the effort placed behind them, in other words marketers act in ways which make the product lifecycle inevitable. For example, whenever Intel develop a new computer chip they publicize the product heavily, they carry out major sales campaigns with the computer manufacturers and they price competitively. Inevitably this means that the new chip has a rapid growth rate, but loses money at first – just as the product lifecycle model predicts. As the chip becomes established, Intel invariably begin developing the next generation of chip, thus ensuring that the current model must go into a decline when the new chip hits the market. Thus the product lifecycle becomes a self-fulfilling prophecy. A further criticism of the PLC is that there is no way to determine the timescales, so there is no way of knowing whether the product still has another year to go in the growth stage or whether it is heading into maturity. The maturity stage might last anything from a few weeks (in the case of some electronic products) to a period of centuries (in the case of, say, iron ore). Finally, there is no doubt that the lifecycle is affected by marketing activities. A product which is heading into a decline might be repositioned into a new market (commonly a foreign one), or might be nursed back to life with some clever promotional campaigns. Finally, the product lifecycle is nearly irrelevant for particular brands. Thus the product lifecycle is a better descriptor than it is a predictor.

Despite the criticisms, the product lifecycle is a useful shorthand tool for considering the most effective strategy at a particular time.

As can be seen from Table 7.1, in the introduction stage, by necessity only a few product variations are offered. Pricing can be high to recoup large investments (skimming) or low to establish market share (penetration). A marketer in this stage attempts to build channels of distribution. They use promotion to build primary demand, that is, to explain to customers why they need this particular innovation. The overall objective here is to create awareness and have individuals try the product. An example of this can be seen from the computer industry. There are many software houses producing desktop publishing suites, but most have a problem when it comes to publishing on the Internet. The software used to create the website content needs to be compatible with the software used by the potential users of the website, or they will be unable to read the content. Adobe overcame this problem by giving away free copies of their Acrobat Reader software (free being the ultimate low price), allowing web users to read material produced by Adobe customers. In turn, this encourages firms to use Adobe's desktop publishing systems and other software. In order to use the Adobe approach, a firm must be very well funded, since the cost of developing software simply to give it away is high and of course there is no reason why competitors should not copy the tactic and thus negate the benefits. Therefore, most B2B firms would probably be forced to use a skimming approach in order to recoup heavy development costs. Worldwide competition and opening markets make imitators of the new product a foregone conclusion. Firms who cannot afford to use a penetration strategy may look for a strategic alliance with an established firm in order to gain access to an established distribution network.

In the Growth stage, the firm attempts to add some extensions and accompanying services to the basic product. Pricing may continue at either a skimming or penetration level but in general firms are

TABLE 7.1 Product lifecycle and marketing strategies

Variable	Introduction	Growth	Maturity	Decline
Product	Basic, little choice	Some extensions, services	Many offerings serving many segments	Far fewer competitors
Price	Skimming or penetration	Meet competition	Meet competition or cut with specific deals	High or low depending on competition
Place	Build channels	Continue to build channels	Move toward intensive distribution	Selective or direct sales
Promotion	Build primary demand	Begin to build selective demand	Persuading and reminding, stressing differences between brands	Reduced to necessary minimum
Overall Objective	Create awareness and trial	Maximize market share or return on investment	Hold market share or maximize profits	Reduce costs, maximize remaining sales and profits

Adapted From: Kotler 2003

forced to respond to new competitors who come into the market, so prices will need to reflect the new competitive environment. Distribution continues to be a key aspect of growth and firms look to build channels of distribution, possibly by forming strategic alliances. Promotion changes in this stage from convincing a customer that their firm needs this particular product, to establishing the benefits of one particular brand versus another. The overall objective in this stage is to maximize market share through low pricing and heavy promotion or to maximize return on investment through a high price strategy.

In the Maturity stage, competition is rampant with many different kinds of product and service offerings serving many different segments. In this stage, firms usually don't have much choice in setting prices because the price is set by the market – in other words, the interplay between suppliers and customers is what sets the prices, not the decisions of the marketing managers. Distribution tends to become intensive in many markets where the most important thing is to sell through as many channels as possible. Intensive distribution for global B2B products will often mean finding one qualified distributor in each country market, rather than selling through discount stores on every corner as it does in consumer marketing. Promotion focuses on persuading and reminding customers, stressing the differences between brands. In this stage the firm's overall objective is to hold market share through aggressive pricing, communications and distribution or to maximize profits by focusing on key segments.

In the Decline stage, there may be fewer competitors as many firms drop out of a slowing market. Price may be kept high or low depending on the number of competitors. Once only a few competitors exist, a firm may have the capability to raise prices on products nearing obsolescence. Place moves toward selective distribution, or in many cases, direct sales through an Internet website or catalog. Promotion is reduced to the absolute minimum. The overall objectives here are to reduce costs and to maximize the remaining sales and profits in this product market. In some countries (especially in the Developing World) obsolete technology is serving the needs of many customers – a firm must decide how to provide parts and service for these markets in order to maintain a positive reputation with customers who may later wish to user newer products.

It is, of course, dangerous for a firm to have all its products in one stage of the lifecycle. Many start-up firms find themselves in this position, since they often only have one product to sell, but if all products are in the Introduction stage, the firm has no sources of cash to finance growth. On the other hand, if all products are in the Maturity stage, there are no oncoming new products to replace those heading toward decline.

Products move differently through stages of the product lifecycle in various country markets. For example, one might surmise that the progress of the personal computer through the various stages was quite different in the US, the countries of the EU and China back in 1990. This is shown graphically in Figure 7.4.

It is extremely important that a manager understands where in the product lifecycle a particular product is when entering any market, since as we have seen this position strongly affects the entire marketing strategy for the firm. It is not infrequent that a firm may bring a new, technologically-advanced product to a market and find virtually no distribution capable of installing and servicing the product. This is exactly what happened with PCs in China in the late 1980s and early 1990s.

TALKING POINT

The product lifecycle gives us a model of what should happen to a product after it is introduced – but the emphasis here is on the word 'should'. Some products simply flop as soon as they are launched – others grow rapidly, then disappear without trace as a smart competing product appears.

So how can we time the launch of the next new product? How do we know for sure that the last product launch will go according to plan? Or that the current one will? The answer is of course that we have no way of knowing, because we can't predict the future. So what's the point? Why not just launch when we feel like it, or when the product is ready for market and let the products take their chances?

Or maybe any planning is better than no planning? An educated guess is better than a stab in the dark.

Diffusion of innovation

The product lifecycle is based upon findings by Rogers (1962) which showed that innovations move through markets in an orderly manner. Customers can be classified according to their willingness to accept new ideas. These firms can generally be classified following Rogers as:

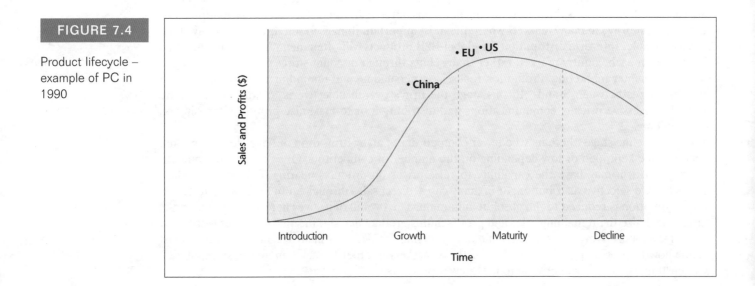

FIGURE 7.4

Product lifecycle – example of PC in 1990

Innovators: companies who will be wiling to try new products or services and are willing to be the first ones. Rogers identified 2.5 per cent of customers as falling into this category. These firms are the ones who accept the product during the earliest stages of the product lifecycle.

Early adopters: After the innovators try a product, these companies will also try it. They are generally open to new ideas but want some proof that the product will work. These firms would be responsible for the growth seen in the Growth Phase of the product lifecycle.

Early Majority: Firms who will buy the product once it is thoroughly tried and tested. These firms form the backbone of the Maturity Phase of the product lifecycle.

Late Majority: Firms who generally do not wish to try new services or products and wait until many other firms have accepted the innovation. Firms like this would be responsible for maintaining the growth of the product in the latter stages of the Maturity Phase of the product lifecycle.

Laggards: Those who would adopt the product only under duress or not adopt at all.

Rogers also identified attributes of innovations which affect the speed of their acceptance:

Relative Advantage: the perception that the idea is better than the one it supercedes.

Compatibility: consistency with existing values, past experience and needs of a firm's buyers and influencers.

Complexity: more complex ideas are adopted more slowly.

Trialability: if a firm can try out a small aspect of a new idea it will be accepted more quickly than if a firm has to make a major switch. For instance, the trialability of a new company-wide computer system would be extremely low and therefore acceptance very slow.

Observability: if the effects of an innovation can be easily observed this innovation may be adopted more quickly.

The underlying reason for the product lifecycle is the constant development of new technologies and processes which create opportunities but also pose threats to firms established with the currently accepted technology. In addition, the globalization of trade throughout the world, including the lowering of barriers to market entry, has allowed new technologies to penetrate into markets which were formerly blocked. No firm can succeed without assuming that its current approach to products and services is in danger of being replaced by newer, better and less costly alternatives.

Geoffrey Moore (1995) introduced the idea of the technology adoption lifecycle. Here he showed that in early stages of a market, technology enthusiasts and visionaries who represented the innovators and early adopters in the adoption process, are willing to accept new technologies enthusiastically. But moving to the next step in the Early Majority phase requires convincing what he called the *pragmatists* to accept the innovation. Moore identified a huge 'chasm' which stopped products from crossing over from minimal acceptance by the enthusiasts and visionaries into the mainstream market dominated by the pragmatists and the next group (Late Majority, he called the *conservatives*). The 'chasm' is defined by Moore as a 'time of great despair when the early market's interest wanes but the mainstream market is still not comfortable ... with the solutions available'. In order to get over the chasm, Moore recommends a focus on vertical market segments that have specific needs for this particular technological innovation, convincing those in the majority mainstream market that the new solution will be beneficial to them. He reiterates the basic idea that only a full understanding of the customer's business can enable a firm to successfully sell a new technology to this customer.

It is obvious that many firms understand this lesson and are assigning considerable resources to the product development process. A proxy for the level of spending on new product development can be established by examining the R&D expenditures of the 300 largest global firms in Table 7.2 (Bowonder and Yadav 1999). The total represented by these large global firms is over US$200 billion. As can be seen, in some industries the percentage of sales spent on R&D is quite high. For instance, in pharmaceuticals and health care, these large global firms averaged R&D spending at 12 per cent of sales. On the other hand, the largest global petroleum companies averaged less than 1 per cent of sales on R&D spending. The US continues to dominate in terms of R&D expenditures. The forecast total for 2003 of all US R&D including federal, industrial and university and non-profit expenditures is US$302 billion (Battelle 2003).

TABLE 7.2 Largest global firm R&D expenditures (US$) (1997)		
Industry	**Total Spending**	**% of Sales**
Electronics	51.5	6.3
Automobiles	40.3	4.2
Pharmaceuticals and Health Care	33.3	12.0
Computers	18.3	5.9
Chemicals	12.5	4.8
Telecommunications	11.5	3.6
Aerospace	7.6	4.6
Software	6.4	13.7
Petroleum	4.7	0.7
Heavy Industry/Farm Equipment	4.2	2.5
Scientific, Photo & Control Equipment	3.1	6.4
Gas/Electricity	2.3	1.0
Metal/Metal Products	2.2	1.2
Food	2.1	1.3
Medical Instruments	1.2	9.7
Building Materials/Glass	0.7	2.1
Forest and Paper Products	0.5	0.9
Engineering/Construction	0.4	0.7
Total	204.2	n/a

Adapted from: Bowonder and Yadav 1999

Bowonder and Yadav (1999) report that innovation is coming from newer firms in Taiwan, China, Korea, Singapore, Ireland, India and Israel. All of this indicates that a firm must establish a systematic approach to new product development.

New product development time has been reduced radically over the last few years. Topfer (1995) showed the difference in development time for selected products as seen in Table 7.3.

In many cases, development time has been cut in half and in some cases even to one-third. Managers are well aware of this trend and are organizing to move more quickly to get from idea to market.

TABLE 7.3 New product development times

Company	Product	Development time in years	
		1980	1990
Honda	Automobiles	8	3
Volvo	Trucks	7	5.5
Rank Xerox	Copiers	5	3
Brother	Printers	4	2
Apple	Computers	3.5	1
AT&T	Telephone Systems	2	1

Adapted from: Topfer 1995

New product development process

Product development is defined succinctly as 'the transformation of market opportunity and a set of assumptions about product technology into a product available for sale' (Krishnan and Ulrich, 2001). Crawford (2003) has been a pioneer researcher in the new product development process. He first poses the question 'what is a new product?' and provides these categories:

New-to-the-world products: These are inventions such as the first automobile or computer.

New category entries: Products introduced by firms into a product category where the firm had not been doing business up to this time.

Additions to product lines: These are line extensions in the firm's current markets such as a lap-top computer introduced by Dell.

Product improvements: Current products made better in some way.

Repositioning: Taking a current product and attempting to find a new use for it. Although not a B2B example, the most famous of this is Arm and Hammer Baking Soda which was repositioned many times as a refrigerator deodorant or carpet cleaner.

Some simplify this by saying that new products are simply any product new to the firm providing it. In any event as we have seen it is important to have a formalized new product process.

Crawford identified five phases in the new product process:

Opportunity Identification & Selection: where new product opportunities are identified and selected for further development.

Concept Generation: where an attractive opportunity includes research with customers and preliminary analysis takes place.

Concept Evaluation: Careful review of new product concepts on technical, marketing and financial variables. This phase also requires ranking to choose the most promising concepts to move forward to the next phase.

Development: In this phase, both technical and marketing development take place. Prototypes are designed and tested and the production process must be established. Marketing must develop a full marketing and business plan, including all additional services and products required by this concept.

Launch: In this final phase, the product is finally commercialized. Distribution and sale of the product begins and the marketing launch plan is put into effect.

Underlying the entire new product development process is the overall strategic direction of the firm. The firm must be sure that the new product development is congruent with its strategy. For instance, an aerospace firm decides that it has a high level of software expertise. However, before beginning the development process to offer a software product the firm must fully understand the differences between the market for software and the current aerospace business it is familiar with.

When business marketing firms attempt to find sources for new ideas, they can look to unmet needs or problems. Table 7.4 presents some ideas for approaching unmet needs.

Firstly, routine market contacts often unearth areas where a firm may provide a product or service not available currently. Secondly, the firm may undertake specific problem analysis through discussions with experts or with users themselves through surveys, focus groups or observation. Finally, a firm may employ scenario analysis, attempting to establish the most likely scenarios for the future and to anticipate what problems their customers may face because of new developments identified in the scenarios.

Von Hippel *et al.* (1999) say firms fail to develop breakthrough products for two reasons:

(1)   companies have built-in incentives to focus on the short-term, and

(2)   developers really don't know how to get to product breakthroughs.

These researchers arrived at an approach to gaining excellent new ideas by studying the 3M Corporation. A most important source of new ideas for 3M is lead users. The process encompasses four major steps:

(1)   *Laying the Foundation*: A team is formed which identifies the markets to target and kinds of innovations they may wish to pursue. In this stage the team must gain the support of key managers within the company.

(2)   *Determining the Trends*: In this step, the team talks to experts in the field and attempts to understand the newest technologies and applications in the area.

(3)   *Identifying Lead Users*: The team identifies the most important users who are on the leading edge of a particular target market. They will then gather information from these lead users and develop preliminary product ideas.

(4)   *Developing the Breakthroughs*: The final step is to move the preliminary concepts through toward completion. The first portion of this step is hosting a workshop with several lead users and in-house marketing and technical people. During these workshops, all participants work to design final concepts which will fit the company as well as the customers' requirements.

Crawford and DiBenedetto (2003) have supplied a checklist of idea stimulators for B2B products. An abbreviated version of this list is presented in Table 7.5.

TABLE 7.4 Approaches used to discover unmet needs and problems

Routine Market Contacts
    Sales call reports
    Service department
    Complaint files

Problem Analysis
    Develop a list of user problems
    Expert opinion
    Published sources
    Direct inquiry of heavy users, individually or in focus groups
    User panels
    User observations

Scenario Analysis

TABLE 7.5 Checklist of idea stimulators for B2B products

Change the physical, thermal, electrical, chemical or mechanical properties of this product.

Any new electrical, electronic, optical, hydraulic, mechanical or magnetic way of performing a function?

Is this function really necessary?

Can we change the power source to make it work better?

Can standard components be substituted?

How might the product be made more compact?

What if it were heat-treated, hardened, alloyed, cured, frozen, plated?

Who else could use this operation or its output?

Has every step been computerized as much as possible?

How can we use the Internet to improve this product/service?

Adapted from: Crawford and DiBenedetto 2003

The key to a successful new product process is that a few real winners emerge while most of the potential losers are eliminated. However, no process can eliminate all failures. Many managers are quite wary about the highly visible step of introducing a new product. If a manager is hoping to have 100 per cent success then this process will eliminate most of the potential successes while eliminating every potential failure.

Determinant attributes

Hansiota *et al.* (1985) described a determinant attribute as one which is both important and differentiating. The task of the business marketer is to understand both the importance of each attribute of a product and or service as it is perceived by their customers and also to understand whether a particular attribute differentiates the offering from competitors. As can be seen by Figure 7.5, attributes must be important and differentiating in order to be determinant.

A determinant attribute is one on which customers will make choices about which products or services to purchase. To properly design products, the manager must know which aspects of a particular offering are important to customers. But that is not enough information. In addition, the manager must determine whether one attribute or a group of attributes make a particular competitor stand out from others. Only this combination of high importance and differentiation will yield the determinant attributes, the upper right corner of the matrix shown in Figure 7.5.

One of the authors has completed many research projects for industrial firms which showed clients' rating very high on unimportant attributes shown in the upper left hand corner of the matrix or very low on the most important and differentiating attributes, placing the firm in the lower right portion of the matrix. Neither of these ratings will result in a firm offering products with determinant attributes which are clearly preferred by its customers.

Testing the new product concept

Crawford and DiBenedetto (2003) define a new product concept as a statement which describes the benefits the new product will give to customers versus other products or solutions they are currently using with the description of the form and/or technology through which these benefits will be realized. Once the new product concept has been honed it is ready for testing by customers. These

FIGURE 7.5

Attribute analysis

Adapted from: Hansiota
et al. 1985

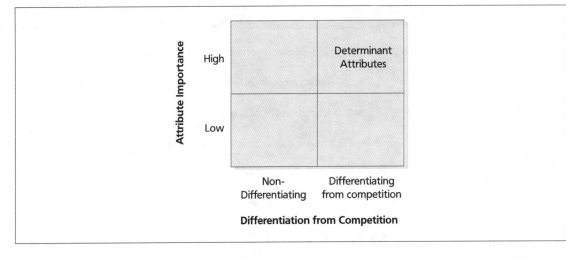

researchers offer a warning which is already well-known to market researchers. In business products, radical new technologies are difficult to test when customers cannot visualize the benefits. One author of this text completed focus groups with MIS managers in the early 1980s, offering various forms of personal computers. One manager stated 'I have no time to fool around with those toys. I have a mainframe to run'. Customers are often not equipped to react to product concepts which solve problems they are not aware of. A better approach for developing product concepts would be finding new ideas with customers, based on potential or possible problems. Generally speaking, concepts are tested using some form of market research. If the product is easily visualized, mail surveys may suffice. But when the product needs to be experienced by potential customers, actual prototypes may be required and personal experience through focus groups may be the best method for concept testing. In some cases, web-based surveys may be used where a product may be seen but direct experience with it is not required to understand customers' reactions. (For a more detailed discussion, see Chapter 4).

After the concept testing, detailed screening of the concept is necessary to see whether it should be moved into the next step. When a firm wishes to fully examine the attractiveness of various new product alternatives, it will review each of these alternatives using some form of a scoring model. A brief example of this is included in Table 7.6.

A firm should develop its own scoring model relevant to its own business and past successes and failures realized through the new product process. The factors and the scales should be adapted for each particular firm's situation, but the process should be used to determine which is worthy of further effort and which should be abandoned. Ames and Hlavacek (1984) offered a figure similar to Figure 7.6, showing how 100 new product ideas might yield only one new product.

In evaluating potential product, Crawford and DiBenedetto have pointed out the possible errors which could be made, summarized in the risk/payoff matrix. This is seen in Figure 7.7.

As they point out, the AA decision (stopping development of a product which would fail as soon as you can) and the BB decision (continuing the development of a product which would succeed) are obviously correct decisions. The incorrect decisions are AB and BA. AB means a product which would succeed is stopped before it has a chance to enter the market. BA allows a product which will fail to continue through the process. Often, the worst error is not the BA, which obviously can waste resources on a possible failure, but the AB-type error which aborts successes before they reach the market. In many business marketing firms, managers have been trained to avoid making mistakes and therefore they often make the AB error and hardly any new products reach the market. At a certain point, aggressive competitors make these managers pay dearly for this too-restrictive product innovation program.

Project teams

It is important that the marketing plans work with the development plans on parallel paths toward launch. This is represented graphically in Figure 7.8.

TABLE 7.6 Scoring model factors and scales					
Factor	**Scale**				
Technical Aspects:	1	2	3	4	5
Technical task difficulty	Very difficult				Easy
Research skills required	Have none required				Perfect fit
Development skills required	Have none required				Perfect fit
Technical equipment/processes	Have none required				Have all
Rate of technological change in market	High/erratic				Stable
Design superiority assurance	None				Very high
Security of design (patent)	None				Have patent
Manufacturing equipment/processes	Have none required				Have them now
Vendor cooperation available	None in sight				Current relationship
Likelihood of competitive cost	Well above competition				Over 20 per cent less
Likelihood of quality product	Below current levels				Leadership
Speed of market	Two years or more				Under six months
Team people available	None right now				All key ones
Investment required	High				Low
Commercial Aspects:					
Market volatility	High/erratic				Very stable
Probable market share	Fourth at best				Number one
Probable product life	Less than a year				Over ten years
Similarity to product line	No relationship				Very close
Salesforce requirements	Have no experience				Very familiar
Promotion requirements	Have no experience				Very familiar
Target customer segment(s)	Perfect stranger(s)				Close/current
Distribution Channels	No relationship				Current/strong
Target Cost	Very unsure of meeting				Meet target
Importance of task to user	Trivial				Critical
Degree of unmet need	None/satisfied				Totally unmet
Likelihood of filling need	Very low				Very high
Competition to be faced	Tough/aggressive				Weak
Technical/Field service requirements	No current capability				Ready now
Environmental effects	Only negative ones				Only positive ones
Global applications	No use outside national markets				Fits global
Market diffusions	No other uses				Many other areas
Probable profit	Break even at best				ROI > 40%

Adapted from: Crawford and DiBenedetto 2003

As can be seen, product and marketing plans have to be developed together. A firm which wishes to move quickly must arrange for simultaneous creation of the product and the marketing plan. In fact, this is an iterative process since the product marketing, especially pricing, is highly dependent upon the cost and features that make up the product offering.

The evaluation of a global product concept presents additional difficulties. Cross-functional teams must be established, which include representatives from a firm's most important markets throughout the world. Despite electronic communications, some face-to-face meetings are probably necessary and there is no question that this can slow down the new product process. Nevertheless, complete 'buy-in' is required from all concerned country organizations in order to ensure that the product will be successful throughout the world.

Project teams are the heart and soul of success for B2B new products. These teams generally include engineers, pure scientists, finance experts and marketing people, most often product managers. In some large firms, members of the market research team may also be included. Both manufacturing and design engineers are generally on the team and many teams include outside consultants

FIGURE 7.6

New product funnel

Adapted from: Ames
and Hlavacek 1984

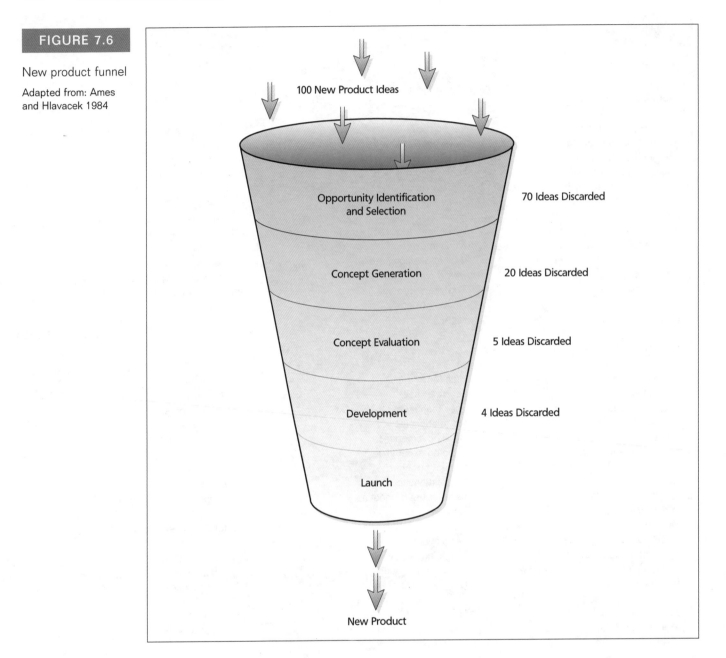

100 New Product Ideas

Opportunity Identification
and Selection   70 Ideas Discarded

Concept Generation   20 Ideas Discarded

Concept Evaluation   5 Ideas Discarded

Development   4 Ideas Discarded

Launch

New Product

FIGURE 7.7

Risk/payoff matrix

Adapted from:
Crawford and
DiBenedetto 2003

Decision is to: If the product were marketed:	A Stop the project immediately	B Continue product development process
A. It would fail	AA	BA
B. It would succeed	AB	BB

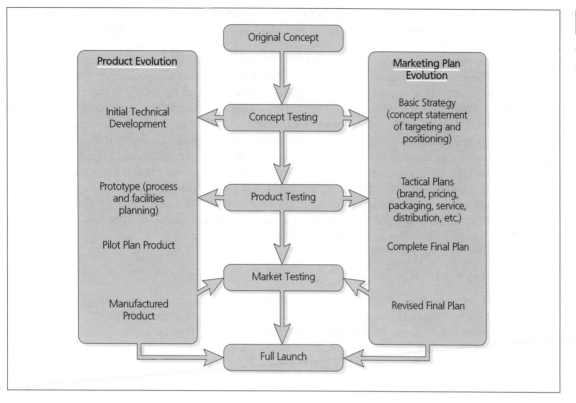

FIGURE 7.8

The twin streams of
development

such as independent product designers or consulting engineers. As was discussed earlier, this multi-function team for a global corporation can be complex. Problems of language and culture sometimes interfere with communications on these teams. One cure is to initiate cross-functional meetings with representatives from various country markets on a regular basis to increase trust and understanding.

McDonough (2000) found that 97 per cent of the firms in his study have used cross-functional teams and that one-third of the teams used them 100 per cent of the time. The study further showed that the use of this approach did not depend upon size of firm or revenue, that cross-functional teams were widely used across many different kinds of organization. McDonough *et al.* (2001) found the use of global NPD (new-product development) teams is increasing. They define global NPD teams as those including individuals who work and live in different countries and are culturally diverse. Companies in the study reported that they expect at least one out of five of their NPD teams to be global. Achieving and sustaining trust between team members, developing effective interpersonal relationships and fostering effective communications of members are more difficult with global teams than with other kinds of teams. In addition, there are some indications that global teams find it more difficult to identify customer needs, ensure that project goals remain stable and stay on budget, keep on schedule and have sufficient resources. These researchers also found that teams of people at one location realize better performance than global teams.

McDonough (2000) identified three major categories which contribute to the success of cross-functional teams. First, is stage setting: developing appropriate project goals, empowering the team with needed decision-making power, then assigning the required human resources and creating a climate which will be productive. Appropriate project goals are the most important of these factors associated with success. Second, there is a category of factors which relates to enablers. These are team leaders, senior managers and product champions. Team leadership is the most important of these factors. Finally, team behaviors such as cooperation, commitment to the project, ownership of the project and respect and trust among team members are important to cross-functional team success. Cooperation is the most important of these factors. Of all of the factors mentioned, the one most frequently cited in the research as important to cross-functional team success is cooperation among team members. Setting appropriate goals was second in relative importance. As mentioned, obtaining cooperation and trust among those with vastly different cultural backgrounds can be a challenge, yet it is a worthwhile goal since cross-functional teams do create projects with higher success rates. In view of these findings, it is important that firms spend more time training managers to handle the problems that arise with global teams and to be sure that the organizational structure ensures these teams the proper resources.

These cross-functional teams enable a firm to respond to the shortening global product lifecycles and quicker time to market exhibited by most competitors. Instead of approaching the new product development process in a sequential way where one stage needs to be totally completed before the second stage begins, more sophisticated firms are using an overlapping approach, the so-called 'rugby' approach to new product development (Takeuchi and Nonaka 1986). In this approach, teams are self-organized and have substantial freedom. This process avoids rigid controls and encourages transfer of knowledge through the team as well as throughout the organization. Here, while one function of a firm may be leading one stage, another function has already taken up another task. For instance, while marketing may be developing and testing concepts for a new roofing product, the technical staff would be working simultaneously at examining the feasibility of the new roofing material formulation. At specific checkpoints, all functional participants must review their progress in order to determine whether to move toward the next stage.

The Internet and NPD

Global teams rely heavily on the instant communication available through the Internet. Ozer (2003) offered a number of propositions related to the use of the Internet in the new product development process. A summary of some of the key ideas offered by Ozer is seen in Table 7.7. Among these suggestions, there is no question that the increased collaboration available through the Internet is critical to the success of global cross-functional teams.

■ Global products

Yip (2003) identifies common customer needs and global customers as key drivers for firms attempting to develop global products. By common customer needs he means 'the extent to which customers in different countries have the same needs and taste'. Global customers are those who wish to have the same products in all their locations throughout the world. In addition, high product development costs and fast changing technologies as well as scale economies are driving firms to consider developing global products. Yip advises firms to begin by identifying the most important strategic markets and then attempting to find commonalities rather than differences in the needs of these customers in various markets around the world.

TABLE 7.7 Use of Internet in the NPD process

NPD Activity	Internet Role
Opportunity Identification	More ideas from more sources
Concept Generation and Screening	Improve flexibility of process More comprehensive screening process
Development	Improve quality and efficiency of manufacturing development Facilitates collaboration among team members
Launch	Faster feedback of results Quicker changes of tactics

Adapted from: Ozer 2003

What is so important about the new product development process for globalized B2B firms? Most firms just react to what customers ask for and then cobble together something new. It seems to work for most small- to medium-sized firms, so why should they spend all their time and effort developing a process including a scoring model and also doing research to find out what customers really want? Why not do it like we always did it – make a new product when we need it?

Extension versus adaptation

For many years a key discussion in international marketing has been the question of whether a product can be taken as it is to many international markets or whether the product must be modified. In the case of business products, generally speaking, products are not acceptable without modification throughout the world. The basic fact that electrical systems vary, the difference between the metric and non-metric measurement systems and simple costs of fuel and space availability make modification nearly always necessary. Keegan and Greene (2003) have identified three major strategies for product development:

Extension strategy: offering a product virtually unchanged from its home market version to all other markets throughout the world.

Adaptation strategy: changing design, function or packaging for particular countries.

Product invention: inventing new products from scratch for the world market.

The decision to extend, adapt or invent depends upon many factors including cultural, economic and political environments as well as internal capabilities of the firm. Keegan and Greene believe that product decisions are linked with marketing communications decisions so that a strategy may be devised in which a product offering is not changed while a communications offering is. This they call Product Extension/Communication Adaptation. In this case, a firm would use its existing product, but position it differently for the market segment to be approached. Similarly, a firm may use the same communication strategy, but change the product. This occurs where technical requirements' mandate changes, but the marketing strategy is otherwise similar. For example, a firm offering the fastest micro computer would not have to change its marketing appeal simply because the product is designed to run on 50Hz electricity instead of 60Hz.

Country of origin

In marketing international products, an additional factor is quite important. This is the country of origin. Buyers' perceptions of a product may relate strongly to the source of that product. Many years ago the Westinghouse Electric Corporation was virtually forced to make an acquisition of a circuit breaker manufacturer in Germany. German buyers were convinced that only German manufacturers made circuit breakers of the quality they required.

According to Anholt (2000), countries often represent particular aspects of a brand. But perceptions are not held forever. The most striking turnaround has been for Japan, which in only one generation has changed the meaning of the words 'Made in Japan' from a negative to a positive. Any firm marketing a product which is made in Japan will have a slight benefit because buyers believe Japanese products embody advanced technology and quality. Korea is making the same transformation. Some countries evoke no response in the minds of buyers. Anholt cites Slovenia which elicits no perceptions at the present time. When a product manufactured in a particular country is quite successful, it can aid other manufacturers in that country. For instance, Nokia has given Finland the opportunity to establish itself as a high-quality source of products.

Choosing the location of various activities related to new product development in a global corporation is a difficult decision. It is important that a particular managing unit be established. But this managing unit, wherever it is located, must work with all the affected divisions and subsidiaries in order to develop a fully acceptable product.

■ Managing the global product

A brand is a set of perceptions which a consumer has about a particular product from a particular manufacturer. A brand essentially is a promise from a manufacturer to a customer about the benefits his or her firm will receive from a particular product. While there are many local brands known only in a particular market, there are also international brands which have been successful in several markets or in a region. A global brand has the same name and positioning throughout the world (Keegan and Greene 2003). A key product strategy decision is the branding decision. Firstly, a marketer must decide whether or not the product will have a brand name. This is especially important for products which are ingredients or components of other products. The well-known 'Intel inside' is an example of branding of a component which has been successful. Kotler (2003) identifies four major branding decisions:

The Brand Sponsor Decision: whether the brand will be a manufacturer, distributor, or licensed brand.

Brand Name Decision: whether to have individual names, one overall, a 'family' name, or several family names.

Brand Strategy Decision: whether to extend the line or develop new brands.

Brand Repositioning Decision: when a firm needs to change the perceptions of customers about a particular brand.

Court *et al.* (1996) report that the brand was responsible for as much as 26 per cent of the purchase decision for various B2B products. Brand importance is far more significant for consumer products (in the same study the brand of computer was responsible for 39 per cent of the purchase decision by consumers). Nevertheless one can see that the brand is responsible for one-sixth to one-quarter of the purchase decision in the study conducted by these McKinsey consultants (see Figure 7.9).

For B2B firms, the development of a global brand is not always appropriate. Where strong local brands exist a global firm may be able to take advantage of the benefits these strong local brands offer through acquisition or strategic alliances. The establishment of a global brand is usually only cost effective for firms who can afford very high marketing communications investments. Generally speaking, B2B firms would not be in this position. If a firm cannot realize major economies of scale from a global brand they should avoid the effort.

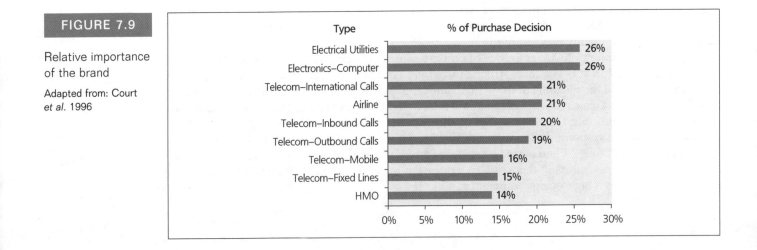

FIGURE 7.9

Relative importance of the brand

Adapted from: Court *et al.* 1996

Packaging and labeling

In worldwide markets, packaging and labeling assume a high level of importance. Packaging serves three major functions: protection, promotion and convenience for the user. For worldwide marketers, the most important of these is protection. Since the product is often transferred through various transportation modes, it usually requires special packaging. In many facilities, this special packaging can cause manufacturing output to slow down considerably. In some cases, pilferage is a problem and products must be packaged to prevent this.

A special consideration related to packaging is a need for waste reduction mandated by governments. In some cases, firms are responsible for disposal both of the packaging and the product after its useful life is completed. This focus on waste reduction has caused many managers to rethink their approach to packaging. For instance, the typical delivery of an office building-full of furniture would create several container loads of cardboard packaging. Many office furniture manufacturing firms have now switched to plastic shrink wrap to reduce the very large amount of cardboard left over once new office furniture is installed.

Labeling is also important as business products are shipped around the world. Managers must be aware that they face both language and literacy problems. A box clearly labeled in English would be of relatively little use in Saudi Arabia. In addition, the Filipino workers in Saudi Arabia who might be unloading and installing a particular product may be illiterate, even in their own language. Therefore, clever use of sign language is required to communicate clearly such important messages as 'this side up' or 'do not puncture with a forklift'.

Quality

Much has been written about the concept of quality. Research in many product areas completed by one of the authors shows that customers always value quality but are not always specific about what the term means to them. It is most important to define the determinant attributes which usually make up a particular buyer's definition of quality. Internationally, firms are relying on the standards established by the International Standards Organization (ISO). Frequently, buyers request that vendors meet particular ISO standards in the 9000 series. When a firm receives certification, it can meet the needs of buyers who use ISO 9000 as a basic requirement. The term TQM, total quality management, means that the firm is dedicated to focusing on customer needs and delivering the quality customers want. Firms who are practicing marketing as we understand it will meet TQM standards. For the Intel corporation, total quality means 'level of service to the customer, responsiveness to the customer, delivery performance, competitive pricing, comprehension or anticipation of where the customer is going in the marketplace – all of the things that define your worth in the mind of the customer', according to Thomas Hogue, VP Materials and Services, Intel Corporation (Porter 1996). Hogue goes on to say that Intel asks their customers to tell them how they are doing in the customers' supplier rating system. In fact, a recent study reported by *Purchasing* showed that 67 per cent of 700 firms surveyed believed their supplier measurement system noticeably improved the performance of suppliers who were measured. Nearly three-quarters of those surveyed thought these improvements were worth the time and money spent developing, deploying and maintaining the measurement system (Porter 1999).

General Electric Corporation applies the Six Sigma approach to quality to its vendors. Six Sigma means that a product would have a defect level of no more than 3.4 parts per million. GE Medical Systems asks its suppliers to use the Six Sigma approach to reduce product defects. In fact, GE even provides what they call Six Sigma 'black belts' who are experts in the methodology to help suppliers find problems in their manufacturing process and correct them in order to move toward the Six Sigma level of defects (*Purchasing* 1999).

Global sourcing

Sophisticated buyers understand that in almost every case they have a 'make or buy' decision. That is, a firm can choose to internally develop and produce all necessary products and services or it can outsource those not considered part of their core competencies. Firms look to outsource in order to lower their costs or gain access to better technologies. Outsourcing of services will be discussed in some detail in the next chapter. A survey by *Purchasing* shows that nearly two-thirds of firms have been outsourcing for more than five years. In this survey, 60 per cent of buyers said they outsourced to avoid expensive capital investments and more than half said they outsourced to gain the technical expertise of a contract manufacturer. Respondents found on-time delivery and detailed knowledge of the product to be problems they experienced in the outsourcing process. While it is difficult to determine what the term core competency involves, Quinn and Hilmer (1995) provide seven characteristics that identify the core competencies of a firm (see Table 7.8)

Core competencies are areas in which the firm will be able to outperform its competition. But the firm must be careful to choose just a few of these activities for management attention. For instance, 3M has focused on four critical technologies which it supports with a very effective innovation system. As has been noted earlier, managers should focus their efforts on activities which affect the determinant attributes those customers use to choose one vendor over another. Once these core competencies are selected, the company must focus its efforts on maintaining superiority so it is obvious that outsourcing of core competencies will not be acceptable. However, a clear definition of these competencies allows a firm to look to outsourcing as a way of cutting costs and letting management focus more of its efforts on what is really important to the company's success. While outsourcing involves costs for seeking and managing firms, where these costs are exceeded by benefits the firm should look closely at an outsourcing alternative.

The question of outsourcing becomes critical in the global setting. Cost to manufacture, package, transport and install products as well as training, relevant import duties and value added taxes must all be included to determine a final landed price for any product in any market. Once this price is determined, the marketing plan may be profoundly affected. In fact, product sourcing and marketing should be viewed as an iterative process since a firm may arrive at the conclusion that domestic manufacturing and an export market entry strategy will yield uncompetitive pricing in a selected market. A solution to this may be outsourcing of some portions of the product manufacturing or changing the location of manufacture while revising the marketing plan. For instance, a firm manufacturing water purification plants may find that shipping large and bulky components from its home market may make it uncompetitive in the Middle East. Therefore the firm might review the manufacturing of these components in a lower-cost Eastern European nation such as Hungary to reduce both manufacturing and shipping costs. Since this firm may not have an ongoing need for this manufacturing, the firm may choose contract manufacturing for selected components.

Quinn and Hilmer (1995) say three questions should be asked when considering outsourcing:

- What is the potential for obtaining competitive advantage?
- What is the potential vulnerability from outsourcing?
- What can be done to alleviate this vulnerability through arrangements with suppliers?

TABLE 7.8 Characteristics of core competencies

1. Skill or knowledge – not a product or function

2. Flexible, long-term platforms

3. Limited number

4. Sources of value chain leverage

5. Company can dominate

6. Important to customer

7. Embedded in company systems

Adapted from: Quinn and Hilmer 1995

These three questions affect the option to be chosen by managers. In some cases a firm may choose to make a product or component in a partnership such as a strategic alliance. Where vulnerability is lower and tight control is not as important, a firm may choose to simply contract with a manufacturer to get the products completed.

A dissenting view of the importance of core competencies is presented by Khanna and Palepu (2000). These researchers point out that while focusing on key competencies may be a correct strategy in Western economies, in emerging markets firms may do better by diversifying. In emerging markets, there are information gaps between labor, investors and consumers and the firm along with misguided and poorly enforced government regulations and inefficient contract enforcement. Therefore, firms must take on a number of basic functions which normally would be left to the institutions in well-developed markets. Firms who do take on these functions can ensure that their marketing efforts are successful.

SUMMARY

It is highly important that every firm have a new product development process. Managers must decide what their core competencies are and develop programs to improve their products and services for customers while carefully considering outsourcing non-essentials. The key points from this chapter are:

- A product is an offering of the firm which satisfies the needs of customers. A product is a bundle of benefits including brand name, design, country of origin, price, packaging and services.

- The product lifecycle is the underlying reason for the necessity of a product development process since products are usually replaced by newer technologies over some period of time. The logic for the product lifecycle is based on diffusion of innovation which specifies various customer types who are more or less willing to accept new products in more or less time.

- Managers must develop a product strategy which includes understanding how many products should be included in a line and how many product lines are necessary.

- Various products may be in different stages of the product lifecycle in specific countries. Managers must understand where each product stands along that curve in order to manage its marketing properly.

- New product development times are shrinking and global customers are looking for the latest technology throughout the world.

- A firm must work hard to excel on the determinant attributes, ones which customers use to make decisions about products or services to purchase.

- A good new-product development process will weed out the poor ideas while allowing the successful ones through. A too-tight process will eliminate all new ideas and a too-loose process will allow costly failures to come to market.

- Marketing plan development and product development must be simultaneous. The forming and managing of new product teams across world markets is a challenging task which requires team leadership and cooperation.

- Country of origin can have a significant effect upon a product's success. A manager must develop an overall world strategy for his or her brands, seeking global brands only where economies may be realized.

- Packaging and labeling are especially important in international business because of shipping requirements and the need to recycle packaging.

- Quality plays a key role in business purchasing decisions. ISO 9000 is a basic requirement in many industries and the Six Sigma approach is becoming more important to many buyers.

- Firms must decide whether to make or buy all the products and services they use. Global outsourcing requires sophisticated analysis of all costs. Where vulnerability from outsourcing is low and tight control of particular suppliers is not important, outsourcing may be the best choice.

REVIEW QUESTIONS

1 Describe the total product including support services, product attributes and core product benefits.

2 Describe the differences between consumer product strategy and business to business product strategy.

3 How does diffusion of innovation relate to the product lifecycle?

4 What are the strategic choices a firm can make in each stage of the product lifecycle?

5 What are the main factors which affect the speed of acceptance of an innovation?

6 Describe the differences between the product lifecycle and the technology adoption lifecycle.

7 Name the five phases in the new product process and describe each.

8 What are some ways of getting ideas for new products?

9 What is a determinant attribute and why is it important to a firm in the new-product development process?

10 Describe a scoring model. What role does it play in the new-product development process?

11 What is meant by AB and BA decisions? How can you tell if a new product development process is working correctly through this approach?

12 How do product evolution and marketing plan evolution relate to one another?

13 What are the rules for developing effective global cross-functional project teams and how does the Internet relate to this?

14 What is a global product and what kinds of strategies may be employed for global product development?

15 Describe country of origin and its effect on global products.

16 List the most important branding decisions. Should a firm always have a global brand?

17 Why are packaging and labeling especially important in global business to business markets?

18 How do customers define quality and what role does ISO 9000 play?

19 Relate core competencies to global sourcing. What costs must be included in this decision and what major problems would a firm possibly encounter in outsourcing?

'Ted' Mahendra is the manager of a small chain of hotels called Southeast Asia Hotels. In addition to the flagship in Jakarta, the chain also includes hotels in Singapore, Kuala Lumpur, Hong Kong and Vietnam. Mahendra, only on the job for six months, had been asked by the owners to increase the occupancy rate of these hotels. Preliminary research shows that the main market segment for each is managers who work for small- to medium-sized (SME) international firms. In fact, one of the first activities he undertook upon gaining this new job was to commission a survey of the needs of his target market segment. The results are shown below:

NEEDS OF SME INTERNATIONAL MANAGERS

Favourite Hotels
Marriott   72%
Hilton   60%
Hyatt   56%

Hotel Selection Factors: (% identifying as very/moderately important)

Fair price	60%
In-room high speed Internet access	53%
Morning wake-up call	46%
Hotel loyalty (mileage/points) program	44%
Quick check-in, check-out	38%
Fitness center	34%
Newspaper delivered to door	32%

Based upon: Sharkey, 2003

The same survey asked for the main associations with the brand name 'Southeast Asia Hotels'. These are shown in the table below.

SOUTHEAST ASIA HOTELS

Associations
Old World
Comfortable
Cheap
Low tech

Mahendra then convened a meeting of the managers of each of his hotels and asked them to tell him what the strongest points of each of the hotels were. Up to now, the managers of each hotel were very proud of the fact that they were self-sufficient. Each hotel baked its own bread every day and did all of its own laundry. The hotels even employed in-house painters and carpenters to make repairs. He summarized this list:

SOUTHEAST ASIA HOTELS

Strengths
Friendly staff
Excellent restaurants
Self-sufficient
Downtown locations

Comparing the common strengths of his hotel chain with the needs identified in survey gave him pause. Mahendra was now faced with the problem of developing a new 'product' which would be able to compete with the big chains. One thing he knew for sure was that Southeast Asia Hotels have no loyalty program and couldn't begin to match those of the major chains.

Questions

1 How do you think Mahendra should go about instituting a 'product development' process in this hotel chain?
2 How does the global product lifecycle apply to the hotel chain?
3 What do you believe are the determinant attributes for selecting one hotel over another?
4 What changes in the total product offering must be made by Southeast Asia hotels in order to improve their occupancy rate?
5 What actions should be taken related to the brand name? If you were to change the name, what might you change it to and what associations would you like to develop for any new brand name?
6 How might the concept of core competencies and outsourcing relate to this case?

REFERENCES

—— 'R&D Funding Forecast for 2003 Predicts Major Shift Ahead', http://www.battelle.org/news/03/01–02–03_RDFunding.stm, accessed 8/20/03.

—— (1999) 'Using Six Sigma to Manage Suppliers', *Purchasing* 127: January 14: 90.

Ames, B. C. and Hlavacek, J. D. (1984) *Managerial Marketing for Industrial Firms*, New York: Random House.

Anholt, S. (2000) 'The Nation as Brand', *Across the Board* 37: 10: 22–27.

Bowonder, B. and Yadav, S. (1999) 'R&D Spending Patterns of Global Firms', *Research Technology Management* 42: 6: 45–55.

Court, D., Freeling, A., Leiter, M. and Parsons, A. J. (1996) 'Uncovering the Value of Brands,' *The McKinsey Quarterly* 32: 4: 176–178.

Crawford, C. M. and DiBenedetto, A. (2003) *New Products Management*, New York: McGraw-Hill/Irwin.

Hansiota, B. J., Shaikh, M. A. and Sheth, J. N. (1985) 'The Strategic Determinancy Approach to Brand Management,' *Business Marketing* 70: 66–83.

Hollensen, S. (1998) *Global Marketing*, Hertfordshire, UK: Prentice-Hall Europe.

Keegan, W. J. and Green, M. C. (2003) *Global Marketing*, Upper Saddle River, NJ: Prentice-Hall.

Khanna, T. and Palepu, K. (2000) 'Why Focused Strategies May Be Wrong For Emerging Markets', in *World View: Global Strategies for the New Economy*, Garten, J. E., ed., Cambridge, MA: Harvard Business Review Books.

Kotler, P. (2003) *Marketing Management*, Upper Saddle River, NJ: Pearson-Prentice-Hall.

Krishnan V. and Ulrich, K. T. (2001) 'Product Development Decisions: A Review of the Literature', *Management Science* 47: 1: January: 1–21.

McDonough, E. F. III (2000). 'Investigation of Factors Contributing to the Success of Cross-Functional Teams', *Journal of Product Innovation Management* 17: 3: 221–235.

McDonough, E. F. III, Kahn, K. B. and Barczak, G. (2001). 'An Investigation of the Use of Global, Virtual and Collocated New Product Development Teams', *Journal of Product Innovation Management* 18: 2: 110–120.

Moore, G. A. (1995) *Inside the Tornado*, New York: Harper-Collins Publishing.

Ozer, M. (2000) 'Process Implication of the Use of the Internet in New Product Development: A Conceptual Analysis', *Industrial Marketing Management* 32: 517–530.

Porter, A. M. (1996) 'Intel Corp Takes on Big Q', *Purchasing*: 119: January 11: 54–55.

Porter, A. M. (1999) 'Quality Report – Raising the Bar', *Purchasing* 127: January 14: 44–50.

Quinn, J. B. and Hilmer, F. G. (1995) 'Strategic Outsourcing', McKinsey Quarterly, 1: 48–70.

Rogers, E. M. (1962) *Diffusion of Innovations*, New York: MacMillan.

Sharkey, J. (2003) 'Consultants Are On the Go Despite Economic Woes', *New York Times*: August 26: C6.

Takeuchi, H. and Nonaka, I. (1986) 'The New New Product Development Game', *Harvard Business Review* 64: 1: 137.

Topfer, A. (1995) 'New Products – Cutting the Time to Market', *Long Range Planning* 28: 2: 61–78.

VonHippel, E., Thomke, S. and Sonnack, M. (1999) 'Creating Breakthroughs at 3M', *Harvard Business Review* 77: Sept–Oct: 47–57.

Yip, G. S. (2003) *Total Global Strategy II*, Upper Saddle River, NJ: Prentice-Hall.

8

SERVICES FOR BUSINESS MARKETS

Learning objectives
After reading this chapter, you should be able to:

- Understand the differences between tangible products and intangible services
- Explain how these differences affect the management and marketing of services
- Outline the important considerations in product support services
- Understand the importance of corporate culture in services marketing
- Describe how service quality is measured
- Explain the process of blueprinting
- Describe the best way to develop new services
- Describe the pitfalls and opportunities in transitioning from a product to a service orientation
- Know how to deal with international services trade barriers

■ Introduction

On the surface there appear to be many similarities between the marketing of tangible products and the marketing of intangible services. But there are a number of important differences as well. Nearly every successful B2B firm offers a combination of products and services and often the services are more profitable than the products. This chapter will help you understand the differences and improve your skills in marketing services.

Services and international trade

According to the World Trade Organization (2003), commercial services accounted for 19.4 per cent of world exports in 2001, an increase from 18.8 per cent in 2000. Exports of commercial services totaled US$1.46 billion in 2001. The share of services exports for each region of the world is shown in Table 8.1 below.

It is clear that services are becoming a more important component of every firm's business, even if the firm's main business is physical products.

As the largest clients become more global, they often seek to reduce the number of suppliers from whom they purchase services. They also wish to standardize these services. Yip (2003) says that large firms may wish to reduce the number of auditors they use and choose only the largest accounting firms who can apply a 'consistent worldwide approach (within the contexts of national rules within each country of operation)'. These large global customers want common procedures and standards.

International services are 'traded' in four different ways according to the General Agreement on Trade in Services (GATS 2001). The GATS 'modes of supply' are:

1 Services supplied from one country to another (e.g. international telephone calls), officially known as 'cross-border supply'.

2 Consumers from one country making use of a service in another country (e.g. tourism), officially known as 'consumption abroad'.

3 A company from one country setting up subsidiaries or branches to provide services in another country (e.g. a bank from one country setting up operations in another country), officially known as 'commercial presence'.

4 Individuals traveling from their own country to supply services in another (e.g. an actress or construction worker), officially known as 'movement of natural persons'.

Services definitions

There is no agreed definition of services. Many describe services as deeds, processes and performances. According to the American Marketing Association's Dictionary of Marketing Terms, services are:

'. . .intangible or at least substantially so. If totally intangible, they are exchanged directly from producer to user, cannot be transported or stored, and are almost instantly perishable. Service products are often difficult to identify, because they come into existence at the same time they are bought and consumed. They comprise intangible elements that are inseparable; they usually involve customer participation in some important way; they cannot be sold in the sense of ownership transfer; and they have no title. . .'
(Bennett 1995)

TABLE 8.1 Share of services exports by region in 2001

Region	Percentage of Share
North America	23.2
Latin America	14.1
European Union	21.6
Africa	17.3
Asia	15.5
World	19.4

The most succinct definition is presented by Semenik and Bamossy (1993): 'Activities, benefits or satisfactions offered for sale where there is no exchange of tangible goods involving a transfer of title.'

The CEO of an oil field lubricant firm convened a meeting of his senior staff. "The competition is killing us in Latin America and in the North Sea. All of a sudden, they have specialists arriving at customer drilling rigs. But we have the best product at the most attractive prices. Why don't the customers see that we are giving better value?"

Is the CEO right in his approach to the product/service continuum? What would you say to the CEO if you were the director of marketing? And if service is so important that a firm with an inferior product can outperform this company, why bother producing a good product in the first place?

The goods/services continuum

In truth, there are few pure goods or pure services. Most offerings contain some portion of service and some portion of good. This can be seen graphically in the good-service continuum presented below in Figure 8.1 using selected examples. While the nearest thing to a pure good may be salt, many firms offer some form of service with the salt. This may include recipes or telephone help with cooking. And while surgery and consulting service may seem to be nearly pure services, often there is a tangible output such as an X-ray or report. A mainframe computer or an elevator system is often provided with a maintenance contract tying tangible goods and intangible services together. Whether the business is classified toward the pure good (tangible) or the pure service side (intangible) of the continuum depends entirely on how it is perceived by the customer. The more the business is characterized by intangible aspects, the less applicable will be the standard goods-oriented marketing approach.

Five different categories (Kotler 2003) of combinations of services and tangible goods have been identified:

1 *Pure tangible good* This includes products far on the left side of our Goods/Services Continuum such as paper or diskettes. In general, a very limited amount of service is offered with this purely tangible product.

2 *Tangible good with accompanying services* This is a tangible product with services added. Highly technical products usually are more dependent upon services such as planning, installation, training and maintenance.

3 *Hybrid* In this case there is an equal offering of goods and services. So, the service portion of the offering is of equal importance to the tangible product offering.

4 *Major service with supporting goods and services* In this case, the most important part of the offering is the service, but some goods and supporting services are required. The best example of this would be business travelers on an airline who buy transportation service but also need some tangibles such as food and seating. While the service requires a capital-intensive good (an airplane) to be effective, the primary portion of the offering is a service.

5 *Pure service* This offering is primarily a service, such as consulting or advertising. Very little tangible goods are required.

FIGURE 8.1

The goods/services continuum

Adapted from:
Shostack 1977

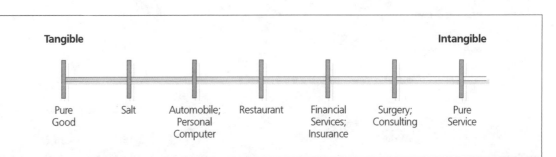

Services are marked by unique characteristics which affect their marketing. A summary of the unique characteristics is listed below in Table 8.2 with the explanation related to each. Some authors use different terms to describe the same characteristics. The idea of inseparability is the same as the 'consumed when produced' concept and the often-used term 'heterogeneity' is the same as variability.

The unique characteristics of services add considerably to the risk perceived by customers in buying services. In some cases, customers do not possess the technical knowledge required to make adequate judgments in the services area (Zeithaml and Bitner 1996). In fact, customers are often unable to judge the quality of the service even after using it (Choi and Scarpa 1994).

Management implications

As a business moves toward the intangible side of the Goods/Services Continuum, new management concerns become paramount. Table 8.3 below summarizes the implications growing from each of the factors unique to service businesses. Since the fact that services are intangible makes it difficult for customers to evaluate the quality of a proposed service, management should attempt to focus on 'tangible clues' of the service to give messages to potential customers about what to expect. These clues can be in the form of uniforms, written contracts, guarantees and brochures describing the service, or a consistent logo to be used in promotion.

Since services are consumed when they are produced, the role of the so-called 'part-time marketers' becomes critical (Gummesson 1991). Part-time marketers are people who carry out marketing activities but do not belong to the marketing or sales department. But they are the people who handle the 'moments of truth' (the moment when the buyer-seller interaction takes place). These part-time marketers often outnumber the full-time marketers who report to sales and marketing departments. Careful selection and training for these people is critical to managing these moments of truth.

Because the user participates in the production of the service along with the provider of the service, it is critical to understand customer expectations for the particular service. In addition, in some cases in order to manage demand, some firms ask customers to do more. An example would be self-service shopping in an office supply superstore such as Staples, which has implications for reducing the satisfaction of the clients as well.

Since services are perishable and cannot be inventoried, management must work to alter the demand or supply side of the equation to attempt to keep customers satisfied. Sasser (1976) described two extremes of services management, one called 'chase demand', and the other, 'level capacity'. The first approach requires consistently adding or subtracting equipment and people to

TABLE 8.2 Unique services characteristics	
Factor	**Description**
Intangibility	Services cannot be touched, felt or even tried out.
Consumed When Produced	Production and consumption of services take place at the same time.
User Participation	Even when the user is not required to be at a location where the service is performed, users participate in every service production.
Perishability	Services cannot be inventoried.
Variability	Because of the labor-intensive nature of services, there is a great deal of difference in the quality of service provided by various providers, or even by the same providers at different times.

Adapted from: Shostack 1977; Lovelock 1992; Semenik and Bamossy 1993

TABLE 8.3 Service characteristics/management implications

Factor	Implications
Intangibility	Enhance and differentiate the 'tangible clues', establish tangible evidence of service.
Consumed When Produced	Careful selection of and training for 'part-time marketers'. Must handle 'moment of truth' correctly the first time.
User Participation	Fully understand customer expectations of service. Involve customer more in service performance where appropriate.
Perishability	Work to alter demand or supply to avoid extremes of 'chase demand' or 'level capacity' strategies. Plan capacity at a high level of demand. Use marketing tools (price, promotion) to control demand. Use part-time employees, cross-training or other methods to control supply.
Variability	Either standardize completely for low cost, low-skilled employees or recruit higher-cost, higher-skilled employees and allow them latitude to deliver customer satisfaction.

Shostack 1977; Grönroos 1990; Sasser 1976

meet an unpredictable flow of demand. The second requires that provisions be made at the highest possible demand level with resulting periods of non-productivity. A better approach is the attempt to control either demand or supply. Managers can use price as well as promotion to shift demand from peak periods to non-peak periods as airlines and hotels do. Some even create reservation systems so that customers can reserve a firm's service production capacity in advance.

On the supply side, managers may use part-time employees to fill in during peak demand periods or attempt to maximize efficiency and ignore non-essential tasks during peak times. Another suggestion is to cross-train employees so that they can perform more than one job and relieve bottlenecks during peak periods.

Finally, services are variable by their very nature. Each performance of a service by an employee, whether a full-time or part-time marketer, will not be perceived in the same way by the customer. Each moment of truth is unique. Managers have reacted to this in two different ways. Some attempt to standardize the operations as completely as possible and then use low-cost, low-skilled employees. In some cases, automating as much of the service as possible is an additional attempt to standardize. Another approach, depending upon the complexity of the service, is to recruit higher-cost, higher-skilled employees, allowing latitude for these employees to provide customer satisfaction. The latter is seen in the case of Marriott, where employees are 'empowered' to give customer satisfaction. These employees are given a wide range of authority to gain this overall result.

Lovelock (1992), describes the service management trinity, the three key functional areas actively involved in making services work: marketing, operations and human resources. The operations function includes the people, facilities, and equipment that run the service operation. Much of this is invisible to the customer. The marketing system shares with operations the delivery of the service, but marketing, in addition, provides other components such as billing, advertising, sales personnel and research.

As has been mentioned, much of the customer interface in services is handled by part-time marketers who normally report to an operations department. Therefore, operations must understand the importance of the interfaces with the customer and human resources must be able to recruit and train individuals who will meet the overall objectives of the corporation for satisfying customers. Grönroos (1990) (see Figure 8.2) identifies the interactive portion of a service, in other words, the portion where customers interact with the firm in contrast to the invisible support portion of the service.

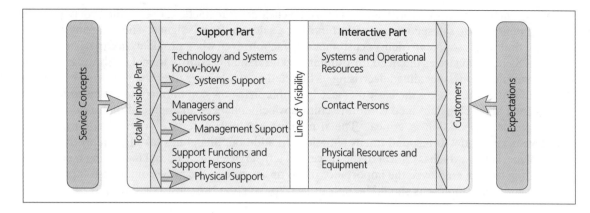

FIGURE 8.2

Interactive vs invisible aspects of service

Adapted from Grönroos 1990: 208

Product support services

Product support is an often overlooked marketing tool. In many B2B markets, the support of the equipment sold is at least as important as the equipment itself. Kotler (2003) states that Caterpillar Tractor and John Deere make more than 50 per cent of their profits from these services. In addition, the support services offered can frequently set a vendor apart from its competitors. As we have seen, the failure to provide service can create major problems for providers in international markets.

Frequently customers use a lifecycle approach to the purchasing of equipment and related services. In this area, customer needs can be defined as follows (Lele and Karmarakar 1983):

- frequency of failure
- downtime experienced
- cost of the downtime
- uncertainty about all of the aspects listed above.

Lele and Karmarakar point out that a customer's reaction to particular events is non-linear. For instance, a farmer might accept a downtime of four hours for a combine harvester. But by the time this downtime reached eight hours during harvesting season, the farmer might actually be compelled to buy a new combine to keep the harvest going. Customers react in the same way to the frequency of failure. Using Lele and Karmarakar's example, a farmer may accept an average of one or two failures per season but react negatively to three or four failures. Customers incur costs to repair items as well as lost wages for idle employees during failures.

In a later article, Lele (1986) identifies three major support service strategies:

- design-related strategies
- support-system-related strategies
- strategies that reduce customer risks.

The design-related strategies include increasing product reliability or changing the product to make it more modular in construction or to build in redundancy. As Lele points out, product design and product support service need to be considered at the same time. Support-system-related strategies attempt to change how service is provided to customers. This may include improving response time by adding more technicians or improving repair time by better training or built-in diagnostics. Strategies that reduce customer risks include warranties and service contracts. In choosing a specific service strategy, manufacturers must weigh speed and cost of product developments, manufacturing and service costs as well as the needs of customers and their willingness to pay for services.

Corporate culture

A critical aspect of the success of a service business is the overall corporate culture established by top management. Tom Siebel, CEO of Siebel Systems, says that 'absolute commitment to 100 per cent customer satisfaction . . . is a cornerstone of our corporate culture' (Fryer 2001). Siebel says his firm uses a scoring system to determine customer satisfaction, and incentive compensation for the entire company, including the salesforce, is given based on customer satisfaction. In fact, the firm pays incentive compensation to salespeople four quarters after a sales contract is signed. The company has spent freely in time and resources to deliver customer satisfaction, even when problems occurred not of their making. Siebel emphasizes the need for training and total quality control to make this work. He adds that communications, including advertising, is directed to *employees* rather than external customers. Communications reinforces the basic message by emphasizing the commitment to the customer.

A strong and well-established corporate culture which enhances an appreciation for good service and customer orientation is critical. The firm must establish a service-oriented culture so that employees know how to respond to any situation. In addition, Siebel has taken to heart the idea of internal marketing, which is critical to the success of any service firm. Internal marketing means communicating to each employee the importance of his or her role in the provision of customer satisfaction. In addition, employees should be encouraged to have the broadest possible view of their own jobs.

Heskett *et al.* (1994) show a direct relationship between employee satisfaction, employee retention and productivity and customer satisfaction which directly relates to financial performance. Inherent in the success of marketing services is the idea of relationship marketing (Grönroos 1990). The foundation of this concept is that customer relationships, whether long- or short-term, are the essence of success in marketing. The basis of a successful relationship is a mutual exchange and fulfillment of promises. The seller makes certain promises related to the goods and services it will provide and the buyer gives a set of promises as well. If the promises are kept on both sides, the relationship grows and strengthens. Successful relationship marketing will rely strongly upon the leadership and corporate culture established by top management. This will be explored in depth in Chapter 12.

■ Measuring service quality

The subject of service quality has been studied extensively over the last 20 years. The leading thinkers have reduced the measurement of service quality to five major dimensions. These are seen in Table 8.4 below.

A critical point to note here is that customers measure satisfaction based on their *expectations* versus their *perceptions* of the actual service performance. This re-emphasizes the need for cooperation between marketing, operations and human resources. Where the marketing and/or sales department over promise, the customer may perceive the service as unsatisfactory; therefore marketing and operations should agree on the capabilities of the service and should be working together on this service from planning through to execution.

Research completed over many years by Radley Resources (a B2B market research firm owned by one of the authors) for a major business travel firm reinforces the idea that promises made by the salesforce can often lead to customer dissatisfaction. Raising the expectations of customers to an

TABLE 8.4 Service quality dimensions

Dimension	Description
Tangibles	Appearance of physical facilities, equipment, personnel and communications materials
Reliability	Ability to perform the promised service dependably and accurately
Responsiveness	Willingness to help customers and to provide prompt service
Assurance	Knowledge and courtesy of employees, ability to convey trust and confidence
Empathy	Caring, individualized attention to customers

Source: Berry, Zeithaml and Parasuraman 1992

unsustainable level means that no amount of hard work can make these customers satisfied where promises at a more reasonable level and then out-performing these promises would yield very satisfied customers.

Repeated testing of these dimensions has shown that reliability is most important. In business marketing, reliability means delivering what was promised on time. It may be noted here that studies completed by Radley Resources in various industries confirm that this factor is most important in customer satisfaction. A general study of industrial firms (Kierl and Mitchell 1990) indicates that the largest gaps in customer satisfaction are in communications, one aspect of assurance, and knowledge of customer needs, a dimension of empathy.

When customers judge the quality of a service, they examine two aspects of the experience, the process and the outcome. The outcome, or the result, may be satisfactory, but customers will judge the overall service as unsatisfactory if the process they have been exposed to is unsatisfactory. Grönroos (1998) gives an example of elevator repair and maintenance. The largest repair and maintenance provider in the Scandinavian market completed some research to determine why, despite being the largest firm with the best products, they were losing business to competitors. After two rounds of research (quantitative and qualitative), the company found that, although the customers were satisfied with the end result of the work being done, they were uncomfortable with the manner in which the work was completed. Grönroos observes, 'top management and the marketing and sales group thought that the company provided products (the results of repair and maintenance) whereas the customers considered the company to be offering processes'. Both the product (the outcome) as well as the process has to be well executed to gain complete customer satisfaction for services. In fact, some say that any firm engaged in relationship marketing is essentially providing services marketing in which products are only a means to an end and the processes are most important to building and sustaining the customer relationship which leads to long-term profitability.

Research by Xerox Corporation found that there was an extreme difference in the attitudes toward the company between customers who said they were merely satisfied and those who said they were *completely* satisfied. The latter were six times more likely to repurchase Xerox products over the next 18 months than were satisfied customers (Jones and Sasser 1995). High levels of satisfaction lead to increased customer loyalty and according to Jones and Sasser, increased customer loyalty is 'the single most important driver of long-term financial performance'.

A final note on measurement: should there be problems in executing a service, prompt problem resolution not only satisfies the customer, but can strengthen the relationship. One way to make this happen is to designate specific employees to handle customer problems and to give those employees authority to resolve those problems.

Quality of e-services

Measurement of customer perceptions of services delivered through the Internet is at an early stage. Recent research shows that somewhat different dimensions form the core of customer perceptions of website services. These are differentiated between a 'no problem' setting and a situation where problems have occurred. These dimensions are listed in Table 8.5 below.

As can be seen, efficiency, fulfillment, reliability and privacy are the key e-service quality dimensions when no problem has occurred in a transaction. Zeithaml *et al.* (2002) show that after a problem has occurred, three new factors become important in a customer's assessment of a website. These include responsiveness, compensation and contact.

Other differences exist between the measurement of the quality of services in general and the measurement of e-service quality. Customers do not have well-developed expectations for service from websites. Where providing more of any dimension in a non-Internet based service results in greater satisfaction, this does not appear to be true with an e-service. There appears to be a satisfaction point beyond which customers find providing more service intrusive. For example, customers want to have an e-mail acknowledging an order and another notifying them that a shipment has taken place. More e-mails than this seem to decrease satisfaction rather than increase it.

The research completed by Zeithaml *et al.* (2002) has shown three major gaps in planning Internet sites. The first is the information gap, which is the discrepancy between 'customers' requirements concerning a website and management's beliefs about those requirements'. The second gap identified is the design gap, which means 'the failure to fully incorporate knowledge about customer requirements into

TABLE 8.5 e-service quality dimensions

Dimension	Description
No problem	
Efficiency	Ability to get to website, find desired product/info and check out
Fulfillment	Accuracy of service promises, product in stock, on-time delivery
Reliability	Availability and proper functioning of the site
Privacy	Assurance that shopping and credit card info is secure
After a problem	
Responsiveness	Providing necessary info, mechanisms for returns, on-line guarantees
Compensation	Return of payment, shipping and handling costs
Contact	Ability to contact live customer service agent by phone or e-mail

Adapted from: Zeithaml, Parasuraman and Malhotra 2002

the structure and functioning of the website'. The final gap is the communication gap, which comes about because marketing does not clearly understand a website's features, capabilities and limitations. This gap often occurs because of a lack of understanding between marketing and operations, a problem identified above. As we have seen, customers judge service based on expectations and these expectations are often raised or lowered by promises made by the firm (especially through the marketing people). It seems a frequent occurrence that marketing people do not understand what a website can or cannot do and tend to over promise.

Overall, there is a final gap, the fulfillment gap, which is the net result of the gaps in information, design and communication and is the overall discrepancy between a customer's expectations and their actual experiences. Finally, one other interesting finding is that a customer's ability to handle technology, called 'technology readiness', also affects satisfaction of Internet-based services. It is therefore important that a firm understand the technological sophistication of its customers when designing an Internet-based service. No research has yet been conducted which attempts to apply these general e-service quality dimensions to the B2B setting. So, for now we must adapt these general findings. The authors believe it is fair to expect business and institutional customers to judge an e-service using these same dimensions. We find the same range of technology readiness in B2B customers. So that there will probably be a wide range of satisfaction with e-business sites partially depending on customer capabilities and partially depending upon website performance.

■ Developing or improving services

Blueprinting

An important part of developing or improving a service is the development of the blueprint. The basic idea is to lay out all the steps required to make a service successful so that a firm can understand who is involved in the service and most importantly where the service passes the 'line of visibility' which divides the backstage, or invisible portions, of the service performance from the front stage portions of the process that are visible to the customer. By developing a blueprint, one can estimate the time required to complete each process and isolate possible bottlenecks or fail points which need to be strengthened before the service is implemented (Shostack 1984). While some observers have

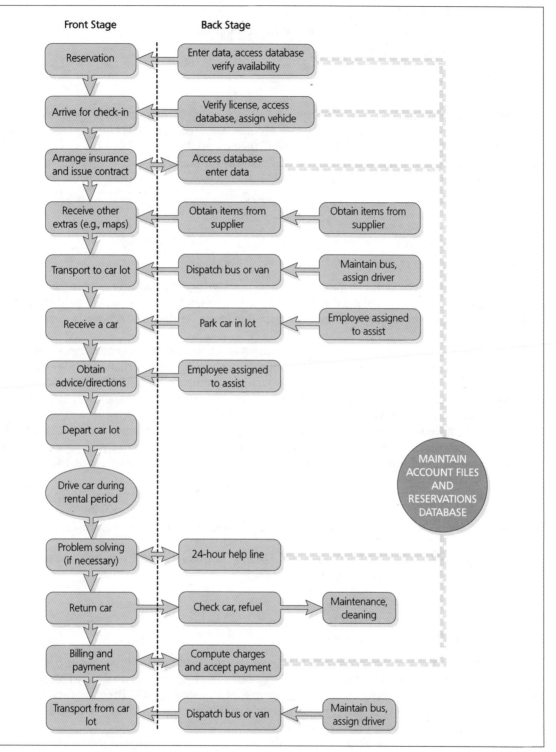

FIGURE 8.3

Flow chart of
rental car process

Lovelock 1992

developed a horizontal method for blueprinting, others have used a vertical method. Included here
is an example of a simple blueprint for a car rental process developed by Lovelock (1992).

Designing new services

Blueprinting is a key part of developing a new service. However, often new services result from trial
and error. Heskett (1986) has suggested steps to enhancing new service development:

- Establish a culture for entrepreneurship.
- Create an organization to foster new service development.
- Test ideas in the marketplace.
- Monitor results.
- Reward risk takers.

While it is difficult to develop a prototype of a service, many of the same steps used in developing new products can be applied to developing new services. Once the service is blueprinted, it should be possible do a detailed business analysis to estimate the potential profitability of the service. The service can then be organized and introduced in a limited way for market testing before moving on to full commercialization. Berry (1989) established four rules for the development of a new service:

- Give people a good reason to change.
- Start strong.
- Market to employees.
- Make the service real.

The first rule is based on the idea that customers perceive higher risks for new services because of the very nature of services explained earlier. They are intangible and untestable by the purchaser. Therefore, a simple and clearly explainable reason for trying out the new service is required to get customers to use it.

A firm must 'start strong' because first impressions are lasting impressions, especially when it comes to services. Word of mouth is critically important, especially in international business markets where industries are small and professional associations dominate. It is most important to test the service performance before offering it to customers so that the first impression will be an excellent one and create positive word of mouth.

Since, as we have seen, employees are critical to the success of any service, it is vital that the firm market to its employees, letting the employees know exactly what the service is designed to do, giving them clear limits of authority and encouraging them to do their best. Once again, the importance of corporate culture cannot be over emphasized.

Since services, as we know, are intangible, they should be made 'real' as much as possible. One strategy is to emphasize tangible benefits as much as possible or to create tangibles and to connect them to the service. As mentioned, specially designed packages, brochures, and guarantees can help in this regard.

De Brentani (1995) described certain types of service projects that generally succeed while others usually fail in B2B markets. Types that succeed are:

- The Customized Expert Service.
- The Planned Pioneering Venture.
- The Improved Service Experience.

The Customized Expert Service is one that leverages the firm's capabilities, but is customized to fit the needs of customers. Expert personnel who can find out from buyers what they require in order to tailor the service to them are crucial to the success of this strategy. De Brentani found this to be the most successful new service offering. An example of this strategy is a model used to select media developed by a marketing communications firm.

In the Planned Pioneering Venture, a firm develops a new service around its core competencies but in an unfamiliar competitive environment. This is usually complex and expensive and requires a formal and carefully planned service development process. Tangible evidence is required here to convince customers to try the new venture. An example of this service is a PC-based system payroll managers could use to input salary payments.

In the Improved Service Experience, a firm makes improvements to a current service-offering using new equipment to enhance the speed and reliability of the service process. While responding to the needs of customers, this scenario is based upon the established facilities and resources of the firm. An example of this service is a new high-speed cargo loading system provided by a shipping company.

New service projects that often fail fall into two categories:

- The Peripheral Low Market Potential Service.
- The Poorly Planned Industrialized Clone.

The first of these is just what it sounds like, peripheral to the firm's core capabilities and not yielding any visible value-added for a customer. This is the proverbial 'quick and dirty' addition to the line made with little effort to understand customer needs. This approach is a common type of service failure in B2B markets.

The second failure mode is based on equipment that is too complex. These are also often clones of competitive service offerings and usually do not meet customer requirements nor match very well with the capabilities of the offering firm. These are the 'me-too' projects launched without the research and planning necessary to fully understand customer needs and to deliver the extra benefit versus competition.

To sum up, new service offerings that are successful meet the needs of customers, leverage a firm's capabilities and are introduced through a careful and well thought out process.

Marketing services

As in tangible products, the most important first step in marketing services is to identify the relevant segment. There is some evidence that service segments tend to be narrower than product segments. For instance, as we have seen in e-commerce, one must segment by technological readiness. In addition, business services may have to be customized for individual customers, yielding a segment of one. Some segmentation may be accomplished along level of expectation since this is a key determinant of the perceived success of a particular service (i.e. those with lower expectations versus those with higher expectations may be placed in different segments).

The product is the service offering, including all of the processes and outcomes which customers will see. Earlier discussions emphasize the importance of bringing together human resources, operations and marketing in developing the proper approach to the service offering.

Distribution of services is often not possible. In fact, customers will often travel to the supplier's location to obtain a very important service from a highly differentiated vendor. While tangible goods are often sold throughout the world through intermediaries, highly intangible services like management consulting or architecture are nearly impossible to pass through steps of distribution.

Pricing for services revolves around managing demand, as has been explained above. Moorthi (2001) says that pricing the most intangible of services (like consulting) is difficult. Despite very strong competition, a renowned consultant might receive a premium price. In the case of the most intangible services quality becomes more important than price. In fact, price is often seen as a surrogate for quality.

Promotion for services has some unique aspects. The most important is the need for internal marketing to employees. This must be a key part of the success of any services offering. To customers, Moorthi (2002) emphasizes the need for education. Word of mouth is also critical among customers and developing satisfied customers who will speak positively to others is very important. This point cannot be emphasized enough. In small countries like Denmark, the communities of specialists in various industries are especially small. Poor service for one customer can easily sour an entire country market for a service provider. A firm wishes to develop loyalty, creating, as Jones and Sasser (1995) call them, 'apostles', who can convert others to the firm's product or service offering. A firm wants to avoid creating so-called 'terrorists', those who are so dissatisfied that they will give negative feedback to colleagues. This is especially easy with the advent of chat rooms, unauthorized websites and mass e-mail.

■ The transition from product to service orientation*

Many managers see the intriguing possibilities in moving their firm from a product-centric orientation

*This section based upon information provided by IBM Institute for Business Value and IBM Business Consulting Services.

to more concentration on the services aspects of their business. Services seem attractive because they often require less capital investment and provide higher margins. However, the difficulties of moving from product to service orientation can be daunting. A first step many firms take is to offer warranties, installation or maintenance services for their basic products. In this case, competitors quickly match the offerings. Then, when faced with a large sales opportunity a firm often sacrifices margins in a bundled offering, thereby setting a dangerous precedent of essentially giving away services. Changing to a services orientation is a real challenge and many firms have found it difficult to succeed in this transformation because of poor strategy or execution.

Greenberg (2002) recommends that instead of becoming a 'solutions provider', meaning adding a range of services to traditional products, a firm should seek to become a customer value provider (CVP). A CVP attempts to aid its clients in providing value to *their* customers throughout the value-chain. The firm may look 'up-chain' in procurement or research and development. Examples are vendor-managed inventory and electronic data interchange (EDI) order capability. A new up-chain area for helping customers create value is collaborative product design. There are obvious benefits including the new knowledge of the customer's business and establishing strong relationships.

'In-chain' aspects of the business relate to manufacturing and include asset management. Down-chain aspects of customer value include marketing/sales and distribution/logistics. In one case cited by Greenberg, a firm that produced custom-designed packaging offered to receive its customers' products, package them and distribute the goods to retailers. In changing the firm from a product provider to a CVP, management must realize that important transformations must be made in corporate culture, organization design and metrics (ways of measuring success for individuals and groups). In addition, the firm may have to change the way it measures return on assets and its technology infrastructure.

In implementing this strategy, Majewski and Srinivas (2002) point out that managers often

FIGURE 8.4 Professional services business model Adapted from: Majewski and Srinivas 2002

	Product-centric	Professional services	Outsourcing	Information services	Financial services
Service value proposition	• Aftersales support • Warranty services • Maintenance offerings	• Installation and support services • Consulting services • Other professional services	• Lower fixed and/or variable costs • Access to enhanced capabilities • Increased flexibility • Reduced headcount	• Information based for: – Maintenance – Inventory management – Supply chain – Trading • Remote monitoring and data aggregation	• Financing for product purchases • May include other value-added financial services • Move assets from balance sheet to income statement
Operating model	• Network or depot repair • In-bound call center • Field service force • Integrated salesforce	• Traditional leveraged engagement model • Separate services org. • New channels to market	• Headcount transfer of client • Technology transfer or updating • Scale economies • Service level tracking	• Solution selling skills • Installed base of networked products • Technology platforms and integration	• Separate financial services organizations • Financial operational processes (risk mgmt, billing, etc.) • Internal balance sheet

underestimate the resources necessary to change their firm's orientation. These researchers point out five services business models as seen in Figure 8.4.

In moving from product-centric to services oriented, firms often come upon the following issues: operational inefficiencies, offering development problems, channel conflict, sales redesign and pull-through issues. To overcome these problems a firm will need to develop a formalized product development system for the service business and the ability to develop clear assignments for channel members based on capabilities. Often, firms fail to redesign their salesforces in the proper way. Consultative selling may be required, but this requires a major cultural shift for a salesforce which is comfortable selling products only. In addition, the firm must change its incentive program to be sure the goals of the salespeople are congruent with the goals of the new organization. Pull-through often requires that a member of the firm use products not manufactured by the firm in order to satisfy customer needs. Again, cultural change is required to make this work.

In short, moving from a product-centric to a services oriented business is difficult and requires understanding the customer's entire business and attempting to become a CVP to help your customer provide more value to its customers.

International services delivery

Service delivery in foreign markets is dictated by the nature of the service and the customers, the attitudes of the host governments and the frequent need for high control of operations. Vandermerwe and Chadwick (1989) developed a six-sector matrix based on the relative involvement of goods and the degree of consumer/producer interaction. For services with a high consumer/producer interaction level and a low involvement of goods, these authors find that the internationalization strategy is to gain high control through direct investment, mergers or acquisitions. In most instances, the management of the people who provide the service by the 'exporting' company is the critical factor for success of the business.

In addition, since services cannot be protected through patents, they can be imitated and therefore speed is essential in finding and moving into foreign markets (Nicolaud 1989). Carman and Langeard (1980) argue that internationalization is more risky for a service firm than for a goods manufacturer since host governments tend to view these firms as taking from the host country and leaving little. Grönroos (1990) adds that service firms have to enter foreign markets 'all at once' rather than moving through various stages like a goods producing firm.

Since services are perishable, responsiveness to demand is critical. Unsold services 'perish'; they cannot be inventoried, or stored for later. Therefore, the service manager must use all marketing tools at his command to adjust for increases and decreases in demand. An early study of services managers found that 'successful services managers are managing the capacity of their operations and the unsuccessful ones are not' (Sasser 1976). The main implication here is the freedom to add or lay off workers if needed, including bringing in home country management or workers on short notice. The ability to manage demand also means pricing flexibility is critical. Short channels of distribution to keep close to the customer as well as tight control over personnel selection are also required (Czinkota and Ronkainen 2004). These characteristics of managing services tend to make service firms prefer the establishment of their own subsidiaries or branch offices, mergers and acquisitions,

---

TALKING POINT

How is it that a US$20-billion Italian-based company with very good products failed to gain any real market position in the United States despite an effort lasting over 15 years? Olivetti Corporation, maker of many technical products which were well accepted throughout the EU failed to overcome its US and Japanese-based competition.

Management focused on aggressive pricing and product quality. But when a customer buys a number of copiers, what is most important to the customer? What is the customer really buying? How could a firm like Olivetti have better established itself in the US Market?

joint ventures, licensing or franchising (Erramilli and Rao 1993; Vandermerwe and Chadwick 1988). However a study of the insurance industry (Zimmerman 1999) indicates that managers are sophisticated in finding ways into markets without the need for establishments. The Internet is an especially powerful way for a services firm to enter a market without a physical presence.

Overcoming trade barriers

The rapid growth in services has caused governments to react. While tariff barriers have declined, non-tariff barriers (NTBs) against services have increased. The barriers take any number of forms ranging from establishment requirements to restrictions on ownership to limitations on services to be offered to different tax treatment. The World Bank counted an increase of 2,500 NTBs from 1986 to 1988 (Lee and Nayam 1988). UNCTAD estimated that 20 per cent of world trade encounters NTBs (Laird and Yeats 1990). The critical test of a barrier is that it is discriminatory. Mukherjee (1992) identifies government measures which discriminate based on source of production as true barriers to trade.

The General Agreement on Trade in Services (GATS), part of the Uruguay Round GATT agreement, is the first multilateral agreement covering trade and investment in service sectors. The GATS also provides a specific legal basis for future negotiations aimed at eliminating barriers that discriminate against foreign services providers and deny them market access. While the GATS agreement is attempting to reduce services trade barriers, the agreement includes many loopholes and exceptions (White 2002). Therefore, firms are often faced with the task of getting around these barriers though their own ingenuity. Managers wishing to overcome barriers generally approach the problem in two major ways – international negotiations and management actions.

Basche (1986) found that service company executives favored negotiations through existing general multilateral organizations like GATT or bilateral industry-specific negotiations for overcoming barriers.

Kotler (1986) described 'blocked' markets as those with high entry barriers caused by governments, labor unions and other interest groups. He prescribed the use of 'megamarketing' to overcome blocked markets, adding two P's (power and public relations) to the familiar four P's of marketing. Kotler described five bases of power a firm might use to influence critical decision makers in its favor – reward, coercion, special expertise, legitimacy and prestige. He recommended that international executives map the existing power structure, develop a strategy and an implementation plan. The firm should choose one of three broad strategies: neutralize opponents, organize allies, or turn neutral groups into allies. Kotler also specifically mentions 'at home' lobbying – using the home government to pressure a foreign government into opening a market.

Dahringer (1991) suggested five key management actions which can be taken to combat barriers to international trade in services. These are:

embodying – including services in physical goods, to move the total product toward the more tangible domain;

superior management – developing strategic alliances, most particularly franchising, which permit a partnership between a locally knowledgeable partner and the foreign organization;

customizing – developing the most attractive package of benefits so that customers will pay a higher price or move to the service rather than have the service brought to them;

technology – using communications and computer technologies (technology transfer is another way of overcoming barriers);

micromarketing – working with governments to relieve discrimination through government actions.

Dahringer also includes superior services quality as a management action. This seems better included in customizing and superior management rather than a separate category.

A manager's choice of market entry strategy is affected by the trade barriers he or she sees. A thoughtful manager may elect not to enter a market or to modify their strategy. These successful international services executives take a long-term view of their effort (Zimmerman 1999). They engage in multiple levels of strategic actions working with home and host governments as well as other local decision makers.

SUMMARY

While there appear to be many similarities between the marketing of tangible products and the marketing of intangible services, there are quite a number of differences. Managers must be aware of the unique characteristics of services which make their marketing quite different. The key points from this chapter are:

- Services are intangible, consumed and produced at the same time, perishable and variable in the quality provided at various times. In addition, users participate in the production of the service.

- There are a few pure goods or services. Usually in business markets, goods are offered with attendant services.

- Managing the service aspect of the business can be very profitable and can help the firm secure a very favorable position with the customer.

- To manage services, marketing, operations and human resources must plan and operationalize services together.

- Successfully changing a firm from product-centered to service-oriented requires leadership by management, especially in the area of corporate culture.

- The assessment of service quality has been well-established, however measurement of e-service quality is still in the developing stage.

- Firms often introduce 'me too' services with no value added. This usually results in a failure of the services business.

- While some researchers claim services businesses must have establishments in-country to market services internationally, there is some evidence to suggest that this is not true. The Internet allows services to be marketed throughout the world with no 'bricks and mortar' investment.

- Governments attempting to protect local businesses have been very creative in developing barriers, creating major problems for services marketers. Marketers must take a long-term view and approach various constituencies to get these barriers lowered.

REVIEW QUESTIONS

1 What are the unique aspects of services and how does this affect management and marketing of these services?

2 List the various combinations of services and goods which may be offered by a firm.

3 How do marketing, operations and human resources work together in a services business?

4 Describe the most important customer needs in product support services.

5 What is the role of corporate culture in services marketing?

6 Name the five key dimensions used to measure service quality and describe each.

7 How do process and outcome relate in customer judgment of service satisfaction?

8 What are the most important e-service quality measurements?

9 Describe blueprinting. Develop a blueprint for a local service business.

10 If you were developing a new service for an oil field lubricant firm, what are the key steps you might use and what rules would you apply to make this new service successful?

11 Name the major differences in marketing services versus products.

12 What are the key problems in moving from a product-centric to a service-oriented business and how would you overcome them?

13 What are the critical problems in marketing services internationally and how would you deal with them?

SPOTLIGHT ON B2B MARKETING

ColorRight Corporation, based in Switzerland, is a marketer of color measurement equipment. The firm was the originator of a particular approach using special technology also invented by the company which is now more than 50 years old. At the beginning of its history, the firm concentrated on equipment for medical laboratories, film processors and printing firms. For instance, the firm supplies equipment to measure the color on film and press for newspapers and other printers and provides equipment to the largest automobile manufacturers so that they can be sure the paint on one part of the automobile matches the paint on another or on replacement parts. At the present time, ColorRight is doing business in more than 60 countries and serves many of the largest multinationals throughout the world.

The new CEO appointed just last year, Mervin Lacroix, reviewed the results for the latest fiscal year. He saw flat year-on-year turnover for each of his seven major end-use market segments:

- graphic arts
- printing and packaging
- digital printing
- photo processing
- retail color matching
- industrial color
- medical/dental.

Lacroix contemplated the results and also some disturbing news from the salesforce. Apparently, SunColor, a Japanese-based competitor, had proposed to a number of large customers that they offer some new services such as reviewing the product requirements so that color measuring equipment could be tailored to the assembly line of an automotive plant. These offers were made at no cost to the customers.

Lacroix assembled his management team and asked each to comment on this new development and also to assess ColorRight's current problems which were resulting in no growth. Each department head spoke in turn. The engineering manager spoke about improving response time of the equipment, lowering the weight and improving portability. The manufacturing manager talked about increasing reliability and lowering manufacturing costs. The director of marketing asked for six new salespeople for North America, three for Europe and ten for Asia as a way of solving the problem. The chief financial officer warned everyone that budgets could not be expanded unless sales began to rise.

Lacroix thanked his staff and pondered their answers. He had recently come upon the idea of services as the main driver of the firm and he wondered what would be involved in changing ColorRight from a product-centric to a services-oriented firm.

Questions

1 If you were Lacroix, which of the department heads' advice would you find most useful?
2 How would you respond to the moves of your competitor, SunColor?
3 What possible obstacles might Lacroix face if he moves forward on changing ColorRight from a product-centric to a service-oriented business?
4 What steps could he take to move in that direction?
5 Assume you were hired by Lacroix and asked to start a services business. What advise would you give him as you began to establish this business?
6 What motivation do you think SunColor has in offering services to some of its major customers?

REFERENCES

—— (2001) *GATS – Fact and Fiction*, Geneva, Switzerland: World Trade Organization.
—— (2003) http://www.wto.org/english/res_e/statis_e/ accessed August 4, 2003.
Basche, J. R. (1986) 'Eliminating Barriers to International Trade and Investment in Services', *Research Bulletin*, 200, New York: The Conference Board.
Bennett, P. D. ed. (1995) American Marketing Association, *Dictionary of Marketing Terms*, Lincolnwood, IL: NTS Business Books.
Berry, L. L. (1989) 'How to Sell New Services', *American Demographics*, October: 42–43.
Berry, L. L. (2001) 'The Old Pillars of New Retailing', *Harvard Business Review*, April 2001: 131–137.
Berry, L. L., Zeithhaml, V. A. and Parasuraman, A. (1992) 'Five Imperatives for Improving Service Quality', in C. Lovelock *Managing Services*, Englewood Cliffs: Prentice-Hall.
Carman, J. M. and Langeard, E. (1980). 'Growth Strategies for Service Firms', *Strategic Management Journal* 1: 7–22.
Chase, R. and Stewart, D. (1995) 'Mistake Proofing: Designing Errors Out', *Productivity Press* (excerpt).
Choi, C. J. and Scarpa, C. (1994) 'A Note on Small vs Large Organizations', *Journal of Economic Behavior & Organization* 24: July: 219–224.
Czinkota, M. R. and Ronkainen, I. A. (2004) *International Marketing* (7th edn), Mason, Ohio: Thomson-Southwestern.
Dahringer, L. D. (1993) 'Marketing Service Internationally: Barriers and Management Strategies', *Journal of Services Marketing*. Summer: 5: 3: 5–17.
De Bretani, U. (1995) 'New Industrial Service Development: Scenario for Success and Failure', *Journal of Business Research* 32: 93–103.
Erramilli, M. K. and Rao, C. P. (1993) 'Service Firms' International Entry-Mode Choice: A Modified Transaction-Cost Analysis Approach', *Journal of Marketing* 57: July: 19–38.
Fryer, B. (2001) 'High Tech the Old Fashioned Way', *Harvard Business Review*, March 2001: 119–125.
Greenberg, D. (2000) *Product Provider to Customer Value Provider: Escaping the Services Maze*, Somers, NY: IBM Institute for Business Value, IBM Global Services.
Grönroos, C. (1998) 'Marketing Services: The Case of a Missing Product', *Journal of Business and Industrial Marketing* 13: 4/5: 322–338.
Grönroos, C. (1990) 'Relationship Approach to Marketing in Service Contacts: The Marketing and Organizational Behavior Interface', *Journal of Business Research* 20: 3–11.
Grönroos, C. (1990) *Services Management and Marketing*, Lexington, Mass: Lexington Books.
Gummesson, E. (1991) 'Marketing-orientation Revisited: The Crucial Role of the Part-Time Marketer', *European Journal of Marketing* 25: 2: 60–75.
Heskett, J. L. (1986) 'Managing in the Service Economy', Boston: *Harvard Business School Press*, 1986.
Heskett, J. L., Jones, T. O., Loveman, G. W., Sasser, W. E. Jr. and Schlesinger, L. A. (1994) 'Putting the Service-Profit Chain to Work', *Harvard Business Review* 72: 2: 164–174.

Jones, T. O. and Sasser, W. E. Jr. (1995). 'Why Satisfied Customers Defect', *Harvard Business Review* 73: Nov/Dec: 88–99.

Kierl, C. and Mitchell, P. (1990) 'How to Measure Industrial Service Quality', *Industrial Marketing Digest* 15: 1: 35–46.

Kotler, P. (1986) 'Megamarketing', *Harvard Business Review* 64: 2: March/April: 117–124.

Kotler, P. (2003) *Marketing Management*, Upper Saddle River, NJ: Pearson-Prentice-Hall.

Laird, S. and Yeats, A. (1990) *Quantitative Methods for Trade-Barrier Analysis*, New York: New York University Press.

Lee, C. H. and Naya, S. ed. (1988) *Trade and Investment in Services in the Asia-Pacific Region*, Boulder: Westview Press.

Lele, M. M. (1986) 'How Service Needs Influence Product Strategy', *Sloan Management Review*, Fall: 63–70.

Lele, M. M. and Karmarkar, U. S. (1983) 'Good Product Support is Smart Marketing', *Harvard Business Review*, November–December: 124–132.

Lovelock, C. H. (1992). 'A Basic Toolkit for Service Managers', in Lovelock, C. *Managing Services*, Englewood Cliffs: Prentice-Hall.

Majewski, B. M. and Srinivas, S. (2003) *The Services Challenge: Operationalizing Your Services Strategy*, Somers, NY: IBM Global Services.

Moorthi, Y. L. R. (2002) 'An Approach to Branding Services', *Journal of Services Marketing* 16: 3: 259–274.

Mukherjee, N. (1992) 'Multilateral Negotiations and Trade Barriers in Service Trade – A Case Study of US Shipping Services', *Journal of World Trade* 26: 5: October: 45–58.

Nicolaud, B. (1989) 'Problems and Strategies in the International Marketing of Services', *European Journal of Marketing* 23: 6: 55–66.

Parasuraman, A., Berry, L. L. and Zeithaml, V. A. (1991) 'Understanding Customer Expectations of Service', *Sloan Management Review*, Spring: 39–48.

Parasuraman, A., Zeithaml, V. A. and Berry, L. L. (1988) 'Servqual: A Multiple Item Scale for Measuring Consumer Perceptions of Service Quality', (Exec. Summary), *Journal of Retailing* 64: 1: 5–6.

Sasser, W. E. Jr. (1976) 'Match Supply and Demand in Service Industries', *Harvard Business Review*, Nov–Dec: 133–140.

Semenik, R. J. and Gary J. B. (1993) *Principles of Marketing: A Global Perspective*, Cincinnati: South-Western Publishing Co.

Shostack, G. L. (1977) 'Breaking Free From Product Marketing', *Journal of Marketing*, April 1977: 73–80.

Shostack, G. L. (1984) 'Designing Services that Deliver', *Harvard Business Review*, Jan-Feb 1984: 133–139.

Vandermerwe, S. and Chadwick, M. (1989) 'The Internalization of Services', *The Service Industries Journal*, January: 79–93.

White, L. J. (2002) Unpublished Paper 'International Trade in Services: More than Meets the Eye'.

Yip, G. S. (2003) *Total Global Strategy II*, Upper Saddle River, NJ: Pearson – Prentice Hall.

Zeithaml, V. A. and Bitner, M. J. (1996) *Services Marketing*, Singapore: McGraw-Hill.

Zeithaml, V. A., Parasuraman, A. and Malhotra, A. (2002). 'Service Quality Delivery Through Web Sites: A Critical Review of Extant Knowledge', *Journal of the Academy of Marketing Science* 30: 4: 362–375.

Zimmerman, A. S. (1999). 'Impacts of Service Trade Barriers: A Study of the Insurance Industry', *Journal of Business & Industrial Marketing* 14: 3: 211–226.

PRICING IN BUSINESS MARKETS

Learning objectives

After reading this chapter, you should be able to:

- Describe how organizational buyers look at price from a value point of view
- Understand the most important factors in B2B pricing
- List the factors impacting upon pricing strategy development
- Understand the importance of cost to pricing decisions
- Describe how firms manage the competitive bidding process
- Describe key factors affecting customer price sensitivity
- Explain the issues in transfer pricing

Introduction

Price is the only activity marketers engage in that produces revenue for the firm. All other marketing activities represent expenditures while pricing managed properly can make a major difference in the firm's revenue and income. Pricing for products and/or services must be congruent with the rest of the marketing plan. Managing price properly also means thoroughly understanding costs as well as customers.

■ The magic of price

As has been pointed out above, price is the only place where marketers have a chance to directly improve the bottom line. They do this by carefully pricing products for maximum profitability. Let us look at the simplified example shown in Figure 9.1.

With the original price of US$10 a firm sells one million units for a total revenue of US$10 million. The direct cost for manufacturing the product (including all of the variable costs) at US$6/unit adds up to US$6 million. Administrative costs are US$3 million. In this case, as can be seen from our simple example, the profit to the firm is US$1 million. Now let us assume that the marketing vice-president decides to raise the price 5 per cent. Therefore, the product will now be sold at US$10.50. If one million units are sold, the total revenue would be US$10.5 million. The direct cost for making one million units remains US$6/unit for a total of US$6 million and the administrative costs also remain the same at US$3 million. This example shows how a 5 per cent increase in price results in a 50 per cent increase in profit from US$1 million to US$1.5 million.

This example is given only to show how a small movement in price can result in very large benefits to the firm. However, this example has some obvious flaws. Firstly, the example boldly assumes that the firm will sell one million units at a higher price that it has sold at the original price. Basic economics teaches us that demand curves slope downward toward the right as seen in Figure 9.2.

If one raises the price, the quantity sold declines. This demand curve certainly holds true for commodity products where all the offerings are exactly the same, such as sand or milk. However, in some consumer markets and in almost all B2B markets, the demand curve actually looks more like that shown in Figure 9.3.

		Original Price	**New Price** (increase price 5%)
Sales Revenue (1 million units @ $10)		$10,000,000	$10,500,000
Direct Costs (Labor, materials, etc) (@ $6.00 per unit)		$6,000,000	$6,000,000
Administrative Costs (Overhead)		$3,000,000	$3,000,000
Profit		$1,000,000	$1,500,000

FIGURE 9.1

The magic of price

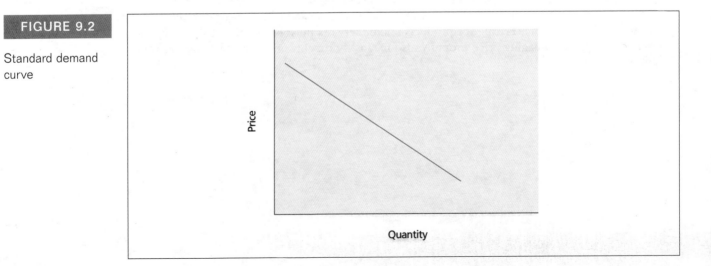

FIGURE 9.2

Standard demand curve

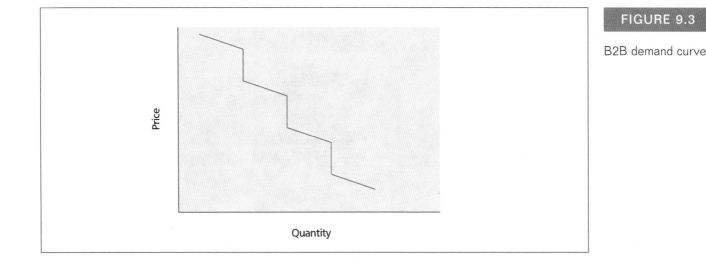

FIGURE 9.3

B2B demand curve

Here we see a 'stepped' demand curve. This illustrates the point that there are ranges of prices at which the demand will not change. If our marketing director is clever enough to determine that customers are not price sensitive to a difference between US$10 and US$10.50, he or she would realize the increased revenue from changing the price.

A second possible criticism of our example is that the increased price may require increases in administrative expenses, such as hiring more salespeople or increasing advertising or trade show promotion. Here again our example would fail. So, while we see that the simple example in Figure 9.1 is an oversimplification of most situations, it does serve to illustrate the point that business marketers must be fully aware of their capability to increase the profitability of their firm through the judicious use of pricing.

◼ The pricing process

Figure 9.4 shows an overview of the pricing process. Firstly, the firm must set pricing objectives in line with its corporate objectives. Secondly, the manager will develop the pricing strategy to be used in each relevant segment. Then the manager will determine what the demand will be at various pricing levels. Following this, they will estimate costs then review the competition, select a pricing method and policy and finally determine the exact prices to be assigned to each individual product and product line.

> **TALKING POINT**
>
> There is a lot of data to support the idea that a firm who has the largest market share also is the most successful in a particular industry. And what is the most effective way to gain the largest market share? Certainly to lower prices below competition. If this is true, wouldn't a smart marketing manager lower prices to below that of competitors to get the biggest market share possible? What could possibly prevent the marketing manager taking this action?

Pricing objectives

Generally speaking, pricing objectives can be divided into three major types (McCarthy and Perrault 2002): profit-oriented, sales-oriented or status-quo oriented. Profit-oriented objectives include pricing to realize a target return on investment or to maximize profits. Sales-oriented objectives aim to increase sales either in currency or unit terms or to penetrate markets and increase share. Status-quo oriented pricing includes meeting competition or choosing to compete on a non-price basis. In some

FIGURE 9.4

The pricing process

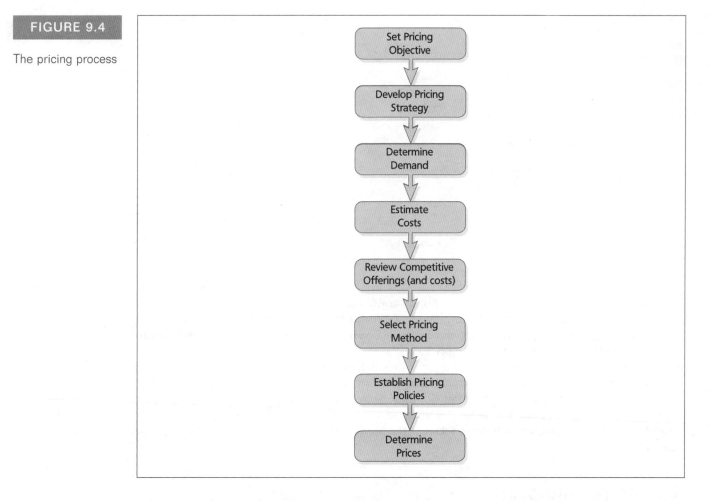

cases, a firm does not have the luxury of pricing to maximize its profits but only to survive in the face of an industry with very strong competition and overcapacity.

Some firms set an internal rate of return for particular product lines and price to achieve this. Others seek a particular margin on sales. The choice depends upon the nature of the industry. In a business where few sales are made per year, the target return on investment is most likely the best approach, whereas, in a high volume business, the margin on sales becomes more important. These accepted versions of pricing strategies do not include the most favorable approach which is to establish pricing based on the value customers place on the product. As has been described above, this requires an in-depth knowledge of the customer's business and the ways in which the product is put to use by the customer.

■ Pricing strategy

To develop a pricing strategy, the manager must consider many factors. An overview of pricing strategy development is seen in Figure 9.5.

The major factors relate to the firm, the environment, distribution channels, competitors and customers. Firm considerations are first the corporate objectives that the firm has established. In addition, costs are critical. In this case, we mean costs not only of the product but the costs of marketing as well, including the market entry costs of various foreign locations. One very important factor in the cost of production is where the production facility is located. Sourcing is very important to the overall decision in marketing products outside the home country, as we have seen. One very important factor will be the costs realized by a foreign factory and the shipping costs inherent in that location.

Finally, the marketing program in the firm is critical since price must match up with the rest of the marketing. For instance, a firm decides that it wishes to offer a laptop computer which will withstand the rigors of a construction site. If the firm designs the product to be the most durable available, then

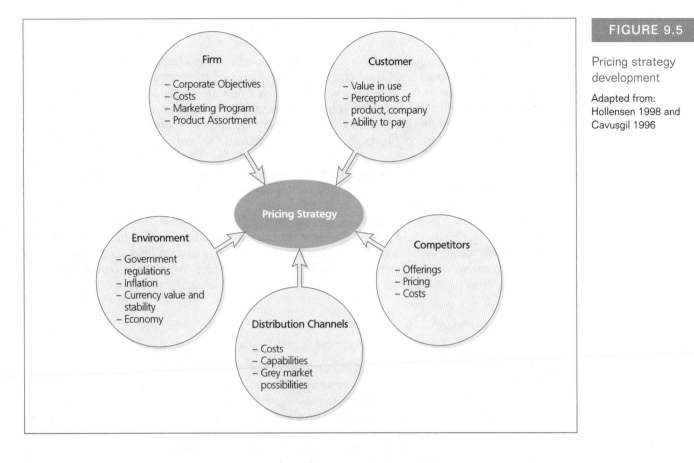

FIGURE 9.5

Pricing strategy
development

Adapted from:
Hollensen 1998 and
Cavusgil 1996

advertises it as such and trains its distribution channels to place the product in the most difficult environments, it would hardly make sense to price the product below ordinary competing laptops.

One important consideration which should not be overlooked is the relationship of the price to be set to the pricing of other products in the line and to other product lines. For instance, a firm may choose to price a large order of ink jet printers at very low prices in order to realize large margins from the sales of exclusive ink cartridges to be contracted for by the customer over a significant period of time. When pricing electric motors, specific horse-power to price ratios may be established by long tradition in the industry and therefore prices must be set to match these customer expectations even though they are not based on costs.

The environment impacts the pricing strategy in many ways: government regulations including price controls, import duties and quotas as well as taxes will have a major effect upon pricing possibilities. Inflation is another important factor in pricing strategy. In countries with hyper-inflation where governments do not allow rapid price increases, a firm should be most aggressive, assigning the highest possible price to any product which is new or modified. The value of a currency in a particular market and the stability of that value will again impact whether a firm can feel comfortable with a particular price level, or whether the firm must be vigilant about changing the price as often as possible. Finally, the relative growth or decline in a particular economy will have an obvious effect on pricing.

Distribution channels also have a large impact on the pricing strategy. The costs associated with the services performed by distributors will have a major effect upon the final price paid by the customer. Therefore, a marketing manager must be fully aware of the costs to be added by the distribution channel and take actions to reduce those costs or even move the services in-house in order to meet required pricing on the customer level. This relates to the capabilities of distribution. Should they be unable to install, train and service a particular product, those costs would be passed to the manufacturer and this would be included in the overall pricing approach. Finally, some distributors may see an opportunity for gray market re-export. This occurs when a manufacturer prices a product at a very low level to meet competition. But sharp distributors in that market overbuy and sell the excess to another market, beating the latter market's much higher prices and turning a neat profit.

Dealing with these 'gray market' products is an ongoing problem for many international marketing managers.

Of course, competitors have a major effect upon pricing strategy. First, one must examine their offerings in detail to understand the benefits and drawbacks of their approaches versus the firm's approach. Where products are sold in markets where bidding is not required to be made public and sales are infrequent it may be difficult to obtain competitors' pricing. Nevertheless, an effort should be made. Finally, competitors' costs are a very important factor in your pricing strategy. Here again it may be quite difficult to obtain these costs, but the manager should attempt at the very least to estimate.

The most important factor in the pricing strategy is obviously the customer. As has been pointed out, it is vital for marketing managers to understand how customers go about doing their business. This will enable the marketing manager to establish a true value-in-use price. Also important in this mix are the perceptions customers have of not only the product but the manufacturer of that product as well. Of course, the ability to pay is important. In some cases, a firm may wish to have a product but be unable to secure necessary funds to obtain it. In this case, a marketing manager may have to resort to alternative payment schemes, accept goods or services in payment (countertrade) or establish long-term payment programs to aid customers to get the products they need.

Determining demand

Customer perceptions of price

As we have seen in Chapter 7, customers perceive a total product including core benefits, product attributes and support services yielding a package of benefits they need. These benefits must be balanced against the costs customers will experience to gain them. Of course, the most important cost is the net outlay of funds required from the customer firm to gain these benefits. This outlay is perceived by the customer not simply in terms of the initial price, but in terms of the value received for the expenditures over the useful life of the product. Customer firms are rather sophisticated in their application of discounted cash flow to pricing offered by vendors and they understand the net difference between one offer and another. Here also, customers may choose to lease rather than own products, thereby increasing the value of the offering to them. Customer perceptions of costs and benefits are shown graphically in Figure 9.6.

Customer perceptions of costs and benefits

As can be seen in Figure 9.6, customer benefits fall into functional, operational, financial and personal categories. The functional are those that come to mind most readily, related to the physical aspects of the product. But also important are operational benefits such as reliability and durability, financial aspects such as the payback period and, not least of all, personal benefits which some

FIGURE 9.6	
Customer perceptions of costs and benefits	

Adapted from: Shapiro and Jackson 1978 and Cespedes 1994

BENEFITS	COSTS
Functional (physical aspects of product)	**Acquisition** (initial price, less discounts, plus freight, installation, taxes)
Operational (reliability/durability)	
Financial (payback period)	**Internal Costs** (training, lost production, disposal)
Personal (commendation for choosing right product)	**Potential Risks** (to operations, personal)

member of the buying center may realize because of his or her choice of a particular product. Customer costs include acquisition costs, which include the initial price less discounts plus freight, installation and taxes; the internal costs, including training, lost production and disposal eventually of the products purchased; and finally, costs related to risk. These include both the risk to the firm which might be caused by a product which did not function correctly and personal risks, once again, related to the failure of the product. In order to price a product correctly, a manager must understand exactly how the customer perceives all these costs and benefits. As we have mentioned in earlier chapters, it is critical for the marketer to fully understand the customer's business, to be aware of the risks the customer faces and the ways in which the customer realizes success. Pricing in this way means setting price based on *value-in-use*. Shapiro and Jackson (1978) give an example of a DuPont pipe made of a particular resin. The pipe was introduced at a far greater price than its competition based on the fact that its life expectancy was much higher than the competitor's pipe. Since this product is buried below ground in many applications the cost to the customer of failure is significantly higher than the difference between DuPont's and the competitor's offerings. The company could then price the product based on its value to the customer or its value-in-use. Value-in-use pricing means the vendor captures some of the benefits realized by the customer.

Price sensitivity

We have already discussed the importance of segmentation in market planning. It should be obvious that establishing the needs of each segment is a precursor to developing appropriate pricing for each segment. In some cases, a product can be customized to meet the specific needs of a segment and priced quite profitably because of the customization. In setting prices for specific segments, the marketing director must estimate the price sensitivity of that particular market segment. Dolan (1995) listed factors that affect customer price sensitivity (see Table 9.1).

The major categories are customer economics, search and usage and competition. Customers will be more sensitive, therefore decreasing the ability of the marketing manager to change the price if the percentage of the particular item is large in comparison to the total expense that the customer is making to achieve a particular end. Pricing flexibility will also be reduced if the customer has to resell the product into a very competitive market. Should the item be of extreme importance to the successful operations of the customer's firm, price sensitivity will tend to decline because reliability becomes paramount.

Reviewing the search and usage category, customers will be more price sensitive if information search is easy and inexpensive and competitive offerings are easily compared. In addition, the

TABLE 9.1 Factors affecting customer price sensitivity

Economics
Percentage of total expense
Parts supplier, OEM or end user
Importance to operations
Search and Usage
Cost of information search
Ease of comparing competitive alternatives
Switching costs
Competition
Differentiation
Perception of Price

Adapted from: Dolan 1995

customer's price-sensitivity is increased substantially where switching costs are low. Switching costs are all the costs associated with changing from one particular product or service to another. For example, a firm might be standardized on a particular IBM computer system. A competing manufacturer, let us say Fujitsu, offers the customer a new computer system with demonstrably better features. However, the customer would hesitate to change knowing that the switching costs, including down-time, training and the inevitable problems caused by such a major change would be substantial. These costs may, indeed, outweigh the benefits seen from a potential new system. Finally, price sensitivity is decreased where the manufacturer's offering is clearly differentiated from its competition and where price perception gives an aura of quality to a particular product.

In Chapter 4, we discussed methods of estimating the total demand by market segment. One should employ these methods to develop an aggregate number for demand based on various pricing levels using the techniques described in that chapter.

Costs

For marketing managers, developing reliable costs to use in pricing decisions is often a frustrating process. Often, many products are made in the same factory and the allocation of costs by the finance department is often arbitrary. Products which are easy to manufacture and have low material costs often assume too much of the overhead of a facility, making the marketing manager's task in pricing to meet market conditions quite difficult. In this regard, marketing people are advised to study the costing process used at a particular facility in-depth so that they can convincingly present their case for proper costing of particular product lines.

Activity based costing (ABC) is a relatively new approach to establishing cost which allows hope for more accurately determining what costs should be assigned to particular product lines and customers. According to Narayanan and Sarkar (2002), under ABC, managers separately keep account of expenses required to produce individual units and batches, to design and maintain and produce and to keep the manufacturing facility running. ABC requires that costs be allocated not only to products but also to customers so that a manager can determine the cost to serve a particular customer. In Narayanan and Sarkar's study, Insteel Corporation tracked overheads needed to serve special customer needs including packing and loading, order processing and invoicing, post-sales service and the cost of carrying receivables. These costs were attributed to each customer and allocated to product based on the volume of each product purchased by a particular customer. Through the ABC approach, Insteel discovered that at a particular plant studied, freight represented 16 per cent of the total people and physical resources cost. After the detailed analysis, management decided to increase the weight shipped per truck load, resulting in a 20 per cent reduction in freight expense. The visibility of the ABC system also allowed Insteel to change the product line and increase prices for less profitable products.

Although the high risks associated with it have been well-established, the idea of 'pricing down the learning curve' is one which has persisted for at least two decades. Learning curve (or experience curve) theory simply states that costs decline rapidly with each doubling of output of a particular product. Experience curve effects come from three major sources (Day and Montgomery 1983):

- Learning: increased efficiency because of practice and skill or finding new and better ways to do things.
- Technological improvements: new production processes and product changes which improve yield.
- Economies of scale: increased efficiency resulting from larger operations.

These improvements are especially relevant to investment and operating costs. Day and Montgomery found significant limitations of the strategic relevance for experience curve approaches and they warn against an all out dedication to this approach. While it may give some advantages in some markets, it also introduces rigidity that may make the firm slower and less flexible in its ability to respond to customer or competitive changes. The experience curve will only be strategically relevant when the three major effects identified above are important in the strategic environment of a particular firm. Ames and Hlavacek (1984) point out that slavishly following the experience curve approach has yielded disastrous results, especially for established or mature products where gains through experience diminish rapidly.

Generally the aggressive (penetration) pricing approach to gain market share is justified in three circumstances. First, in new or underdeveloped markets where customers are very price sensitive, price may be the weapon of choice to establish a secure market presence before competitors can move. Second, where fixed and variable costs will assuredly drop with a rapid increase in volume. Finally, where competitors are weak or have rigid high costs a firm may use pricing to place a severe strain on its competitors who will probably not be able to match the firm's lower prices (McKinsey 2003).

Competition

Needless to say, understanding competitive offerings, including their prices, is critical. To begin with, a firm must be careful about setting its prices higher than competition. This obviously depends upon the strategic position the firm finds itself in. Should the company be a leader in its market, it probably will price higher than competitors. In monopolistic competition situations, smaller firms would realize no benefit by attempting to price lower than the dominant competitor since the large firm could easily match the smaller firm's prices or even retaliate by lowering prices further, putting a much larger financial strain on the smaller firm than it would realize itself. In high growth or hyper-competitive markets, some firms may attempt to simply disturb the status quo as we have seen in Chapter 3. An important tool in these markets is the race to the next price point. While this is more common in consumer markets, there is a strong effect in B2B markets as well. Moore (1995) points out that when workstation prices were lowered to under US$50,000 and then under US$10,000, the result was 'huge boosts in sales volumes'. He continues, 'the vendor who hits the next lowest price point engages a large new market segment who previously could not afford to take advantage of a particular product or technology. When a market leader does not move toward that price point rapidly, new aggressive competitors will do so'. This is true even in the case where these smaller competitors have to sell below their costs. In the hyper-competitive situation, the learning curve has its most telling effect.

Countering direct competitive efforts requires creativity to differentiate the firm's offering from its competitor's. In Chapter 8, we described the transition from a product-centric company to a solutions provider and beyond that, to a customer-value provider. One commodity chemical firm set up a new business unit to provide solutions selling to its customers. While expenses increased (selling, general and administrative costs rose 5 per cent), gross margins rose to 20 per cent from 9 per cent (Johanssen *et al.* 2003).

Understanding your competitors' current position is an important factor affecting the price but an equally important aspect of this decision is competitor reaction. Certainly, this aspect of pricing requires experience and knowledge. A correct assessment of competitors' reaction to increasing or decreasing price may determine whether the strategy chosen by the company is the correct one. Sophisticated companies are able to include in their data warehouse information about past competitive reactions to pricing moves. This knowledge can help the manager make more informed decisions about potential competitive actions.

TALKING POINT

International marketing director James Calvano suddenly received a phone call from Ahmed Markat, his sales manager in Istanbul. 'Jim, what's going on? I just visited our customer, Cukuroba Electric, and they have been able to source transformers in Croatia at a 25 per cent reduction from the prices we charge. Please let me know what to do.' Calvano had been faced by this problem before. The company has a good distributor in Croatia who was taking advantage of the rebuilding in the Balkans. To get the business, Calvano had offered a very low price and the distributor had bought 100 large transformers.

Why doesn't the company just have the same price everywhere? Surely this type of price discrimination damages the reputation of the firm – so why make problems for yourself? Or maybe the new market makes it worth the small risk that someone will take advantage!

■ Pricing methods

Pricing methods are closely related to pricing objectives. Firms who wish to assure profits start their pricing on the basis of cost. International exporters use three basic methods (Cavusgil 1996):

- Rigid cost-plus pricing: where the price is set simply by adding all the costs incurred for serving an international customer to the costs of manufacturing the product plus a margin.
- Flexible cost-plus pricing: is similar to rigid cost-plus pricing but allows for some price variation, such as discounts for large orders or to meet local competition.
- Dynamic incremental pricing: assumes that fixed costs are incurred whether the firm sells outside its home market or not, so that the exporter seeks only to recover international variable costs.

Stottinger (2001) showed that most exporters use either the rigid cost-plus or flexible cost-plus approach, focusing on costs and competition rather than customer value in their pricing method.

More sophisticated firms analyze cost and demand and develop prices for a target return on investment. This method generally assumes demand at a certain level and does not sufficiently take into account the changes in demand resulting from changes in price or potential competitive moves.

Firms using sales-oriented objectives attempt to set prices which will grow their sales in units or currency or increase market share. These approaches have been discussed in some depth above. Those with status quo objectives generally set prices to meet competition. Finally, firms who attempt to use value-in-use pricing base their pricing decision upon extensive work with customers. While it would be naïve to say that they should ignore costs entirely, marketing managers who wish to be successful must price from the market in, knowing customer needs and willingness to pay as well as competitors' offerings, current and future possible pricing. Should market prices in a particular country fall below the costs to serve customers in that country, management must re-examine the entire marketing strategy for that particular market and take steps to lower costs or decide not to serve customers in that particular market at that particular time.

A special consideration for exporters is the escalation of price which can take place because of the additional costs of exporting, the import duties and value added taxes (VAT) applied in various markets.

As can be seen from Table 9.2, a domestic product which is sold at the factory for US$5 and is subject to the normal mark-ups by distributors and retailers might be sold to consumers for US$9.38. This same product sent to an export market may be subject to the various costs escalations shown in Table 9.2, resulting in a consumer price 72 per cent higher than that of the domestic price. (This table makes the assumption that the domestic market has no VAT.) Even adding VAT for the domestic market, export pricing can often be much higher. Firms can take several actions to reduce this price escalation. As recommended by Czinkota and Ronkainen (2004), first the firm may attempt to eliminate some steps of distribution. In the example shown in Table 9.2, for simplicity, a number of wholesale steps were eliminated. But in some markets, especially in Japan, multiple steps of wholesaling are the norm. A marketer must examine eliminating some of these steps to keep the price escalation within reason.

A second method to reduce a final price in exporting is to adapt the product using lower cost components or ingredients and taking out costly additional features which can be made optional in particular markets. A third way to reduce escalation is to change tariff or tax classifications. This may require local lobbying of the taxing or importing authorities. A final method would be to assemble or produce overseas. Once foreign sourcing is established with far lower cost components, all costs applied to the product will be reduced. Shipping components to the local market for assembly is often a good cost-cutting approach. For instance, in Venezuela completed furniture products were subject to a punitive tariff of over 50 per cent. An office furniture manufacturer decided to ship the product unassembled and then contract with a local assembler to put the pieces together. Unassembled components were subject to a tariff of only 10 per cent. So, while assembly costs had to be added, the resulting market price was far lower than that realized when shipping in the completed product.

TABLE 9.2 Escalation in export markets

Cost Factors	Domestic	Export Markets
Manufacturer's price at factory	5.00	5.00
+ Insurance, shipping (15%) (CIF)	–	0.75
Landed costs (CIF Value)	–	5.75
+ Tariff (20% of CIF Value)	–	1.15
Importer/distributor's cost	–	6.90
+ Importer/distributor's margin (25% of cost)	1.25	1.72
Subject to VAT (Full cost + margin)	–	8.62
+ VAT (18% on cost + margin)	–	1.55
Retailer's cost	6.25	10.17
+ Retailer's margin (50% on cost)	3.13	5.08
+ VAT (18% on margin)	–	0.91
Consumer price (Retailer's cost + margin + VAT)	9.38	16.16
% Escalation over domestic price	–	72%

Adapted from: Becker 1980

Pricing policies

Pricing policies include deciding upon list price and discount levels, allowances, rebates, and geographic differences (standardization vs differentiation).

The question of list price varies by industry. In some industries, list prices are set in such a way that no customer ever pays that price. The list prices for a product line are set in order to provide various levels of discounts. Discounts can be given for volume purchases, whether cumulative or based on individual order, or based on time of order. As we have seen in Chapter 8, pricing for services is often used to manage demand.

Allowances and rebates are simply price reductions given to dealers or distributors to help them promote a particular manufacturer's product. Some firms give advertising allowances to their distributors in order to encourage them to promote their particular product or even for identifying their facilities such as showrooms or service vehicles with a particular brand name. A firm may choose to offer a trade-in allowance for older products in order to replace them with newer versions. A rebate is a fee paid to a purchaser once the product is bought and installed.

A firm must decide on its geographic policies. First and foremost will be whether one standard price will be established in all markets with the final local price determined by varying import duties, currency and local laws. Differentiated pricing allows local distributors or sales agents to set prices. In Stottinger's study of 45 industrial firms heavily involved in exporting, all but three made pricing decisions centrally and the largest firms were more likely to have centralized pricing decisions. Firms that used a company salesforce internationally tended to standardize price while those with independent distributors tended to allow differentiation.

Keegan (2003) describes three global pricing policy alternatives:

- *Ethnocentric* (extension): where a price per unit is the same no matter where in the world it is sold.
- *Polycentric* (adaptation): which allows local managers or independent distributors to establish whatever price they feel is acceptable. In this case, prices are not coordinated between countries.
- *Geocentric*: where the firm does not use a single price worldwide or allow local managers or distributors to make independent pricing decisions. This is an intermediate approach which recognizes that there are unique local market factors which impact the pricing decision and that price must be integrated with all elements of the marketing program across the world. In this case, headquarters may decide to use a market penetration approach for a particular market in order to gain short-term market share and a skimming approach elsewhere to reap profits used to offset low margins in markets where penetration is used.

Keegan points out that in global marketing, 'there is no such thing as a normal margin'. The geocentric approach is one which allows a true global competitive strategy in which a firm can take into account competitors and markets on a worldwide basis.

Legality of pricing policies

Many nations regulate pricing in various ways. The most obvious controls relate to anticompetitive actions. In the EU and the United States, firms cannot collude to set prices and these kinds of laws are widely enacted although intermittently enforced in various other markets throughout the world. In the United States, a manufacturer must generally treat each class of customer equally. That is, the customer who buys a particular quantity of product should receive the same discount as another customer buying that same quantity. However, some exceptions to this rule are allowed. Manufacturers can use discriminatory pricing to meet a competitive threat in a particular market or if it can be proved that their costs to serve one customer are lower than another.

In setting international prices, another important issue is that of dumping. Dumping simply means that a product is sold in a particular market at a level less than its cost of production plus a reasonable profit margin. Anti-dumping penalties have increased in the United States, the EU, Canada and Australia and this will continue to be a key issue in international marketing. Managers must be careful that their pricing decisions can be defended against anti-dumping accusations.

Transfer pricing

Transfer pricing can have an important effect on pricing decisions. Transfer prices are those set for goods or services which are bought by one division of a firm from another division. These are inside or intra-corporate prices. As might be expected, local tax authorities are quite interested in the transfer prices set inside corporations. Creating artificial profits by pricing high from a low tax jurisdiction may raise the attention of taxing authorities in the receiving higher tax nation.

Transfer pricing can also have a significant effect upon the motivation of local partners. If for tax reasons prices are set in such a way as to reduce the profits of a local subsidiary or joint venture, managers of this entity may become de-motivated. This 'softer' portion of the pricing decision between entities of a particular firm must also be taken into account.

Determining prices for products and product lines

The final step in our pricing process is to determine the actual prices. This requires an alchemy of customer perception, company needs, competition, environmental factors and distribution. As seen in Figure 9.5, managers must decide how prices within a product line relate to one another and how total product line pricing relates to another product line's pricing. Setting the price for a product and attendant service requires a full analysis of all factors which may affect the customer decision and profitability as has been described above. Of course, a manager must be ready to react to competitive pricing moves. A useful exercise is to establish possible scenarios of competitive pricing moves, develop cost and customer information needed to make a decision in reaction to a competitor and then make a hypothetical decision.

Terms of sale and payment

Key items which can affect pricing internationally are the terms of sale and terms of payment. Incoterms are standard terms of sale set by the International Chamber of Commerce.

Incoterms specifically define the responsibilities of the buyer and the seller in any transaction. Table 9.3 shows some selected terms along with their explanations. As can be seen, EXW means Exworks. This is the minimum obligation of the seller to the buyer. In this case, the seller just makes the goods available, usually at the factory loading dock, and the buyer is responsible for all costs and risks from that point on. Other terms parcel out the risks and costs to the buyer and the seller in different ways as can be seen in Table 9.3. DDP – delivered duty paid – is the maximum obligation that the seller can take. In this case, the seller pays all the costs and assumes all the risks until delivery is made to the buyer. In addition, the seller is responsible for getting the product through customs, paying import duties, related taxes and so on. As one might guess, these terms of shipment and risk can be a source of competitive advantage and must be part of the overall equation including the product price and the export payment method offered.

Financing foreign trade

Although there are many terms of payment in international business, Figure 9.7 shows those most often used.

In Figure 9.7, the buyer's risk has been placed on the vertical axis and the seller's risk on the horizontal axis. As can be seen, cash in advance reduces the risk of the seller while increasing the risk of the buyer while consignment or open account are high-risk strategies for the seller but low-risk for the buyer. Open account terms include payment by check, direct debit, electronic funds transfer or any other method that relies heavily on the buyer's eventual willingness to settle the debt after the goods have arrived. From the seller's viewpoint, this is risky since the buyer is in a foreign country and therefore enforcing the debt by legal action would prove extremely difficult. Once a relationship of trust has been established between a buyer and a seller, or in cases where the seller has reliable representation in the importing country, open-account is simple to use and may become inevitable.

A large percentage of international business is completed using letters of credit. With a documentary letter of credit, the importer's bank will pay for goods providing certain conditions are met, in most cases the presentation of a bill of lading or air waybill. There may be other requirements: an insurance certificate, pre-inspection certificate, dangerous goods notice, bank indemnities and so

---

TABLE 9.3 Selected Incoterms

Term	Explanation
EXW	Exworks – the seller needs only to make the goods available to the buyer at a specific place, usually the seller's factory. The buyer takes on all costs and risks from that point on.
FAS	Free Alongside Ship – seller delivers the goods alongside a vessel at a particular port. The buyer takes on all costs and risks from that point.
FOB	Free on Board – seller delivers when the goods 'pass the ship's rail' at a particular port. Some mistakenly use FOB as a synonym for EXW but according to Incoterm definitions it is quite different. Buyer takes all risks and pays all costs from the delivery point.
CIF	Cost, Insurance, Freight – same as FOB but seller pays transportation, freight and insurance costs to the destination. The buyer has the risk of loss once delivery to the ship is made.
DDU/DDP	Delivered Duty Unpaid/Delivered Duty Paid – seller delivers when the goods arrive at destination. Seller pays all costs and assumes all risks until delivery is made. Under DDU, the buyer is responsible for import duties, taxes, etc. Under DDP, the seller is responsible for import duties, taxes, etc.

Adapted from: Incoterms 2000

FIGURE 9.7

Export payment
methods

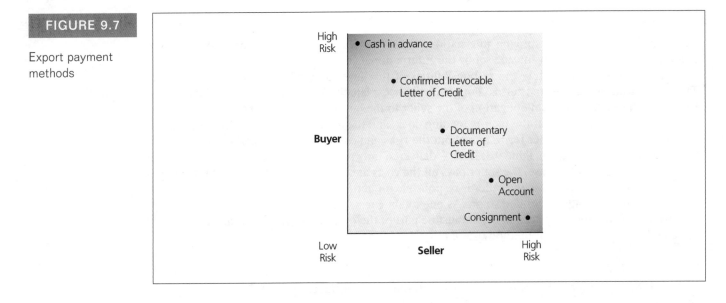

forth. The drawback of this method is that the bank can, and indeed must, refuse payments unless all the conditions have been met exactly, even if the goods have been delivered on time and in perfect condition. The most common type is a confirmed irrevocable letter of credit in which the seller's bank as well as the buyer's bank are involved in the transaction. This allows the seller full confidence that his or her firm will be paid regardless of the creditworthiness of the buyer or the buyer's bank. Of course, the buyer will have to apply for a confirmed, irrevocable letter of credit and the issuing bank in the buyer's country will be sure that the buyer will have sufficient funds to cover it. Since the buyer often must borrow the funds to insure the letter, this approach, while comforting to the seller, may be a commercial drawback to completing a negotiation and may have a strong impact upon the price a seller can command from a buyer.

Effect of the Internet

Because the Internet has become so pervasive, a marketing manager must assume that any facts placed on the Internet will quickly be obtained by buyers throughout the world. Because there are price-oriented search engines, many firms are wary about putting their prices on the Internet because where prices are posted, the Internet makes comparisons quite easy and therefore would dictate a standardized pricing policy rather than a differentiated one. If differentiated prices must be used, the website should explain why there is a price difference in a particular market based on additional costs for freight or distribution.

Competitive bidding

Business-to-business sales are often completed through competitive bids. This is especially true for government institutions and non-profit organizations such as hospitals. Some non-governmental firms also use competitive bids. In some cases, a firm may require a bid to a particular specification and then reserve the right to negotiate further with the winning bidder. Firms use specification buying especially for large projects. These firms develop detailed specifications either based on the performance or description of a particular product, service or a combination of both. Firms supplying military product or large power plants or other major projects need to develop an expertise not only in the bidding process, but also in the specification process. 'Specmanship' means a firm's salesforce is expert at helping a customer develop specifications which will limit the bidders. The most successful salespeople can develop specifications with requirements that can be met only by their firm. When faced with a potential competitive bidding situation which will be based on specifications to be developed by a large customer, it is necessary to spend the required time to gain the most favorable specifications possible before bidding documents are released.

The development of a competitive bid should be viewed as equal in effort to developing a total business plan. It is not unusual for a firm to spend well over €100,000 to complete the analysis required to provide responsive bids to a particular customer. Before a firm decides to take on this major effort, a screening procedure should be completed. Table 9.4 shows a procedure for evaluating bid opportunities.

In this procedure, eight pre-bid factors should be examined. These factors are shown in Table 9.4. An analysis tool such as suggested in Table 9.4 can be used to assign a weight to each factor and then rate the firm's capability for this particular bid. Multiplying the weights by the ratings gives a value for each factor and adding all of the values together gives the firm some idea of whether they should pursue this particular bid. Of course if there are other opportunities, these can be compared using this same tool.

The factors include first plant capacity. The firm must consider whether winning this bid will place an unusual strain on the plant required to make the product or whether the plant is running at a relatively low level and can use additional capacity. Competition must be considered as well, both in terms of the number of competitors and their possible bids. Past experience with competitors will serve as a guide here. A third and most important area is the possibility for follow-up opportunities. In some cases, a firm winning a bid will be placed on a preferred supplier list (such as with a government) and many additional orders may follow. In addition, a firm may receive orders for associated products. Here, the marketer must be careful because many sophisticated purchasers will indicate a large follow-up to a particular order with the goal of pushing the supplier to reduce the initial price. A next factor is quantity. Obviously, a very large order is more attractive than a smaller one. Large orders for standard products with the same features are more attractive than orders for a mix of products. If the quantity can create economies of scale for a supplier, it will be more attractive than one which simply pushes a supplier past a point of diminishing returns. Delivery is a key consideration as well. In some cases, a large quantity of a product is required to be delivered all at once. This may put an undue strain on the manufacturer's facilities. Another important consideration is the effect of accepting this order on customers, both from a delivery and plant capacity point of view. If a large order has the potential of reducing the manufacturer's capability to satisfy loyal customers in the future, it may not be as attractive. Obviously, profit is critical in deciding whether or not to move ahead. While this analysis must take place before final prices are determined, a general idea of the prices required to gain an order should be employed so that the firm can make an estimate of the possible profit to be realized. In some cases, a firm may decide that profit is not the overriding concern and that in order to fill the plant it will move ahead with a relatively unprofitable bid. Another key factor is experience. As has been said, developing a winning bid for a particular project may take as much effort as an entire business plan for a new venture. If the firm has experience in developing bids of this particular kind, it should be looked upon more favorably. Finally, the bid capability means the availability of people and financial resources to actually complete the work. There may be times when the firm simply does not have the capability to do the required work and therefore the project becomes less attractive.

Table 9.4 shows a hypothetical bid situation where the firm has assigned weights to each of these factors and then rated the attractiveness of this bid along each one of the factors. The total value is then added and as can be seen for this particular bid opportunity, the number is 820. It may be that the firm has set a minimum hurdle for proceeding with a bid. If we assume that hurdle might be 700 for this firm, it would proceed with the bidding process based on this score.

Once a firm has decided to move ahead, the firm must develop a pricing strategy. Pricing strategy for bids is the same as the general pricing strategy shown above. In some cases, a firm may price simply for survival in order to get some business to keep the plant running. In most cases, the firm will decide whether it wishes to gain market share, increase profitability or use any of the other strategies described above.

Internationally, insisting on competitive bidding can be a problem in a high-context culture, where the project will probably be given to the firm the buyers feel is best positioned to do it based on the past establishment of trust. However, in a low-context culture a firm would develop specifications and push the supplier to meet the specifications as written (Hall 1976).

TABLE 9.4 Evaluating bid opportunities

Pre-bid Factor	Weight (%)	Rating (1–10)	Value
Plant capacity	20	10	200
Competition	10	8	80
Follow-up opportunities	10	7	70
Quantity	10	7	70
Delivery	10	5	50
Profit	20	9	180
Experience	10	9	90
Bid capability	10	8	80
TOTAL	100%	N/A	820

Adapted from: Paranka 1971

SUMMARY

As we have seen, price is a critical aspect of the overall marketing plan and must be totally congruent with the rest of the levers of the marketing machine.

The most important points from this chapter are the following:

- Marketing managers should attempt to give the highest possible price along the 'stepped' demand curve to maximize the revenues for their firm.

- Exceptions to this occur only in high-tech, fast developing markets, where the quick race to the next price point is critical.

- The overall pricing process moves through eight steps starting with setting the pricing objective and ending with determining prices.

- Pricing objectives may be profit oriented, sales oriented or status quo oriented.

- The pricing strategy must be developed considering firm, customer, competitor, distribution and environmental variables.

- Customers weigh functional, operational, financial and personal benefits against acquisition and internal costs as well as potential risks in determining whether a price is fair.

- Some customers are more price sensitive than others. This is affected by the economics of the particular purchase, the cost of search and usage including switching costs and competitive offerings available.

- Developing reliable costs for product pricing is a difficult task for marketing people. Activity-based costing helps marketing people assign costs to particular product lines and customers to get more accurate costs for their pricing.

- Experience curve pricing is a dangerous strategy except in very limited circumstances.

- Countering lower competitive costs may require the firm to look creatively at offering and dictate that the firm attempt to become a customer value provide rather than a product-centric company.

- International exporters generally use rigid cost-plus or flexible cost-plus approaches, but more sophisticated firms work from the customer in using valu in-use pricing.

- The firm must set pricing policies related to list price and discounts, allowances, rebates and standardization versus differentiation for geographic areas. Most international firms seem to price centrally.

- Geocentric pricing, a blend of polycentric and ethnocentric pricing approaches, allows a basic price worldwide integrated with the global marketing program but also allows for local factors which may change individual market prices. When pricing, a firm must be careful to understand local laws regarding competition and dumping.

- Transfer or intra-corporate prices are often scrutinized by local taxing authorities and may have a significant effect upon the motivation of local partners.

- In setting prices, the marketing manager must decide upon the terms of sale and terms of payment. Standard terms of sale are provided by the International Chamber of Commerce. Frequently in international business, letters of credit are used to assure suppliers they will be paid. But other approaches may be required by commercial necessity.

- Competitive bidding is a major factor in B2B markets. A wise firm employs knowledgeable salespeople to influence the specifications on which bids will be made.

- Firms should employ an evaluation procedure to decide whether or not to move ahead with particular bids.

REVIEW QUESTIONS

1 Describe the 'magic of price' as it is explained in the text.

2 List the factors in the pricing process.

3 What are the three major types of pricing objectives firms may use?

4 In developing a pricing strategy, what factors should a manager consider?

5 How does the customer perceive costs and benefits in weighing whether a price seems fair?

6 What affects a customer's price sensitivity?

7 Explain the concept of switching cost.

8 How can a manager develop accurate costs to be used in his pricing decision?

9 When should the experience curve be used as a basis for pricing and when not?

10 What are the most common pricing methods used by international exporters? What are the drawbacks to these methods?

11 In developing pricing policies, what should an international firm consider?

12 How can transfer pricing affect the results realized by local partners?

13 List the most common Incoterms and the most common export payment methods. What are the advantages and disadvantages of each and how do they relate to one another?

14 When a firm enters a competitive bidding situation, how might they analyze the attractiveness of entering a particular bid?

Czech glass is a particularly attractive product in the chandelier industry. In northern Bohemia, glassworks have been in existence since the mid-14th century and Czech crystal, which is colorless and ideal for engraving and cutting has been particularly attractive to chandelier makers. In 1724, Josef Palme began making chandeliers in northern Bohemia. These chandeliers were acquired by King Louis XV, Maria Theresa and the Russian Czarinas and some have been placed in La Scala in Milan and Versailles.

Thomas Klaus, president of Crystal Components, had established his firm as a major supplier of Czech glass components to the chandelier makers in the Czech Republic. Now, he is thinking of moving into foreign markets. Preliminary research shows large numbers of chandelier makers in the EU, US and China. While they are quite capable of making chandeliers to equal the quality of those made in the Czech Republic, they need the Czech glass to make these chandeliers world class in quality. Klaus is also well aware of the recent Czech accession into the EU. So, he is most interested in establishing relationships with chandelier manufacturers as quickly as possible. A key question in his mind is the proper pricing for these components. He established costs for spheres and ovals in crystal formations used in the chandeliers and also determined the import duties into each of the target markets. These are seen in Exhibit 9.1.

EXHIBIT 9.1	Crystal Components

Costs (all labor and materials)

Size:	Spheres:	Ovals:
1 cm	3.00 euro	4.00 euro
3 cm	5.00 euro	6.00 euro
5 cm	7.00 euro	8.00 euro

Import Duties

EU	15%
US	10%
China	25%

He knows that final prices of chandeliers range from €500 up to many thousands of Euro and each chandelier uses anywhere from 10 to 100 spheres, ovals or a combination of both. Since Crystal Components is a small firm, he also knows that he will need distributors to import the product in each of these markets and may have to provide some type of technical expertise to the chandelier manufacturers in their own languages. A quick analysis of the marketplace shows existing suppliers providing alternative products (not from the Czech Republic). Klaus has determined that competitors in general have the following prices for a 1 centimeter sphere: US – US$ 4.25; EU – €4.50; China – 30 yuan; and in most cases, these firms are located within the markets he is concerned about.

Questions

1 Which market(s) should Klaus move into first?

2 How should Klaus price his product in each of these markets based on the final pricing for his products?

3 How will this pricing affect the rest of Klaus's marketing strategy?

REFERENCES

_____ (2000) Incoterms 2000, Paris: ICC Publishing, SA.

_____ (2003) 'Penetration Pricing', *McKinsey Quarterly*, 3: 46–47.

Ames, B. C. and Hlavacek, J. D. (1984) *Managerial Marketing for Industrial Firms*, New York: Random House, Inc.

Becker, H. (1980) 'Pricing: An International Marketing Challenge', in *International Marketing Strategy*, Thorelli, H. and Becker, H., eds., New York: Pergamon Press.

Cavusgil, T. S. (1996) 'Pricing for Global Markets', *Columbia Journal of World Business*, 31: 4: Winter: 66–78.

Cespedes, F. V. (1994) 'Industrial Marketing: Managing New Requirements', *Sloan Management Review*, 35: 3: Spring: 45–60.

Czinkota, M. and Ronkainen, I. A. (2004) *International Marketing*, New York: Harcourt, Inc.

Day, G. S. and Montgomery, D. B. (1983) 'Diagnosing the Experience Curve', *Journal of Marketing*, 47: Spring: 44–58.

Dolan, R. J. (1995) 'How Do You Know When the Price is Right', *Harvard Business Review*, 73: 5, Sept-Oct: 174–183.

Hall, E. T. (1976) 'How Cultures Collide', *Psychology Today*, July: 66–97.

Hollensen, S. (1998) *Global Marketing: A Market Responsive Approach*, Hertfordshire, UK: Prentice-Hall Europe.

Johanssen, J. E., Krishnamurthy, C. and Schlissberg, H. E. (2003) 'Solving the Solutions Problem', *McKinsey Quarterly*, 3: 116–126.

Keegan, W. J. and Green, M. C. (2003) *Global Marketing*, Upper Saddle River, NJ: Prentice-Hall.

McCarthy, E. J. and Perrault, W. D., Jr. (2002) *Basic Marketing: A Global Managerial Approach*, New York: McGraw-Hill.

Moore, G. A. (1995) *Inside the Tornado*, New York: Harper Collins Publishing.

Narayanan, V. G. and Sarkar, R. G. (2002) 'The Impact of Activity-Based Costing on Managerial Decisions at Insteel Industries – A Field Study', *Journal of Economics and Management Strategy*, 11: 2: Summer: 257–288.

Paranka, S. (1971) 'Competitive Bidding Strategy', *Business Horizons*, 14: June: 39–43.

Shapiro, B. P. and Jackson, B. B. (1978) 'Industrial Pricing to Meet Customer Needs', *Harvard Business Review*, 56: 6: Nov/Dec: 119–127.

Stottinger, B. (2001) 'Strategic Export Pricing: A Long and Winding Road', *Journal of International Marketing*, 9: 1: 40–63.

10

SUPPLY-CHAIN MANAGEMENT

Learning objectives
After reading this chapter, you should be able to:

- Explain the difference between logistics and physical distribution
- Describe the key elements in managing the supply-chain
- Describe the key terms in exporting
- Explain the role of relationships in supply-chain management
- Explain how to maintain relationships in the supply-chain
- Describe some of the difficulties inherent in managing global supply-chains

▌ Introduction

Ensuring that the goods arrive at the customer's premises at the right time, in the right quantities and at the right price, is at the heart of marketing. In the past, simply ensuring that the delivery truck is reliable and the driver knows where to go was sufficient, but in recent years a much wider-ranging view has been taken of the process of taking raw materials and converting them into customer satisfaction.

Particularly in the global context, this process involves many different companies, often in different countries, each with their own needs. Managing this complex chain of supply efficiently is one of the ways firms can improve their profit margins and competitive position.

Logistics versus physical distribution

Physical distribution is concerned with the movement of goods via road, rail, sea and air. It is the process of organizing transportation which will move the goods in a timely and secure manner, within a reasonable budget taking all factors into account.

Logistics is a word borrowed from military terminology. The logistics approach takes a holistic view of the movement of goods, examining the whole process from raw materials through to final consumer. The intention behind the logistics approach is to integrate the various transport systems involved in order to ensure a smooth flow of goods.

The advantages of taking a logistics approach can be spectacular. For example, until the 1970s goods being transported by sea would often be loaded by hand onto a lorry at the factory, taken to a train station where they would again be loaded by hand onto a railway truck, then taken to the docks where they would be handled again onto the ship. At the destination port, the reverse procedure would apply. Working each hold on a ship required a total of 18 men, not counting the ship's crew: one gang of eight men on the dock, another gang of eight in the hold, and two men operating winches. One ship's officer would also be needed to supervise loading, in order to ensure that the ship's trim was not disturbed.

Looking at the problem from a logistics viewpoint led to the widespread introduction of containers. These are filled at the factory, then transported by train, lorry or ship to the destination warehouse in the foreign country. Loading onto a ship now requires only five men: two on the dock to attach the lifting gear, one man in a container hoist, and two more men in the hold to detach the lifting gear. In some container ports the lifting cranes are designed to eliminate the need for the men on the ground, thus reducing the former 18 men to only one, who is able to load several hundred tons an hour. The result of this has been a dramatic drop in the number of ships needed, since ships only spend hours in port instead of days and a corresponding drop in the number of dock workers needed.

Logistics and supply-chain management

The concept of supply-chain management is central to logistics. Place, time and value are central features of logistics management, with transport and warehousing functioning as the intermediate links rather than the central concern. It is in the transport and warehousing operations that costs can be reduced and the recent rapid development of information technology has greatly increased the possibilities for doing this. For a logistics operation to be successful on the international scale, two main criteria must be satisfied: firstly, the people working in the various countries need to be coordinated in an effective and professional manner. Secondly, there must be a high level of specialist knowledge of the laws, conventions, product quality controls and regulations in each country the goods must pass through.

Coordinating the professionals requires the following factors to be in place:

1 Data communication needs to be transparent, with all those involved being kept informed as to what is happening to the goods.

2 There must be a coordinating philosophy or set of rules to which all those involved should subscribe.

Logistics coordinators are now able to track consignments in real time, wherever they are in the world, by using IT systems. This enables effective use of resources: aircraft can always fly full, ships can be loaded swiftly and spend more time at sea, warehouses can be smaller because goods stay for shorter periods of time. For example, Chevron Oil introduced SAP logistics software in 1992 at a total cost of US$160m. By 1997 the software had been responsible for reducing purchasing-related costs by 15 per cent. In addition, purchase transactions were facilitated electronically instead of using paper transactions, which greatly improved the reliability of the process and improved response times (Fortune 1997).

Another use of IT has been to minimize wasted journeys or part-full journeys. An example of how IT has been successful in facilitating this is the Delego company of Sweden. Delego was started by two truck drivers who met by chance on a ferry from Denmark to Germany. Chatting to other drivers over a few beers, the two truckers realized that several of their erstwhile colleagues were traveling between the same two points, but with only half-full or even empty trucks. The two truckers planned a new system for organizing part-loads, and eventually gave up their trucking jobs, borrowed some capital, and started the Delego website. The system works through the Internet: when a transport company has an empty or part-empty truck on a given route, the company enters its details on the Delego website (or by telephone) and Delego tries to match up the truck with a cargo, providing an estimate of the financial return for the trucker.

Logistics facilitators and managers

Logistics has become widely-adopted by global firms. Shipping and trucking companies are therefore redefining themselves as logistics facilitators. This means that such companies take responsibility for the whole process, moving goods from the factory gates to the final destination by whatever means are available. This leads to even greater savings for the businesses involved, since the process operates much more smoothly.

Logistics managers are responsible for some or all of the following interfaces:

1 Collaboration with physical distribution. Selecting transportation methods such as road, rail, sea or air.
2 Optimization of the material flow within the work center.
3 Planning and organizing the storage area layouts, and the type of handling equipment involved.
4 Selection of suppliers for raw materials, price levels and specifications.
5 Selection of subcontractors to perform specific tasks.
6 Organizing after-sales activities, including problem resolution with supplied products.
7 Verifying that sales forecasts accord with the real needs of the client.
8 Developing delivery schedules.
9 Developing packaging to meet the need for physical strength and security.

Not all elements of the logistical system are controllable by the logistics manager. Transport delays, changes in legislation requiring new documentation, the bankruptcy of distribution channel members, or even the weather can play havoc with the best-laid logistical systems. This means that even greater care should be taken with those elements that are controllable.

Table 10.1 shows the elements that are controllable.

As with many other complex decisions, each element of the logistics system impacts on every other element. If the supplier fails to become reliable, the customer may have to bear the extra cost of holding large buffer stocks: additionally, if supplies fail, the customer may lose production or even customers. Clearly customers in many markets will favor reliable suppliers and will even pay premium prices for this, so a good logistics system is likely to have pay-offs on the bottom line in terms of improved profits and possibly improved competitor advantage.

In practice, two main variables must be traded off against each other (see Figure 10.1). The first is the total distribution cost, which would generally be regarded as something that should be kept to

TABLE 10.1 Controllable elements in a logistics system

Element	Description
Customer service	Customer service is the product of all logistics activities. It relates to the effectiveness of the system in creating time and place utility. The level of customer service provided by the supplier has a direct impact on total cost, market share and profitability.
Order processing	This affects costs and customer service levels, because it is the starting point for all logistics activities. The speed and accuracy of order processing clearly affects customer service: this is particularly true in global markets, where errors or delays become multiplied by distance, and by the time which it takes to make corrections.
Logistics communications	The way in which information is channeled within the distribution system affects the smooth running of the logistics. For example, a good progress-chasing system will allow deliveries to be tracked and therefore customer reassurance will be greater.
Transportation	The physical movement of the goods is often the most significant cost area in the logistics process. It involves the most complex decisions concerning carriers and routes and is therefore often most prone to errors and delays.
Warehousing	Storage space serves as the buffer between production and consumption. Efficient warehousing reduces transportation costs by ensuring that (for example) containers are shipped full and transport systems are fully utilized.
Inventory control	This ensures that the correct mix of products is available for customers and also ensures that stocks are kept at a reasonable level to avoid having too much capital tied up.
Packaging	The purpose of packaging is primarily to protect the contents from the environment and vice-versa. It also serves as a location for some shipping instructions, e.g. port of destination.
Materials handling	Picking stock to be included in an order is potentially a time consuming and therefore expensive activity. Some warehouses have the capacity to automate the system, so that robots select the products and bring them to the point from which they will be shipped.
Production planning	Utilized in conjunction with logistics planning, production planning ensures that products are available in the right quantities and at the right times.
Plant and warehouse location	The location of the firm's facilities should be planned so as to minimize delivery times (and therefore minimize customer response times) as well as ensure that the costs of buying or renting space are minimized. This will often result in difficult decisions, since space near customers is likely to be more expensive than space in (for example) remote rural locations.

a minimum. The second variable is the level of logistical service given to customers. As service improves costs will rise and there is likely to be a diminishing return for extra expenditure: in other words, there is a point at which further expenditure is unlikely to make a material improvement in service levels.

Firms need to trade off these cost and service level considerations in such a way as to maximize the firm's ability to achieve its strategic objectives. The total-cost approach to logistics management attempts to balance these by assuming that all logistical decisions impact on all other logistical problems, so management needs to look at the efficiency of the system as a whole rather than only concerning itself with individual elements of the structure. The interactions between the elements are described as cost trade-offs, because an increase in one cost may be matched by a decrease in another. Reducing overall costs is the aim of this approach, but there are difficulties.

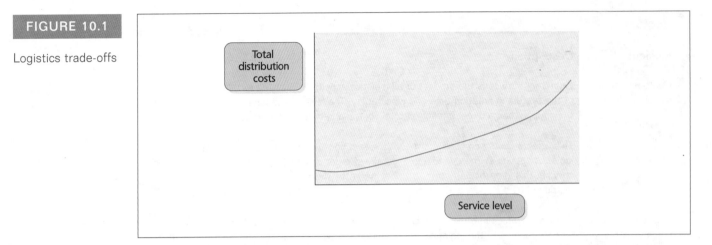

FIGURE 10.1

Logistics trade-offs

For example, the separate elements of the logistical system will almost certainly be controlled by different firms, each with its own cost structure and strategic aims. Thus an increase in cost for one element of the system will not be offset by a reduction in cost elsewhere, since the gainer and the loser are actually different firms. Even within a single firm, different departments will have their own budgetary constraints – managers may not be prepared to lose out so that someone else in the organization can gain. Any attempt to organize the logistical system as a seamless whole must take account of these problems, which of course places a premium on supply-chain integration.

In some cases, the business must maintain the highest possible service levels whatever the cost. For example, delivery of urgent medical supplies is not cost-sensitive, but it is highly service-sensitive. At the other extreme, delivery of paper for recycling is unlikely to be service-sensitive, but almost certainly will be cost-sensitive.

Determining the level of service is a complex problem because it is difficult to calculate the possible revenue gains from an improvement in customer service levels. This calculation needs to be made in the light of competitive pressures, customer preferences, industry norms and so forth. The cost element is much easier to calculate, and the net result needs to be a trade-off between the two elements. One study found that a 5 per cent reduction in customer service levels resulted in a 20 per cent decrease in sales (LaLonde *et al.* 1988)

■ Managing the supply-chain

Supply-chain management has been described as the integration of business processes from end user through original suppliers to provide products, services and information that add value for customers (Cooper *et al.* 1997). The critical element in managing the supply-chain is to ensure that value is added for customers: in order to do this, the supply-chain needs to be coordinated and needs to become as seamless as possible.

For B2B marketers this has two implications. Firstly, it implies that the marketer needs to work at establishing relationships with both suppliers and customers, and in most cases will need to be prepared to change the firm's working practices in order to accommodate the needs of other firms in the supply-chain. Secondly, it means that seeking new customers will mean fitting into an existing supply-chain, where the rules and practices are already well-established.

In order for relationships to work at optimum efficiency within the supply-chain, the members need to share information about strategic plans, new product development, customer profiles and much else. This information is commercially sensitive, so a great deal of trust is necessary. Goods flow down the supply-chain, but information flows up it, enabling the various members of the chain to plan around the reality of existing market conditions. Effective supply-chain management is a powerful tool for creating competitive advantage for the following reasons (Quinn 2000):

1 it reduces costs

2 it improves asset utilization

3 it reduces order cycle time, thus speeding up delivery of customer satisfaction.

Effective supply-chain management can also shut out competitors by denying them access to sources of components or raw materials. For example, when CD players were first marketed the only source of supply for the CD drives were three factories in Taiwan, all of whom were under exclusive contract to Japanese electronics manufacturers. This effectively shut out European and US manufacturers until they could develop the manufacturing capacity themselves – a somewhat ironic position for the Europeans, since the technology was originally developed in the UK.

The goals of supply-chain management are shown in Table 10.2.

If the supply-chain is properly managed, it should create tangible benefits for customers in terms of reduced waste, more flexible and reliable deliveries and improved costs. For the members of the supply-chain, it should increase security of supply, make planning easier, reduce costs, and reduce competitive pressures. There have been many studies which have demonstrated the advantages of integrating the supply-chain: Ferguson (2000) demonstrated that best-practice SCM companies have a 45 per cent cost advantage over median supply-chain competitors. On the other hand, supply-chain glitches have been shown to cause an average 9 per cent drop in the value of the company's shares on the day the problem is announced and up to 20 per cent decline in the six months following the announcement (Bowman 2001).

In global supply-chain management, there are four strategic marketing challenges (Flint 2004). These are:

1 *Customer value learning.* Finding out what customers regard as valuable is complex in the global environment, because supplying firms need to consider differing decision-making processes, differing decision-maker values, different importance rankings of service versus physical attribute values and so forth. The value-chain may span several different cultures, so that each link in the chain must be considered separately as well as how it fits into the whole.

2 *Understanding customer value change.* Customers often change what they value as changing circumstances dictate. Because changes happen at different times in different countries, customer value is a moving target.

3 *Delivering value in a world of uncertainty.* Because change is constant and may even be accelerating, it is virtually impossible to integrate the strategies of firms which are often thousands of miles apart and being pulled in different directions by local changes in the business environment.

TABLE 10.2 Goals of supply-chain management	
Goal	**Method used to achieve goal**
Waste reduction	By minimizing duplication, harmonizing operations and systems, and by reducing inventories, waste is reduced. For example, harmonizing materials handling equipment reduces the need for loading and unloading components and also creates economies of scale in purchasing equipment and containers.
Time compression	Improved information flows about market conditions enable supply-chain members to predict demand more accurately and thus make response times quicker. Also, preferred-customer status within the supply-chain means that each member responds more quickly to the needs of other members than to the needs of non-members. Reducing response times improves cash flow for all members because deliveries happen faster so invoices are paid sooner.
Flexible response	Ensuring flexibility in the supply-chain means that all the members are able to adjust more quickly to changing market conditions. This can lead to major improvements in competitive advantage.
Unit cost reduction	Good supply-chain management seeks to reduce unit costs, which will either allow the firms in the chain to make more money or will allow them to reduce the price to the end consumer, which again offers a competitive advantage. Cost is not necessarily the same as price: a customer operating a just-in-time manufacturing system may accept a slightly higher price for receiving small daily deliveries rather than paying a lower price for one large monthly delivery, because the savings in terms of holding stocks will outweigh the extra outlay.

4 *The customer value process*. In order to meet the problems raised by the first three challenges, marketers may need to shift from a functional towards a process orientation. This may be difficult, in that shareholders believe that they have invested in a company rather than in a supply-chain, which makes it difficult for the process to be seamless.

These challenges will differ in importance from one firm to another and the solutions will be widely varying, but these are not challenges which a global firm can ignore. Success in integrating the supply-chain provides an important competitive advantage and given that globalization also provides the best opportunities for minimizing total costs, managing the global supply-chain effectively is a powerful route to growth.

Establishing and maintaining relationships

Relationships exist not only between suppliers and purchasers, but also across several other categories of partner. Morgan and Hunt (1994) offered the following categorization:

1 Supplier partnerships

- Goods suppliers
- Services suppliers.

2 Lateral partnerships
- Competitors
- Non-profit organizations
- Government.

3 Buyer partnerships

- Intermediate customers
- Ultimate customers.

4 Internal partnerships

- Business units
- Employment
- Functional departments.

From a marketer's viewpoint, the most important set of relationships here will be the buyer relationships, but this does not mean that the other relationships can safely be ignored. In terms of supply-chain management, these relationships are important as they ensure that the firm's place in the supply-chain and its ability to contribute effectively are assured. For Morgan and Hunt (1994), relationship marketing refers to all marketing activities directed towards establishing, developing and maintaining successful relational exchanges. This led them to develop the commitment-trust theory, which states that those networks characterized by relationship commitment and trust engender cooperation, a reduced tendency to leave the network, the belief that conflict will be functional rather than damaging and reduced uncertainty.

All relationships (whether business or personal) are affected by the degree of trust which exists between the parties. Establishing a relationship of trust between businesses can be a complex affair, since many different individuals will need to be part of the process and consequently part of the outcome. There is more on this in Chapter 13.

Channel system orientation

In order to overcome some of the problems inherent in having a logistical system made up of several companies, supply-chain management seeks to synchronize channel activities through a series of negotiations which divide up the overall profits between members. At least in theory, this should make all members better off, since overall costs will fall and service levels will rise. In this scenario, relationships between the channel members must be seen as long-term, permanent, totally honest and highly cooperative if savings are to result.

Companies with effective logistics systems grow 8 per cent faster than those without, realize a 7 per cent price premium, and are 12 times as profitable as firms with inferior service levels (Novich 1992). Setting the service level may or may not be a function of profitability: much depends on the strategic aim of the company involved. This means that it may be possible to help a partner firm to achieve a strategic aim in exchange for a concession on profitability.

Key elements in welding the channel into a single system are as follows:

1 Develop information systems which provide realistic sales forecasts for channel members.
2 Standardize packaging and handling systems (for example by using palletization or containerization).
3 Provide services (e.g. warehousing or data handling services) which improve efficiency for everyone (usually provided by the channel leader).
4 'Pooling' of shipments to avoid the 'empty truck' problem.

Since the service level is often the only strategic advantage the channel has, there are obvious advantages in coming to an agreement and integrating the system. Unfortunately, such integration may take some years to achieve, since relationships of trust take time to establish. Supply-chain management implies a greater degree of integration than does logistics management: SCM implies integration of all the business systems of the channel members, whereas logistics is only concerned with integrating the systems relating to the movement of goods.

Inventory management

Inventory management is the buffer in the logistical system. Inventories are essential in B2B markets because production and demand never quite match. This means that there are times when the producers need to stockpile products and times when the demand outstrips supply and stockpiled products are released onto the market. This ensures a smooth flow of goods to the final users.

Operating deficiencies in the system will sometimes result in delays in delivery, in which case stocks can be used: also, industrial buyers cannot predict demand accurately because they are themselves relying (ultimately) on consumer demand, which is volatile. As we saw in Chapter 1, demand in B2B markets is much more volatile than that in consumer markets because of stocking and de-stocking effects.

The attempt by some firms to introduce just-in-time purchasing in which the purchasing firm does not hold stocks, but instead shifts the responsibility for maintaining inventories onto the suppliers does not accord with the systems approach to logistics, since it does not take account of the whole supply-chain. Some have questioned the efficiency of JIT recently because of the tendency for it to contribute to traffic congestion as trucks make more frequent deliveries and also its tendency to increase costs for suppliers. See Table 10.3 for a summary of the impact of just-in-time on the marketing firm.

TALKING POINT

Just-in-time inventory management means arranging for components to arrive almost exactly at the moment when they are needed at the customer's factory. This obviously results in savings for the customer – but what about the supplier? Suppliers need to deliver small amounts frequently rather than large amounts periodically – so they use smaller vehicles and more of them, and often park just outside the customer's gates until the exact minute for delivery.

Fine for the customer, of course, but wouldn't the supplier pass those costs on? Somebody has to keep the inventory – and somebody has to pay for it. Ultimately it's the end customer. And what about the impact on the environment? All those extra vehicles clogging the streets and parking spaces cannot be a good thing!

Yet if all firms could arrange the logistics in a JIT manner, wouldn't the flow of goods from raw materials to finished products be a real process, instead of a lot of starts and stops? Maybe JIT has something to offer after all!

TABLE 10.3 Effects of JIT on marketing firms

Activity	Impact
Transportation	Because the number of shipments increases, the quantity ordered each time decreases. The shipments also need to meet the exact demands of the customer and are non-negotiable, so the supplier must be flexible. In one study, 49 per cent of companies using JIT said that the inability of suppliers to deliver to their specifications was a problem (Celley *et al.* 1986).
Field warehousing	Shipping over long distances may not be feasible because of the inherent unreliability of transportation, so smaller, more numerous warehouses will be needed. In addition, the use of third-party warehousing may be unsuitable because the customer will require absolute reliability: the supplier may not feel that a third party can be trusted sufficiently.
Field inventory control	Inventory levels of producers may need to be increased as customers will be totally unable to tolerate stockouts under any circumstances. Because of the need for 100 per cent control of inventory, the producer may need to take over all the distribution functions.
Protective packaging	Packaging may be changed or even eliminated in some cases because the goods will be used immediately in production. This is a rare case where just-in-time might benefit the vendor.
Materials handling	There may be few changes here, but because quantities delivered are much smaller, it may not be feasible to use (for example) containerization as a way of reducing handling.
Order processing	The simplest way of dealing with this is electronically. The situation will inevitably become more complex as more frequent deliveries, at clearly-specified times, become necessary.

Estimates of future sales are the key element in controlling the logistics system. These estimates need to be far more accurate than the general ones used for planning sales promotions or other long-term marketing plans: the logistics and inventory forecast needs to be flexible enough to operate on a day-to-day basis if necessary. This requires some fairly sophisticated computer technology, which should be linked throughout the supply chain so as to enable firms further up the chain to predict demand. Falling inventory at the retailer means increased demand at the wholesaler, the manufacturer, the component supplier and the raw material supplier in that order, but delays in the system mean that increased demand at the retail level will perhaps take several months to filter through to the raw material level.

International trade

Table 10.4 shows the most common documents used in international trade.

This comprehensive list of paperwork may not be necessary for all shipments. There is considerable duplication, in other words. Having said that, trucks traveling through Europe may need to carry large amounts of paperwork to satisfy the formalities at each border, once the truck has left the European Union. Standardizing the documentation for trucks was a major issue within the EU in its attempts to maximize the free flow of goods throughout the Union, but of course the system is not perfect because Member States are still permitted to ban imports from other Member States if their governments believe that the imports represent a threat to human or animal life. This was the justification for the French ban on British beef imports during the late 1990s and is the justification for the British ban on the import of live shellfish from the rest of the European Union. In the United States virtually all border controls between the states have been abolished, but differences in state taxation mean that some products (for example cigarettes) are still worth smuggling internally and California maintains restrictions on imports of plants and fruit, for fear of importing an epidemic which would damage the state's lucrative fruit farming.

Export document	**Description**
Ocean bill of lading	The contract between the shipper and the carrier. The bill of lading is a receipt given by the carrier (often issued by the ship's purser) which proves that the goods were loaded. It is often used as proof of ownership, so that it matches with the cargo unloaded and can be bought and sold.
Export declaration	This includes complete particulars of the product and its destination, and is used to control exports and compile statistical information about exports.
Letter of credit	This is a financial document issued by the importer's bank, guaranteeing the exporter's payment subject to certain conditions (often the presentation of bill of lading to prove that the goods were shipped).
Commercial invoice	The bill for the goods from the seller to the buyer. Often used by customs officials to determine the true value of the goods.
Certificate of origin	This document assures the buyer that the goods have not already been shipped from a country with which, for example, a trade embargo applies. These certificates are often provided by a recognized chamber of commerce in the exporting country.
Insurance certificate	This assures the importer that insurance is in place to cover the loss of, or damage to the goods in transit.
Transmittal letter	A list of the particulars of the shipment and a record of the documents being transmitted, together with instructions for disposition of documents.
Customs entry	This provides information about the goods, their origin, estimated value, and destination. This is for the purpose of assessing customs duty.
Carrier's certificate and release order	A document to advise customs of the details of the shipment, its ownership, port of loading and so forth. This certificate proves the ownership of the goods for customs purposes.
Delivery order	The consignee, or customs broker, issues this to the ocean carrier as authority to release the cargo to the inland carrier. It includes all the data necessary to ascertain that the cargo may be released.

TABLE 10.4 Trade documentation

The most important document from the international marketer's viewpoint is the bill of lading, since this is proof of ownership. It is a document of possessory title, which means that only the holder of the bill of lading can collect the goods. There are exceptions to this general rule: if perishable goods arrive before the bill of lading has arrived (for example if the bill of lading has been posted but the goods were sent via airfreight) the shipper can release the goods to a third party on receipt of a letter of indemnity from the party collecting the consignment. Possession therefore passes when the bill of lading is transferred, but ownership only passes when the parties intend it to pass, as evidenced by the sales contract.

As receipts, bills of lading provide only *prima facie* evidence that a certain quantity was received on board, that packaging marks were in order and that the goods were apparently in good condition. Nevertheless, it is up to the carrier to prove that the items stated were not put on board, or that they were loaded in good condition. Obviously a ship's master is only required to attest that the goods appeared to be in good condition: with a few exceptions the ship's officers are not expected to carry out detailed internal inspections of cargoes to investigate their inner qualities.

TALKING POINT

Obviously world trade is important. We can each make what we are good at making and we can profit from ideas from other countries. Also, of course, more trade usually means less war – it is not a good idea to shoot the grocer. So why not just remove all trade restrictions immediately? Certainly there would be a painful period of readjustment, but after that, wouldn't life be so much easier? After all, poor countries frequently complain that they don't have fair access to rich markets while wealthier countries complain that they are paying too much for goods.

Or is free trade just a rich country's response? Do we only consider this approach because we know we have the economic power to clobber any opposition? A 10 per cent drop in our standard of living during a period of readjustment would hardly be noticed – but in Mali or Ethiopia it would mean millions of deaths. So how DO we control trade? Simply by more paperwork? Or by a controlled and calculated regime of duties and documents? And if so, who does the controlling and calculating?

Another problem in international transport is ensuring that everyone involved is clear about what is meant by specific terms. As discussed in Chapter 9, Incoterms have been agreed upon internationally to describe specific types of shipping conditions, so that importers and exporters know exactly who is paying for what.

■ Transportation methods

Selecting a transportation method for a global market can be complex. As a general rule, the faster the shipment, the higher the cost, but standby air freight (in which the shipment is sent on the next available aircraft with spare capacity) can be relatively cheap and when the costs of having capital tied up in goods in transit is also taken into account, can actually be cheaper than surface transportation. Obviously for perishable or highly valuable goods such as computer chips air freight is almost always cheaper, because there is less spoilage and the capital is tied up for a shorter period.

Five basic modes of transportation are used in B2B marketing. Goods are shipped by sea, by air, by road, by rail, or in some cases by pipeline. Often combination systems are used, for example the ro-ro (roll-on, roll-off) ferries which transport lorries (or even just the trailers) across the English Channel, Irish Sea and North Sea routes.

Figure 10.2 shows the factors which a marketing manager will typically take into account when choosing a transportation method.

In most cases, each of the factors will trade-off against each of the others in some way. For example, sea transport (or indeed inland waterway transport) will be substantially cheaper than air freight, but will be much slower. Equally, the reliability of rail transport may compare unfavorably with road transport, but may protect the goods better.

Accessibility

In some circumstances accessibility is an issue. The city of Iquitos, in Peru, is only accessible by water or air – there are no rail or road links into the city. This obviously limits the choices somewhat. Less obviously, some towns in Australia which are accessible by rail may only see one freight train a week and are much better served by road transport, since Australian buses tow trailers for limited amounts of freight and usually offer a daily service.

Costs

Costs obviously vary in different countries. Inland waterways are widely used in Continental Europe, but are not commercially viable within the UK. Railway systems are heavily subsidized in Switzerland

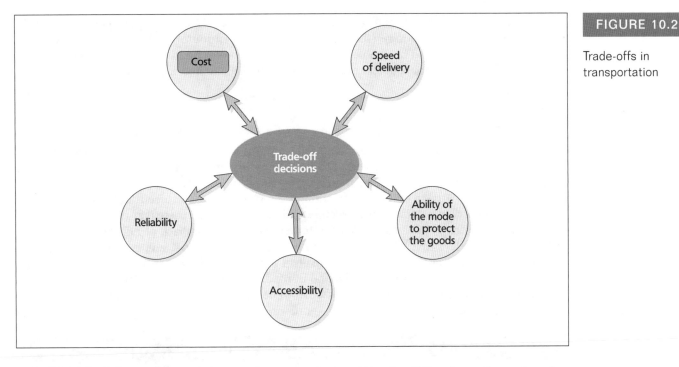

FIGURE 10.2

Trade-offs in
transportation

and the United States for environmental reasons, but not in the UK, where the system has deteriorated dramatically in the last 15 years or so.

Sea freight

Sea freight includes scheduled services (liners) which operate according to a fairly strict schedule, visiting specific ports at specific dates, and tramp services which sail once they have a full cargo for a specific destination. Liner services charge fixed rates, tramp ships (which are frequently modern, fast vessels) have variable rates which are almost always cheaper than the scheduled rates. Sea freight charges are based on either volume or weight, with extra charges for extra services, for example tallying cargo on and off (tallying means that a ship's officer counts the units of cargo as they are loaded).

Shipping agents will carry out all the functions of booking space on the ship and arranging for the loading of the cargoes: they are paid commission by the ship owners. The details of the shipment are contained on a standard shipping note (SSN) which advises the shipping company on what is to happen to the goods on arrival at the foreign port.

Air freight

Air freight used to be an expensive option, but is now much cheaper due to increased efficiency of aircraft and the introduction of standby air freight. Speedy delivery means less stockholding, more rapid settlement of invoices, less insurance and therefore faster turnover of working capital. International airlines' cargo rates are fixed through the IATA (International Air Transport Association), but carriers such as DHL are free to fix their own prices and of course it is feasible to charter a cargo aircraft for a particularly large shipment. For air transport, the air waybill is the equivalent of the bill of lading, but it does not prove title to the goods. One of the problems with air transport, however, is that aircraft do not carry the standardized containers used by road and sea transport, so cargo has to be repacked, increasing handling costs.

Road transport

Road transport is usually very flexible in that goods can be collected and delivered door-to-door, a factor which offsets the sometimes high costs per mile (when compared with sea or even air). In combination with roll-on roll-off ferries truckers can operate throughout Europe, much of the United

States seaboards, the Far East and North Africa, but for longer distances containers are more useful. Many countries restrict cabotage (the collection of cargoes en route) so that a vehicle may make a delivery in one country and be unable to pick up a return cargo. Road cabotage has been abolished within the European Union, but still exists in most of Africa and non-EU countries.

Rail transport

Rail transport varies greatly between countries, largely due to the differences in rail and road infrastructure. In some countries (e.g. Germany) rail transport is well-developed and competes well with road transport. In other countries (e.g. Thailand) the rail network is by no means national, but is effective and efficient over the routes it does cover. In yet other countries (e.g. the UK) the rail network is capable of carrying only a tiny fraction of the freight transport needs of the country, due to an aging and poorly-maintained infrastructure and an emphasis on passenger transportation, which pushes the system close to capacity on many routes. The main drawback of rail transport in a small country like the UK is that the goods need to be loaded onto a lorry, unloaded onto a train, then reloaded onto a lorry at the other end. Normally it is simpler and quicker to drive the lorry directly to the customer's premises. Within continental Europe, the United States and Australia, distances are great enough to make transferring cargoes worthwhile, although in all three cases the long-distance truck (or road-train, in Australia) are much more widely used.

SUMMARY

The physical distribution of products has marketing implications. Managing the supply-chain effectively enables all its members to maximize their efficiency and hence their profits – or of course to pass on savings to customers and therefore be more competitive.

The key points from this chapter are as follows:

- Logistics takes a holistic view: physical distribution refers to particular elements of the process.

- The main trade-offs in logistics are cost and service level.

- Just-in-time purchasing may be counterproductive unless the supply-chain is well run.

- Air freight can be cheaper than other forms of transport when all costs are taken into account.

- Relationships exist across several categories of partner, not just buyers and sellers.

- The crucial elements in welding together the supply-chain are information systems, packaging and handling, effective services, and pooling of shipments.

- Accurate sales estimates are the key to successful supply-chain management.

REVIEW QUESTIONS

1 Why might an exporter prefer to deal on open account?
2 What are the main advantages of air freight over rail freight?
3 Why might just-in-time be damaging to a logistics approach?
4 Why might an exporter use a tramp ship rather than a scheduled liner?
5 What are the main problems in establishing a logistics approach?

Cyprus is an island in the Eastern Mediterranean, perhaps best known as a holiday destination: the party-and-package holiday resort of Ayia Napa, the Troödos Mountains, the family resort of Paphos in the west and the ancient Greek and Egyptian ruins on the island are world famous. Cyprus has a considerable military presence also: since 1974, the island has been divided between the Turkish Cypriots in the North and the Greek Cypriots in the South, with the United Nations maintaining an uneasy truce between the two along the Green Line, which divides Nicosia (the capital) in two. The island's strategic situation, close to the Middle East, means that the British Army and the RAF maintain large bases on the island at Akrotiri and Dhekalia.

Cyprus has a small population (around 760,000 people) but is economically highly-successful, with a high standard of living and low unemployment (around 3.4 per cent). It thus represents a desirable, though small, market for most consumer goods. The island is small: the Greek part of the island is less than 70 miles from end to end and around 30 miles wide at the widest point.

CA Papaellina & Co. Ltd. is one of the island's most important distributors. CAP was founded in 1930 and has since grown to the point where the company distributes into most of the retail outlets on the island. The company is well aware of the peculiarities of the Cypriot distribution system: for example, the island has many small street-corner kiosks which sell everything from newspapers to bootlaces, as well as several huge hypermarkets (retail stores of over 5000 square meters selling area). CAP handles many international brands, such as Chanel, Davidoff, Jean Paul Gaultier, Kleenex, Lucozade, Ribena, Aquafresh, Maclean's, and even Tabasco Sauce. In 2002, the company opened its new pharmaceuticals center, and in 2001 it signed a contract for new warehouse software worth CYP170,000 (approximately US$300,000). This software was supplied by the UK software house, JBA Automated Systems of Durham.

CAP is divisionalized into five separate areas. These are:

1 Personal care and household products.

2 Consumer health-care products.

3 Paper products and foodstuffs.

4 Cosmetics and Fragrances.

5 Pharmaceuticals.

CAP employs 150 people, runs its own salesforce and supplies in every retail sector in Cyprus. This means that the firm is equally able to supply huge hypermarkets and corner kiosks – in itself, this presents considerable logistical and accounting problems. Using its own fleet of trucks and vans, the company distributes throughout the Greek portion of the island.

Because the Cypriot market is so small, distribution chains are short and are often integrated: CAP owns 30 per cent of the AlphaMega Hypermarket in Nicosia, 100 per cent of Beautyline (the cosmetics retail chain) and 50 per cent of Demetrides and Papaellinas, the distributors for the Swiss pharmaceutical giant, Novartis. CAP opened its own specialist pharmaceutical distribution center, PharmacyLine, in March 2002. This distribution center can carry out daily deliveries to every pharmacy in Cyprus, an important service considering that many medicines have extremely short shelf-lives, or may be in infrequent demand and therefore may not be stocked by the pharmacies.

Foreign companies appreciate the way CAP uses its intimate knowledge of the Cypriot market to facilitate distribution. For example, CAP has a relabeling and repacking unit in which imported products are relabeled in Greek to meet local labeling requirements and if necessary are also repackaged. CAP's knowledge of the local distribution systems means that the company is able to distribute in bulk to hypermarkets with the same ease with which its small vans distribute small quantities to kiosks: the mountainous topography of Cyprus and its constant influx of foreign visitors, present special problems which only a local firm can solve.

Cyprus is a small island dependent on foreign trade. It can no longer be self-sufficient, but it is rich, so it imports most of what it needs from day-to-day and exports some agricultural products and a lot of tourism. CA Papaellina is at the forefront of facilitating this exchange.

Questions

1 What advantages does Novartis gain from dealing through CAP?

2 Why might CAP have bought into retail outlets?

3 What specific problems might a confectionery manufacturer have when approaching the Cypriot market? How might CAP be able to help?

4 What are the major differences between supplying hypermarkets and supplying kiosks?

5 Why would competing manufacturers such as Chanel and Jean Paul Gaultier be prepared to use the same distributor?

REFERENCES

Bowman, R. J. (2001) 'Does Wall Street really care about the supply chain?', *Global Logistics and Supply Chain Strategies*, April: 31–35.

Celley, A. F., Clee, W. H., Smith, A. W. and Vonderembese, M. A. (1986) 'Implementation of JIT in the United States', *Journal of Purchasing and Materials Management*, 22: Winter: 13.

Cooper, M. C., Lambert, D. M. and Pugh, J. D. (1997) 'Supply chain management: more than a new name for logistics', *International Journal of Logistics Management* 8: 1: 1.

Ferguson, B. (2000) 'Implementing supply chain management', *Production and Inventory Management Journal*, Second Quarter: 64.

LaLonde, B. J., Cooper, M. C. and Noordweir, T. G. (1988) *Customer Service: A Management Perspective*, Oak Brook, Ill, Council of Logistics Management.

Novich, N. S. (1992), 'How to sell customer service', *Transportation and Distribution*, 33: January 1992: 46.

Quinn, F. J. (2000) 'A supply chain management overview', *Supply Chain Yearbook 2000*: Jan: 15.

Morgan, R. M. and Hunt, S. D. (1994) 'The commitment-trust theory of relationship marketing', *Journal of Marketing*, 58: July: 20–38.

Flint, D. J. (2004) 'Strategic marketing in global supply chains. Four challenges', *Industrial Marketing Management* 33: 1: January.

MANAGING DISTRIBUTION CHANNELS

Learning objectives

After reading this chapter, you should be able to:

- Explain the main issues in designing a suitable distribution policy

- Explain the role of distribution in gaining competitive advantage

- Describe ways of integrating the distribution network

- Describe the advantages of different types of distribution system

- Show how 'cutting out the middleman' reduces efficiency and increases costs

- Describe some of the techniques used for efficient customer response

■ Introduction

Finding and managing distributors and dealers around the world is often the most time consuming task of the B2B marketing manager. Yet many have said the distribution network is a key strategic resource which takes a great deal of time and effort to build and serves as an important competitive advantage. This Chapter describes the process of discovering and managing channel partners in a global setting.

■ Strategic issues in distribution

Strategy is about creating competitive advantage. The following factors are the key issues in the ways that distribution affects strategy:

1 Distribution can add value to the product by increasing utility.
2 The channel is the firm's major link to its customers.
3 Choice of channel influences the rest of the marketing mix, so affecting overall strategy.
4 Building appropriate channels takes time and commitment, particularly in a global context, so distribution decisions are difficult to change.
5 The distribution system determines segmentation and targeting issues in many cases.
6 Conflicts may arise between the firm's strategic goals and those of the distributors, particularly in global markets where timescales may be very different.
7 Intermediaries in foreign countries may weaken the control of the supplier over the way the product is marketed.

Distribution adds utility to the product in the ways shown in Table 11.1.

The distribution system often determines the targeting rather than the other way round. This is particularly true in Third World countries where the transport infrastructure means that some parts of the country are inaccessible: there was more on this in Chapter 10.

Obtaining strategic advantages

Strategic advantage can be obtained by the way distributors serve customers. Although it is part of received wisdom that 'cutting out the middleman' reduces costs because the 'middleman' profit is removed from the equation, it turns out that the services provided by the middleman are actually useful and necessary and would have to be carried out by someone else. For example, a motor mechanic needs rapid delivery of spare parts: ordering each part for each car directly from the manufacturer would mean complex ordering and some very lengthy delays. Carrying out a routine service on

TABLE 11.1 Added utility

Utility	Explanation and Examples
Place utility	Making the product available in a place which is convenient for the customer. For example, Snap-On Tools offers a tool service to light engineering companies, using large Mercedes vans as mobile tool warehouses and calling on the firms on a weekly basis.
Time utility	Making goods available at a time which suits the customer's needs. Just-in-time ordering and delivery is an example of this: deliveries are planned in such a way that stocks of components arrive at regular intervals, thus eliminating the need for the purchaser to hold stocks.
Ownership utility	Goods are transferred to the purchaser rapidly after ordering, so that the purchaser can benefit immediately from ownership. This can involve the supplier in stockholding, however, which may be counterproductive: equally, the fact that stocks have to be held in a foreign country rather than delivered from the home country has allowed several companies to gain a competitive advantage in a foreign country, where the local competitors manufacture to order instead.
Information utility	Distributors are able to answer questions directly, providing faster answers than can be obtained from the supplying company. For example, a firm may set up a helpline for its users, but arrange for the distributors to operate the helpline so as to take advantage of local knowledge and experience.

someone's car might need 10 or 15 different spare parts, from light bulbs to brake linings, all manufactured by different companies in different parts of the country (or even different parts of the world). So the motor mechanic orders all the parts from a motor factor, who keeps stocks of the commonest parts and can deliver within an hour or so. The middleman's profit is almost always covered amply by the savings in time made by using the service.

Serving the customer

Distributors serve customers in some or all of the following ways:

1 *Provide fast delivery*. Local distributors will hold buffer stocks of products, so should be able to supply customer needs rapidly.

2 *Provide a segment-based product assortment*. Like the motor parts factor mentioned above, a distributor may well be able to supply a wide range of products which are suitable for the needs of a specific market segment.

3 *Provide local credit*. A distributor may be able to provide credit facilities for firms. Having local knowledge, the distributor will be able to decide who is creditworthy and who is not. An overseas manufacturer may have no idea where to start obtaining credit ratings.

4 *Provide product information*. Local distributors may have knowledge of other products which are useful to the customer and which are complementary to the firm's products.

5 *Assist in buying decisions*. Distributors are often able to advise on the availability of components, or are able to research availability from among the manufacturers they act for. This can backfire from the manufacturer's viewpoint, since distributors may (and often do) carry several alternative components, some of which are likely to be 'generic' components which are substantially cheaper than the manufacturer's own offerings.

6 *Anticipate needs*. Because the distributors know the local market, they are often able to anticipate the needs of their customers and advise manufacturers accordingly.

These advantages to the customer mean that judicious choice of a distributor provides access to an existing group of committed customers. It also means that the distributor adds value to the product offering by giving advice, assistance and rapid response. Distributors also serve the manufacturers in the following ways:

1 *Buy and hold stocks*. Distributors are the customers of the manufacturers, since they select, buy and pay for the goods. The manufacturer is thus relieved of much of the financial and logistical responsibility of holding stocks.

2 *Combine manufacturers' outputs*. Since customers almost always buy from a number of manufacturers, they will be exposed to the firm's products when they order products from other manufacturers. This in effect provides a 'piggy back' promotional method.

3 *Share credit risk*. The distributor may offer credit to their own customers and carry the risk for this: even though the manufacturer will offer credit to the distributor in order to allow them to stock the products, this is a much smaller risk.

4 *Share selling risk*. The distributors have a stake in making the sales, since they have committed to purchasing the products. Obviously there is an assumption that the products are saleable and an assumption that the manufacturer will play a part in marketing the products, but both parties have a clear stake and commitment in the success of the product.

5 *Forecast market needs*. Distributors are much closer to the market than the manufacturers are and are therefore in a much better position to forecast demand.

6 *Provide market information*. Likewise, the distributors are a good source of information about possible new needs of their customers. This can be helpful in new product development.

Setting up distribution channels

Setting up the right channels for getting the product from its source to the customer involves a combination of direct selling and the use of various intermediaries and facilitators. Intermediaries include distributors, wholesalers and retailers who are classified as merchants. The channel also may include manufacturers representatives or sales agents who find customers and even negotiate for the supplying firm. This group are classified as agents. The major difference between agents and merchants is that merchants purchase and resell product while agents do not. As has been pointed out in Chapter 6, a manufacturing firm will have far more control over an agent than over a merchant since the merchant owns the product. In formulating the firm's channel design, a marketing director must take into account a number of environmental influences as well as company resources and capabilities. These are shown in Figure 11.1.

First and foremost, the firm must look at customer segment requirements. Is the segment sophisticated enough to deal with remotely located distribution outlets, or is training and maintenance a necessity requiring local, on-the-scene distributors? As we will see later in this chapter, various kinds of customers require different levels of service.

TALKING POINT

How can customers require different levels of service? Why shouldn't everybody get the best service we can provide? Surely if we're truly customer-oriented, we should be providing the best service we can for everybody all the time!

Or maybe some customers are not as valuable as others. Maybe we don't make enough money out of some of them, so they get second-class service!

Or just maybe we have some customers who actually prefer us to leave them alone? Maybe they aren't prepared to pay for all that extra service – and would just like a basic, cheap arrangement.

For firms selling software, this may mean direct sales to large multinational corporations wherever they are located, one-step wholesale distribution to local small computer centers, direct sales to large computer retailers and two-step distribution through distributors and retailers or direct sales through the Internet to the smallest clients. The way customers are segmented will have a major effect upon the distribution alternatives chosen. For instance, customers who are highly price-sensitive will not buy through even one-step of distribution and will demand direct sales from the manufacturer.

FIGURE 11.1

Influences on channel design

Adapted From:
Czinkota & Ronkainen
2004

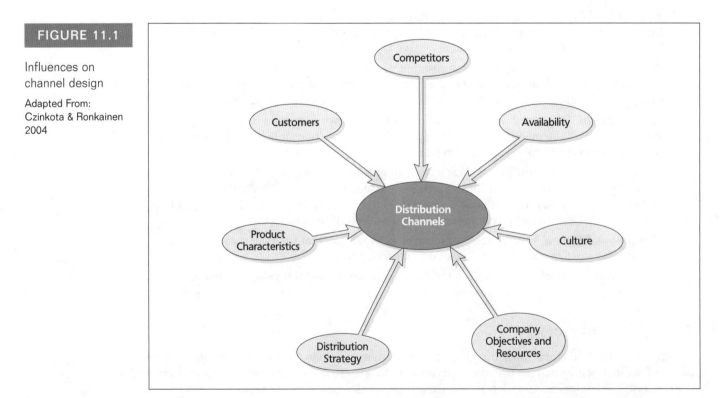

Competitors may also determine channels to be chosen. If an entrenched competitor has already set a pattern of distribution which customers have become accustomed to, it will be difficult for a newcomer to change that pattern unless it can show efficiencies and cost savings to its customers as a result of these changes. The functions handled by distributors may also be set by the competitors. Here again, a newcomer would have difficulty changing what customers have come to expect.

Availability of distributors

Competition also may affect the next influence shown in Figure 11.1 – availability. In many small markets, there are few qualified distributors for products requiring technical knowledge. Most or all of these distributors may have already established agreements with competitors. If a new firm moves into a particular market, it may find that the most desirable distributors are not available. In this case, the marketing manager is faced with the difficult choice of offering a product to a distributor who is already handling a competitive product or finding a distribution firm in a related field and training that distributor to represent the product. In many industry segments in many countries the lack of qualified distribution is the rule rather than the exception.

Influences on channel design and distribution

Culture can have an important effect upon channel design as well. In some countries, an established way of distributing all products has grown up and become the norm. The well known case in Japan, in which many levels of distribution sell to one another before the product reaches the final consumer is a daunting challenge for many non-Japanese marketers. In some markets, distribution firms are owned by manufacturers or close relationships have been established. Changing these culturally-driven distribution patterns can be quite difficult.

Company objectives and resources also have a significant effect upon distribution choices. It should be obvious that the distribution strategy must be in congruence with the marketing strategy, which, in turn, should be in agreement with the overall company objectives and strategies. Equally important will be company resources. Should the firm decide to establish a large network of distributors in over 100 countries, the management of this network will require a large commitment of human resources. Since most distributors need to be trained and motivated by headquarters staff, frequent visits are usually necessary. Because of the travel time required to reach all parts of the globe, it is impossible for a limited staff to properly supervise and motivate a worldwide distribution network in multiple countries. A common problem discovered by the authors during years of consulting work is the over-reliance on electronic communication as a substitute for personal training and motivation. Disappointment with distributor results can usually be traced to under-resourcing selection, training and motivation of distributors.

Distribution strategy will also have an important influence on channel design. A firm must decide whether it requires intensive, selective or exclusive distribution. Intensive distribution means selling through as many outlets as are available and qualified. Selective distribution means choosing a limited number of firms as intermediaries. Exclusive distribution means choosing one intermediary in each market. Products that have few customers, such as nuclear power plants or aircraft engines, are obviously candidates for exclusive distribution. Carefully selected individual firms who can represent the manufacturer both in follow-up service as well as customer training is critical. A firm selling file folders to be used in offices will probably choose intensive distribution, hoping to market the product to as many possible users through as many possible channel types as is practical.

Finally, product characteristics must be a part of the equation. If a firm has decided to market its product as a high-priced, high-service product, this will dictate choosing exclusive or selective distribution through well-financed, prestigious outlets. While a firm which identifies its product as a 'value alternative' using lower prices will probably opt for the 'warehouse' approach. As we have described above, the distribution strategy, such as that for nuclear power plants or aircraft engines, is directly related to the product characteristics as well.

Although directors of marketing hope to see neat looking distribution charts, they often find that their actual distribution patterns are quite messy. Figure 11.2 shows how a manufacturer might distribute its product depending upon the considerations discussed above and shown in Figure 11.1.

Most firms use multiple distribution channels to reach customers in order to deliver the required satisfaction to any particular customer segment. In Figure 11.2, we see a manufacturer selling

FIGURE 11.2

Marketing channels

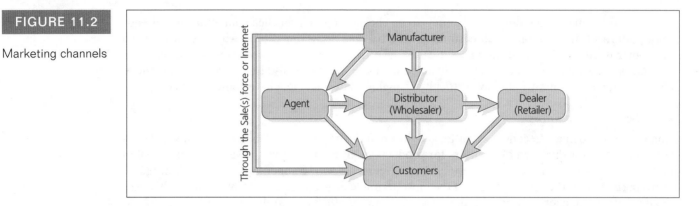

directly, either through its own salesforce or through the Internet to certain customers. These might be the largest or the smallest customers. In addition, the manufacturer is using an agent and while agents as we know do not take title to the product, they may be the main intermediary in a particular market. This manufacturer also uses a distributor (wholesaler) who sells to customers as well as dealers (retailers) who also sell to customers. Also shown is a relationship between the agent and distributor. A manufacturer may choose to have independent sales agents who call on distributors helping with the sale. Any one manufacturer may very well have distribution patterns that look just like those shown in Figure 11.2. Firm management must frequently re-evaluate its choices, changing the distribution patterns to suit the needs of new market segments that it identifies.

Many firms divide their customers into A, B and C-type customers, with the As usually the top 10 per cent by number accounting to up to 50 per cent of the firm's volume. The B-type customers are medium-sized and frequently 25 per cent of customer by number and may account for 25–30 per cent of all sales. The remaining nearly two-thirds of customers in the C category probably account for this smallest percentage of sales and their per-order volume is small. If a firm uses this approach, its distribution alternatives will be clear. The A-types will be served by direct sales from the manufacturer, the B-types through some form of distribution, and the C-types thought the Internet or mail order.

Selecting a distributor

In selecting a distributor, the first step is to use the Partner Profile shown in Chapter 6 in Table 6.9. This can easily be applied to any possible distribution partner to determine whether this partner is the best choice. Unfortunately, choosing intermediaries often is approached under unrealistic deadlines during quick trips to multiple markets. Experience has shown that spending one day in a country and finding a firm through informal discussions over dinner or at a local pub usually results in a poor choice. A marketing executive then finds that the intermediary signed-on in haste is very difficult to remove.

Because many countries have passed legislation steeply in favor of local distributors, the marketing manager should be sure that all distribution partners sign carefully drawn agreements. A list of the most important contract areas which should be included in any agent or distributor agreement is seen in Table 11.2

The type of relationship refers to whether a firm will be taking title to the product or not, in other words, if the distribution partner is an agent or a merchant. The second contract area describes the type of entity the intermediary will be. It is preferable to make agreements with corporations rather than individuals. The latter leaves a firm open to the interpretation that the firm has an employer–employee relationship which is entirely different than that of an arm's length distributor and allows far less protection in the event of disagreement. In the case of taxes, the location of the establishment will determine the tax jurisdiction. It is best to appoint an intermediary with multiple lines so that it does not appear to be a branch of a manufacturing firm. The duration of the agreement should be limited – one to two years – and not indefinite. New agreements should be developed and signed periodically to show that the relationship is being renewed. Next, termination: should the agreement say that an intermediary can be terminated with or without cause as is permitted in the United States,

TABLE 11.2 Agent/distributor agreements	
Key Contract Areas	
Type of Relationship	Terms/Conditions of Sale
Corporation vs Individuals	Facilities and Personnel
Taxes	Inventory
Duration of Agreement	Confidentiality
Termination	Proprietary Information (Trademarks,
Product Sale or Service Agreement	Tradename and Copyright)
Territory/Exclusivity	Records and Communications
Arbitration and Governing Law	Advertising/Promotion
Payment and Compensation	Other Provisions

Source: Fitzpatrick & Zimmerman 1985

this clause will usually be unenforceable in most other countries. The most solid basis for termination will be failure to reach goals. These goals must be established on a periodic basis by agreement of the manufacturer and the intermediary. Should the agreement be terminated, it is important to include in the document how the termination will take place. Important items such as disposition of inventory, return of literature and other materials, ownership of customer lists and so on should be described in this agreement.

The product sale or service agreement identifies what product or service areas the intermediary will be responsible for. Territory refers to the areas where the intermediary is to represent the manufacturer. Sophisticated manufacturers attempt to include in this agreement a retention of rights to distribute the product independently of the distributor. Most distributors will want exclusivity in a particular country. In some cases, this will be the only logical course since a market may be too small to support multiple distributors. However, this course also leaves the manufacturer with no other alternative should the intermediary prove to be inadequate. The next area to include is whether or not disputes will be submitted to arbitration and what jurisdiction will be governing. It is always better to pre-establish an arbitration method in these agreements so that disputes can be settled without going to court. Payment and compensation relates to the way commissions will be calculated for agents and the way payments will be made through distributors. Because of anti-corruption laws, more fully discussed in Chapter 18, it is necessary to establish clear accounting pathways to trace payments.

Other important items listed above include the terms of sale such as ownership of the goods, the facilities and personnel to be applied to the distribution of the particular product line and inventory to be carried. An important clause to include in an agreement is confidentiality and marketers should be sure that confidentiality survives the termination of the agreement. The dealer should be required to acknowledge that the manufacturer retains the rights to all proprietary information. The intermediary should be granted limited use of this intellectual property, especially including trademarks and copyrights. Records and communication should be specified so that the intermediary will know the reporting requirements of the manufacturer. Some manufacturers carefully describe the kinds of advertising and promotion to be used and even retain a right of approval before advertising is placed. Some other provisions may also be necessary in the agreement. The most important one is *Force Majeure* which allows a firm freedom from the provisions of the agreement because of so-called 'Acts of God'. One may also wish to include a section requiring dealers to comply with all local laws.

This listing, while a good starting point, is not complete for every situation and a marketing director developing a distributor or agent agreement must be careful to be sure all clauses required for his or her particular business are included.

International and multinational distribution

Arnold (2000) has identified many problems which surface in international distribution. While his research focused on developing markets, the experience of the authors confirms that the problems identified are often experienced in developed as well as developing countries. The multinational corporations Arnold studied wanted control over their businesses and often used distributors just to get started in a particular area. The managers had the idea that these distributors would be replaced or acquired as the business expanded. However, in many cases a more efficient and economical means of getting to market is through local distributors. These international distributors must be carefully chosen and managed. Based on Arnold, some rules of international distribution are listed in Table 11.3.

As has been mentioned, many firms do not spend enough time choosing distributors. Often, distributors are chosen simply because they make contact with the manufacturer asking for the line. As Arnold (2000) says, 'in fact, the most eager potential distributors may be precisely the wrong people to partner with'. Carefully identifying the needs of the segment and the capabilities required in a particular country will lead a manufacturer to spend the required time to select the best possible candidate. Above all, this is the most important task in distribution management.

Distributors who have key contacts in a country but are unable to develop a market usually are not the best long-term partners. Having said that, it is the author's experience that most distributors will spend only a limited amount of time developing a market. A manufacturer must understand its commitment to market development and cannot rely entirely upon the distributor to 'pioneer' in a new market without significant help.

Although many multinational firms see distributors as simply market entry vehicles, a more effective strategy will be to choose distributors who will become partners. When a large firm shows that it will not partner with the local distributor on a long-term basis, the local distributor management often become defensive and look to short-term gains rather than long-term market development.

As has been mentioned above, a full effort is required to enter a new market. Resources of all kinds, including people, are required to make a distributor successful. Training in selling and technical aspects of the product is usually a minimum and on-site visits to help in real situations are often what make the difference between success and failure. Arnold suggests that some multinationals have taken minority equity stakes in distribution companies. While this increases a multinational's exposure to market downturns and political risk, it also signals a level of commitment to local distributors. It can be a very effective way to gain cooperation and full effort from local intermediaries.

While distributors can implement strategy, adapting it to the local culture, the multinational should maintain control over the marketing strategy. In some cases, employees from the manufacturer should be sent to work in the distributor's location to ensure the implementation is following the strategy.

The need for market and financial data is obvious. Where cooperation has been established, distributors will be more forthcoming with these data. However, should the distributor suspect that the manufacturer is not committed to a long-term relationship, information flow is usually the first aspect of the relationship to dry up.

Some have suggested the setting-up of distributor councils to increase cooperation among national or regional distributors. Based on the experience of the authors, distributor councils should be approached with caution. While they can serve as a vehicle for increasing cooperation, they can also reinforce dissatisfactions among distributors, especially in periods of downturn or where a manufacturer experiences product problems. A less formal approach may achieve the same results. In other words, holding annual or semi-annual meetings with regional or even worldwide distributors (should the number not be unwieldy) can serve as a good vehicle for education and motivation.

TABLE 11.3 Guidelines for successful international distribution

Rules of International Distribution

1 Select distributors – don't let them select you.
2 Find distributors with market development capabilities.
3 Treat distributors as long-term partners.
4 Fully resource the market entry effort.
5 Keep control of marketing strategy.
6 Require detailed market and financial data.

Adapted from: Arnold 2000

Supplier relations are important for any organization, not least because around 50 per cent of the average firm's turnover is channeled back to suppliers of one sort or another (Hakansson 1992). These relationships are dynamic, because they are built up through human contact and human effort. In fact, business is about people – only people buy and sell, hire and fire and make decisions. From the perspective of the buyer, the seller's salesperson actually is (in effect) the selling company. Likewise, from the salesperson's perspective the buyer is the buying company. This means that any sign of dishonesty or even unpleasantness on the part of the individuals concerned will affect the other party's perception of the company as a whole. Since the relationships a firm has are actually interrelated, a bad reputation can spread extremely quickly: salespeople, engineers, customers and others meet each other at forums outside the organization and pass on opinions and information about their own firm and others.

Selecting and motivating distributors

Here is a checklist for selecting and motivating distributors.

1 Ask potential customers to recommend possible distributors. This will help ensure a smooth logistical flow.
2 Determine which distributor fits the company's overall strategy the best. Goals and strategic aspirations of the distributor should be close to those of the company, so that the relationship remains close. For example, a conflict might arise between an aggressive company seeking rapid growth and a distributor which prefers high profit margins at the expense of growth.
3 Visit the distributor regularly. This helps to build the relationship by keeping the company up-to-date with developments in the market and allows the distributor to raise issues. It is probably also advisable to allow the distributor access to staff at all levels in the organization – technical people, administrators and financial managers – as well as marketers, since this will also strengthen the relationship.
4 Visit the overseas customers with the distributor. Provided the distributor or agent has no objection, joint visits to the overseas customers also help to support the distributor and build the relationship. Customers usually welcome the opportunity to have direct contact with the company.
5 Provide training and support. If the distributor's staff can be trained at the company's premises this will make a major difference to the smooth running of the relationship, since the distributor will make useful contacts for informal resolution of minor problems and will develop a better understanding of the corporate culture.

▋ Managing distribution channels

Channels can be led by any of the channel members, whether they are producers, wholesalers, or retailers, provided the member concerned has channel power. This power comes from seven sources (Bitner 1992), as shown in Table 11.4.

Channel cooperation

Channel cooperation is an essential part of the effective functioning of channels. Since each member relies on every other member for the free exchange of goods down the channel, it is in the members' interests to look after each other to some extent. Channel cooperation can be improved in the following ways:

1 The channel members can agree on target markets, so that each member can best direct effort towards meeting the common goal.
2 Define the tasks each member should carry out. This avoids duplication of effort, or giving the final consumer conflicting messages.

TABLE 11.4 Sources of channel power

Economic sources of power	Non-economic sources of power	Other factors
Control of resources. The degree to which the channel member has the power to direct goods, services or finance within the channel.	Reward power. The ability to provide financial benefits, or otherwise favor channel members.	Level of power. This derives from the economic and non-economic sources of power.
Size of company. The bigger the firm compared with other channel members, the greater the overall economic power.	Expert power. This arises when the leader has special expertise which the other channel members need.	Dependency of other channel members.
Referent power emerges when channel members try to emulate the leader.		Willingness to lead. Clearly some firms with potential for channel leadership prefer not to have the responsibility, or are unable to exercise the potential for other reasons.
Legitimate power arises from a superior–subordinate relationship. For example, if a retailer holds a substantial shareholding in a wholesaler, it has legitimate power over the wholesaler.		
Coercive power exists when one channel member has the power to punish another.		

Co-marketing

A further development is co-marketing, which implies a partnership between manufacturers, intermediaries and retailers. This level of cooperation involves pooling of market information and full agreement on strategic issues (Marx 1995).

Channel conflict arises because each member wants to maximize its own profits or power. Conflicts also arise because of frustrated expectations; each member expects the other members to act in particular ways and sometimes these expectations are unfulfilled. For example, a retailer may expect a wholesaler to maintain large enough stocks to cover an unexpected rise in demand for a given product, whereas the wholesaler may expect the manufacturers to be able to increase production rapidly to cover such eventualities.

Channel management techniques

Channel management can be carried out by cooperation and negotiation (often with one member leading the discussions) or it can be carried out by the most powerful member laying down rules which weaker members have to follow. Table 11.5 shows some of the methods which can be used to control channels.

TABLE 11.5 Channel management techniques

Technique	Explanation	Legal position
Refusal to Deal	One member refuses to do business with one or more other members; for example, hairdressing wholesalers sometimes refuse to supply mobile hairdressers, on the grounds that this is unfair competition for salons.	In most countries suppliers do not have to supply anybody they don't wish to deal with. However, grounds may exist for a lawsuit if the refusal to deal is a punishment for not going along with an anti-competitive ruling by a supplier, or is an attempt to prevent the channel member from dealing with a third party with whom the manufacturer is in dispute.
Tying Contracts	The supplier (sometimes a franchiser) demands that the channel member carries other products as well as the main one. If the franchiser insists that all the products are carried, this is called full-line forcing.	Most of these contracts are illegal in the UK, but are accepted if the supplier alone can supply goods of a given quality, or if the purchaser is free to carry competing products as well. Sometimes they are accepted when a company has just entered the market.
Exclusive Dealing	A manufacturer might prevent a wholesaler from carrying competitors' products, or a retailer might insist that no other retailer be supplied with the same products. This is often used by retailers to ensure that their 'price guarantees' can be honored – obviously consumers will not be able to find the same product at a lower price locally if the retailer has prevented the manufacturer from supplying anybody else.	Usually these are legal provided they don't result in a monopoly position in a local area; in other words, provided the consumer has access to similar products, there will not be a problem.
Restricted Sales Territories	Intermediaries are prevented from selling outside a given area. The intermediaries are often in favor of this idea, because it prevents competition within their own area.	Courts have conflicting views about this practice. On the one hand, these deals can help weaker distributors and can also increase competition where local dealers carry different brands; on the other hand, there is clearly a restraint of trade involved.

Most attempts to control distribution by the use of power are likely to be looked on unfavorably by the courts, but of course the abuse of power would have to be fairly extreme before a channel member would be likely to sue.

Sometimes the simplest way to control a distribution channel is to buy-out the channel members. Buying-out members across a given level (for example, a wholesaler buying-out other wholesalers in order to build a national network) is called horizontal integration. Buying-out members above or below in the distribution chain (for example a retailer buying-out a wholesaler) is vertical integration. An example of extreme vertical integration is the major oil companies, which extract crude oil, refine it, ship it, and ultimately sell it retail through petrol stations. At the extremes, this type of integration may attract the attention of government monopoly regulation agencies, since the integration may cause a restriction of competition.

Presumably vertical integration greatly increases the efficiency of the supply-chain. After all, if each stage of the supply-chain is operated by a separate firm, with its own strategies and agendas, conflict is inevitable.

So why not run everything this way? Why don't monopolies regulators encourage vertical distribution rather than investigating it and punishing it? If we argue that a vertically-integrated industry concentrates too much power in a few hands, is it really any different from the kind of integration that happens with a well-run supply-chain? We ban oligopolistic collusion – why not ban the very open, bare-faced collusion that happens between members of a supply-chain?

Producers need to ensure that the distributors of their products are of the right type. The image of a distribution agent can damage (or enhance) the image of the products sold (and vice-versa). Producers need not necessarily sell through the most prestigious distributor and in fact this might be counter-productive for many cheap, everyday items such as office stationery or nuts and bolts. Likewise a prestigious product should not be sold through a downmarket distributor.

Distribution methods in the global markets

This is particularly important in global markets, where the producing company may not be familiar with the distribution methods in the target country. For example, manufacturers' agents in Germany tend to be highly-professional and committed and expect the same level of commitment from the firms they represent: they will expect regular visits from the selling company, marketing support, and above all reliability of delivery. In most cases a German agent will make a thorough investigation of the foreign company before accepting the task of selling its products. In other countries (notably the UK) manufacturers' agents are rarely as assiduous in checking out the client company – they are much more likely to take on the product, see if it sells and if it fails to sell the agent will simply drop it from the range. For the German agent, the company represented is integral to the agent's reputation: for the UK agent, the relationship is not regarded as being as direct.

■ Efficient customer response

Efficient customer response seeks to integrate the activities of manufacturers and distributors using computer technology; the expected result is a more responsive stocking system for the distributor, which in turn benefits the manufacturer. Some of the features of ECR are as follows;

1 *Continuous replenishment*: under which the supplier plans production using data generated by the distribution network.

2 *Cross-docking*: attempts to coordinate the arrival of suppliers' and retailers' trucks at the distribution centers so that goods move from one truck to the other without going into stock. Although transport efficiency falls because a supermarket truck collecting (say) greengrocery might have to wait for several suppliers' trucks to arrive, the overall speed of delivery of products improves, which can be crucial when dealing with fresh foods.

3 *Roll-cage sequencing*: allows storage of products by category at the factory; although this adds to the labor time at the factory, it greatly reduces labor time at the distributor or warehouse.

The main problem with ECR is that it relies on complete cooperation between members of the distribution chain. In any channel of distribution where the power base is unequal, this is less likely to happen; despite the overall savings for the channel as a whole, self-interest on the part of channel members may lead to less than perfect cooperation.

Some manufacturers try to use several different channels in order to distribute products (Perry 1989). This can be helpful in meeting different market segments, but has the major drawback that the various distributors may resent the existence of the others and may feel that their own positions are being undermined. Care needs to be taken to ensure that the segments really are clearly defined and overlap is kept to a minimum.

Having said that, many firms manage to operate successfully through multiple distribution channels for different segments: for example, 3M have a total of five separate channels just for audio-visual equipment. In each case the distribution channel addresses a specific customer group, so that the distribution network does not compete with itself even though they all carry the same product lines.

Using distribution networks strategically will always involve consideration of the strategies of the distributors themselves. These may conflict with the strategy of the supplying firm: harmonizing these strategic differences and generating synergies from them, is a challenge for most firms.

SUMMARY

Distribution policy is a major contributor to strategy in B2B marketing. The purpose of the exercise is to ensure that goods arrive in the right condition, at the right time and in the right place: good distribution makes it easy for potential customers to buy.

The key points from this chapter are:

- Distributors provide a wide range of services to both customers and to suppliers. These services have to be provided by somebody.

- Distribution can be a critical success factor in B2B markets.

- Distribution might be intensive, selective or exclusive: each has its advantages in specific markets.

- Distributors should be treated as partners.

- Conflict within distribution networks is inevitable, since the firms involved all have separate agendas.

- Channel management is carried out by cooperation and negotiation.

- Cutting out the middlemen is likely to increase costs and reduce efficiency of the network as a whole.

REVIEW QUESTIONS

1 How might a company evaluate a relationship with a distributor?

2 What types of conflict are most likely in distribution networks?

3 What are the main ways of controlling distributors?

4 How might a distributor control the distribution network?

5 Negotiation implies power. What power might a distributor have when dealing with a supplier?

Tyron Automotive Group Ltd., manufactures, distributes and services a comprehensive range of safety systems for vehicle tires. The main customers for the systems are police forces, security companies, emergency services, armies, trucking companies and even the general public via a system of distributors. The products allow the vehicle to continue to be driven even if the tires burst or are shot out.

Founded in 1979, Tyron developed, in conjunction with Avon Tyres, the first commercially available products for steel drop center rims as a direct result of a request from the UK's Ministry of Defence to overcome the immobilization of vehicles by having the tires shot out or deflated by running over booby-traps. These first 'well filler' bands were sold throughout the world, primarily to military, government and security organizations. The systems vary from an economical 'run-flat' system which allows the vehicle to continue for a short distance so that the driver does not lose control in the event of a blowout, through to military systems which allow the vehicle to be driven for 50km or more on flat tires. The latest version of the Tyron product can cope with a blowout at 150 mph and is expected to be a big seller to police forces.

The company was founded in 1979, and in 1984 it allowed its patented products to be manufactured under license. This gave the company a worldwide presence, but in late 1990 these licensing agreements ran out, leaving Tyron with a major gap in its marketing program. From 1991 to 1993 the company made considerable efforts to develop new products, working closely with tire, wheel and vehicle manufacturers, and investing substantial sums of money in new plant and machinery to produce the improved products. The difficulty the company faced was in finding suitable distribution for the products, especially in foreign markets.

The company salesforce eventually recruited more than 1,000 distributors throughout England, Wales and Scotland: typical distributors are tire fitting companies, caravan suppliers, automotive parts suppliers and garages. These are mainly small firms, but they ensure a very wide distribution throughout the mainland UK: there is even one distributor in Northern Ireland. These distributors fit the systems to existing customers' vehicles.

For international sales, the company eventually contacted Trade Partners UK, through its local chamber of commerce. Trade Partners UK (TPUK) is a Government organization set up to help small firms to export. TPUK provided training for Tyron's salesforce and also arranged for the company's managing director, Tony Glazebrook, to attend two trade fairs – Meplex in Dubai, and Intersec. The second of these trade fairs was followed up by a visit to Australia and New Zealand under the guidance of TPUK's export experts, the trade attachés of the British embassies in those countries.

As a result of these initiatives, Tyron appointed several new distributors in the Middle East, resulting in immediate orders worth over £110,000 each. This is a substantial sum for a firm employing only 10 people. The company went on to appoint distributors in France, Benelux, Australia, Trinidad and Tobago, Germany, the USA, Indonesia, Singapore, Sweden, and Oman. These lead distributors are expected in turn to appoint sub-distributors within their own regions and countries (although the USA distributor has yet to leave California). Recruiting sub-distributors is a slow process and in some cases the national distributors have made little progress, but in the long run the company expects substantial growth from these foreign distributors.

Tyron now expects 70 per cent of its total sales to come from exports in 2003/04 and is also pushing ahead with new products. By approaching caravan and vehicle manufacturers the company is hoping to have its products fitted as original equipment. Tyron tends to be a product-oriented company, so the help given by TPUK has proved invaluable: managing director Tony Glazebrook said, 'Getting help from Trade Partners is the best business decision I ever made'.

Questions

1 Tyron are relying heavily on distributors. What other methods might be appropriate?

2 What are the advantages for Tyron of using overseas distributors rather than setting up a subsidiary in the target country?

3 How might Tyron's dealers respond to the news that the company is seeking to have the systems fitted as original equipment?

4 For a major market such as the USA, how might Tyron speed up the process of acquiring distributors?

5 What other approaches might Tyron have for dealing in the USA?

REFERENCES

Arnold, D. (2000) 'Seven Rules of International Distribution', *Harvard Business Review*, 28: 7: Nov-Dec: 131–137.

Bitner, M. J. (1992) 'Servicescapes: the impact of physical surroundings on customers and employees', *Journal of Marketing*, April: 57–71.

Czinkota, M. R. and Ronkainen, I. A. (2004) *International Marketing* 7th ed., Mason, Ohio: Thomson-Southwestern.

Fitzpatrick, P. B. and Zimmerman, A. S. (1985) *'Essentials of Export Marketing'*, New York: AMACOM.

Hakansson, H. and Gadde, L-E. (1992) *Professional Purchasing*, London, Routledge.

Marx, W. (1995) 'The co-marketing revolution', *Industry Week*, 2 October: 77–79.

Perry, D. (1989) 'How You'll Manage your 1990's Distribution Portfolio', *Business Marketing*, June.

12

BUSINESS-TO-BUSINESS MARKETING COMMUNICATIONS

Learning objectives
After reading this chapter, you should be able to:

- Describe communications theory
- Describe the main problems in planning a campaign
- Explain how attitude-change models can be used in planning a campaign
- Explain the difference between push and pull strategies
- Explain the use of models in B2B communications

▋ Introduction

This chapter is about ways of communicating in B2B markets. The major difference between B2B and consumer marketing communications is the lack of mass media for businesses. Consumer marketing communications are heavily dominated by television, radio and press advertising, but B2B advertising is less likely to use these media due to the much smaller number of buyers involved.

Business-to-business versus consumer communications

Because B2B markets are smaller than consumer markets, some restrictions will apply. Table 12.1 shows the main differences.

Of course, B2B and consumer advertising also have a great deal in common. Advertising aims to reach people with its message and change its target market in some way – changing attitudes or behavior, increasing level of knowledge, or whatever. Ultimately advertisers hope to change behavior, because they hope to influence the audience to buy the products on offer. Other marketing communications are intended to have a similar effect.

There is a greater emphasis on personal selling in B2B markets than there is in consumer markets, largely due to the larger order values and the smaller numbers of buyers in each market segment. Because the buyers and sellers are much more likely to establish a long-term relationship in a B2B environment, there is also a greater emphasis on the personal contact which selling entails.

Communications theories

Communications theory has been dominated by the Schramm or conduit model of communications (see Figure 12.1), a model which is familiar to most students of communication.

In this model, the sender of a message first needs to code the message in order to send it. The code will need to be something the receiver can understand, for example it must be in a language the receiver knows. There must be a medium for the message to travel through (for example television or print) and the recipient must be able to decode the message. Interference and noise will affect the way the message is transmitted and interpreted (Schramm 1948, 1971).

The problem with this model is that it implies that communication is something that is done to people, rather than a cooperative process. A more modern view of communication is that it is a co-construction of meaning in which the person receiving the message interprets it in the light of previous experience. In this model, communication is an active process on both sides: the input from the receiver is at least as great as that from the transmitter and the message is likely to be interpreted in many different ways by each different receiver.

TABLE 12.1 Differences between B2B and consumer communications

Consumer markets	B2B markets
Availability of mass media	Mass media of little use
Greater use of emotional appeals	More rational approach used
Greater tendency on the part of consumers to avoid the message	Greater preparedness to seek out information
Selective retention means that communications are quickly forgotten	Communications are frequently stored for future reference – brochures advertisements and leaflets may be filed away
Copy is almost always short and punchy usually just ten or a dozen words	Copy is frequently long even a thousand words or more
Communication is aimed at individuals who are in most cases solely responsible for purchasing decisions	Communication is aimed at groups who in most cases need to agree on purchasing decisions
Characterized by mass media reaching broad market segments	Characterized by industry-specific media widely read by DMU members

FIGURE 12.1

Conduit model of communications

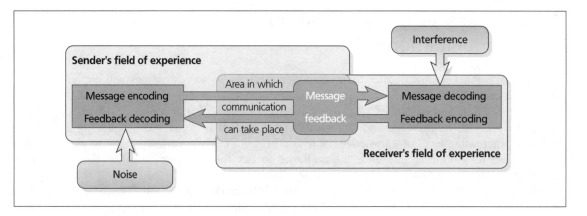

The model implies that communication creates a pool of meaning between the parties. Each person puts something into the pool, each person takes something out and the pool changes slightly each time (see Figure 12.2).

To stretch the analogy further, when either party puts something into the pool the new input mixes with everything that is already in the pool. What the other party draws from the pool therefore includes some of what already existed. Provided the new material is not wildly at odds with what is already in the pool, the shared meaning will remain close. If the new material is very different from that which already exists between the parties, the person who put the material in may have to add a lot more before the meaning becomes clear.

This model of communications is particularly relevant to personal selling. The personal selling function is, by its nature, a dialogue in which the seller may control the process, but the bulk of the communication comes from the buyer. Salespeople who lose sight of this end up doing most of the talking and lose the sale.

The model also explains another phenomenon in communication, which is that some communications are actively sought out by customers, whereas others are not (Blythe 2000). Unsought communications are those which the seller sends out in the optimistic hope that a buyer will respond: display advertising, TV advertising, billboards and so forth. Sought communications are those which a buyer specifically looks for: classified advertising, exhibitions, brochures and even sales pitches. It is important to distinguish between the two, since the approach needs to be very different – an unsought communication needs to be persuasive and attention grabbing, whereas sought communication should be informative and factual, because the buyer is already persuaded to a large extent.

Considered in terms of the decision-making process (see Chapter 2), buyers who are at the need-identification stage may be approached using unsought communication. A business publication

FIGURE 12.2

Pool of meaning

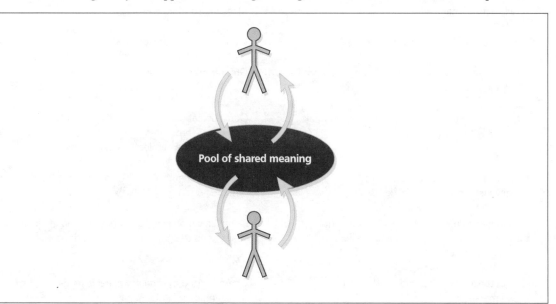

advertisement, suitably placed, may make companies realize that they have a problem that had not previously been identified. For example, in the wake of the September 11th attacks on New York, British Airways ran a highly-successful campaign on UK television aimed at encouraging business travelers back onto BA North Atlantic services. The advertisements contrasted one company pitching for business by sending a beautifully-produced glossy brochure to its New York customer, with another company whose executive arrives in person. The executive making the personal visit is quickly on first-name terms with the customer, and is greeted as a friend: the brochure is left on the table. The executives who sent the brochure, meanwhile, are congratulating themselves because, in the course of a telephone call, the New York customer said that he 'liked the spreadsheets'.

This advertisement was unusual in several respects. Firstly, it appeared on television, which is rare for B2B advertising. Secondly, it was aimed at a general problem for any business, which is the failure to attach enough importance to personal contacts. Thirdly, the product itself is generic – airplane rides across the Atlantic are provided by a very large number of airlines, any of whom might benefit from BA's advertising, since all it did was flag up the problem. Later BA advertising became much more brand-specific, delineating the advantages of using BA rather than its rivals.

Buyers who are at the information-search stage may use display advertising because they will be sensitized to look out for it, but will rapidly move towards seeking out communications such as brochures or sales presentations in order to obtain hard facts on which to base decisions. At this point an emotive sales pitch is likely to be of a lot less interest than a factual presentation.

Signs and meaning

A sign is anything that stands for something (its object) to somebody (its interpreter) in some respect (its context) (Pierce 1986). Signs fall into three categories:

- icon
- index
- symbol.

Icon

An icon is a sign that looks like the object, or represents it visually in a way that most people would relate to. For example, as shown in Figure 12.3, an agricultural machinery manufacturer might use a stylized picture of a tractor as a symbol or might use a picture of a head of wheat.

Index

An index is a sign that relates to the object by a causal connection. A man dressed in a checked shirt wearing a hard hat represents construction or possibly lumberjacking. Most people are familiar with the image of a manual worker.

FIGURE 12.3

Agricultural icons

Symbol

A symbol is an artificial sign which has been created for the purpose of conveying meaning. The intertwined arrows used to indicate recycled or recyclable materials are familiar to most people: they convey an impression of greenness or environmental friendliness. Likewise many global companies use symbols to identify their brands. For example, the diamond logo of Hong Kong and Shanghai Banking Corporation is familiar worldwide.

Semiotics

The study of signs and their meaning is called semiotics. The spoken language is the prime example of a sign system, but semiotics is not limited to language. Semiotics pays attention to the recipient of the message because meaning can only be derived socially: it is an interaction between the recipient and the text. In the first instance, texts are created by reworking signs, codes and symbols within the sign system in order to generate myths, connotations and meanings. The social process involved should create pleasure as well as cognitive activities.

For example, a trade fair uses the sign systems of the spoken word, the written word, the 'market stall' format and the besuited stand personnel to generate its meaning. The visitor then filters the information and adds it to their pre-existing attitudes to create a meaning.

Syntactics

Syntactics is about the structure of communications. Symbols and signs change their meaning according to the syntax: for example, a picture of a tiger might symbolize danger, aggression, endangered species, or the mysterious Orient according to the context of the communication.

Semantics

Semantics is concerned with the ways in which words relate to the external reality to which they refer. Semantics is not actually about the study of meaning, although it is often interpreted this way: it is only really concerned with the appropriateness of the words themselves.

In fact, communication is carried out in many other ways than simply the words themselves. Only around 30 per cent of communication uses words: companies communicate by using pictures, non-verbal sounds (e.g. the Intel four-note jingle), smell, touch, numbers, artifacts, time and kinetics. Salespeople know the value of body language and non-verbal communication: facial expressions and gesture are widely used to create meaning in advertising. Silent communication may take place through any of the following media;

1 *Numbers*. Brand names frequently use numbers to imply that the brand is the latest in a long series. Boeing use this method to identify their aircraft models.
2 *Space*. Images of people standing close together imply that they have a close relationship: some companies have placed their logos in close juxtaposition to indicate that they have a close relationship.
3 *Artifacts*. Small gifts and free samples convey a sense of obligation to the recipient.
4 *Time*. Images of a person in a hurry might convey an image of success and energy to Northern Europeans or Americans, but might convey arrogance, or someone who has no time for anyone else to an African audience.
5 *Kinetics*. Gesticulating, facial expressions and body language all convey meaning.

Meaning

Meaning is conveyed not just by words, but by the way the words are used and by the peripheral cues that surround them. Much human communication is made for effect, rather than as a literal statement: people become adept at reading between the lines.

The main problem with silent languages is that they are not culturally universal. Body language and gesture does not transfer well to other cultures, even when the cultures are relatively close. Some well-known examples are the two-finger sign used in the UK, which means nothing to people elsewhere in Europe apart from France: the circle of forefinger and thumb which means 'OK' in the US but is a rude gesture in Brazil, as is showing the soles of the feet in Thailand.

More subtly, Japanese people tend to show their emotions less in public than Americans, Indians tend to regard shabby clothes as denoting poverty whereas Northern Europeans associate this with freedom and independence and numbers which are considered lucky in some cultures are considered unlucky in others (Costa and Pavia 1992). Unfortunately, these cultural differences often go unrecognized because people tend to regard body language and so forth as universal. While a foreigner might easily be forgiven for an error in speaking the language (in fact such errors might even be seen as charming), the same courtesy does not usually extend to errors of body language or behavior.

The problem of misunderstanding arises because of ethnocentrism, which is the belief that one's own culture is the 'right' one and everyone else's is a poor copy. Ethnocentrism is one of the few features of human behavior that belongs to all cultures (Shimp and Sharma 1987). In practice marketing communications can be applied worldwide only with great care.

Attitude and attitude change

Attitude is a learned tendency to respond in a consistent way to an attitudinal object. Attitudes are made up of three components:

- cognition – which is what is consciously known of and thought about the attitudinal object
- affect – which is what is felt emotionally about the attitudinal object
- conation – which is the intended behavior towards the attitudinal object.

Provided these three components are in balance the attitude is stable and is therefore unlikely to change much. For example, a buyer might say, 'I like Corus Steel. They are nice people to deal with, the products are always up to specification and I think we'll probably always buy from them rather than from anyone else'. The first part of this statement is affective – 'I like them, they are nice people', the second part is cognitive – 'the products are always up to specification' and the third part is conative – 'we'll probably always buy from them'. Note that conation is only *intended* behavior – other factors may intervene to prevent the behavior being carried out.

Because attitudes tend to be stable, the first essential for attitude change is to destabilize the attitude. This means changing one or more elements of the attitude.

The cognitive element of attitude comes about because the individual develops salient beliefs about the company and its products. Salient beliefs are those which are the most important to the buyer and which relate to the products concerned. For example, a buyer may believe that a company is 100 per cent reliable on its delivery times and because this is important to the buyer it will be a salient belief. The buyer may also believe that the same company provides very good working conditions for its staff, but may not care about this particularly and therefore the belief is not salient. If the company subsequently becomes unreliable, the salient belief will change and thus the attitude will change: if the company behaves badly towards its staff, this will not affect the buyer's attitude.

Changing attitudes

There are three ways to change attitudes, as follows:

1 Add a new salient belief – For example, the BA advertisement mentioned earlier tried to add the belief that a personal contact is worth far more than even the glossiest brochure.

2 Change the strength of a salient belief – If the belief is a negative one, it can be discounted or played down. If it is a positive one, it can be given greater importance. For example, a buyer may believe that a firm is reliable and this may be important, but a set of statistics showing that the firm is 99.7 per cent reliable will strengthen the belief by providing factual evidence.

3 Change the evaluation of an existing belief – The importance of an existing belief can be strengthened. Using the reliability example, a buyer may accept that the firm is reliable, but has not realized that this in turn means that the buying firm's production has never been halted due to a failure on the part of the supplier – unlike other suppliers whose unreliability has resulted in large losses of production. This type of argument moves reliability much higher in the buyer's perception.

Changing a salient belief

Changing a salient belief is not always about factual presentations aimed at cognition. Changes in salience can also come about through emotive appeals. For example, in the BA advertisement mentioned earlier, the executive who traveled to New York appeared smart, confident, young, organized and generally admirable. The group who did not travel were huddled round a table in a poorly-lit room, appeared disorganized, unattractively dressed, overweight, and lacking in confidence. This was clearly intended as an emotional appeal, implying that all the sensible people use British Airways. This type of association would help in some ways to overcome the problem of promoting travel generally rather than the BA brand (there is more on modeling later in the chapter).

Obviously new information does not always change attitudes. As the inconsistency between the existing attitude and evidence, brought about by reality, increases, there will come a point where the individual buyer needs to re-evaluate the attitude and go through some kind of mental readjustment to restore stability. This can come about through three main mechanisms:

1 Stimulus rejection – The individual discounts the new information or rejects it entirely. This can easily come about if the new information is presented by an incompetent sales person who manages to come across as unreliable.

2 Attitude splitting – This involves only accepting that part of the new information which does not cause an inconsistency. The individual might accept that the new information is true, but that the firm's own circumstances are exceptional.

3 Accommodate the new attitude – Essentially this means accepting the new attitude in its entirety.

Elements of attitude

The three elements of attitude are so closely linked that a change in one is likely to lead to a change in both the others (Rosenberg 1960). Attitudes can basically be changed via two routes (Petty and Caccioppo 1983). The first route (the central route) involves an appeal to the rational, cognitive element of attitude. This generally will be more prevalent in business marketing than in consumer marketing (see Chapter 2). The second route is the peripheral route, which involves an appeal to the affective element, usually by associating the brand with another attitudinal object. For example, B2B marketers often refer to their products as the Rolls Royce of the product category, in order to tap into buyers' perceptions of the quality and reliability of Rolls Royce (or Cadillac for example). Presumably younger marketers might begin tapping into the reputation of BMW, Lexus or Mercedes. In the BA example, the peripheral route is used by associating the brand with the smart looking individual who is using it. No-one would believe that flying with BA will make someone more confident, better dressed and 30 pounds lighter, but the emotional association is clearly drawn. Because of the interdependence of the elements of attitude the peripheral route is effective in changing attitudes.

Obviously new information may conflict with the information the buyer already holds. Cognitive dissonance theory states that if an individual holds two conflicting cognitions, he or she will experience discomfort and will try to resolve the dissonance either by changing one or other of the views, or by introducing a third viewpoint which will reconcile the differences (Festinger 1957).

The most interesting aspect of dissonance theory is that attitudes can apparently be changed more easily by offering low rewards than by offering high ones. Festinger and Carlsmith (1959) induced students to lie to each other by telling them it was part of a psychological experiment and offering them payment varying from US$1 to US$20. The students who were offered the lower amount actually began to believe the lie, whereas those offered the higher amount tended not to. The higher-paid students were able to justify lying on the basis that they were receiving a substantial reward (at 1959 prices). The lesser-paid students had no such external justification and therefore had to resolve the dissonance by believing the lie themselves.

The reason for the power of cognitive dissonance is that the arousal of dissonance always contains personal involvement. Therefore, the reduction of dissonance always involves some form of self-justification (Aronson *et al.* 1974). Self-justification is necessary because the individual usually feels that the dissonance has arisen as a result of an action or thought which is immoral or stupid, or both. In the marketing context, cognitive dissonance may reveal itself as post-purchase dissonance. Here, the buyer of the product may find that information previously gathered about the product is inaccurate – the cognition based on the pre-purchase information-search conflicts with the direct experience of using the product. In these circumstances the buyer can take one of four general approaches to reducing the dissonance:

1 Ignore the dissonant information and look for positive (consonant) information about the product. This means that it is important for salespeople to call back on customers after the order has been delivered in order to check that all is well. If the customer is experiencing post-purchase dissonance, this is an opportunity to provide reassuring information.

2 Distort the dissonant information, perhaps by considering the source of the information as unreliable.

3 Play down the importance of the issue. Buyers may decide that the particular aspect of the product which causes the problem is really not very important after all.

4 Change the behavior or the situation. From the marketer's viewpoint, this can be the most dangerous, since the buyer may change behavior by placing future orders elsewhere.

In most cases, post-purchase dissonance can be eliminated entirely by intelligent use of sales-people. In extreme cases, buyers may take action against the vendor. These responses fall into three categories (Singh 1988):

● voice responses – complaints to the supplier

● private responses – complaints to colleagues, business contacts and even family

● third-party responses – complaints through trade associations or litigation.

Of the three, the most damaging is likely to be private responses, because these damage corporate reputation without the supplier having the opportunity to put their side of the case. The least damaging is a voiced response, so it may be advisable for companies to encourage customers to complain if anything is even remotely wrong with the products (see Chapter 2).

▊ Developing the marketing communications program

In order to devise a marketing communications program which will meet the needs of the firm, the steps shown in Figure 12.4 should be followed. Firstly, as can be seen from the figure, marketing communications objectives must be completely congruent with the overall corporate objectives and the

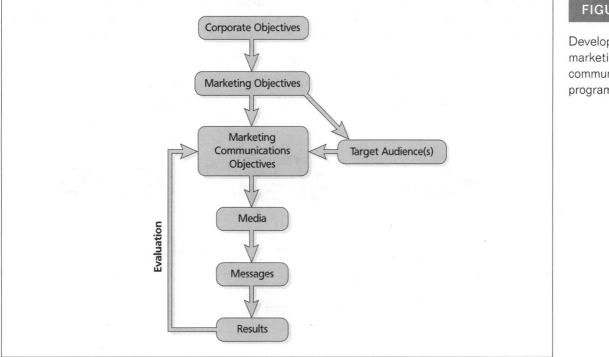

FIGURE 12.4

Developing the marketing communications program

marketing objectives of the firm. Some managers make the error of stating marketing communications objectives in imprecise terms. For example, some have offered objectives such as 'help the salesforce increase market share' or 'find new distributors in the EU'. A marketing communications manager who offers these kinds of objectives will be at a disadvantage once the budget is spent, because it will be unclear whether objectives have been met. The authors strongly feel that marketing communications objectives should be measurable. Examples are: 'increase market share for high-powered semiconductors to 10 per cent in the transportation market segment' or 'develop 10 new distributors in the EU for financial software products'.

Target audiences and marketing communications objectives are rarely established simultaneously. In order for the objectives to be set, the audiences must be identified. Once the objectives and the audiences have been established, the proper media must be chosen. In business marketing, media may be electronic but is more often print (either business or trade publications), exhibitions, brochures or mailings. A very important media outlet will be the firm's website. Next, messages must be established. While business marketing communications focuses on transmitting more fact than emotion, well-turned, interesting phrases will always attract more attention than simple declarative statements. Therefore, as much creativity must be applied to business marketing communications as is applied to consumer marketing communications.

Once the messages have been established and placements made, results must be measured. If the objectives have been set as has been described above, the manager will be able to compare the results with the objectives, evaluate any shortfalls and change the objectives, audiences, media or messages in order to improve results. Approaching business marketing communications in this way makes the effort an investment rather than simply an expense.

Marketing communications consists of advertising, public relations, sales promotion and personal selling. How the effort is divided between these tools relates to the budget available. As can be seen in Figure 12.5, other important factors also have an effect upon the mix of tools to be used.

An important area is media and/or services availability and cost. While a firm might feel comfortable placing advertisements in a trade publication in large markets such as the United States or the EU, it may find that no such publication exists in a particular foreign market. For instance, while there may be a publication focusing on hospital waste disposal in the large markets, it would be unusual to find such a publication in Swedish or Danish. Also to be considered are services availability and cost. For example, a firm might be comfortable with rapid public relations help or the ability to hire a firm to make videos. In Nigeria, firms like this might be far less available. The cost of these media or services may also be quite prohibitive where there is little competition in smaller markets.

A second factor determining the marketing communications mix is channel preferences. Distributors and agents often have strong opinions about how communications should be conducted. In some cases, these individuals wish to review and rewrite advertising messages. While they often have technical knowledge, many are not capable of clear communications using the written word.

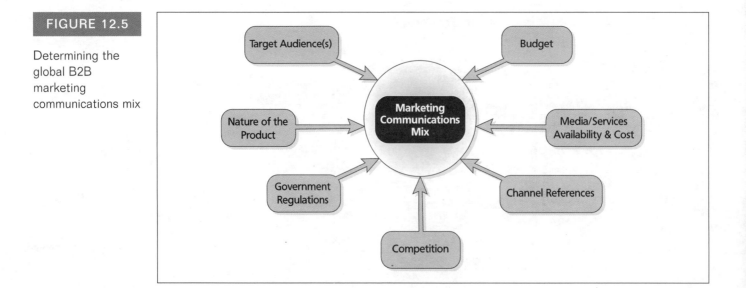

FIGURE 12.5

Determining the global B2B marketing communications mix

Nevertheless, a prudent manager will take into account the opinions of agents and distributors in local markets. A third determining factor is competition. Should a major competitor advertise heavily in a particular journal or establish a major presence at a particular trade exposition, a marketing manager may be forced to match that competitor. Government regulations have some effect upon communications, although this is more prevalent in the consumer area. In some countries, direct comparisons between products are not permitted and certain kinds of promotions are not allowed. The marketing manager must be acutely aware of these regulations so as not to violate one of them. The next influence is the nature of the product itself. Some products are easily explained in print media while others need direct demonstration either at a trade fair or through the salesforce. Using inappropriate media is simply a waste of expenditure.

Target audiences are not the same as target segments. Segments are those to who the firm will sell. But target audiences also include those who influence the purchase. For instance, a firm may have decided its target segment for computer access flooring products is managers in large multinational corporations. However, the firm may also find that independent consultants, whether for interiors, security or computer design may be equally important in making the buying decision. In other words, these are influencers in the buying center. These consultants must be included as target audience members, even if they are not identified as part of the segment design. The target audience is obviously of critical importance. Should a particular target audience in a particular market seem to gather all its information from one source, a marketing manager would be wise to place heavy emphasis on that source in the communications budget. Determining the preferences of target audiences is often somewhat difficult but can be accomplished through primary research.

The firm may also face some other obstacles in its global communications program. Firstly, language can have a major effect upon the size and shape of print ads and catalogs. English is an economical language which takes up less space on a page than most others. Should the firm choose to develop television commercials, no on-screen spokesman should be used. Adequate time must also be allowed for translation and insertion of 'voice-over material' with no spokesman on-screen.

Advertising

Advertising is a non-personal communication inserted in a medium. This means that it is not personal selling, or word-of-mouth communication, or messages on T-shirts. It is characterized by its impersonal quality and also by its one-way approach: it is not interactive except in a very limited way.

Business advertising is aimed at organizations rather than at individuals. As we have seen, though, organizations do not make purchasing decisions: people do. Business advertising therefore needs to appeal to a wide spectrum of people, each with differing personalities and attitudes and most especially, each with a different role within the organization. This means that any advertising may need to have a wide appeal to reach people operating to different agendas. Organizational buyers rarely buy goods and services through advertising alone (Plank and Fernandez 1984) so advertising generally acts as a support mechanism rather than a primary means of communication.

If the cost of advertising is calculated on the basis of the cost of campaign divided by the number of people it reaches, it is very much cheaper than any other communication method, with the possible exceptions of PR and word-of-mouth. On the other hand, it is considerably less effective than, for example, personal selling. Since each communications medium has its particular strengths and weaknesses, it is important to integrate the marketing communications so as to build on the strengths of each. The sales manager who fails to realize that advertising is essential to support the sales team, and the advertising manager who fails to realize that advertising cannot do everything, will each be heading for disaster. Yet often these two managers might be in conflict as they fight for budgets. There is more on this later in the chapter.

Advertising has the following roles in business-to-business marketing:

1 To create a favorable climate for personal selling – Salespeople whose companies advertise widely, rarely have a problem with making appointments: a prime example of this is IBM. Their salespeople can arrive at a firm without an appointment and still be shown the way to the IT manager's office: they can safely say that 'Nobody ever got fired for buying from IBM'. In fact, McGraw-Hill magazines division ran a highly successful press advertisement which showed a grumpy looking buyer saying 'I don't know who you are. I don't know your

company. I don't know your company's products. I don't know what your company stands for. I don't know your company's customers. I don't know your company's record. I don't know your company's reputation. Now – what was it you wanted to sell me?' It is easy to imagine the discomfort of a salesperson faced with this situation.

2 To reach inaccessible buying influences – Some of the members of the buying unit are inaccessible to salespeople (see Chapter 2). In some cases the salesperson may never meet the final decision-maker (see Chapter 13). One estimate states that salespeople may only reach an average of three out of ten buying influences that should be reached (*Sales and Marketing Management* 1984). These people may, however, read the business press and may well have formed an opinion about the company and its products. Clearly advertising can help the process of establishing the brand in the minds of people who have little or no contact with salespeople.

3 To reach unknown buying influences – In many cases it is impossible to know who are the influencers in the buying decision. The managing director's golf partner might be a stronger influence than the chief engineer, but the salesperson might be concentrating attention on the engineer. Again, the golf partner may well become aware of the company and its products through the firm's advertising activities.

4 To generate leads for salespeople – Particularly in the case of sought after communications the buyer may well contact the company for more information as a result of seeing an advertisement. These leads need to be qualified as serious leads, not merely casual enquiries. The advantage of these leads is that the salesperson can spend more time on visiting live prospects and less time on cold-calling or other lead-generating devices.

5 To supplement field sales communications – Salespeople usually cannot call on their customers as often as they would like. In many cases, advertising is able to keep the company and its products fresh in the minds of buyers in between calls from salespeople.

6 To inform channel intermediaries – Both present and prospective channel intermediaries can be stimulated by advertising. These advertisements might be used to promote new products or to remind the distributors of the firm's existence and product lines.

7 To stimulate derived demand – Because demand in B2B markets is derived from consumer markets, it may sometimes be worthwhile for a supplier to stimulate demand among its customers' markets in order to create a derived demand. An example of this was the UK's glass manufacturers who ran a joint campaign aimed at consumers, the strap line for which was 'You can see what you're getting with glass'. This helped to slow down the trend towards using steel cans, but did not help much in the parallel switch to plastic bottles.

8 To project a favorable corporate image – Sometimes a firm which only supplies other firms may need to improve its public image. For example, a firm may need to re-establish its environmental credentials, or may wish to stimulate a consumer demand to include its products in the final product. An example of this is Intel, a firm which does not supply the public but which has established its brand name in the public consciousness in such a way that most computer users want an Intel chip in their machines. This means, in turn, that computer designers and manufacturers are compelled to include Intel chips in their machines.

9 To provide the most economical promotional mix – Advertising can be much more cost-effective at the need-recognition and information-search stages than a sales call or even an exhibition (see Chapter 14).

Media in business advertising

One of the major advantages of B2B marketing is that each industry has its own trade publications. This makes targeting easy, especially since members of the industry tend to read the publications (and the advertisements) more assiduously than most consumers read consumer magazines. Some trade journals are vertical, in other words they are read by all firms in the same industry, while other journals are horizontal (for example *Marketing Business*) and are read by a specific group of professionals across a wide range of industries.

Trade journals tend to be kept, sometimes for long periods. Any regular visitor to corporate waiting rooms will have noticed that some of the trade journals on the table are several years out of date. Buyers frequently save articles from trade journals for future reference and in some cases (notably professionals such as architects) the trade journals become part of the corporate library, used for information searches sometimes years later.

Selecting an appropriate trade journal follows the sequence shown in Table 12.2.

Trade journal advertising is a relatively low-cost form of advertising. Also, it is usually fairly closely targeted, which means that less of the advertising budget is wasted in advertising to people who are not interested in the product category and never will be. Trade journals also have considerable credibility with their target audiences and are often used as the major source of information for buyers. Trade journals have the advantage of being a sought communication, so advertising is often read.

TABLE 12.2 Sequence of choosing trade journal

Stage of process	Explanation
Determine target markets	Use industrial classifications or trade directories to identify targets. Brainstorming with salespeople and other marketers may be helpful at this stage.
Define members of the DMU (Buying Center)	Job titles, professional qualifications and sometimes trade association membership can help in defining the membership of the DMU.
Determine what DMU members seek in the publications they read	This may be determined as a result of formal market research, or of simply asking people from the professions concerned. There is unlikely to be a definitive answer to this question, however, since different people will have different aims and indeed any individual DMU member will have different needs at different times.
Develop messages to communicate to the DMU members	The problem here is that different DMU members will have different needs and therefore different messages. On the other hand, the messages should have a common theme since DMU members will need to speak with each other in order to arrive at a decision.
Determine which journals best fit the needs of the campaign	This can be determined using rating services such as BRAD (British Rate and Data) or BPA in the USA.
Rank the publications	This can be done using the cost of advertising, the circulation figures, the editorial content and article value and the degree of fit with the needs of the campaign.
Select the appropriate publication for each DMU member group	This will involve a judgment regarding the best penetration of buying influence for the money expended.
Evaluate the effectiveness of each publication	This is a complex area. Unless the firm is prepared to spend large amounts on formal market research, much of the evidence is likely to be hearsay. Also, given that many DMU members will keep trade journals for a long period, it may be some years before the impact of the advertising is felt. This is, of course, a general characteristic of advertising.

Direct response advertising

Direct response advertising involves a communication from the selling company to the purchasing company in a personalized and often tailored manner. The intention of direct response advertising is to open a dialogue between buyer and seller, so the medium needs to communicate effectively. Its main appeal is that it is easily monitored and controlled: databases help the monitoring process in the following ways (O'Malley *et al*. 1999).

- Tracking responses.
- Recording speed of fulfillment of the sale.
- Tracking responses in different sectors.
- Comparing conversion rates to response rates.
- Assessing the effectiveness of media in reaching the target audiences.
- Comparing response levels in different media.
- Recording customer data captured in the course of the campaign.

Unfortunately, much direct mail is poorly targeted so it is frequently destroyed without even being read. The key to success in direct response advertising is to target carefully and to make the message itself appropriate and worthwhile for the recipient. The main media used for direct response advertising are the Internet, telesales and direct mail.

Direct marketing has been defined as 'A cybernetic marketing process which uses direct response advertising in prospecting, conversion and maintenance'. (Bauer and Miglautsch 1992). Direct marketing is therefore neither a more sophisticated mail-order system, nor is it merely a communication device in the manner of mailshots.

Direct marketing is not a mass medium: it communicates with consumers as individuals, rather than as a group of segments (Bird 1993). It is interactive, meaning that prospects respond directly (and measurably) to direct communications. Provided the communication is targeted accurately, responses will result.

The rapid growth of direct marketing in recent years has been the result of the falling cost of information technology and also the fragmentation of markets.

The impact of technology on direct marketing is shown in Table 12.3.

Databases come in three basic varieties:

1 Hierarchical databases – Data is stored under a single criterion, for example an account number. This makes it easy to call up details on a specific individual, but hard to generate lists of (for example) customers who are habitual late payers. Hierarchical databases are essentially derived from manual filing systems: they are quicker, but not much more sophisticated.

2 Network databases – These use 'tags' to identify records needed for analysis. For example, a customer's records might include a tag for the postcode (so that records can be sorted geographically), another tag for the date of the last transaction (so records can be sorted by recency of use) and a set of tags for other business variables such as type of customer or industry. Network databases are generally more useful than hierarchical databases, but are more expensive and harder to operate since the user must understand the structure of the data in order to manipulate it.

3 Relational databases – Currently the dominant system, relational databases store the data in two dimensions: the data for a given customer lies in one dimension, the data on a given attribute across all customers lies in another. For example, a bank might store information on a loan under both the customer's records and the bank's loan records, including a record of late payment or extra borrowing. A relational database allows the information to be added to both records at once and be accessed either way.

When deciding on database design, managers should ask themselves the following questions (Linton 1995):

TABLE 12.3 Impact of technology	
Technological factor	**Explanation and examples**
Addressability	This is the ability to identify and reach individuals (Vavra 1992). Computers allow marketers to record thousands of names and addresses, and also to search for information about firms rapidly, in order to identify the appropriate recipients for mailings.
Measurability	Computers enable marketers to record the purchasing behavior of companies and to analyze purchasing patterns in order to tailor communications (Vavra 1992).
Flexibility	The ability to approach each customer with a uniquely tailored approach, using desktop publishing or data mining (Vavra 1992).
Accountability	The ability to track expenditure and monitor returns (Vavra 1992). Computer technology allows marketers to track each mailing individually if necessary, and record follow-ups.
Increased processing power	The ever increasing data processing capabilities of equipment allow faster and more detailed analysis of customers and their purchasing behavior.
Analytical software	The availability of analysis software has made statistical analysis of customer records extremely simple.
Telephone systems	Until the mid-1980s telephones could only realistically be used for outbound telesales. With the advent of 0800 numbers, respondents to mailings can call free. This greatly improves response rates. Another labor-saving innovation for firms has been the advent of IVR (interactive voice response) systems which allow many calls to be handled entirely by computer. Many callers find these systems irritating, however: business is about people, not economics.

1 How will the database support business objectives?
2 What is expected from the system?
3 What are the main requirements?
4 What applications will it be used for?

Sometimes a firm might find it worthwhile to outsource management of the database, although this is less common nowadays than previously, because powerful computers are cheap enough for firms to be able to manage the database in-house. The advantages of outsourcing database management are as follows:

1 The database will not affect the capacity of the firm's internal systems.
2 There will be no need to recruit or train extra staff.
3 The database will be managed by specialists, who may be able to make useful suggestions for its management.
4 Outsourcing may be more cost-effective due to economies of scale.

Populating the database may come from internal sources, such as the firm's own sales records (also form returns, exhibition enquiries, sales promotions and so forth), or it may come from bought-in databases. Lists of names can be bought from list brokers, and electronic directories can be used to identify prospects.

It is tempting to use market research records to populate the databases, but unless the respondents have specifically agreed to allow this, it is extremely dangerous to do so. Within the UK such practices may be illegal under the Data Protection Act and many countries have enacted similar laws to prevent invasion of privacy. In any event, use of information which was provided under an assurance of confidentiality is unethical and will result in greater refusals by respondents to take part in market research, which would of course be detrimental to the accuracy of research.

Cleaning the list will result in greater levels of response. Respondents can easily be irritated by misspellings of their names, wrong addresses and so forth. The commonest errors are shown in Table 12.4 (Bradford 1995).

Cleaning the list can be difficult. Visual checking of the list might remove some of the more obvious errors, but checking whether someone has left a company may be harder. The salesforce may be able to assist with this.

De-duping (removing duplicate names) can be carried out in six stages (Mander 1993).

1 Identify and examine key elements of the name and address – for example, title, initials, surname, position in the company and each line of the address.

2 Form access keys – When two or more records share the same combinations of parts of names and addresses they should be identified and 'pulled'.

3 Develop a scoring system for potential duplicates – the higher the score, the greater the similarity. This allows the machine to compare records for similarity and 'pull' the most similar ones.

4 Identify the acceptable level of duplication – this gives the machine a cut-off point beyond which the records are regarded as suspect.

5 Prioritize duplicates – If two people from the same company are receiving mailings, for example, the company can decide which of them should receive the mailing, or whether both of them should continue to do so.

6 Change the records – Delete unwanted records, merge data from duplicated records and so forth.

TABLE 12.4 Common errors in databases

Error	Explanation
Incorrect name	Even seemingly minor errors such as wrong initials might result in someone else with the same surname receiving the mailing. In a large organization, this is likely to result in the mailing being destroyed, since the mailing may well go to the wrong division.
Titles	In some cases the recipient might be offended by the omission or addition of a title. For example, the medical profession is often touchy about being addressed as Doctor and in the international context it is sometimes considered polite to use all the individual's titles (for example, this is typical in Germany, where someone might be addressed as Frau Professor Doktor Schmidt).
Duplicate entries	Sometimes the same person is listed under different versions of the same name. Someone might be listed as Alan Reynolds, A.J. Reynolds, Mr A. Reynolds, or any of several other combinations. Multiple mailings are not only wasteful for the company, they are irritating for the recipient and also give the impression that the company sending the mailing is careless and impersonal.
Gone-aways	Sometimes mail continues to be sent to individuals who have left the firm, retired, or even died. People change jobs on average every four or five years, so it is difficult for marketers to keep track of them.

The first three stages of this process can be carried out by computer: the final three require intervention by a human being. For small lists, the de-duping process is probably more easily carried out manually: a small engineering firm might only have a mailing list of a few hundred, whereas an airline frequent-flyer program might have a list running into millions.

Segmentation in direct marketing also operates differently from that in traditional marketing. Traditionally, segmentation is a top-down process, beginning with a mass of possible customers and breaking them down into suitable groups. In direct marketing segmentation is often carried out by examining the characteristics of customers on the database and then aggregating them into segments. This means that each supplying company will develop its own segmentation approach, often behaviorally-based. In common with other forms of marketing, direct marketing has two main aims: customer acquisition, and customer retention.

Customer acquisition can be aided by database combination, in which prospects are identified by mining the databases for information about them and their companies. Hot prospects can be identified by their propensity to respond to the mailings.

Customer retention is a process of first finding out why customers defect (Reichhold and Sasser 1990). There is an assumption that satisfied customers will be loyal and dissatisfied customers will defect, but research shows that this is not always the case. Attitude is not necessarily a clear guide to behavior: conditions may prevent someone from carrying out intended behavior. Loyalty has been defined as 'the relationship between the relative attitude towards the entity and patronage behavior' (Dick and Basu 1994). There are four categories of loyalty:

- no loyalty – in which the relative attitude is low and there is no consistent patronage behavior
- spurious loyalty – in which the patronage behavior is high but the customer does not really believe that there is any real difference in product offerings
- latent loyalty – in which the high relative attitude to the brand is not reflected in patronage
- loyalty – in which high patronage and high relative attitude go together.

Business to business marketers should be aiming to create relationships in which loyalty is high. Direct marketing can help here by ensuring that the customer is regularly contacted at all stages of the relationship in order to maintain a two-way flow of communication.

Standardization versus adaptation

The basic problem facing the global marketer is whether to seek to standardize the marketing communications, or tailor them to local cultural differences. The advantages of standardizing are cost, consistency across borders and avoidance of creep in terms of brand values. The disadvantages are that the campaign is likely to have to be produced to 'lowest common denominator', in other words will have to offend nobody rather than please everybody.

There are four basic strategies for international communications (Keegan 1984):

1 Same product, same communication – This can be used where the need for the product and its use are the same as in its home market. This applies to most engineering products such as nuts and bolts or sheet steel.

2 Same product, different communication – This can be used when the need for the product differs in some way in each of its target markets, or when cultural differences mean that the product has a different connotation. This may be the case with finished products such as, for example, drilling equipment, which may be used in Africa to drill water wells or in Europe to drill drainage holes. Although the basic function of the equipment is to poke holes in the ground, the conditions under which it is used and the advantages of using it will differ considerably.

3 Different products, same communication – Sometimes the product formula has to be changed to meet local conditions, but the promotion can remain the same. For example, safety regulations may differ between countries, but the basic product remains the same. An agricultural tractor may need to be adapted to run on the local fuel, but remain the same to all outward appearances.

TABLE 12.5 Translating advertising copy

Rule	Explanation
Avoid idiom, jargon or buzz-words	These can be difficult to translate and easily adopt different meanings in the foreign language. Translators are rarely perfect in both languages, so such problems are likely to occur.
Check local legal requirements and codes of conduct	Foreign countries frequently have unfamiliar regulations. Sometimes these seem unreasonable or unlikely, but it is their country – you need to play by their rules.
Ensure that translators speak the everyday language of the country	Spanish spoken in Spain differs from that spoken in Latin America, just as American English and British English differ. Portuguese differs between Portugal, Brazil, Angola and Mozambique, and French differs between France, Belgium, Côte D'Ivoire, Réunion and so forth. For obvious reasons, people who are not native speakers should never be used.
Brief the translators thoroughly	Translating copy is not a one-for-one proposition. Phrases, style and even content may need to be adapted in order to read well in the foreign language. A good translator will need to understand what your company and products are about in order to know how to translate.
Check the translation with customers and distributors in the local market	This gives the local users the chance to become involved and also gives the opportunity to raise any criticisms of the material before it goes into production.
Re-translate the material back into the original language	This provides a final safety check. This is especially important, since the translators are almost certainly not part of your company and therefore probably do not understand the company philosophy, culture and style and may therefore use inappropriate phraseology.

4 Different products, different communications – Many markets require products which are unique to that market and also have cultural differences which dictate changes in the communications mix. For example, computer software for Arabic markets needs to adapted for language and keyboard configuration and also the marketing communication needs to be changed entirely for language and cultural parameters.

Translating advertising copy, brochures, leaflets and other promotional materials is also prone to error and misunderstanding. Table 12.5 shows a checklist for translating advertising copy (Majaro 1982).

Provided that a universally recognized icon is available and it is possible to produce meaningful hooks in each language, it should be possible to produce good international copy. Factual communications and sought communications are much more likely to translate successfully than are emotional communications.

Tactical considerations

The tactical possibilities are obviously very large in number. Most of the tactics of marketing communication demand creativity on the part of the marketers, so it is virtually impossible to lay down any hard and fast rules about approaching different marketing problems. However, the following list may provide some guidelines:

1 Marketers should always try to do something which is different from what the competitors are doing.

2 It is essential to consult everybody who might be involved in the day-to-day application of the plans. Salespeople in particular do not like to be told what to do by somebody back at Head Office.

3 Most marketing activities do not produce instant results, but they will need to be monitored anyway.

4 The messages given to the customers, distributors, agents and indeed all the other publics need to be consistent.

5 Competitors will almost always make some kind of response to any marketing initiative, so marketers should try to anticipate any likely responses and have tactics in place to meet them.

Tactical aspects of marketing communications are dealt with in later chapters.

Integrating marketing communications

Currently, there is considerable interest in seeking to integrate marketing communications. The reasons for this are as follows:

1 Greater consistency of message will increase the impact of the communication.

2 Communications can reinforce each other.

3 Different people respond more, or less, positively towards some media than to others.

4 Economies of scale in terms of message formulation and delivery can be achieved.

5 Integrated communications have a strategic effect: members of the organization become clearer about what the organizational aims are.

The aim of integration is to ensure that the basic messages which are sent out by the organization are consistent throughout and that everyone is 'singing from the same song sheet'. In practice, integration is difficult to achieve, for the following reasons:

1 The salesforce may not be able, or prepared, to deliver the corporate message if they do not think that it meets the needs of the specific customer they are talking to.

2 Employees often talk about their work when they go home and may not keep to the corporate message.

3 Firms in a global environment will need to adapt the message for different cultures.

4 Communication is not a magic bullet: recipients interpret messages and often confuse the message with the medium.

There may even be an argument for NOT integrating communications. If a company is dealing with several different market segments, some of which exist in overseas markets, it may actually be more desirable to differentiate the communications and offer a different message to each group. The problem with this approach, of course, is that different groups may have very different perceptions of the messages, since it is almost impossible to ensure that the messages only reach the specific segment and no-one else.

SUMMARY

Communication is rather more complex than at first appears. The communication that the company intends to send often bears little relationship to the communication which is actually received: this is because communication takes place in a large number of ways and at many different levels. The medium often has as much effect as the message itself and the way the message is conveyed alters the meaning. Finally, the message combines with the recipient's existing knowledge and prejudices to create an entirely new (and possibly unintended) message.

The key points from this chapter are as follows:

- Business buyers actively seek out information.

- Messages are not a magic bullet: communication is a cooperative process.

- Sought communications are those which the buyer looks for: unsought communications are those which the seller sends out.

- Meaning is conveyed by more than words and pictures.

- Cultural differences in communication are often misinterpreted.

- Attitude consists of conation, cognition and affect. Attitude change begins by changing one of these.

- Cognitive dissonance causes breakdowns in communication.

- Business buyers rarely buy as a result of advertising alone.

- Direct mail must be carefully targeted if it is not to end up in the bin.

- The main trade-off in international communications is the decision whether to standardize or to tailor.

REVIEW QUESTIONS

1 How might advertising be used as a catalyst for attitude change?
2 Why might a firm wish to tailor its international marketing communications?
3 How might a supplier company measure the effectiveness of its marketing communications?
4 What are the main differences between B2B and B2C marketing communications strategies?
5 What is the difference between the peripheral and the central routes to attitude change?

SPOTLIGHT ON B2B MARKETING

Google is one of the world's best established search engines. Within seconds the system can search through literally billions of pages to find the key words entered, listing some thousands of web pages in order of best fit. Google's AdWords Select system allows website owners to pay for top ranking in search results: these results are offset to the top right-hand corner of the search results page, so that the person conducting the search still obtains the list of pages in the correct order, but additionally the advertiser's pages will appear on Page One. Since most searchers rarely go beyond the first page, this gives Google's advertisers a major advantage over the other web pages further down the list.

Early in 2002 Google introduced a new system allowing advertisers to pay only when visitors click onto the link. This aroused the anger of rival search engine Overture, to the extent that Overture have filed a lawsuit alleging patent infringement. Overture is the number one paid search engine in the United States and claims 80 per cent reach in the UK and 73 per cent in Germany. This is largely due to partnership agreements with AOL, Freeserve in the UK, and T-Online in Germany.

Google's sites operate in 82 languages, it has offices in Tokyo and London and has annexes in Germany and France. Google spokesman David Krane said, 'The release of AdWords was a soft launch. AdWords Select brings one of our recently-introduced advertising products to our customers in their own language and currency'.

Meanwhile Overture are not sitting still. Jim Olson, company spokesman, says 'We're aware of all of our competitors regardless if they are overseas, and we take these competitors seriously. We've been doing this longer and are bigger than anyone else doing paid search – we offer superior economics, service and product quality than anyone else.'

In August 2002 Google signed a contract worth an estimated UK£1m with Lloyd's TSB Insurance. Lloyd's is paying for placement in search results related to more than 1,000 insurance-related keywords. This highlights the advertisers' view of the importance of web-based marketing and especially search-based marketing. Damian Burns, digital account director with London-based Zenith Interactive Solutions, says: 'From the perspective of the advertiser, search engines are becoming increasingly important to target consumers because the general public filters advertising deliberately. With people in research mode, you can target in a relevant listing and their propensity to listen will be far higher'.

So far, Google has signed on British Telecom, British Airways, Ford Motor and Virgin. Overture has signed up much the same list of UK blue-chip companies, but has the problem that it does not host its own websites. It therefore relies on partnerships with ISPs (Internet service providers) in each country they wish to enter. Google is already worldwide, or nearly so, and therefore has no such limitations. For Google, signing up partners in new countries is an addition to the existing business: for Overture, it is a basic necessity.

As the Internet grows worldwide, it might be assumed that there would be plenty of business for everybody, but Google and Overture seem to be determined to grab as much as they can while the market is growing. The battle for market leadership is likely to be a tough struggle, but in the meantime the business customers of these search engines can only gain from the battle.

Questions

1   Why might Google's AdWords system be of particular interest in a B2B environment?

2   What would be the most appropriate communications method for Google to use when approaching potential customers?

3   How might Overture best communicate with its potential customers?

4   Why would B2B advertisers want to be attached to a search engine?

5   What problems might Google encounter when operating in a global context?

REFERENCES

Aronson, E., Chase, T., Heinrich, R. and Ruhnke, R. (1974) 'A two-factor theory of dissonance reduction: the effect of feeling stupid or feeling awful on opinion change', *International Journal of Communication Research*, 3: 340–52.

Bauer, C. and Miglautsch, J. (1992) 'A conceptual definition of direct marketing', *Journal of Direct Marketing*, 6: Spring: 7–17.

Bird, D. (1993) *Commonsense Direct Marketing* (3rd edn), London: Kogan Page.

Blythe, J. (2003) *Essentials of Marketing Communication*, Harlow: Financial Times, Prentice Hall.

Bradford, G. (1995) 'Targeting technology', *ADMAP*, January: 32–4.

Costa, J. A. and Pavia, T. M. (1992) 'What it all adds up to: culture and alpha-numeric brand names', in Sherry, J. F. and Sternthal, B. (eds) *Advances in Consumer Research*, 19: 40, Provo, Utah: Association for Consumer Research.

Dick, A. S. and Basu, K. (1994) 'Customer loyalty: towards an integrating framework', *Journal of the Academy of Marketing Science*, 22(2): 99–103.

Festinger, L. (1957) *A Theory of Cognitive Dissonance*, Stanford, CA: Stanford University Press.

Festinger, L. and Carlsmith, J. M. (1959) 'Cognitive consequences of forced compliance', *Journal of Abnormal and Social Psychology*, 58: 203–10.

Linton, I. (1995) *Database Marketing: Know what your customer wants*, London: Pitman.

Mander, G. (1995) 'De-duplication', *Journal of Database Marketing*, 1(2): 150–61.

O'Malley, L., Patterson, M. and Evans, M. J. (1999) *Principles of direct and database marketing*, London: Financial Times Pitman.

Petty, R. E. and Caccioppo, J. T. (1983) 'Central and peripheral routes to persuasion: application to advertising', In Percy, L. and Woodside, A. (eds), *Advertising and Consumer Psychology*, Lexington, MA: Lexington Books.

Pierce, C. S. (1986) in Mick, D. G. 'Consumer research and semiotics: exploring the morphology of signs, symbols and significance', *Journal of Consumer Research*, 13: September: 196–213.

Reichheld, F. F. and Sasser, W. E. (1990) 'Zero defects: quality comes to service', *Harvard Business Review*, September/October: 105–11.

Rosenberg, M. J. (1960) 'An analysis of affective-cognitive consistency', in Rosenberg *et al.* (eds) *Attitude Organisation and Change*, New Haven, CT: Yale University Press.

Schramm, W. A. (1948) *Mass Communications*, Urbana, Ill: University of Illinois Press.

Schramm, W. A. (1971) 'The nature of communication between humans', in Schramm, W. A. and Roberts, D. F. (eds) *The Process and Effect of Mass Communication*, Urbana, Ill: Illinois University Press.

Shimp, T. and Sharma, S. (1987) 'Consumer ethnocentrism: construction and validation of CETSCALE', *Journal of Marketing Research*, August: 280–89.

Singh, J. (1988) 'Consumer complaint intentions and behaviour: definitions and taxonomical issues', *Journal of Marketing*, 52: January: 93–107.

Vavra, T. (1992) *Aftermarketing*, Homewood, Ill: Irwin.

CUSTOMER RELATIONSHIPS AND KEY-ACCOUNT MANAGEMENT

Learning objectives

After reading this chapter, you should be able to:

- Describe the key issues in buyer-seller relationships

- Explain the role and function of personal selling

- Describe the sales process

- Structure a sales presentation

- Describe ways of motivating the salesforce

- Describe the basic remuneration packages for salespeople, with their advantages and drawbacks

■ Introduction

Business is largely about personal relationships. Even though business people often aim to be totally rational in their buying behavior, the personality of the people they see conveys an image about the personality of the supplying corporation: for the buyer, the sales representative IS the corporation.

Personal selling has a special place in B2B transactions. Because of the higher order values and fewer number of buyers, suppliers feel the need to offer a personal service, supplied by the salesforce.

▊ Buyer-seller relationships

Figure 13.1 shows the key issues in relationships between buyers and sellers.

- Trust versus formality – refers to the degree to which the relationship is bounded by contractual agreements. This issue can be affected by culture in the global context: most negotiators are less likely to trust foreigners than they are to trust people from their own cultural background , but also different cultures have different attitudes towards the role of trust in business. Often this comes from the legal codes of the countries involved: in the UK, for example, trust is of high importance because written contracts are not always enforceable – parties to the contract can claim that they were induced to sign by verbal reassurances which subsequently did not materialize. This means that a written contract is not the whole story and may prove to be unenforceable. In Japan, written contracts are enforceable, but only after expensive and prolonged litigation, which means that written contracts are not regarded as highly as good relationships of trust. In Germany and the United States the written contract forms the basis of the agreement, so business relationships tend to be more formal.

- Power and dependence – refers to the degree to which either party can make life difficult for the other party. If one firm is heavily dependent on the other, the second firm can dictate the terms of the relationship.

- Complexity – this is likely to be a function of the closeness of the relationship. The more points of interaction which exist between the buyer and the seller, the more complex the relationship becomes, but at the same time the relationship also becomes closer.

- Supplier relations – concern the coordination of suppliers with each other and the relationships which may develop from this.

- Conflict and cooperation – these are at the opposite ends of a spectrum. Conflict is inevitable when companies with different aims, backgrounds and agendas attempt to work together: if the conflict is resolved in a reasonable manner, cooperation is the end result.

- Adaptations – is a longer-term result of conflict resolution. As the relationship develops, the parties will need to adapt their business practices in order to cooperate better.

- Relationships as investments – a relationship might be considered as a long-term investment. Each party will need to expend effort which is not immediately rewarded in order to enjoy longer-term benefits.

Business transactions may differ greatly from one another. At one end of the scale, there may be a one-off transaction involving relatively little decision-making and only limited contact between the

FIGURE 13.1

Issues in
relationships

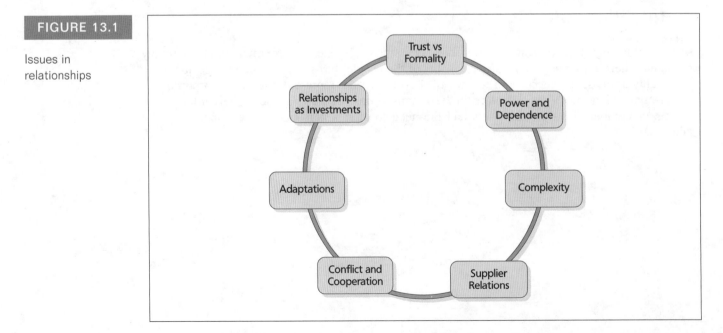

buyer and the seller (for example, if the office manager needs to buy some emergency photocopier paper from a local office supplies company and simply sends a junior member of staff out with some petty cash). At the other end of the spectrum a purchase decision might involve establishing a long-term relationship between the firms, operating at many levels and with frequent contact between members of both organizations. For example, a major insurance company might switch its business from IBM to Unisys and consequently need to retrain its staff, establish a training program for new staff, alter its internal systems, establish new protocols for dealing with its existing customers and so forth. Such a relationship would be expected to continue at all levels within the organization for the foreseeable future, as new software and hardware are developed and introduced and internal systems adapt to external environmental changes.

Within this complex relationship there will be distinct interactions between the parties: these are called episodes (Hakansson and Gadde 1992). The way each episode is handled will depend largely on the past history between the organizations (if any). If the parties know and trust each other, the episode will be handled in a different way from the way it would be handled if the parties have no previous relationship, or have reasons for mistrust. The possible cases for handling episodes can be broadly categorized as follows:

1 Simple episode with no previous relationship – These episodes would involve simple purchases, often in small quantities, or regular purchases of basic raw materials which are of a fairly standard nature (for example, sales representatives buying petrol).

2 Simple episode in a well-developed relationship – Here the relationship facilitates the process: for example, a firm's relationship with its bankers may mean that borrowing money becomes much simpler because the firm already has a track record.

3 Complex episode with no previous relationship – This type of transaction involves the most negotiation, because complexity in itself generates uncertainty and this is exacerbated by the unknown qualities of the other party to the transaction. Often these purchases are one-offs: for example, a power generating company may only buy one hydro-electric dam in its entire existence, so there is no opportunity to build a long-term relationship with the civil engineers who build the dam.

4 Complex episode in well-developed relationships – This may mean that many people from both organizations will need to interrelate (as in the case of the insurance company and the IT supplier mentioned earlier). Again, the previous relationship will inform the progress of events and the nature of the interaction.

Investing in relationships

Investing in a long-term relationship will therefore almost certainly pay dividends in reducing trans-action costs, since there is little or no time wasted on learning about the other party. It also reduces risk by reducing complexity. The difference between an investment and a cost is simple: a cost is expected to yield returns within the same accounting period, whereas an investment is expected to yield a stream of returns spread across several accounting periods.

Relationships clearly have at least some of the characteristics of investments. In the early stages of the relationship, the main costs of establishing the relationship will be most evident. In the first few years, outgoings are likely to exceed revenues for the selling firm. In one study, this situation prevailed for the first four years of the relationship and the selling firm only moved into profit in the relationship after seven years. This means that it is far more profitable to retain and improve existing relationships than it is to seek out new ones and it is well-known that firms which expand too rapidly frequently encounter cash flow problems. From the purchasing firm's viewpoint, there are costs attached to dealing with a new supplier, particularly when the purchase is complex: similar savings are likely to accrue over long periods.

Where relationships differ from most other investments is that the relationship is not transferable in the way that (for example) an investment in plant and machinery would be. If one firm acquires another firm and takes over its operations, the relationship may continue as part of the package, but this in itself poses an obstacle to implementing change.

Advantages of establishing a relationship

One of the major advantages of establishing a relationship is the possibility for making adaptations. Classical economics assume that all products are identical, but of course this is not the case in the real world and firms adapt their offerings in order to accommodate purchasers. To a lesser extent, purchasers sometimes adapt their requirements in order to take advantage of special offers from suppliers. An example of this is the Land Rover, originally designed in the late 1940s as a utility vehicle for farmers and landowners. The vehicle was designed around the availability of aluminum, which was then in oversupply in comparison to steel, which was strictly rationed. The rust-free qualities of aluminum quickly became a major selling-point for the vehicle, but this was a side-effect of the Rover Car Company's ingenuity in making use of a plentiful material to replace a scarce one.

Adaptation

From the seller's viewpoint, adaptation may take place in order to satisfy one purchaser's needs, or a group of purchasers. If the adaptation is intended to meet the needs of a group of purchasers, this is an example of segmentation and targeting. If the adaptation is intended to meet the needs of one purchaser, this is customization. Research shows that the commonest type of adaptation is in technological collaboration with materials suppliers (Hakansson 1989). Adaptations involving components, equipment and processes are less common.

Knowledge-based adaptation

Knowledge-based adaptation gains in importance as development issues increase in importance. Buyers who encourage their suppliers to learn about their systems and applications of technology will give the suppliers the opportunity to make potentially useful suggestions: the downside of this is that the buyer becomes more committed to the suppliers and may find it harder to switch suppliers at a later date, for example to take advantage of better deals elsewhere. In addition, the differences between supplier and purchaser are likely to lead to creative solutions for mutual problems.

Research shows that, at least in some cases, firms are not always aware of the extent of contacts made between themselves and their suppliers (Hakansson and Gadde 1992). In some cases, engineering staff might meet regularly to discuss technical issues, or marketing people might consider joint promotional campaigns, without necessarily bothering to notify other departments that this is happening. Some interactions occur informally – individuals might meet at seminars or trade fairs, or on training courses, or even on the golf course.

The result of this is that many long-term relationships between firms rely much more strongly on mutual trust than on formality. This approach is strongly evidenced in Japanese firms, where contracts are regarded as an adjunct to the business agreement rather than as its main pillar: Japanese executives spend a great deal of time establishing informal relationships with suppliers and purchasers and try to create an atmosphere of trust before being prepared to do business. This can be frustrating for American executives and to some Northern European executives, who are used to doing business at a much faster pace and even (in the case of Americans especially) involving their legal advisers from the outset. Partly this difference in attitude is rooted in the Japanese culture, which is strong on issues such as duty and honesty and partly it is a result of the Japanese legal system, which actively discourages corporate lawsuits by making them expensive and extremely long drawn out.

TALKING POINT

Business is a risky business. Firms make mistakes, run out of money, buy the wrong goods, go broke with monotonous regularity. Yet we are apparently being advised to rely on trusting someone who is trying to sell us something – trying to get money from us, in other words!

If business is risky, shouldn't we be getting everything nailed down as tight as possible in a contract? Yet, if the Japanese don't worry too much about contracts (and they are, after all, the world's second largest economy, despite having virtually no natural resources), shouldn't we be learning from them and relying on goodwill and a low golf handicap? Maybe we can all trust each other – but equally, we may be kidding ourselves!

Buyer-supplier relationships

Power and dependence are important aspects of buyer-supplier relationships. The most important supplier relationships are likely to involve large volumes of goods or materials, but may involve relatively low volumes of key supplies. From a purchaser's viewpoint, establishing a long-term relationship with a supplier carries the risk of becoming over-dependent on that supplier. Spreading the risk by using several suppliers means diluting the advantages of establishing a relationship.

Power-dependence relationships

Power-dependence relationships are seldom symmetrical. In many cases the purchaser will be holding most of the power, but in some cases the reverse is true – suppliers may even band together in order to exercise power over purchasers, as is the case with OPEC, the Organization of Petroleum Exporting Countries. OPEC operates by controlling the supply of oil to the rest of the world and was originally set up (at the instigation of Venezuela) to redress the power balance between the largely Third World oil producers and the industrialized countries who are the main users of oil. Sellers may have more power during a boom, when supplies may be limited, whereas buyers have more power in a recession. Abuse of the situation may very well lead to reprisals when the positions are reversed, of course, so maintaining a long-term relationship may rely on looking after good customers (or suppliers) when times are hard.

Conflict in relationships

Although a good business relationship is characterized by cooperation, conflict will inevitably arise. Broadly speaking, conflict is a psycho-social outcome of interaction (Ruekart and Walker 1987) and can be described as a breakdown or disruption in normal activities in such a way that the organizations concerned experience difficulty working together (Reitz 1977: Hellreigel and Slocum 1988: Hodge and Anthony 1991: Robbins 1991: Daft 1998: Hatch 1997). The traditional view of conflict is that it is dysfunctional, so that all conflict is seen to impact negatively on both organizations and should therefore be avoided at all costs. In other words, conflict is a bad thing, reducing the efficiency of organizations by focusing attention on the conflict rather than on the original purpose of the interaction.

An alternative view is that conflict is inevitable where people have a diversity of background, interests and talents. The interactions or functional view of conflict is that it can be a positive force which helps effective performance and encourages creativity and that far from diverting attention away from the aims of the organization, conflict ultimately generates more effective ways of achieving those aims.

If the degree of conflict is low, the relationship is probably not particularly meaningful or important to either party. Low conflict probably means low interaction: as interaction between the organizations increases, it seems likely that conflict will also increase. Equally, there should be a high degree of collaboration. Figure 13.2 illustrates the trade-offs involved.

	High degree of conflict	Low degree of conflict
High degree of collaboration	Well-developed relationship, probably highly-productive and highly-creative in solving mutual problems.	Pleasant, easy relationship with no exciting synergies. Low-risk, low-return environment.
Low degree of collaboration	Poor environment for achieving anything: a relationship which is probably short-lived.	Hardly a relationship at all. Not productive in any sense, this relationship is also unlikely to last.

FIGURE 13.2

Trade-offs between conflict and collaboration

Note from the figure that the relationships with low degrees of collaboration are unlikely to be long-lived, but relationships with low degrees of conflict are unlikely to be creative or dynamic.

Overall, the most desirable outcome is one in which conflict is handled constructively, so that the outcomes are achieved which are acceptable to both parties. Conflicts should not be smoothed over, nor should they be allowed to escalate, so there is a premium placed on maintaining routes of communication.

In short, conflict is inevitable when there are two or more organizations which are independent of each other and therefore having different goals. The problem is exacerbated when one considers that the profits from the encounter will be divided according to negotiation. Increased openness will reduce the conflict and give an understanding that the relationship is dependent on mutual profitability. Provided all parties accept this, agreements which allow for mutual gain will be more likely to occur.

■ The role of personal selling

Personal selling is probably the largest single budget item in most B2B markets. Salespeople earn high salaries and need expensive back-up: company cars, administration assistance, expensive brochures and sales materials and so forth. Allowing for traveling time, preparation time, etc. salespeople spend only a fraction of their time actually making sales presentations. This therefore begs the question: why have we not been able to find a cheaper way to get business?

The reason is that salespeople provide a personal touch. A salesperson is able to meet a buyer (or indeed anyone else in the buying corporation), discuss the buying corporation's problems and develop a creative solution. The buyer understands the corporation's problem, the salesperson understands the capabilities of the supplier and their products and (usually) the two share knowledge about the industry and the environment in which it operates. This relationship is illustrated in Figure 13.3.

The key point in this is that selling is about establishing a dialogue: it is not about persuading people to buy things they don't really want, it is not about fast-talking a buyer into making a rash decision and it is most definitely not about telling lies about the firm's products.

Functions of selling

Salespeople exist to carry out the following functions:

- Identify suitable possible customers.
- Identify problems those customers have or might have.
- Establish a dialogue with the potential customer.
- Refine the view of the problem to take account of the dialogue.
- Identify solutions which are within the supplying firm's capabilities.
- Explain the solution.
- Represent the customer's views to the supplying company.

FIGURE 13.3

The function of
selling

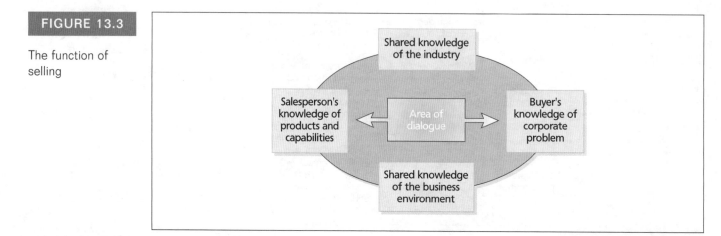

- Ensure a smooth process of supply which meets the customer's needs.
- Solve any after-sales problems which may arise.

Marketers usually think of personal selling as part of the promotional mix, along with sales promotion, advertising and publicity. Personal selling is different from the other elements in that it always offers a two-way communication with the prospective customer, whereas each of the other elements is usually a one-way communication. This is partly what makes personal selling such a powerful instrument; the salesperson can clarify points, answer queries and concentrate on those issues which seem to be of greatest interest to the prospect. More importantly, the salesperson is able to conduct instant 'market research' with the prospect and determine which issues are of most relevance, often in an interactive way which allows the salesperson to highlight issues which the prospect was not aware of.

As with other forms of marketing communication, selling works best as part of an integrated campaign. Salespeople find it a great deal easier to call on prospects who have already heard something about the company through advertising, publicity, or exhibition activities and many salespeople regard it as the main duty of the marketing department to deliver warm leads (or even hot ones). Equally, marketers regard it as part of the salesperson's responsibility to 'sing from the same song-sheet' by communicating the company's core message, in conjunction with the other communications methods.

Salespeople and marketers often have divergent views about the relationship between selling and marketing and this is occasionally a source of conflict between them (Dewsnap and Jobber 1998).

A marketer's view

Salespeople are able to find, inform and persuade customers in a way that has yet to be bettered by any other communications medium.

This view of personal selling emphasizes heavily the provision of information and the element of persuasion. Personal selling is one of several possible options available to the marketer for communicating the company's messages to the customers; its major advantage over other communications is that the message can be tailored to fit the prospect's need for information. This is very much a marketer-oriented view; marketers appear to be working to the model shown in Figure 13.4.

Marketers and writers about marketing seem to be unanimous in their belief that personal selling is the most powerful promotional shot in the locker; equally, they seem to be unanimous in believing that it is the most expensive.

FIGURE 13.4 Marketer's view of the role of personal selling

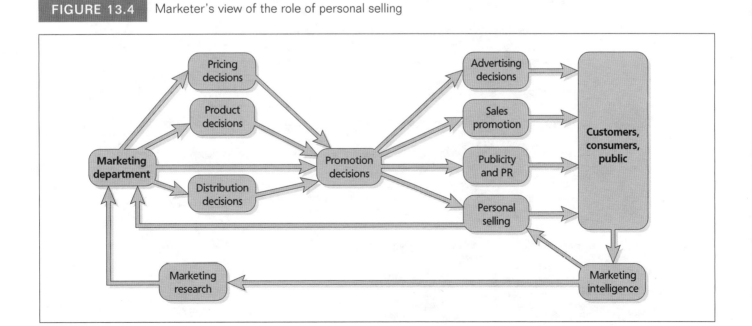

Because of the supposed high cost of personal selling and the knowledge that there are many other ways of communicating effectively with customers, marketers will sometimes look for ways of eliminating the salesforce.

To summarize the marketers' eye view, the salesforce functions and their potential replacements are shown in Table 13.1.

At first sight the marketer's model of the role of personal selling appears to allow for the replacement of selling with other (often IT-based) techniques. Since personal selling is regarded as an expensive option, this viewpoint is wholly understandable. A mailing which contacts 5,000 good prospects for a cost of UK£15,000 is a great deal cheaper than a sales representative, who would contact around half that number of prospects in a year at a cost of UK£50,000; even allowing for the sales rep's much better success rate, the cost advantage is obvious. If the marketers are right in thinking of selling as a communication tool, it is obviously cost-effective to seek other ways of communicating.

Undoubtedly personal selling does have a major communications element, involving as it does a two-way dialogue between salesperson and prospect, but there is a great deal more to personal selling than this. An examination of what salespeople actually do will make this clearer.

The salesperson's eye view

Research into sales practice shows a somewhat different picture from that conveyed by most marketing texts.

The emphasis in selling practice is not on telling prospects about the products, but on asking questions about the prospect's needs. The salesperson's role in the sales presentation is not about delivering a persuasive sales talk, but rather is about using appropriate questions. The questions not only help in finding out what the prospect actually needs, but also help to lead the discussion and the subsequent negotiations in a particular direction. DeCormier and Jobber (1993) found a total of 13 different types of question in use by salespeople; some of these were for information-gathering purposes, others serve to control and direct the discussion. Rackham (1991) categorized questions in four dimensions; situation, problem, implication and need-payoff. In each case the emphasis is on asking the prospect about his or her situation, with a view to finding a solution from among the salesperson's portfolio of products. The three key elements in this are firstly, that the needs of the buyer are paramount, secondly, that the salesperson is asking questions not making statements, and thirdly, that communicating the marketing department's 'message' is not relevant to this core process.

TABLE 13.1 Replacements for salesforce functions

Salesforce function	Marketer's replacement method
Prospecting	Bought-in database; database combination.
Evaluating prospects	Database scrutiny, credit referencing technology, response to direct mail.
Preparing	Combining databases to find most effective approach to the individual customer.
Approaching the customer	Initial mailing, Internet advertisement, direct-response advertising.
Making the presentation	Tailored direct-mail, Internet or e-mail negotiation.
Overcoming objections	Interactive computer-based (Internet-based) information system.
Closing	Internet-based close, credit transfer, e-mail order forms.
Following-up	Direct mail.

Sales trainers and writers have emphasized the problem-solving aspects of selling for many years now and salespeople are usually told that the most successful presentations are those in which the customer does most of the talking (Lund 1979). Problem-solving is at the core of the activity rather than communication; if the customer is allowed to talk, he or she will (in effect) tell the salesperson how to sell the product.

In the case of services, the marketer and the salesperson will also be concerned with the people, process and physical evidence (Booms and Bitner 1981). Salespeople have a role to play here as well; for example, it is common practice for salespeople to leave something with the customer once the sale is closed (a copy of the order, a brochure about the product, etc.) The salesperson is the main individual in the 'people' element, at least in most service industries and also often has considerable input into the process.

Comparison between selling and marketing

In fact, a comparison of the salesperson's activities and the marketer's activities reveals considerable common ground, as Table 13.2 shows.

The main difference between selling and marketing is that selling is concerned with individuals and individual relationships, whereas marketing is concerned with market segments. Although direct marketing and database marketing seek to target very small segments (even a segment of one) by using information technology, salespeople already do this, face-to-face and in real time, without the benefit of the marketing department's range of resources.

The salesperson's model

The salesperson's model of the relationship between marketing and sales will look more like that shown in Figure 13.5. From the salesforce viewpoint, it is the salesforce who do the 'real' work of finding out the customer's needs and fulfilling them, with the marketing department providing the back-up services of advertising, public relations and sales promotion. Marketers provide information (gained by market research) to the salesforce and also to the production department, but the salesforce exists to identify and solve customer's problems. They do this using the range of products supplied by the production department.

TABLE 13.2 Comparison of marketers' and salespeople's activities

Marketer's activities	Salesperson's activities
Research into the needs of consumers.	Needs analysis based on situation and problem questions.
Gap analysis.	Analysis of needs to identify problems.
New product development, designed to meet the consumers' needs.	Selection from among the existing range of products to find closest fit for prospect's needs.
Pricing: selecting a price which meets the needs and expectations of both the customer and the firm.	Price negotiation: negotiating a price which meets the needs and expectations of both the customer and the firm.
Promotion: developing an appropriate promotion strategy which will equate to the consumers' psychological and behavioral characteristics.	Promotion: explaining the features and benefits of the product in terms of the customer's needs, psychology and behavioral characteristics.
Distribution decisions: ensuring that the product is in a convenient place for the consumer to buy it.	Distribution negotiations: ensuring that the product reaches the customer in the right quantities and at the right time.

FIGURE 13.5

Salesperson's
model of the
relationship
between marketing
and selling

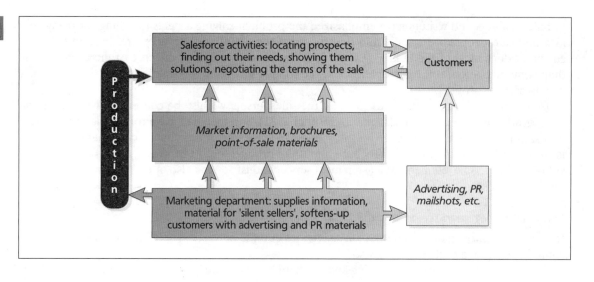

In the salesperson's model, the marketing department occupies a subservient role. Since the sales-force are in the 'front line', dealing directly with the customers, it is clear that every other department in the firm depends on them to bring in the business. They are, in fact, the only department which brings in money; everything else generates costs. Sales training programs sometimes emphasize this; salespeople are told that the average salesperson supports five other jobs, they are told that 'nothing happens until somebody sells something' and they are encouraged to think of themselves as the most important people in the firm.

Many salespeople regard their relationship with their customers as being more important than their relationship with the firm that pays their salaries – further evidence that salespeople regard themselves as being the most important people in the firm. Research shows that salespeople are often defensive of their good relationships with customers even when this conflicts with instructions from the marketing department (Anderson and Robertson 1995). This may be due to the belief that it is easier for salespeople to find a new company to work for than it is to find new customers.

While there may be some justification for the salesperson's model, the model ignores the interrelated nature of the firm's activities. Salespeople would have nothing to sell were it not for the efforts of the production department, would have no pay-packet and no invoicing without the finance department, would have no deliveries without the shipping department and so forth. Salespeople may have been given a false view of their own importance, but trainers may feel justified in doing this in order to counteract the often negative image and low status that selling has in the eyes of other departments.

In this model, the salesforce collects information about the market from the marketing department's research and information about the individual customer directly from the customer. Information about the product range, prices and discount structures, delivery lead times and methods, sales promotion and the use of advertising and PR materials (contained in the salesperson's 'silent seller') are all used in negotiation with the customer. This is done with the aim of obtaining an acceptable solution for both parties, regarding both information exchange and product and price exchange.

For many salespeople, the marketing department also has the role of 'softening-up' prospective customers by providing publicity and advertising; the salesperson feels more confident about making a call knowing that the prospect has already heard of the company and has had the opportunity to form some favorable impressions. In this model the marketing department performs a support function, providing a set of products for the customer to choose from, a price structure for the sales-person and the customer to negotiate around, a distribution system which can be tailored to suit the customer and promotional back-up in the form of advertising and publicity. Sales promotions might be useful as ways of closing sales (they are sometimes called deal-makers) but the basic problem-solving and decision-making is done by the salespeople when they are with the customer.

TALKING POINT

If customers are aware of their problems, why do we need salespeople at all? Why not simply provide all the information on a website, make it as interactive as possible and let people get on with it? After all, the social side of selling is hardly worth bothering with – buyers are paid to buy, not to sit chatting to sales reps!

Not to mention that too cozy a relationship between salespeople and customers might lead to all sorts of complications – favoritism and so forth. So isn't it far and away the best and cheapest option to get rid of the salesforce and use the money to buy a really good website?

On the other hand, most of us like to socialize in work. We are social animals, are we not? If that's the case, why do we limit corporate contacts just to salespeople and buyers? Why not expand out and get everybody to meet up?

In fact, it is this problem-solving and decision-making function that distinguishes the salesforce from other 'promotional tools'. The salesforce do not think of themselves as being primarily communicators; they think of themselves as being primarily decision-makers.

If the salespeople are correct in this view, then it would be impossible to replace them with a database (at least, given the current state of the art). Computers can hold and manipulate information very effectively, but they are unable to solve problems creatively or negotiate effectively, or indeed establish a long-term relationship on a human level. For these functions a human being is necessary.

A problem that arises from this perspective is that salespeople tend to identify very much with the customers. They will, and indeed should, be prepared to represent the customers' views back to the company and even fight the customer's corner for them within the firm, because this leads to a more customer-oriented attitude within the company. On the other hand, the firm is entitled to expect a certain amount of loyalty from its employees, so the salesforce's over-identification with the customers is likely to lead to conflict between salespeople and their colleagues back at Head Office.

For these reasons salespeople find it is easier and more beneficial to begin by finding out the customer's needs, and then apply a solution to those needs based on the firm's product range. Although marketing writers commonly refer to 'the product', it is very rarely the case that a salesperson will only have one product to offer; in many cases, salespeople even have the capacity to vary products or tailor them to fit the customer's needs. For example, computer software houses selling to major customers are able to write customer-specific software for the client; services salespeople (for example selling training services) will almost always have to tailor the product.

Types of salesperson

Newton's typology of salespeople states that there are, in general, four types of salesperson: trade, missionary, technical and new-business (Newton 1969). These are defined as follows:

- Trade salespeople build long-term relationships with customers, using low-key selling techniques to increase business as the relationship develops. They tend to be older, make careful use of reporting techniques and tend to be paid at least partly on commission. The main objective of these salespeople is to increase sales volume with existing customers.

- Missionary salespeople have the task of liaising with recommenders, who often do not actually buy the products. For example, missionary salespeople are used extensively in the ethical pharmaceuticals industry, encouraging doctors to prescribe specific drugs. The doctors do not buy the drugs: this is the role of pharmacists, but pharmacists will not stock drugs that doctors do not prescribe, so the missionary salesperson needs to close this gap. The problem for managers is relating reward to effort and skill: clearly these salespeople cannot be paid on a commission basis, since they make no actual sales. Turnover of personnel tends to be high in missionary selling, since it is difficult for the salespeople to be confident that what they are doing actually works.

- Technical salespeople exist to persuade engineers and other technical people to use the product. Typically, they call on users and influencers and may be called in by other salespeople to provide a stronger technical input. Technical salespeople have a technical qualification: thus they can speak the same language as the people they call on. They tend to be paid on a salary-only basis and there also tends to be a low turnover of technical salespeople.

- New-business salespeople seek out business from firms which are not currently customers. This suits people who like challenge and variety, but the downside is that this type of selling involves regular rejection by prospects, which some salespeople find difficult to handle. New-business salespeople are difficult to find and retain.

Because Newton's classification is almost 40 years out of date, some categories of salespeople have been omitted from it, in particular key-account salespeople. A key-account salesperson has a much more complex role than any other salesperson, because of the lengthy negotiations which must be undertaken in a key-account scenario. This involves dealing with many different decision makers as well as (potentially) dealing with decision makers in different countries and with different cultural backgrounds. There is more on key-account selling later in the chapter.

Donaldson (1998) established a more modern classification of selling types, as follows:

1 *Consumer direct* – These salespeople deal with consumers and are therefore outside the scope of this book, but they are order-getters who rely on selling skills, prepared presentations (canned presentations) and conditioned response techniques to close sales.

2 *Industrial direct* – These salespeople are also order-getters, but operate on a much larger scale. Usually these salespeople deal with one-off or infrequent purchases such as aircraft sales to airlines, machine tools, greenfield civil engineering projects and so forth. The emphasis for these salespeople is on negotiation skills.

3 *Government institutional direct* – Similar to industrial direct, these salespeople specialize in dealing with institutional buying. Because institutions typically operate by putting purchase contracts out to tender, these salespeople need special techniques: on the other hand, many of these organizations issue publications which explain how to sell to them, sometimes specifying the rules of business and acceptable profit levels. Often the salesperson's main hurdle is to become accepted as an approved supplier.

4 *Consumer indirect* – These salespeople call on retailers. Selling is normally on a repeat basis to established customers, but the main thrust of the salesperson's effort goes into understanding the consumer market. This means that the salesperson needs to help the retailer sell more of the product, by using creative merchandising, by advising on sales techniques and (in the case of fast-moving consumer goods) negotiating with the retailer for extra shelf-space for the products.

5 *Industrial indirect* – Most of the activity of these salespeople is in supporting distributors and agents. They need strong product knowledge and will need to concentrate on defending existing business from incoming competition: this is because it is typically the case that product and price are similar between competitors. The service level the salesperson offers is therefore the main competitive tool.

6 *Missionary sales* – Missionaries have already been described under Newton's classification. This type of selling is most effective when the selling cycle is long but the information/needs of potential specifiers are immediate, when other forms of communication cannot convey the whole picture and when the buying process is complex.

7 *Key-account salespeople* – A key-account is one which is of strategic importance, which represents a substantial proportion of the supplier's turnover, or which is likely to lead to a change in the way the firm does business. Key-account salespeople need very strong negotiating skills, a high degree of confidence and the ability to relate to people at many different levels in the organization (Cespedes 1996, Millman and Wilson 1995, 1996).

8 *Agents* – A manufacturer's agent represents many different suppliers, but does not take title to the goods. Agents typically call on the same regular group of customers, but offer a wide range of goods: the skills required are therefore the ability to understand a wide range of products, the administrative ability to keep track of the orders and to meet the

differing order formats of client companies and the ability to work efficiently often on low margins. Good agents do not carry products which compete directly, although there are exceptions to this general rule.

9   *Merchandisers* – Merchandisers call on large and small retail outlets specifically for the purpose of maintaining in-store displays and point-of-sale materials. In some cases (for example, Procter and Gamble) suppliers have their own employees stationed in supermarkets so as to improve the coordination of their supply operations. These salespeople are sometimes called customer account managers, which more accurately describes the breadth of their role.

10   *Telesales* – Telephone selling can be either inbound or outbound. Inbound telesales involves responding to customer enquiries, often generated by advertising or exhibitions. Outbound telesales usually involves cold-calling prospects, or replacing a personal visit with a telephone call. The main advantage of telesales is that it is very much cheaper than personal calls: the main disadvantage is that it is considerably less effective on a call-for-call basis. Telesalespeople need good communication skills, including a clear speaking voice: on the plus side, the telesales operator usually has better access to customer information than a field salesperson would have, due to the availability of computers.

11   *System selling* – This involves teams of salespeople, each of whom brings a different skill to bear on the problem. Missionary salespeople, new-business salespeople, and technical salespeople may all be involved in selling to the same account.

12   *Franchise selling* – Franchising is much the same as licensing, but is much more extensive. The franchiser grants the franchisee the right to use its business system and provides extensive support services and promotional input. In exchange, the franchisee pays a substantial royalty and an up-front franchise fee and agrees to conduct the business exactly according to the instructions from the franchiser. An example of this in the B2B field is Snap-On Tools, which supplies tools to the light engineering and motor trade.

There are, of course, many other ways of describing types of salesperson. Suggestions have included customer partner, buyer-seller team coordinator, customer service provider, buyer behavior expert, information gatherer, market analyst, forecaster and technologist (Rosenbloom and Anderson 1984, Wilson 1993). As personal selling develops in complexity, other classifications may well emerge.

The selling cycle

Figure 13.6 shows the selling cycle.

The selling sequence is drawn as a circle to indicate that it is an ongoing process, although in practice each salesperson will divide up their day in such a way as to carry out several, or even all, of the separate processes at once.

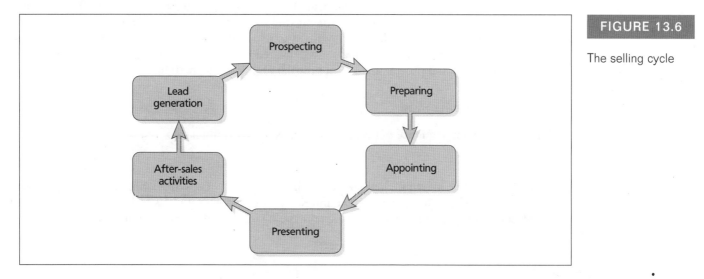

FIGURE 13.6

The selling cycle

Lead generation

Lead generation activities are sometimes also called prospecting, although in fact they differ considerably. Lead generation is concerned with finding people who are prepared to meet the salesperson and hear what he or she has to say. Prospects are potential buyers who have a need for the product and the means to pay for it. Lead generation is a process of establishing first contact: leads are generated via advertising, cold-calling (making visits or telephone calls without an appointment), by running exhibition stands, by sending out mail-shots, or by personal recommendation.

Prospecting

Prospecting is about establishing that the lead has a need for the product and also has the means to pay for it. In some cases these issues cannot be clearly determined in advance of meeting the potential customer, but a good salesperson will try to investigate a prospect as thoroughly as possible before wasting time on making a sales call.

Preparing

Preparing for the sale involves preparing both physically and mentally: wearing the right clothes, having the right presentation materials to hand, having the right mental attitude and having the appropriate knowledge of the prospect's company and circumstances. Preparing is likely to be complex, since in many cases the salesperson will be calling on several firms in one day, each with a separate set of data to remember and each with a separate set of needs.

Appointing

Appointing means making appointments to see the appropriate person or people in the firm. Salespeople are often advised to ensure that all the decision-makers are present, but in the modern business climate this is unlikely to be possible. Therefore the salesperson may well go through a process of using one appointment to generate the next until all the decision-makers have been seen.

Presenting

The sales presentation is a process of conducting a directed conversation in which the prospect's need is established and agreed, the supplier's solution is explained and the sale is closed. Closing the sale may mean that the order is placed or it may not: the purpose of the presentation is to get a decision, which may or may not be in favor of purchase. There is a section on the sales presentation below.

After-sales activities

After-sales activities include calling on the customer afterwards to ensure that the process went smoothly, to learn lessons for the future and perhaps to correct any shortcomings in the delivery or the product. Often salespeople are apparently afraid of carrying out follow-up calls, perhaps because of a fear that the customer will have a complaint: however, it is far better to find out from the customer that there is a problem than to be informed that the customer has complained to the company. After-sales visits also offer opportunities for making further sales or asking for recommendations. Other after-sales activities include ensuring that the paperwork is correctly completed for the company's systems, ensuring that the products are delivered on time, representing the customer's views back to the company and providing other appropriate market information.

The sales presentation

Figure13.7 shows the sequence of events which leads to an eventual sale.

Opening the sale

Particularly when first meeting a new customer, the salesperson needs to establish a personal rapport. This is established by a showing a genuine interest in the customer and his or her problems; the traditional view of the salesperson as being a backslapping individual with a fund of good jokes is a long way from the truth.

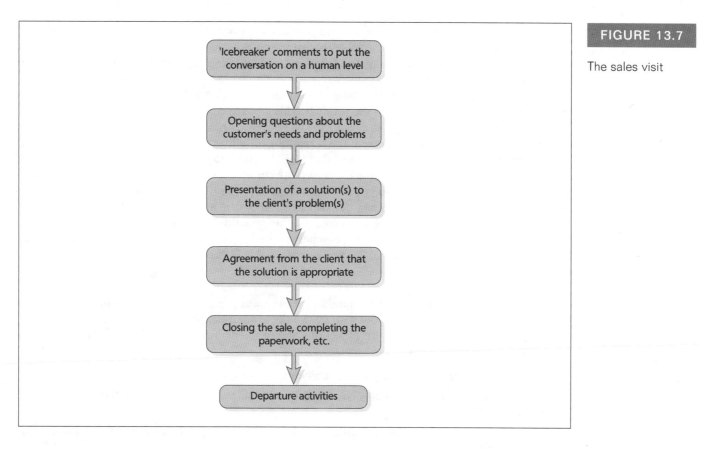

FIGURE 13.7

The sales visit

Typically salespeople begin with an 'icebreaker'. This is an opening remark or series of comments which tend to put the relationship on a human level; they are the common politeness which anybody might use when meeting someone new.

Comments about the weather or the state of the traffic help to put both parties at ease before getting down to business, but it is usual to proceed fairly quickly to the business at hand. Often the aim of the exercise is to create a perceived similarity between the salesperson and the prospect; if the prospect feels that they have something in common, this will increase the level of trust in what the salesperson has to say (Dion *et al*. 1995). Salespeople seek to establish relationships with their prospects, because this is a more certain way of making sales (McKenna 1991); it is also a way of making the working day more pleasant.

The presentation

The following quotation is taken from a sales training manual used by Extras Ltd., a sales training consultancy.

There are some golden rules for the presentation, as follows:

1 You have two ears and one mouth; use them in that proportion.
2 Don't flatly contradict a customer. There's always another way of pointing out a misunderstanding or misconception.
3 Think about the customer's needs at all times.
4 Don't tell lies, porkies, fibs or half-truths and don't make promises you can't keep. You'll get one sale this way, but only one.

Adapted from: Extras Ltd's Sales Training Manual.

In the first instance, salespeople should be prepared to listen to what their customers have to say; selling is not about talking well, it is about listening to people's problems and finding solutions.

Secondly, salespeople need to be ultra polite and very aware of the customer's sensibilities. The overall impression should be that the salesperson is a 'friend in the business' – and in fact most salespeople will agree that it easier to find another company to work for than it is to find new customers. Good salespeople look after their customers.

As in any other area of marketing, the best way to encourage people to buy a product is to ensure that it meets their needs as fully as possible.

Finally, telling lies to customers is counter-productive, since the lie will inevitably come to light once the customer takes delivery of the product. This leads to cancellation of contracts, return of the goods, and even lawsuits – which the customer will almost certainly win. Unfortunately, the same is not true when the situation is reversed; it is a paradox of selling practice that the customer is free to tell any number of lies but the salesperson must tell the truth, despite popular belief to the contrary.

Although some customers regard salespeople with suspicion, the evidence is that salespeople actually seek to develop and maintain good relationships with their customers even when this conflicts with instructions from their marketing departments (Anderson and Robertson 1995).

For the customer, the salesperson is a source of information, a source of help in problem-solving and is an advocate back to the supplying company. Good salespeople are also adept at helping their customers through the decision-making process; often this is the hardest part of making a sale.

Canned presentations

In the past, companies have tried to standardize the sales presentation and in some cases this has advantages. Salespeople were sent out with a carefully worded 'script' to work from and a set of ready-made answers for the most common objections and problems raised by customers. The advantages of this approach are as follows:

1 The salesperson can be trained fairly quickly.

2 The company can be reasonably confident that the salesforce are giving all their customers the same basic message.

3 The sales presentation can be written so that it closely mirrors the company's other marketing communications.

Such an approach often comes across as a 'hard sell', since the customer is not being treated as an individual, but rather as a unit in a mass market. Although a 'hard-sell' approach might work for some products and some companies (Chu *et al.* 1995), this generally only applies to low-risk, low-cost products. In most other cases (which means most cases in which a salesperson is involved) the sale will only be successful if the customer's needs are being met and (more importantly), the customer perceives that these needs are being met. By using the salesperson as a mere mouthpiece for the marketing department, the company is losing the main strength of personal selling, which is the ability to tailor an approach to fit the customer's individual situation.

For these reasons salespeople find it is easier and more beneficial to begin by finding out the customer's needs and then apply a solution to those needs based on the firm's product range. Although marketers commonly speak of 'the product', it is very rarely the case that a salesperson will only have one product to offer; in many cases, salespeople even have the capacity to vary products or tailor them to fit the customer's needs. For example, a machine-tool salesperson would have considerable latitude in redesigning the products to fit a particular task.

Asking questions

The obvious way to find out the customer's needs is by asking questions. The traditional approach, which was developed by E. K. Strong in the 1920s is to divide questions into two types; open questions and closed questions. An open question has a number of different possible answers, whereas a closed question can only be answered yes or no (Strong 1925). Here are some examples of open questions:

- What sort of maintenance bills are you paying at the moment on your equipment?
- Who is in charge of the budgets for maintenance?
- Where should the shipment be delivered?

And some examples of closed questions:

- Would you like me to show you how you can save on maintenance?

- Shall I put you down for the 24-hour call-out service?
- Should we deliver to the main warehouse?

Open questions are actually opening questions; they are the main tool the salesperson has for finding out about the customer's needs. Closed questions tend to be closing questions, used towards the end of the sales presentation to bring the customer to the decision point. Questions have a further important function in that they enable the salesperson to keep control of the direction in which the presentation is going. Questions are powerful in directing people's thoughts; anybody with small children knows that the constant stream of questions is both distracting and wearing because the child keeps triggering the adult's mind to think of a response. Questions demand attention in a way that statements do not.

The presentation itself is, in part, the transfer of knowledge from the salesperson to the prospect. Salespeople will, of course, have considerable knowledge about the products in the range and probably of the industry in general.

One method of structuring the presentation to the customer's needs is to adopt the NASA structure, shown in Table 13.3.

Agreement

If at any stage the salesperson is unable to get an acceptance, he or she should go back to the Needs (see Table 13.3 below) and review what the prospect's problem is. The NASA system places the emphasis on finding solutions to the prospect's need problem; researchers have demonstrated that this is the most effective way to achieve success in selling (Lund 1979).

During the solution part of the presentation, the salesperson is explaining about the particular product which seems to fit the prospect's needs. Because the presentation revolves around the specific customer, it is essential to refer back to those needs at each stage. People do not buy physical products, they buy what the product will do for them. The classic example is the hot water bottle; people do not buy a rubber bag with a stopper in it, they buy a warm bed.

This means that a simple description of the product's features is entirely inadequate; the features must be converted to benefits if a sale is to result. Features are about what the product is; benefits are about what it will do for the customer.

Handling objections

Objections are queries or negative statements raised by the prospect in the course of the presentation. The prospect may, for example, say that a particular feature of the product is not wanted, or is an expensive frill. In most industries the same objections tend to crop up over and over again; common ones are 'We can't afford it', and 'I need to consult someone else about this'.

Although objections are often seen as being barriers to making the sale, good salespeople recognize them as requests for further information. Provided the objection is successfully answered, the negotiation can continue until a mutually acceptable solution is reached. Objections can be handled in the following ways:

TABLE 13.3 The NASA model

N	*Needs* – The salesperson asks the prospect about their needs; what problems does the prospect have?
A	*Acceptance* – Having ascertained the needs, the salesperson confirms with the prospect that these are in fact the needs and obtains the prospect's acceptance of the problem.
S	*Solution* – The salesperson shows the prospect how the solution will meet their problem.
A	*Acceptance again* – This time the salesperson seeks the prospect's acceptance of the proposed solution.

1 Repeat the objection back to the prospect, to confirm that both the salesperson and the prospect understand each other and the nature of the problem.

2 Isolate the objection; in other words, confirm that it is the only problem with the product.

3 Apologize for not having explained properly. This avoids making the prospect lose face, or feel silly.

4 If the objection is false (i.e. has no basis in fact), explain how the product actually meets the problem; alternatively (if the objection is real), show how the benefits of the product outweigh the disadvantages.

5 Confirm with the prospect that the objection has been overcome.

Objections should be distinguished from conditions; a condition prevents the sale going ahead. The commonest ones are as shown in Table 13.4.

Often, conditions do not really exist and are being used to cover up another objection which the prospect would prefer not to raise. Hidden objections need to be brought out into the open if the salesperson is to be able to answer them; this can sometimes be a difficult process and relies heavily on the trust of the prospect. Salespeople can sometimes use the direct approach of simply saying 'I get the feeling there's something else troubling you about the product – what's the problem?' Commonly the objection will be expressed as a desire to 'think about it'. In this case, the salesperson can say 'Yes, I understand that. But just to clarify things for me, what is it you particularly want to think about?' Often this will lead to a statement of the real objection.

Objections can also be classified as real and false. A real objection is a genuine problem with the product; a false objection arises from a misunderstanding, or refers to something that has not yet been covered in the presentation.

Objections can sometimes be used for a trial close; the salesperson says 'If we can overcome that problem for you, are we in business?' This can sometimes mean closing the sale early, but at the very least it brings out any other objections. As a general rule, it is advisable to deal with objections as they arise; leaving them all to the end of the presentation means that the prospect is sitting with negative feelings about the product for a long time. Objections must always be taken seriously; even if the salesperson feels that the problem is a small one and the prospect is getting too concerned over a triviality, it may not seem that way to the prospect.

Closing the sale

Once all the objections have been answered, the sale can be closed. Closing techniques are ways of helping the prospect over the decision-making hurdle. Perhaps surprisingly, most people are reluctant to make decisions, even more so if they are professional buyers. This is perhaps because of the risks attached to making a mistake, but whatever the reason buyers often need some help in agreeing to the order. Salespeople use a number of closing techniques to achieve this; Table 13.5 has some examples.

TABLE 13.4 Common conditions

Condition	What the salesperson should do
The prospect has no authority to make the decision	Find out who does have the authority and ask the prospect to make an appointment to see that person.
The firm has no money	If this is true, the sale cannot go ahead. In most cases it is not true; buyers will often say that the budget has run out as a way of getting rid of the salesperson. Astute salespeople will find out who has the authority to increase the budget, or will arrange for payment to be deferred into the next financial year.
No need for the product	Unless there is a need, no purchase will take place. This is a problem which the salesperson has caused by not properly identifying the needs in the first place.

TABLE 13.5 Examples of closing techniques

Technique	Explanation	Example
Alternative close	The prospect is offered two alternatives, each of which leads to the order.	'Would you like them in red, or in green?'
Order-book close	The salesperson writes down each feature in the order book as it is agreed during the presentation.	'OK, you want the green ones, you want four gross, and your best delivery date is Thursdays. If you'll just autograph this for me, we'll get it moving for you.'
Immediate gain close	The prospect is shown that the sooner he or she agrees to the deal, the sooner he or she will get the benefits of the product.	'Fine. So the sooner we get this paperwork sorted, the sooner you'll start making those savings, right?'

There are, of course, many other closing techniques. Salespeople will typically use whichever one seems most appropriate to the situation.

Incidentally, salespeople usually avoid asking prospects to 'sign' the order. This has negative connotations because it implies a final commitment – people talk of 'signing your life away' or 'signing your death warrant'. It is better to ask people to 'OK that for me' or 'Autograph this for me'.

TALKING POINT

We are told that selling is about solving problems. All well and good, but what happens when the customer says that the solution being offered isn't good enough? Does the salesperson give up? No. Apparently he or she then heads in objection-handling mode, then rapidly into closing mode using all sorts of psychological gymnastics to get the buyer signed-up.

Is this behavior peculiar to salespeople, though? How about when we are persuading a friend to come out for the evening, or to go on a trip together? Even more so, when we are persuading our wife or husband (or girlfriend, or boyfriend) to lose weight or give up smoking? We know it would be good for them to do this and they know it too, but can they make a firm commitment?

Could it be that we are all salespeople at heart, just some of us are not trained enough to do it well?

The astute reader will have recognized that the above sequence of events ties in closely with the NASA model described earlier. During the face-to-face part of the salesperson's job the prospect's needs always come first, followed by an acceptance of the needs, followed by the presentation of the solution to the need problem. Acceptance of the solution, or rejection of it, determines whether the sale goes ahead or not.

Post-presentation activities

It would clearly be rude simply to pack up the order forms and leave immediately after making the sale, so it is good practice to stay for a few moments and discuss other matters, or at the very least to recap on the sale and make sure the customer is happy with everything. In most cases the customer has (so far) only bought a promise to deliver, so it is also a good idea to leave behind some information about the product, a set of contact telephone numbers and copies of the documentation. This serves two purposes; firstly, it ensures that problems can be nipped in the bud because the customer can contact the firm at any time. Secondly, it gives the customer a sense of security and tends to reduce the incidence of cancellations. Buyer's remorse is the term for post-purchase regrets; some of these second thoughts come about because the buyer acquires new information or remembers something important which wasn't covered in the presentation and some of them come from a feeling of mistrust which arises because the customer has nothing tangible to show for the commitment made at the close.

Sometimes salespeople are afraid that, by leaving information and contact telephone numbers, the customer will be encouraged to cancel. The reverse is the case. Customers who are able to telephone are:

(a)   more confident that they don't need to, and

(b)   able to do so if there is a problem, which means that the problem can be solved before the goods are delivered.

After-sales service

Sometimes salespeople are nervous about going back to customers they have sold to, for fear of cancellations or for fear of having to deal with complaints. The reason for this is that salespeople need to maintain a positive outlook about the company, the products and themselves and dealing with customer complaints may mean that the salesperson becomes infected with negativity.

In fact it is always worthwhile revisiting customers once the delivery of the product has been made. The reasons for this are as follows:

- If there is a problem, the visit offers the opportunity to rectify matters. Research shows that customers whose complaints are dealt with to their complete satisfaction become more loyal than those who didn't have a complaint in the first place (Coca Cola Company 1981). Perhaps salespeople should actually encourage customers to complain, so that they can demonstrate how well they can handle complaints!

- If the customer is completely satisfied with the product (which is usually the case), this helps the salesperson feel even more positive about the firm and the products.

- Repeat sales often result and a longer-term relationship can develop.

Salespersons could, for example, make an appointment to see both the buyer and the users of the product to check that everybody is happy with the purchase. Only good outcomes are possible.

■ Key-account selling

A key-account is one which possesses some or all of the following characteristics:

- It accounts for a significant proportion of the firm's overall sales. This means that the supplying firm is in a vulnerable position if the customer goes elsewhere. This in turn means that the supplier may be expected to negotiate significant changes in its methods, products and business practices, in order to fit in with the customer's business practices and needs.

- There is cooperation between distribution channel members rather than conflict. This places the emphasis strongly on good, effective channels of communication, with the salesperson in the front line.

- The supplier works interdependently with the customer to lower costs and increase efficiency. This again implies lengthy negotiations and frequent contact between the firms.

- Supply involves servicing aspects such as technical support as well as delivery of physical products. Servicing aspects will often fall to the salesperson and because of the intangible nature of services, good communication is at a premium.

Key-account selling has the following features:

1   There will be many decision-makers involved, with very little likelihood of being able to meet all of them at one time.

2 It is frequently the case that the salesperson is not present when the final decision is made and he or she may never meet the most senior decision-makers.

3 The problems which the salesperson is expected to address are complex and often insoluble in any permanent sense.

4 The consequences of the problem are often much more important than the immediate problem would suggest.

Traditional selling emphasizes objection handling, overcoming the sales resistance of the buyer and closing the sale. This naturally tends to lead to a focus on the single transaction rather than on the whole picture of the relationship between the supplier and the buyer.

In itself, this may not matter for many purchases. A firm selling photocopiers, for example, has many competitors who are supplying broadly similar products. This means that a quick sale is essential, since otherwise the buyer will be getting several quotes from other firms and will probably make the final decision based on the price alone. In addition, repeat business will be unlikely to materialize and will be a long time coming if it does, so the salesperson is not looking to establish a long-term relationship with the buyer, nor is the buyer particularly interested in establishing a long-term relationship with the salesperson. Both parties are mainly interested in solving the customer's immediate problems, then moving on to other business.

Selling to major accounts cannot follow the simplistic approach of finding out needs and closing which is used in traditional selling situations; it involves a much more drawn-out procedure. Buyers who are considering a major commitment to a supplier, either for a single large purchase or for a long-term stream of supplies, are unlikely to be impressed with a one-hour presentation followed by an alternative close. Also, the salesperson will need to sell the solution to his or her own firm, since major changes in products and practices are often needed.

In major account selling the emphasis shifts from objection handling towards objection prevention. The salesperson is concerned to ensure that objections do not arise, or at least if they do that the answers are already in place. This means that the questions that need to be asked are a little more sophisticated than just the open-or-closed dichotomy. The system of classifying questions as open or closed is inadequate in a key-account situation. Neil Rackham (1995) identified four groupings of question types, as follows:

1 *Situation questions* – These questions are about finding out the current situation of the prospective customer, in terms of the customer's strategic direction, financial position, status of the problem and so forth.

2 *Problem questions* – These questions relate to the specific problem the buyer has at present. These questions help to develop mutual understanding of the problem and reveal the implied needs.

3 *Implication questions* – These explore the wider implications of the problem, and often reveal that the problem has much greater ramifications than were at first apparent. This makes the buyer feel the problem much more acutely.

4 *Need-payoff questions* – These questions enable the buyer to state explicit needs, which allows the seller to explain the benefits of the product.

This classification of questions has been registered as SPIN by Huthwaite Research Group Ltd. The process of working through these questions and covering all the implications of the proposed solution is time consuming and will involve many people; this means that the one-call approach to selling which is typical of small sales will not apply to major accounts.

From a sales management viewpoint this has major implications. In small-account sales, the one-call sale is the norm; typically, sales managers operate on the basis that the more calls the salespeople make, the more sales will result. On the face of it, this is perfectly logical. If a salesperson has a closing rate of 1 in 4 (1 sale for every 4 calls) then 20 calls will produce 5 sales, 40 calls will produce 10 sales, but 12 calls will only produce 3 sales. Therefore most sales managers apply pressure to their salesforces to make more calls.

In major account selling this approach would be disastrous. Encouraged (or compelled) to call on more customers, the salesperson will inevitably begin to call on only those customers who can be sold to quickly and easily, in other words the smaller accounts.

Sales productivity actually comes from two components; sales efficiency and sales effectiveness. Efficiency is about getting in front of the maximum number of prospects for the minimum cost; sales effectiveness is about maximizing the sales potential once in front of the prospects. Both elements are important, but small-account selling puts more emphasis on efficiency, whereas major account selling puts more emphasis on effectiveness.

In small-account sales, managerial involvement is not usually hands-on. The managers who are most successful concentrate on managing sales-team activities, but do little or no selling themselves and do not become involved directly with customers unless there is a major problem (Rackham 1995). In major-account selling, though, the sales manager is almost certain to become directly involved with the customer at some stage, if only because such a large commitment on the part of the customer demands that they should speak to the senior management of the supplier firm. Sales managers should follow these principles when becoming involved in major sales:

- Only become involved when your presence makes a unique difference. The salesperson involved on the account is probably very deeply immersed in it and will know a lot about the customer and the state of the negotiation; you cannot possibly know as much.
- Do not make sales calls on a customer unless your salesperson is with you. You could upset a delicate stage of the negotiation, or at the very least introduce new factors.
- Before any joint call, agree on specific and clear selling roles with your salesperson. Again, control needs to be strongly with the salesperson who is responsible for the account, so it is essential to trust that person's judgment.
- Be an active internal seller for your salespeople. The solution arrived at for the client is likely to involve internal changes for the supplier, some of which will not be popular with the other people in the firm. They will need to be convinced and the sales manager is the best person to do this.
- Always have a withdrawal strategy that prevents any customer becoming too dependent on you personally. Customers may prefer to deal with 'the boss' rather than with the salesperson, but a sales manager cannot afford to spend all their time out of the office, selling to major accounts.

Problems arise for the sales manager in coaching major sales. In small sales, where the salesperson is perhaps making four or five calls a day, it is easily possible for the sales manager to accompany the salesperson for a day and observe what happens in calls. Corrections can be made to the salesperson's approach and within a week or so the improvement in sales should become apparent. In major sales, the lead times between first contact with the client and the final agreement to the sale are likely to be very long indeed, often months and sometimes years; in those circumstances, coaching becomes difficult, to say the least. Improvements in methods may not show results for years and therefore it may be difficult to motivate salespeople to make changes in their practices.

One of the biggest problems for the sales manager is that it is relatively easy to get people to work harder – extra incentives will usually motivate people to put in more hours, or otherwise increase sales efficiency. Increasing sales effectiveness, though, means getting people to 'work smarter' and since most people are working as 'smart' as they know how to already, extra incentives will probably not help.

The KAM/PPF model

For the purposes of discussion, the Millman and Wilson definition of a key-account will be used. For Millman and Wilson, a key-account is a customer in a B2B market identified by a selling company as being of strategic importance (Millman and Wilson 1994). This definition avoids the problem of linking key-account status to size, geographical location or volume of business. The implication is that an account can be small in volume terms, or can be a small company, but can represent a major breakthrough for the selling company, perhaps because the account opens the door to other, larger volumes of business. Key-account management (KAM) encapsulates all those activities intended to establish or maintain a relationship with a strategically important customer.

The PPF model

The Millman-Wilson (1995) Relational Development model is a tool for examining the initiation, growth and eventual demise of the relationship between firms. Linked to the PPF (Product Process Facilitation) model of relational interaction (Wilson 1993), as shown in Table 13.6, it is possible to show that the types of problem being addressed and resolved by the partners in the relationship will vary according to the stage of the relationship.

The PPF model postulates that the nature of dyadic organizational relationships is directly related to the nature of the problems that the parties focus on resolving. In dyadic business relationships these problems are hierarchical, in that a more distant relationship between the parties will only generate problems related to products. The higher order problems of process and facilitation will only become apparent as the relationship becomes closer.

The KAM model

The Millman-Wilson Stages of Relational Development model describes the stages firms go through as the relationship achieves key-account status (Millman and Wilson 1995). In the pre-KAM stage, the firms do not have a relationship but are assessing whether there is potential for establishing key-account status. In the early-KAM stage the supplying firm might develop preferred-supplier status. In the mid-KAM stage the partnership builds further, consolidating the preferred-supplier status. In the partnership-KAM stage the firms develop a spirit of partnership and build a common culture and the supplier locks in the customer becoming the external resource base. In the synergistic-KAM stage the firms share rewards and become quasi-integrated. The final stage is the uncoupling-KAM stage in which the firms disengage.

The combined KAM/PPF model

The combined KAM/PPF model categorizes the types of problem and shows how these can be related to the stages that firms go through when establishing a key-account relationship. Table 13.7 shows the PPF strategies mapped against the stages of the relational development model (Wilson 1999).

The strategic issues raised at different stages of the relationship connect with the firm's communication strategies and particularly with the stated strategies of firms at trade fairs. In the early stages, communication might be dominated by outbound messages from the selling company, but in the later stages a true dialogue is likely to be the prevailing paradigm.

Negotiation

'You don't get what you deserve in this life; you get what you negotiate.'

Negotiation is about coming to a mutual agreement, where each party is prepared to give up something in order to obtain concessions from the other party. The emphasis on negotiation that is so apparent at present has come about largely because of the emphasis on establishing long-term relationships between customers and suppliers, and is particularly important in major account selling.

TABLE 13.6 The PPF model of problem characteristics

Problem Category	Nature of Problem
Product	Availability, performance, features, quality, design, technical support, order size, price, terms.
Process	Speed of response, manufacturing process issues, application of process knowledge, changes to product, project management issues, decision-making process knowledge, special attention in relation to deliveries, design, quotes, cost reduction.
Facilitation	Value creation, compatibility and integration of systems, alignment of objectives, integration of personnel, managing processes peripheral to customer core activity, strategic alignment.

TABLE 13.7 KAM/PPF strategies

Development stage	Objectives	Strategies
Pre-KAM	Define and identify strategic account potential. Secure initial contact.	Identify key contacts and decision-making unit. Establish product need. Display willingness to address other areas of the problem. Advocate key-account status in-house.
Early-KAM	Account penetration. Increase volume of business. Achieve preferred supplier status.	Build social network. Identify process-related problems and signal willingness to work together to provide cost-effective solutions. Build trust through performance and open communications.
Mid-KAM	Build partnership. Consolidate preferred-supplier status. Establish key-account in-house.	Focus on product-related issues. Manage the implementation of process-related solutions. Build inter-organizational teams. Establish joint systems. Begin to perform non-core management tasks.
Partnership-KAM	Develop spirit of partnership. Build common culture. Lock in customer by being external resource base.	Integrate processes. Extend joint problem-solving. Focus on cost reduction and joint value-creating opportunities. Address key strategic issues of the client. Address facilitation issues.
Synergistic-KAM	Continuous improvement. Shared rewards. Quasi-integration.	Focus on joint value creation. Create semi-autonomous project teams. Develop strategic congruence.
Uncoupling KAM	Disengagement.	Withdraw.

The basis on which negotiation rests is that both parties will benefit as a result of the trade. In everyday terms, a shopkeeper would prefer to have money than to have the goods on the shelves, whereas the customers would prefer to have the goods than have the money. If this were not the case, trade would be impossible. The contract results at any point along a line drawn between the maximum amount of money the customers are prepared to pay and the minimum amount the retailer is prepared to accept. In a Middle Eastern bazaar, the price would be subject to negotiation by the parties, with the shopkeeper trying to get the highest price and the customer trying to pay the lowest. In Western shops there is only an indirect negotiation, with the customer going to the retailer who offers the best deal; this can scarcely be called negotiation at all.

Negotiating follows eight stages, as shown in Table 13.8.

Negotiation takes practice, and a considerable degree of empathy; good negotiators need to be able to judge other people's behavior accurately and reliably and do this in real time with the customer present.

Techniques of negotiation vary from one individual to the next, but the list shown in Table 13.9 gives a useful overview (and some interesting names) for some of the main ones. Some of these tactics are used by buyers, some by salespeople, some by both; some are acceptable bargaining ploys, some are somewhat dubious ethically and are intended to get the best deal in a one-off selling or buying situation.

Ultimately, the deal that is struck will depend on the relative strength of each party in terms of their firms' negotiating positions and on the skills and charisma of the negotiators. The process is not a mechanical one; as pointed out at the beginning of this chapter, business is not done by companies, it is done by people. The chemistry between two individuals is at least as important as the final economics of the deal itself.

TABLE 13.8 Eight stages of negotiation

Stage	Explanation
Preparation	Good negotiators set targets; what is the maximum they might achieve, what is the minimum they are willing to accept, and what is the most probable outcome. This may mean working out detailed costings. More importantly, the negotiator needs to work out what it is the other side are likely to want and be prepared to give – this avoids surprises in the discussions.
Discussion	Listening carefully to what the other party is saying usually gives a clue as to how to express a counter-offer, or even to what it is the person really wants from the negotiation.
Signals	Negotiators need to give clear signals when the discussion is going in the right direction. This encourages further movement and helps the negotiation to proceed.
Proposition	The proposition being offered needs to be fair, and flexible. Nelson Rockefeller's business maxim was 'Always leave something for the next guy'. In following this, he ensured that everybody wanted to do business with him, because they knew they would always benefit from it.
Presentation	It is essential to communicate effectively so that both parties are clear about exactly what is on offer and what each is going to gain.
Bargain	Bargaining is about getting something back for what one is prepared to offer. If the other party says, 'Can you cut the price another 5 per cent?' the salesperson should not just agree to do it. The salesperson needs to say 'OK, we'll cut it if you'll guarantee to order 20 per cent more goods'. In other words, salespeople should negotiate, not donate.
Close	At some point both parties will need to summarize their positions and come to an agreement. This should be done once both parties are happy with the deal they are getting, so the close need not be aggressive or manipulative.
Agreement	Any agreement made needs to be put in writing to ensure that there is no misunderstanding. Salespeople should also seek some kind of formal commitment from the other party, either in cash or as a contract.

Managing the salesforce

Possibly the most expensive marketing tool the company has, the salesforce is in some ways the hardest to control. This is because it is composed of independently minded people who each have their own ideas on how the job should be done and who are working away from the office and out of sight of the sales managers.

Sales managers are responsible for recruitment, training, motivation, controlling and evaluating salesforce activities and managing sales territories.

Recruitment

Recruitment is complicated by the fact that there is no generally applicable set of personality traits that go to make up the ideal salesperson. This is because the sales task varies greatly from one firm to another and the sales manager will need to draw up a specific set of desirable traits for the task in hand. This will involve analyzing the company's successful salespeople and also the less successful ones, to find out what the differences are between them.

Some companies take the view that almost anybody can be trained to sell and therefore the selection procedures are somewhat limited, or even non-existent; other companies are extremely selective and subject potential recruits to a rigorous selection procedure.

TABLE 13.9 Negotiating tactics

Tactic	Description and Explanation
Act Crazy	Moving around from one topic to another can sometimes disorient the other party and cause their carefully prepared position to collapse. This is a tactic sometimes used by buyers in traditional selling situations, where they want to confuse the salesperson.
Big Pot	Here the salesperson quotes a high price initially, in order to have room to maneuver later. Equally, a buyer may imply that a very large order will be placed in order to negotiate a better deal.
Prestigious Ally	Mention of an existing customer who has influence over the prospect may sway the sale. For example, a computer salesperson selling to a car component manufacturer is more likely to get the sale if they are is already selling to Ford.
The Well is Dry	The negotiator says that there is no further room for negotiation; the deal must either go ahead as it is, or not at all. This is a somewhat dangerous tactic, since the other party might well call a halt at that point; it is advisable to leave the door open, perhaps by appealing to senior management to allow a little more room for negotiation.
Limited Authority	This is similar to The Well is Dry. Here the negotiator says that the deal has gone as far as they are authorized to take it. This can have the effect of producing a little more from the other party, or it could lead to a demand to speak to someone who does have the authority to negotiate.
Whipsaw!	This needs two negotiators, one to play 'good cop' and the other to play 'bad cop'. The 'bad cop' tries to drive as hard a bargain as possible, then when that is rejected the 'good cop' (the other negotiator) speaks privately to the other party and says 'Maybe I can talk him round. Can we go just a little bit higher?'
Divide and Conquer	This is very commonly used in industrial selling due to the large number of people involved in the buying process. The salesperson approaches each one in turn, separately, and gets some kind of agreement to go ahead 'provided the others agree'. Finally there is no-one left to veto the deal.
Get Lost	Very common in the legal profession, the negotiator simply is unavailable for comment. This tactic is intended to unnerve the other party, who then may offer more than was intended in order to secure the deal.
Wet Noodle	The negotiator simply doesn't respond to anything. This tends to make the other party improve the offer in the hopes of provoking a reaction and kick-starting the negotiation.
Be Patient	Just being quiet and letting the other person keep talking will often lead them into persuading themselves.
Split the Difference	Probably the most common bargaining tactic of all, 'Let's split the difference'. The person who first suggests it probably has the most to gain; it is worth waiting it out to get an even better deal.
Play Devil's Advocate	The negotiator gives the other party some good reasons NOT to accept the deal. Often this will provoke the other party into justifying why the deal should go ahead – the tactic works by using reverse psychology.
Trial Balloon	'I suppose you'd go ahead if we were to offer . . .' This type of statement allows the negotiator to judge whether the other party is open to an offer, without actually committing to making the offer.
Surprise!	The negotiator suddenly slips in some new information which puts everything else in a different light and re-starts the negotiation on different lines. Sometimes this is done in order to unsettle the other party, more often it is done to re-start a stalled negotiation.

Sources of potential recruits are; advertising, employment agencies, recommendations from existing sales staff, colleges and universities and internal appointments from other departments.

Training

Training can be long or short, depending on the product and the market. Table 13.10 illustrates the dimensions of the problem.

The role the salesperson is required to take on will also affect the length of training; *missionary salespeople* will take longer to train than *order-takers*, and *closers* will take longer than *telephone canvassers*.

Typically, training falls into two sections; *classroom training*, in which the recruits are taught about the company and the products and may be given some grounding in sales techniques, and *field training*, which is an ongoing training program carried out in front of real customers in the field. Field training is often the province of the sales managers, but classroom training can be carried out by other company personnel (in some cases, in larger firms, there will be specialists who do nothing else but train salespeople).

People tend to learn best by performing the task, so most sales training programs involve substantial field training, either by sending out rookies (trainees) with experienced salespeople, or by the 'in-at-the-deep-end' approach of sending rookies out on their own fairly early in their careers. The latter method is indicated if there are plenty of possible customers for the product; the view is that a few mistakes (lost sales) won't matter. In industrial selling, though, it is often the case that there are fewer possible customers and therefore the loss of even one or two could be serious. In these circumstances it would be better to give rookies a long period of working alongside more experienced salespeople.

Ultimately, of course, salespeople will lose more sales than they get. In most industries, fewer than half the presentations given result in a sale; a typical proportion would be one in three.

Payment

Payment for salespeople traditionally has a commission element, but it is perfectly feasible to use a *straight salary* method, or a *commission-only* method. Although it is commonly supposed that a commission-only salesperson will be highly motivated to work hard, since otherwise he or she will not earn any money, this is not necessarily the case. Salespeople who are paid solely by commission will sometimes decide that they have earned enough for this month and will give themselves a holiday; the company has very little moral power to compel them to work, since there is no basic salary being paid. Conversely, a salesperson who is paid salary-only may feel obligated to work in order to justify the salary.

Herzberg (1960) says that the payment method must be seen to be fair if de-motivation is to be avoided; the payment method is not in itself a good motivator. Salespeople are out on the road for most of their working lives and do not see what other salespeople are doing; whether they are

TABLE 13.10 Factors relating to length of training of sales staff

Factors indicating long training	Factors indicating short training
Complex, technical products	Simple products
Industrial markets with professional buyers	Household, consumer markets
High order values (from the customer's viewpoint)	Low order values
High recruitment costs	Low recruitment costs
Inexperienced recruits – for example, recruited direct from university	Experienced recruits from the same industry

competent at the job, whether they are getting some kind of unfair advantage, even whether they are working at all. In these circumstances a commission system does at least reassure the salesperson that extra effort brings extra rewards. The chart in Table 13.11 shows the trade-offs between commission-only and salary-only; of course, most firms have a mixture of salary and commission.

Motivation

Motivation, perhaps surprisingly, tends to come from sources other than payment. The classic view of motivation was proposed by Abraham Maslow (1954). Maslow's Hierarchy of Needs' theory postulates that people will fulfill the needs at the lower end of a pyramid (survival needs and security needs) before they move on to addressing needs at the upper end (such as belonging needs, esteem needs, and self-actualization needs). Thus, once a salesperson has assured his or her basic survival needs, these cease to be motivators; the individual will then be moving onto esteem needs, or belonging needs. For this reason sales managers usually have a battery of motivational devices for salespeople to aim for.

For rookies, the award of a company tie might address the need to belong; for more senior salespeople, membership of a Millionaire's Club (salespeople who have sold more than a million pounds' worth of product) might address esteem needs. Many sales managers offer prizes aimed at salespeople's spouses or partners. This can be a powerful incentive since salespeople often work unusual hours and thus have disrupted home lives; the spouse or partner is sometimes neglected in favor of the job, so a prize aimed at them can help assuage the salesperson's natural feelings of guilt.

Sales territory management

Sales territory management involves ensuring that the salesforce have a reasonably equal chance of making sales. Clearly a garage tools salesperson in a major city will have an easier task than one in a rural area, simply because of the shorter distances between prospects; such a salesperson would spend more time in presentations and less time driving. On the other hand, the city salesperson would probably face more competition and might also have to spend more time caught in traffic during rush hour periods.

Territories can be divided *geographically* or by *industry*; IBM divide territories by industry, for example, so that salespeople get to know the problems and needs of the specific industry for which they have responsibility. IBM salespeople might be given responsibility for banks, or insurance companies, or local government departments. This sometimes means that salespeople have greater distances to travel in order to present IBM products, but are more able to make sensible

TABLE 13.11 Trade-offs in salesperson's pay packages

Mainly Salary	Mainly Commission
Where order values are high	Where order values are low
Where the sales cycle is long	Where the sales cycle is short
Where staff turnover is low	Where staff turnover is high
Where sales staff are carefully selected against narrow criteria	Where selection criteria for staff are broad
For new staff, or staff who have to develop new territories	For situations where aggressive selling is indicated (e.g. selling unsought goods)
Where sales territories are seriously unequal in terms of sales potential	Where sales territories are substantially the same

recommendations and give useful advice. Geographical territories are more common, since they minimize travel time and maximize selling time.

It is virtually impossible to create exactly equal territories. Thus it is important to discuss decisions with salespeople in order to ensure that people feel they are being treated fairly. For example, some salespeople may be quite happy to accept a rural territory because they like to live and work in the country, even if it means earning less.

SUMMARY

The salesforce is a major part of B2B budgets. In many cases, salespeople spend relatively little time actually selling and a great deal of time filling in paperwork, traveling between appointments and so forth. This means that much sales management effort is directed towards ensuring that the salespeople spend as little time on administration as possible and that they are effective when in front of a customer.

The key points from this chapter are:

- Relationships between firms operate at many levels.
- Conflict is not necessarily a bad thing: it often leads to creative solutions.
- Trust and person-to-person relationships are essential components of successful B2B relationships.
- Selling is about solving problems for customers, it is not about persuasion.
- Selling may not belong in the communications mix at all.
- Salespeople often identify with customers.
- Salespeople should remember they have two ears and one mouth and use them in that proportion.
- Canned presentations are unlikely to be successful because they ignore customer individuality.
- Objections are requests for information: conditions are states of affairs which make the sale impossible.
- After-sales activities are essential, but are often neglected.
- Techniques used in small-scale accounts are counter-productive in key-account selling.
- The same is true of management techniques.
- Commission is a way of ensuring fairness: it is probably not a strong motivator.

REVIEW QUESTIONS

1 What are the main differences between key-account selling and small-account selling?
2 Which remuneration system would you expect to be more highly-motivating: a commission-only system, or a straight-salary system?
3 Why is ice-breaking important?
4 Why do salespeople tend to identify with customers more than with the firms they work for?
5 Why are after-sales activities often neglected?

Bristol Myers Squibb is one of the leading pharmaceutical companies in the United States. The company is well-known for its commitment to staff training and to developing people's skills: as one sales manager put it, 'What's kept me here for 15 years is the BMS culture. It's a culture that's directed towards its people. BMS wants to take care of those who are willing to work hard and do the right things'.

This commitment to the staff is indicated in the company's mission statement, which contains the following statement:

We pledge personal respect, fair compensation and honest and equitable treatment. To all who qualify for advancement, we will make every effort to provide opportunity. We affirm our commitment to foster a globally diverse workforce and a company-wide culture that encourages excellence, leadership, innovation and a balance between our personal and professional lives. We acknowledge our obligation to provide able and humane leadership and a clean and safe work environment.

While most companies have similar wording in their mission statements, most do not live up to the ringing phrases: Bristol Myers Squibb invest substantial sums in supporting and training salespeople and other staff on the organization.

Pharmaceutical selling is dominated by missionary selling. The salesforce are rarely in front of a buyer: usually they talk to doctors, hospitals, and even State organizations which have influence over the decisions made. Pharmaceutical selling can almost be seen as a public-relations exercise, except that the results (in terms of sales) are much more tangible. The pharmaceutical industry is also characterized by a continuous training need as new, ever more complex products arrive on the market.

During the summer of 2002 BMS revamped its entire hardware and software support systems for its salesforce. This included the M-Power automation system, including the field-force automation system CallMex. This system enabled BMS to manage sample distribution, capture doctors' signatures electronically, record and analyze data on prescribers, prepare reports and use pen-tablet systems to communicate with Head Office. The new software also complied with new legislation (the Prescription Drug Marketing Act).

These changes were revolutionary for a salesforce used to a paper-based system, so the entire salesforce (almost 4,000 people in all) had to be trained to use the new equipment and software.

The BMS salesforce is widely scattered geographically. They are divided into 350 districts across five time zones, so bringing them together for a training program would have been impossible. The company therefore opted for a web-based training program, enabling the salesforce to learn in spare time and at their own pace.

The e-learning system was set up by Dendrite Inc., a specialist firm in e-learning. Dendrite's WebSession Manager is an integrated software and service product designed for distance learning. It enables software application sharing, user training and coaching, and document preparation collaboration. Web sessions are led by moderators who direct the class, and co-moderators who field questions and generally play a behind-the-scenes role. The participants log-on via a standard modem at specific times for classes and are able to interact with the instructors on-line in real time.

The system was piloted with 300 representatives and managers during the week of May 6th 2002. This was sufficient to train these participants successfully, so the system was rolled-out to the entire salesforce: as a result of the pilot, the class times were adjusted and the submission process for on-line assessments was streamlined. Dendrite had to ship 40,000 individual pieces of hardware to participants in advance of starting the training program, including a videotape from BMS's senior management stressing the importance for corporate strategy of adopting the system. Another video provided the participants with instruction on using the tablet PC.

The scale of the program was vast. Dendrite used over 100 instructors, who had themselves to be trained beforehand: the company used 20 virtual training studios at its headquarters and provided more than 50,000 hours of virtual training. Students submitted 280,000 assessment questions and over 20,000 pieces of training material were distributed.

Participants worked through six self-paced pre-recorded sessions before joining a live session and during each week of the training program the participants only needed to commit two days out of the field. This minimized the disruption to BMS's sales program. In follow-up participant evaluation studies, 90 per cent of participants said that the program had met or exceeded their expectations, 97 per cent said that moderators and co-moderators enhanced the virtual learning experience, and 89 per cent said that they could use CallMex successfully in their sales territory activities.

For BMS, the program was a resounding success. It saved approximately 5,500 field sales days as well as an estimated US$10m in travel expenses, but the most important aspect of its success was the way in which it succeeded in motivating the salesforce to learn and use the new systems.

Questions

1 To what extent do you think this training system would work for other types of selling, for example technical salespeople?

2 What problems might arise from surveying participants afterwards?

3 Why might salespeople not participate in a program such as this?

4 What problems arise from the 11 per cent of BMS salespeople who say that they are unable to use CallMex successfully?

5 How might BMS build on this scheme for further salesforce training?

REFERENCES

Anderson, E. and Robertson, T. S. (1995) 'Inducing Multi-line Salespeople to Adopt House Brands', *Journal of Marketing* 59: 2: April: 16–31.

Booms, B. H. and Bitner, M. J. (1981) 'Marketing Strategies and Organization Structures for Service Firms', in 'Marketing of Services', J. Donnelly and W. R. George, eds, American Marketing Association.

Cespedes, F. V. (1996) *Managing marketing linkages texts, cases and readings*, Upper Saddle River, N. J.: Prentice-Hall.

Chu, W., Gestner, E. and Hess, J. D. (1995) 'Costs and Benefits of Hard Sell', *Journal of Marketing Research*, XXXII: February: 97–102.

Daft, R. L. (1998) *Organization Theory and Design*, (6th edn), Ohio: South Western College Publishing.

DeCormier, R. and Jobber, D. (1993) 'The Counsellor Selling Method; Concepts, Constructs, and Effectiveness', *Journal of Personal Selling and Sales Management*, 13(4): 39–60.

Dewsnap, B. and Jobber, D. '*The Sales and Marketing Interface; Is It Working?*' Proceedings of the Academy of Marketing Conference, Sheffield: 1998.

Dion, P., Easterling, D. and Miller, S. J. (1995) 'What is really necessary in successful buyer seller relationships?', *Industrial Marketing Management*, 24: 1–9.

Donaldson, W. (1998) *Sales Management Theory and Practice*, London: MacMillan.

Drucker, P. F. (1973) '*Management; Tasks, Responsibilities, Practices*', New York: Harper & Row.

Hakansson, H. (1989) *Corporate Technological Behaviour – Co-operation and Networks*, Routledge: London.

Hakansson, H. and Gadde, L-E. (1992) *Professional Purchasing*, London: Routledge.

Hatch, M. J. (1997) *Organization Theory – Modern Symbolic and Postmodern Perspectives*, Oxford: University Press.

Hellreigel, D. and Slocum J. W., Jr. (1988) *Management*, (5th edn), London: Addison-Wesley.

Herzberg, F. (1966) *Work and Nature of Man*, London: William Collins.

Hodge, B. J. and Anthony, W. P. (1991) *Organization Theory – A Strategic Approach*, (4th edn), London: Allyn and Bacon.

Levitt, T. (1960) 'Marketing Myopia', *Harvard Business Review*, July-August: 45–56.

Lund, P. R. (1979) *Compelling Selling*, London: Macmillan.

Maslow, A. (1954) *Motivation and Personality*, New York: Harper and Row.

McKenna, R. (1991) *Relationship Marketing*, London: Century Business.

Millman, T. and Wilson, K. J. (1994) '*From key account selling to key account management*', Proceedings of the Tenth Annual IMP Conference, University of Groningen, Netherlands.

Millman, T. and Wilson, K. J. (1995) '*Developing key account managers*', IMP 12th International Conference Proceedings, Manchester Federal School of Business and Management.

Millman, A. F. and Wilson, K. J. (1996) 'Developing key account management competencies', *Journal of Marketing Practice*, 2(2): 7–22.

Newton, D. A. (1969) 'Get the most out of your sales-force', *Harvard Business Review*, Sept-Oct: 16–29.

Rackham, N. (1991) *The Management of Major Sales*, Aldershot: Gower.

Rackham, N. (1995) *Spin Selling*, Aldershot: Gower.

Reitz, H. J. (1977) *Behaviour in Organizations*, Homewood Ill: Richard D. Irwin Inc.

Robbins, S. P. (1991) *Organizational Behaviour – Concepts, Controversies and Applications* (5th edn), London: Prentice Hall.

Rosenbloom, B. and Anderson, R. E. (1984) 'The sales manager: tomorrow's super marketer', *Business Horizons*, Mar-Apr: 50–6.

Ruekert, R. W. and Walker, O. C., Jr. (1987) 'Marketing's Interaction with Other Functional Units: A Conceptual Framework and Empirical Evidence', *Journal of Marketing*, 51: January: 1–19.

Strong, E. K. (1925) *The Psychology of Selling*, New York: McGraw-Hill.

The Coca Cola Company (1981) 'Measuring the Grapevine: Consumer Response and Word of Mouth'.

Wilson, K. J. (1993) 'A problem-centered approach to key account management', Proceedings of the National Sales Management Conference, Atlanta.

Wilson, K. J. (1993) 'Managing the industrial sales-force of the 1990s', *Journal of Marketing Management*, 9(2): 123–39.

Wilson, K. J. (1999) 'Developing key account relationships: the integration of the Millman-Wilson relational development model with the problem-centered [PPF] model of buyer-seller interaction in business-to-business markets', *The Journal of Selling and Major Account Management*, 1: 4: Summer.

SALES PROMOTION, EXHIBITIONS AND TRADE FAIRS

Learning objectives

After reading this chapter, you should be able to:

- Describe the key benefits and drawbacks of using exhibitions

- Explain how exhibitions can be used in key-account management

- Explain ways of making exhibitions more effective

- Describe the key benefits of sales promotions

- Explain how sales promotions smooth out fluctuations in demand

- Describe the main types of sales promotion, with their advantages and disadvantages

- Describe ways of improving the effectiveness of sales promotions

▌ Introduction

Exhibitions and trade fairs are among the most widely-used B2B marketing tools and yet at the same time they are the least well-researched. Even experienced exhibitors have very little idea of how, or even whether, exhibitions are effective.

Sales promotions allow free rein to the imagination of the manager. So many sales promotion activities are used by clever managers, yet this area has received only limited attention from academics. In B2B marketing, sales promotions are often played down, yet they still have a potentially important role to play.

■ Exhibitions and trade fairs as communication

Exhibitions and trade fairs represent a substantial commitment on the part of marketers. Total expenditure on exhibitions and trade fairs in the UK is consistently higher than the spend on advertising in the trade press and is also higher than the combined expenditure on outdoor, cinema and radio advertising. Yet few exhibitors assess the effectiveness of this activity in any realistic way, and there is continuing academic debate about whether exhibitions are actually effective in communicating with target markets. Attitudes are polarized among exhibitors: some believe strongly that exhibitions are excellent promotional tools, whereas others believe exhibitions are marginal at best (Blythe and Rayner 1996).

One of the areas of dispute is the split between activities relating directly to making sales (generating leads, identifying prospects, even making sales pitches on the stand) and the non-sales benefits of exhibitions (public relations, enhancing corporate reputation, carrying out market research, etc.). Most exhibitors are concerned mainly with immediate sales (Shipley *et al.* 1993, Kijewski *et al.* 1992, Blythe 1997). Having said that, some exhibitors are more concerned with non-selling activities.

Exhibitions occupy a key role in B2B marketing, since they allow contact with buyers who otherwise might never meet due to geographical or time constraints. This is particularly the case with international trade fairs such as those held in Germany, where exhibitions occupy a more important role than in most other countries. Exhibitions such as these can bring together people who might otherwise not have known of each others' existence. Since contact at a fair takes place on neutral territory, both parties can feel more relaxed, so exhibitions offer an opportunity for the relationship between buying company and selling company to develop more fully and perhaps develop in unexpected directions. Since many visitors are technical people or administrators rather than buyers, there are many opportunities for establishing contacts at all levels of the organization.

As a public relations exercise, exhibitions have much to offer. Since buyers are only a tiny minority of visitors to exhibitions (less than 10 per cent at most) (Blythe 2000, Gramman 1994), selling objectives are probably not considered to be the most important activities to be undertaken. Yet, almost everybody who visits has some interest in the industry for which the exhibition is organized. This means that many of them will be influential in the buying decision, or at the very least might talk to people who are influential.

In terms of semiotics, trade fairs provide signs about the company and its products. For some firms, the sign is the main reason for exhibiting – being at the exhibition at all gives a signal that the company is at the forefront of the industry, or at least is not one of the laggards. In most cases, though, trade fairs are the vehicle by which signs are delivered. Sign systems of trade fairs are well-known – the stand, the suited personnel, the product samples, the free gifts, the product demonstrations and set-piece displays are typical of trade fairs. Each system has an accepted etiquette, so that visitors and exhibitors know what their role is when attending the show.

Syntactically, trade shows tend to be stylized. The meaning of a brochure offered at a trade show is not the same as the meaning of a brochure offered by a salesperson at a customer's office. Because trade shows have a cultural context of their own, the resulting meanings differ from those encountered outside the exhibition hall.

Research into exhibitions

Most research into managers' perceptions of exhibitions confirms that most managers see them in terms of making sales. This is true of both US and UK shows: even when managers do not expect to take orders at the exhibition, they do see the exhibition as an opportunity to generate leads, qualify prospects and open sales. This is particularly apparent in the staffing of stands: managers predominantly staff them with salespeople, even though there is evidence to suggest that visitors do not like this (Tanner and Chonko 1995, Skerlos and Blythe 2000).

Shipley, Egan and Wong (1993) identified 13 reasons for exhibiting, of which seven were directly related to selling while six represent non-selling activities. Research conducted by Blythe (1997) showed that the selling aims were ranked highest in importance by the majority of exhibitors (see Table 14.1).

Attempts to determine whether exhibitions are effective or not are also colored by the assumption that they are primarily selling devices. Sharland and Balogh (1996) defined effectiveness as the

TABLE 14.1 Ranking of exhibition aims

Reason for Exhibiting	Ranking
Meeting new customers	1
Launching new products	2
Taking sales orders	3
Interacting with existing customers	4
Promoting existing products	5
Enhancing the company image	6
General market research	7
Meet new distributors	8
Keeping up with the competition	9
Getting information about the competition	10
Interacting with existing distributors	11
Getting an edge on non-exhibitors	12
Enhancing the morale of the staff	13

number of sales leads generated, followed up and successfully closed and efficiency as the comparison between the cost of trade show participation versus other sales and promotion activities. United States' research by the Trade Show bureau in 1988 put the cost of a trade show lead at US$132 compared with US$251 per call in the field (Trade Show Bureau 1988). United Kingdom research showed the comparable figures to be UK£30 per useful contact at a trade show, compared to UK£150 for a field call (Centre for Leisure and Tourism Studies 1994). Although a 'useful contact' may not be the same as a sales lead, the general conclusion of researchers is that trade shows and exhibitions generate leads more cheaply than other methods.

The problem lies in determining the strength of these 'leads'. A useful contact may not be a buyer at all – which is not a problem if the individual might act as a gatekeeper or influencer in reaching the decision-makers. Even a qualified lead from a buyer may not be strong, since such a buyer will almost certainly be visiting the firm's competitors, who will undoubtedly be at the same venue.

Some early research by Kerin and Cron (1987) showed that some exhibitors do pay attention to the possibilities of non-selling activities. Although the emphasis was still on selling, other aims were present (see Table 14.2).

For this particular group of respondents, corporate image came out highest, although the next two highest scoring aims were selling aims. The dissidents may well be right, since there is a discrepancy between the exhibitors' view of exhibitions and the visitors' view. If exhibitions are about communicating, it would seem reasonable to suppose that the visitors and the exhibitors should have compatible aims in attending: that is to say, their aims will not be the same, but they should be complementary. In the case of exhibitions, visitors are quite clearly seeking out at least some of the communication. Figure 14.1 shows the comparison between visitors' tactics and strategies, and exhibitors' tactics and strategies.

Personal selling clearly happens on exhibition stands, although probably not to the extent that exhibitors believe it does.

TABLE 14.2 Importance of trade show aims

Aim	Mean score (out of 10, with 10 as highest)
Enhancing corporate image	5.32
Introducing new products	5.14
Identifying new prospects	5.08
Getting competitive information	4.94
Servicing current customers	4.69
Enhancing corporate morale	3.75
Selling at the show	2.79
New product testing	2.17

FIGURE 14.1

Exhibitors and visitors strategies and tactics

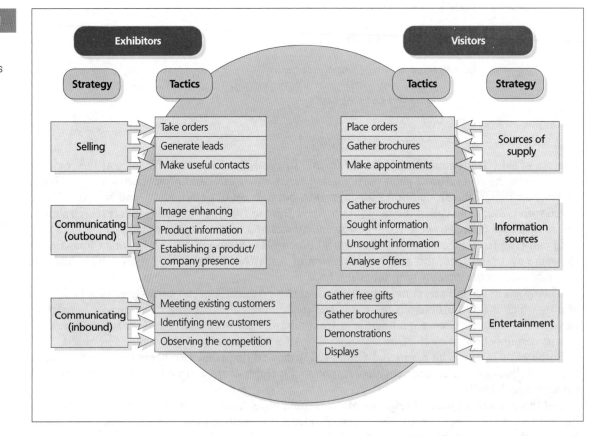

Visitor expectations

Research conducted among visitors to trade fairs shows that most of them are not directly involved in purchase decisions and many of them have no role whatsoever in purchasing. (Skerlos and Blythe 2000, Gramman 1993, Bello and Lohtia 1993, Munuera and Ruiz 1999). The Skerlos and Blythe (2000) research showed the breakdown of job titles illustrated in Table 14.3.

TABLE 14.3 Visitor job profiles

Job	Percentage of respondents
Sales and marketing	24%
General administration	26%
Design	14%
Engineering	22%
Research and development	14%

TABLE 14.4 Reasons for visiting

Reason for visiting	Percentage citing
To see new products and developments	54%
To try new products and go to demonstrations	23%
To obtain technical or product information	21%
To see new companies	12%
To discuss specific problems and talk with the experts	10%
To compare products and services	7%
To make business contacts	6%
To see a specific company or product	5%

When asked about their role in purchasing, 40 per cent of the respondents said they had no role whatsoever. The respondents' reasons for visiting the exhibition were as shown in Table 14.4. Respondents were allowed to state more than one reason.

Those who stated that they had no role in purchasing were substantially more likely to be there to see new products and developments: this is not surprising, since they are likely to be technical people.

Visitors were invited to rate their overall satisfaction with the exhibition in terms of the extent to which their aims were met. Research and development people were significantly less satisfied with the outcomes than were the sales and marketing people, and engineers showed a similar pattern. Visitors' experience of the trade show is therefore clearly related to their jobs, since the job will tend to dictate the visitor's needs and requirements from the show. Failure to meet these needs will result in visitor dissatisfaction with the show.

■ Exhibitions and key-account management

Key-account management is about creating long-term relationships with other firms. As we saw in Chapter 13, relationships go through stages, at each stage of which the focus is on a different type of problem.

In the context of key-account management, exhibitions offer few opportunities to make immediate sales. What they do offer is an opportunity to initiate relationships by approaching influencers and users, for example technical people and administrators: these opportunities are much greater than the opportunity to meet buyers, simply because of the numerical preponderance of these people. Opportunities to deepen existing relationships by meeting key-account firms' technical or administrative people are obviously present and may represent the real strength of exhibitions. In some cases these people may not have been involved directly with the supplying company as the relationship is being established, but are able to become part of the process by meeting people on the exhibition stand.

The KAM/PPF model

Using the KAM/PPF model (Wilson 1999) outlined in Chapter 13, it is possible to map visitors' and exhibitors' reasons for attendance (Blythe 2002). Table 14.5 shows this mapping.

For key-account managers, trade fairs offer three main opportunities:

1 First contact at the pre-KAM or even early-KAM stage.
2 Building partnerships and establishing a common culture at the mid-KAM and partnership-KAM stages.
3 Offering an opportunity for a shared voice at the synergistic-KAM stage.

TABLE 14.5 Exhibitions and the KAM/PPF model

Development Stage	Visitors' Reasons for Attendance [percentage citing in brackets]	Exhibitors' Reasons for Attendance [importance ranking in brackets]
Pre-KAM: defining and identifying strategic account potential	See new companies [12%], to make business contacts [6%], to compare products and services [7%]	Meet new customers [1], launch new products [2], meet new distributors [8], promote existing products [5]
Early-KAM: account penetration, seeking preferred-supplier status	Obtain technical or product information [21%]	Interact with existing customers [4], interact with existing distributors [12], enhance the company image [6], take sales orders [3]
Mid-KAM: building partnership, consolidate preferred-supplier status	Discuss specific problems/talk with the experts [10%]	Interact with existing customers [4], interact with existing distributors [12]
Partnership-KAM: develop spirit of partnership, build common culture, lock in customer	Discuss specific problems/talk with the experts [10%]	Interact with existing customers and distributors [possibly by sharing exhibition space]
Synergistic-KAM: continuous improvement, shared rewards, quasi-integration	No real role. At this stage the companies are very close together and may even be sharing their promotional activities, including exhibiting at trade fairs	No real role
Uncoupling-KAM: disengagement	To see new customers, products, developments and companies	To meet new customers and distributors and to take sales orders

Pre-KAM stage

The first contact is far more likely to be with a technical person or an administrator than with a buyer or decision-maker, which means that the key-account manager needs to use these people as product champions in order to enter the prospective customer's firm. Given that these technical people are at the trade fair for the purpose of finding out what is new in the field, exhibitors might be well advised to put some of their own technical people on the stand in order to explore possible synergies. In the pre-KAM stage, when the parties are feeling each other out, it appears that exhibitors place a high importance on finding new customers and launching new products. Unfortunately, only 12 per cent of visitors cite seeing new companies as a reason for attending, only 6 per cent cite making business contacts, and 7 per cent cite comparing products and services.

Early-KAM stage

At the early-KAM stage, when the parties are aiming to increase the volume of business and build a social network, the exhibitor's aim of interacting with existing customers will be most appropriate. The 21 per cent of visitors who cited obtaining technical information as a reason for attending will also probably be catered to. Where the prevailing strategy is concerned with building networks, the trade fair offers a neutral territory on which people who would not normally have the chance to meet are able to network with the exhibiting firm. For the exhibitor, the key strategy here is to ensure that the partner firm's technical, administrative and marketing people are specifically invited to the stand, possibly with the objective of meeting their opposite numbers. Interaction between these individuals is likely to encourage the identification of problems, the finding of creative solutions and a closer relationship between the organizations. However, research indicates that many technical people's needs are not being met – the opportunity to discuss specific problems, which is a common reason for visiting the exhibition, is unavailable because the exhibiting firms tend to concentrate mainly on selling activities.

Mid-KAM stage

In the mid-KAM stage, visitors may wish to discuss specific problems [and 10 per cent gave this reason for attending]. Exhibitors will wish to interact with existing distributors and customers, the latter of which aims is rated fourth in importance by exhibitors.

Partnership-KAM stage

At the partnership-KAM stage the two parties are probably too closely intertwined to need to meet in an exhibition hall and may even be sharing stand space. Nevertheless, social activities built around the exhibition such as dinners together can help cement relationships.

Synergistic-KAM stage

At the synergistic-KAM stage, firms develop strategic congruence. At this point, trade fairs provide the opportunity to share a voice. This is, of course, true of other communications media, but trade fairs allow congruence across a broader spectrum of activities than most because of the interactive nature of the medium. For example, trade fairs can be used for concept testing of new products, allowing the partners to obtain quick feedback on the market viability of the product.

Uncoupling-KAM stage

At the uncoupling-KAM stage, when the partnership is dissolving, the parties are likely to use the trade fair to seek new partners. Obviously there is likely to be considerable overlap between the separate stages and activities, but as the relationship deepens the role of trade fairs is likely to become less.

Effective use of trade fairs

Using trade fairs effectively as a tool in key-account management means understanding how trade fairs work and who the visitors are. As in any other area of marketing, the key issue is to meet the needs of those visitors effectively in order to facilitate exchange. Using a courtship analogy, the exhibition hall is the business equivalent of the dance hall. It is a place for chance encounters that may lead to romance, or it is a place to go to on a date. Whether chance or pre-arranged, the key-account manager can only make the best of the event by setting objectives and being clear about achieving them.

An important issue here is to ensure that the right people are on the stand in order to discuss issues with the visitors. If the exhibitor intends to relate to technical people, it would seem sensible to ensure that some of the exhibitor's technical people are on the stand to answer questions. If the intention is to establish links with key-accounts at other levels in the organization, it may be sensible to arrange for senior managers to be on the stand, at least for part of the time: these people frequently have few opportunities to meet customers.

■ Why exhibitions fail

Exhibitions frequently do not work for firms. In most cases, this is because exhibitors have not thought through their strategies clearly enough, have not set objectives, and have not evaluated their activities sufficiently rigorously (or at all, in many cases) (Blythe 2000). As in any other area of marketing, failure to meet the needs of the customer (in this case the visitor) will result in a failure to communicate effectively and hence a failure of the exhibition.

In other cases, exhibitions fail because the exhibitors have inappropriate objectives. Although orders are sometimes placed at exhibitions or shortly afterwards, going to an exhibition with the sole objective of making sales is almost certainly unrealistic in most cases because so few buyers are present as a proportion of visitors. Even when buyers are present, they are likely to be in the information-gathering stage of the buying process and are unlikely to be in a position to place an order anyway.

As in other areas of business, much of the risk of failure can be reduced by planning ahead. Unfortunately, many exhibitors leave the planning of the exhibition to the last minute and do not prepare sufficiently in advance.

Planning for exhibitions

Failure to plan an exhibition may be caused by the view that exhibitions are merely flag-waving exercises aimed at showing the corporate face and nothing more. In other cases, companies do not plan because they regard the exhibition as a one-off event, and so do not wish to impose extra burdens on the marketing team. In other cases, however, failure to plan is simply a result of lack of knowledge or lack of the will to take trouble over ensuring that the exhibition is successful.

Planning an exhibition properly can easily take up six months or more, if pre-preparation and post-exhibition activities are taken into account. The stages of planning an exhibition are as follows:

1 *Decide on the objectives* – This goes beyond merely deciding what the reasons are for exhibiting: the objectives need to be measurable (and systems need to be in place to do this), achievable (within the context of the firm's resources), and realistic (considering the visitor profile and competitive pressures at the exhibition).

2 *Select which exhibition to attend* – This relies on the range of choice, the visitor profiles (obtainable from the organizers, though the figures may have been massaged), the cost of exhibiting, the availability of suitable space in a good location, the timing of the exhibition relative to the firm's business cycle, the competitive level and the prestige value of the exhibition. One author always attended an exhibition in person before committing to a corporate effort (usually the following year).

3 *Plan the staffing of the stand* – Most managers tend to use the salesforce to staff the stand, but often this is inappropriate: much depends on what the objectives of exhibiting are. Using salespeople also has the disadvantage of taking them off the road at a time when enquiries are likely to be at their highest. Since visitors are likely to be in the information search stage of the buying process, it is probably too early to involve salespeople anyway.

4 *Plan the support promotions* – These may include direct mail-shots to visitors, advertising campaigns in advance of the exhibition, press releases in the trade press and salesforce activity before the exhibition (inviting existing customers to visit the stand) and afterwards (following up on enquiries), including a wide variety of social events.

5 *Decide on the layout of the stand and its contents* – Since visitors are usually information-gathering, the layout needs to be attractive and eye-catching but should also convey solid information. It is often a good idea to have an area so that customers can discuss business in private: this area can double as a rest area for stand personnel. Refreshments can be made available within this area: opinions are mixed as to whether alcoholic drink should be available.

6 *Arrange the follow-up activities after the exhibition* – A surprising number of exhibitors fail to do this, with the result that the salesforce is not able to follow up on leads generated, the company is not prepared to send information out to those who requested it, and the PR momentum obtained from the exhibition is wasted (Blythe and Rayner 1996). The biggest problem with delaying follow-ups is that prospective customers will almost certainly have contacted the firm's competitors at the same exhibition, so a delay is likely to mean that the competitors will get the business.

7 *Plan the logistics of the exercise* – Ensure that sufficient promotional material has been produced, that the staff are transported to the exhibition, that the hotels are booked and are of a suitable standard, that stand personnel are briefed and prepared, that equipment, furnishing, samples and so forth all arrive at the right time and in the right condition.

Evaluation

Once the exhibition is over, evaluation needs to take place. Many firms do not evaluate their activities effectively (or at all) which seems perverse considering the amount of money and effort which is expended on exhibition attendance. The reasons for not evaluating might be as follows (Blythe 1997):

1 The firm lacks the resources to carry out the evaluation.
2 The activity is not important enough to warrant evaluation.
3 The evaluation would be too difficult or expensive.
4 The firm is owner managed and therefore the owner feels able to estimate the effectiveness of the exhibition without formal evaluation.

Managing the exhibition stand

Stand management is straightforward provided the planning has been carried out effectively and the necessary equipment and staff have arrived. Designing the layout of the stand is an important part of the process; most exhibitors tend to make the company name the most prominent feature of the stand, with brand names and product specifications lower on the list of priorities. This is a reasonable policy if the purpose of the stand is to raise the corporate profile, but in most circumstances the visitors' need for solid information will dictate the design and layout of the stand.

In many cases, firms assume that the visitors will recognize the company's name and will know what products are available. This is something of a leap of faith; overseas visitors to exhibitions may not be familiar with the firm and its products and even domestic visitors may be more familiar with brand names than with company names, since that is what is usually given the heaviest promotion.

Exhibition visitors

Exhibitions are tiring for the visitors as well as for the exhibitors, so visitors usually only spend significant time at a few stands. This may be as few as 10 or 12, and this figure does not rise if the exhibition is larger since most visitors only spend one day at an exhibition. This means that large exhibitions with many stands do not increase the number of visitors who will see the stand; statistically, large exhibitions actually reduce the chances of particular visitors seeing a particular stand since there are more to choose from. The problem of clutter is probably greater at exhibitions than in any other environment, as exhibitors all compete for the visitors' limited attention. For this reason the stand must be designed with the visitors' and exhibitor's objectives in mind.

Exhibition staff

For example, if the exhibition objective is to raise corporate awareness the company name needs to be prominent and a plentiful supply of brochures and leaflets needs to be available. Temporary promotion staff could be employed to hand out leaflets in other parts of the exhibition so that exhibitors who do not plan to visit the stand might be encouraged to do so, or at least go away with some information about the firm. The stand might have some kind of stunt or gimmick to raise awareness; a product demonstration or some spectacular event will attract attention.

On the other hand, if the aim is to make sales or generate leads the stand should show the brand names prominently, with plenty of information on product benefits. The stand should be staffed with some technical people and some salespeople and brochures should only be given to visitors who are prepared to leave their names and addresses (some exhibitors will only mail out brochures rather than give them out on the stand). This ensures that follow-up calls can be carried out. Promotions and stunts should be used to collect names and addresses; for example, a free draw for a prize. Special 'exhibition-only' discounts or promotions can be used, and pre-publicity can reflect this in order to get buyers onto the stand. In these circumstances, casual non-buying visitors are less important and might even be actively discouraged – although (for the reasons outlined earlier in the chapter) this may be a short-sighted policy since most exhibitions are probably not good selling venues and the casual visitors may be the exhibitor's best future customers.

Organizing the stand

The following is a checklist for organizing the stand itself.

- Ensure that displays are easily accessible and are informative.
- Check that stand members have a clear brief.
- Have clear objectives in place and, where possible, set targets for stand members.
- Have an area where prospects can be taken for a private conversation if necessary.
- Ensure an adequate supply of drinking water and other refreshments.
- Establish a rota for stand staff to ensure regular breaks.
- Have a record-keeping system for leads and useful contacts.
- Have a feedback system for visitors' comments.
- Set up some 'fun' activities for stand staff.

It is useful for stand staff to have the opportunity to tour the rest of the exhibition (this also gives them a break) and it is worthwhile to give them objectives in doing this, for example, making it the time for gathering information about competitors. Staff will need a break at least every hour; long periods of standing, smiling and relating to large numbers of people is both physically and psychologically exhausting. This requires careful planning to ensure that there are enough suitably-qualified people left to man the stand during breaks.

The main problem concerning stand staff is maintaining their motivation over the period of the show. After a few hours on the stand the visitors seem to meld into a single mass, most of the enquiries seem like a waste of time and the smile begins to wear a little thin. For this reason it is a good idea to have some activities running which keep the stand personnel interested. For example, a competition for collecting business cards, with an appropriate small prize, can keep staff interested.

Demonstrations throughout the day can help to break the monotony for staff as well as visitors, particularly if the demonstrations are given by stand members in rotation. Again, a small prize could be offered for the best demonstration.

Exhibitions are often held away from the firm's home base and therefore away from the staff's homes and families. Sometimes it might be appropriate to allow staff to bring their partners with them, but in most cases this is problematical, so every opportunity should be given for staff to telephone home and it almost goes without saying that their accommodation and meals should be of a high standard – this compensates to a small extent for being away from home, but in any case it reflects better on the firm.

Overall, exhibitions need to be planned in fine detail, with everything leading towards the planned objectives. Choice of exhibition, pre-publicity and post-exhibition follow-ups, stand design, staffing and choice of what to exhibit should all be chosen with clear objectives in mind.

■ Alternatives to exhibitions

Because of the cost and commitment attached to exhibiting, not least the disruption to the exhibitors' normal routine, firms are beginning to look for alternative routes for meeting buyers and promoting their products. Since one of the major advantages of exhibitions is the 'neutral territory' aspect, allowing buyers and sellers to discuss matters in a more relaxed way, many exhibitors are moving towards private exhibitions or road shows to exhibit their products.

Private exhibitions

Private exhibitions are sometimes run at venues near to the public exhibition and coinciding with the main event. Typically such events are held in hotels or small halls where the buyers are invited.
The main advantages are as follows;

- The atmosphere is usually more relaxed and less frenetic than that in the main exhibition.
- No competitors are present to distract the visitors.
- The exhibitor has much more control over the environment than would be the case at the public exhibition, where the organizers may impose irksome regulations.
- Superior refreshment and reception facilities are available.
- If the event is held in an hotel the staff will have access to their rooms and can easily take breaks.
- Sometimes the overall cost is less.

The main drawback of the private event is that visitors will only come to it if they are given advance warning and even then may decide only to visit the main exhibition. The invitations need to be sent out early enough so that visitors can make allowance for the event, but not so early that they forget about it, and some incentive to make the necessary detour may also need to be in place. It is extremely unlikely that the list of desirable visitors will be complete – one of the main advantages of the public exhibition is that some of the visitors will be unknown to the exhibiting company and a first contact can be made.

Private exhibitions work best in situations where the company has a limited market, where the costs of the main exhibition are high and where a suitable venue is available close to the main site.

Road shows

A road show is a traveling exhibition which takes the product to the buyer rather than the other way round. In some cases these are run in hotels, in other cases trailers or caravans are used. Road shows are useful in cases where large numbers of buyers are concentrated in particular geographical areas and where many of them would not make the journey to visit a national exhibition. In some countries (for example the United States) industries may be geographically concentrated (e.g. the film industry in California or the steel industry in Pennsylvania) making a road show more economical.

Like private exhibitions, road shows allow the exhibitor to control the environment to a large extent. Road shows can be run in conjunction with other firms, which reduces the cost and increases the interest level for the visitors; this can be particularly effective if the firms concerned are complementary rather than competing.

In common with private exhibitions, the roadshow's organizer is entirely responsible for all the publicity. In the case of a major public exhibition the exhibition organizers and even the firm's competitors will ensure that a certain minimum level of visitors will attend; in the case of a road show the exhibitor will need to produce considerable advance publicity and even send out specific invitations to individual buyers and prospects. This adds to the risk as well as the cost.

Sales promotion

Sales promotions are intended to create a short-term increase in sales. They can take many forms, from short-term discounts through to extra quantities, free packs and free gifts. These extra incentives should be aimed at the corporation, not at the buyer in person, of course.

Sales promotions are typical of push strategies. A push strategy is one in which the goods are heavily promoted to distributors rather than to the end customer: the theory is that the distributor will, in turn, promote the product heavily, thus pushing the goods through the distribution chain. The converse of a push strategy is a pull strategy, in which the goods are promoted heavily to the final users in order to create demand which will pull the goods through the distribution chain.

Sales promotion expenditure has increased in recent years as producers find that push strategies can be more accurately targeted and are less prone to clutter (the effect of too much advertising vying for the customer's attention). One of the major benefits in a B2B scenario is that it deflects interest away from price as a competitive tool, particularly if the promotion is not of the 'extra discount' variety. Creating the campaign should be based on the 'who do I want to do what?' question. (Cummins 1998).

Sales promotions can be used to encourage trial, to trade up (buy the more expensive version of the product), or to expand usage: when aimed at distributors, they can encourage them to increase stock levels (load up). This may only move sales from the future to the present: when the promotion is over, the distributor may de-stock and therefore reduce purchases for a period. This may not matter if the purpose of the promotion is to even out demand in order to schedule factory production better, or if the purpose is to lock out competitors from shelf space at the warehouse, but it is important to understand that sales promotions usually have a short-term effect.

Business-to-business sales promotion

Sales promotions can sometimes be used in creative ways. An example is the promotion run by Osram, the light bulb manufacturer, when the company first began to produce long-life light bulbs. These bulbs were much more expensive than ordinary filament bulbs, but lasted many times longer. Osram identified a market among factory and warehouse operators, where the cost of replacing a light bulb is often high: apart from the man-hours involved just in changing light bulbs, the bulbs were often inaccessible, high in the roof spaces of the company premises. The problem in marketing the bulbs lay in the fact that many factory maintenance managers had a fixed budget allowance for buying light bulbs and were unable to exceed this even when the labor savings were obvious. Appeals to the finance directors to increase the budget were usually met with a flat referral to the maintenance manager. Osram somehow had to get the two individuals together to discuss the new bulbs, so they used a creative sales promotion. Osram mailed a cashbox to the finance directors with a note saying that there was information inside which would save them 50 per cent on light bulb replacement: Osram mailed the key to the cash box to the maintenance manager. This meant that both parties had to get together to access the information and would presumably discuss the outcome.

Another creative approach used in B2B sales promotion was that adopted by the German hair cosmetics manufacturer, Goldwell. Goldwell deals exclusively with hairdressing salons and when the firm entered the UK market they found themselves facing an established market in which L'Oréal, Schwarzkopf, Wella, Clynol and Clairol had sewn up the bulk of the market between them. Goldwell countered this by giving away free samples of product – but if a salon placed an order, the free samples would be of a different product in the Goldwell range. Salon owners would use the products and perhaps order them next time – thus obtaining free samples of yet another product. This approach bought Goldwell a substantial share of the professional market in the UK and coupled with its rapid delivery system made the company a major player within five years of entering the market.

Reducing costs of promotions

Joint promotions are a way of reducing the costs of promotions by sharing them with another (related) firm. Entering into a joint promotion agreement with another company allows the firm to gain in several ways: the cost of the promotion is reduced, the scope of the promotion is increased because the other firm will contact its own customer base and the customer's perception of value is often increased. For cxample, a firm manufacturing engineering lubricants might offer a joint promotion with a firm selling industrial cleaning materials. The products are complementary in that using lubricants often creates a cleaning problem, but they may be dealing with different firms and therefore might open up a new customer base for each other.

In capital-goods markets, reduced-interest or zero-interest deals can be powerful incentives, as can leasing deals. These incentives can overcome situations where the corporate budget is spent out, or where the finance director has declared a moratorium on expenditure. The problem for the supplier can lie in working out the cost of such deals, so many firms involve an outside bank or finance company to handle the details. Finance companies judge the supplier against the following criteria:

1 The goods need to be durable, identifiable and movable (in case of repossession).
2 The goods should have a value greater than the outstanding debt at all times, which means there should be a well-established second-hand market.
3 The supplier must itself be a reliable, well-established business.

Some suppliers are large enough to act as their own finance companies. This was notably the case for IBM, which from its foundation up until the mid-1980s did not sell any of its equipment outright: everything was leased. This meant that IBM retained ownership of all its equipment throughout the world, which gave the company a substantial measure of control over its customers, though at the cost of cash flow problems in the early years.

Categories of sales promotion

Sales promotions in the B2B environment fall into three categories: promotions aimed at the sales team, promotions aimed further down the value-chain at middlemen and promotions aimed at the customer.

Promotions aimed at the salesforce are part of the motivational program, covered in Chapter 13. Prizes, cash rewards and extra benefits such as 'salesman of the month' status all come under this category and can be considered as sales promotions since they are aimed at gaining a short-term increase in sales. Such promotions work well in single-transaction type selling, but can be seriously counterproductive in key-account management, since salespeople are encouraged to go for quick results rather than build long-term relationships.

Sales promotions aimed at channel intermediaries form part of a push strategy. Early in the product life cycle, incentives to middlemen may be necessary to gain acceptance of new products by channel members. This can be an important consideration for the customer, since onward sales of the goods needs to be assured. Incentives to encourage distributors to carry the product will also help in shutting out later competition. For example, a manufacturer of an artificial sweetener may want to encourage food manufacturers to incorporate the sweetener. In order to do this, a sales promotion encouraging retailers to stock products containing the sweetener would clearly help. Promotions aimed at customers might be used to shift the time of purchase, stimulate trial, or encourage continued use of a product. These probably represent the mainstream of sales promotions.

Sales promotion is less widely used in B2B markets than it is in consumer markets. The reasons for this are obscure: it may be that business buyers are less likely to be swayed by temporary promotions, or it may be that a sales promotion is not conducive to building long-term relationships. There is, however, a role for sales promotion in the B2B arena, even if only in the form of 'deal sweeteners' which are available to salespeople to cement orders and build relationships.

SUMMARY

Although exhibitions and trade fairs are often considered as a form of sales promotion, they do in fact have totally separate features and advantages. Exhibitions offer a wide range of communications possibilities between all levels of the organizations which exhibit and those which attend. Like an old-fashioned marketplace, exhibitions allow all interested parties to meet if they so wish, but this opportunity is often squandered by an over-emphasis on making immediate sales.

Sales promotions occupy a small but useful role in B2B marketing by smoothing and facilitating the decision-making process.

The key points from this chapter are as follows:

- Buyers are very much in the minority at most, if not all, exhibitions.

- Most visitors are on an information search, not on a shopping trip.

- Most exhibitors are focused strongly on selling, whereas they should be focused on making useful contacts.

- The dissonance between exhibitors' aims and visitors' aims often results in disappointment for both parties.

- Exhibitors should establish objectives for their activities, but rarely do so.

- Sales promotions can be useful as deal sweeteners or facilitators.

- Sales promotions can be used for the salesforce, for intermediaries, for customers, or for the customers of customers.

REVIEW QUESTIONS

1 How might an exhibitor evaluate the aim of enhancing the company image?
2 What objectives might be appropriate for a first-time exhibitor?
3 What would be the most appropriate staffing approach for an exhibitor seeking to relate to existing customers?
4 What type of sales promotion would be most effective for a firm entering a new market?
5 How might salespeople use sales promotions to close deals? What might be the dangers of doing this?

SPOTLIGHT ON B2B MARKETING

Each year in January Earl's Court hosts the Toy Fair. This exhibition is attended by toy buyers from all over the UK and the world – and is one of the premier showcases for British toy manufacturers.

Because 80 per cent of toys are sold at Christmas, the toy industry needs to operate on long lead times and needs to have orders booked well in advance in order to schedule production. For some firms, the difference between a successful exhibition and an unsuccessful one is the difference between surviving the year and not surviving. The Earl's Court exhibition and another one in Harrogate, are widely believed to be the most important in the industry.

Apart from the buyers there are a number of other types of visitor. Some are there to sell things to the exhibitors: marketing consultants, machine tool manufacturers and financial services salespeople are all likely to be among those present. Also, many students attend the exhibition. Some are design students, looking to pick up ideas and contacts, some are business students observing the process of exhibiting. Another large category of visitor is the technical people, the engineers and programmers who build mechanical and electronic toys for rival firms and are simply on a spying mission to see what is happening with the competition. There are even some visitors who are having a day out of the office or are retired from the industry altogether – in other words, have no power to buy anything at all and are simply there for the entertainment value of spending all day in a giant toy shop.

In fact, only a relatively small number of the visitors is engaged in buying anything at all. This presents a problem for the exhibitors, many of whom are small firms who are staking their year's profits on doing business at the show.

For AM Games Ltd the show is particularly crucial. As a small company starting out in the board games business, AM Games needs the showcase that the exhibition provides, but can barely afford to attend. The company produces a grand total of three board games and is hoping that (eventually) they will be bought out by one of the bigger games manufacturers. The directors of AM Games realize that they are unlikely to strike it rich with only three games – but establishing them in the market is a way of attracting the attention of the larger manufacturers.

The games themselves are all of the traditional board variety. There are no electronic gadgets involved, just dice and counters: each game has an educational aspect as well as the excitement of a game of chance and each game was invented and tested by the managing director's son-in-law, a mathematics professor at a university in the Midlands. AM Games Ltd's managing director, Colin Rogers, is a retired Army officer who has funded the company out of his Army savings. He wouldn't be destitute if the company failed – but equally he is anxious not to lose his investment. To this end he hired a firm of exhibition consultants to help him plan and run the stand. The consultants advised him on the design of the stand and on what he might reasonably expect from an exhibition – and in fact the advice proved to be very useful, because he obtained more than 20 good sales leads from interested buyers in the course of the first day.

Afterwards, Colin considered whether the exhibition had been worthwhile. Of the total of 70 sales leads obtained, he managed to follow up on 50 in the first week after the exhibition, making telephone calls and appointments to see the firms' buyers. The 50 leads actually resulted in 14 firm appointments, which seemed to be a reasonable result. Colin thought it would probably be worthwhile booking a stand at the exhibition for the following year – the sales figures should be enough to carry the company through until then at least. Overall, his gut feeling was that exhibitions are a good way forward for his fledgling company.

Questions

1 What else might Colin have achieved from the exhibition, apart from sales leads?

2 How might Colin have ensured that the right kind of people visited the stand?

3 How might Colin have evaluated the success or otherwise of the stand?

4 What other activities might have been advisable to ensure that the exhibition went well?

5 Should Colin consider going to other toy exhibitions?

REFERENCES

Bello, D. C. and Lohtia, R. (1993) 'Improving trade show effectiveness by analyzing attendees', *Industrial Marketing Management*, 22: 311–18.

Blythe, J. (1997) 'Does size matter? Objectives and measures at UK trade exhibitions', *Journal of Marketing Communications*, 3: 1: March.

Blythe, J. and Rayner, T. (1996) 'The evaluation of non-selling activities at British trade exhibitions – an exploratory study', *Marketing Intelligence and Planning*, 14(5).

Blythe, J. (2000a) 'Objectives and measures at UK trade exhibitions', *Journal of Marketing Management*, 16: 1.

Blythe, J. (2002) 'Using Trade Fairs in Key Account Management', *Industrial Marketing Management*, 31: 627–635.

Cummins, J. (1998) *Sales Promotion: How to Create and Implement Campaigns That Really Work*, London: Kogan Page.

Exhibition Industry Federation (1989) *EIF Exhibition Effectiveness Survey*, London: Centre for Leisure and Tourism Studies.

Gramann, J. (1994) 'Independent market research', Birmingham: Centre Exhibitions with National Exhibition Centre.

Kerin, R. A. and Cron, W. L. (1987) 'Assessing trade show functions and performance: an exploratory study', *Journal of Marketing*, 51: 87–94.

Kijewski, V., Yoon, E. and Young, G. (1992) 'Trade Shows: How Managers Pick their Winners', Institute for the Study of Business Markets.

Munuera, J. L. and Ruiz, S. (1999) 'Trade Fairs as Services: A Look at Visitors' Objectives in Spain', *Journal of Business Research*, 44: 1: 17–24.

Sharland, A. and Balogh, P. (1996) 'The value of non-selling activities at international trade shows', *Industrial Marketing Management*, 25: 1: 59–66.

Shipley, D., Egan, C. and Wong, K. S. (1993) 'Dimensions of trade show exhibiting management', *Journal of Marketing Management*, 9: Jan: 55–63.

Skerlos, K. and Blythe, J. (2000) 'Ignoring the Audience: Exhibitors and Visitors at a Greek Trade Fair', Proceedings of the Fifth International Conference on Corporate and Marketing Communication, Erasmus University, Rotterdam 22nd and 23rd May.

Tanner, J. F. and Chonko, L. B. (1995) 'Trade show objectives, management and staffing practices', *Industrial Marketing Management*, 24: 257–64.

Trade Show Bureau (1988) *Attitudes and Opinions of Computer Executives Regarding Attendance at Information Technology Events*. Study, No. 1080, East Orleans, Massachusetts: Trade Show Bureau.

CORPORATE REPUTATION MANAGEMENT

Learning objectives
After reading this chapter, you should be able to:

- Identify the features that characterize an organization's reputation

- Explore the key events and characters that create and influence an organization's reputation

- Understand how reputation is valued and the significance it has on the performance of the enterprise

- Identify different categories of image

- Explain how image is managed

- Understand the interplay between different categories of image within the organization

Introduction

Corporate reputation has been defined as the aggregate perceptions of outsiders about the salient characteristics of firms (Fombrun and Rindova 2000). In other words, an organization's reputation is composed of the overall view that people have about the organization. Reputation is important for two reasons: firstly, it has a direct effect on the bottom line because organizations with good reputations are more likely to attract customers. Secondly, a good reputation acts as a buffer should a crisis occur.

■ Creating and managing a reputation

Reputation, along with image, is a component of the attitude people have towards the organization (see Chapter Twelve for more on attitude formation and change). Reputation is the set of expectations which the organization's publics have of its future behavior and is therefore closely related to the cognitive element of attitude. Organizations with a good reputation are expected to act well: organizations with a bad reputation are expected to behave badly.

Of course, reputation is more than simply good or bad. In some cases the organization's reputation will be good in some respects and bad in others, or it may be that the organization has a reputation for a particular type of behavior that is perceived as good by some people and bad by others. For the manager, therefore, the problem is not so much one of creating a good reputation instead of a bad one. It is rather a problem of creating the right reputation so that the organization's publics are clear about what to expect. Attempts to create the wrong reputation (good or bad) will result in frustrated expectations.

Managing reputation is more than just an exercise in spin-doctoring. Spin-doctoring is a process of putting a good face on unacceptable facts, whereas managing reputation is a process of ensuring that the facts themselves are acceptable. It is about ensuring that everyone's experience of the organization is in keeping with the reputation the organization has or hopes to build. This means that everyone within the organization has a role to play: each member of staff has the power to work well or badly, each shareholder has the power to affect the share price, each customer has the power to buy or not to buy. More importantly, each stakeholder has the power to make or break the organization's reputation, simply by saying or doing the right things, or the wrong things, when dealing with those outside the organization.

The sources of knowledge which influence reputation are:

1 Direct experience of dealing with the organization.

2 Hearsay evidence from friends, colleagues and acquaintances.

3 Third-party public sources such as newspaper articles, TV documentaries and published research.

4 Organization-generated information such as brochures, annual reports and advertising.

The degree to which the corporate communications officer has influence over these sources is in inverse proportion to the influence on attitude. This is illustrated in Figure 15.1.

Reputation affects decision-making on the part of all stakeholders, so the reputation of an organization is both created and consumed by its members. There is an element of positive feedback involved – a particular reputation will attract people who feel positive about the organization and will repel those who feel negative about it. Once inside the organization, people will act in ways which reflect the reputation. For example, a company with a reputation for treating its staff well will attract managers who like to work in that type of managerial paradigm and will therefore in turn treat their staff well. Figure 15.2 shows how these elements relate.

One of the problems with reputation management is that different reputations may be attractive to different stakeholders. Stakeholders are people or groups of people who are affected directly or indirectly by a firm's activities and decisions (Post, Lawrence and Weber 2002). An employee may be attracted by an organization's reputation for paying its staff generously, but this same attribute might repel a shareholder. Likewise, customers might be attracted to a firm with a reputation for keeping its prices and profits at rock bottom, but this would hardly attract either staff or shareholders.

FIGURE 15.1
Hierarchy of information sources

Ability of the corporate communications officer to control the information is greater lower down the scale

Direct experience
Hearsay from friends
Third-party sources
Organization-generated information

Influence on attitude is greater the higher up the scale

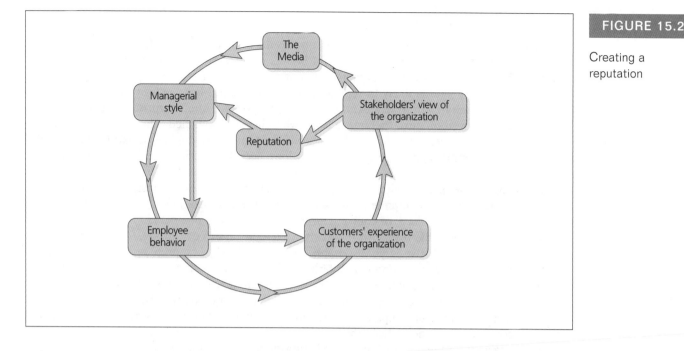

FIGURE 15.2

Creating a
reputation

Ultimately it is not possible to please everybody, so managers need to identify who are the key players and should seek to establish a good reputation with those people.

In practice, organizations acquire reputations rather than develop them. While it may be possible to re-establish a better reputation (or at least a more appropriate one) this is likely to be off-putting to some stakeholders, even if it is attractive to others. In practice, managers are unlikely to create a reputation from scratch – they are much more likely to be tinkering with the organization's existing reputation to make it more attractive to some people, or to make it more explicit to the stakeholders.

Maintaining a strong reputation pays direct dividends for the enterprise. Research shows that investors are prepared to pay higher share prices for companies with good reputations, even when risks and returns are comparable with other firms in the same industry. Cordeiro and Sambharaya (1997) showed earnings forecasts made by financial analysts were heavily influenced by the non-financial component of the corporate reputation. Surveys of MBA students show that they are attracted to companies with good reputations, which means that companies which are larger and more visible are apparently better to work for. Part of this attraction is the reflected glory of working for a high-profile company and part of it is about a perception that working for a major company is likely to be more secure and better rewarded.

The reputation of the organization is important to all stakeholders, but there may be conflicts between the groups: what is good for shareholders may not be good for staff, and what is good for the board of directors may not be good for customers. This means that the board of directors often finds itself in the position of being a clearing house for pressures from different stakeholder groups. Even when stakeholders are in broad agreement as to where the company should be heading there will be differing opinions on how to get there.

For companies, there is a problem in meeting the differing needs of different market segments while still maintaining a consistent corporate reputation. For example, British Airways now offers a fully-reclining seat in business-class, effectively giving each passenger a bed. While this provides an image of luxury for the business traveler (as anyone who has ever tried to sleep on an airplane can testify), it means less space in Economy, which is where many backpackers book seats. Yet backpackers are usually seen as a long-term investment by airlines, since they are often students taking time out from university and are therefore the business-class travelers of the future.

Image

Image is the affective component of attitude towards the organization. It is the gut feeling or overall impression that the organization's name and brands generate in the minds of the organization's publics. There are five basic types of image, as shown in Table 15.1.

None of these images is likely to represent the whole truth. Mirror image can be confirmed by external market research, but members of the organization are often surprised or disappointed to find that the organization's external image is not what they had imagined. The current image may be more or less accurate according to whether it is based on misunderstanding or half-truths. It is likely to be less than accurate because outsiders do not have access to the information that people on the inside have.

Wish image is the image desired by management. Often it equates to a vision statement, defined when the organization was founded and is the image the organization is working towards. Wish images are not always realized, of course. During the 1960s, town planners in Spain had the idea of creating a quiet respectable resort for the wealthier middle classes of Europe, foreseeing (correctly) that these people would have large disposable incomes and would be prepared to spend increasing amounts of their money on leisure, particularly as air travel became more widely available. The wish image of the resort was that of a peaceful town with an old quarter at its heart and up-market, comfortable hotels around it. The result of these careful deliberations was Benidorm – now widely regarded as the epitome of rampant over-development and used as a byword for appalling resorts even by people who have never been there.

Corporate image is the image of the organization, as opposed to the image of its products and services. Corporate image is composed of organizational history, financial stability, reputation as an employer, history of corporate citizenship and so forth. It is possible to have a good corporate image and a poor reputation for products and vice versa. For example, IBM has an exemplary corporate image although its products are not greatly different from those available elsewhere, whereas Rolls Royce has an outstanding image for its products despite a somewhat checkered corporate history involving several bankruptcies and re-launches.

The multiple image occurs when separate branches of the business or even individuals within the business create their own image within that of the overall corporation. An obvious example is that of sales representatives, who each have a personal image and reputation with customers which may or may not accord with the overall corporate image. Organizations such as IBM try to overcome this by using very strict selection criteria when employing salespeople: at one time, IBM salespeople wore a company uniform of blue blazers and gray trousers, but this was discontinued after a 'revolution' by French IBM salespeople, who simply refused to wear the uniform. Even now though, IBMers tend to have a similar appearance, conforming to the strong corporate culture.

TABLE 15.1 Types of image

Mirror image	How we think others see the organization. Sometimes this image is the result of self-delusion.
Current image	The actual view of us held by outsiders. This is not always as positive as we might wish it to be.
Wish image	How the organization wishes others to see it. This is something to strive for – often embodied in the mission statement.
Corporate image	The image of the organization, rather than the images of its brands.
Multiple images	The many images put forward by the individuals working within the organization.

TALKING POINT

Creating a standard corporate image is obviously desirable. Yet for most purchasing firms, the only real contact they have with the supplier is through the sales representatives – who are all individuals.

We are told that the strength of the sales function is the ability to provide a personalized, individual service. But if we insist on hiring a group of clones, how are we to individualize what we do? And even if the salespeople are very similar, the simple fact of tailoring the company's service to each customer is bound to lead to variations in the image.

So is it really possible EVER to generate a consistent corporate image? Or are we left with the unpalatable truth that we cannot force our employees into neat little molds?

Corporate image and added value

Corporate image is not a luxury. The image of a corporation translates into hard added value for shareholders. This is partly because of the effect that image has on the corporation's customers, but is also a function of the effects it has on staff and is very much a result of the influence the image has on shareholders. High-profile companies are more attractive to shareholders, even if the firm's actual performance in terms of profits and dividends is no better than average. Since the central task of management is to maximize shareholder value, image must be central to management thinking and action.

Maximizing shareholder value is not the same as maximizing profits (see Figure 15.3). Profit maximization tends to be short-term, a matter of cutting costs, reducing investment, downsizing, increasing sales volumes at the expense of long-term customer loyalty and so forth. Adding value to the shareholders' assets is about creating a secure, growing long-term investment. Since the dot.com bubble burst investors have become painfully aware that investment in firms with spectacular profits but little underlying solidity is a quick way to lose money. City analysts look more and more towards using measures such as customer loyalty, brand awareness and investment levels in judging the long-term prospects for firms.

The counter argument for this is that the shifting global marketplace has reduced survival prospects for companies. The life expectancy of a firm is now less than 20 years (De Geus 1997). Maintaining a profitable competitive advantage is also problematical. If a firm finds a profitable market niche, competitors respond rapidly and profits fall to the point where it is almost impossible to maintain an adequate return on the original capital investment (Black *et al*. 1998).

FIGURE 15.3   Comparison between adding value and maximizing profits

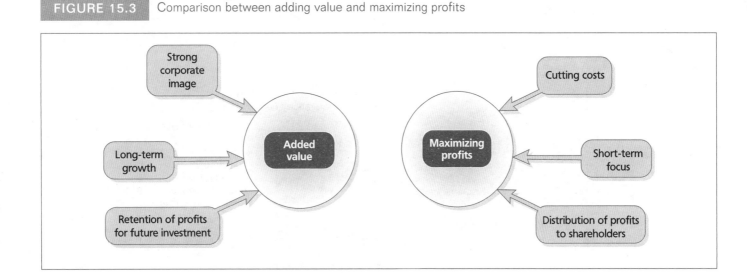

The value which accrues from image management has always been accounted for under the heading of 'goodwill' on the firm's balance sheet. The goodwill element of the firm's value is the difference between the value of the firm's tangible assets and its value on the stock market. For some firms, the value of goodwill is actually the bulk of the firm's overall value. For example, Coca Cola's goodwill value is more than 80 per cent of the firm's total value. Much of this goodwill value comes from the Coca Cola brand itself. This approach to valuing the firm's reputation and image is now regarded as being somewhat crude and new measures are being developed to take account of brand value, customer loyalty values and so forth, to move away from the reliance on financial measures when assessing firms' successes.

TALKING POINT

Boards of directors often use the stock market valuation of the company's shares as a barometer of the company's success. Yet this is rarely reflected in the corporation's mission statement. Most of these talk about caring for staff and customers.

Does this mean that the mission statement is not strictly true? Or does it mean that staff and customers are mere instruments in attaining the goal of share value? And if a higher share value is independent of profit, does that mean that the wool is being pulled over shareholders' eyes? In short, are most boards of directors behaving in some Machiavellian way in order to shore up their own positions?

Or are they perhaps merely trying to balance the needs of a wide group of people?

◼ Public relations and external communication

Public relations or PR is the management of corporate image through the management of relationships with the organization's publics. Roger Hayward (1998) offered an alternative definition, as follows.

Those efforts used by management to identify and close any gap between how the organization is seen by its key publics and how it would like to be seen.

Public relations has more than just a role in defending the company from attack and publicizing its successes. It has a key role in relationship marketing, since it is concerned with building a long-term image rather than gaining a quick sale. As shown in Figure 15.4, there is a strategic relationship between publicity, PR, and press relations. Public relations occupies the overall strategic role in the relationship.

FIGURE 15.4

Publicity, PR and press relations

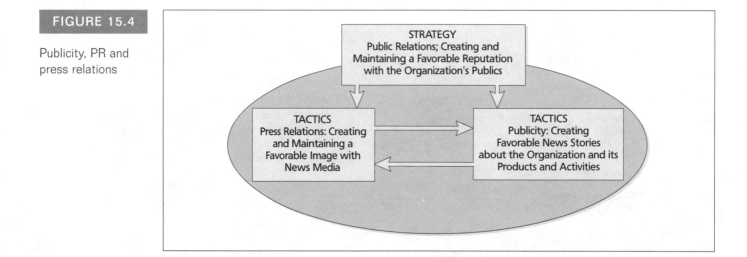

In some cases, firms use PR solely for crisis management, either by employing somebody with a nice smile and a friendly voice to handle complaints, or by waiting for things to go wrong and then beginning to formulate a plan for handling the problem. This is a fire-fighting or reactive approach to public relations and is generally regarded as being far less effective than a proactive approach, which seeks to avoid problems arising.

Public relations managers have the task of coordinating all those activities which make up the public face of the organization and will have some or all of the following tasks to handle.

- organizing press conferences
- staff training workshops
- social events
- handling incoming complaints or criticism
- grooming senior management for TV or Press interviews
- molding the internal culture of the organization.

Public relations people talk about 'publics' rather than 'the public'. This is because they are dealing with a wide range of people, all with differing needs and preconceptions. The following publics might be part of the PR manager's remit.

- customers
- suppliers
- staff
- government and government departments
- local government
- neighbors
- local residents
- the general public
- pressure groups such as environmentalists or trade unions
- other industry members.

In each case the approach will be different and the expected outcomes will also be different. The basic routes by which PR operates are word-of-mouth, Press and TV news stories and personal recommendation. The aim of good PR is to put the name of the firm and its products into people's minds in a positive way.

Public relations is not advertising, because it is not directly paid for. Advertising can also be both informative and persuasive, but PR can only be used for conveying information or for placing the company before the public eye in a positive way. Public relations does not generate business directly, but achieves the company's long-term objectives by creating positive feelings. The ideal is to give the world the impression that this is 'a good firm to do business with'.

Tools of public relations

Public relations people use a number of different ways of achieving their aims. The list in Table 15.2 is by no means comprehensive, but does cover the main tools available to PR managers.

Of these, the press release and sponsorship are probably the most important.

A press release is a favorable news story about the organization, which originates from within the organization itself. Newspapers and the trade press earn their money mainly through paid advertising, but they attract readers by having stimulating articles about topics of interest to the readership. Editors need to fill space and are quite happy to use a press release to do so if the story is newsworthy and interesting to the readership. The trade press relies heavily on press releases, since industry news would be difficult to collect in any other way, but even business-oriented newspapers such as the *Financial Times* need companies to send news in, which is of course the essence of the press release.

The advantages of writing a press release are that it is much more credible than an advertisement, it is much more likely to be read and the space within the publication is free. There are, of course, costs attached to producing press releases.

TABLE 15.2 Tools of PR

Tool	Description and Examples
Press releases	A press release is a news story about the organization, usually designed to put the firm in a good light but often intended just to keep the organization in the public eye. For example, a firm might issue a press release about opening a new factory in a depressed area of the country. Newspapers print this as news, since it is about creating jobs.
Sponsorship	Sponsorship of events, individuals or organizations is useful for creating favorable publicity. For example, many firms are sponsoring golf tournaments which provide opportunities for personal interaction as well as favorable publicity.
Publicity stunts	Sometimes firms will stage an event specifically for the purpose of creating a news story. Again, this is less common in B2B markets, since mass-media publicity is of less value.
Word-of-mouth	Generating favorable word-of-mouth is an important aim of PR. For example, Alex Lawrie Factors, a UK business financial services company, frequently invites financial intermediaries such as bank managers, business consultants and financial advisers to sports events such as horse racing. The intermediaries are likely to raise this in conversation with clients and thus remember to promote Alex Lawrie services.
Corporate advertising	Corporate advertising is aimed at improving the corporate image, rather than selling products. Such advertising is very common in the trade press, but occasionally appears in the mass media. British Airways have successfully used television to promote the company's image, aiming specifically at business-class sales.
Lobbying	Lobbying is the process of making representations to members of Parliament, congressmen, or other politicians. For example, an industry association might lobby Parliament to persuade MPs not to introduce new restrictions on the industry.

Table 15.3 shows the criteria under which the press stories must be produced if they are to be published.

Increasing skepticism and resistance to advertising has meant that there has been a substantial growth in the use of press releases and publicity in recent years. Press stories are much more credible and although they do not usually generate business directly, they do have a positive long-term effect in building brand awareness and loyalty. It should be said that advertising alone also does not usually generate business immediately.

TABLE 15.3 Criteria for successful press releases

Criterion	Example
Stories must be newsworthy, i.e. of interest to the reader	Articles about your new lower prices are not newsworthy; articles about opening a new factory creating 200 jobs are.
Stories must not be merely thinly disguised advertisements	A story saying that your new processing equipment is a bargain at only £23,000 is not news. A story saying that you have concluded a partnership agreement with a machine-tool manufacturer in Poland probably is, in trade press. A story that you are financing a new training initiative for underprivileged teenagers is probably news in the national press.
Stories must fit the editorial style of the magazine or paper they are being sent to	An article sent to *Cosmopolitan* about your new machine tools would not be published. An article about your new female marketing director probably would.

Editors do not have to publish press releases exactly as they are received. They reserve the right to alter stories, add to them, comment on them or otherwise change them around to suit their own purposes. There is nothing substantial that press officers can do about this. Cultivating a good relationship with the media is therefore an important part of the press officer's job.

Sometimes this will involve business entertaining, but more often the press officer will simply try to see to it that the job of the Press is made as easy as possible. This means supplying accurate and complete information, it means writing press releases so that they require a minimum of editing and rewriting and it means making the appropriate corporate spokesperson available when required.

When business entertaining is appropriate, it will often come as part of a media event or press conference. This may be called to launch a new product, to announce some major corporate development such as a merger or takeover or (less often) when there has been a corporate crisis. This will involve inviting journalists from the appropriate media, providing refreshments and providing corporate spokespeople to answer questions and make statements. This kind of event only has a limited success, however, unless the groundwork for it has been very thoroughly laid.

Journalists are often suspicious of media events, sometimes feeling that the organizers are trying to buy them off with a buffet and a glass of wine. This means they may not respond positively to the message the PR people are trying to convey and may write a critical article rather than the positive one that was hoped for.

To minimize the chance of this happening, media events should follow these basic rules:

1 Avoid calling a media event or press conference unless you are announcing something that the press will find interesting.

2 Check that there are no negative connotations in what you are announcing.

3 Ensure that you have some of the company's senior executives there to talk to the Press, not just the PR people.

4 Only invite journalists with whom you feel you have a good working relationship.

5 Avoid being too lavish with the refreshments.

6 Ensure that your senior executives, in fact anybody who is going to speak to the Press, have had some training in doing this. This is particularly important for TV.

7 Be prepared to answer all questions truthfully. Journalists are trained to spot lies and evasions.

8 Take account of the fact that newspapers (and indeed broadcast media) have deadlines to adhere to. Call the conference at a time that will allow reporters enough time to file their stories.

It is always better from the Press viewpoint to speak to the most senior managers available rather than to the PR people. Therefore, the senior managers will need some training in handling the Press and answering questions and also need to be fully briefed on anything the Press might want to ask. In the case of a press conference called as a result of a crisis this can be a problem. Many major firms establish crisis teams of appropriate senior managers who are available and prepared to comment should need arise. Press officers should be prepared to handle queries from journalists promptly, honestly and enthusiastically and arrange interviews with senior personnel if necessary.

The role of PR in the organization

Organizations, just like people, have needs. Some of these needs are common to all organizations and have different levels of importance according to the circumstances of the organization, or the particular stage in its development. A hierarchy of organizational needs was developed by Pearson (1980). Table 15.4 shows how PR can help in satisfying those needs.

Pearson's hierarchy is useful as a concept but less useful as a practical guide because so many firms deviate from the order in which the needs are met.

TABLE 15.4 The hierarchy of organizational needs

Organizational Need	Requirements	Typical PR Activity
Output	Money, machines, manpower, materials	Staff programs to attract the right people
Survival	Cash flow, profits, share performance, customers	Publicity aimed at customers; events publicizing the firm and its products
Morale	Employee job satisfaction	Staff newsletters, morale-boosting activities, etc.
Acceptability	Approval by the external stakeholders (shareholders, Government, customers, suppliers, society in general)	External PR, shareholder reports, lobbying of Government departments and MPs, events for suppliers and customers, favorable press releases
Leadership	Having a respected position in the company's chosen field; this could be customer satisfaction, employee involvement, industry leadership in technology, or several of these	Corporate image-building exercises, customer care activities, publicity about new products and technological advances, sponsorship of research in universities, sponsorship of the Arts

Adapted from: Pearson 1980

Internal communications media

House journal

House journals are printed information books or sheets, which are made available to employees. Journals may be of any of the following types.

- *Magazines* – Containing feature articles and illustrations, these magazines are relatively expensive to produce but have a professional, credible feel about them.
- *Newspapers* – These can be produced to resemble a tabloid newspaper, which makes them more accessible to some groups of employees. Content consists of news articles about the firm, with some feature articles.
- *Newsletter* – Common in small firms, a newsletter would probably be A4 or foolscap size and will contain brief items, usually without illustration. Newsletters are cheap and easy to produce, especially in small numbers.
- *Wall newspaper* – These look like posters and are fixed to walls. They are useful for brief communications about events or changes in company policies.
- *Electronic newsletter* – Internal e-mail systems offer great potential for disseminating newsletters. The medium is cheap to use, effective and often increases the likelihood that the newsletter will be read. Furthermore, it is possible to tell who has opened the newsletter and who had deleted it without reading it – although, of course, opening it is not the same as reading it.

When planning a house journal, you need to consider the issues shown in Figure 15.5.

- *Readership* – Different groups of staff may have different needs, so it may be necessary to produce different journals for each. Research workers are likely to have different needs from truck drivers, for instance.

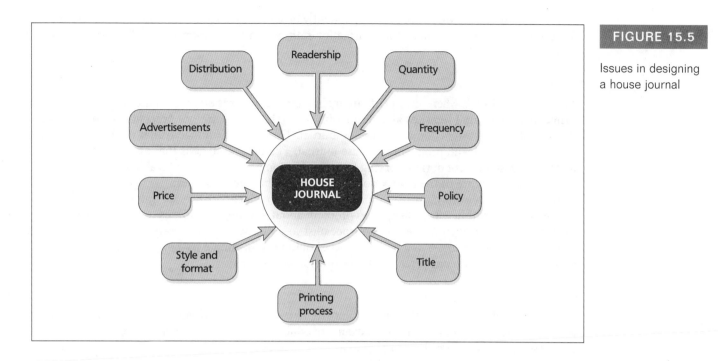

FIGURE 15.5

Issues in designing a house journal

- *Quantity* – The greater the number of copies, the lower the production cost per copy. If the number of employees is large, a better-quality journal can be produced. If the numbers are small, the firm may need to produce newsletters or wall newspapers instead.
- *Frequency* – Frequent publication means that the journal is more likely to become part of the daily routine of staff. Some large firms even publish such journals daily.
- *Policy* – The journal should be more than simply a propaganda device for senior management. It should fit in with an overall PR program and should have a clear editorial policy to ensure the quality of content.
- *Title* – The title should be characteristic of the organization. Changing the title is difficult once it has become established, just as with any other brand name.
- *Printing process* – To an extent the printing process will affect the content, since simple, cheap printing processes cannot reproduce some illustrations. Cost will also affect the choice of process, as will the desire for a good-quality, credible journal.
- *Style and format* – Credibility is linked to the degree to which the journal resembles a commercial magazine. Style and format are part of the communication in the same way that packaging is part of a product.
- *Price* – Obviously the vast majority of house journals are free to staff, but it is feasible to make a charge if the journal is sufficiently interesting. There is no reason why a cover-price should not be put on the journal in any case, even if it is free. This conveys to the staff that the journal is valuable and thus is more likely to be read.
- *Advertisements* – Carrying advertising may be a useful way to reduce costs. If the circulation is sufficiently large, outside organizations might be prepared to place advertising – this is particularly true if the firm is large and in a single location, since local shops, restaurants and entertainment venues might well wish to promote their products. Employees may well want to advertise items for sale or forthcoming social events and this also increases the readability of the journal.
- *Distribution* – Journals can be delivered by hand, by post to the employee's home address, or at distribution points within the firm (for example mail pigeonholes). The decision rests on the frequency of the journal, the location of employees and the type of journal involved. Distribution via e-mail is probably the quickest and cheapest method.

House journals are often edited independently of senior management in order to ensure that the focus is on the employees' need for information rather than on the management's need to control or manipulate.

Websites

Most firms' websites, where they exist, are mainly geared towards external marketing. In some cases, firms operate internal websites aimed at employees. These sites are not accessible by outsiders and they fulfill the same function as the house journal. The main advantage is that the costs are greatly reduced compared with producing a house journal. The disadvantage is that employees are unlikely to access the site except during working hours and in some cases may not be able to access the site at all because the nature of their work does not involve using the computer.

Internal websites are most useful in organizations in which virtually all employees are provided with computers and in which there is no problem about allowing employees to scan the website during working hours. Website design is a specialist area, but some rules have been developed. Sites need to be simple to access and use, graphics should be kept simple to minimize download time and articles should fit onto one screen as far as possible.

Internal briefings and open meetings

Some organizations give staff the opportunity to have access to senior management at open meetings or briefings. These briefings have the advantage of allowing senior management to gain direct access to grass-roots views from the workforce, as well as allowing the workforce the chance to question senior managers about company policies.

The overall effect is to increase openness within the firm and break down barriers. Employees (in general) work better if they understand why things are being done the way they are being done. This also enables them to use their initiative better if the system breaks down for any reason.

Sponsorship

Sponsorship has been defined as 'An investment, in cash or kind, in an activity in return for access to the exploitable commercial potential associated with this activity' (Meenaghan 1991). Sponsorship of the Arts or sporting events is an increasingly popular way of generating positive feelings about firms.

Sponsorship in the UK grew a hundredfold between 1970 and 1993, from UK£4m to UK£400m. It has continued to grow ever since, with estimates for 2004 ranging between UK£1500m and UK£2000m. A large part of this increase has come from tobacco firms, due to global restrictions on tobacco advertising. Sponsorship of Formula One motor racing, horse racing, cricket and many arts events such as the Brecon Jazz Festival would be virtually non-existent without the major tobacco companies. Companies sponsor for a variety of different reasons, as shown in Table 15.5 (Zafer Erdogan and Kitchen 1998).

The basis of sponsorship is to take the customers' beliefs about the sponsored event and link them to the company doing the sponsoring. Thus a firm wishing to appear middle-class and respectable might sponsor a theatre production or an opera, whereas a company wishing to appear to be 'one of the lads' might sponsor a football team. As far as possible, sponsorship should relate to the company's existing image.

Sponsorship will only work if it is linked to other marketing activities, in particular to advertising. Hefler (1994) estimated that two to three times the cost of sponsorship needs to be spent on advertising if the exercise is to be effective. The advertising should tell customers why the firm has chosen this particular event to sponsor, so that the link between the firm's values and the sponsored event is clear. A bank which claims to be 'Proud to sponsor the Opera Festival' will not do as well as they would if they were to say 'We believe in helping you to enjoy the good things in life – that's why we sponsor the Opera Festival'. A recent development in sponsorship is to go beyond the mere exchange of money as the sole benefit to the sponsored organization or event. If the sponsored organization can gain something tangible in terms of extra business or extra publicity for their cause, then so much the better for both parties.

TABLE 15.5 Reasons for sponsorship

Objectives	% Agreement	Rank
Press coverage/exposure/opportunity	84.6	1
TV coverage/exposure/opportunity	78.5	2
Promote brand awareness	78.4	3
Promote corporate image	77.0	4
Radio coverage/exposure/opportunity	72.3	5
Increase sales	63.1	6
Enhance community relations	55.4	7
Entertain clients	43.1	8
Benefit employees	36.9	9
Match competition	30.8	10
Fad/fashion	26.2	11

For example, Lincoln-Mercury (a Ford subsidiary) sponsored a mini-tour of the Canadian circus company, Cirque du Soleil. The tour was linked to the new-model Lincoln luxury car, but Cirque du Soleil were able to use the mini-tour as a publicity exercise for their later major tour of the United States. This in turn led to more publicity for Lincoln, so that the two organizations developed a symbiotic relationship beneficial to both. This type of sponsorship is a way of creating a new type of B2B relationship in which neither business is a customer of the other.

There is evidence that consumers feel gratitude towards the sponsors of their favorite events, but there is no evidence regarding business buyers. Any feelings of gratitude may be an emotional linking between the sponsor and the event rather than a feeling of gratitude that the sponsor made the event possible. The difference between these emotions is merely academic in any case – if sponsorship leads to an improvement in the firm's standing with customers that should be sufficient. There are also spin-offs for the internal PR of the firm; most employees like to feel that they are working for a caring organization and sponsorship money also often leads to free tickets or price reductions for staff of the sponsoring organization.

The following criteria apply when considering sponsorship (Hefler 1994).

- The sponsorship must be economically viable; it should be cost-effective, in other words.
- The event or organization being sponsored should be consistent with the brand image and overall marketing communications plans.
- It should offer a strong possibility of reaching the desired target audience.
- Care should be taken if the event has been sponsored before; the audience may confuse the sponsors and you may be benefiting the earlier sponsor.

In the B2B arena, one of the main benefits of sponsorship of sports and arts events is the availability of tickets or reserved seating for sponsors. This enables the sponsoring firms to offer seats as a relationship-builder or deal-sweetener to possible customers.

TALKING POINT

Anyone watching a major sporting event such as the Wimbledon tennis tournament will have noticed many empty seats. Anyone wanting to obtain tickets for such events finds them hard to get. So why does this happen?

Corporate sponsorship is the culprit. Corporations are given many free seats which they are unable, or unwilling, to use on the days they are available and therefore seats are empty while real sports fans are unable to obtain tickets. This naturally causes a degree of resentment among fans – and a feeling that 'Big Business' is acting against the interests of ordinary people.

So how to corporations gain by this? What does this achieve for enhancing the corporate reputation? Perhaps in the B2B environment there is no need to care about Joe Public, but isn't that attitude somewhat cynical?

Or perhaps there is an opportunity for someone. Could corporations make unwanted seats available to the public on a first-come-first-served basis?

Crisis management

No matter how carefully PR activities are planned and prepared for, crises will develop from time to time. Preparing for the unexpected is therefore a necessity. Some PR agencies specialize in crisis management, but a degree of advance preparation will certainly help if the worst should happen. Preparing for a crisis is similar to organizing a fire drill. The fire may never happen, but it is as well to be prepared.

Crises may be very likely to happen, or extremely unlikely. For example, most manufacturing firms can expect to have a product-related problem sooner or later and either need to recall products for safety reasons, or need to make adaptations to future versions of the product. On the other hand, some crises are extremely unlikely. Assassination or kidnapping of senior executives is not common in most parts of the world, nor are products rendered illegal without considerable warning beforehand.

Crises can also be defined as within the firm's control, or outside the firm's control. Many firms have been beset by problems which were really not of their making: however, very few problems are entirely outside the firm's control. In most cases, events can at least be influenced, if not controlled. Sometimes, however, the cost of such influence is out of all proportion to the level of risk involved. Figure 15.6 shows the elements which make up good crisis management.

FIGURE 15.6

Elements of good crisis management

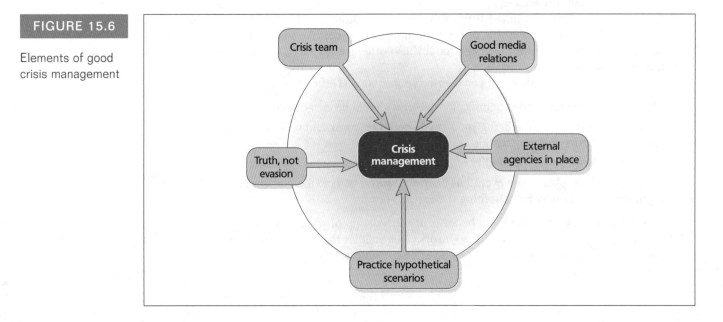

Establishing a crisis team

Ideally, the organization should establish a permanent crisis management team of perhaps four or five individuals who are able to take decisions and act as spokespeople in the event of a crisis. Typical members might be the personnel manager, the safety officer, the factory manager, the PR officer and at least one member of the Board of Directors. Keeping the crisis team small means that communication between members is easy and fast.

The team should meet regularly to review potential risks and formulate strategies for dealing with crises. It may even be possible to rehearse responses in the case of the most likely crises. Importantly, the team should be trained in presentation techniques for dealing with the media, especially in the event of a TV interview.

The team should be able to contact each other immediately in the event of a crisis and should also be provided with deputies in case of being away on business, on holiday, off work sick or otherwise unavailable. The essence of planning for crises is to have as many fall-back positions as possible. Having a Plan B is obvious, but it is wise to have a Plan C or even Plan D as well.

Dealing with the media in a crisis

One of the main PR problems inherent in crisis management is the fact that many crises are newsworthy. This means that reporters will be attracted to the company and its officers in the hope of getting comments or newsworthy statements which will help to sell newspapers.

Provided the groundwork has been laid in advance, the company should have a good relationship with the news media already. This will help in the event of a crisis. However, many managers still feel a degree of trepidation when facing the press at a crisis news conference. The journalists are not there to help the company out of a crisis, they are there to hunt down (or create) a story. Their objectives are probably not compatible with those of the company, but they are under an obligation to report the news reasonably accurately.

Preparation is important. As soon as the crisis breaks, the crisis team should be ready to organize a press conference, preferably on the company's own territory. The press conference should be held as soon as is reasonably possible, but it allows the spokespeople sufficient time to prepare themselves for the journalists and gives a reasonable excuse for not talking to reporters ahead of time. The crisis team should remember that they are in charge. It is their information, their crisis and their story. They are not under an obligation to the news media, but they are under an obligation to the company's shareholders, customers, employees and other publics. The media may or may not be helpful in communicating with these publics in a crisis situation.

Another important consideration is to ensure that the situation is not made worse by careless statements. Insurance and legal liability may be affected by what is said, so this should be checked beforehand.

Crisis teams need to have a special set of talents, as well as the training needed to perform their ordinary jobs. Rapid communication and rapid response, is essential when the crisis occurs. Good relationships with the news media will pay off in times of crisis.

Crisis management should not be left until the crisis happens. Everyone involved should be briefed beforehand on what the crisis policy is. This enables everyone to respond appropriately, without committing the company to inappropriate actions – in simple terms, being prepared for a crisis will help to prevent panic reactions and over-hasty responses which might come back to haunt the company later.

Using outside agencies to build corporate image

Outside public relations agencies are frequently used for developing corporate image. The reasons for doing this might be as follows:

1 The firm is too small to warrant having a specialist PR department.
2 External agencies have expertise which the company lacks.
3 The external agency can provide an unbiased view of the firm's needs.
4 External agencies often carry greater credibility than internal departments or managers.

5 Economies of scale may make the external agency cheaper to use.

6 One-off events or campaigns are more efficiently run by outsiders, without deflecting attention away from core activities.

The Public Relations Consultants' Association lists the following activities as services that a consultancy might offer.

- Establishing channels of communication with the client's public or publics.
- Management communications.
- Marketing and sales promotion related activity.
- Advice or services relating to political, governmental, or public affairs.
- Financial public relations, dealing with shareholders and investment tipsters.
- Personnel and industrial relations advice.
- Recruitment training and higher and technical education.

This list is not exhaustive. Since outside agencies often specialize, the firm might need to go to several different sources to access all the services listed above. Even firms with an in-house public relations department may prefer to subcontract some specialist or one-off activities. Some activities which might involve an outside agency could be as follows.

- *Exhibitions* – The infrequency of attendance at exhibitions (for many firms) means that in-house planning is likely to be disruptive and inefficient. Outside consultants might be setting up four or five exhibitions a week compared with the average firm's four or five a year, so they will quickly acquire strong expertise in exhibition management.
- *Sponsorship* – Outside consultants will have contacts and negotiating expertise which is unlikely to be available in-house. In particular, an outside firm will have up-to-date knowledge of what the 'going rate' is for sponsoring particular events and individuals.
- *Production of house journals* – Because of the economies of scale available in the printing and publishing industry, house journals can often be more cheaply produced by outsiders than by the firm itself.
- *Corporate or financial PR* – Corporate PR relies heavily on having a suitable network of contacts in the finance industry and the financial press. It is extremely unlikely that a firm's PR department would have a comprehensive list of such contacts, so the outside agency provides an instant network of useful contacts.
- *Government liaison* – Lobbying politicians is an extremely specialized area of public relations, requiring considerable insider knowledge and an understanding of current political issues. Professional lobbyists are far better able to carry out this work than a firm's public relations officer would be.
- *Organizing one-off events* – Like exhibitions, one-off events are almost certainly better subcontracted to an outside agency.
- *Overseas PR* – Firms are extremely unlikely to have the specialist local knowledge needed when setting up public relations activities in a foreign country.

Choosing an agency or consultancy

Choosing an appropriate agency or consultancy begins with the agency's ability to carry out the specific tasks you need. Deciding which tasks the agency should do can be a process of elimination (see Figure 15.7). Begin by deciding which tasks can be completed in-house, then whatever is left is the task of the agency.

Table 15.6 below was developed as a checklist to aid in choosing a PR consultancy.

Unless the outside agency has been called in as a result of a sudden crisis (which is possibly the worst way to handle both PR and consultants), the consultancy will be asked to present a proposal. This allows the consultancy time to research the client's situation and its existing relationships with its publics. The proposal should contain comments on the following aspects of the problem:

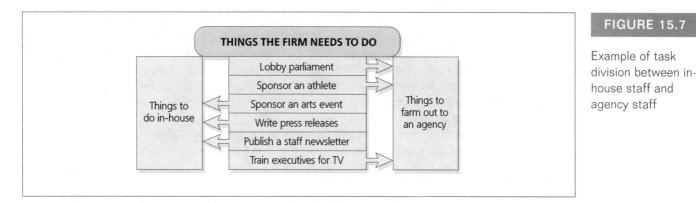

FIGURE 15.7

Example of task division between in-house staff and agency staff

- Analysis of the problems and opportunities facing the client company.
- Analysis of the potential harm or gain to the client.
- Analysis of the potential difficulties and opportunities presented by the case, and the various course of action (or inaction) which would lead to those outcomes.
- The overall program goals and the objectives for each of the target publics.
- Analysis of any immediate action needed.
- Long-range planning for achieving the objectives.
- Monitoring systems for checking the outcomes.
- Staffing and budgets required for the program.

TABLE 15.6 Checklist for choosing a PR consultancy

Competence and Reputation

- Years in business
- Size – people and billings
- Full service or specialisms
- Reach – local, national, international
- Growth pattern and financial stability
- Types of accounts
- Experience with accounts similar to yours, or conversely conflicts of interest with competitors' accounts
- Samples of work
- Sample list of suppliers used

Staff

- List and qualifications of staff – full time, project clients, freelance/consultants
- Names of several former employees
- Staff to be assigned to your account – qualifications and length of time with the firm
- Percentage of their time to be devoted to your account – other accounts they will handle
- Staff or personnel back-up available
- Staff turnover in the past two years

Clients

- Existing client list
- Past clients
- Average number of clients during the last five years – retainer clients, project clients
- Oldest clients and length of service
- Average length of client-firm relationship
- Clients lost in the last year

Results and measurement

- Does the firm understand your objectives and needs?
- How will progress be reported?
- How will results be measured?
- What will it cost – billing process, hourly rate, expenses billed, approval process?

Harley W. Warner, APR, Fellow Warner Communication Counselors Inc. Reprinted with permission of *Public Relations Review*.

Client firms will often ask several agencies to present, with the aim of choosing the best among them. This approach can cause problems, for several reasons. Firstly, the best agencies may not want to enter into a competitive tendering situation. Secondly, some agencies will send their best people to present, but will actually give the work to their more junior staff. Thirdly, agencies in this position may not want to present their best ideas, feeling (rightly in some cases) that the prospective client will steal their ideas. Finally, it is known that some clients will invite presentations from agencies in order to keep their existing agency on its toes.

Such practices are ethically dubious and do no good for the client organization's reputation. Since the whole purpose of the exercise is to improve the firm's reputation, annoying the PR agencies is clearly not an intelligent move. To counter the possibility of potential clients stealing their ideas, some of the leading agencies now charge a fee for bidding.

Relationships with external PR consultancies tend to last. Some major firms have used the same PR consultants for over 20 years. Changing consultants frequently is not a good idea. Consultants need time to build-up knowledge of the firm and its personnel and the firm needs time to develop a suitable atmosphere of trust. Consultancies need to be aware of sensitive information if they are not to be taken by surprise in a crisis and the firm is unlikely to feel comfortable with this unless the relationship has been established for some time.

Developing a brief

The purpose of the brief is to bridge the gap between what the firm needs and what the consultant is able to supply. Without a clear brief, the consultant has no blueprint to follow and neither party has any way of knowing whether the exercise has been successful or not.

Developing a brief begins with the firm's objectives. Objective setting is a strategic decision area, so it is likely to be the province of senior management. Each objective needs to meet SMARTT criteria, as follows.

1 *Specific* – in other words it must relate to a narrow range of outcomes.
2 *Measurable* – if it is not measurable, it is merely an aim.
3 *Achievable* – there is no point in setting objectives which cannot be achieved, or which are unlikely to be achieved.
4 *Relevant* – to the firm's situation and resources.
5 *Targeted* – accurately.
6 *Timed* – a deadline should be in place for its achievement.

The objectives

The objectives will dictate the budget if the firm is using the objective-and-task method of budgeting. This method means deciding what tasks need to be undertaken to achieve the final outcome and working out how much it will cost to achieve each task. Most organizations tend to operate on the all-we-can-afford budgeting method, which involves agreeing a figure with the finance director. The SMARTT formula implies that, in these circumstances, the budget will dictate the objectives since the objectives must be achievable within the available resources.

Setting the objectives is, of course, only the starting point. Objectives need to be translated into tactical methods for their achievement and these tactics also need to be considered in the light of what the company is trying to achieve.

The brief will be fine-tuned in consultation with the PR agency itself. From the position of their specialist knowledge, the agency will be able to say whether the budget is adequate for what needs to be achieved, or (conversely) say whether the objectives can be achieved within the budget on offer. The agency can also advise on what the appropriate objectives should be, given the firm's current situation.

Measuring outcomes

If the outcomes from the PR activities do not match up with the budgeted objectives, conflict between the client and the agency is likely to be the result. The most common reason for the relationship

Activity	Possible evaluation methods
Press campaign to raise awareness	Formal market research to determine public awareness of the brand/company
Campaign to improve the public image	Formal market research; focus groups for perceptual mapping of the firm against competitors; measures of attitude change
Exhibition or trade show	Records of contacts made; tracking of leads; formal research to determine improvements in image
Sponsorship of a sporting event	Recall rates for the sponsorship activity

TABLE 15.7 Evaluating PR

breaking down is conflict over the costs and hours billed, as compared with the outcomes achieved. From the agency's viewpoint, much of what happens is outside their direct control. Sponsored events might not attract sufficient audiences, press releases might be spiked as a result of major news stories breaking and special events might be rained off. Many a carefully planned reputation-enhancing exercise has foundered, for example, when the celebrity athlete involved has been caught taking drugs.

Measuring outcomes needs to be considered at the objective setting stage. A good PR agency will not offer any guarantees of outcomes, but it should be feasible to assign probabilities to the outcomes and to put systems in place for assessing whether the objectives were achieved.

Table 15.7 shows some possible evaluation methods.

Evaluating activities is never an easy task. It is difficult to be objective, and some activities are too difficult or expensive for evaluation to be worthwhile, but without evaluation, managers have no way of knowing what corrective action to take

SUMMARY

Corporate reputation goes beyond merely putting spin on the corporation's activities. It is a coordinated effort to influence communications to and from stakeholders and also between them, in order to improve the corporation's position in the minds of its publics. In this sense, corporate reputation has a strategic role, because it involves positioning the corporation in the public consciousness: this has real pay-offs in terms of share values, employee satisfaction and behavior, and customer perceptions of the firm.

The key points from this chapter are as follows:

- Corporate reputations are not built through spin-doctoring.
- Corporate reputation has a stock-market valuation.
- Public relations has an internal role.
- Crises will happen: having a crisis team in place is prudent.
- Outside agencies are often cheaper and more effective than carrying out PR tasks in-house.
- Between two and three times the cost of sponsorship should be devoted to other communications efforts in order to support the sponsorship expenditure.

REVIEW QUESTIONS

1   Why might a firm prefer to handle its corporate reputation activities in-house?
2   What are the key issues in building a crisis team?
3   If corporate reputation has such a strong effect on the firms' stock-market valuation, why bother with any other activities?
4   What are the main criteria for deciding to sponsor an event or organization?
5   How might a company avoid PR disasters such as that resulting from the Bhopal tragedy (below)?

SPOTLIGHT ON B2B MARKETING

On December 2nd 1984 over 40 tons of lethal chemical gas was released into the air from the Union Carbide chemical factory in Bhopal, India. The accident was caused by water entering a tank containing chemicals: the resulting reaction generated great heat and vented the poisonous gases into the atmosphere. As a result, many thousands of people in the Bhopal area were killed – estimates vary between 3,800 and 8,000 – and hundreds of thousands have suffered ill health ever since.

Such a disaster was bound to make headlines throughout the world. Union Carbide were held accountable in the world's press and the company was widely criticized by environmental groups. As years went by after the disaster, the situation grew no better: Union Carbide were seen as being slow to pay compensation, slow to make reparations at the plant and slow in implementing a clean-up operation. In particular, the US parent company was accused of not caring about the victims simply because they were Indians.

Twenty years on, the story has not gone away. Campaigners are still seeking further compensation: an Indian court ordered Union Carbide to pay US$470m in 1989 (five years after the disaster) as a full settlement of all claims arising from the disaster and the company did so, but campaigners say that the damage has been underestimated and that the high incidence of birth defects in the region is a result of the leakage. Union Carbide argue that the birth defects are caused by close interbreeding, a feature of marriages in the area. Campaigners claim that contamination of local water supplies has come from the plant: Union Carbide say that the type of contamination could not have been caused by anything they used at the plant and the pollution must be coming from somewhere else.

Union Carbide's main argument, though, is that the Bhopal plant was only owned 51 per cent by the company (26 per cent was owned by the Indian Government, the rest being privately-owned shares) and the Bhopal plant was staffed and managed entirely by Indians. The US company therefore denies any legal liability whatsoever and has the backing of the Second Circuit Court of Appeals, Manhattan, which ruled in 1987 that the case belongs in India and the US company has no liability. The Indian Government was held partly liable and was ordered to purchase health insurance for the 100,000 people who are thought to have been affected by the incident.

The case was further complicated in 2001 when Dow Chemical bought the US Union Carbide company. Dow (not unreasonably) do not accept any responsibility whatsoever for the disaster and are refusing to consider any further claims. Meanwhile, campaigners have persuaded the Indian criminal court to issue a warrant for the arrest of the former Union Carbide CEO, Warren Anderson, on charges of culpable homicide and assault. This arrest warrant has been issued and moves are afoot to have Anderson extradited from the USA to stand trial in India. This is unlikely to be implemented, of course – the US justice system is unlikely to give up a US citizen without very solid evidence of direct (and personal) responsibility.

Meanwhile, in Bhopal the survivors of the disaster wait for something to happen. The compensation amounted to less than US$500 each, which may be a substantial sum of money to people who earn only US$2 a day, but still won't cover the medical bills. The ebb and flow of corporate takeovers means that Union Carbide (India) is now owned entirely by a different corporation, as is Union Carbide USA. Neither of the new owners have any interest or desire to pay compensation and certainly do not feel liable for the disaster. Yet the campaigning still continues, presumably until the last of the survivors has died.

Questions

1   If Union Carbide in the USA has no connection with the Indian subsidiary, why should they do anything?
2   Why is this a potential problem for Dow Chemical?
3   Union Carbide supplies chemicals for industry. The company does not deal with the general public, so why should the company worry about the news media?
4   What might Union Carbide have done to reduce the level of protest?
5   What could Union Carbide (or Dow) do now to reduce the negative publicity which still occasionally crops up?

REFERENCES

Black, A., Wright, P. and Bachman, J. E. (1998) *In Search of Shareholder Value*, London: Pitman.

Cordeiro, J. J. and Sambharaya, R. (1997) 'Do corporate reputations influence security analyst earnings forecasts?' *Corporate Reputation Review*, 1: 2: 94–98.

De Geus, A. (1997) *The Living Company*, Boston MA: Harvard Business School Press.

Fombrun, C. J. and Rindova, V. in Schultz, M., Hatch M. J. and Larsen M. H. (2000) *The expressive organisation*, Oxford: Oxford University Press.

Hayward, R. (1998) *All About PR*, London: McGraw-Hill.

Hefler, M. (1994) 'Making sure sponsorship meets all the parameters', *Brandweek*, May.

Meenaghan, J. A. (1991) 'The role of sponsorship in the marketing communications mix', *International Journal of Advertising*, 10: 1: 35–47.

Pearson A. J. (1980) *Setting Corporate Objectives as a Basis for Action*, Johannesburg: National Development and Management Foundation of South Africa.

Post, J. E., Lawrence, A. T. and Weber, J. (2002) *Business and Society: Corporate Strategy, Public Policy, Ethics*, New York: McGraw-Hill.

Zafer Erdogan, B. and Kitchen, P. J. (1998) 'The interaction between advertising and sponsorship: uneasy alliance or strategic symbiosis?', Proceedings of the 3rd Annual Conference of the Global Institute for Corporate and Marketing Communications, Strathclyde Business School.

SAP

SAP (Systeme, Anwendungen, Produkte in der Datenverarbeitung GmbH) was founded in 1972 in Mannheim, an industrial city in Western Germany. The company produces and designs computer software exclusively for businesses and has built up from early beginnings to being the world's largest B2B software corporation. In fact, SAP is the world's third largest independent software producer overall. With almost 30,000 employees in more than 50 countries, SAP has certainly come a long way in 30 years.

The original five founders were all ex-IBM systems consultants who had noticed that many of their clients were developing the same, or at least very similar, computer programs. Their vision was to develop and market standard software which would integrate all business processes, thus creating economies of scale which would allow the fledgling company to compete with IBM and the other major companies (Groupe Bull and ICL). The other part of the vision was that data processing should occur in real time, so that the computer screen would be the focal point for all data handling. This was a novel idea in 1972 – at the time, corporate computers were room-filling machines that accepted data on punch cards and by huge reels of tape and gave results in hard copy on special computer print-out paper. Computers were much slower, with typical memory capacities of around 500 kilobytes (even on a large mainframe computer) so results could take anything from minutes to hours to be produced. Operating in real time, from a screen, was therefore a ground-breaking idea.

From signing-up their first customer (the German subsidiary of ICI in Ostringen), the company moved on to sign-up cigarette manufacturer Roth-Handle and pharmaceutical company Knoll. SAP's financial management system was the first package available, but this was quickly followed by its materials-handling software which flowed seamlessly into the financial package, emphasizing SAP's commitment to integrating the software.

The company became a GmbH (a private corporation) in 1977, and moved to Walldorf, a small town outside Mannheim, conveniently located at the junction of three autobahns. The same year, the company signed its first foreign customers – two companies from Austria. The company introduced a new module, Asset Accounting, which again plugged into the earlier software to make an integrated whole. Late in the year the company launched a French version of its accounting system, in order to enter the French market: part of the problem with accounting software is that accounting law and practice varies between different countries, so that the software needs to be rewritten (to a greater or lesser extent) whenever the product is sold abroad.

In 1980 SAP introduced order history software, making the package even more attractive and by the end of that year, 50 of Germany's top 100 companies were SAP customers. 1980 was the beginning of the rapid expansion of computer power as technology developed for the Space Shuttle became available: SAP launched its Cost Accounting module and exhibited for the first time at the Systems trade fair in Munich. In 1982 sales rose by 48 per cent to over DM24 million. By the end of 1982, 236 companies in Germany, Austria and Switzerland were using SAP standard programs, and in 1983 sales rose by a further 45 per cent.

In 1984 SAP went truly international, establishing SAP (International) AG in Switzerland. The focus of this new subsidiary was to expand the company's sales into international markets. Development teams began work on Personnel Management software and Plant Maintenance software, integrated (of course) into all the other software. By the end of 1985, SAP had customers throughout Western Europe and had begun to penetrate markets outside Europe with customers in South Africa, Kuwait, Trinidad, Canada and the USA.

During the second half of the 1980s the company established subsidiaries in Denmark, Sweden, Italy and the USA. It established partnerships with Arthur Andersen, opened an International Trade Center in Walldorf, and signed Dow Chemical as its 1,000th customer. Rapid expansion left the company short of working capital, so SAP launched itself on the Frankfurt and Stuttgart stock exchanges, becoming SAP AG and increasing its capital stock from DM5 million to DM60 million.

In 1989 the company further demonstrated its international commitment by organizing user conferences in Lausanne and the USA. The company's direct contact with its international customers proved to be crucial to its success in the following years.

The collapse of communism in Eastern Europe in 1989 proved to be a perfect opportunity for SAP. With Seimens Nixdorf, SAP founded SRS GmbH in Dresden during 1990, thus gaining a strong foothold in the new East German market and opening the door to expansion throughout the former Communist countries. In 1991 SAP collaborated with a Russian software house to produce Russian versions of SAP software: in the same year, the first Japanese installation was completed. By 1992 SAP was firmly established as a global company, with subsidiaries in 15 countries including Malaysia, South Africa and Japan.

During 1993 the company established a software development center in Foster City, California – in the heart of Silicon Valley. In 1994 sales jumped 66 per cent: in 1995 the company pulled off a major coup by signing Microsoft as a customer.

During the late 1990s SAP began to distribute through intermediaries, using value-added resellers to distribute to the small and medium-sized businesses that had previously not had access to SAP software. The late 1990s were also characterized by the fear of the Millennium Bug – the supposed software problem which would cause computers to crash when the date reset to zero on 1st January 2000. Although these fears were not realized, software companies enjoyed an unprecedented boom at this time, writing links to adapt old software and (of course) selling new packages which were guaranteed Y2K compatible.

Throughout the 1990s product development continued, with SAP developing customer relationship management, supply-chain management, and industry-specific software solutions. In the new century, SAP formed SAPHosting, a subsidiary dedicated to the Internet applications service provider and application hosting businesses. They also formed a strategic alliance with Commerce One to create SAPMarkets, a subsidiary aimed at creating globally-interconnected B2B marketplaces on the Internet. During 2000, the company sponsored the United States Grand Prix, aiming for a worldwide audience. The sponsorship was backed up by an advertising campaign developed by Ogilvy and Mather which was rumored to have cost more than US$100m. Formula 1 racing has the advantage of being held every other week for eight months of the year.

'That kind of brand exposure is almost impossible to get', said SAP public relations director Bill Wohl. 'Sports marketing is one of the tried-and-true methods of true brand exposure.'

'The global appeal of Formula One is consistent with our efforts to expose millions of people to the SAP brand, continuing our ongoing efforts to build awareness for one of the world's leading technology brands, and to symbolize that SAP is racing to the pole position of e-business solutions', said Martin Homlish, executive vice president and chief marketing officer at SAP.

Trade fair attendance remains a strong part of SAP's European efforts: the company exhibits at CeBIT, the world's largest IT trade fair, where visitors from all over Europe come to see the latest developments. In the United Sates the company decided to use a roadshow. The SAP E-Business Solutions Tour is mounted on a 53-foot truck and is taken to the customer's premises, taking up a large proportion of the car park in most cases, but providing customers with all the information they need to take advantage of e-business opportunities. The truck is linked by satellite directly to the Web and customers are immersed in the technology as soon as they enter the vehicle. SAP salespeople are on hand to guide customers through the customizing process and to explain how SAP can tailor the software to meet their specific needs. SAP has, in general, been a sales-oriented company, but the Tour is intended to make the company more market-led: in conjunction with the other customer participation schemes the company has. SAP is becoming much more customer-led as time goes by.

Through its history the company's branding developed. In common with most of the companies in the early days of software development, branding was not an issue because the software was virtually invisible – the computer screen was only used by programmers, with inputs and outputs being limited to punch cards or tape and hard copy. SAP merely followed the look and feel of the dominant operating systems such as OSF/Motif and later the Microsoft Windows graphical user interface. The major turning point for the company came in 1998 when it decided to move away from the Microsoft look and create its own branding. The development of high-definition color monitors enabled the company to produce a much more exciting look to the programs: SAP developed (in conjunction with the design team at Frogdesign) a new design called 'Enjoy'. This design incorporated motifs from nature (water, stones, leaves, etc.) to give a visual breath of fresh air to the office workers using the system. Enjoy made SAP software instantly distinguishable from other brands.

During the late 1990s SAP focused on its Web-enabled product lines. The look and feel of SAP software was unified under the Enjoy design, but what the company found was that customers wanted to have their own designs. The concept of flexible visual design was a novelty at the time, but SAP embraced this fully. The change was also catalyzed by the development of SAP's Internet products. In order to encompass both the Internet products and the customers' desire for customization, SAP dropped Enjoy and established a more vibrant, flatter look which enabled the customers to rebrand the product with their own images and colors. This more minimalist design enabled SAP to offer customized designs, but also allowed the company itself more flexibility when developing new products and brands. Through the mySAP Enterprise Portals solution, customers were able to use the Theme Editor software to redesign the look of the screens. During 2002 SAP again consulted with Frogdesign to develop a new, sophisticated, but user-friendly design.

Providing design flexibility without compromising performance is a tall order for any software company, but SAP appear to have done it: some clients have been able to redesign the appearance of the software to the extent that it would not be recognizable as a SAP product, but instead appears as if it has been produced in-house. This is clearly an important consideration for companies that need to establish their own brands on the Internet and elsewhere. In this way SAP can fulfill its goal of aligning its own products under one cohesive visual brand, while allowing its customers to do the same with SAP products aimed at their own customers. Henning Kagermann, the CEO of SAP AG, said recently:

> *According to the experts, software development is reaching maturity as a product for the mass market. Today, and more so tomorrow, software products are expected to offer more than just usability and efficiency; they must be enjoyable to use as well as reflect the individual branding goals of each customer.*

Developments on the Internet include the American SAP Users' Group (ASUG) which provides mutual advice and assistance for SAP users. This is a remarkable innovation, because it is run almost entirely by volunteers. SAP also has a SAPfans website, run by people who are simply enthusiastic about SAP products, and the SAP Design Guild which offers advice and information on redesigning SAP graphics to meet customer specifications. SAP believes that it is essential to involve users in software design: to some extent this is a hangover from the founders' days at IBM, where the software was almost entirely custom-written for each new client. Despite SAP's commitment to the idea of standardizing software, the company still insists on consulting and facilitating communication as fully as possible with customers.

This commitment to customer participation extends to the SAP Customer Appreciation Program, run in the United States by ASUG. The Customer Appreciation Program offers rewards (free consultation hours, free training programs, etc.) in exchange for participation in SAP market research, for speaking at SAP-organized events, and for offering testimonials to be used in SAP advertising. Participants might be asked to provide a reference to a prospective customer, provide information to a SAP staff-writer for a case study to be used in attracting new customers, or might be asked to give a testimonial quote to be used in advertising. In all, SAP identify 13 ways in which existing customers can help in attracting new customers, winning bonuses for themselves as they do so.

Such advertising has proved extremely effective. In June 2003, SAP's US rivals, Oracle and Peoplesoft, became embroiled in a takeover war which also included J. D. Edwards and Co. As the battle raged, SAP announced that it would seize the opportunity to run a major advertising campaign in the world's financial press and via mailshots in order to grab business while its rivals' backs were turned. Within a few days of this announcement, SAP shares had risen 13 per cent, before an advertisement had even been placed. This was against a background of a general rise of 0.6 per cent in technology shares, and a flat European market.

As the software industry enters the 21st century, there is a strong feeling that the boom times are over. Many of the fortuitous strokes of fate that contributed to SAP's success were one-offs – the fall of the Berlin Wall, the Y2K bug, the exponential increase in computer power during the 1990s. Additionally, the initial rush for companies to automate their management information systems has died down as the systems are in place and are being used. After all, there are only so many major blue-chip companies around and most of those are quite happy with their present solutions. Finally, the industry is not recession-proof. The drop in world trade, and particularly the damage done to the US economy as a result of September 11th and the Iraq war has meant that the last thing on most CEOs minds is updating the software. Thus there is a feeling that there may be too many companies in a market which is topping out or even shrinking.

SAP has now been operating for more than thirty years. Probably the vast majority of the general public have never heard of the company – yet it is one of the major players in the software industry, and its products affect the lives of almost everyone on the planet, directly or indirectly.

Case study questions

1 To what degree is SAP marketing-oriented? What evidence is there for this?
2 To what extent do you think luck played a part in SAP's success?
3 How did SAP integrate their marketing communications?
4 Why might the company be using trade shows in Europe and road shows in the United States?
5 What new product policy is SAP using?
6 Why might the Customer Appreciation Program work in the States, but be less effective in Europe?
7 How might SAP protect itself from recession?
8 How is SAP seeking to control corporate reputation?

MANAGING THE
MARKETING PROGRAM

The final section of this book introduces you to the tactical issues involved in managing the interface between businesses, and looks at some of the broader issues which affect B2B trading in the 21st century.

Chapter 16 looks at planning, implementation and control. In this chapter, the strategic issues raised in Chapter 3 are revisited and translated into practical tactics for running the business. The chapter shows how to combine elements of the marketing mix in order to achieve corporate objectives and outlines methods for obtaining feedback on the success (or otherwise) of marketing programs.

Chapter 17 deals with the organization of marketing effort and examines issues of staff empowerment, ways of structuring the organization for maximum effectiveness and change management.

Chapter 18 considers ethical issues. In recent years, anti-globalization issues, the environment and considerations of what constitutes fair and unfair competition, have come to the forefront. This chapter enables you to understand the background of these ethical considerations and to understand what it means to be a good corporate citizen in a global context.

Chapter 19 examines future developments in business marketing, both in terms of tactical and business environment issues and in terms of the philosophy which underpins marketing thinking. Post-modern marketing and the emergence of value-based marketing represent some of the latter trends, while considerations of the effects of globalization and the impact of new communications technology represent some of the former issues which are covered.

16

MARKETING PLANNING, IMPLEMENTATION AND CONTROL

Learning objectives
After reading this chapter, you should be able to:

- Explain the processes involved in planning

- Describe ways of obtaining feedback

- Explain how to combine elements of the marketing mix to attain goals

- Describe some of the problems of implementing marketing plans

- Describe ways of implementing marketing information systems

▊ Introduction

Coordinating marketing activities has been a problem for marketers since the beginning of marketing thinking. In any organization, individuals act according to ideas of their own: media buyers operate with one set of rules, salespeople and advertising planners with another. Since all employees go home and almost all talk about their work and their company, the possibilities for controlling all marketing communications are strictly limited. Having said that, planning is essential if there is to be any common direction in the organization.

■ Marketing planning

As we saw in Chapter 3, planning is an essential part of management. Having said that, much planning is carried out in a haphazard or ad-hoc manner: strategic plans are often produced and then ignored (a practice which Nigel Piercy has dubbed SPOTS, or 'strategic plan on the shelf').

The basic process of marketing planning is shown in Figure 16.1. Having decided on a strategic direction and position, marketers need to consider how to marshal the tools at their disposal in order to achieve the strategic outcome.

The firm will already have made the basic strategic decisions, which are:

● Which market should the firm be in?
● What strengths and weaknesses is the firm bringing to the marketplace?
● Where does the firm intend to be in 5 to 30 years' time?
● What will the firm's competitors do in response to the market and to the firm's activities?
● Does the firm have sufficient resources to achieve the objectives decided upon?

This in turn will have led to setting more specific objectives, giving the detail of how the strategy is to be achieved. The next stage in the planning process is to determine where the firm is now. This can be carried out by using the marketing audit.

The marketing audit

The marketing audit is a comprehensive review of the firm's current position in terms of its marketing activities (Kotler *et al.* 2003). It is, in effect, a snapshot of the firm's marketing, but like a snapshot it inevitably represents a past position since matters will have progressed while the situation is being analyzed. This means that the audit should be carried out on a regular basis if the firm is to be

FIGURE 16.1

Marketing planning process

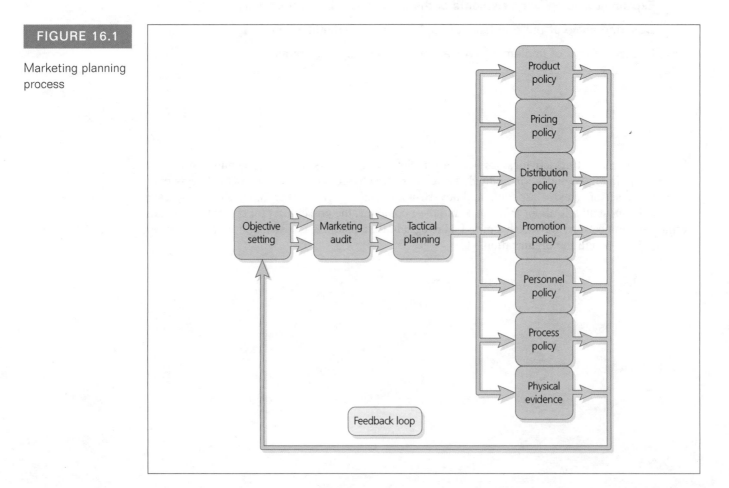

able to see whether progress is being made: obviously the frequency of the audit will depend on a number of factors, as follows:

1 The amount of time that can be spared from actually carrying out marketing tasks.
2 The cost of carrying out the audit, in both man-hours and resources generally.
3 The nature of the market. In a volatile market, the audit may need to be carried out more frequently than would be the case in a stable, mature market.
4 The nature of the corporate objectives. Some objectives need constant monitoring and also some objectives impact greatly on other parts of the marketing effort.

Audit break-down

The audit breaks down into seven main areas, with several sub-sections in each. The main areas are:

1 *The macro environment audit* – This takes account of all the factors which impact on the industry as a whole, including the economy, technology, political, legal, cultural and ecological factors.
2 *The task environment audit* – This is concerned with factors which impact on the company itself, for example markets, customers, competitors, distribution and dealers, suppliers, facilitators and publics.
3 *The marketing strategy audit* – This area is concerned with the appropriateness of the business mission, marketing objectives and strategic aim.
4 *The marketing organization audit* – This area is about the formal structure of the marketing function, functional efficiency and interface efficiency.
5 *The marketing systems audit* – This is concerned with the marketing information systems, marketing planning systems, control systems and new product development systems.
6 *The marketing productivity audit* – This section brings in financial measures such as profitability analysis and cost-effectiveness analysis.
7 *The marketing function audit* – This audits the 7-Ps and determines how effective the company is in each of those areas.

The marketing audit can be time-consuming: it involves a degree of subjectivity and a considerable amount of introspection. This can make it an expensive exercise, both in time and in emotional labor. For the audit to be effective, it has to be more than a simple 'tick the box' exercise.

Criticism

The marketing audit has been criticized because it tends to lead people into the trap of thinking of all the activities as being separate from each other, whereas of course everything impacts on everything else. This means that problems are likely to be complex: such complexity has three characteristics, as follows (Mason and Mitroff 1981):

1 Any policy-making situation comprises many problems and issues.
2 These problems and issues tend to be highly interrelated, so that the solution to one problem creates other problems elsewhere, or at least requires a more global solution.
3 Few if any problems can be isolated effectively for separate treatment.

Complex and wicked problems

Complex problems cannot be solved by simple means. Variations in one element of the system causes reverberations throughout the system: many corporate problems display this level of complexity. Rittel (1972) referred to this type of problem as a wicked problem. Wicked problems have the properties shown in Table 16.1.

The existence of wicked problems means that the marketing-mix approach, sometimes called the 'silo' approach because everything is placed in separate containers, falls far short of providing a useful model for problem-solving. In the same way, the marketing audit implies that each activity is separate and can be treated in isolation.

TABLE 16.1 Properties of wicked problems

Property	Explanation and Examples
Ability to formulate the problem	Tame problems can be formulated and written down. Wicked problems have no definitive formulation. For example, the problem of buying a house can be formulated in terms of writing down price range, location and size. Desirable (but not essential) features such as a south-facing garden might be added. This is a tame problem. On the other hand, planning to buy a house to retire to in 30 years' time is a wicked problem because of the huge number of variables that will affect the individual and the property market.
Relationship between problem and solution	Tame problems can be formulated separately from any implied solution. The formulation of wicked problems cannot be separated from statements of the solution, in other words understanding the problem in itself creates the solution.
Testability	Solutions to tame problems can be tested and judged either correct or false. There is no single way to tell whether the solution to a wicked problem is correct or false, because solutions can only be good or bad relative to each other.
Finality	Tame problems have a closing point at which they can be deemed to have been solved. The stopping-point can be tested, in other words. Wicked problems, on the other hand, have no end: there is always room for improvement and each solution generates more problems.
Tractability	There is a large range of possible solutions for a tame problem and these can be listed. For a wicked problem, there is no exhaustive, numerable list of possibilities.
Explanatory characteristics	A tame problem can be stated as a gap between what is and what ought to be and there is a clear explanation for every gap. Wicked problems have many possible explanations for the same discrepancy.
Level of analysis	Tame problems have identifiable, natural form: there is no argument about the level of the problem. The proper level of generality can be found for bounding the problem and identifying its root cause. Wicked problems are symptoms of another problem, and have no identifiable root causes. Would-be problem solvers cannot be sure that they are not attacking the symptoms rather than the root causes of the problem.
Reproducibility	A tame problem can be abstracted and modeled and attempts to solve it can be tried out until one is found that appears to fit. Wicked problems are all one-shot propositions: there is no trial and error.
Replicability	Tame problems tend to repeat themselves in different organizations or at different times. Wicked problems are essentially unique.
Responsibility	No-one can be blamed for failing to solve a tame problem and in fact people are often praised. Would-be solvers of wicked problems are often blamed for causing other problems, but are unlikely to be praised because wicked problems are rarely solved in any final sense.

Another criticism of the audit is that it tends to view the company as a discrete entity, surrounded by an environment which is mainly hostile. In the B2B world, it is more likely that the company has a number of strategic alliances and long-term relationships which are largely benevolent in nature. On the other hand, any assessment of the organization's current position needs to start somewhere.

TALKING POINT

The marketing audit, like the balance sheet, offers an instant picture of where the company is. Of course, by the time the audit has been carried out and all the information has been collated, several months might have elapsed and the company will have moved on greatly. The audit therefore tells us where we used to be, not where we are now.

Yet shouldn't we be looking forward? What is the point of looking backwards? This would be a poor way to drive a car, so why do we think it's a good idea when we are driving a company? If the world is changing as fast as we are told it is, we can't afford to be backward looking!

On the other hand, what choice do we have? We can never know exactly where we are and the future is always hard to predict.

Despite the criticisms, the marketing audit does have the advantage of focusing the minds of the marketers and it is certainly a useful checklist.

Tactical planning

Because marketers are looking for a competitive edge, they will usually try to offer their customers something that is unavailable elsewhere. In this respect, marketing differs from other business disciplines. If the legal directors were swapped from one competing firm to another, they would have little difficulty in continuing with their jobs. The law remains the same throughout the industry. The same is true for financial directors, personnel directors, production managers and so forth. If the marketers were swapped, however, they may well feel completely lost since each firm within an industry adopts its own approach to the market. Each firm should be addressing the needs of different segments, dealing with different distributors and different clients, and using different promotional campaigns.

The tactical possibilities for a marketing campaign are huge in number. Most of the tactics of marketing involve creativity on the part of marketers, so it is virtually impossible to lay down any hard and fast rules about approaching different marketing problems. However, the following is a list of useful guidelines for practitioners:

- Try to do something that the competition has not thought of yet.
- Always consult everybody who is involved in the day-to-day application of the plans.
- Do not expect instant results from anything you do – but monitor the results anyway.
- Ensure that the messages you give to customers, suppliers and other publics are consistent.
- Be prepared for a competitive response and try to anticipate what it might be when formulating plans.
- Communication tools cannot be used to achieve marketing objectives. They can only achieve communications objectives.

The dividing line between strategy and tactics is often blurred. One of the key identifying features of tactical decisions is that they are relatively easy to reverse, which means that tactics can be adapted in unstable circumstances. For a strategy to be converted into tactics, the following four elements need to be put in place:

1. A specific action – what is to be done.
2. An accountability – who is to do it.
3. A deadline – when is it to be done by.
4. A budget – what it will cost to do it.

Usually a set of tactics is developed to implement the strategy and these tactics will need to be coordinated. An example in marketing is the development of an integrated marketing communications package, which will involve the coordinated efforts of a great many individuals. In the B2B environment the process is similar but the elements include the salesforce, trade shows, catalogs and websites rather than relying mostly on media advertising.

Cost effectiveness will always be an issue in promotional campaigns and it is for this reason that there has been a rapid growth in direct mailing in B2B markets. The accurate targeting of customers that direct mail allows has enabled marketers to refine the approach and hence increase the response rate.

Having decided what is to be done, managers are in a position to implement the program.

■ Developing core competency

Competency to achieve a given strategic objective is derived from the way resources are combined and utilized. Efficiency in the use of resources is the key to effectiveness in strategic success (usually expressed as competitive advantage). If resources are to be adequately utilized, managers must know what resources are available: in order to ensure that those resources are being used effectively, competency auditing is also essential. But, there are problems in translating theory into practice.

Research into companies' resources

There has been considerable research into the importance of resources for the firm (Penrose 1959, Wernerfelt 1984, Barney 1991). There is a problem of definition here, however: some authors prefer not to use the term 'resources' when writing of the range of means at the disposal of the planners and managers, but instead refer to 'assets'. This means that there is currently no generally agreed classification of resources (or assets) within the strategic management field.

Certainly some major distinctions can be made. Firstly, resources may be tangible or intangible. Tangible resources are those assets such as machinery, buildings, vehicles, stock of raw materials, work in progress and so forth which can be touched and handled. Intangible resources are intellectual property such as patents or software, brand equity, goodwill and the intellectual resources of the employees. Of the two, it is the tangible assets which are the easiest to identify, value, buy and sell: the intangible assets are more fragile (in that they can easily be lost) and are harder to value (since future income streams can be hard to predict). Intangible assets often represent the major part of a firm's stock market valuation, on the other hand.

The second classification which can be made is to divide intangible resources into relational resources and competences. Relational resources are all of the means available to the firm derived from its relationship with its environment (Lowendahl 1997). These might include special relationships with customers, distributors and consumers and also the firm's reputation and brand equity.

Competence refers to the firm's fitness to perform in a given field and is based on the effective use of resources. Durand (1996) has drawn a distinction between knowledge, capability and attitude. These are shown in Table 16.2.

Table 16.2 Knowledge, capability and attitude	
Knowledge	The set of rules (know-how, know-what, know-where and know-when) and insights (know-why) that are used to make sense of information (Dretske 1981). This knowledge is contained in the heads of the employees for the most part, but is collective: examples are marketing insights, knowledge of competitors, technological expertise and understanding of political issues.
Capability	This is the organization's potential for carrying out specific activities. Capability bases might include rapid response to market changes, or specific abilities to create new products (Stalk *et al.* 1992).
Attitude	This is the shared tendency to respond in a particular way to outside stimuli. Some firms are known for an aggressive attitude, or a litigious attitude, or even a caring and sharing attitude (Hewlett-Packard being an example of the latter). This attitude is shared by the employees, at least during working hours. Such attitudes, when seated firmly within the organizational culture, can represent substantial assets (Barney 1986).

There is some confusion between the terms 'competences' and 'capabilities'. Durand's (1996) view is that a competence in a certain area will arise when the firm's knowledge, capabilities and attitudes are aligned in such a way that synergies are created. For example, Virgin Airways' service competence is a combination of knowledge of customers, the capability to adapt and a customer-oriented attitude.

Auditing resources and competences

From the viewpoint of auditing resources and competences, there are considerable conceptual difficulties. As far as tangible assets go, accountants have evolved some straightforward techniques for arriving at a value: however, these values are only valid in particular circumstances. For example, a fixed asset such as a piece of machinery might be valued in one of three separate ways. Firstly, its value in terms of what it can produce, or the income stream that might be expected from it. This is also a function of the business environment, since the value of the production might vary or the demand for the product may shift dramatically. For example, a mold which produces plastic components is only valuable as long as the demand for those components continues – as soon as the demand is removed, the value of the mold drops to zero.

Secondly, tangible assets might be valued in terms of their purchase price and expected life. Thus a vehicle might depreciate by a calculable amount over a given period: the firm's accountants are usually able to calculate the value of, for example, the salesforce's company cars in this way.

Thirdly, tangible assets can be valued according to their resale value. This can be higher than the original purchase price (for example, buildings or office premises) or lower than the original purchase price (for example vehicles or machinery), or in some cases might be virtually zero (for example, some of the tunneling machinery used to build the Eurotunnel).

Each of these valuation methods will arrive at a different answer. Clearly the difficulties inherent in auditing intangible assets are likely to be greater, particularly if there is pressure to audit in financial terms. Therefore few organizations do this: this is one of the problems faced by marketers when trying to justify expenditures on (for example) brand-building.

Auditing knowledge

Auditing knowledge is likely to be judgment-based, since knowledge has a high rate of decay in a changing environment. A linked audit might be to consider the firm's ability and disposition towards maintaining its knowledge base: this is a function of the training of staff, of staff development initiatives and of the firm's propensity to spend money on research and development. This audit can be assessed qualitatively by making benchmarking comparisons with other firms in the same industry.

Auditing capability

Auditing capability is likewise a judgment-based activity, though there may be some objective elements involved. Capability might be judged by events in the recent past (for example, an exceptionally effective new product development and launch) or might be judged by assessing the individual capabilities of the firm and aggregating them to give an overall view of capability (i.e. what we should be able to accomplish). This latter method has the advantage of being more up-to-date, but has the major drawback of not taking account of possible synergies or unforeseen weaknesses.

Corporate attitude is probably subject to more instances of self-delusion on the part of senior managers than any other element in the competences framework. Often the attitude of senior management is not reflected further down the hierarchy and (worse) employees may be at some pains to conceal their real attitudes for fear of appearing to be out of step with the management. This is likely to have a severely damaging effect on the coordinating function of the strategy, since employees are likely to act in one way while trying to convince senior management that they are in fact acting in a different way. For this reason, corporate attitudes need to be monitored at grass-roots level: attitudes are difficult to measure at best, because behavior is not a good guide and self reports may conceal political agendas.

TALKING POINT

Corporate attitude is an interesting concept. It seems to imply that the whole organization has the same attitude – yet how can this be? Organizations are not separate from their members: each member presumably has a set of attitudes on all sorts of issues. In some cases they will agree with their workmates, in other cases not – this is what makes those round-the-photocopier discussions interesting!

So how can we talk about a corporate attitude? Do people perhaps have one set of attitudes in private and another set when in work? Does the organization have that much influence over us?

If so, doesn't each member's attitude affect the whole corporation to some small extent? How can we possibly expect to control that?

Resource audits

Relational resources are even harder to pin down: with whom does the organization have a relationship and what is the value and status of the relationship? Relationships often break down, in business as in real life. What is the value of the firm's reputation? This can sometimes be arrived at in general terms by looking at the difference between the firm's balance sheet asset value and its stock market valuation, but this is a somewhat nebulous measure, relying as much on factors such as the general state of the economy, the general state of the industry and the state of competing investments, as on the current state of the firm.

Valuing a brand is not as straightforward as might at first appear, either. A well-established brand tends to have a less elastic demand curve: in other words, they are less price-sensitive (Hamilton *et al.* 1997). This means that a price increase on a strong brand will have less effect than a price increase on a weak brand. This implies that a strong brand will have a much better chance of weathering a recession, for example, than a weak brand: this is in itself a valuable characteristic and is one that is well worth investing in.

The resource audit will cover the areas shown in Table 16.3.

The resource audit should include all the resources the firm can tap into, even when these are not actually owned by the firm: intangible resources and financial resources which can be called upon if needed fall into this category. Particular weight should be given to unique resources – those resources

Table 16.3 Elements in the resource audit	
Element	**Examples and explanation**
Physical resources	A list of the fixed assets of the organization, for example machinery, buildings and equipment. The audit needs to include the age and condition of the assets, their location and their capability, as well as their financial value (which is often calculated in an arbitrary manner in any case). This is to determine their usefulness in achieving strategic advantages.
Human resources	This can be a problematical area, since much of the value of staff depends on their motivation and commitment rather than on their paper qualifications and the numbers of them within the organization.
Financial resources	This should include the sources of money (whether equity or loan), the liabilities the organization has and the possible availability of capital or loans should it become necessary to acquire more funding – this is essentially the firm's credit rating.
Intangibles	From a marketer's point of view, intangible assets such as brands, patents, reputation and relationships with customers (goodwill) are at least as important as any of the firm's other assets, since these are the capital from which marketers derive competence.

which competitors are unable to duplicate, for example patented products or other intellectual property.

Competence analysis cannot be measured in absolute terms: it always has to be measured against competitors' provision and customers' expectations. In particular it is important to identify the organization's core competences – the particular competences that ensure that the organization can outperform its competition in some respects.

Core competences

Identifying core competences will vary from one industry to another. Threshold competences are those which any business in the industry would need to have in order to survive: any machine-tool manufacturer needs a threshold competence in engineering and in design, but some manufacturers have developed core competences which single them out from the competition. For example, Abbott Toolfast Pvt have a core competence in producing clamping equipment, Sharma Machine Tools has a competence in presses and Galaxy Machinery Pvt has a core competency in lathe manufacture. All of these companies are Indian and in the global context they share a competency in low-cost manufacture. Core competences only have relevance when compared with competitors and with market segments.

Core competences might also be linked to critical success factors. The critical success factor in an industry is the basic elements that have to be right if the firm is to succeed, rather than merely survive. For example, Internet-based firms need a threshold competency in information technology, but the critical success factor is likely to be the design of the web page. A well-designed page will encourage business, whereas a poorly-designed one is frustrating to visit. Examples of poor design abound: websites which use complex images which take too long to download, websites which require in-depth knowledge of the company's systems in order to navigate, websites which do not give hard information but instead concentrate on sales pitches and websites which do not allow the visitor to escape by any other means than rebooting the computer.

Sustaining the lead

Maintaining a lead in the market means establishing a competence which cannot easily be copied by others. Strategists should consider three questions (*Coyne et al.* 1997):

1 *How rare is our competence?* In other words, can the competence be easily copied and does it exist among other firms in the industry?

2 *How long will it take our competitors to develop the competence?* Imitators may need months or years to produce equivalent technology: on the other hand, if the competence resides in the expertise of staff members, a competitor need only headhunt key individuals. Competences involving cross-functional processes are difficult to emulate, as are competences which involve external groups such as suppliers and key-customers.

3 *Can the source of our advantage be easily understood by the competition?* Some skills may be deeply embedded in the company's culture, such as (for example) high levels of service responsiveness. A core competence involving only a few elements is easier to understand and emulate than one relying on the combination of many elements.

Because competences involve combining many elements, the process involved is perhaps crucial to a successful outcome. For example, a chef may take basic ingredients such as flour, eggs, apples, sugar and so forth and make an apple pie. A great chef will use the same ingredients to create a confection which is a work of art: a bad chef might create an inedible mess. In the business world, every process combines the following four resources:

1 *Basic assets*: These are the tangible and intangible assets of the business, as expressed in the financial reporting systems. Tangible assets would include plant and machinery, cash, work in progress, buildings, fixtures and fittings. Intangible assets include reputation of the firm, reputation of brands and goodwill.

2 *Explicit knowledge*: This is knowledge which can be written down or otherwise recorded. Much of this would be in the public domain: the legal restrictions that companies in the industry

need to work within, the technical problems associated with the industry, or the published market research which forms the basis of the tactical marketing planning. Some explicit knowledge might be in the form of customer databases or patents.

3 *Tacit knowledge*: This is knowledge which is difficult or impossible to codify and usually resides in the heads of employees. For example, skilled workers or professionals within the organization may have particular abilities which cannot be written down: skilled welders, toolmakers or machinists have honed their skills over many years of practice. Likewise, a skilled buyer or corporate lawyer will develop skills (such as the ability to read another person's true intentions) which cannot be taught in college. Some tacit knowledge might be disseminated throughout the organization, for example customer-care skills.

4 *Procedure*: This is the mechanism by which the basic assets, explicit knowledge and tacit knowledge are brought together.

Procedure

Procedure can easily be mistaken for process, but the two differ. A good procedure which lacks the necessary staff skills to carry it out will not produce an effective process, nor will a bad procedure be compensated for by (for example) an abundance of basic assets. The procedure must therefore take account of the available assets, explicit knowledge and tacit knowledge.

Procedure is the element which is most easily changed by management and therefore it is the element which most commonly changes. This is often unsettling for staff and requires a degree of re-learning and re-ordering of knowledge. From a tactical point of view, this can prove to be severely counter-productive.

Linking processes

When processes are linked together to deliver a set of benefits to customers they become the components of a capability. A capability should be more than the sum of the individual processes: synergies should result from the combination of the processes. This will not happen if the processes are inappropriately linked or mutually damaging in some way (Stalk *et al.* 1992). An organization may combine its processes in different ways in order to develop different capabilities, either at the same time or in order.

For example, a company may have developed effective processes for recruitment, stock purchasing, delivery and efficient invoicing. These processes might all arise from having combined an asset-base of state-of-the-art computer equipment and the tacit knowledge of a group of IT experts within the firm. This is shown diagrammatically in Figure 16.2.

FIGURE 16.2

Developing resources into processes and capabilities

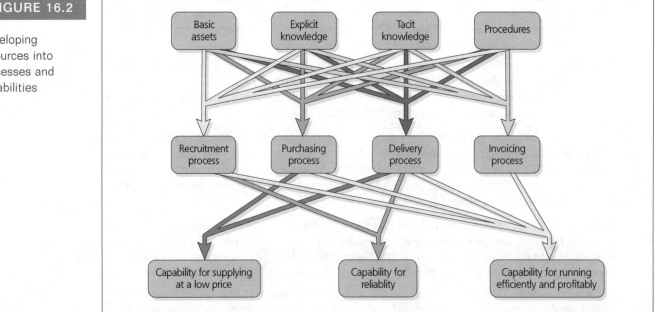

Obviously different managers might combine the same components in a different way in order to generate new processes and competences. This is a more complex management task than simply altering procedures, so is somewhat rarer and also is a valuable ability for a manager to have. An example of this is the nuclear waste reprocessing plant at Sellafield in Cumbria. Originally this was a facility which was used in conjunction with the nearby nuclear power plant, but managers realized that the firm's resources would be better spent on developing the waste reprocessing facility rather than expanding the power plant. British Nuclear Fuels now has a world reputation for reprocessing nuclear waste.

Generating new capabilities from existing components is in itself a process, involving creative thought as well as the ability to identify which components are available and which processes they can be diverted from in order to strengthen other components. From the viewpoint of the end customer, the process is a major part of the benefits of the product and forms a large part of the perception of both company and brand. For most firms, improving the firm's competitive position will mean developing new capabilities, which in turn means either changing processes in some way or recombining processes in order to generate new capabilities.

For example, a computer software company moving into a foreign market will need to develop the capability to service that market. This may mean changing the process of recruitment to include foreign language speakers, it may mean changing the training process to encompass training in the foreign software protocols (or at least learning the usual jargon in the foreign language). Conversely, it may mean combining an existing process for translating foreign language documents into English with an existing capacity for writing software, so that the translation is simply carried out in reverse. In practice, it probably means a combination of all these changes, plus several more.

■ Monitoring and evaluating marketing performance

Feedback is essential for monitoring performance and (in an ideal world) no marketing activity would be undertaken without having a monitoring and evaluation system in place beforehand.

There are two basic groups of approaches for performance analysis; sales analysis and marketing cost analysis. Sales analysis looks at the income generated by the firm's activities, whereas marketing analysis looks at the costs of generating the income. Table 16.4 illustrates some sales analysis measures.

Considerable amounts of information will be needed if the firm is to make effective use of sales analysis to monitor activities. This may involve the firm in substantial market research expenditure, since market research is the cornerstone of monitoring and evaluation.

The other part of the picture is to examine the cost of achieving the goals which have been specified. Marketing cost analysis is a set of techniques for breaking down the costs of the firm's activities and associating them with specific marketing objectives. Costs can be broken down (broadly) into direct costs such as salespersons' salaries, which can be directly attributable to a given activity, traceable common costs such as costs of advertising, which can be traced back to specific products and non-traceable common costs such as the cost of PR or corporate advertising, which cannot be allocated to any particular product range or brand.

The main problem with marketing cost analysis lies in organizing the firm's accounting systems in such a way as to permit analysis. For example, payroll records may not be easily broken down by job function; it may be difficult to sort out which of the administration staff spend most of their time on marketing-related tasks, or even to find out what the pay bill is for the salesforce. Likewise, defining which jobs constitute marketing jobs and which do not also presents problems. Clearly the cost of servicing customers in remote areas is a marketing cost – so should the transportation costs be taken into account as well as the salesforce mileage costs? Also, if a given product is not performing well, should we be looking at the costs of production?

For the dyed-in-the-wool customer-oriented firm these answers are obvious, since all the activities of the firm are regarded as marketing activities. In other firms, not all managers agree with the basic premises on which marketing is based. At the very least, many people find it difficult to translate the theory into practice and to gear the organization's activities towards a consumer orientation.

A problem with all of the above approaches is that they are financially-based and predicated on the assumption that marketing is about making sales rather than about achieving strategic

Table 16.4 Methods of sales analysis

Analysis Method	Explanation
Comparison with forecast sales	The firm compares the actual sales achieved against what was forecast for the period.
Comparison with competitors' sales	Provided the information is available, the firm can estimate the extent to which marketing activities have made inroads into the competitors' business. The problem here is proving that the difference has been caused by the high quality of the firm's marketing activities, rather than by the ineptness of the competitor.
Comparison with industry sales	Examination of the firm's performance in terms of market share. This is commonly used in industries where a relatively small number of firms control the market; for example, the car industry.
Cash volume sales analysis	Comparison of sales in terms of cash generated. This has the advantage that currency is common to both sales and costs; it has the disadvantage that price rises may cause the company to think it has done better than it has.
Unit sales analysis	Comparison of sales in terms of the number of units sold, or sometimes the number of sales transactions. This is a useful measure of salesforce activities, but should not be taken in isolation; sometimes the figures can be distorted by increased sales of cheaper models.
Sales by geographic unit	Sales are broken down regionally so that the firm can tell whether one or two regions are accounting for most of the sales and whether some less-productive regions are not worth what they cost to service.
Sales by product group or brand	This is particularly important for judging the product portfolio. This serves two purposes; it is possible to identify products which should be dropped from the range and it is also possible to identify products which are moving into the decline phase of the product lifecycle and should therefore be revived.
Sales by type of customer	Can reveal, for example, that most effort is being expended on a group of customers who make relatively few purchases. May reveal that the firm's customers tend to be ageing and may therefore be a declining group in years to come.

marketing objectives. For example, a firm may have a legitimate marketing objective to improve customer loyalty. While this may increase sales in the long run, the appropriate measure of success would be the degree to which customers make repeat purchases, which in the short term may actually lead to a reduction in sales as the firm shifts the emphasis away from recruiting new customers towards retaining existing ones.

Balanced scorecards

The balanced scorecard approach was suggested by Kaplan and Norton (1992). The authors suggest that the organization should measure performance using a limited specific set of measures, that are derived from the success factors which are most important to the stakeholder groups.

The measures to be used can be grouped in the following categories:

1 Financial measures – These would include return on capital employed, cash flow, growth in share value and so forth.

2 Customers – These measures would include perceived value for money (not necessarily cheapness), competitive benefits package and so forth.

3 Internal processes – These might be enquiry response time, conversion rate from enquiry to order.

4 Growth and improvement – This would include the number of new products on offer, the extent of employee involvement and empowerment, employee attitudes to the firm and so forth.

The balanced scorecard is an attempt to integrate all the factors which would impact on the organization's long-term success so that the strategy does not become unbalanced. To be most effective, managers need to apply some weighting to each of the factors in order to ensure that attention is paid to those areas which are most closely allied to the corporate mission or vision.

Feedback systems

When a discrepancy appears between the expected performance and the actual performance, the marketing manager will need to take action. This will usually take the following sequence:

- Determine the reason for the discrepancy – Was the original plan reasonable? Have the firm's competitors seized the initiative in some way, so that the situation has changed? Is someone at fault?

- Feed these findings back to the staff concerned – This can be in the form of a meeting to discuss the situation, or in the form of memos and reports.

- Develop a plan for correcting the situation – This will probably involve the cooperation of all the staff concerned.

Feedback should be both frequent and concise and any criticisms should be constructive; for example, managers should never go to a sales meeting and offer only criticisms since this sends the salesforce out with negative feelings about themselves and the company.

Marketing strategy and planning is much like any other planning exercise; it relies on good information, a clear idea of where the organization is going and regular examination of both outcomes and methods to ensure that the plan is still on target.

■ Control systems

The purpose of any strategic control system is to decide whether the current strategy is correct and should therefore be retained, or whether circumstances have altered in such a way that the strategy should be scrapped and a new one formulated.

Most control is reactive: it seeks out variances in performance and applies a correction to redress the variance. Such feedback is called negative feedback, because it acts against the trend of the variance in order to reduce it. Feedback which tends to increase the variance is called positive feedback and is generally considered to be counter-productive since it creates a situation where the system runs away with itself entirely in one direction. In some cases, a variation which is self-correcting, i.e. a temporary blip in performance, may be over-compensated for so that variance increases rather than decreases. This comes about because of time delays in the feedback systems. Figure 16.3 illustrates how this works in practice.

In Figure 16.3, the first arrow shows how feedback applied too late will send sales rocketing too high. This may seem like a good outcome, but it is likely that the feedback applied will have been a costly sales-boosting exercise such as a major sales promotion or an advertising campaign. The result is a fall in profits, possibly a fall in competitive position and at worst, provokes an insupportable competitive reaction. The second arrow shows a correctly-applied negative feedback, which helps the fall in sales to bottom out and return to normal.

FIGURE 16.3

Positive and
negative feedback

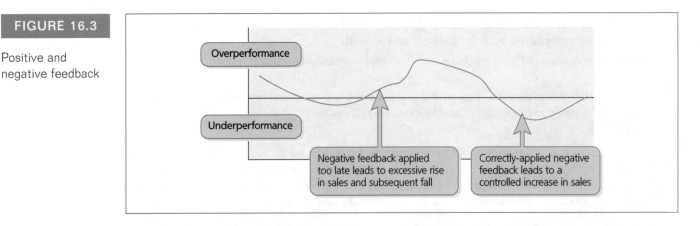

Feeding back into the system seems to be fraught with risks. Too early a feedback increases the problem, too late a feedback seems to be wasted effort. If we look at the most important fluctuation of all, the economic cycle, we must wonder whether it's worth bothering at all.

Since the 1930s, governments have sought to control the boom-and-bust cycle, taking the credit when the economy booms and passing the buck when the economy crashes. Yet all the feedback, government initiatives, job-creation schemes and rhetoric seem to have done nothing whatsoever to cure the problem.

Maybe there is no problem. Maybe fluctuations are just a natural part of life: the process of sleeping and waking applied to business. In which case, why are we bothering with feedback at all?

Some fluctuation is inevitable. Minor deviations from the plan will always occur sooner or later: the difficulty for managers lies in judging the extent to which such deviations are permissible before action must be taken.

The concept of feedback and control is borrowed from engineering. The controls for a machine are intended to maintain the status quo: some controls are automatic (for example the governor on a steam engine) while others are designed for use by a machine operator (for example the accelerator on a car). In either case the machine will obey the control systems, because that is what it has been designed to do.

Human beings are not machines. The most difficult management issues concern the control of human beings and this is the area where the feedback systems most often break down. For the purposes of feedback and control, processes can be divided into systematized processes such as repetitive clerical or assembly-line tasks and unstructured processes, which are activities requiring judgment (Dermer 1977).

Examples of the second type would include professional activities such as the law or accountancy and within the firm they would include senior managerial tasks and one-off projects. For most 21st century firms, unstructured processes are in the majority, simply because repetitive clerical work has been taken over by computers and most factory work has been automated. Since Dermer first formulated this division in 1977, the number of people working in manual jobs has more than halved: at the same time, the number of clerical tasks such as filing and typing has dramatically reduced due to the use of computers. It is unlikely that any firms nowadays have a typing pool, but in the 1970s such systems were commonplace.

Difficulties with control systems

The type of thinking that applies to engineering problems is not necessarily applicable to human problems. Each has its own set of assumptions which may not hold true for the other: certainly many of the assumptions made by managers prove to be false when attempts are made to put them into practice. Finlay (2000) says that there are four assumptions borrowed from engineering which do not transfer to management. These are shown in Table 16.5.

Because of these problems, firms need to use adaptive controls. While much of the control system can be automatic, managers need to use human judgment to override the system when necessary, otherwise long-term change is unlikely to happen. Hofstede (1978) uses a biological analogy to explain this in terms of a living cell, but it may be more appropriate to think of a more complex organism. Fluctuations in outside temperature can be compensated for by the body's natural homeostatic mechanisms – sweating when the temperature is too high, shivering when it is too cold – but beyond certain limits of comfort a human being will exercise judgment and either go somewhere cooler or wear something warmer, as appropriate. In a similar way, organizations need to exercise judgment when the environment behaves in a way that is beyond the control system's capacity.

Two methods of control exist: firstly, to change the organization's behavior in some way to overcome the difficulty and reach the objective, or secondly to change objectives and aim for something that is achievable rather than something that is not. The ancient Greek philosopher Diogenes was perhaps the greatest exponent of the latter course: in order to avoid the problems of earning enough money to live in a house, he chose to live in a barrel instead. This option may not always be the optimum one.

Controls come in hierarchies and levels of control are exercised at different levels of the organization. Three generic ways of controlling the course of events in the business are available: firstly, changing the inputs to the system. Secondly, the process itself can be controlled. Thirdly, the objective of the organization can be changed.

Table 16.5 Assumptions underlying control systems

Assumption	Problems with this view
Objectives can be devised and can be stated precisely	Most organizations do not have clear objectives, but rather have broad goals. For example, it is almost impossible to set objectives for a personnel department or a legal department and in many cases it is difficult to do so for a marketing department. Companies led by visionaries neither have nor need objectives – the vision is sufficient.
Achievement can be measured and a measure of variance can be calculated	Without measurable objectives, achievement cannot be measured. Even if there is a measurable objective, the reason for the variance may be difficult to calculate – a fall in sales may be due to a great many factors, some of which are beyond the marketer's control.
Variance information can be fed back	Unstructured activities involve judgment and are often unique, so feedback for one activity is unlikely to be directly applicable to another. Indirect feedback is about accumulating knowledge and extrapolating from it, not about applying a set, known correction.
The feedback is sufficient to maintain control	The system will only work if the applied feedback is bigger than the environmental shift. For example, a company selling carburetors might decide that a fall-off in business should be followed by a major advertising campaign, but if the fall-off has been caused by a dramatic fall in the demand for cars, the campaign is unlikely to be effective.

Tactics of control

There are three basic types of control, as shown in Table 16.6.

Administrative control

Administrative control is often exercised through planning systems which control the allocation of resources and monitor the utilization of resources against the plan. Planning systems might be top-down, centralized systems in which the standardization of work procedures is paramount. Such centrally planned systems often use a formula approach, for example setting budgets as fixed percentages of turnover or allocating resources on the basis of numbers of customers dealt with. This tends to place an emphasis on bargaining within the organization to vary the formula in some way.

Within a devolved organization structure, administrative control is more likely to center on bottom-up planning, carried out within an overall set of budget constraints. In these circumstances, each division needs to reconcile its activities with other divisions in order to ensure consistency: this becomes the main role of senior management within the organization. The risk of bottom-up planning is that key strategic issues are left out of the equation, because each division focuses on its own part of the problem without seeing the overall picture. Again, coordination is a function of senior management: the center needs to establish the boundaries and reconcile the plans of the divisions, which may in turn mean that the center should benchmark in order to establish best practice.

Control through direct supervision is common in small organizations, where one person is able to control resources effectively. In large organizations it is only really possible in conditions of stability, or during times of crisis (for example if the survival of the organization is threatened). Autocratic direct control by one person might be the only way the necessary changes can be forced through – although, of necessity, this is a route which is likely to lead to considerable resentment among lower-grade staff who are displaced or undermined.

Control through performance targets became popular during the 1990s, especially as a way of controlling the newly-privatized monopolies of power supply, railways, telephone systems and so forth. Setting the correct performance indicators is far from easy: indicators often give only a partial view of the overall situation and it is usually the case that activities which are measured are the ones that get done, regardless of the real-life situations faced by the staff and managers in the organization.

Responsibility for marketing is likely to be devolved to the divisions, since marketing (in a customer-oriented firm) pervades all the activities of the organization. An organization given to using financial controls is likely to establish such divisions as profit centers, which rather complicates the issue for the divisions since they will be working towards marketing-based objectives, but will be judged on a finance-based objective. Strategic planning based organizations will be more likely to use cost or revenue centers, with marketing planning being carried out at the center.

Table 16.6 Types of control

Type of Control	Explanation and Examples
Administrative control	Based on systems, rules and procedures, administrative control is typical in hierarchical organizations which often have large numbers of rules and regulations.
Social control	The control exercised by workmates and the organizational culture. This is common in organismic organizations and smaller organizations.
Self-control	Control exercised by individuals on themselves, based on their own interpretation of correct behavior. This is common in organizations composed of professional people, who may be working to a professional code of ethics rather than a set of rules laid down by the employer.

Adapted from: Johnson and Gill 1993

Social and cultural control

Social and cultural control comes from the standardization of norms of behavior within the organization. In such organizations, administrative controls have a lower priority: people behave in the way they do because it is the right way to behave, not because they have a boss applying the yardstick at every stage. In the 21st century organization, this type of control is likely to become much more prevalent: people are becoming more individualistic, more idealistic and less inclined to obey orders blindly. Also, social controls are much more effective in organizations which are facing chaotic situations or circumstances of rapid environmental change, in which it is impossible to lay down fixed procedures for dealing with every possible eventuality.

Social controls can sometimes work the other way, by hindering senior management when changes become necessary. The reason is that cultural norms are difficult to change and people who regard themselves as professionals are likely to prove difficult if asked to do something which they feel impinges on their professional prerogatives.

In some respects, the 21st century workplace is likely to be less about controls and more about influences. Managers may not be able to impose fixed procedures on workers, partly because such procedures will be difficult to formulate and partly because a well-educated, independently-minded workforce is unlikely to be as prepared to accept management by diktat as workers were 50 or 100 years ago. Influence can come from many sources, but the greatest influences are likely to be social ones, created by, and in turn creating, obligations between the staff. This implies that managers will need to be charismatic rather than autocratic and lead rather than drive the workforce.

SUMMARY

Planning and implementing marketing tactics is complex because too many activities impinge on each other and almost all the activities of the firm and its employees impact on customers in one way or another. Controlling the process is far from simple and planning in advance often seems to be a Herculean task, when one considers the number of factors to be taken into account.

Of course, planning has to happen and it has to be sufficiently flexible to allow for change: it also needs to be flexible enough to allow individuals some leeway in what they do for the organization.

The key points from this chapter are:

- The marketing audit is a snapshot and is therefore out of date as soon as it is completed.

- Wicked problems are common in marketing and may not have a single, final solution.

- Feedback and control are essential for the success of the plan, but concepts borrowed from engineering may be inappropriate.

- Combining resources creates competency: resources may be tangible or intangible.

- Strong brands are valuable, but evaluating them is difficult.

- Activities divide into systematized processes and unstructured processes. In the 21st century, the latter are becoming more common.

REVIEW QUESTIONS

1 What are the factors which would determine the frequency of marketing audits?

2 What are the key factors in establishing a feedback system?

3 Why is brand evaluation difficult?

4 What are the differences between tame problems and wicked problems?

5 How would you classify employees: as tangible resources, or as intangible resources?

British investment banking always used to be a gentlemanly profession, regulated by the old school tie and marketed through networks and word-of-mouth. The banks funded such activities as mergers and acquisitions, share issues and underwriting corporate launches. The lack of anything recognizable as marketing activity was never a problem – everybody in the money markets knew who the leading banks were and in an era when money was in short supply the customers came almost cap-in-hand to the investment banks.

During the 1990s all that changed. The world money supply increased dramatically and competition began to come in from American and Japanese banks as well as banks from elsewhere in the European Union. Aggressive marketing approaches, coupled with a range of mergers and sell-outs, means that there are now more US banks in London than there are in New York and more Japanese banks than there are in Tokyo. At first, the differentiation between the companies was minimal – after all, money is money and the ways in which it can be used for corporate investment are often strictly controlled by legislation and Stock Market regulators. After a while, though, banks began to realize that they would have to become more innovative and indeed aggressive in their marketing approaches if they were to find good homes for their money.

UBS Warburg, for example, began running a global campaign focusing on what it claims to be the bank's key brand attributes – vision, performance and efficiency. Using images of innovative products and services, the bank hopes to link its brand to innovative ideas: the head of Publicis, the bank's advertising agency, said 'The campaign recognizes the reality of a tougher world and links the UBS Warburg brand by analogy to exceptional capability in a defined range of brand attributes . . .These are individually dramatized by deliberately futuristic images to reflect UBS Warburg's commitment to pushing back the boundaries of conventional thinking to achieve more success for its clients'.

Sponsorship has also proved to be a useful shot in the promotional locker, with banks sponsoring art and sporting events. Credit Suisse First Boston (CSFB) sponsored the Royal Academy's 2001 'Genius of Rome' exhibition, on the basis that the subject of the exhibition – the cultural upheavals in Rome between 1592 and 1623 – reflected the upheavals currently affecting the financial markets of the world. The main reason for sponsoring these high-profile events is, of course, to provide corporate hospitality – one investment banker is reported to have said 'All the investment banks are targeting the same very small pool of clients. If you invite them to a high-profile prestigious event you can develop very close personal relationships. It's much more cost-effective than running an ad campaign'.

It is early days for investment banks, though. Most of them have only hazy notions about establishing their brand values, or of differentiating themselves: in the past, differentiation had come about through the use of various industry league tables and the like. Alec Rattray of international branding consultants Landor says, 'All of them are similar in terms of technology and the quality of their analysts. We try to help find the difference and the relevance of their brand because often they can't see it for themselves'. When working with Japanese bank Nomura, Rattray found that he could not focus on the bank's size because it is not the biggest. Instead, he focused on the qualities of Nomura's UK head, Guy Hands, whom Rattray characterizes as being entrepreneurial and innovative.

It seems that investment banks are going to have to concentrate much more on deciding who they are and what their brand values are if they are to stay ahead in the game. Much of what they have to offer is advice and experience – but many accountancy firms and even law firms are filling this gap, using money guaranteed or borrowed on the open market to fund the takeover or merger process. Often these firms are much slicker at marketing themselves and already have a foot in the door because they are already acting for one or other of the client firms.

In investment banking, as in so many other areas, it seems that the old school tie must be replaced with real relationship building. Meanwhile, it is paradoxical that so much effort needs to be made in order to sell money – but that's the City in the 21st century.

Questions

1 If the key factor in investment banking is relationships, why do the banks need to consider their brand values?
2 How might investment banks differentiate themselves?
3 Why might Nomura's branding policy be dangerous?
4 If sponsorship is more powerful than advertising, why bother advertising?
5 How might Nomura plan its marketing activities?

REFERENCES

Alexander, L. D. (1985) 'Successfully implementing strategic decisions', *Long Range Planning*, 18(3).

Barney, J. B. (1986) 'Organisational culture: can it be a source of sustained competitive advantage?', *Academy of Management Review*, 11: 656–65.

Barney, J. B. (1991) 'Firm resources and sustained competitive advantage', *Journal of Management*, 17: 1: 99–120.

Coyne, K. P., Hall, S. J. D. and Clifford, P. G. (1997) 'Is your core competence a mirage?', *The McKinsey Quarterly*, 1: 40–54.

Dermer, J. (1977) *Management Planning and Control Systems: Advanced Concepts and Cases*, Irwin.

Dretske, F. (1981) *Knowledge and the flow of information*, Cambridge MA: MIT Press.

Durand, T. (1996) 'Revisiting key dimensions of competence', Paper presented to the SMS Conference, Phoenix: Arizona.

Finlay, P. (2000) *Strategic Management*, Harlow: Financial Times Prentice Hall.

Hamilton, W., East, R. and Kalafatis, S. (1997) 'The measurement and utility of brand price elasticities', *Journal of Marketing Management*, 13: 4: 285–298.

Hofstede, G. (1978) 'The poverty of management control philosophy', *Academy of Management Review*, 3: 3: July: 450–61.

Johnson, P. and Gill, J. (1993) *Management Control and Organisational Behaviour*, Paul Chapman Publishing.

Kaplan, R. S. and Norton, D. P. (1992) 'The balanced scorecard – measures that drive performance', *Harvard Business Review*, Jan-Feb.

Kotler, P., Armstrong, G., Saunders, J. and Wong, V. (2003) *Principles of Marketing*, (4th European ed.) Harlow: Financial Times Prentice Hall.

Lowendahl, B. R. (1997) *Strategic management of professional business service firms*, Copenhagen: Copenhagen Business School Press.

Mason, R. and Mitroff, I. (1981) *Challenging Strategic Planning Assumptions*, New York: Wiley.

Penrose, E. T. (1958) *The theory of the growth of the firm*, New York: Wiley.

Rittel, H. (1972) 'On the planning crisis: systems analysis of the first and second generations', *Bedriftsokonomen* 8: 390–6.

Stalk, G., Evans, P. and Shulman, L. (1992) 'Competing on capabilities', *Harvard Business Review*, March/April.

Wernerfelt, B. (1984) 'A resource-based view of the firm', *Strategic Management Journal*, April/June: 171–80.

17

ORGANIZING FOR MAXIMUM EFFECTIVENESS

Learning objectives

After reading this chapter, you should be able to:

- Describe organization structure alternatives

- Discuss the strengths and weaknesses of centralization versus decentralization

- Discuss the advantages and disadvantages of the product or market manager form of organization

- Discuss the benefits and drawbacks to the matrix form of organization

- Understand the considerations in choosing the most effective structure

- Explain how to react to turbulent markets

- Know when to restructure the marketing department

- Understand how to manage organizational change

■ Introduction

Once the hard work of segmentation has been completed and a strategy has been chosen, the basics of marketing must be put in place. Nothing is more basic than the organization structure. The design and implementation of this structure can empower employees to make the strategy work or place insurmountable obstacles in the way of this success. As Day (1990) says, 'above all, the structure must mirror the segmentation of the market so that responsibilities for serving each major market segment are well defined'.

■ Structural alternatives

Marketing can be organized around functions, product lines, target markets or some combination of these. The five broad ways to organize marketing tasks, are shown in Table 17.1.

TABLE 17.1 Organizational alternatives

Alternative	Description
Functional (Figure 17.1)	Each marketing activity has a specialist in charge of it. This structure would have an advertising manager, a product development manager, a market research manager and so forth.
Product (Figure 17.2)	Each manager is responsible for all the marketing decisions concerning a particular product. The firm may also employ specialists to advise and assist, but each product manager would have overall responsibility.
Segment or Market (Figure 17.3)	Here each manager is responsible for a given market segment. For example, a glass manufacturer might have one manager in charge of marketing to the automotive industry, another for marketing to the building trade, another marketing to the bottling industry and so forth. Each manager would thus be able to develop specialist knowledge of the customers' needs.
Geographic or Area (Figure 17.4)	This approach usually is used in international markets, but can be used elsewhere. Managers are each responsible for all the marketing activities within their own geographical region.
Matrix (Figure 17.7)	Here there is joint decision-making between the specialist market researchers, sales managers, product managers and all the other functional managers. No one manager is in overall control, and decisions are made by balancing each person's role and demands.

Functional and product designs in organizations

In smaller firms, there may be no specific marketing department and of course in some firms marketing is not very high on the agenda because the firm has little control over the variables of the marketing mix. Such firms may have a marketing department, but it may only be concerned with running the occasional advertisement and organizing trade fairs. Figure 17.1 shows a simple functional organization normally used in businesses which provides single product lines to a limited number of markets.

A major advantage of this approach is simplicity. Decision-making is centralized. However, where a firm has multiple products or markets to be addressed, this approach becomes unwieldy. In the functional design, it is difficult for a particular product or market to get the attention it needs from the various functions in marketing. This has led to the establishment of product or market-based organizations as shown in Figure 17.2.

While this seems to solve the problem of the functional organization it also puts a great amount of strain on the top marketing executive who needs to be an expert in several different lines of business or differentiated market segments. This approach creates a great deal of duplication.

Organizations using the market segment approach

A combination approach is shown in Figure 17.3 where marketing is organized on a functional basis but the sales organization is organized by product.

The difficulty with this organization is the obstacles it presents for functions such as manufacturing and engineering to interact with product line experts. It should be noted that this structure would be the same organized around markets rather than products.

FIGURE 17.1

Simple functional
organization

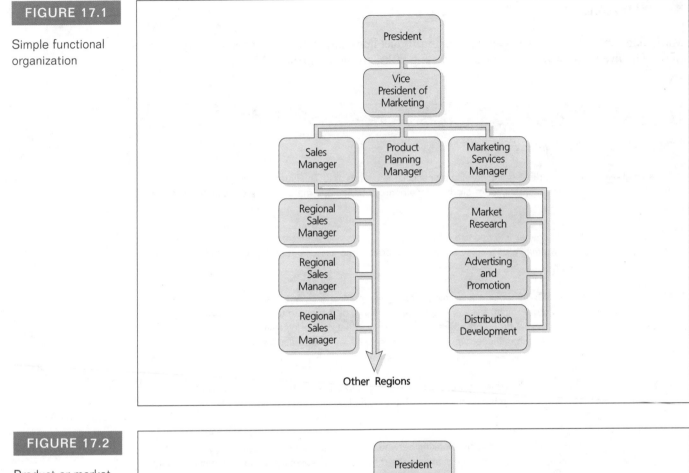

FIGURE 17.2

Product or market
organization

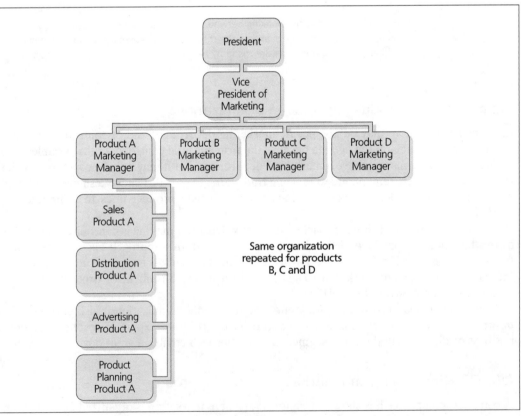

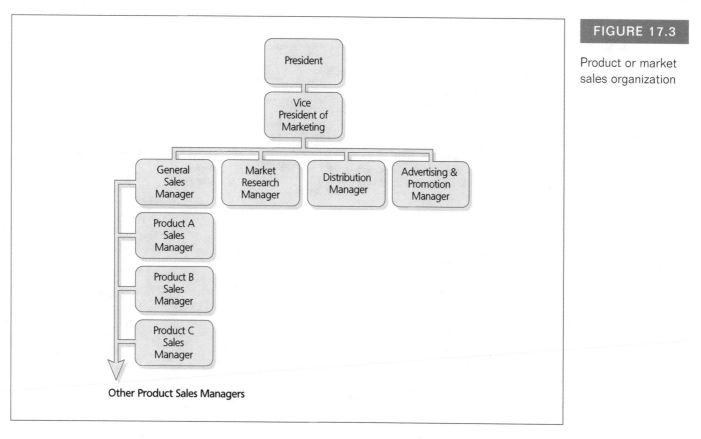

FIGURE 17.3

Product or market sales organization

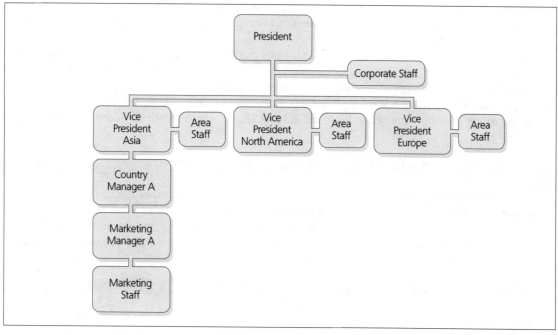

FIGURE 17.4

Geographic or area organization

Geographic or area organization

The geographic or area organization is represented in Figure 17.4.

This structure is best employed by companies with short or similar product lines with vastly different conditions in its geographic markets. The structure allows local managers to adapt their marketing programs very well to specific markets. However, it limits the exchange of information from one area to another and adds a level of complication to rationalizing the product line. Once again, duplication and inefficiency are evident.

FIGURE 17.5

Mixed market
organization

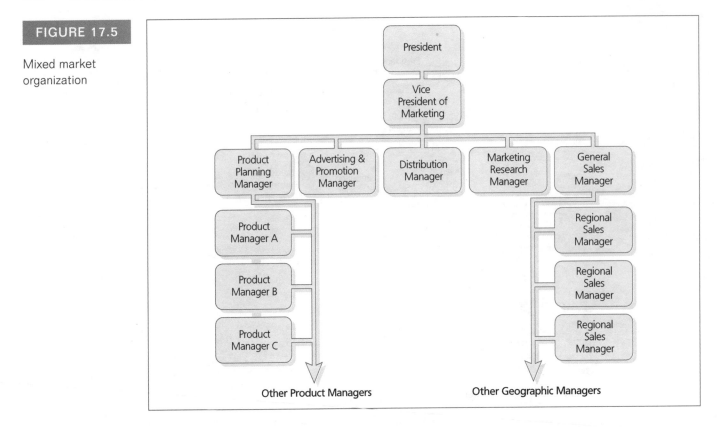

Figure 17.5 shows yet another permutation where the sales organization is organized in the traditional geographic way, but product managers are established to focus attention on the needs of the particular product line.

This organization is best used where a single sales organization serves one set of customers with a varied line of products. Again, this structure may be organized around markets rather than products. While this organization's approach is quite common in B2B firms, the difficulty here is that product managers do not report to a level high enough in the organization, in order for them to affect the basic decisions of other functions. We shall discuss this in some depth in another section of this chapter.

TALKING POINT

The least expensive way to organize is to keep the functions together – all sales grouped in one department and all the marketing functions in another and so on.

If this is true, then why do some firms devise such complex organization structures? Why not just tell the functional managers to cooperate with one another to serve the most important product areas and market segments?

The overlay of serving international markets adds more complexity to the organization design. The simplest approach for handling international business is the export department as an extension of a functional organization. This is seen in Figure 17.6.

This organization is effective only for a firm with very limited sales outside its home market. Once a firm begins to have significant international sales, the export sales department is overwhelmed and the firm may move to various other types of organizations. There are six basic types of international organization structures according to Czinkota and Ronkainen (2004):

- *Global product* – product divisions are responsible for all manufacturing worldwide.
- *Global area* – geographic divisions are responsible for all manufacturing and marketing in their areas.

FIGURE 17.6

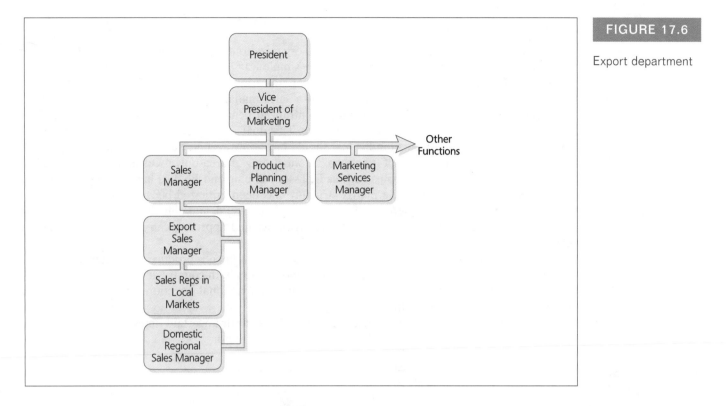

Export department

- *Global functional* – each functional area is responsible for worldwide operations.
- *Global market* – similar to the global product structure.
- *Mixed or hybrid* – combining features of all the alternatives listed above.
- *Matrix* – for large multinational corporations attempting to give equal emphasis to functional and geographic aspects of the organization.

These organizations look similar in a general way to the simple organizations shown in Figures 17.1 through 17.7.

The most common structure used by multinational organizations is the product structure. The benefit of this approach is centralization and ease of decision making. A global product structure assigns the international responsibility to each product division, therefore, there is no central pool of international expertise. In many cases, several product-oriented organizations in the firm are marketing simultaneously to the same customer with little or no coordination between them. In addition, some activities such as market research are often not given adequate attention, especially on an international basis since the critical mass of projects does not develop within each product organization. Centralizing functions like research is sometimes the solution to that problem. The market structure allows the firm to focus on specific market segments and has the same advantages and disadvantages as the product structure.

Day (1990) calls the product-oriented organization an impediment to 'market-driven thinking'. He says these organizations tend to be competitor-centered and to over-emphasize cost. Day prefers the market-oriented organization with its ability to clearly align sales and marketing towards customer segments. He adds that functionally-organized firms who have semi-related products suffer because no individual takes the responsibility for a customer group or a prospective new segment.

The area or regional structure is the second most frequently used approach internationally. In this case, the firm is divided geographically and all activities related to the particular area are planned and executed within the area organization. For firms with narrow product lines and similar customers, this approach can work well. Here again, duplication is a possible negative effect. Another problem is a possible lack of information transfer from one regional organization to another. Cost-effective product standardization is often downplayed in favor of regional differences.

The matrix organization

The mixed structure combines aspects of all the organizational types mentioned above. It is similar to Figure 17.5, which presents this form in a very simple way.

Figure 17.7 shows the essentials of the matrix organization.

In this case, a French product manager and a sales manager located in France report to their respective managers located in a regional or centralized headquarters location. At the same time, they also report to a country manager for France. This dual reporting relationship violates the basic principle of management that an individual should have only a single supervisor. But this approach has been devised to cure the ills of functional, product-only or area-only focus in the other organizational alternatives. Many large firms such as Eriksson, Boeing and Phillips have used this approach successfully over many years. The matrix structure has been criticized because the dual reporting causes problems with each supervisor (functional and country) demanding different actions from an individual. The very complexity of the matrix organizational approach can make decision-making clumsy.

Yip (2003) graphically shows the matrix at work. This has been reproduced in Figure 17.8.

As can be seen, the structure allows for integration across both country and business dimensions. Yip says that many corporations are heading in this organizational direction. This approach allows true integration of the global strategy.

Hunt (1998) claims the matrix structure is the best design for uncertain times. To make the matrix organization work, he recommends these points be kept in mind:

FIGURE 17.7

Matrix organization

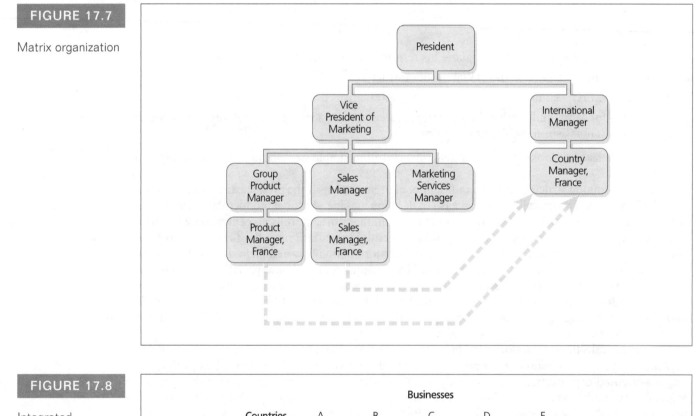

FIGURE 17.8

Integrated corporate strategy

Adapted from: Yip 2003

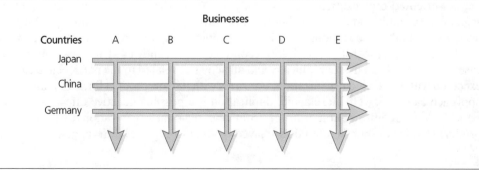

- Matrices work best in demanding markets.
- People working in matrices must accept this as an ambiguous structure.
- Clear ground rules must be established but without massive manuals.
- This approach is dependent on the people involved – the design must suit the people involved, not the reverse.
- In some cultures, it is unwise to introduce the matrix approach. Smaller units or segmentation into divisional or local units is a better approach.

Bartlett and Ghoshal (1990) provide three principles for changing organizational psychology in a way that will make the matrix organization work:

- The development and communication of a clear and consistent corporate vision.
- Using human resources to broaden individual perspectives and develop identification with corporate goals.
- Integration of individual thinking into the overall corporate agenda. Success lies in developing in a manager's mind flexible perspectives and relationships that allow individuals to make the proper judgments and trade-offs to achieve an overall strategic objective.

In 1999 Boeing regrouped its design and manufacturing engineers in the commercial transport area into a matrix organization based around five specific aircraft model teams (or platforms) (Proctor 1999). Boeing made the change from a product-based organization after a year of benchmarking with various other firms including BMW, Daimler-Chrysler and Toyota. The new organization is responsible for the design, planning, parts and tools required to build a specific aircraft type such as a 717. To keep the platform teams from going off in their own direction, experts from each function interface with the teams to aid in consistency and knowledge transfer. In this organizational structure, an individual employee belongs both to a functional group such as structures, payloads or systems and also belongs to a platform team such as that for the 717.

An extension of the matrix organization structure is the organismic structure. Unlike the traditional mechanistic or bureaucratic pyramid, there is no clear 'boss'. Each individual contributes expertise (and effort) towards achieving the organization's objectives. The leader for each task is determined by the project being tackled at the time. This type of structure is typical of small consultancy firms who may be dealing with a wide range of disparate tasks, but can be found in larger organizations or departments of larger organizations. The main advantage of the organismic structure is that it is extremely flexible, which makes it a more appropriate structure for dealing with changing environments.

Organismic structures have the following characteristics:

1 Communications flow evenly between all the members of the organization.
2 There is no fixed leadership: leadership devolves to the person best fitted to deal with the situation facing the organization at the time.
3 Status in the organization comes from knowledge and skill rather than from qualifications and experience.
4 The organization makes use of a broader range of skills from each individual than would be the case in a hierarchical organization.

These characteristics mean that an organismic structure is able to react quickly to external changes and thus does not need to go through the painful readjustments that a hierarchical organization would need. Organismic organizations can react extremely quickly, but they also have drawbacks, as follows:

1 A great deal of time is spent in discussions and in resolving leadership issues.
2 Career paths can be difficult to identify.
3 The bigger the organization, the more complex the communications become.
4 In periods of stability, managers tend to become confirmed in their leadership roles. In other words, the organization tends to become hierarchical if conditions remain stable.

TALKING POINT

Change is a constant, or so we are told. If that is the case, why aren't all organizations organismic? How can hierarchical organizations survive at all? And yet most organizations are hierarchical – this seems to be a natural law!

So why do we like hierarchies? Is it because we like to think someone else will take responsibility? Do we feel more comfortable being told what to do? Are people really that lacking in initiative? Or (moving to the dark side of the Force) is it that we like to boss people around, show our power over others, not allow other people to have their say in decision-making?

There is an old saying – 'uneasy sits the butt that bears the boss'. So why not let someone else share some of the responsibility? Maybe because we are afraid to let go!

■ Centralization versus decentralization

One key decision to be made in international marketing is the degree of independence to be given to local organizations. Decentralized organizations allow a high degree of independence for local subsidiaries while highly centralized organizations concentrate decision-making at the head office. In reality, firms are a mix of centralization and decentralization often by function. Some functions, such as R&D or human resources may lend themselves to centralization while local marketing functions are often decentralized. Wise management allows a high level of local marketing decision-making so that products and approaches can be adapted to the needs of the local customers. If a firm faces severe challenges by competitors on a global basis, it may wish to set strategy on a global basis while allowing local decision-making within that strategy. This is called coordinated decentralization (Czinkota and Ronkainen 2004).

In the past, country managers played a significant role in international organizations. But as Yip (2003) says in a semi-serious way, 'the country manager has been made obsolete by the fax machine and the Internet'. In truth, the role of the country manager while continuing to be important has changed significantly. Today, rather than having unquestioned power, the country manager is often the most visible representative of the parent company especially under matrix organizations. In general, the hierarchical, colonial form of management organization has pretty much disappeared and has now been replaced by a mix of organization types more suited to the particular needs of individual firms.

While most marketing organization theories show the sales department reporting to a senior marketing executive, in truth sales often does not report to marketing. In a study of 47 German and US firms, Workman *et al.* (1998) did not find one sales manager reporting to a marketing manager.

■ Choosing the most effective structure

In deciding how to design the organization, several factors come into play. These are seen in Figure 17.9.

Obviously the products offered have a significant effect upon the organization. Should the products require installation and maintenance with highly skilled technical people, a more centralized firm would be required. Firms with single or a limited number of products can use the least costly and easiest to manage functional approach. Firms with multiple product lines selling to multiple segments will more than likely have to use the product or market-based organizational structures.

For international firms, the degree of internationalization is an important factor in making the structure decision. A firm that simply sells a few products outside its home market can have an export department within a functional organization and this will work perfectly well. But a firm with a global strategy will eventually move to a complex matrix or other hybrid type of organization with all of the advantages and disadvantages this provides.

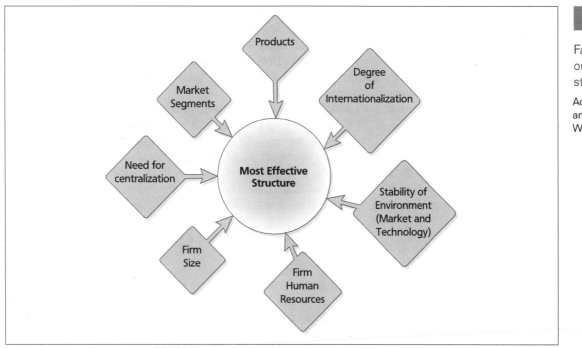

FIGURE 17.9

Factors affecting
organizational
structure

Adapted from: Czinkota
and Ronkainen 2004,
Workman *et al.* 1998

Both market and technological environments can have a major effect upon the structure decisions. Where rapid and unpredictable changes in government regulation, customer needs, competitive actions or distribution are occurring frequently, the need is for a structure that can respond rapidly. This may take any of the forms described depending on the other variables the firm must face (human resources, size of firm, products, segments, etc.). Firms facing hyper competition especially need adaptable organizational structures.

A key question affecting firm organization is its human capabilities. As we have seen, the matrix organization works best where employees understand how to make it work. The experience, knowledge and capabilities of individuals must be understood when an organization type is chosen.

Firm size was found to be a key determinant by Workman *et al.* (1998). In their study, smaller firms tended to have marketing and sales together in one unit which was functionally organized. Medium-sized firms organized marketing and sales in a strategic business unit along with a corporate marketing group. The largest firms placed marketing in a business unit but employed shared salesforces which sold more than one business unit's product. Alternatively they placed sales and marketing in a 'distribution business unit', an entity essentially devoid of R&D and production capabilities. We have discussed the need for centralization or decentralization in a previous section.

Yip (2003) points out that there are national differences in organization. European-based companies were familiar with multi-nationalization and generally have given more autonomy to foreign subsidiaries. American firms, with their large domestic customer base, often had separate domestic and international organizations and are now faced with the problem of integrating global strategy and developing the proper level of local autonomy. Japanese-based multinationals began mostly as exporters. When costs rose in Japan, they relocated production activities to foreign markets. The Japanese have a long history of success using a worldwide strategy. But Japanese multinationals face the problem of allowing local autonomy as they continue to operate as global firms.

Nohria *et al.* (2003) found that despite the fact that management spent hours trying to find the ideal structure for their firms, the keys to success were simplicity, cooperation and exchange of information across the company, putting the best people 'closest to the action' and establishing systems for easy knowledge sharing.

In the 1950s the Westinghouse Electric Corporation, one of the world's first global conglomerates, established an international company in New York City. This subsidiary in effect purchased and resold products for more than 100 product divisions. Westinghouse International established country organizations throughout the world and hired individuals both at headquarters and outside the US who were experts in their respective markets. By the late 1960s, it was clear that the corporation was losing share to firms with more product expertise in the local markets. So the firm dissolved the international company and placed all international activities within each product division. While this improved the product focus for the larger divisions such as nuclear power, the smaller divisions ignored international opportunities since the critical mass required to address these opportunities was lacking in those smaller divisions. Ten years on, the firm realized that a new organization was required and so a matrix approach was instituted.

None of these organizational alternatives was entirely satisfactory. Obviously, the changes were significant and costly, both in terms of resources and morale and yet no final ideal organization had been achieved. Some firms, such as GE, have successfully used the matrix approach but have adapted it to give lead responsibility in a particular country to the product group with the most interest in that country. For instance, in the late 1980s, the lead divisions for GE in the People's Republic of China were the aircraft engine and nuclear power divisions. While the company had a strong country manager organization, these divisions also provided leadership and had a major input into decision-making for the PRC.

Product-market manager considerations

As has been pointed out, functional organization often underplays the importance of particular products or markets, since each functional manager has to allocate his or her human and financial resources among many competing products and markets without detailed knowledge of any of them. Therefore, the product manager form of organization was instituted some years ago, first in consumer products firms and then more commonly in business marketing organizations. This form of organization is most often used by firms with a number of uniquely different products produced in the same facilities, marketed by a functional marketing organization and sold through a common salesforce. Where the product line is quite similar but the products are sold to a number of highly differentiated market segments, the market manager approach would be more appropriate. However, there is little difference between these approaches in terms of organization. In both cases an individual is assigned to the task of getting special attention for either a product or a market without any direct authority over any of the line managers needed to accomplish the objective.

There are a number of cases where the product management form of organization is not ideal. Firstly, where a product group has grown to the size where it can support its own production and marketing, it is more appropriate to set up a separate division for that product. In some cases where divisionalization is not feasible but marketing requirements for each product are quite different, it may make sense to set up separate marketing groups but keep all other operations centralized. In other cases, separate sales groups are the most logical approach where specific customer segments must be served or when the business of each product is too small for divisionalization.

Using product managers successfully

Often firms begin to use product managers with the hope that they will focus the company on improving the product. But firms have frequently been disappointed with the change to the product manager approach. A most important aspect of success for this approach is setting realistic expectations. The product manager is by definition an anomaly. In many firms he or she has the responsibility for the profit and loss of a particular product line without the authority over any of the departments required to deliver that profitability. A firm must carefully construct the product manager's job description and explain to all other departments how this product manager will function. Another major problem is selecting the wrong person. Since the product manager has no authority to order anyone to do anything, he or she must convince other managers to act on programs which they may not be enthusiastic about. Thus the product manager must have extraordinary powers of persuasion and be able to assemble the most information about the product line available anywhere in the company.

Another key to success is proper orientation and training for product managers. One should think of a product manager as a mini-general manager, especially in a B2B firm. These individuals must develop an understanding of all the functional aspects of the firm including engineering, manufacturing, finance and human resources, as well as marketing and sales. A well experienced person has a good head-start on success.

Realistic tests for the success of a product manager include an ability to:

- Accurately interpret the changing needs of the product line business.
- Draw together complete and imaginative plans.
- Develop specific programs for product improvements.
- Devise a follow-up system so that plans can be modified should the objectives not be met.

In some firms, neither product managers nor market managers adequately serve the needs of customers. In these firms, both market and product managers have been established. While this creates more complexity, it is possible to make this organization work well. The critical factor in the success of a combination product and market manager organization is to clearly define the activities each should concentrate on. Product managers should focus on protecting the pricing integrity of their product, maintaining product leadership and providing in-depth technical or product knowledge to support sales efforts. In general, product managers should be held accountable for long-term profitability for their product line.

Using market managers

Market managers, on the other hand, should be responsible for developing a full understanding of customer needs, identifying opportunities and developing a reputation for industry expertise among key customers. The inevitable conflict which arises from having both product and market managers can be regarded as a positive force if properly managed. This approach both uncovers market opportunities and provides a mechanism for sorting those opportunities and pursuing only the most potentially rewarding ones.

Customer focused organizations

Recently, organizations have been dissatisfied with results of traditional formal organization structures and have felt the necessity to change these organizations so that they are more customer focused. No consensus has emerged of the best approach but some recent examples follow. Homburg *et al.* (2000) describe the organization requirements for a 'customer-focused' business. While there are similarities to the dual product/market manager approach, the key difference is that profit and loss responsibility shifts to customer (market segment) focused SBUs and more of the marketing activities take place within these SBUs.

George *et al.* (1994) show the importance of cross-functional teams dedicated to major customers rather than the traditional product or brand manager approach. Cross-functional teams can include individuals from sales, manufacturing, R&D, finance and several marketing functions. Challenges identified in instituting this approach include:

- Roles and responsibilities of each team member must be sharply defined.
- Team members often need to learn new skills.
- Information systems need to be improved so that all can get information quickly.
- Cross-functional career paths must be developed.
- Incentives for success must be carefully aligned with team results.

■ Reacting to turbulent markets

Aufreiter *et al.* (2001) report that some e-businesses are doing quite well. Those firms are able to redirect their marketing very quickly. These researchers give the example of Staples.com which changes its marketing campaigns several times a day based on feedback from its websites. These authors recommend this for e-based businesses. They structure their marketing organizations to reflect stages of the customer lifecycle. One unit focuses on acquisition, another on retention/development. Individual managers are assigned to customer segments ranging from initial or casual respondents to the website versus frequent buyers. E-commerce businesses are seeking skills common in product managers. That is, the ability to integrate the functions across the company and since selling through the web yields instant feedback, highly flexible organizations and individuals are required for success.

Patching

Eisenhardt and Brown (1999) recommend 'patching' – the strategic process by which corporate executives remap businesses in response to changing market opportunities. This is done by adding, dividing, transferring, exiting or combining parts of businesses. According to these researchers, 'when markets are turbulent, patching becomes crucial'. Managers in highly turbulent markets do not see organization structure as stable but as temporary. They are ready to make many small changes to keep their businesses flexible enough to respond to changing market conditions. These managers keep business units small and make changes quickly. They attempt to get the change approximately correct but the emphasis is on moving quickly rather than having all the details of an organization change worked out.

Patching does not work well in organizations with many shared services or cross-divisional committees and the success depends upon clear business level measurements and consistent company-wide compensation. Managers must have the basic facts of their business readily available so they can understand how to change and those involved in the change understand the rationale for it. Company-wide compensation is critical to allow the movement of individuals from one organization to another with a minimum of problems. Patching is a result of a detailed understanding of market segmentation and then the ability to create new products or services to address the needs of these market segments. Also important to success of this approach is picking the correct general manager and developing a detailed plan for the first 30 to 60 days after the patch is made. Often it is necessary to reward and recognize managers whose businesses have been cut or restructured.

■ When to restructure

Whether strategy dictates structure, or structure dictates strategy, is a somewhat vexing question. In most organizations, each will influence the other so that it will be difficult or impossible to tell which is cause and which is effect. From a planning perspective, the type of organizational structure that is most appropriate will depend on the volatility of the market and the degree of control the organization has over its environment. If the organization is hierarchical or mechanistic, a strategy that maintains the status quo is most likely to be effective, since the structure cannot cope with rapid change. A very large firm, such as British Petroleum, has considerable control over the environment in which it operates, even at the level of being able to influence national governments. This allows BP to operate with a very hierarchical structure. Managers need to ask the following questions in order to know when to restructure the marketing department:

- Is the marketing structure capable of implementing the plans?
- Does the marketing focus the organization on priority markets or products?
- Are managers suitably empowered?
- Does the firm meet its sales and profit objectives?
- Is the organization responding to customer needs or competitive actions?
- Does the marketing department produce creative business strategies and plans?

If the answer to any of these questions is a negative, then either the structure of the organization is wrong or the strategy is wrong. Either one can be changed, but obviously the decision will rest on which is the easier (or safer) to change in order to ensure the organization's survival in the long run.

Before moving into a restructuring mode, a manager must determine whether the structure is the problem or whether the people filling the positions have been misplaced. Reorganizations are by necessity very disturbing and often cause productivity to plummet for a significant period of time. So all other alternatives should be reviewed before a extensive reorganization is undertaken. Some shifting of individuals to better utilize their inherent skills may solve the problems without formal reorganizing. Expecting reorganization alone to solve basic business problems can be quite naïve and lead to depressing results.

■ Managing change

Continual tinkering with the structure is not an optimum solution in most cases, because employees will become unsettled by the changes: it is probably better to build in the required degree of flexibility when first designing the corporate structure. The downside to changes in the structure (from the staff viewpoint) are as follows;

1 Changes in structure mean that people's career paths become unclear.
2 Effort which has been put into building relationships with colleagues can be wasted.
3 Changes often mean learning new roles. This means that the benefits of the structural changes will be slow in arriving.
4 Learning new roles means that more mistakes will be made at first.
5 If a staff member is being forced through a change, this might be seen as an opportune moment to change jobs.
6 The people who are most able to change jobs are usually the most talented.
7 Changes in structure inevitably mean changes in status: those whose status improves might be happy about this, but those whose status is lowered will not.

If staff does not support required changes, or feels threatened by them and feel that their status or job security is threatened, they are likely to sabotage the changes. This may happen officially, through industrial action or through union representation, or it may happen covertly through non-cooperation with the changes. Managements in hierarchical organizations can easily acquire the reputation of being bullies and it is common for firms in trouble to bring in 'hatchet men' who use force of personality to push changes through, often with little regard for casualties. The tactics outlined in Table 17.2 might be useful in reducing the problems outlined above.

Sometimes replacement of staff is unavoidable. Some skills become obsolete; others become essential and are unavailable from within.

Strategic changes will be easier to implement if managers (and indeed staff) feel that they own the mission and corporate strategy. Suitably empowered managers and staff will be able to be more innovative, more flexible and more able to take risks in order to improve the outcomes of environmental threats and opportunities.

Failure to predict the amount of time implementation will take and the problems which will arise, failure to take account of other problems which will divert attention and resources elsewhere and failure to forecast correctly the bases on which the strategy was formulated will also affect the outcomes (Alexander 1985).

Quinn (1989) shows that managers use an approach of 'logical incrementalism' in making major strategic changes such as a reorganization. Managers must move more slowly and opportunistically toward an overall goal while keeping in mind the capabilities of the people and the requirements of new roles they may be placed in. They will selectively move people trying to meet an organizational goal that will be modified along the way and rarely publicly announced or discussed.

TABLE 17.2 Tactics for improving the acceptance of structural change

Problem	Tactical alternatives
Career paths become unclear	New career opportunities under the new regime will exist and these should be pointed out early in the process. For example, a document which begins, 'Due to our ongoing commitment to improving the organization, a restructuring will be implemented. This will mean that the following new posts will be created and priority will be given to existing staff in making appointments to these posts'. This positive approach is more likely to be supported than an approach which says that posts will disappear.
Networks with colleagues will disappear	Time spent in building networks is never wasted. People who are well-networked should be identified, as they are often the best drivers for the new structure since they are usually influential in the organization.
New roles take time to learn	Before the new structure is implemented, an audit should be taken of staff to find out who already has the necessary skills for the new structure. These people should be given status and preferably also the task of teaching others whenever this is possible. Obviously managers should be tolerant of mistakes at this early learning stage.
More mistakes will be made	Tolerance of mistakes is of course essential, but also managers need to be extra vigilant during transition periods. Training is only partly effective: often people will do well in the training sessions, but only apply the learning correctly once they have actually started trying to do the job they have trained for.
Staff may feel that this is an opportune moment to leave	Change is always disruptive, even when it is beneficial. Staff who can see that the change will be beneficial to themselves are more likely to accept the changes: emphasizing the career benefits and medium-term improvements that the changes will bring will certainly help. Emphasizing the ways in which the firm will benefit is likely to be counter-productive, since it signals that the management are more concerned with the shareholders than with the staff. Although this might be obvious to staff anyway, it is tactless to make it explicit.
The most talented people will find it easiest to leave	Any strategic changes should (ideally) benefit the most talented staff most directly. These people need to be brought into the confidence of senior management: in fact, if possible everybody in the organization should be kept as fully informed as is reasonable.
Some people will lose status	Ideally, this should not happen but if it does happen then such people should either be compensated in some way, or should be offered the chance to take redundancy payments. They would almost certainly be entitled to this anyway, as a reduction in status would be regarded as a constructive dismissal by an industrial tribunal. Perhaps surprisingly, however, some people may be prepared to downshift in status if this also means a quieter life.

SUMMARY

Achieving the optimum marketing organization is a difficult task. Many approaches have been tried and each has its advantages and disadvantages. Understanding the capabilities of the individuals in your firm will go a long way to improving the results, but designing the proper structure is a key way that individuals can be empowered to do their best.

The most important points from this chapter are as follows:

- Organization ranges from the simple functional structure where all similar functions such as market research, advertising or distribution are gathered together, to the complex matrix or organismic organization structure where lines of authority are blurred.

- The trade-off in organization design is usually simplicity versus a proper level of concentration on product or market segment.

- Many combinations of organization are possible and managers tend to develop their organization in an incremental way to satisfy an overall idea of the most effective organization form.

- The needs of the global firm add another layer of complexity to organization.

- A major question in global organizations is the need for centralization versus decentralization of marketing functions.

- Decisions about the most effective organization are based upon a number of internal and external factors.

- The best organization structures probably have these characteristics: simplicity, easy exchange of information and putting the best people closest to the customers.

- The debate about product or market managers has evolved into the 'customer focused organization' where market segment oriented organizations take precedence over product organizations.

- For fast-moving markets, major reorganizations have been replaced by 'patching' where small changes are made quickly to meet the needs of a rapidly changing market.

- It is often more effective to leave the structure the way it is and to move individuals into positions where they can succeed.

REVIEW QUESTIONS

1 Describe the major alternative forms of organization.

2 How do the export manager and matrix forms differ? Why would a firm choose the matrix organization?

3 When is it appropriate to use product or market managers?

4 What are the most important considerations in deciding how to design the organization structure?

5 What is patching? When is it best used? Describe how patching might be employed.

6 What questions would you ask before changing the organization structure?

7 What tactics could you use to improve the acceptance of structural changes?

SPOTLIGHT ON B2B MARKETING

Dr Khaled Ibrahim is a successful entrepreneur in Cairo. Ten years ago he saw an opportunity to use the scientific knowledge being developed in Egyptian Universities to start a scientific instrument business. That firm, KI Scientific (KIS), provides scientific instruments in many areas, focusing on hospitals and industrial processing as well as environmental monitoring. KIS is a manufacturer of a number of these instruments, but purchases and resells instruments from various other manufacturers as well.

During the past year, their turnover reached US$40 million, with most of the revenues coming from markets in the Middle East and Africa. Dr Ibrahim was now dissatisfied with the level of success he was achieving in several key markets. When KIS began, it had a clear lead over competitors both in cost of manufacture and in technology. The firm was easily able to make in-roads with the most important customers in Nigeria, South Africa and several of the smaller African nations as well as Jordan, Iran and Saudi Arabia. Now the competition appears to be moving forward more quickly and closing the gap and in some cases even developing superior products to those produced by KIS. The current organization of KIS is shown in Exhibit 17.1.

EXHIBIT 17.1 KIS organization

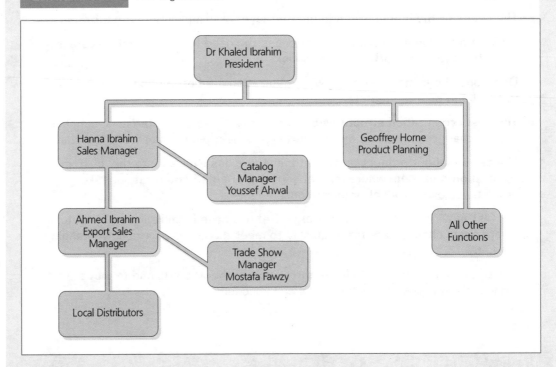

Dr Ibrahim has been reading lately about the importance of organization to success and wonders whether he should change the organization. His daughter is the sales manager. She is a 35-year-old doctoral student at Cairo University. His brother is in charge of international sales and a number of young people populate the various marketing departments. He has recently hired an ex-patriate British manager to oversee product development and suspects that this individual may be able to handle more responsibility.

Questions

1 What should Dr Ibrahim do first in his quest to improve the results for his firm?

2 What organizational alternatives might there be for KIS?

3 If Dr Ibrahim decides not to reorganize, what other moves might he make to improve his firm's competitiveness?

REFERENCES

Alexander, L. D. (1985) 'Successfully Implementing Strategic Decisions', *Long Range Planning*, 18: 3: 91–97.

Ames, B. C. (1963) 'Payoff from Product Management', *Harvard Business Review*, 41: 6: 141–152.

Ames, B. C. (1971) 'Dilemma of Product/Market Management', *Harvard Business Review*, 49: 2: 66–74.

Aufreiter, N., Ouillet, P-Y. and Scott, M. K. (2001) 'Marketing Rules', *Harvard Business Review*, 79: 2: 30–31.

Bartlett, C. A. and Ghoshal, S. (1990) 'Matrix Management: Not A Structure, A Frame of Mind', *Harvard Business Review*, 68: 4: 138–145.

Czinkota, M. R. and Ronkainen, I. A. (2004) *International Marketing*, Mason, Ohio: South-Western Publishing.

Day, G. S. (1990) *Market Driven Strategy*, New York: The Free Press.

Eisenhardt, K. M. and Brown, S. L. (1999) 'Patching: Restitching Business Portfolios in Dynamic Markets', *Harvard Business Review*, 77: 3: 72–82.

George, M., Freeling, A. and Court, D. (1994) 'Reinventing the Marketing Organization', *The McKinsey Quarterly*, 4: 43–62.

Homburg, C., Workman, J. P. and Jensen, O. (2000) 'Fundamental Changes in Marketing Organization: The Movement Toward a Customer-Focused Organization Structure', *Journal of the Academy of Marketing Science*, 28: 4: 459–478.

Hunt, J. W. (1998) 'Is Matrix Management A Recipe for Chaos?', *Financial Times*, Jan 12: Management: 14.

Nohria, N., Joyce, W. and Roberson, B. (2003) 'What Really Works', *Harvard Business Review*, 81: 7: July: 43–52.

Proctor, P. (1999) 'Boeing Shifts to Platform Teams', *Aviation Week and Space Technology*, 150: 20: 63.

Quinn, J. B. (1989) 'Strategic Change: Logical Incrementalism', *Sloan Management Review*, 45: Summer: 45–60.

Workman, J. P., Jr., Homburg, C. and Grunner, K. (1998) 'Marketing Organization: An Integrative Framework of Dimensions and Determinants', *Journal of Marketing*, 62: 21–41.

Yip, G. S. (2003) *Total Global Strategy II*, Upper Saddle River, NJ: Prentice-Hall Inc.

18

ETHICAL CONSIDERATIONS FOR BUSINESS MARKETERS

Learning objectives

After reading this chapter, you should be able to:

- Describe various approaches to corporate responsibility

- Explain the concepts of ethical principles and business ethics

- Describe how ethical standards impact the various functions of marketing

- Understand the special considerations affecting ethical behavior in a global economy

- Describe the best way to analyze ethical problems

- Explain methods for making a firm more responsive to ethical matters

■ Introduction

Establishing the proper ethical conduct for employees and managers is an important yet difficult task. Recently, both the business and general press have been filled with stories exposing ethical lapses in corporations across the world. In this chapter, we will attempt to clarify the most important issues in global ethics and provide tools to help you establish ethical guidelines for the marketing department.

■ Ethical environment

Any marketing department is operating in many environments that affect its ability to establish and maintain ethical conduct. These various influences are shown in Figure 18.1.

Terpstra and David (1991) describe the corporate environment as including formal administrative structures such as organization charts and the assignment of authority, responsibility and information flow as well as informal administrative systems such as methods for controlling operations and evaluation and rewards systems and the corporate culture. Corporate culture is defined by Terpstra and David as, 'a learned, relatively enduring interdependent system of meanings that classify, code, prioritize and justify activity both within the organization and toward the external environments it has defined as relevant'. They point out that the symbols and meaning of corporate culture are usually imperfectly shared by organizational members.

The societal environment includes social relationships and cultural definitions of life. Two of the most important aspects of this environment are the infrastructure, such as technical, educational and research; and government regulation. Because doing business outside the home country can so often be dependent upon cultural differences, the diagram has specifically identified cultural influences as a separate item. The main elements of a definition of culture include these characteristics:

- shared set of beliefs
- learned and passed on from one generation to another
- used to distinguish one group from another
- provides solutions to problems every individual faces – how he/she should properly relate to another individual of the same or opposite sex, the physical world and the universe.

Adapted from: Terpstra and David 1991; Keegan and Greene 2003; and Czinkota and Ronkainen 2004

The physical environment includes climate, geography, plant and animal life and natural resources. The view of the physical environment has a major impact upon what is considered proper behavior. For instance, citizens of Western Europe are far more concerned about air pollution than are most individuals in the Peoples' Republic of China.

Finally, the industry environment is also an important influence on the ethical behavior of individuals. Acceptable behaviors which become industry norms are often considered to be the standards by which actions should be judged. Competitive forces are often at the heart of questionable actions taken by individuals.

■ Business ethics

Ethics means a standard of behavior, a conception of right or wrong conduct (Post, Lawrence and Weber 2002). Ethical principles are guides to moral or immoral behavior. Ideas of right and wrong are derived from religious beliefs as well as industry and professions, families, friends, school and the media. All of these influences help an individual develop a specific concept of morality and ethics.

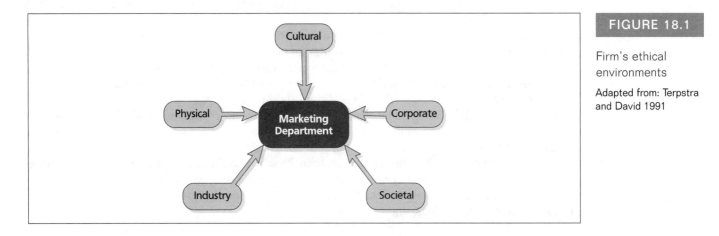

FIGURE 18.1

Firm's ethical environments

Adapted from: Terpstra and David 1991

Business ethics is simply the application of the foregoing ideas to business settings. Developing the proper guiding principles for business ethics has been the subject of discussion over many years. Three basic competing views of corporate responsibility have been put forward (Goodpaster and Matthews 1992). These can be defined succinctly as:

- the invisible hand
- the hand of government
- the hand of management.

The invisible hand, most strongly expressed by Milton Freidman, assigns to business the sole responsibility of making profits within the law. In this conception, the marketplace will punish immoral behavior and the overall common good results from each firm pursuing competitive advantage. Self-interest is the most important factor in this view.

The hand of government view, expressed by John Galbraith, describes a system in which corporations pursue economic objectives while governments and political processes force firms to set objectives which will result in the common well-being. As Goodpaster and Matthews explain, the similarities of these two views are interesting. In both, morality and ethics are the responsibility of rules and incentives rather than that of independent judgment by individuals or corporations.

The third view, called the hand of management, assigns the corporation an important role in setting moral behavior and developing a corporate conscience. This approach expects managements not to ignore profit and business survival but to 'coordinate imperatives, not deny their validity'. In this view, the presence of ethical or intelligent individuals will not ensure an ethical corporation. Therefore, these standards must be structured to coordinate and organize individuals for the purpose of achieving an overall moral responsibility.

Although there remain some who would take the Freidman, invisible hand, position, there appears to be a trend toward more corporate responsibility in nearly every part of the world. The reasons for this are self-evident. Firstly, the negative publicity resulting from revealed unethical behavior is swift and overwhelming negative reaction can boil up quickly in the form of protests and boycotts. Secondly, as will be explained later in this chapter, tighter regulations are being adopted by a number of countries. Thirdly, some studies indicate that firms which emphasize ethical and socially responsible behavior have better financial performance (Verschoor 1998 and Kurschner 1996).

Two basic approaches form the basis for ethical thinking. The first, deontology, embodies the view that ethical decisions follow absolute principles. Actions are inherently right or wrong, independent of their consequences. These principles are often derived from a religious base such as the traditions of Judaism, Christianity, Islam or from philosophies such as Confucianism (Newton 2004). The most familiar derivative of deontology is Kant's Categorical Imperative. The Categorical Imperative requires that for an action to be proper it would have to be acceptable as a general or universal law, all people are respected and an individual considers the decision both as a rule-maker and a rule-follower.

Another approach is consequentialism (also known as teleology) which bases its judgment of any action on the goodness of its consequences. The most well-known form of this school is utilitarianism which favors actions that generate 'the greatest good for the greatest number'. Many managers use a version of the utilitarian principle in their ethical decision-making, since it is similar to the familiar cost-benefit analysis.

In reality, managers find it difficult to make decisions based only on one school of ethics or another. It is easy to see that applying the utilitarian principle runs into problems in such simple decisions as attempting to decide whether to make a large investment in new plant and equipment versus paying dividends to shareholders. An analysis of costs and benefits are difficult when various stakeholders' interests are in competition. In addition, the utilitarian principle might lead a manager to operate an unsafe insecticide plant which might benefit a large population with better crops and therefore better nutrition, while harming a few hundred people located nearby the plant site. Utilitarianism often leads managers to ignore minority rights.

Using deontology also creates problems. Jean Paul Sartre illustrated the problem which arises when two universal principles conflict with one another. During World War II, he was forced to choose between staying home to comfort his ill and aging mother or fighting for the freedom of France (Donaldson, Werhane and Cording 2002).

A third approach is that of 'virtue' theory ethics in which individual character plays a major role. The teachings of Aristotle are at the heart of this theory, which states that individuals should learn good habits in order to live a virtuous life. Further, virtuous people should be role models as well. This approach has been criticized because it does not provide clear rules and decision-making methods. (Above based on Donaldson *et al*. 2002; Whysall 2000 and Schlegemilch 1998.)

Post *et al*. (2002) offer a slightly different view describing three methods of ethical reasoning:

- Utilitarian.
- Rights.
- Justice.

The utilitarian approach has been explained above. The rights method says an action is ethical when basic human rights are respected. Here again, it is difficult to balance the various stakeholders' rights. In the justice method, an attempt is made to distribute benefits and costs fairly. The major problem with this approach is similar to that of utilitarianism in that it is difficult to measure benefits and costs and hard to agree on which group should be the recipient of each (Smith 1995).

Marketing and ethics

Smith (1995) says that marketers often rely on simple rules or maxims such as those shown in Table 18.1.

TABLE 18.1 Ethical maxims for marketing
Do unto others as you would have them do unto you.
Would I be embarrassed if the media publicized my decision?
Good ethics is in the firm's long-term best interest.
Would colleagues view this action as proper?
When in doubt, don't.

Adapted from: Smith 1995

By its very nature, B2B marketing places the buyer-seller relationship at its center. Many ethical issues arise from the dynamics of this relationship. In addition, there are issues related to product, pricing, marketing communications, channels of distribution and market research. A list of possible ethical issues which face B2B marketers is presented in Table 18.2.

TALKING POINT

A salesperson for an etching machine manufacturer has placed his equipment with a firm in Singapore. After several weeks of attempting to get the equipment to operate properly, the customer demands that the machine be removed and replaced with a new one. Management decides to replace the machine with a refurbished model which is undetectable from a newly-manufactured product.

Should the salesman tell the customer that this product is remanufactured? Would he risk losing the sale? Or his job? If the machine really is indistinguishable from a new one, who cares about being economical with the truth?

Or would that be the equivalent of a woman lying about her age to a man she is about to marry?

TABLE 18.2 Ethical issues in International B2B Marketing

Selling

Bribery
Gifts/favors/entertainment
Misrepresentation/overselling
Conflicts of interest
Compensation and bookings

Product

Safety
Obsolescence/elimination
Service/warranty
Manufacturing – environmental impact
Disposal

Marketing Communications

Deceptive/misleading advertising and/or sales promotion
Violations of confidential information (direct, Internet marketing)

Pricing

Price-fixing
Reciprocity
Violation of secrecy in bidding
Unjustified price discrimination
Unfair pricing
Questionable invoicing
Artificial transfer pricing

Distribution

Discrimination
Dishonesty
Inflated 'commissions'

Market Research

Respondent participation
Researcher responsibilities

Personnel

Discrimination in hiring
Unfair treatment of employees

Selling

In the selling function, many difficult ethical problems emerge. An obvious one is bribery. In some countries, bribery is practically non-existent and is legally and culturally frowned upon. But in others, payments ranging from small 'dash' or 'grease' payments to large special commissions have been the norm. The cost of bribery can be a major expense. Hong Kong firms said that bribes accounted for 5 per cent of the cost of doing business in China. In Russia, the cost ranged to 20 per cent and in Indonesia as high as 30 per cent (Hollensen 1998). In Albania, businesses pay an average of 8 per cent of their sales (*Economist* January 16, 1999). A salesperson confronted with this has an ethical decision to make depending upon home country and host country laws and customs.

According to Terpstra and David (1991), both frontstage and backstage culture exist in every country. Frontstage culture includes the standard, normal, proper ways of doing things that insiders *are* willing to share with outsiders. It is easy for a visiting business person to determine what frontstage culture is all about. This includes the question of formality versus informality in addressing new acquaintances, gift giving traditions, the relationship between social engagement and business negotiations and so on. What is more troubling is backstage culture, defined as knowledge that insiders see as standard ways of doing things that they are *not* willing to share with outsiders. Insiders may not want to share knowledge because the activities may be illegal or because the special knowledge gained gives the insider a competitive advantage. Very often, the most carefully guarded backstage cultural activity is the bribe or so-called 'commission'.

For many years, the United States was alone in enforcing strict anti-bribery regulations. The Foreign Corrupt Practices Act (FCPA), which took effect in 1977, provides for fines up to US$2 million for corporations and up to US$100,000 for officers, directors, stockholders, employees and agents in addition to a prison term of up to five years for those who bribe government officials to gain advantage in securing contracts in countries outside the US. The immediate effect was a steep drop in US business in several developing countries. In 1997, the Organization for Economic Cooperation and Development (OECD) adopted the Convention on Combating Bribery of Foreign Public Officials in International Business Transactions. The Convention recommended that OECD members enact laws to criminalize bribery activity. As of 2003, all 35 countries who signed the convention did enact the recommended laws (Report to the Senate and House of Representatives 2003). It should be noted that both the OECD Convention and the FCPA do not relieve a firm from responsibility when managers use a third party such as an agent to actually deliver the 'commission' to a government official. The OECD Convention also includes the proviso that legislation be adopted to eliminate the tax deductibility of bribes paid to public officials. This has been accomplished by the 35 original participant countries (see Table 18.3).

A distinction is made between 'dash' or 'grease' payments and large scale bribery. The former are small payments such as those made to customs officials in airports. These kinds of traditional payments are not violations of the laws in most countries.

In the case of bribery, laws in developed countries may obviate the ethical issues. What is illegal is usually clearly unethical and this makes the manager's decision an easy one. Nevertheless, we have seen recent examples of questionable activity in many industries. For example, according to the *Economist* (June 14, 2003), a fraud squad descended on Airbus headquarters in Toulouse, France to

TABLE 18.3 Signatory countries – OECD Anti-bribery Convention

Argentina	Japan
Australia	Korea
Austria	Luxembourg
Belgium	Mexico
Brazil	The Netherlands
Bulgaria	New Zealand
Canada	Norway
Chile	Poland
Czech Republic	Portugal
Denmark	Slovak Republic
Finland	Slovenia
France	Spain
Germany	Sweden
Greece	Switzerland
Hungary	Turkey
Iceland	United Kingdom
Ireland	United States
Italy	

Report on Anti-Bribery Convention 2003

'check whether there was possible falsification of documents, bribery or other infractions as part of a [1997] sale of Airbus aircraft to Sabena' (the Belgian Airline). Sabena had purchased 34 A320s which it did not need and which 'helped trigger the airline's collapse four years later'. Until France ratified the OECD Convention in 2000, Airbus would have been permitted a tax deduction for any bribery (if it is proven they had done so). Airbus's major competitor, Boeing, has repeatedly felt it was the subject of unfair competition from Airbus but Boeing has not been immune to questions of impropriety. In November 2003, Boeing dismissed its chief financial officer and a vice president for discussions they had about a possible job offer for the latter while she was a US Government official negotiating a contract with the firm (Wayne 2003).

Though not members of the OECD, managers in Islamic nations are prohibited from engaging in bribery or other forms of 'marketing dishonesty' by religious principles (Saeed *et al.* 2001).

Research shows that gift-giving can be an effective tool for B2B marketers, with more expensive gifts relatively more effective in generating a positive and sustained increase in customer intent to repurchase and actual sales (Beltramini 2000). A study of more than 300 industrial buyers showed that 50 per cent had a firm policy to accept no gifts. Another 24 per cent had policies which limited the value of a gift to under US$50. Of those firms with no limits on gifts, most were smaller (under 200 employees) (Bird 1989). Gifts are also fraught with danger in foreign markets. Kathleen Reardon (1984) recites a number of embarrassing instances where an uninformed salesperson gave inappropriate gifts such as a gold bracelet from Tiffany to his Saudi customer's wife (acknowledging the wife is not acceptable), insisting his Japanese counterpart open a gift in his presence (embarrassing since it is not customary) or providing a clock to a buyer in China (a symbol of bad luck). Judgment is also required in deciding upon entertainment or providing favors. Taking customers to lunch or dinner or to a concert or sporting event certainly is within the ethical bounds of nearly every society. But other provisions for entertainments may tax the ethical limits and should be reviewed carefully.

The question of favors is more complex. In China, the concept of *guanxi* is culturally ingrained. This means developing personal relationships by doing favors for another party and thus obligating them. The other then feels they should do reciprocal favors. *Guanxi* is a fact of life in China and in a number of other societies as well and must be viewed as a necessary part of doing business. In a later part of this chapter we will discuss ways of responding to various ethical challenges such as this.

Misrepresentation and/or overselling a product, especially by puffing up specific aspects in a not entirely accurate way, or by omitting possible critical problems, also creates ethical issues. In the selling function, individuals also face conflicts of interest, not only because they may be required to sell products which are not suited for a particular client, but also because some agents and distributors may handle competing products. Finally, in the selling area, compensation and bookings can create ethical problems. Most salespeople are well aware of the most effective way to increase their compensation and this is certainly within the prescribed limits of any ethical system. However, when sales are manipulated to yield unjustified compensation, ethical issues come to the fore. In one case a firm owned by a single proprietor was about to sell to a large multinational. The owner instructed his salespeople to generate phantom orders to increase the order book and therefore the acquisition price by the multinational. Salespeople were compensated on unreal sales and therefore participated in this unethical behavior.

Product

Marketers must be primarily concerned with the safety of their products. Ethical issues often come to the fore when buyers are unaware of potential safety problems which may result from the use of a manufacturer's product. In B2B marketing, most governments do not establish laws and governmental agencies to protect buyers. The rule of *caveat emptor* (buyer beware) is generally applied to business buyers. This places an additional ethical burden on suppliers of business products to be sure their products are safe when used in the proper way. In some cases, instructions must be supplied in local languages and even in sign language when the installers or service people are illiterate.

A second product area is that of obsolescence or elimination. While 'sloughing off' product has been recommended by Peter Drucker and others for many years, an ethical issue is how quickly products are eliminated or made obsolete. A corollary issue is that of follow-on service of these products.

In some cases, a firm eliminates a product and also makes no arrangement for supplying spare parts or service. While it may seem obvious that this can create negative reactions in the marketplace, some firms neglect this important assurance.

One author experienced this problem in Chile. Local managers were angry at the multinational represented by the author because the firm had pulled out of Chile when the world copper price rapidly declined. The desertion left owners of mining equipment without spare parts or service, creating major problems for them. Here, an ethical approach would have also been good business as Chile rebounded and the firm wished to sell not only additional mining equipment, but many other products in a market which was now holding quite a negative opinion of the firm. When a firm offers a warranty, it should be sure that any claims can be satisfied.

While not specifically a marketing problem, the environmental impact caused by manufacturing may be weighed in the decision by a customer to choose one product versus another. In the building products business industry, for instance, some architects are now asking for detailed information about manufacturing processes of interior walls (drywall or gypsum board) in order to establish whether a particular product meets established 'green' standards.

Disposal can also pose a difficult problem for marketers. In the EU, disposal is an integral part of the overall product cycle and products must be designed with disposal in mind. An interesting and difficult problem arose in the UK in 1995 (Zyglidopoulos 2002). The Brent Spar, a very large floating oil-storage buoy, had been decommissioned several years before. After reviewing the various alternatives, the Shell Corporation decided to dispose of the Spar through sinking it in deep water. However, Greenpeace, the environmental group, objected on a number of grounds and organized protests throughout continental Europe, including calling for a boycott. Faced with these protests and a negative reaction from the general public as well as governments, Shell had to change their disposal plans.

Marketing communications

Advertising is a large area in which ethics standards need be applied. Ordinary 'puffery' of product is expected in consumer advertising. But in business marketing, generally speaking, this will backfire. Nevertheless, some managers who have spent the majority of their careers in the consumer area have felt the need to over-emphasize benefits in advertising.

A new area of concern is the violation of confidential information. Some business marketers have collected a great deal of personal information about customers and potential customers through the Internet. The use of this information must be carefully thought through if ethical standards are not to be violated.

Pricing

In the area of pricing, obvious illegal activities such as price fixing is prohibited by anti-trust laws in most of the developed countries and price fixing is prevented in the developing world if harm comes to participants who make their homes in countries where anti-trust laws are strictly enforced.

Reciprocity is an interesting problem. This simply means giving preference to a vendor who is also a customer. In a hypothetical example, General Electric may be selling plastics to an electronics manufacturer while also buying computers from that same firm. In this case, a salesman might be tempted to use that relationship to gain an advantage with the electronics firm. An unscrupulous buyer at GE might threaten to cut off computer purchases unless the electronics firm purchased plastics from the company. In many firms, this practice is frowned upon and even specifically prohibited by the firm's code of ethics. However, it is sometimes described in basic texts as one of the marketing tools.

Since business marketers often are required to provide sealed bids for a contract, they should have the confidence that these prices are not shared with others. However, in public bidding it is expected that all bids will be revealed. The timing of these discussions is often a sticking point. An unethical buyer might share pricing with a supplier before bids are officially opened and an ethical problem may arise for the salesperson given this special look at the pricing of his or her competitors.

Unjustified price discrimination and unfair pricing occurs when a firm decides to price differently for the same class of customer buying the same quantity. While this kind of discrimination is illegal in the US and in other developed countries, problems can arise where pricing discrimination is used unfairly from one country to another. At the extreme, this can cause the shipment of gray goods back to an unwanted market.

International trade seems to be plagued by questionable invoicing resulting in money laundering. It is a rare international business person who has not been approached by some firm asking for inflated invoices as a way of transferring funds out of a particular country. A similar but not as frequently encountered problem is transfer pricing where prices are set artificially high in order to avoid taxation in a particular market.

Distribution

A vexing problem is attempting to set the same requirements and giving the same benefits to distributors around the world. Meeting local market conditions can often result in a hodgepodge of distribution policies. It is important that a firm apply its ethical standards to the distribution policies it employs in various markets. Finally, related to the bribery discussion above, inflated commissions should be viewed as suspect by any manufacturer's marketing department. The Foreign Corrupt Practices Act requires that accounting procedures be in place to detect unusually large commissions which may eventually result in bribes.

Market research

Craig and Douglas (2000) advise that respondents' participation in research must be entirely voluntary and it is unethical to mislead them in order to gain their cooperation. Respondents must be told that their responses will be held in strict confidence and that their identity will be anonymous. Respondents must not be harmed in any way by the research process and should be informed if recording devices or other observations, which may not be evident, are being used. Researchers should be truthful about their skills and experiences. They should take care to design and conduct research in the most cost-effective way. Researchers should be careful to provide security for the data and provide findings only supported by the data. Researchers also should clearly define work they are doing which is not related to research. Contracts should follow the guidelines provided by ESOMAR or the American Marketing Association or other professional associations.

Personnel

Certainly a firm must be careful in applying requirements for hiring individuals. Discrimination is proscribed by law in many countries and yet discrimination may be the best course of action in particular markets. For instance, it would not be feasible to hire a woman as a salesperson in Saudi Arabia. Nevertheless, the proper application of law and ethics is required in choosing employees. Some firms in the quest to reduce cost have established unsafe or unfair working conditions. While this does not impact directly on an international marketing person's area of responsibility, it does affect the ability of the marketer to sell products in those markets where ethical concerns are important. Closer to the marketing responsibility is the treatment of local salespeople, other marketing specialists and clerical staff. While personnel policies may not transfer completely from the home office, reasonable expectations of employees should be considered when setting local policies.

According to Chonko and Hunt (2000), ethical conflict occurs when individuals see their duties toward one group as inconsistent with their duties toward another (including one's own self). The most important conflicts found by these researchers were balancing corporate interests against the interests of: customers, self, society and subordinates (in that order). These researchers, in completing a study of nearly 1100 marketing professionals found that more than one-half said 'there are many opportunities for marketing managers in their *industry* to engage in unethical behaviors' while 41 per cent agreed with the statement that 'there are many opportunities for marketing managers in *my company* to engage in unethical behaviors' (italics added). However, only 12 per cent said that managers in their firms engaged in unethical behavior, while 25 per cent said that managers in their industries engaged in unethical behaviors. Interestingly, Chonko and Hunt report that only 8 per cent of those interviewed believed that 'successful managers in my company are generally more unethical than unsuccessful managers'.

In their study, Chonko and Hunt found the ten most difficult ethical problems identified by marketing professionals were (in frequency of mention):

- bribery
- fairness
- honesty
- pricing
- product
- personnel
- confidentiality
- advertising
- manipulation of Data
- purchasing.

Issues not identified by these authors but which also have received much attention are

- pollution
- budget considerations
- non-reporting of violations
- refusing to help customers.

(Chonko and Hunt 2000).

■ Ethics in global business

Zyglidopoulos (2002) states that multinationals have to maintain higher levels of social and environmental responsibility because of the severe corporate reputation effects of lapses in these areas. He further states that matters impacting the firm's reputation should not be left to the discretion of national subsidiaries but should be coordinated centrally at headquarters who would set a global set of norms.

Chan and Armstrong (1999) identify problems by their importance in a study of 300 Australian and Canadian firms (150 each). The five most frequently *mentioned* international marketing ethical problems were ranked as follows:

- large scale bribery
- cultural differences
- involvement in political affairs
- pricing practices
- ilegal/immoral activities.

The five most frequently *occurring* categories of ethical problems were:

- cultural differences
- gifts, favors and entertainment
- pricing practices
- questionable commissions to channel members
- large scale bribery.

Chan and Armstrong define cultural differences as those involving potential misunderstandings related to traditional requirements of the exchange process, including what may be called a bribe by one culture but not by another, different practices related to gifts, payments, favors, entertainment and political contributions. Interestingly, these authors found differences between Australian and Canadian managers in both their perceptions of importance of ethical problems and in their listing of the frequency of the problems.

There is no question that there are different conditions in various markets when it comes to the concept of corruption. Transparency International, an independent non-governmental organization, publishes an annual corruption perceptions index. The list for 2003 is presented as Table 18.4.

A brief review of the table will show that corruption is perceived to be rampant in Bangladesh, Nigeria, Haiti, Paraguay, Myanmar, Tajikistan, Georgia, Cameroon, Azerbaijan, Angola, Kenya and Indonesia. Each of these countries scored lower than 2.0 in this index. Markets which are perceived to have very low levels of corruption include Finland, Iceland, Denmark, New Zealand, Singapore and Sweden, each of which scores above 9.0 in the index.

TALKING POINT

The SS United States was probably the swiftest most luxurious ocean liner in the 1950s and 60s. Because it was designed to be lightweight and fireproof, the ship probably contained more asbestos than any other. In 1992, it was purchased by a consortium planning to refurbish it for luxury cruising. However, the asbestos would have to be removed first. In the United States, this project would cost an estimated US$100 million. So, the liner was towed to Turkey where the same job could be completed for about US$2 million. The Turkish Government refused to allow the removal there. Subsequently, the owners were looking at other locations such as Sevastopol in the Ukraine where laws about the environment were less strict.

If the country's laws don't prohibit a particular action, is it ethical to have the ship towed to Sevastopol and the asbestos removed in a way which might cause cancer among workers and nearby residents, even if there aren't any laws against it in the Ukraine? Shouldn't a corporation be able to take that action? How can a manager reconcile his or her beliefs with those in a particular nation?

From a practical viewpoint, some of the countries where this work could be carried out are very poor. People are starving without the work (and foreign currency) that this type of job offers. Maybe we are willing to starve rather than compromise our ethics – but are we justified in letting others starve because of them? (This talking point based upon Stachell 1994.)

The widely varying environments in countries throughout the world have lead some to postulate that no one set of ethical guidelines can be established for marketing people which will be effective in every market. This leads inevitably to cultural relativism which contradicts the idea that there are universal moral truths. Rachels (2002) says cultural relativism is based on the idea that since cultures have varied practices, any one of these practices may be acceptable. For instance, if in one culture large bribes are a matter of course while in another no bribes are permitted in gaining contracts, cultural relativism would say that no rules regarding bribes would be proper. Cultural relativism says that if a society is living up to its own moral standards, that is all that is required of it. It does not allow for the idea of moral progress and change for the better.

It is obvious that managers in different cultures have different ethical attitudes toward the situations they face everyday. For instance, MacDonald (1988) showed that Hong Kong managers believed taking credit for another person's work was more unethical than bribery or gaining competitor information, a finding completely at odds with the beliefs of Western managers.

Donaldson and Dunfee (1999) say accepting 'whatever prevails in the host country' is a mistake because this can result in both corruption and public relations disasters – i.e. 'substitutes unmitigated relativism for good sense'. As we have seen earlier in this chapter, absolute adherence to one theory or another does not provide a manager with the guidance required to face ethical problems they encounter in the conduct of business. This is especially true when varying cultural standards are at play as well.

TABLE 18.4 Transparency international corruption perceptions index 2003

Country rank	Country	CPI 2003 score	Surveys used	Standard deviation	High-low range
1	Finland	9.7	8	0.3	9.2–10.0
2	Iceland	9.6	7	0.3	9.2–10.0
3	Denmark	9.5	9	0.4	8.8–9.9
	New Zealand	9.5	8	0.2	9.2–9.6
5	Singapore	9.4	12	0.1	9.2–9.5
6	Sweden	9.3	11	0.2	8.8–9.6
7	Netherlands	8.9	9	0.3	8.5–9.3
8	Australia	8.8	12	0.9	6.7–9.5
	Norway	8.8	8	0.5	8.0–9.3
	Switzerland	8.8	9	0.8	6.9–9.4
11	Canada	8.7	12	0.9	6.5–9.4
	Luxembourg	8.7	6	0.4	8.0–9.2
	United Kingdom	8.7	13	0.5	7.8–9.2
14	Austria	8.0	9	0.7	7.3–9.3
	Hong Kong	8.0	11	1.1	5.6–9.3
16	Germany	7.7	11	1.2	4.9–9.2
17	Belgium	7.6	9	0.9	6.6–9.2
18	Ireland	7.5	9	0.7	6.5–8.8
	USA	7.5	13	1.2	4.9–9.2
20	Chile	7.4	12	0.9	5.6–8.8
21	Israel	7.0	10	1.2	4.7–8.1
	Japan	7.0	13	1.1	5.5–8.8
23	France	6.9	12	1.1	4.8–9.0
	Spain	6.9	11	0.8	5.2–7.8
25	Portugal	6.6	9	1.2	4.9–8.1
26	Oman	6.3	4	0.9	5.5–7.3

TABLE 18.4	*(cont.)*				
Country rank	Country	CPI 2003 score	Surveys used	Standard deviation	High-low range
27	Bahrain	6.1	3	1.1	5.5–7.4
	Cyprus	6.1	3	1.6	4.7–7.8
29	Slovenia	5.9	12	1.2	4.7–8.8
30	Botswana	5.7	6	0.9	4.7–7.3
	Taiwan	5.7	13	1.0	3.6–7.8
32	Qatar	5.6	3	0.1	5.5–5.7
33	Estonia	5.5	12	0.6	4.7–6.6
	Uruguay	5.5	7	1.1	4.1–7.4
35	Italy	5.3	11	1.1	3.3–7.3
	Kuwait	5.3	4	1.7	3.3–7.4
37	Malaysia	5.2	13	1.1	3.6–8.0
	United Arab Emirates	5.2	3	0.5	4.6–5.6
39	Tunisia	4.9	6	0.7	3.6–5.6
40	Hungary	4.8	13	0.6	4.0–5.6
41	Lithuania	4.7	10	1.6	3.0–7.7
	Namibia	4.7	6	1.3	3.6–6.6
43	Cuba	4.6	3	1.0	3.6–5.5
	Jordan	4.6	7	1.1	3.6–6.5
	Trinidad and Tobago	4.6	6	1.3	3.4–6.9
46	Belize	4.5	3	0.9	3.6–5.5
	Saudi Arabia	4.5	4	2.0	2.8–7.4
48	Mauritius	4.4	5	0.7	3.6–5.5
	South Africa	4.4	12	0.6	3.6–5.5
50	Costa Rica	4.3	8	0.7	3.5–5.5
	Greece	4.3	9	0.8	3.7–5.6
	South Korea	4.3	12	1.0	2.0–5.6

TABLE 18.4 *(cont.)*

Country rank	Country	CPI 2003 score	Surveys used	Standard deviation	High-low range
53	Belarus	4.2	5	1.8	2.0–5.8
54	Brazil	3.9	12	0.5	3.3–4.7
	Bulgaria	3.9	10	0.9	2.8–5.7
	Czech Republic	3.9	12	0.9	2.6–5.6
57	Jamaica	3.8	5	0.4	3.3–4.3
	Latvia	3.8	7	0.4	3.4–4.7
59	Colombia	3.7	11	0.5	2.7–4.4
	Croatia	3.7	8	0.6	2.6–4.7
	El Salvador	3.7	7	1.5	2.0–6.3
	Peru	3.7	9	0.6	2.7–4.9
	Slovakia	3.7	11	0.7	2.9–4.7
64	Mexico	3.6	12	0.6	2.4–4.9
	Poland	3.6	14	1.1	2.4–5.6
66	China	3.4	13	1.0	2.0–5.5
	Panama	3.4	7	0.8	2.7–5.0
	Sri Lanka	3.4	7	0.7	2.4–4.4
	Syria	3.4	4	1.3	2.0–5.0
70	Bosnia & Herzegovina	3.3	6	0.7	2.2–3.9
	Dominican Republic	3.3	6	0.4	2.7–3.8
	Egypt	3.3	9	1.3	1.8–5.3
	Ghana	3.3	6	0.9	2.7–5.0
	Morocco	3.3	5	1.3	2.4–5.5
	Thailand	3.3	13	0.9	1.4–4.4
76	Senegal	3.2	6	1.2	2.2–5.5
77	Turkey	3.1	14	0.9	1.8–5.4

TABLE 18.4 *(cont.)*

Country rank	Country	CPI 2003 score	Surveys used	Standard deviation	High-low range
78	Armenia	3.0	5	0.8	2.2–4.1
	Iran	3.0	4	1.0	1.5–3.6
	Lebanon	3.0	4	0.8	2.1–3.6
	Mali	3.0	3	1.8	1.4–5.0
	Palestine	3.0	3	1.2	2.0–4.3
83	India	2.8	14	0.4	2.1–3.6
	Malawi	2.8	4	1.2	2.0–4.4
	Romania	2.8	12	1.0	1.6–5.0
86	Mozambique	2.7	5	0.7	2.0–3.6
	Russia	2.7	16	0.8	1.4–4.9
88	Algeria	2.6	4	0.5	2.0–3.0
	Madagascar	2.6	3	1.8	1.2–4.7
	Nicaragua	2.6	7	0.5	2.0–3.3
	Yemen	2.6	4	0.7	2.0–3.4
92	Albania	2.5	5	0.6	1.9–3.2
	Argentina	2.5	12	0.5	1.6–3.2
	Ethiopia	2.5	5	0.8	1.5–3.6
	Gambia	2.5	4	0.9	1.5–3.6
	Pakistan	2.5	7	0.9	1.5–3.9
	Philippines	2.5	12	0.5	1.6–3.6
	Tanzania	2.5	6	0.6	2.0–3.3
	Zambia	2.5	5	0.6	2.0–3.3
100	Guatemala	2.4	8	0.6	1.5–3.4
	Kazakhstan	2.4	7	0.9	1.6–3.8
	Moldova	2.4	5	0.8	1.6–3.6
	Uzbekistan	2.4	6	0.5	2.0–3.3
	Venezuela	2.4	12	0.5	1.4–3.1
	Vietnam	2.4	8	0.8	1.4–3.6

TABLE 18.4 *(cont.)*

Country rank	Country	CPI 2003 score	Surveys used	Standard deviation	High-low range
106	Bolivia	2.3	6	0.4	1.9–2.9
	Honduras	2.3	7	0.6	1.4–3.3
	Macedonia	2.3	5	0.3	2.0–2.7
	Serbia & Montenegro	2.3	5	0.5	2.0–3.2
	Sudan	2.3	4	0.3	2.0–2.7
	Ukraine	2.3	10	0.6	1.6–3.8
	Zimbabwe	2.3	7	0.3	2.0–2.7
113	Congo, Republic of the	2.2	3	0.5	2.0–2.8
	Ecuador	2.2	8	0.3	1.8–2.6
	Iraq	2.2	3	1.1	1.2–3.4
	Sierra Leone	2.2	3	0.5	2.0–2.8
	Uganda	2.2	6	0.7	1.8–3.5
118	Cote d'Ivoire	2.1	5	0.5	1.5–2.7
	Kyrgyzstan	2.1	5	0.4	1.6–2.7
	Libya	2.1	3	0.5	1.7–2.7
	Papua New Guinea	2.1	3	0.6	1.5–2.7
122	Indonesia	1.9	13	0.5	0.7–2.9
	Kenya	1.9	7	0.3	1.5–2.4
124	Angola	1.8	3	0.3	1.4–2.0
	Azerbaijan	1.8	7	0.3	1.4–2.3
	Cameroon	1.8	5	0.2	1.4–20.
	Georgia	1.8	6	0.7	0.9–2.8
	Tajikistan	1.8	3	0.3	1.5–2.0
129	Myanmar	1.6	3	0.3	1.4–2.0
	Paraguay	1.6	6	0.3	1.2–2.0
131	Haiti	1.5	5	0.6	0.7–2.3
132	Nigeria	1.4	9	0.4	0.9–2.0
133	Bangladesh	1.3	8	0.7	0.3–2.2

Used by Permission of Transparency Inernational

Explanatory notes

CPI 2003 Score

relates to perceptions of the degree of corruption as seen by business people, academics and risk analysts, and ranges between 10 (highly clean) and 0 (highly corrupt).

Surveys Used

refers to the number of surveys that assessed a country's performance.

A total of 17 surveys were used from 13 independent institutions and at least three surveys were required for a country to be included in the CPI.

Standard Deviation

indicates differences in the values of the sources: the greater the standard deviation, the greater the differences of perceptions of a country among the sources.

High-Low Range

provides the highest and lowest values of the different sources.

Hunt and Vitell (1986) proposed a general theory of marketing ethics which takes into account the cultural, industry and organizational environments as well as personal experiences, both deontological and consequential considerations to arrive at the proper behavior. This framework, while useful, does not specifically address the problem of competing cultural norms.

Donaldson and Dunfee (1999) propose a theory based on the Integrative Social Contracts Theory (ISCT). These authors differentiate between pluralism, allowing for tolerance of other cultures' norms and relativism, in which any action undertaken by managers in a particular culture is acceptable simply because it has been undertaken by others in that culture.

Chan and Armstrong (1999) claim that international marketing relativism is becoming a dominant approach and that 'experience and culture have become criteria of what is ethical'. Yet, Husted *et al.* (1996) showed that there was a measure of agreement across various cultures related to questionable business and marketing practices. In the past, the concept of universal ethical standards was looked upon by some as a form of moral imperialism, implying that one set of standards is inevitably more right than another. However, with the coalescing of universal standards, an emerging set of universal norms appears to be forming.

Donaldson and Dunfee (1999) describe three levels of ethical standards or norms. At the most basic level are *hypernorms* – fundamental rights acceptable to all cultures and organizations. Second are *consistent norms*, which are more culturally specific. They must be consistent with hypernorms, however. According to Donaldson and Dunfee, most corporations' ethical codes fall within this category. A third level is called *moral free space*. Here we find norms that are inconsistent with some of the legitimate norms described in the second level, yet are often expressions of strongly held cultural beliefs. Moving even farther away are what these authors call *illegitimate norms*. These are the norms which are incompatible with hypernorms.

Using this approach, hypernorms relate to basic practices such as price gouging in markets where there are no alternatives, or using slave labor to manufacture products. But, the existence of moral free space allows managers to adapt where the norms of a particular country conflict with consistent norms in the home country, but not with the overriding hypernorms. One example given by these authors relates to nepotism. In India, firms often promise employees a job for one of their children when a child reaches the proper age. In the West, this might violate an anti-nepotism policy. But, this kind of action, quite acceptable in India, falls into the moral free space of the model proposed. This approach allows managers to avoid the dangers of ethical relativism which establishes no standards whatever while allowing for adaptation to local cultures when that adaptation does not violate basic moral standards.

■ Analyzing ethical problems

When a manager faces a problem which may raise ethical issues, he or she should be able to apply guidelines that can help in decision-making. Figure 18.2, Analyzing an Ethical Question, combines the thinking of Post *et al.* (2002) and Donaldson and Dunfee (1999).

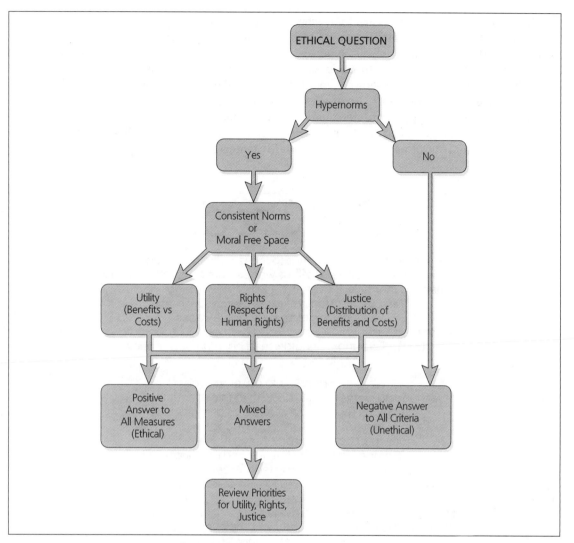

FIGURE 18.2

Analyzing an ethical question

Adapted from: Post *et al.* 2002; Donaldson and Dunfee 1999

An ethical question would first be tested against the hypernorms which form the bedrock of ethical thinking. Violation of these hypernorms would lead to rejecting a possible course of action as unethical. If the action is permissible when compared to consistent norms or falls into moral free space, it would then be subjected to a review in terms of utility (the benefits versus the costs), rights (whether human rights are respected) and justice (related to whether the benefits and costs are fairly distributed). Should the action provide positive answers when viewed from the basis of utility, rights and justice, the action proposed would be ethical. Should the action create negative results when viewed from these three perspectives, it would be unethical. Should the answers be mixed, a manager would have to balance the concerns of all stakeholders as related to utility, rights and justice before deciding on a course of action.

■ Making ethics work

In response to the need for more consistent ethical behavior, corporations have attempted to institutionalize basic corporate values. One very obvious response has been the development of codes of ethics. But the mere existence of codes of ethics are generally ineffective in implementing ethical behavior among managers (Chonko and Hunt 2000). While it is important to have a code of ethics, it is more important that top management make ethical behavior a priority. Chonko and Hunt cite several studies confirming that the commitment of senior management to ethics is essential for promoting ethical behavior and that familiarity with the company code of ethics increases sensitivity to ethical decision making.

A number of firms have been cited for having useful codes of ethics. Smith (1995) states that Johnson & Johnson's Credo is frequently given as 'a high standard and testament to the potential influence of codes of conduct'. According to their homepage, this firm has no mission statement that 'hangs on the wall', but uses a simple 'Credo' to guide employees toward ethical behavior. The Credo has been published in 36 languages and is shown in four languages on the following pages in Exhibits 18.1 to 18.4.

The simple statements in this Credo allow for much interpretation in local markets. Yet, built-in appear to be the hypernorms recommended by Donaldson and Dunfee (1999). Caterpillar Corporation has also published excellent guidelines. In their code of worldwide business conduct, the firm states 'we hold ourselves to the highest standard of integrity and ethical behavior: we must always tell the truth'.

EXHIBIT 18.1

United States credo

Our Credo

We believe our first responsibility is to the doctors, nurses and patients,
to mothers and fathers and all others who use our products and services..
In meeting their needs everything we do must be of high quality.
We must constantly strive to reduce our costs
in order to maintain reasonable prices.
Customers' orders must be serviced promptly and accurately.
Our suppliers and distributors must have an opportunity
to make a fair profit.

We are responsible to our employees,
the men and women who work with us throughout the world.
Everyone must be considered as an individual.
We must respect their dignity and recognize their merit.
They must have a sense of security in their jobs.
Compensation must be fair and adequate,
and working conditions clean, orderly and safe.
We must be mindful of ways to help our employees fulfill
their family responsibilities.
Employees must feel free to make suggestions and complaints.
There must be equal opportunity for employment, development
and advancement for those qualified.
We must provide competent management,
and their actions must be just and ethical.

We are responsible to the communities in which we live and work
and to the world community as well.
We must be good citizens — support good works and charities
and bear our fair share of taxes.
We must encourage civic improvements and better health and education.
We must maintain in good order
the property we are privileged to use,
protecting the environment and natural resources.

Our final responsibility is to our stockholders.
Business must make a sound profit.
We must experiment with new ideas.
Research must be carried on, innovative programs developed
and mistakes paid for.
New equipment must be purchased, new facilities provided
and new products launched.
Reserves must be created to provide for adverse times.
When we operate according to these principles,
the stockholders should realize a fair return.

Johnson & Johnson

EXHIBIT 18.2

United Arab
Emirates credo

مـبـدأنـا

نحن مسؤولون ، أولا اتجاه الأطباء والممرضات والمرضى والأمهات والآباء

وكل من يستعمل موادنا وخدماتنا .

شغلنا الدائم هو الجودة التي تقودنا للعمل لتلبية متطلباتهم .

يجب علينا أن نجتهد باستمرار للنقص من المصاريف

لنحافظ على أثمان مناسبة .

متطلبات الزبناء يجب أن تتم بسرعة ودقة .

مزودونا وموزعونا ، يجب أن نهيئ لهم ظروف الربح المعقول .

نحن مسؤولون اتجاه عمالنا رجالا ونساء ،

الذين يساهمون في أنشطتنا في كل أقطار العالم

كل واحد يجب أن يعامل على أنه فرد وأن يعترف بمستحقاته

يجب أن يكون لهم إحساس بالاطمئنان في عملهم .

يجب أن تكون ترقيتهم متوازية ومعقولة ،

الجميع يجب أن يعمل في ظروف نظيفة ومنظمة وصحية .

يجب أن نكون على علم بحالتهم العائلية ونساعدهم على تحمل مسؤولياتهم .

يجب أن يشعر عمالنا بالحرية في إعطاء اقتراحات وملاحظات .

حظوظ متساوية للعمل والتقدم والترقية يجب أن تعطى لكل من لديهم الأهلية .

علينا أن نكون متأكدين من أن مسؤولينا أكفاء ودليلا للعدل والضمير المهني

نحن مسؤولون اتجاه المجتمعات التي نعيش فيها ونعمل كذلك اتجاه المجتع الدولي .

يجب أن نكون مواطنين صالحين ، نشجع الأعمال الاجتماعية والخيرية

وندفع نصيبنا المستحق من الضرائب .

يجب أن نشجع التقدم في ظروف الحياة والصحة والتعليم .

يجب علينا صيانة الأراضي ، المعامل والمكاتب التي ننعم بها حفاظا على المحيط والموارد الطبيعية .

وأخيرا نحن مسؤولون اتجاه المساهمين في الشركة .

الشركة يجب أن تحقق ربحا معقولا

علينا تطوير أفكار جديدة .

يجب أن يتابع البحث العلمي ، وتنمية برامج خلاقة وتحمل ثمن أخطائنا

علينا أن نجدد أدوات عملنا ، وبناء وحدات جديدة وتقديم منتوجات جديدة .

علينا تكوين احتياطات تحسبا للأزمة الصعبة

عملا بهذه المبادئ علينا أن نضمن لمساهمينا مردودا مستحقا لاستثماراتهم .

جـونـسـون وجـونـسـون

EXHIBIT 18.3

Chinese credo

我们的信条

我们相信我们首先要对医生、护士和病人，
对父母亲以及所有使用我们的产品和接受我们服务的人负责，
为了满足他们的需要，我们所做的一切都必须是高质量的。
我们必须不断地致力于降低成本，以保持合理的价格。
客户的订货必须迅速而准确地供应。
我们的供应商和经销商应该有机会赚取合理的利润。

我们要对世界各地和我们一起共事的男女同仁负责。
每一位同仁都应视为独立的个体。
我们必须重视他们的尊严，赞赏他们的优点。
要使他们对其工作有一种安全感。
薪酬必须公平合理；
工作环境必须清洁、整齐和安全。
我们必须设法帮助员工履行他们对家庭的责任。
必须让员工在提出建议和申诉时畅所欲言。
对于合格的人必须给予平等的任用、发展和升迁的机会。
我们必须具备称职的管理人员；
他们的行为必须公正和符合道德。

我们要对我们所生活和工作的社会，对整个世界负责。
我们必须做好公民—支持对社会有益的活动和慈善事业，
缴纳我们应付的税款。
我们必须鼓励全民进步，促进健康和教育事业。
我们必须很好地维护我们所使用的财产，
保护环境和自然资源。

最后，我们要对全体股东负责。
企业经营必须获取可靠的利润。
我们必须尝试新的构想。
必须坚持研究工作，开发革新项目，
承担错误的代价并加以改正。
必须购置新设备，提供新设施，推出新产品，
必须设立储备金，以备不时之需，
如果我们依照这些原则进行经营，
股东们就会获得合理的回报。

Johnson & Johnson

EXHIBIT 18.4

Argentinean credo

Nuestro Credo

Creemos que nuestra primera responsabilidad es con los médicos,
enfermeras y pacientes, con las madres, padres y todos aquellos
que usan nuestros productos y servicios.
Para satisfacer sus necesidades, todo lo que hacemos
debe ser de la más alta calidad.
Debemos luchar constantemente por reducir nuestros costos
a fin de mantener precios razonables.
Los pedidos de nuestros clientes deben ser atendidos
rápidamente y con precisión.
Nuestros proveedores y distribuidores deben tener la oportunidad
de obtener una ganancia justa.

Somos responsables ante nuestros empleados, ante los hombres
y mujeres que trabajan con nosotros en el mundo entero.
Cada uno de ellos debe ser considerado como una persona única.
Hemos de respetar su dignidad y reconocer sus méritos.
Deben sentirse seguros en sus empleos.
Los salarios deben ser justos y adecuados
y las condiciones de trabajo limpias, ordenadas y seguras.
Debemos ser conscientes de brindar diversas formas de ayuda a nuestros
empleados en el desempeño de sus responsabilidades familiares.
Los empleados deben sentirse libres para hacer
sugerencias y presentar sus quejas.
Debe prevalecer la igualdad de oportunidad de empleo,
desarrollo y progreso de los cualificados.
Debemos proporcionar una gerencia competente y sus acciones
han de ser justas y éticas.

Somos responsables ante las comunidades en las que vivimos
y trabajamos, así como ante la comunidad mundial.
Debemos ser buenos ciudadanos; apoyar iniciativas filantrópicas y caritativas
y pagar nuestros impuestos.
Debemos fomentar las mejoras cívicas y una mejor sanidad y educación.
Debemos mantener en buen estado los bienes
que tenemos el privilegio de usar, protegiendo el medio ambiente
y los recursos naturales.

Nuestra responsabilidad final es con nuestros accionistas.
La empresa debe conseguir un beneficio justo.
Debemos experimentar con nuevas ideas.
La investigación debe continuar, debemos desarrollar
programas innovadores y pagar por los errores.
Debemos adquirir nuevos equipos, proporcionar nuevas instalaciones
y lanzar al mercado nuevos productos.
Han de crearse reservas para los tiempos adversos.
Si obramos de acuerdo con estos principios, los accionistas
recibirán un aporte justo a su inversión.

Johnson & Johnson

Paine (1994) has described two approaches to corporate integrity strategies. The first approach emphasizes compliance which is based on avoiding litigation and liability. A firm pursuing this approach establishes rules for employees hoping to direct employee behavior through the threat of punishment. As Paine points out, however, the emphasis on legal restrictions may allow the perception that 'if it's legal it's ethical'. But actions which are lawful can be unethical, especially in developing countries.

Paine believes a more effective approach is based on individual integrity, emphasizing employee responsibility for proper conduct. In this approach, the firm supplies clear codes of conduct, training for employees, audits and controls to ensure that standards are being met. For instance, in the Johnson & Johnson policy on business conduct, the very first statement describes managers' responsibility for enforcement and compliance with the policy and the managers' periodic certification of compliance.

Paine stresses, as do others (Robin and Reidenbach 1987; Chonko and Hunt 2000) that top management has a critical role to play in establishing the proper ethical climate and behavior. Robin and Reidenbach further state that top management must integrate ethical core values into the organization's corporate culture.

Paine (1994) summarizes an effective integrity strategy as follows:

- The guiding values and commitments make sense and are clearly communicated.
- Company leaders are personally committed, credible and willing to take action on the values they espouse.
- These values are integrated into the normal channels of management decision-making and reflected in the organization's activities.
- Company systems and structures support and reinforce core values.
- Managers throughout the company have the decision-making skills, knowledge and competence to make ethically sound decisions on a day-to-day basis.

The World Bank and the IMF now require that governments fight corruption and countries who do not may suffer consequences. The IMF stopped lending to Kenya and the World Bank reduced its commitments to Kenya and Nigeria because they were not moving quickly enough to fight corruption (*Economist* 1999).

To make ethics work within a corporation, it is important that a training program be established. Some firms also have appointed an ethics officer and/or an ethics committee. Many firms conduct ethics audits to compare actual behavior with the established company standards. In order to implement truly ethical behavior, a firm must establish a comprehensive program including the code of ethics, employee training and an ethics officer as well as audits of conduct.

Associations as well have established codes of ethics. ESOMAR, a worldwide market research association, has a long and detailed code of ethics as does the Chartered Institute of Marketing (CIM) and the American Marketing Association (AMA). The CIM has about 60,000 members, including students and branches in nine nations, as well as headquarters in the UK. The AMA includes 38,000 members. Its code of ethics is shown as Table 18.5.

The CIM code of professional standards, while not as specific as the AMA code, covers most of the same areas.

TABLE 18.5 American Marketing Association's Code of Ethics

Members of the American Marketing Association are committed to ethical professional conduct. They have joined together in subscribing to this Code of Ethics embracing the following topics:

Responsibility of the Marketer

Marketers must accept responsibility for the consequences of their activities and make every effort to ensure that their decisions, recommendations and actions function to identify, serve and satisfy all relevant publics: customers, organizations and society

Marketers' Professional Conduct Must Be Guided By

1. The basic rule of professional ethics: not knowingly to do harm
2. The adherence to all applicable laws and regulations
3. The accurate representation of their education, training and experience
4. The active support, practice and promotion of this Code of Ethics

Honesty and Fairness

Marketers shall uphold and advance the integrity, honor and dignity of the marketing profession by:
1. Being honest in serving consumers, clients, employees, suppliers, distributors and the public
2. Not knowingly participating in conflict of interest without prior notice to all parties involved
3. Establishing equitable fee schedules including the payment or receipt of usual, customary and/or legal compensation for marketing exchanges

Rights and Duties of Parties in the Marketing Exchange Process

Participants in the marketing exchange process should be able to expect that:
1. Products and services offered are safe and fit for their intended uses
2. Communications about offered products and services are not deceptive
3. All parties intend to discharge their obligations, financial and otherwise, in good faith
4. Appropriate internal methods exist for equitable and/or redress of grievances concerning purchases

It is Understood that the Above Would Include But Is Not Limited To, the Following Responsibilities of the Marketer:
In the Area of Product Development and Management

- Disclosure of all substantial risks associated with product or service usage
- Identification of any product component substitution that might materially change the product or impact on the buyer's purchase decision
- Identification of extra cost-added features

In the Area of Promotions

- Avoidance of false and misleading advertising
- Rejection of high-pressure manipulations, or misleading sales tactics
- Avoidance of sales promotions that use deception or manipulation

In the Area of Distribution

- Not manipulating the availability of a product for the purpose of exploitation
- Not using coercion in the marketing channel
- Not exerting undue influence over the reseller's choice to handle a product

In the Area of Pricing

- Not engaging in price fixing
- Not practicing predatory pricing
- Disclosing the full price associated with any purchase

TABLE 18.5 *(cont).*

In the Area of Marketing Research

- Prohibiting selling or fundraising under the guise of conducting research
- Maintaining research integrity by avoiding misrepresentation and omission of pertinent research data
- Treating outside clients and suppliers fairly

Organizational Relationships

Marketers should be aware of how their behavior may influence or impact the behavior of others in organizational relationships. They should not demand, encourage or apply coercion to obtain unethical behavior in their relationships with others, such as employees, suppliers, or customers.

- Apply confidentiality and anonymity in professional relationships with regard to privileged information
- Meet their obligations and responsibilities in contract and mutual agreements in a timely manner
- Avoid taking the work of others, in whole, or in part, and representing this work as their own or directly benefiting from it without compensation or consent of the originator or owner
- Avoid manipulation to take advantage of situations to maximize personal welfare in a way that unfairly deprives or damages the organization of others

Any AMA Member Found to be in Violation of Any Provision of the Code of Ethics May Have His or Her Association Membership Suspended or Revoked

Reprinted with permission from the American Marketing Association

SUMMARY

Establishing an effective ethics program, especially in a firm heavily involved in international business is both a challenge and a necessity. Firms violating societal norms suffer major negative effects to their corporate reputation. Therefore, it is important that managers understand how to deal with ethical problems in all markets throughout the world.

The key points from this chapter are:

- The marketing department is operating within many influences. Corporate culture is an important part of the ethical tone of the firm.

- Today, relying solely on the market's invisible hand or the hand of government leaves the firm vulnerable to actions which may reflect poorly upon it.

- While philosophy gives us deontology (acting based on absolute principles) and utilitarianism as well as virtue ethics, none of these approaches nor the simple rules sometimes used in marketing departments give useful guidelines for managers.

- There are ethical issues in many aspects of marketing, including selling, product, marketing communications, pricing, distribution, market research and personnel.

- Local markets range from highly corrupt to completely honest and in some cases lead marketers to the thought that no established ethical principles can be applied throughout the world – cultural relativism.

- A relatively new theory proposes that fundamental ideas called hypernorms can be accepted by all marketers. Once these are established, adapting to local cultures is less difficult.

- Firms and associations have developed codes of conduct. But codes of conduct by themselves do not ensure ethical behavior. A full program must be established.

REVIEW QUESTIONS

1 Describe the environmental impacts on the marketing department's ethical decision making.

2 What are the major competing views of corporate responsibility? Describe in detail.

3 Compare and contrast the deontological, consequential and virtue theories of ethics.

4 List the key ethical issues in international B2B marketing and describe some key issues in at least three of these areas.

5 How important is the question of bribery in international business? What is being done on an international basis to counter it?

6 What are the most important international marketing ethical problems?

7 What is international marketing relativism? What are the drawbacks to this approach and how can a manager adapt to local cultures while maintaining ethical standards?

8 What are the key elements of a successful corporate ethics program?

SPOTLIGHT ON B2B MARKETING

Jian Ching-yen is the vice president of marketing for Taiwan Office Furniture, a US$50 million manufacturer of office furniture located near Taipei. Today he is faced with a serious problem that needs to be handled properly. Over the past few years the firm has grown rapidly because of a new lightweight material they are using to manufacture binder bins or flipper door cabinets, which hang on office furniture panels and also can be mounted on drywall. Some disturbing news has recently reached Jian and today there will be a meeting to discuss the implications.

Since the new material was introduced for these cabinets, Taiwan Office Furniture had been able to lower its prices and is now at least 30 per cent cheaper than its nearer competitors for the cabinets. Because the cost of the cabinets make up a good percentage of the overall selling price of an office furniture installation, Taiwan has been able to win many bids and therefore sales are growing rapidly.

On a recent trip to Jakarta and Manila where 25 per cent of the furniture has been sold, one distributor mentioned to Jian that in a few instances the new material had lacked the strength to hold a fully loaded cabinet.

As a matter of course, Taiwan Office Furniture issues to its distributors guidelines for cabinet loading. The firm warns that placing more than 100lbs in a four-foot wide cabinet may overload its capabilities. Yet, office workers rarely weigh what they put in a cabinet and binders filled with paper plus large inserts with office supplies like staples and CDs can easily bring the weight beyond that recommended by the company. During his trip, Jian was also told by distributors both in Malaysia and Indonesia that in a few installations, heavily-loaded cabinets had fallen off panels or walls. In no case was an office worker injured, but this seems to be raising a possible problem for the firm.

The meeting today will be with the executive committee, including Jian's boss, the president of the firm, as well as the manufacturing, engineering and financial officers of the firm. Jian has talked to all of them privately and summarizes their positions as follows:

- *Manufacturing* – we are making the product to the specifications given to us by engineering. There are no manufacturing defects.

- *Engineering* – the standards we set are reasonable and when tested the product meets the standards we have set.

- *Finance* – while this may be a problem, we can't get too carried away and cost ourselves a profitable quarter or year.

The company has approximately 20,000 of these cabinets in place. To fully test each unit at approximately US$50 per test would cost the company US$1,000,000. To replace all the units would cost a minimum of US$200 per unit or about US$4,000,000. That certainly would have a major impact upon the bottom line for at least one-quarter and possibly more.

Jian feels the cabinet situation may be an ethical problem since there are no laws regulating this kind of situation. Jian thinks about his options and sketches them on a pad:

1 Ignore the problem since very few instances have been reported.

2 Send out additional warnings to both distributors and office workers.

3 Test all installed units.

4. React to problems only, replacing those units which fail.

5 Replace all units.

Jian knows it's not going to be a pleasant meeting, but he believes something must be done.

Questions

1 How can Jian Ching-yen apply ethical tests to this problem?

2 What are the possible consequences should the firm decide to do nothing?

3 What is the best course of action for Jian to take?

4 How should he present his case to the executive committee meeting that is about to take place?

REFERENCES

_____ (1999) 'A Global War Against Bribery', *The Economist*, 350: 8102: 16 Jan: 22–24.

_____ (2003) 'Airbus's Secret Past', *The Economist*, 367: 8328: 14 June: 55–58.

http://www.iccwbo.org/home/statements_rules/rules/1995/esomcod.asp accessed 11/16/03.

http://www/catepillar.com/about_cat/pdf/worldwide_code.pdf accessed 11/16/03.

http://www/jnj.com/our_company/our_credo/index.htm accessed 11/16/03.

Beltramini, R. F. (2000) 'Exploring the Effectiveness of Business Gifts: Replication and Extension', *Journal of Advertising*, 29: 2: 75–78.

Bird, M. M. (1989) 'Gift-Giving and Gift-Taking in Industrial Companies', *Industrial Marketing Management*, 18: 91–94.

Chan, T. S. and Armstrong, R. W. (1999) 'Comparative Ethical Report Card: A Study of Australian and Canadian Managers' Perceptions of International Marketing Ethics Problems', *Journal of Business Ethics*, 18: 3–15.

Chonko, L. B. and Hunt, S. D. (2000). 'Ethics and Marketing Management: A Retrospective and Prospective Commentary', *Journal of Business Research*, 50: 3: 235–244.

Craig, S. and Douglas, S. P. (2000) *International Marketing Research*, Chichester, W. Sussex: John Wiley and Sons, Ltd.

Czinkota, M. R. and Ronkainen, I. A. (2004) *International Marketing*, Mason, Ohio: South-Western Publishing.

Donaldson, T. and Dunfee, T. W. (1999) 'When Ethics Travel: The Promise and Peril of Global Business Ethics', *California Management Review*, 41: 4: 45–63.

Donaldson, T., Werhane, P. H. and Cording, M. (2002) *Ethical Issues in Business: A Philosophical Approach*, Upper Saddle River, NJ: Prentice-Hall.

Goodpaster, K. E. and Matthews, J. B., Jr. (1982) 'Can a Corporation Have a Conscience', *Harvard Business Review*, 60: 1: 132–141.

Hollensen, S. (1998) *Global Marketing: A Market Responsive Approach*, Hertfordshire, UK: Prentice-Hall Europe.

Hunt, S. D. and Vitell, S. (1986) 'A General Theory of Marketing Ethics', *Journal of Macromarketing*, 8: 5–16.

Husted, B. W., Dozier, J. B., McMahon, T. J. and Kattan, M. W. (1996) 'The Impact of Cross-National Carriers of Business Ethics on Attitudes about Questionable Practices and Forms of Moral Reasoning', *Journal of International Business Studies*, 27: 2: 391–411.

Keegan, W. J. and Green, M. C. (2003) *Global Marketing*, Upper Saddle River, NJ: Prentice-Hall.

Kurschner, D. (1996) 'Five Ways Ethical Busine$$ Creates Fatter Profit$', *Business Ethics*, March-April: 20–23.

MacDonald, G. M. (1988) 'Ethical Perceptions of Hong Kong/Chinese Business Managers', *Journal of Business Ethics*, 7: 835–845.

Newton, L. H. (2004) *Ethics in America: Source Reader*, Upper Saddle River, NJ: Prentice-Hall.

Paine, L. S. (1994) Managing for Organizational Integrity, *Harvard Business Review*, 72: 2: March-April: 106–117.

Post, J. E., Lawrence, A. T. and Weber, J. (2002) *Business and Society: Corporate Strategy, Public Policy, Ethics*, New York: McGraw-Hill, Inc.

Rachels, J. (2002) 'The Challenge of Cultural Relativism', in *Ethical Issues in Business: A Philosophical Approach*, Donaldson, T., Werhane, P. H. and Cording, M., eds., Upper Saddle River, NJ: Prentice-Hall: 410–419.

Reardon, K. K. (1984) 'It's the Thought that Counts', *Harvard Business Review*, 62: 5: 136–141.

Report to Senate and House of Representatives mandated by IAFCA (2003), http://www. tcc. mac. doc. gov/pdf/Bribery2003_text. pdf accessed 11/21/03.

Robin, D. P. and Reidenbach, E. R. (1987) 'Social Responsibility, Ethics, and Marketing Strategy: Closing the Gap between Concept and Application', *Journal of Marketing*, 51: January: 44–58.

Saeed, M., Ahmed, Z. U. and Mukhtar, S-M. (2001) 'International Marketing Ethics from an Islamic Perspective: A Value-Maximization Approach', *Journal of Business Ethics*, 32: 127–142.

Satchell, M. J. (1994) 'Deadly Trade in Toxics', *US News and World Report*, 7 March: 116: 9: 64–66.

Schlegelmilch, B. (1998) *Marketing Ethics: An International Perspective*, London: International Thomson Business Press.

Smith, N. C. (1995) 'Marketing Strategies for the Ethics Era', *Sloan Management Review*, 36: 4: 85–97.

Terpstra, V. and David, K. (1991) *The Cultural Environment of International Business*, Cincinnati, OH: South-Western Publishing Company.

Verschoor, C. C. (1998) 'A Study of the Link Between a Corporation's Financial Performance and Its Commitment to Ethics', *Journal of Business Ethics*, 17: 1509–1516.

Wayne, L. (2003) 'Boeing Dismisses 2 in Hiring of Official Who Left Pentagon', *New York Times*, 25 Nov: A1: C2.

Whysall, P. (2000) 'Marketing Ethics – An Overview', *The Marketing Review*, 1: 175–195.

Zyglidopoulos, S. C. (2002) 'The Social and Environmental Responsibilities of Multinationals: Evidence from the Brent Spar Case', *Journal of Business Ethics*, 36: 141–151.

19

THE FUTURE OF BUSINESS MARKETING

Learning objectives
After reading this chapter, you should be able to:

- Explain the three major trends affecting B2B marketing

- Describe some of the new marketing approaches now developing as a result of those trends

- Explain how postmodernism is affecting marketing thought

- Describe value-based marketing

- List the new insights developed in relationship marketing

▌ Introduction

Predicting the future is easy – predicting it accurately is not. This chapter aims to examine the trends in thinking about B2B marketing and to consider some of the possibilities implicit in current developments.

■ Trends in business-to-business marketing

Business-to-business marketing will be strongly affected by three major trends – globalization, rapidly changing technology and increased visibility. These trends can be seen in Figure 19.1 and, in fact, the trends affect each other as well.

TALKING POINT

A medium-sized manufacturer of hip joint replacements has provided its products to hospitals throughout North America and Europe. The director of marketing suddenly sees comments on various websites accusing the firm of supplying defective products. The director knows these defective units are supplied by a competitor.

How do the major trends in B2B marketing affect this rumor? If the report isn't true why should the marketing director care? Why not just do nothing?

Globalization is made possible in part by rapidly changing technology and these changes in technology measurably increase the visibility of marketing actions and because globalization exists, companies are more visible as well. One can make the case that each of these three trends would be weaker without the other.

Globalization

Globalization is a commonly used but poorly defined term. Definitions range from the all encompassing (Friedman 2000) –

> *Globalization is the inexorable integration of markets, nation-states and technologies to a degree never witnessed before – in a way that is enabling individuals, corporations and nation-states to reach around the world farther, faster, deeper and cheaper than ever before, and in a way that is enabling the world to reach into individuals, corporations and nation-states farther, faster, deeper, and cheaper than ever before;*

to the very succinct (Dunning 2003) – 'connectivity of individuals and institutions across the globe or at least over most of it'. Czinkota and Ronkainen (2004) say that globalization results in the belief that 'distinctions between national markets are . . . fading and, for some products, will eventually disappear'. Dunning makes the distinction between globalization, the global marketplace and global capitalism. He believes that globalization by itself is a neutral concept, but that the global marketplace and global capitalism are criticized for failing to provide goods and services at fair and affordable prices in an equitable way and for allowing multinationals too much power. No matter what the definition, most agree that globalization is a permanent fixture of the 21st century.

Czinkota and Ronkainen (2004) identify drivers of globalization – market factors, cost factors, environmental factors and competitive factors:

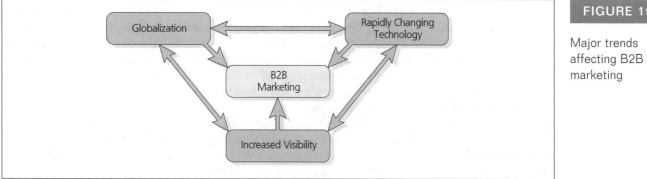

FIGURE 19.1

Major trends affecting B2B marketing

- *Market factors* – More and more the world customer is becoming a real factor and products can be designed to meet similar needs of customers throughout the world. In addition, customers are expecting both higher quality of service as well as customization. They see fewer real product differences and are less brand loyal (Kotler 2003).

- *Cost factors* – cost efficiencies and the avoidance of duplication of effort are two important drivers of globalization. Developing new products has become more and more expensive so that firms must look to a very large market in order to justify the cost of development.

- *Environmental factors* – the removal of various barriers to trade and improved communications are also driving firms toward seeing markets globally.

- *Competitive factors* – when a competitor is marketing its products in many nations throughout the world a firm must react to match these competitive strategies and tactics and prevent the competitor from securing an unassailable advantage. A firm must seek global competitive advantage rather than just national advantage.

Recent developments call into question the continued pace of globalization. Frequently, less developed countries are asking for major changes in the ways that the developed world deals with them in trade agreements. Especially important are:

1 Governmental agricultural subsidies given to farmers in the EU, United States and Japan that essentially keep out agricultural products exported from the developing world.

2 Dumping regulations (that have also been used to protect indigenous industries in developed countries).

3 Intellectual property rules that also have the same effect (Czinkota and Ronkainen 2004).

Protectionist pressure now seen in the US as well as the EU and the new, more aggressive approaches from Asian and Latin American countries may slow the pace of globalization considerably. Should this pace slow, the business marketing manager will have to recognize the opportunities some trade barriers may provide for securing protected markets through intelligent selection of the market entry strategy. While in the long run increasing globalization might make marketing business products around the world more effective, a wise manager will watch these trends carefully and take advantage of opportunities that present themselves.

Rapidly changing technology

A second important trend is rapidly changing technology, especially in electronics and telecommunications. One need only pick up any newspaper or view any television program in nearly any part of the world to see the impact of technology. The Internet, of course, is the most important technological event impacting business marketing. But the advent of the cell phone, faster and lower-cost computers, as well as the continuing reduction in the size of components of every kind are all critical technological advances. These technologies improve communications and management within the firm and with suppliers and distributors. They also allow for higher quality products and customization to meet customer needs.

Technology not only makes products better and adds to visibility, but also provides many more vehicles for contacting the customer. Only a decade ago, tried and true methods of marketing communications like trade shows, catalogues, trade magazine advertising and mailings were adequate to reach potential customers and provide leads to the salesforce. Now, a good website is an absolutely essential weapon in the marketing communications arsenal. Unfortunately, the advent of the website has not reduced the need for the other forms of communications. In fact, one of the ironies of the Internet is that other forms of communications are required to drive customers to the firm's website.

In other words, a website alone is not enough. One of this book's authors carried out research with architects which showed that they expect up-to-date and user-friendly websites while continuing to want printed catalogs and the ability to get specific advice from a manufacturer, either through a local sales rep, or factory technical support on the other end of a toll-free telephone line.

A well-designed website also helps a firm to serve a large number of smaller volume customers in a more effective manner. If these customers can be convinced to order direct from the website, the salesforce can be focused on the largest volume opportunities.

One intriguing new trend is that of webcasting, sometimes called push technology. Webcasting has been defined as a way of updating news or other selected information on a computer user's desktop through periodic transmission over the Internet. However, the Hyper Dictionary (2003), defines webcasting as 'real transmission of encoded video under the control of the server to multiple recipients who all receive content at the same time (in contrast to normal web browsing)'. In some definitions, webcasting implies sending information to be viewed by users at their own convenience. In any event, this new and more powerful way to send information is used by B2B marketers who, once they have established an e-list of their most important customers and other buying center members, can announce new products or services or provide other important information to selected segments as required.

On-line auctions and exchanges have received some attention lately, as providing a model for future B2B dealings. These exchanges allow buyers to source products at the lowest prices and to have access to a very wide range of potential suppliers. However, the exchange model for B2B transactions on the Internet is flawed (Wise and Morrison 2002). Firstly, the emphasis on obtaining the best price runs counter to the relationship marketing paradigm which is regarded as the best current thinking on how buyer-seller relationships should work. Secondly, these on-line exchanges offer little to suppliers. Although they gain access to a wide range of new buyers, the transactions are likely to be unprofitable since the lowest bidder gets the sale. Thirdly, the firms running the on-line exchanges have very little understanding of the needs of the buyers or the sellers.

Increased visibility

There is no question that firms are now being subjected to far greater visibility. The growth in the number of media outlets corresponding to the growing number of investors have made business a popular subject for far more individuals than in the past. Institutions are responding, providing firms with the ability to show their good intentions. The web allows facts or rumors to spread very quickly across the world. Firms concerned about reputation management monitor the web and are pro-active in providing corrective information.

As Whysall (2000) notes, interest in marketing ethics is markedly greater than ever before. Perhaps one of the most obvious ways in which firms' actions are becoming more visible is the establishment of the UN's Global Compact. The Global Compact, first proposed in 2000 by Kofi Annan, Secretary General of the United Nations, lays out nine principles in the areas of human rights, labor and the environment which firms are invited to adapt as core values 'within their sphere of influence' (*International Herald Tribune* 2001). According to the United Nations, over 1000 companies are participating in this compact as of October 2003 (UN Global Compact 2003). While the Compact has no regulatory mechanism or enforcement capabilities, the basic idea is to establish worldwide peer pressure for firms so that the adoption of these principles is a prudent action. According to Jagdesh Bahagwati (*International Herald Tribune* 2001), the Global Compact is one of a series of actions to increase social responsibility by companies. The others include mandatory and voluntary home and host country codes.

Sustainability has become another important issue related to visibility. The World Business Council for Sustainable Development is one business association focusing on this issue and the Global Reporting Initiative allows firms to say what they have been doing to address sustainability or environmental problems throughout the world (Kolk 2002).

Unfortunately, the increasing visibility has also encouraged terrorists. As we have seen, on that terrible day, September 11th 2001, a small band of dedicated suicidal individuals can gain worldwide attention. This is often done by attacking business targets in a particular nation. In today's world, marketing executives must give at least some thought to security when planning events and attempt to balance clever creativity in communications with possible negative reactions.

■ Latest thinking

Partly as a response to the trends described above, marketing scholars and managers have been rethinking some of the basic assumptions about marketing. In the sections that follow, we have described some newer thinking that may change a manager's perspective on the future of marketing.

Product development

The acceleration of the international product lifecycle, that is now reduced to as little as months or even weeks, means firms must accelerate product development. In addition, management must design for a global market when moving new products through the development process. But, this does not necessarily mean complete standardization. As we have mentioned, technology allows for customization even for narrow market segments. Responding to the challenge of faster development requirements, the most advanced firms have reduced the time they need to bring a product from the idea stage to commercialization.

The basis of this new approach, according to Holman *et al.* (2003) is the way product and process information is used throughout the development cycle. Instead of a sequential process, these firms have adopted a flexible approach. Holman *et al.* claim that using a standard product development approach as much as one-third of the time is spent doing unnecessary work or waiting for information. To optimise the process, the team decides on the most important information it will need and attempts to get those answers as quickly as possible.

One example is the development of prototypes. In the standard approach, the prototype team would attempt to make the best possible model of the product. In order to do this the team needs detailed product specifications that are normally only available late in the development cycle. It will then require some time to construct the model. However, in the more efficient approach, the team decides what information it requires from the prototypes and they are designed to elicit this information. This may result in a simpler model that can be produced at a much earlier stage in the cycle.

Another key to the success of this process is the leader. Leaders of the newer process are vital since they must decide which are the most important activities the team should undertake and also which activities are unnecessary. (Above adapted from Czinkota and Ronkainen 2004; Holman *et al.* 2003.)

Post-modern marketing

Post-modernism as a philosophical movement appears to cause considerable confusion; Stephen Brown's (1998) book on this subject makes a brave attempt to clarify the topic, but he admits the difficulty of doing so in a mere 100,000 words. Even the avowed founders of the post-modernist movement have subsequently repudiated their involvement with it, which is in itself a typically post-modernist action.

The modernist view that the world holds certainties which can be discovered by the scientific approach has been called into question; chaos theory implies that the future is unpredictable and that therefore planning should be replaced by preparation, for example. Post-modernism, on the other hand, has the features shown in Table 19.1.

While it is inextricably modernist to do so, it is feasible to examine the marketing philosophy and developments in marketing and recognize post-modernist features. For example, markets have become more fragmented and individualistic and relationship marketing (and database marketing) are attempting to recognize this and provide working day-to-day solutions. De-differentiation is evidenced in marketing campaigns using classical music or great works of art and indeed the reverse (marketing imagery displayed as art – e.g. Andy Warhol's soup cans). The borderline between advertising and entertainment has long been eroded by television and in the B2B arena has been eroded by exhibitions, trade fairs and seminars or conferences which take place in exotic locations. Hyperreality is evidenced by virtual reality and also by retailers who indulge in a hyperreal price war which isn't really taking place (Brown and Quinn 1994).

The chronology issue is increasingly exemplified by some marketers' obsession with the past; the nostalgic recreation of old designs, of 'traditional recipes' and of 'real' products is typified by the replacement of 'new improved' on packages with 'as good now as it's always been'. In business markets, some firms promote themselves as being 'newer than tomorrow' while others (notably financial service providers) emphasize their traditional values and solid background.

In the B2B arena, postmodernism can explain the blurring of boundaries between companies. Traditional thinking has been that one company is a buyer, while the other is a seller. The current trend towards establishing long-term relationships between firms means that some companies are in buyer-seller relationships, whereas others have progressed to the point of being joint-venture partners in establishing a value-chain. This is much more in accord with post-modern views.

TABLE 19.1 Features of post-modernism

Feature	Explanation
Pastiche	Most human activities are composed of elements of many disciplines and are usually made up of previously-known elements. Nothing is new: everything has already been written and we are merely recombining old ideas in different ways.
Fragmentation	There is an omnipresence of disjointed moments and experiences in life and sense of self. The world is dynamic and therefore people cannot be permanently assigned to groups: people shift attitudes, behavior and intentions too frequently. In other words, life is not a coherent dialogue, but is rather a series of sound bites.
Hyperreality	There is a constitution of social reality through hype or simulation and this is powerfully signified and represented. There is a confusion of the borders between reality and simulation (Baudrillard 1983).
Chronology	Time is often reversed: the latest model might be based on an old design (e.g. the Chrysler PSV), or the latest fashion in design becomes futuristic. Much depends on era: in the 1950s and 1960s design fashions were futuristic, whereas in the early 21st century the fashions are retro. The world is not progressing towards anything: everything happens in the 'now'.
De-differentiation	The differences between aspects of society are gradually being eroded. The distinction between chemistry and physics, between art and science, between music and the written word, are all broken down in the post-modern view. In other words, there is a blurring of boundaries.
Reversal of consumption and production	The current cultural assumption is that we define ourselves by what we consume, not by what we produce. Production is low in importance, consumption is high in importance.
Anti-foundationalism	This is also described as anti-authoritarianism. Established rules and models are seen as suitable targets for attack, lampoon and satire.
Pluralism	The acceptance of difference in styles and culture without making judgments about superiority or inferiority. This has become a feature of Western societies, growing out of the hippy movement of the late 1960s and early 1970s.
Acceptance of disorder and chaos	Unlike modernists, post-modernists accept that chaos is a natural concomitant of change. It is therefore the natural order of things, the common state of existence. Modernists seek to create order out of chaos: post-modernists see this as futile.
Emphasis on form and style rather than content	Meaning is determined by the form rather than the content. An academic paper may contain the same information as a novel, but the message to the reader is different and the values conveyed are vastly different.

Boundaries are further blurred by the fact that the same firms may collaborate in one market while they compete in another. No one firm has the ability to fully compete in all markets – as a result, smart managers are choosing their opportunities for both cooperation (through strategic alliances or other arrangements) or competition.

Anti-foundationalism commonly expresses itself in avant-garde marketing techniques and innovative approaches to doing business. Since most marketers aim to differentiate their products by doing something the competition is not doing, there is an emphasis on achieving competitive advantage by breaking the rules – the essence of anti-foundationalism.

The post-modernist view is not easily understood and still less is it easy to apply to marketing issues. As a philosophy it has much to offer in understanding current trends, however.

Value-based marketing

Value-based marketing is the almost single-handed creation of Peter Doyle (2000). Starting from the premise that the central task of management is to maximize shareholder value, the theory goes on to look at how this affects marketing thinking and action.

Maximizing shareholder value is not the same as maximizing profits. Maximizing profits is often a short-term, tactical process involving cutting costs, reducing investment, downsizing, increasing sales volumes at the expense of long-term customer loyalty and so forth. Shareholder value is about creating a long-term, secure and growing investment. Increased sophistication among investors has led them to look for long-term growth prospects rather than short-term profits. The risk of speculating in firms with spectacular profits but little underlying substance has become well-known and stock exchange analysts look more and more towards using measures such as customer loyalty, brand awareness and investment levels in judging whether stocks are likely to increase in value in the long term. Because speculation is so dangerous, investors look for stocks which they will own for the long term.

Unfortunately for the investors, the shifting global marketplace means that companies do not survive long. The life expectancy of a firm is now less than 20 years (De Geus 1997). Maintaining a profitable competitive advantage is likely to be even more elusive: as soon as it becomes apparent that a firm has found a profitable niche, competitors enter the market and profits are rapidly eroded until they reach the point where the company is unable to maintain an adequate return on its original capital investment (Black *et al.* 1998).

Obviously some companies are exceptions to this general trend. Large, well-established firms seem able to maintain their shareholder value year after year, using profits to increase capital value rather than pay dividends. Such blue-chip companies are regarded as safe investments because they maintain steady growth, even if the dividends are unexciting. In fact, for some investors a small dividend is a sign that the company is reinvesting profits rather than distributing them imprudently. Even such companies are not immune from environmental shifts and often the weight of their carefully calculated strategic plans helps to bear them down. Recent examples include the Welsh water supplier, Hyder, which (despite being in an industry that is regarded as virtually bullet-proof) managed to become unprofitable and uncompetitive. The problems faced by Swissair during 2001 are another example.

When an airline gets to the point where planes are grounded because of unpaid fuel bills, matters have become serious. For marketers, the idea that the company exists to increase shareholder value may seem to fly in the face of the customer-oriented, high-service approach which has been advocated by marketing academics for the past 50 years. In fact, customer orientation does not necessarily mean that the company gives the customers everything they want: it does mean that the company ensures that customers are satisfied and loyal in order to maximize the long-term survival potential of the firm.

Because marketers have focused almost exclusively on the customers, while other (often more senior) managers have focused on the shareholders, marketing thinking has not realized its early promise and has been met with suspicion at boardroom level. In fact, marketing can and will fulfill the objective of maximizing shareholder value once marketers accept that the customers and consumers are the means to an end rather than the end in themselves.

Doyle (2000) has offered an alternative definition of marketing that encompasses this view.

Marketing is the management process that seeks to maximize returns to shareholders by developing and implementing strategies to build relationships of trust with high-value customers and to create a sustainable differential advantage.

This definition has the advantage of removing profitability from the equation and substituting shareholder value. It also includes an oblique reference to the relationship marketing perspective. However, it is certainly not hard to imagine successful firms which do not bother to build long-term relationships and which do very nicely from dealing with a large number of low-value customers. The point here is that loyalty is important for building shareholder value (hence the relationship marketing focus) and low-value customers tend not to be loyal.

Relationship marketing has also not fulfilled its early promise in consumer markets, although it has been successful in B2B markets. Establishing relationships of trust is easier in an environment where the benefits are obvious to all concerned: in consumer markets the benefits are often obscured. Consumers do not necessarily want to establish a relationship with the companies who supply their needs and many people are irritated by firms' attempts to move the relationship beyond the business level. In B2B markets, the advantages of forming close strategic alliances are much more obvious.

Growth is essential in a shareholder-driven company, because growth in the value of the shares (rather than the dividends) is what investors seek. Therefore it is the central factor in creating shareholder value. For marketers, this means an emphasis on two possible strategies: firstly, recruiting more customers, and secondly selling more to the customers who are already on board. In the past, transactional marketing has concentrated on the former, whereas relationship marketing focuses on the latter. It seems likely that both are necessary if the firm is to achieve the levels of growth that shareholders require. In these conditions, the use of existing customers as recruiters for other customers becomes a desirable tactic and thus the emphasis again shifts to delighting customers.

This does not necessarily mean offering customers more and more for less and less – that way lies bankruptcy. For example, Viglen is the UKs largest computer manufacturer, but the company only deals with business markets. The computers supplied for educational establishments are cheap and basic, with few frills or refinements – they are widely used in education because budgets are tight and the need for all the 'bells and whistles' is small. Viglen's customers are, however, delighted to be able to obtain the basic equipment at a low price.

Much of the value that will be added to the shareholder's assets will be through growth in the brand value. This is the key area which marketers are able to influence. Increases in brand value reveal themselves in four ways, as shown in Table 19.2.

The difference in orientation between aiming for an increase in shareholder value and aiming for an increase in customer satisfaction is a small one. It is really a difference in focus rather than a new philosophy altogether: a key focus for marketers is the twofold problem of how to increase the brand value and how to cash in on the increased value in the long term. Simply harvesting profits is not the way forward – reinvesting profits in further building of the brand, or in other ventures, is realistic and will increase the shareholder value.

Possibly the most important of the tactical decisions that spring from this difference in perspective is that of deciding which brands to keep and which to drop. Previously this decision would have been made on the basis of the BCG Matrix or some similar tool, but under a value-adding regime the decision will more likely be made on the basis of the growth potential for each brand rather than the current profitability or sales status. This may give different answers from those obtained from a BCG analysis.

TABLE 19.2 Aspects of brand value

Aspect	Examples and Explanation
Obtain higher prices	A well-known brand can command higher prices because it reduces risk for the consumers. Most major brands follow this approach to deriving value from the brand: Mercedes trucks and IBM computers are more expensive than their competitors, but the companies justify this by offering a high-quality, reliable product.
Higher volume growth	By keeping prices competitive, a brand owner can increase the amount of business done. This is the approach taken by Dell, and Iveco trucks.
Lower costs	If a brand achieves a large market share, many of the marketing costs are amortized across a larger production run. The marketing costs for a major brand may well be lower per unit of production than the costs for a less well-known brand.
Higher asset utilization	A major brand which follows a high-volume strategy will make better use of production assets. A brand which goes for a high-price strategy will generate greater returns on assets.

> ### TALKING POINT
>
> Alan Sugar once said 'We just want your money!' This refreshing honesty towards customers is rare – most firms talk about customers as if they owned the place, which of course they don't – shareholders do.
>
> So if shareholders own the firm, why aren't we more honest about this? Why should mission statements not say, 'Our shareholders come first. We want to please them more than anything – so what do we have to do for you so you will help us please our shareholders?'
>
> In business, most people accept that everybody is out for themselves – it's a dog-eat-dog world. Are customers so sensitive that we need to mollycoddle them? Or is it just that we are following the marketing dogma and paying lip service to the idea of customer centrality?

Value-based marketing offers a somewhat different perspective and at the very least a change of emphasis. In fact, earlier definitions of what marketing is all about centered on profit – all value-based marketing has added is the concept of substituting shareholder value for profit. In this scenario, customer satisfaction is seen as a means to an end, but whether the end is profit or capital growth is debatable. Either way, it may explain why the marketing concept has not really been accepted at Board level.

Relationship marketing

Currently, relationship marketing has failed to deliver in consumer markets, but appears to have scored notable successes in the B2B arena. Recent research has offered a number of new insights, as follows:

1 The relationship between satisfaction and customer loyalty appears to be weaker in a highly-relational exchange (Homburg *et al.* 2003). This implies that establishing a long-term, deep relationship has more effect on loyalty than offering customer satisfaction in terms of product or service delivery.

2 Organizational infrastructures have a marked effect on salespeople's ability to establish relationships with other firms (Dubinsky *et al.* 2003).

3 The marriage analogy continues to be used when discussing relationship marketing (Stoltman and Morgan 2002).

4 Relationships can be regarded as an asset of the firm, albeit a risky asset (Hogan and Armstrong 2001). Interestingly, this paper also regards increased shareholder value as being the main aim for the corporation.

This focus on relationship marketing may be a result of an increasing desire to create stability in an unstable world, or it may be a way of simplifying the complex problems created by managing the value-chain.

■ The twenty-first century marketplace

In the B2B area, four formative trends have been identified (Wise and Morrison 2002). These are:

1 *The move from simple to complex transactions* – Twenty years ago, a typical B2B transaction involved a single purchase, paid for with money. Currently, transactions may involve several companies on the supply side (offering a single product made up of service and physical attributes) and even several cooperating companies on the purchasing side, each wanting something different from the deal. For example, consider the position of the consortium of civil engineering companies that built the Channel Tunnel. The financing package for the Tunnel involved corporate shareholders, private individuals and banks. This meant that a wide range of finance industry companies needed to become involved in the deal, each of whom hoped to establish a longer-term relationship with the various consortium members in order

to transact deals in other parts of the civil engineering world. The situation was made more complex by the fact that the consortium was drawn from both French and British companies.

2 *The move from middleman to speculator* – As profit margins are driven down by intensifying competition, the on-line exchanges will need to consider speculating in the products on offer on-line. Instead of merely brokering deals, they are likely to become involved in the actual transactions themselves, as a way of generating revenue. One of the difficulties of trading on the Internet is that people have the perception that it should be free, which leaves Internet providers without an income. Speculation may be the answer.

3 *The move from transactions to solutions* – Creative companies can use the Internet and their relationships with the rest of the value chain to offer more than just a product. Integrated firms can (and will) offer tailored solutions to their customers' problems.

4 *The move towards sell-side swaps* – Rather than go through the procedures for setting up a buy-sell transaction, some firms are now using the Internet to exchange products or services. For example, the trucking business is one in which trucks often travel empty or with part-loads. This is clearly inefficient: the cost of running the truck is virtually the same whether it travels empty or full, so several internet sites now exist where trucking companies, instead of competing against each other for loads, are able to exchange loads to ensure that the trucks run full. This is especially important for small operators, some of whom are owner-drivers with only one truck. These on-line swaps enable them to compete with the major haulage companies.

If these predictions are correct, the B2B world is likely to become less competitive and more cooperative, less transactional and more relational, less secretive and more sharing.

The importance of basics

Despite the trends described above, the findings of one important study focus on the basics. In its Trends Study 2005, the Institute for the Study of Business Markets (ISBM) at Pennsylvania State University asks leading B2B marketers in the US to identify the most important challenges facing them (ISBM 2003). The respondents identified the following (listed in order of importance):

- Better organize and market the marketing function itself.
- Get right the basics of market segmentation, targeting and positioning.
- Refine the marketing budget process and metrics.
- Build markets through higher customer-value solutions.
- Better manage changing distribution channel relationships.
- Deploy the power of business-to-business brands.
- Compete more aggressively in global markets.
- Master e-Business tools.

The Institute for the Study of Business Markets, Smeal College of Business, Penn State. Used with permission.

The need to improve the marketing function, to 'sell' the benefits of the function and to be able to successfully implement the most basic marketing tasks – segmentation, targeting and positioning – have been consistent themes of these studies conducted every other year.

■ Conclusion

Overall, marketing in the 21st century presents many new challenges. Shrinking markets, green issues, runaway advances in communications technology, and rapidly-changing public attitudes towards consumption and communication predicate major changes not only in marketing techniques but in corporate strategy. The role of marketing is still, at the end of the day, to meet customers' needs in the most effective, efficient and sustainable way possible for as long as it is possible to do so. Marketers will need to re-examine their models of marketing strategy many times; in an era where change is the only constant, marketing cannot afford to stand still. Ultimately, the firms who take the greatest care of their customers' interests are the ones most likely to maintain their competitive edge in a cut-throat world. Yet the basics will always be vital to success.

The rapid change in the marketing environment and the many responses to it indicate that a good marketer must have a combination of skills. They will not only need specific knowledge of marketing techniques which we have described throughout this text, but will also need to develop such timeless skills identified by Chonko (2004) as written and verbal communication, decision-making, analytical skills, listening, creative and critical thinking skills. An individual who has these skills and the ability to learn will not be at a disadvantage when new environments present themselves. That individual will be able to combine the skills and knowledge already learned with new skills required to address the problems of these new environments.

SUMMARY

Three major trends will be affecting B2B marketing in the foreseeable future: globalization, rapidly changing technology and increased visibility. Each of these trends will have an impact on how marketing is accomplished and each of the trends affects the others as well.
The key points from this chapter are:

- While described in many ways globalization essentially means improved, less difficult trade and growing similarities of market segments.

- Four drivers of globalization are market, cost, environmental and competitive factors.

- Technologies and improving communications will allow for higher quality products which more closely meet customer needs.

- The website is a critical tool in marketing communications because good or bad information can be passed around quickly.

- A firm must pay more attention to what is said about it on the web. Increased visibility means a firm must think about the impression it is making.

- There are many avenues available to firms to show their good intentions. One important one is the UN's Global Compact.

- Product development is speeding up as a result of the pressures for faster introductions of new products.

- Post-modernism is a factor in today's marketing. According to post-modernism, planning should be replaced by preparation.

- Post-modernism reinforces the idea that good managers know when to collaborate and when to compete.

- Value-based marketing is another important trend which emphasizes the building of long-term shareholder value rather than short-term profit maximization. This requires building customer loyalty and brand awareness.

- Relationship marketing continues to be vital in the B2B area. Relationships should be seen as an asset of the firm.

- The old idea that manufacturers dominate markets is being replaced by the domination of customers.

- The basics of marketing – segmenting, targeting and positioning – remain as important today as at any time.

- The most well-prepared marketing executive will have developed specific skills about marketing but also 'timeless skills' which can be used to learn about new environments as and when they present themselves.

REVIEW QUESTIONS

1   Describe the three major trends affecting B2B marketing.

2   What are the specific effects of each one of these trends?

3   What is post-modern marketing and how can it affect marketing decisions?

4   How has product development been changed to meet the needs of fast-changing global markets?

5   What is the difference between a shareholder-driven and a profit-driven company?

6   What are the essential ingredients of improving shareholder value?

7   What are some of the new developments in relationship marketing?

8   Describe the levels of integration of marketing communications.

9   What marketing basics do B2B marketers feel are critical in 2005?

10   What are the most important timeless skills?

REFERENCES

http://iroi.seu.edu.cn/books/ee_dic/whatis/webcasti.htm, accessed 12/6/03

http://www.hyperdictionary.com/computing/webcasting, accessed 12/6/03

Baudrillard, J. (1983) *Simulations*, New York: Semiotext(e).

Black, A., Wright, P. and Bachman, J. E. (1998) *In Search of Shareholder Value*, London: Pitman.

Brown, S. (1998) *Postmodern Marketing 2,* London: Thomson.

Brown, S. and Quinn, B. 'Re-inventing the retailing wheel: a postmodern morality tale', in P. J. Goldrick (ed) (2000) *Cases in Retail Management*, London: Pitman Publishing.

Chonko, L. B. (2004) 'Marketing Education in the 21st Century: A look to the future of marketing education: observations of one teacher-researcher curmudgeon', *Marketing Education Review*, 13: 1: 1–18.

Czinkota, M. R. and Ronkainen, I. A. (2004) *International Marketing*, Mason, Ohio: South-Western Publishing.

De Geus, A. (1997) *The Living Company*, Boston MA: Harvard Business School Press.

Doyle, P. (2000) *Value-Based Marketing: Marketing Strategies for Corporate Growth and Shareholder Value*, London: Wiley.

Dubinsky, A., Chonko L. B., Jones, E. P. and Roberts, J. A. (2003) 'Development of a relationship selling mindset: organisational influencers', *Journal of Business to Business Marketing*, 10: 1–29.

Dunning, J. H. (2003) 'The Moral Imperatives of Global Capitalism: An Overview', in *Making Globalization Good*, Dunning, J. H., ed., Oxford: Oxford University Press.

Friedman, T. L. (2000) *The Lexus and the Olive Tree*, New York: Anchor Books.

Hogan, J. E. and Armstrong, G. (2001) 'Toward a resource-based theory of business exchange relationships: the role of relational asset value', *Journal of Business to Business Marketing*, 8: 3–27.

Holman, R., Hans-Werner, K. and Keeling, D. (2003) 'The future of product development', *McKinsey Quarterly*, 3: 28–40.

Homburg, C., Giering, A. and Menon, A. (2003) 'Relationship characteristics as moderators of the satisfaction-loyalty link: findings in a business to business context', *Journal of Business to Business Marketing*, 10: 3: 35–61.

Kolk, A. (2002) 'Multinational and Corporate Social Accountability', *Insights* (Academy of International Business), 2: 4: 12.

Kotler, P. (2003) *Marketing Management*, Upper Saddle River, NJ: Prentice-Hall.

Olivia, R. *ISBN Trends Study in 2005,* Unpublished, ISBM.org (used by permission).

Stoltman, J. J. and Morgan, F. W. (2002) 'Extending the Marriage Metaphor as a Way to View Marketing Relationships', *Journal of Business to Business Marketing*, 9: 49–76.

Whysall, P. (2000) 'Marketing Ethics – An Overview', *The Marketing Review*, 1: 175–195.

Wise, R. and Morrison, D. (2000) 'Beyond the exchange: the future of B2B', *Harvard Business Review*, November-December: 86–96.

APPENDIX: FOREIGN EXCHANGE

Marketing managers operating around the world will frequently be faced with the prospect of selling in a local currency. While the letter of credit is a common form of payment (described elsewhere in the text), it is often necessary to sell product in the currency of the buyer. Therefore, an international manager must be familiar with the foreign exchange process.

In the simplest terms, the exchange rate shown everyday in most newspapers is the price of one country's currency in terms of another country's currency.

There is no single foreign exchange rate for trading one currency into another and there is no single place of exchange such as a stock market where this takes place. In reality, the exchange of currency takes place electronically, mostly between banks throughout the world. At any one time the exchange rate between currencies may vary slightly for each transaction. Nevertheless, many newspapers print rates derived from particular sources at a particular time.

TABLE A1 Currency rates

CURRENCIES, BONDS & INTEREST RATES

CURRENCY RATES

FINANCIAL TIMES FRIDAY JANUARY 30 2004

Jan 29

Country / Term	Currency	DOLLAR Closing mid	DOLLAR Day's change	EURO Closing mid	EURO Day's change	POUND Closing mid	POUND Day's change
Argentina	(Peso)	2.9100	-0.0100	3.6001	-0.0756	5.2764	-0.0691
Australia	(A$)	1.3154	+0.0277	1.6274	+0.0065	2.3851	+0.0278
One Month				1.6319	+0.0068	2.3881	+0.0281
One Year				1.6845	+0.0065	2.4153	+0.0287
Bahrain	(Dinar)	0.3770		0.4664	-0.0082	0.6836	-0.0066
Bolivia	(Boliviano)	7.8610	+0.0010	9.7253	-0.1689	14.2536	-0.1353
Brazil	(R$)	2.9440	+0.0650	3.6422	+0.0181	5.3381	-0.0676
Canada	(C$)	1.3350	+0.0109	1.6516	-0.0152	2.4207	-0.0033
One Month		1.3365	+0.0108	1.6521	-0.0154	2.4179	-0.0038
Three Month		1.3396	+0.0109	1.6531	-0.0152	2.4107	-0.0036
One Year		1.3487	+0.0111	1.6553	-0.0143	2.3736	-0.0009
Chile	(Peso)	598.250	+10.8500	740.125	+0.7060	1084.75	+9.4300
Colombia	(Peso)	2743.50	+20.80	3394.12	-33.22	4974.51	-9.80
Costa Rica	(Colon)	421.680	+1.600	521.682	-8.9280	764.590	-7.0660
Czech Rep.	(Koruna)	26.9268	-0.5704	33.3125	+0.1350	48.8237	+0.5743
One Month		26.9462	-0.5703	33.3090	+0.1333	48.7462	+0.5667
One Year		27.1653	-0.5609	33.3394	+0.1307	47.8041	+0.5733
Denmark	(DKr)	6.0213	+0.1037	7.4493	+0.0001	10.9178	+0.0847
One Month		6.0266	+0.1038	7.4496	-0.0001	10.9021	+0.0833
Three Month		6.0371	+0.1037	7.4501	-0.0003	10.8642	+0.0823
One Year		6.0738	+0.1022	7.4543	+0.0003	10.6883	+0.0869
Egypt	(Egypt £)	6.1650	+0.0100	7.6271	-0.1208	11.1784	-0.0892
Estonia	(Kroon)	12.6472	+0.2175	15.6465		22.9319	-0.1775
Hong Kong	(HK$)	7.7743	+0.0073	9.6180	-0.1591	14.0963	-0.1224
One Month		7.7684	+0.0071	9.6027	-0.1595	14.0531	-0.1241
Three Month		7.756	+0.0078	9.5712	-0.1578	13.9573	-0.1222
One Year		7.718	+0.0112	9.4722	-0.1477	13.5818	-0.1001
Hungary	(Forint)	214.364	+5.8960	265.200	+2.7800	388.684	+7.0510
One Month		216.359	+6.0160	267.4469	+2.8764	391.396	+7.1730
One Year		235.429	+6.6910	288.9370	+2.6677	414.296	+7.1510
India	(Rs)	45.3050	-0.0050	56.0491	-0.9871	82.1470	-0.7998
One Month		45.3625	-0.0200	56.0738	-1.0004	82.0614	-0.8364
One Year		45.6425	-0.0825	56.0161	-1.0596	80.3194	-0.8562
Indonesia	(Rupiah)	8430.50	+13.00	10429.80	-166.10	15286.20	-123.30
One Month				10421.17	-166.38	15250.92	-124.87
One Year				10346.58	-160.46	14835.59	-108.00
Iran	(Rial)	8374.00	+10.00	10359.90	-168.70	15183.70	-127.90
Israel	(Shk)	4.4810	-0.0010	5.5437	-0.0983	8.1250	-0.0800
Japan	(Y)	106.020	+0.4850	131.163	-1.6840	192.235	-0.9630
One Month		105.93	+0.4850	130.9390	-1.6897	191.62	-0.9930
Three Month		105.71	+0.4750	130.4491	-1.6929	190.23	-1.0030
One Year		104.485	+0.3300	128.2324	-1.7797	183.87	-1.0380

Country / Term	Currency	DOLLAR Closing mid	DOLLAR Day's change	EURO Closing mid	EURO Day's change	POUND Closing mid	POUND Day's change
Kenya	(Shilling)	76.5000	-0.0400	94.6420	-1.7066	138.710	-1.4080
Kuwait	(Dinar)	0.2948		0.3647	-0.0064	0.5346	-0.0051
One Month		0.295		0.3647	-0.0064	0.5337	-0.0052
One Year		0.2975	-0.0003	0.3652	-0.0065	0.5236	-0.0051
Malaysia	(M$)	3.8000		4.7012	-0.0823	6.8902	-0.0663
Mexico	(New Peso)	11.0955	+0.1755	13.7268	-0.0193	20.1184	-0.1277
One Month		11.1297	+0.1797	13.7578	-0.0151	20.1339	-0.1321
Three Month		11.21	+0.1808	13.8337	-0.0152	20.1733	-0.1315
One Year		11.6405	+0.1925	14.2862	-0.0036	20.4845	+0.1608
New Zealand	(NZ$)	1.4964	+0.0201	1.8514	-0.0070	2.7134	-0.0107
One Month				1.8562	-0.0066	2.7165	-0.0112
One Year				1.9188	-0.0038	2.7514	-0.0170
Nigeria	(Naira)	137.000	-0.1500	169.490	-3.1540	248.408	-2.6660
Norway	(NKr)	7.0610	-0.1639	8.7603	-0.1764	12.8392	-0.7147
One Month		7.0968	-0.1641	8.7602	-0.1747	12.8201	
Three Month		7.0982	-0.1637	8.7595	-0.1727	12.7736	
One Year		7.1378	-0.1591	8.7600	-0.1715	12.5606	
Pakistan	(Rupee)	57.3850	-0.0650	70.9939	-1.1606	104.051	
Peru	(New Sol)	3.4993	-0.0166	4.3292	-0.0549	6.3449	
Philippines	(Peso)	56.0550	-0.2000	69.3485	-0.9618	101.639	
One Month		56.314	-0.1990	69.6113	-0.9703	101.873	
Three Month		56.932	-0.2130	70.2567	-0.9628	102.453	
One Year		59.896	-0.1745	73.5092	-1.0375	105.402	
Poland	(Zloty)	3.8461	-0.0710	4.7582	-0.0061	6.9737	+0.0629
One Month		3.859	-0.0717	4.7703	-0.0066	6.981	+0.0629
One Year		4.0041	-0.0689	4.9142	+0.0021	7.0461	-0.0601
Romania	(Leu)	32873.90	+537.50	40670.00	-35.00	59607.00	+410.50
Russia	(Rouble)	28.5018	-0.0213	35.2610	-0.5903	51.6795	-0.4584
One Month			-0.0001	4.6597	-0.0811	6.8000	-0.0654
One Year			-0.0811	4.6370	-0.0811	6.786	-0.0660
Saudi Arabia	(SR)	3.7503	-0.0001	4.6235	-0.0785	6.6294	-0.0581
One Month		3.7513	-0.0002				
Singapore	(S$)	3.7673	-0.0087	2.1024	-0.0257	3.0812	-0.0176
One Month		1.6993	-0.0086	2.1001	-0.0250	3.0733	-0.0156
One Year		1.6988	-0.0082	2.0773		2.9785	-0.0115
Slovakia	(Koruna)	32.9427	-0.6222	40.7550	-0.7000	59.7317	-0.5642
One Month		33.0652	-0.6272	40.8728	-0.0722	59.8154	-0.5627
One Year		34.1037	-0.5332	41.8548	-0.0492	60.014	-0.4163
Slovenia	(Tolar)	191.915	-3.3250	237.428	-0.0310	347.980	+2.7380
South Africa	(R)	7.0512	-0.1162	8.7235	-0.0063	12.7853	-0.0897
One Month		7.0939	-0.1159	8.7691	-0.0078	12.8331	
Three Month		7.1862	-0.1147	8.8682	-0.0112	12.9322	+0.0622
One Year		7.6012	-0.1200	9.3289	-0.0095	13.3763	

Country / Term	Currency	DOLLAR Closing mid	DOLLAR Day's change	EURO Closing mid	EURO Day's change	POUND Closing mid	POUND Day's change
South Korea	(Won)	1172.50	+10.00	1450.56	-24.12	2125.98	-18.63
One Month		1175.65	+1.10	1453.25	-24.10	2126.77	-18.72
Three Month		1180.40	+1.85	1456.67	-23.18	2124.22	-17.38
One Year		1194.15	+1.70	1465.56	-22.90	2101.41	-15.55
Sweden	(SKr)	7.4203	+0.1618	9.1800	+0.0430	13.4544	-0.1666
One Month		7.4297	+0.1622	9.1840	+0.0429	13.4402	-0.1649
Three Month		7.4485	+0.1621	9.1918	+0.0426	13.404	-0.1635
One Year		7.5148	+0.1593	9.2228	+0.0414	13.3241	-0.1658
Switzerland	(SFr)	1.2624	+0.0152	1.5618	-0.0082	2.2890	-0.0058
One Month		1.2615	+0.0151	1.5594	-0.0083	2.2822	-0.0055
Three Month		1.2596	+0.0151	1.5545	-0.0082	2.2669	-0.0055
One Year		1.2506	+0.0141	1.5348	-0.0087	2.2007	-0.0055
Taiwan	(T$)	33.3000	+0.0050	41.1971	-0.7147	60.3796	-0.5719
One Year		33.2575		41.1105	-0.7209	60.1634	-0.5363
Thailand	(Bt)	32.69	+0.0400	40.1198	-0.6352	57.5263	-0.4373
One Month		39.2450	+0.1980	48.5520	-0.6004	71.1590	-0.3224
Three Month		39.26	+0.0230	48.5304	-0.5830	71.0219	-0.3031
One Year		39.35	+0.2130	48.2935	-0.5588	69.2462	-0.2337
Tunisia	(Dinar)	1.2303	+0.0160	1.5220	-0.0065	2.2306	+0.0077
Turkey	(Lira)	1346000	+15000	1665204	-10259	2440568	+3973
U A E	(Dirham)	3.6730	-0.0001	4.5441	-0.0796	6.6599	-0.0642
One Month		3.6733		4.5407	-0.0796	6.6451	-0.0646
Three Month		3.6765		4.5121	-0.0772	6.4698	-0.0572
UK (0.5515)*	(£)	1.8132	-0.0175	0.6823	-0.0054		
One Month		1.809	-0.0177	0.6833	-0.0053		
Three Month		1.7996	-0.0176	0.6857	-0.0053		
One Year		1.7597	-0.0156	0.6974	-0.0057		
Uruguay	(Peso)	29.4050	-0.0500	36.3784	-0.6996	53.3171	-0.6047
USA	($)			1.2372	-0.0216	1.8132	-0.0175
One Month				1.2361	-0.0217	1.809	-0.0177
Three Month				1.2341	-0.0216	1.7996	-0.0176
One Year				1.2273	-0.0209	1.7597	-0.0156
Venezuela †	(Bolivar)	3027.03	+23.11	3744.89	+23.11	5488.61	-36.44
	(Dong)	15698.00	+9.00	19420.80	+9.00	28463.60	-257.50
Euro (0.8083)*	(Euro)	1.2371	-0.0217			1.4656	+0.0113
One Month		1.2361	-0.0217			1.4634	+0.0112
Three Month		1.234	-0.0216			1.4583	+0.0111
One Year		1.2273	-0.0209			1.4339	+0.0116
SDR		0.67540		0.83560	-0.0079	1.224700	

Rates are derived from WM/Reuters at 4pm (London time). *The closing mid-point rates for the Euro and £ against the $ are shown in brackets. The other figures in the dollar column of both the Euro and Sterling rows are in the reciprocal form in line with market convention. †Official rate set by Venezuelan government is 1598 mid per USD; the WM/Reuters rate is for the valuation of capital assets. Some values are rounded by the F.T. The exchange rates printed in this table are also available on the internet at http://www.FT.com.
Euro Locking Rates: Austrian Schilling 13.7603, Belgium/Luxembourg Franc 40.3399, Finnish Markka 5.94573, French Franc 6.55957, German Mark 1.95583, Greek Drachma 340.75, Irish Punt 0.787564, Italian Lira 1936.27, Netherlands Guilder 2.20371, Portuguese Escudo 200.482, Spanish Peseta 166.386.

The table above was printed in the *Financial Times* on Friday, January 30th, 2004.

The rates are averages taken from a particular source at four o'clock London time. As has been pointed out, rates vary slightly around the world. They also vary from day-to-day. The rates quoted in the table above are called spot rates. The spot rate is that given for immediate delivery of a currency. However, settlement is usually required within two business days.

The formula for converting any amount of currency into US dollars, for example, would be (where S is the spot rate and FC is the amount of foreign currency to be converted):

$$S = \frac{FC}{US\$}$$

So, for instance, if we wish to know what the value of HK$50,000 in US$ would be for spot delivery, we would use the formula as follows:

Take the spot rate for the Hong Kong dollar given on Table A1 as 7.7743. The simple math shown below converts the HK$50,000 to US$6,431.45.

$$7.7743 = \frac{HK\$50,000}{US\$}$$

$$HK\$50,000 = 7.7743 \times US\$$$

$$6,431.45 = US\$$$

In some cases it may be necessary to convert to other currencies rather than the dollar, the euro or the pound shown in the table above. Two calculations using the dollar or the pound vs each currency in question can take the manager to the proper value. These calculations yield the cross rates. The *Financial Times* has added to the convenience by printing the cross rates of some currencies.

Often, when a sale is made, payment will be completed at a later time. Should the contract be negotiated in foreign currency, the manager may wish to assure payment of a certain amount by contracting for currency at a future date. Rates in the future are called forward exchange rates and are also shown on the main currency rate table above (Table A1). Notice that under the Hong Kong dollar are rates for one-month, three-month and one-year terms. A manager may arrange with a financial institution to deliver a certain amount of foreign currency at a particular date and receive a contract or option from the financial institution assuring that a fixed amount of domestic currency will be delivered.

For instance, were a firm to sell 500 computers to Japan at US$500 each, the manager would expect to receive US$250,000 in payment. Let us assume it takes 90 days to make and ship the product and the manager has quoted the contract in yen. To make this example simple, we will assume that the exchange rate when the contract is made is 100 yen per dollar. In this case, the manager expects to receive 25 million yen in payment. Should the yen weaken to 110 per dollar, simple calculation would show that the firm would now only receive US$227,272. So, if the manager wishes to be assured of receiving US$250,000, he or she would arrange for a forward contract or option with a financial institution and pay the required fees. The financial institution will use the forward rates in determining how much currency must be delivered to yield the US$250,000 required by the selling firm.

Having this rudimentary knowledge of foreign exchange can enable a manager to sell in local currency when it is commercially desirable to do so, while also preventing serious erosion in receipts.

TABLE A2

Exchange cross rates

EXCHANGE CROSS RATES

Jan 29		C$	DKr	€	Y	NKr	SKr	SFr	£	$
Canada	(C$)	1	4.510	0.605	79.42	5.304	5.558	0.946	0.413	0.749
Denmark	(DKr)	2.217	10	1.342	176.1	11.76	12.32	2.097	0.916	1.661
Euro	(€)	1.652	7.449	1	131.2	8.760	9.180	1.562	0.682	1.237
Japan	(Y)	1.259	5.679	0.762	100	6.679	6.999	1.191	0.520	0.943
Norway	(NKr)	1.885	8.503	1.142	149.7	10	10.48	1.783	0.779	1.412
Sweden	(SKr)	1.799	8.115	1.089	142.9	9.543	10	1.701	0.743	1.348
Switzerland	(SFr)	1.058	4.770	0.640	83.98	5.609	5.878	1	0.437	0.792
UK	(£)	2.421	10.92	1.466	192.2	12.84	13.45	2.289	1	1.813
USA	($)	1.335	6.021	0.808	106.0	7.081	7.420	1.262	0.552	1

Danish Kroner, Norwegian Kroner and Swedish Kronor per 10; Yen per 100.   Source: FT derived from WM Reuters.

INDEX